# Handbook of Writing, Literacies, and Education in Digital Cultures

At the forefront of current digital literacy studies in education, this handbook uniquely systematizes emerging interdisciplinary themes, new knowledge, and insightful theoretical contributions to the field. Written by well-known scholars from around the world, it closely attends to the digitalization of writing and literacies that is transforming daily life and education. The chapter topics—identified through academic conference networks, rigorous analysis, and database searches of trending themes—are organized thematically in five sections:

- Digital Futures
- Digital Diversity
- Digital Lives
- Digital Spaces
- Digital Ethics

This is an essential guide to digital writing and literacies research, with transformational ideas for educational and professional practice. It will enable new and established researchers to position their studies within highly relevant directions in the field and to generate new themes of inquiry.

**Kathy A. Mills** is a Professor of Literacies and Digital Cultures at Learning Sciences Institute Australia at Australian Catholic University, Australia.

**Amy Stornaiuolo** is an Assistant Professor in the Reading, Writing, and Literacy program of the Graduate School of Education at the University of Pennsylvania, USA.

**Anna Smith** is an Assistant Professor of Secondary Education at Illinois State University, USA.

**Jessica Zacher Pandya** is the Chair of Liberal Studies and Professor of Teacher Education and Liberal Studies at California State University, Long Beach, USA.

# Handbook of Writing, Literacies, and Education in Digital Cultures

Edited by
Kathy A. Mills
Amy Stornaiuolo
Anna Smith
Jessica Zacher Pandya

NEW YORK AND LONDON

First published 2018
by Routledge
711 Third Avenue, New York, NY 10017

and by Routledge
2 Park Square, Milton Park, Abingdon, Oxon, OX14 4RN

*Routledge is an imprint of the Taylor & Francis Group, an informa business*

© 2018 Taylor & Francis

The right of Kathy A. Mills, Amy Stornaiuolo, Anna Smith, and Jessica Zacher Pandya to be identified as the authors of the editorial material, and of the authors for their individual chapters, has been asserted in accordance with sections 77 and 78 of the Copyright, Designs and Patents Act 1988.

All rights reserved. No part of this book may be reprinted or reproduced or utilised in any form or by any electronic, mechanical, or other means, now known or hereafter invented, including photocopying and recording, or in any information storage or retrieval system, without permission in writing from the publishers.

*Trademark notice*: Product or corporate names may be trademarks or registered trademarks, and are used only for identification and explanation without intent to infringe.

*Library of Congress Cataloging-in-Publication Data*
A catalog record for this book has been requested

ISBN: 978-1-138-20630-4 (hbk)
ISBN: 978-1-138-20633-5 (pbk)
ISBN: 978-1-315-46525-8 (ebk)

Typeset in Minion
by codeMantra

# Contents

| | | |
|---|---|---|
| Preface<br>KATHY A. MILLS | | viii |
| Acknowledgments | | x |
| Introduction | Digital Diversity, Ideology, and the Politics of a Writing Revolution<br>KATHY A. MILLS AND AMY STORNAIUOLO | 1 |
| **Section I** | **Digital Futures**<br>KATHY A. MILLS | 11 |
| Chapter 1 | Cosmopolitan Practices, Networks, and Flows of Literacies<br>AMY STORNAIUOLO, GLYNDA HULL, AND MATTHEW HALL | 13 |
| Chapter 2 | Sensory Literacies, the Body, and Digital Media<br>KATHY A. MILLS, LEN UNSWORTH, AND BERYL EXLEY | 26 |
| Chapter 3 | Experiencing Electracy: Digital Writing and the Emerging Communicative Landscapes of Youth Composing Selves<br>ANNA SMITH AND JON WARGO | 37 |
| Chapter 4 | Fostering Impossible Possibles through Critical Media Literacies<br>JESSICA ZACHER PANDYA AND NOAH ASHER GOLDEN | 50 |
| **Section II** | **Digital Diversity**<br>JESSICA ZACHER PANDYA | 61 |
| Chapter 5 | Digital Divides and Social Inclusion<br>MARK WARSCHAUER AND TAMARA TATE | 63 |
| Chapter 6 | Beyond the Techno-Missionary Narrative: Digital Literacy and Necropolitics<br>ELIZABETH LOSH | 76 |

| Chapter 7 | Integrating and Humanizing Knowledgeable Agents of the Digital and Black Feminist Thought in Digital Literacy Research<br>TISHA LEWIS ELLISON | 88 |
|---|---|---|
| Chapter 8 | Global Refugee Crisis: Literacy Concerns and Media Coverage<br>ARIEL LORING AND VAIDEHI RAMANATHAN | 99 |
| Chapter 9 | Race and Racism in Digital Media: What Can Critical Race Theory Contribute to Research on Techno-Cultures?<br>KATHY A. MILLS AND AMANDA GODLEY | 111 |
| **Section III** | **Digital Lives**<br>ANNA SMITH | 123 |
| Chapter 10 | Embodiment and Literacy in a Digital Age: The Case of Handwriting<br>CHRISTINA HAAS AND MEGAN MCGRATH | 125 |
| Chapter 11 | Playful Literacies and Practices of Making in Children's Imaginaries<br>KAREN E. WOHLWEND, BETH A. BUCHHOLZ, AND CARMEN LILIANA MEDINA | 136 |
| Chapter 12 | Digital Geographies<br>TY HOLLETT, NATHAN C. PHILLIPS, AND KEVIN M. LEANDER | 148 |
| Chapter 13 | Youths' Global Engagement in Digital Writing Ecologies<br>DONNA E. ALVERMANN AND BRADLEY ROBINSON | 161 |
| Chapter 14 | Literate Identities in Fan-Based Online Affinity Spaces<br>JAYNE C. LAMMERS, ALECIA MARIE MAGNIFICO, AND JEN SCOTT CURWOOD | 173 |
| **Section IV** | **Digital Spaces**<br>KATHY A. MILLS | 185 |
| Chapter 15 | Assembling Literacies in Virtual Play<br>CHRIS BAILEY, CATHY BURNETT, AND GUY MERCHANT | 187 |
| Chapter 16 | Space, Time, and Production: Games and the New Frontier of Digital Literacies<br>ANTERO GARCIA | 198 |
| Chapter 17 | Digital Metroliteracies: Space, Diversity, and Identity<br>SENDER DOVCHIN AND ALASTAIR PENNYCOOK | 211 |
| Chapter 18 | Critically Reading Image in Digital Spaces and Digital Times<br>PEGGY ALBERS, VIVIAN M. VASQUEZ, AND JEROME C. HARSTE | 223 |
| Chapter 19 | The Quantified Writer: Data Traces in Education<br>ANNA SMITH, BILL COPE, AND MARY KALANTZIS | 235 |

| Section V | **Digital Ethics**<br>AMY STORNAIUOLO | 249 |
|---|---|---|
| Chapter 20 | Digital Ethics, Political Economy, and the Curriculum: This Changes Everything<br>ALLAN LUKE, JULIAN SEFTON-GREEN, PHIL GRAHAM, DOUGLAS KELLNER, AND JAMES LADWIG | 251 |
| Chapter 21 | Digital Youth and Educational Justice<br>LALITHA VASUDEVAN, KRISTINE RODRIGUEZ KERR, AND CRISTINA SALAZAR GALLARDO | 263 |
| Chapter 22 | Composing as Culturing: An American Indian Approach to Digital Ethics<br>KRISTIN L. AROLA | 275 |
| Chapter 23 | Aesthetics and Text in the Digital Age<br>THEO van LEEUWEN | 285 |

List of Contributors — 301

Index — 303

# Preface

Kathy A. Mills

The decision to produce an academic research volume with a distinctive focus on writing and literacies emerged from our service as elected officers of the Writing and Literacies Special Interest Group (SIG) of the American Educational Research Association. It all began one brisk, spring day as we sipped hot coffee in a busy café in Chicago, Illinois, during the 2015 AERA Annual Meeting. Jessica Zacher Pandya was incoming Chair, Kathy Mills the Program Chair, Amy Stornaiuolo the Treasurer, and Anna Smith the Communications Chair. We recognized our shared vision to extend the scope of our international research leadership and bring together our expertise as digital writing and literacies scholars. Encouraged by the outgoing Chair, Leslie Cook, we made a collective commitment that day to produce a volume that synergized research of writing in the digital turn by leading scholars within and beyond the Writing and Literacies SIG, a network that includes nearly 600 members across multiple countries and continents, including the US, Canada, UK, Australia, South Africa, Europe, South America, New Zealand, and Cyprus.

Why writing and why now? The *Handbook of Writing, Literacies, and Education in Digital Cultures* has grown from a vibrant legacy of writing and literacies scholars, such as Steve Witte, Steve Cahir, Shirley Brice Heath, Brian Street, Kris Gutierrez, Glynda Hull, Allan Luke, Colin Lankshear, Michele Knobel, Sarah Warshauer Freedman, Anne Haas Dyson, Linda Flower, Bill Cope, Mary Kalantzis, and many other influential scholars. These scholars had earlier recognized the great potential of attending seriously to writing and literacies as a substantial and significant research field. Reading research had a visible presence at the American Education Research Association (AERA) in the 1970s and early 1980s, with clearly designated forums for research dissemination. However, there were no similar networks or programs of writing and literacies research.

There was a palpable excitement in the establishment of the Writing and Literacy Special Interest Group at AERA, which later became Writing and *Literacies*. As Sarah Freedman has stated in our SIG's series of podcasts, "No longer was writing to follow literacies, but indeed to lead it" (Wargo & Smith, 2015). The interest and anticipation had a ripple effect as writing began to emerge as a distinct research focus both within and beyond AERA members. The use of the term "literacies" became an important inclusive way to reflect the diversity of literacy as social practices across communities, aligned with key international research of the way in which children, young people, and adults participate in multiple spheres of communication. This move was aligned to the emergence of bodies such as the National Centre for the Study of Writing and Literacy (NCSWL) and the National Writing Project in the US.

Why digital cultures? The digitalization of writing and literacies is becoming increasingly apparent and transformational in everyday life. Technologies of inscription are changing in complex ways, and writing cultures take on innumerable forms across all stages of life, across media, and across social contexts. The time is right to recognize research of literacy across diverse digital contexts of use as a mature, yet rapidly expanding field of research in its own right. Research of the multiple digital contexts of writing is no longer positioned at the margins of literacy studies, reserved for young, tech-savvy literacy academics. The field is expanding to include many who appreciate that literacy is no longer dominated by practices that involve eraser fragments and pencil shavings on the desk. In daily life, less of what we now write and read is produced with pen and paper, or distributed as printed text.

In recent years, the Writing and Literacies SIG at AERA has continued to be a significant player in research as theorists from around the world meet to establish and develop new frontiers in new literacy studies, multiliteracies, media literacy, digital literacies, multimodal literacy, and other original approaches to writing and literacies research studies. This is a substantial volume that brings together leading scholars to provide in-depth and authoritative knowledge of this vital research field. This benchmark reference work organizes and systematizes the field of writing and literacies in digital cultures, providing an essential guide for researchers, educators, graduate and post graduate students, librarians, policy makers, and projects—one that can't be ignored. This volume, *Handbook of Writing, Literacies, and Education in Digital Cultures*, will accomplish two significant aims: First, it will bring together new knowledge about digital composition and literacies research that showcases many theoretical contributions and multiple perspectives in this field of education. Second, it will provide an essential guide to the emerging strands of writing and literacies research across diverse digital cultures, generating new themes of inquiry and consolidating others.

This vital research volume addresses the field of digital composition and literacies research beyond literacy uses in classrooms. This is strategic, because social practices involving digital technologies for writing occur in many spheres of our everyday lives, and are generating increased international research interest across many disciplines. The book is primarily aimed to gain the interest of researchers of literacy across all levels of education. However, it may also appeal to academics in fields such as applied linguistics, English and language studies, media and communication studies, composition and rhetoric studies, sociology of education, cultural geography and anthropology, visual arts, creative industries, and other related fields within the humanities.

The book is uniquely conceptualized around essential themes of digital cultures that have become salient in writing and literacies research—digital futures, digital diversity, digital lives, digital spaces, and digital ethics. The book will enable new and established researchers to position their inquiries within relevant directions in the research field, with recommendations for educational and professional practice more broadly. Most importantly, it will enable us to think differently about writing and literacies research.

## Reference

Wargo, J. & Smith, A. (Producers). (2015, December 11). *Writing and literacies on air: Why writing?* [Audio podcast]. Retrieved from https://soundcloud.com/writing-and-literacies.

# Acknowledgments

Kathy, Amy, Anna, and Jessica would like to thank the contributing authors for their thoughtful contributions to the volume and for being important interlocutors in broader conversations about writing and literacies in digital cultures.

The editors thank the anonymous international and professorial reviewers of the book proposal. You have helped to make this volume inclusive of diverse priorities and perspectives of academics across several continents in the field of writing and digital literacies.

We would like to acknowledge the following peer reviewers of the volume who contributed insightful critique of the chapter manuscripts through blinded review:

Donna Alvermann, University of Georgia
Kristin Arola, Washington State University
Beth Buchholz, Appalachian State University
Cathy Burnett, Sheffield Hallam University
Jen Scott Curwood, University of Sydney
Sender Dovchin, University of Technology, Sydney
Tisha Lewis Ellison, University of Georgia
Beryl Exley, Griffith University
Antero Garcia, Stanford University
Matthew Hall, The College of New Jersey
Ty Hollett, Pennsylvania State University
Glynda Hull, University of California, Berkeley
Kristine Rodriguez Kerr, New York University
Jayne Lammers, University of Rochester
Ariel Loring, University of California, Davis
Alecia Magnifico, University of New Hampshire
Kathy A. Mills, Learning Sciences Institute Australia, Australian Catholic University
Jessica Zacher Pandya, California State University, Long Beach
Alastair Pennycook, University of Technology, Sydney
Nathan Phillips, University of Illinois at Chicago
Laura Scholes, Queensland University of Technology
Anna Smith, Illinois State University
Amy Stornaiuolo, University of Pennsylvania
Tamara Tate, University of California, Irvine

Len Unsworth, Learning Sciences Institute Australia, Australian Catholic University
Jon Wargo, Boston College
Mark Warschauer, University of California, Irvine
Karen Wohlwend, Indiana University

We also owe a major debt of gratitude to Naomi Silverman at Routledge, for her vision and support at every stage of bringing this book to fruition.

# Introduction
*Digital Diversity, Ideology, and the Politics of a Writing Revolution*

Kathy A. Mills and Amy Stornaiuolo

For writing and literacies researchers, the opening decades of the twenty-first century seem replete with possibilities, as emerging digital technologies facilitate expanded communicative repertoires and multiple forms of participation, collaboration, and civic engagement. These possibilities motivate three key agendas for writing and literacies research that inform this book. The first is the rapid and increased role of digital technologies that have become ubiquitous in daily life, in schools, in workplaces, and in every sphere of society. Such transformations have led to a groundswell of literacy research to help education keep pace with the changes to the digital communications environment, to ensure that schooling practices continue to be relevant in a world in which we cannot predict the technologies of tomorrow. Writing and literacy education is not simply an agenda of the past—of basic skills, of narrow curriculum, a means through which governments can create good citizens with functional literacies. Rather, literacies are central to education, to society, to human cognition, to human socialization, cultural identities, power relations, and to the very construction of social space.

The second transformation that literacy research must address is the ideological nature of language and literacies. Language is always ideological, located within broader structures of cultural, economic, and political power (Luke, Comber, & Grant, 2003). Writing and literacies research will have a central role in drawing attention to the ideological nature of literacy education. This underpins the political debates that currently circulate in relation to literacy standards in schools, in national literacy testing, and in pre-service teacher education programs. These debates have long existed, and the pressures of literacy achievement and school accountability are not likely to retrocede. Internationally, educational researchers must make a stand to expose the dominant Western or European colonizing powers that use narrow conceptions of skills-based, universal sets of literacy practices to oppress cultures and communities that are positioned marginally in education. Research on writing and literacies is needed to challenge the dominant ideologies in educational practice, in society, and in the media.

Third, and related to the second point, writing and literacies studies must critically account for the role of interrupting subordination of marginalized groups on the basis of race, language, culture, geographical location, class, gender, ability, religion, and national origin. Language is inextricably tied to culture and identity (see Chapter 9). Writing and literacies research needs to continue to address the increasing realities of local difference and global connectedness. It needs to guide educators to know how to respect cultural difference in local and global contexts, and to understand the complexity of literacies against the multiplicity of identities, socio-material relations, textual practices, and labor markets that cross national, state, cultural, and linguistic boundaries. And not only this, we need also to envisage innovative and broadened understandings of the very constitution of literacies, to expand notions of semiotics to take account of the full role of the senses and the body in meaning making, and to challenge the ocularcentrism—the privileging of what is perceived through the eyes—that continues to underpin many conventional definitions of literacy. We need to recognize the diverse bodily ways of making meaning across different communities and social practices, understanding the techniques of the body and pursuing the education of the senses for communicating meaningfully for contemporary social purposes.

In considering the broad scope of these questions, we examine how the three agendas we detailed above can push forward new directions for writing and literacies scholarship even as they raise central challenges for educators and researchers. Each chapter of this book is aimed at theorizing writing and literacies in ways that move the field forward into the future of a world in which concepts, such as globalization, are increasingly inadequate to account for social actions that extend beyond the cosmos. How, for example, will rapid communication be configured for astronauts confined in spacecraft millions of miles away from earth in planned explorations to Mars? To what extent are the complex socio-material relations of communication across time and space changing as objects, digital devices, and voices become networked in the Internet of Things? How are digital childhoods reshaping the future world for babies and toddlers who already interact with an expanded array of digital toys, books, and cold (often slimy) glass screens? What are the implications of changes to writing and literacy pedagogies in schools that blend both old and new(ish) technologies of inscription? What is the role of media sharing platforms, such as YouTube and DeviantArt, in the construction of children and youth identities and futures? How are virtual and augmented reality technologies reshaping potentials for the orchestration of multiple senses in children's online practices? These and many other questions would not have been asked a decade ago. So, what has changed, what has not changed, and what is the role of culture in these transformations?

**Writing and Cultures Past and Present: A Brief Background**

In light of this rapidly evolving communicative landscape, a central task facing writing and literacies scholars involves understanding the recursive nature of the relationship between evolving communication technologies and literacy practices within and beyond schooling. While we may be tempted to characterize these digitally facilitated communicative practices as "new"—and certainly the ways many people use digital technologies to communicate in 2017 looks different to any decade prior—we must also acknowledge that people's writing and literacy practices are always being transformed over time and space in relation to the unfolding rhythms of social and cultural life.

People have always used new technologies to engage in the basic human need to communicate with others, particularly with those who are separated geographically beyond the reach of one's own voice. For example, picture postcards have been a social communication practice from the beginning of the twentieth century in Britain, when beautiful images were combined with a short message around the margins of the card. These were delivered within a few hours through a special rapid postal service that could be described as "near-synchronous" multimodal communication. This occurred a century before Instagram and Pinterest were invented (Gillen, 2016). As Gillen argues, people subverted the etiquette of epistolary writing to send sentiments to loved ones on picture postcards that were less private than the letter, while opening up greater spontaneity in written communication. Today, we still have the rapid consumption of printed books, greeting cards, food packaging, collectable cards, and burgeoning niche markets for stylized writing and stationery materials. Yet these texts exist alongside the growth of texts that are circulated by multinational technology corporations, the Internet, telecommunications and media companies, and broadcasting systems. A primary aim of this volume is to examine how these shifts in people's literacies are tied to emergent social practices in digital cultures.

The focus on writing, on encoding and inscription, in the title of this volume is a response to the salience of textual design in Web 2.0 or "social web" environments and beyond (O'Reilly, 2005), where the ease of production and rapid circulation of texts has reached a greater level than ever before, instantiated by millions of images and sounds that are shared to a plethora of social media sites by groups of users of all ages (Mills, 2016). In comparison with earlier features of the Internet, Web 2.0 technology or the read-write web supports the sharing of music, videos, synchronous document editing, blogging, microblogging, online polls and surveys, wikis, and other collaborative forms of online text production and dissemination (Mills, 2010).

The idea of the public contributing to knowledge and textual production is much older than the invention of the Internet, or the idea of "participatory culture" by the Birmingham School of Cultural Studies (Jenkins, 2006b). Walter Benjamin entitled his 1934 essay "The Author as Producer," observing that media technologies such as newspapers, television, film, radio, and photography were blurring distinctions between authors and consumers. He argued half a century ago that "the conventional distinction between author and public that the press has maintained…is disappearing" (Benjamin, 1968, p. 83). Examples of the day included the way in which newspapers position letters and opinions from readers alongside the journal's editorials. Interestingly, Benjamin already maintained that authors should not only publish revolutionary content, but also aim to revolutionize the means through which texts are produced and circulated (Deodato, 2014). This volume examines how these revolutionary forms of production, participation, and circulation emerge and are practiced rhetorically in contemporary digital cultures.

Such a focus on how writing and literacies are practiced and transformed in relation to intersecting social, historical, political, and economic contexts makes central the notion of *culture*. By appending digital to the terms "writing" and "literacies" in the title, we signal the ways digital technologies influence and create cultural practices, particularly as they cut across traditional divides and facilitate different allegiances and connections. To theorize culture, we draw on Brian Street's (1993) conception of it as "an active process of meaning making and contest over definition" (p. 25). Street argues that understanding culture as a verb moves us away from more reified, static, and neocolonial definitions of culture as a "fixed inheritance of shared meanings" (p. 23). He maintains that traditional conceptions of culture, in addition to essentializing groups of people and disguising the active forms of semiosis involved, obscure the ways power operates in reinforcing racial and ethnocentric divisions. Instead of examining what culture *is*, Street suggests focusing on what it *does*. Such an emphasis on culturing as an active process of production (Chapter 22; cf. Lyons, 2010) draws attention to the ways people's literacy-making practices are rooted in collective histories. If, as Geertz (1973) suggests, culture is made from "webs of significance" that we collectively create through semiotic activity (p. 4), literacy researchers are well positioned to study how people's emergent social semiotic practices and digital cultures are co-constructed over time.

### Looking Forward: Emerging Directions in Writing and Literacies Research

A book about digital practices runs the risk of becoming quickly dated in a constantly evolving communicative landscape; we sought to mitigate that possibility by highlighting enduring issues that we predict will only grow more prominent for writing and literacies researchers over time. Throughout the volume, readers will find the agendas we identified above taken up in significant ways. As the authors suggest innovative theoretical, methodological, and pedagogical directions for the field of writing and literacies research that take up the challenges of ubiquitous communication technologies, questions of ideology in communicative practice, and the persistence of racism in digital cultures. We highlight here several theoretical contributions we found particularly generative for animating the field in important ways for years to come.

*Emergence*

As people connect across devices, platforms, spaces, and geographies at a scale and pace previously unimagined, a central question revolves around how people and things move, associate, and intersect across space and time. In other words, in light of the ways texts and people circulate in unpredictable fashion across global networks (Appadurai, 1996; Jenkins, Ford, & Green, 2013), how can writing and literacies scholars account for the ways meaning *emerges* from and in relation to the world? While multiliteracies research (New London Group, 1996) helpfully emphasized the patterned, designed aspects of literacy practices, it is equally important to attend to the more improvisational, idiosyncratic, and contingent dimensions of meaning making that are amplified in digital cultures (Stornaiuolo, Smith, & Phillips, 2017). One of the most important implications of an emergent perspective on literacy practices is an emphasis on the affective dimensions of literacies—their emotional, sensorial, and embodied nature (see Chapters 2, 10, and 11) as well as their aesthetic qualities (see Chapters 18 and 23). A focus on emergence also highlights the constraints to connecting, as algorithms, software, and corporate infrastructures all influence how texts flow and circulate in online spaces (Lynch, 2015). Moving forward, we anticipate significant scholarship will attend to how meaning emerges in these material-semiotic assemblages, including the rise of the Internet of Things, that can both enfranchise and marginalize individuals and groups in different measure.

These emergent dimensions of writing and literacy practices are often particularly challenging to identify and study, as they are always situated in and responsive to the interactional flow of people and materials in a given moment, fleeting and ephemeral. Look only to recent practices of using technologies to geolocate oneself for entertainment or navigation, including the use of wearable tech to collect personalized data and situate and re-situate the self in relation to unfolding activity in the world (see, for example, Chapters 12 and 16). Such practices suggest the need for new methodologies that take into account big and small data (see Chapter 19), and allow more fine-grained tracing of literacies across material/immaterial assemblages (see Chapter 15). Scholars might productively draw on interdisciplinary methods from fields such as the arts and human geography that are sensitive to the emergent ways people make meaning in and across spaces in response to other people, texts, and data.

*Diversity*

Decades ago, the New London Group (1996) identified the diversity of peoples and communicative forms as a central aspect of making meaning in a globally connected world, but in the years since then, issues of diversity and "superdiversity" have been at the center of theorizing the challenges of communicating across multiple cultural, national, and linguistic contexts (Blommaert, 2010; Canagarajah, 2012; see Chapter 5). Some of the most important contributions in this area have come from critical, postcolonial scholars who examine issues of power and oppression in how diversity is conceptualized (see Chapter 4). We see scholarship that pushes back on the ways nationalism and standardization continue to marginalize communities of color, an important avenue for writing and literacies scholars. The scholarship highlights perspectives that begin with assumptions of diversity as a resource and positions communities and individuals as knowledgeable (see Chapter 7) and as already cosmopolitan intellectuals with unique vantage points on the world (Campano & Ghiso, 2011). A number of scholars are exploring the role of digital media in contexts of forced migration and transnational rhetorical practice, both in maintaining connections across borders and in imagining how to create equitable conditions in the face of inequitable and unjust treatment (see Chapter 8).

Some of the greatest challenges for writing and literacies researchers studying how diversity is imagined, practiced, and regulated across mobile, digital cultures revolve around issues of power and privilege, requiring not only critical but also ethical frameworks for theorizing diversity now (see Chapter 20). Scholars involved in anti-racist, coalition-building work with communities have explored how methodologies must endeavor to take better account of the ways power and privilege influence research design and participation (see Chapter 9). Many researchers interested in intersections of language and literacy in mobile contexts are attempting to attend to these complexities by working to privilege multiple languages and voices in more equitable and reflexive ways (see Chapters 13 and 17). We are heartened by scholarship that puts justice and equity at the forefront, positioning young people and their everyday experiences as central to understanding how community partnerships and activist practices can create more just contexts for writing and literacies (see Chapter 21).

*Performativity*

Over the past decade, the face-to-face "presentation of self in everyday life" (Goffman, 1959) plays out in new ways online, as users curate their digital selves through multiple and online profiles for different professional, familial, interest-driven, or peer-oriented virtual audiences, who may or may not ever meet face-to-face (see Chapter 14). The Internet has become the new stage, while Goffman's (1959) "back-stages"—the hidden or private places—are no longer very private, as users display images of the meals they eat, their pregnant belly diaries, or details of reduced price underwear sales to their followers. The flip side is that social media sites, such as Facebook, also become sites of curating the self in plastic and sanitized ways that obscure the real pain and everyday realities of people's lives. Theorists such as Jenkins (2006a, p. 3) argued about the nature of "participatory culture" that can be facilitated through the web, when there are relatively low barriers, technical or otherwise, to artistic expression and civic engagement. Various concepts have been put forward to encapsulate this mega production of texts, calling it "produsage" (Bruns, 2008), "designing" (New London Group, 1996), "Edutainment" (Buckingham, Scanlon, & Sefton-Green, 2001), or new technologies for "multimodal communication" (Jewitt, 2006). All of these frameworks recognize the centrality of performing the self online through rhetorical practice (see Chapter 3), with the attendant risks and opportunities for participating in visible ways in networked publics (boyd, 2011).

One of the most pressing questions for the future involves the uncertain implications of composing in public, with interactive audiences who not only collaborate in the production of texts but comment, critique, and circulate materials in impactful ways (see Chapter 1). Writing and literacies researchers are well positioned to ask about the identity politics of participating in these public writing and literacy practices, including possibilities for digital activism (Bonilla & Rosa, 2015; Stornaiuolo & Thomas, 2017) as well as the consequences of reinscribing and even magnifying oppressive practices against already marginalized groups (Love & Bradley, 2013). With the technological means of production in the hands of the public, one could argue that "cultural hegemony"—the ideological "common sense" worldviews of society that were controlled by the ruling class, along with the means of material production (Gramsci, 1971)—has been eroded. Yet while the Internet has enabled more users to become co-creators of culture and public discourse, the extent to which users simply reproduce or alternatively resist dominant culture is always dynamic, shifting, and constantly contested (see Chapter 6).

What is now at stake in online participation is a loss of privacy that has become embedded in millions of digital footprints that can be traced by others. The production of writing on the Internet is not so participatory that users can escape from power relations and online corporate surveillance. For example, in the participation of individuals in online markets, they become economic subjects associated with the commodification of privacy. Internet advertising servers and infomediaries are third parties that compile economic profiles of web users to classify and target consumers with ads that are tailored to their patterns of use (Campbell & Carlson, 2002). Digital footprints are ever-expanding, raising new questions about digital ethics, online surveillance, and the performance of identities. Future directions for scholarship in this area must include attention to the commodification of users, as online production increasingly translates into free labor for corporate interests and a new means of governmental surveillance and control. For scholars interested in examining how people's identities are shaped across digital cultures, there is great need for the development of critical and intersectional perspectives sensitive to the less visible and machine-driven dimensions of composing and creating digitally.

**Conclusion**

This chapter has outlined some key theoretical directions important for studying writing and literacies in digital cultures. In suggesting that emergence, diversity, and performativity represent promising directions for future scholarship, we hope also to illuminate new tensions and challenges that require writing and literacies scholars to build on previous scholarship while continuing to innovate theoretically and methodologically. We explore the themes and challenges discussed in the introduction across the five sections of the book, which are organized around central dimensions of writing and literacies scholarship in socially and linguistically heterogeneous contexts of global communication and education: digital futures, digital diversity, digital lives, digital spaces, and digital ethics.

Section I: Digital Futures articulates new perspectives concerning the ethical, sensorial, and critical elements of writing and literacies, and contemporary debates at the nexus of literacies and digital rhetoric that have direct relevance to the social construction of authorial identities for youth and other writers in education contexts. It outlines an ethically oriented approach to contemporary writing and literacies practices in a world in which privacy is often exchanged for participation. It provides a new perspective of the forgotten sensorial dimensions and role of the body in writing and literacy practices in the digital and non-digital contexts of use, with a particular focus on the education of touch or haptics in schooling. This book section also explores how multimodality, techne, and praxis emerge and resonate as youth write the self in relation to place, trope, and culture across new communicative platforms and in transmediated contexts. The section concludes with debates about the potentials and limitations of participatory politics in new spaces for writing and literacies, providing critiques of representation and collaborative design in contemporary ecologies and power relations.

Section II: Digital Diversity brings together the work of scholars from around the world to address issues of inclusion in contemporary writing and literacies research, from race to gender, and to the geographical displacement of refugees. Our approach to issues of social justice and diversity in this volume is that structural inequality in society is absolutely core to all writing and literacies research and should not be compartmentalized. It is the warp and woof of this volume woven throughout the handbook, but several issues are foregrounded explicitly in this section. Continual changes to the digital communications environment interplay with social inclusion and marginalize groups in complex ways that do not remain static over time, raising specific agendas of urgency. For example, how does the ongoing massive refugee displacement of this century intersect with digital inclusion? We can pursue research interventions with computer coding, 3D printing, and augmented reality goggles, but do we understand the real barriers to literacies and social inclusion for children and adolescents who live in contexts of abject poverty, violence, and the struggle for daily survival?

Section III: Digital Lives brings together leading scholars of digital practices to theorize the contemporary dimensions of everyday writing and literacies across the life course from digital childhoods to adolescence, including materiality, play and imagination, mobilities, global citizenship, and fan-based affinity practices. This section includes new ideas about the role of the material world in structuring thought, outlining promising pathways for future research on writing as material and embodied practice. It explores the relationships between global imaginaries, children's digital play, and innovative making in contemporary childhoods, seeing imagination and making as sites of collective cultural production that can both rupture and mobilize youth and materials. The fundamentally mobile and digital nature of techno-social practices is theorized in relation to people on the move, and the implications for literacies, education, recreation, and civic engagement. It explores how young people's involvement as global citizens creates intersections with digital media and literacy practices that carry baggage, often unexamined, but directly related to sociocultural, political, and economic contingencies. With the rise of fandoms, this section explores how the role of fan-based affinity spaces allow young adults to explore literacy practices related to reading, writing, reviewing, and designing in interest-driven spaces.

Section IV: Digital Spaces shifts the focus to social spaces that discursively shape, and which are shaped by, writing and literacies practices. From play in virtual worlds and sandbox games like Minecraft, to "metroliteracy" spaces of urban youth and to institutionally marginalized court-involved adolescents or trouble-makers, this section critically interweaves game theory and pedagogies of care, design, and social justice. For example, it demonstrates through research how virtual worlds provide opportunities for new kinds of interaction and new forms of textual practice, play, and learning. The chapters collectively provide a compelling argument to see the potentials of these everyday contexts of meaning making for children today. For example, the section explores the role of writing and literacies within a range of games, including first-person shooter games, alternate reality games, and online roleplaying games, interrogating new game theory concepts, from the "magic circle" to "gamification," and the implications for communities of practice and education. Later work in this section elaborates parallels between writing and literacies that become bound together through physical urban space as metrolingualism with social media practices, such as Facebooking, which similarly constitute the urban fabric. It theorizes the varied ways in which linguistic and cultural resources, spatial repertoires, and online activities are bound together to make meaning. The critique of art in digital texts, and how image-text relations position readers, then extends critical literacy to analyze artistic and design choices in digital composition. These authors bring knowledge of design principles of art to enable educators and students to interrogate their own and others' digital text production with a critical reading of the image. Finally, the complexities of "big data" in information-rich societies are cross-examined along with its potentials for education and assessment.

Section V: Digital Ethics debates current ethical concerns associated with the social and ethical risks of children and young people's access to information on the Internet. The earlier waves of euphoria and hype about the potentials of the Internet are becoming weaker, leaving the digital shore awash with contemporary questions about how students as citizens can live ethically and productively in globalized networked communications environments. This section critically interrogates the philosophical and educational questions about the relationships between ownership of information, profit, state control, and power, asking questions about how to induct students into responsibly exercising their rights to privacy, and to discern truth from fiction. Illustrating the ways in which young people put to use a range of digital composition technologies at hand, this section theorizes the nexus between social justice and the act of composing that works against oppression. It narrates young people's use of technologies for digital authoring toward fostering belonging. This is vital in the lives of court-involved youth, or for those who are undocumented, and who often experience education as marginalizing. An ethical perspective of digital writing and literacies for an Indigenous community—American Indian Anishinaabe people—is also presented, acknowledging the need to approach digital production with care within textual ecologies of craftsmanship and composition. The book concludes by turning to concerns of aesthetics, which are no longer exclusive to the domain of poetry writing and art, but which are features of previously unembellished transactional texts of the digital age.

In sum, *Handbook of Writing, Literacies, and Education in Digital Cultures* reflects a major scholarly contribution by leading scholars in the field to re-envisage the future of writing and literacies research in compelling, dynamic, and critical ways. Our aim is to encourage scholars to think differently about writing and literacies research, questioning our familiar approaches to expand and critically explore our established imaginations of inscription in digital and diverse lives.

## References

Appadurai, A. (1996). *Modernity at large: Cultural dimensions of globalization*. Minneapolis: University of Minnesota Press.

Benjamin, W. (1968). The work of art in the age of mechanical reproduction. In H. Arendt (Ed.), *Illuminations: Essays and reflections* (pp. 217–251). New York, NY: Schocken Books (Original work published 1936).

Blommaert, J. (2010). *The sociolinguistics of globalization*. Cambridge: Cambridge University Press.

Bonilla, Y., & Rosa, J. (2015). #Ferguson: Digital protest, hashtag ethnography, and the racial politics of social media in the United States. *American Ethnologist, 42*(1), 4–17.

boyd, d. (2011). Social network sites as networked publics: Affordances, dynamics, and implications. In Z. Papacharissi (Ed.), *Networked self: Identity, community, and culture on social network sites* (pp. 38–57). New York, NY: Routledge.

Bruns, A. (2008). *Blogs, wikipedia, second life, and beyond: From production to produsage*. New York, NY: Peter Lang.

Buckingham, D., Scanlong, M., & Sefton-Green, J. (2001). Selling the digital dream: Marketing educational technology to teachers and parents. In A. Loveless & V. Ellis (Eds.), *ICT, pedagogy and the curriculum: Subject to change* (pp. 20–40). London, UK: Routledge.

Campano, G., & Ghiso, M. P. (2011). Immigrant students as cosmopolitan intellectuals. In S. A. Wolf, K. Coats, P. Enciso, & C. A. Jenkins (Eds.), *Handbook of research on children's and young adult literature* (pp. 164–176). New York, NY: Routledge.

Campbell, J. E., & Carlson, M. (2002). Panopticon.com: Online surveillance and the commodification of privacy. *Journal of Broadcasting & Electronic Media, 46*(4), 586–606.

Canagarajah, S. (2012). *Translingual practice: Global Englishes and cosmopolitan relations*. New York, NY: Routledge.

Deodato, J. (2014). The patron as producer: Libraries, web 2.0, and participatory culture. *Journal of Documentation, 70*(5), 734–758.

Geertz, C. (1973). *The interpretation of cultures*. London, UK: Fontana.

Gillen, J. (2016). *Antique Instagrams or Snapchats? Multimodal composition of early twentieth century British postcards*. Paper presented at the American Educational Research Association Annual Meeting 8–12 April 2016, Washington, DC.

Goffman, E. (1959). *The presentation of self in everyday life*. New York, NY: Doubleday.

Gramsci, A. (1971). *Selections from the prison notebooks* (Q. Hoare & G. N. Smith, Trans.). New York, NY: New York International Publishers.

Jenkins, H. (2006a). *Confronting the challenges of participatory culture: Media education for the 21st century*. Cambridge, MA: The MIT Press.

Jenkins, H. (2006b). *Convergence culture: Where old and new media collide*. New York, NY: New York University Press.

Jenkins, H., Ford, S., & Green, J. (2013). *Spreadable media: Creating value and meaning in a networked culture*. New York: New York University Press.

Jewitt, C. (2006). *Technology, literacy and learning: A multimodal approach*. Abingdon, UK: Routledge.

Love, B., & Bradley, R. (2013). Teaching Trayvon: Teaching about racism through public pedagogy, hip hop, black trauma, and social media. In J. L. Martin (Ed.), *Racial battle fatigue: Insights from the front lines of social justice advocacy* (pp. 255–268). Santa Barbara, CA: Praeger.

Luke, A., Comber, B., & Grant, H. (2003). Critical literacies and cultural studies. In M. Anstey & G. Bull (Eds.), *The Literacy Lexicon* (2nd ed., pp. 15–35). Frenchs Forest, NSW: Pearson, Prentice Hall.

Lynch, T. L. (2015). Where the machine stops: Software as reader and the rise of new literatures. *Research in the Teaching of English, 49*(3), 297–304.

Lyons, S. R. (2010). *X-marks: Native signatures of assent*. Minneapolis: University of Minnesota Press.

Mills, K. A. (2010). A review of the digital turn in the new literacy studies. *Review of Educational Research, 80*(2), 246–271.

Mills, K. A. (2016). *Literacy theories for the digital age: Social, critical, multimodal, spatial, material and sensory lenses*. New Perspectives in Language and Education. Bristol, UK: Multilingual Matters.

New London Group (1996). A pedagogy of multiliteracies: Designing social futures. *Harvard Educational Review*, 66(1), 60–92.

O'Reilly, T. (2005). What is web 2.0? Design patterns and business models for the next generation of software. Retrieved May 30, 2016, from www.oreillynet.com/pub/a/oreilly/tim/news/2005/09/30/what-is-web-20.html.

Stornaiuolo, A., Smith, A., & Phillips, N. (2017). Theorizing a transliteracies framework for a connected world. *Journal of Literacy Research*, 49(1), 68–91.

Stornaiuolo, A., & Thomas, E. E. (2017). Disrupting educational inequalities through youth digital activism. *Review of Research in Education*, 41.

Street, B. V. (1993). Culture is a verb: Anthropological aspects of language and cultural process. In D. L. Gradoll, L. Thompson, & M. Byram (Eds.), *Language and culture: Papers from the annual meeting of the British Association of Applied Linguistics held at Trevelyan College, University of Durham* (pp. 24–44). Clevedon, UK: BAAL and Multilingual Matters.

# I
# Digital Futures

Kathy A. Mills

This section sets up the theoretical foundations of the volume, advancing new perspectives that foreground the ethical, sensorial, and critical directions in writing and literacies research. It engages with contemporary debates at the nexus of literacy studies and digital rhetoric that have direct relevance to the social construction of authorial identities for youth and other writers in education contexts.

First, the ethical dimension is particularly central today because flows of digital writing now pervade our contemporary lives via an expanded array of networked textual ecologies that amplify writers' ethical participation in social life. These textual ecologies create different affordances for collaboration and social interaction, as users navigate interactions with others across time and space—others with whom they may or may not share common ethical ground. Second, the forgotten sensory dimension of writing and literacies in digital contexts is similarly vital, because writers and readers attend to sensory information in their worlds and in their texts actively, selectively, and with discernment. As Haas (1996, p. 226) argues, "The body is the mechanism by which the mediation of the mental and the material occurs." Third, digital rhetoric emerges in this discussion as a player in humanizing the effect of technologies and the role of humans in directing them, positioned as a syncretic practice that generates new knowledge by asking questions differently. Finally, research of writing and literacies in digital spaces is recognized to be a field of struggles, underscoring the need to examine the ideological and practical ramifications of viewing digital composition as a "field." Central to this analysis is the unveiling of the power dynamics that exclude or include certain people from defining fields, and to name what Bourdieu (2000) has termed "impossible possibles."

In Chapter 1, Amy Stornaiuolo, Glynda Hull, and Matt Hall theorize an ethically oriented approach to contemporary writing and literacies practices in a world in which privacy is often exchanged for participation, and in which negotiating cultural differences through open dialogue requires cosmopolitan literacies that bring together different ensembles of emotional, aesthetic, cognitive, and ethical proficiencies.

Moving away from the privileging of sight in literacy studies, Kathy Mills, Len Unsworth, and Beryl Exley draw attention to the sensorial dimensions and role of the body, such as haptics and use of the breath, in digital practice (Chapter 2). Extending both sensory anthropology and social semiotics, these authors demonstrate how material and sensory relations are altered when the same story is instantiated across different media—from picture book to iPad e-book. They similarly consider a writing lesson and process drama to demonstrate the sensorial dimensions of touch across a range of digital and nondigital communication contexts. This work opens up new ways of thinking about the relations between bodies, minds, digital environments, and textual representation.

Anna Smith and Jon Wargo, in Chapter 3, extend new forays in research by examining undergirding theories of digital rhetorics and digital literacies to understand youths' contemporary composing. Using examples from longitudinal research, they illustrate how multimodality, techne, praxis, and mobilities emerge and resonate as youth write the self in relation to place, trope, and culture across new communicative platforms in transmediated contexts. They posit that theoretical apparatuses like "electracy" can mitigate the tensions between contemporary mobile, digital making, and the logics of many analytical approaches to digital writing derived from alphabetic print.

Interrogating critical media production and consumption across the life span, Jessica Zacher Pandya and Noah Asher Golden outline a way forward through the potentials and limitations of participatory politics in new spaces for writing and literacies (Chapter 4). Central to this work is the theorization of power and agency in relation to multimodal practices in digital spaces. They are careful not to evoke utopian claims, while providing critiques of representation and collaborative design in contemporary ecologies.

The integration of these refreshingly different yet complementary outlooks results in original work of a deeper kind, characterized by heterogeneity and new possibilities for the expanding parameters of writing and literacies research in digital cultures.

**References**

Bourdieu, P. (2000). *Pascalian Meditations*. Cambridge, UK: Polity Press.
Haas, C. (1996). *Writing technology: Studies on the materiality of literacy*. New Jersey: Laurence Erlbaum Associates.

# 1
# Cosmopolitan Practices, Networks, and Flows of Literacies

Amy Stornaiuolo, Glynda Hull, and Matthew Hall

It is easy to point out the myriad ways writing now permeates our lives: We dash off texts as we wait for a bus, write a report for work with a colleague via Google Docs, update our blogs on our tablets, and post on social media to protest unfair social conditions. Writing now occupies the interstices of our everyday lives, flowing in and across increasingly globalized networks (Appadurai, 1996; Jenkins, Ford, & Green, 2013), as a central means of participating in contemporary life (Freedman, Hull, Higgs, & Booten, 2016). Digitally networked writing practices expand and amplify participation in the social world, as people compose, remix, orchestrate, and assemble symbolic artifacts in ways that connect them with others (Lankshear & Knobel, 2011). Networked writing can be understood as a principal way of participating in textual ecologies, built through the collaborative creation, curation, and circulation of artifacts linked with people in complex networks. As a fundamental part of these ecologies, writing now includes more and more spatially oriented and aesthetically inclined forms across multiple modes, media, and languages (Bezemer & Kress, 2008; Canagarajah, 2012), affording new opportunities for people to collaborate with others to take action in areas of local and global concern (Flower, 2008; Stornaiuolo & Jung, in press).

As people participate in the world by writing with, for, and about others under multiple configurations, they must navigate interactions with those with whom they do not share common ground. Examples of these complicated configurations abound: People can easily comment on news articles and YouTube videos, but the comments sections can also serve to dehumanize, reproducing and exacerbating racist, patriarchal, and homophobic discourses; social media sites allow people to connect across geographical distances, but just as often polarize across ideological ones; blogs provide opportunities for people's voices to be shared and amplified, but those voices can operate outside of mainstream media, speak only to the choir, and be lost amid the sea of online content. As people attempt to communicate across increasingly widening ideological and material divides, such engagements require an ethical set of practices that create space for the kind of dialogic interaction at the heart of humanizing practices (Freire, 1970).

This chapter explores implications of these shifting and unstable practices for writing in digital spaces, particularly the ethical dimensions of writing in relation to others across linguistic, cultural, and ideological diversities. How does networked writing—which includes translingual, multimodal, and collaborative practices, emerging digital tools, and networked spaces for curating and sharing—require people to take other people, ideas, and materials into account in new ways? How do people engage in writing online as a form of action, to transform themselves and the world around them, for purposes of social good? What rhetorical approaches do people take in recognizing, navigating, and challenging different forms of power and privilege online across asymmetrical and unequal global conditions? We take up these questions throughout the chapter as we explore the ethical ramifications of writing in digital spaces and cultures, particularly the role that new forms of networked writing can play in creating equitable social change that recognizes people's full human potential and challenges conditions of injustice.

**Cosmopolitanism in Education: From Shared Humanity to Humanizing Practices**

To theorize how people engage in ethically attuned literacy practices, education scholars have increasingly turned toward cosmopolitanism (e.g., Campano & Ghiso, 2011; Hansen, 2010; Harper, Bean, & Dunkerly, 2010; Hull & Hellmich, in press; Hull, Stornaiuolo, & Sahni, 2010; Juzwik & McKenzie, 2015; Papastephanou, 2002; Rizvi, 2009; Stornaiuolo, 2016; Vasudevan, 2014). Often defined as a form of global citizenship, cosmopolitanism involves "membership in and identification with a world community that transcends locality—whether that locality be tribe, culture, race or nation—and which respects differences nonetheless" (Go, 2013, p. 210). In other words, cosmopolitanism orients us to the ways we understand ourselves in relation to others with whom we are not immediately or visibly connected, as we navigate the moral, ideological, and physical distances between us (Hull & Stornaiuolo, 2014). For literacy scholars concerned with the ethical dimensions of digital practices, cosmopolitanism offers a generative lens for understanding how people rhetorically negotiate multiple localities and distances while recognizing "the essential humanity we all share—not so much despite our differences but by virtue of our differences" (Fine & Boon, 2007, p. 8). Chouliaraki (2016a) calls this effort to understand across differences—by "recognizing the humanity of others and acting upon them without demanding reciprocation"—a "moral project" at the center of a cosmopolitan ethic (p. 3). The idea of recognizing our shared humanity rests at the heart of most definitions of cosmopolitanism (see Kleingeld & Brown, 2013).

What it means to recognize our shared humanity, however, is not an uncomplicated endeavor. Scholars theorizing posthumanism have framed the "human" as a historical construction, pushing back on liberal humanism and undermining human exceptionalism (Hayles, 1999). As technological systems become more visibly intertwined with and inseparable from our bodily ones (Haraway, 1991), posthumanist scholars are questioning what constitutes "human" qualities and where those boundaries fall (and fail), rendering problematic cosmopolitanism's universal ethical commitment to humanity (Pin-Fat, 2013). Of course, critical scholars have long challenged normative conceptions of humanity in cosmopolitanism by rejecting "universalizing" models rooted in Western, elitist, and colonial moral imaginaries (e.g., Appiah, 2006; Bhabha, 1994; Delanty, 2012; Mignolo, 2002; Werbner, 2008). In focusing on grassroots, grounded, everyday forms of negotiating difference and diversity, these critical scholars have theorized a "collective effort to humanize" (Fine & Boon, 2007, p. 8) as a key aspect of cosmopolitanism "from below" that must be paired with critical reflection about social inequality to avoid becoming an uncritical celebration of global togetherness (Chouliaraki, 2016a).

These critical cosmopolitan approaches move scholars away from more static notions of shared *humanity* and toward consideration of the dynamic process of *humanizing* oneself and others through everyday actions paired with critical reflection. Such efforts to understand and historicize "cosmopolitan activity" (Stornaiuolo, 2016) are well aligned with Freirean notions of humanization that center around taking reflective action in the world—because, as Freire (1985) notes, "to transform the world is to humanize it" (p. 70). The process of becoming fully human, for Freire (1970), involves people acting agentively and consciously to shape the world as historical actors in particular social, cultural, and political contexts (cf. Del Carmen Salazar, 2013). A key practice in this process of becoming fully human is dialogue. In cosmopolitanism, dialogue has the potential to transform and humanize the world, with the goal not being consensus or agreement, but mutual learning, enrichment, and reciprocity (Appiah, 2006; Hansen, 2010). We turn now to explore how networked writing practices can serve humanizing ends, not only by functioning as a form of reflective action that can challenge conditions of injustice, but also in fostering conditions under which mutually enriching dialogue can flourish. To do so, we first consider central challenges to that enterprise.

**Central Challenges**

Perhaps the gravest challenge to a cosmopolitan ethic and practice as a framework for networked writing is the vexed historical moment in which we live. Discourses of populism and nativism abound, fueled by fears of increased immigration and a resulting super-diversity, and economic uncertainties and a frustrated awareness of the vast divides that separate the wealthy and the few from the rest. Ironically, the very forces of globalization, which propel the movement of capital and labor and ideas and people across political borders, and which strongly, urgently signal the need for outward facing polities, have inspired an inward turn, as nations grapple each with their own aftermath of vast demographic, economic, and ideological shifts; eruptions; and realignments. Schooling, traditionally a national enterprise, is typically designed to socialize individuals for participation in local communities and in autonomous nation-states, shoring up a labor force for international competition. There have been inroads in recent years, to be sure, as nonprofits and international schools attempt to globalize education, exploring the development of "international mindedness," but these are exceptions that prove the rule of an inward national focus. In such an environment, positioning networked writing as a key site for cosmopolitan practice is both an uphill struggle and a crucial one, a humanizing effort in a dehumanizing time.

So too is the reclamation of cosmopolitanism as a suitable framework for this enterprise. Conventional cosmopolitanism has already been roundly critiqued for its Western origins and elitist associations, and some disciplines have found ways to move past those perceived limitations and embrace cosmopolitanism almost as a given. But in education we've just begun to explore how this philosophy and set of values can usefully be taken up, not only by the privileged but by the marginalized, and not through assumptions of welcome and gratitude but through positions of reciprocity. Silverstone opined eloquently about the moral responsibility of the West and of media to listen to and hear the other. Surely such an attitude of openness is an important gesture of solidarity, but it cannot be the only or the last one, and the positionality of the privileged can't always or usually be the place we start.

As Freire (1970) reminded us long ago, an "authentic education is not carried on by 'A' for 'B' or by 'A' about 'B', but rather by 'A' with 'B.'" What does this admonition mean for writing, for youth, and for teachers in a digital and global age? Pratt (1999) gave us alternatives twenty-five years ago by helpfully naming some of the "literate arts of the contact zone" that might be used by those who must struggle in asymmetrical relations of power: "autoethnography, transculturation, critique, collaboration, bilingualism, mediation, parody, denunciation, imaginary dialogue, vernacular expression" (p. 37). But she also reminded us of the "perils" of writing in the contact zone: "miscomprehension, incomprehension, dead letters, unread masterpieces, absolute heterogeneity of meaning" (p. 37). A central challenge, if we are to embrace cosmopolitanism as a humanizing framework for understanding networked writing in practice, is resisting the paternalism inherent in being privileged to choose to listen, and concomitantly, resisting the insularity of writing in ways that only one's own community can hear and comprehend. Imagine confronting these challenges, which have forever existed, in a digital age, and they become magnified and intensified, but perhaps also offer potential solutions.

## Cosmopolitan Practices in Networked Writing

We turn now to consider three networked writing practices with cosmopolitan potential—literate arts of the contact zone (Pratt, 1999) that we suggest can serve humanizing ends. These are practices we have observed and studied in our work with young people, which we illuminate further in the next section. While certainly subject to the challenges we outline above, these networked writing practices—negotiating visibility, expressing solidarity, and critiquing systems of power—each foster the possibility of reflective action and dialogue. As people imagine and discursively create spaces of inclusion or counternarrate oppressive or marginalizing discourses, these rhetorical acts can work to humanize participants and foster critical reflection. And as people take up positions of reciprocity and openness with one another in their writing, opportunities for mutually enriching dialogue to take root become expanded. While we recognize that these three practices always unfold in particular contexts and under specific historical, political, and cultural conditions, we hope they serve an illustrative purpose here: To suggest that literacy researchers remain attuned to writing practices that position people as historical actors who shape the world around them, especially those practices with cosmopolitan potential, turned to ethical ends.

The first networked writing practice we highlight here is "autoethnographic" (Pratt, 1999, p. 37) in nature and involves people making themselves—or, more precisely, narrated versions of themselves—visible to others. Many times these practices of visibility involve first-person accounts or critical autobiographies (Gutiérrez, 2008), as individuals add their voices to the public sphere. Expressing one's voice publicly—and expecting that one's voice matters—is now a central way young people participate in civil, political, and cultural life (Rheingold, 2008; Zuckerman, 2014). Stornaiuolo and Thomas (2017) have explored how these participatory practices of visibility online represent new forms of youth activism that can disrupt or counternarrate deficit discourses about marginalized youth. One example of how young people are engaging in these practices of visibility to counternarrate dehumanizing discourses is Beltrán's (2015) study of undocumented young people narrating their immigration stories online. As young people created and circulated first-person accounts about being undocumented in the United States, Beltrán shows how their networked writing served to humanize undocumented young people, making their stories visible as a form of collective witnessing of oppression. These young people's efforts to document their everyday realities of injustice were acts of courage and risk, as they made themselves vulnerable in multiple ways by sharing their stories publicly. Certainly not all autoethnographic networked writing practices are ethically alert, particularly those that reproduce or exacerbate conditions of injustice—but we do think the act of making oneself visible, and therefore often vulnerable, can serve the social good: To witness acts of injustice, document lived realities that may be invisible, or counternarrate mainstream discourses that dehumanize (for further discussion of this networked writing practice, see Bakhti's example in Hull et al., 2010).

The second practice we suggest has cosmopolitan potential is the use of networked writing to express solidarity. Chouliaraki's (2013) work on solidarity is instructive here; she argues that while people are now exercising their voices in more democratic fashion, these expressions do not always lead us to recognize others' humanity because of "the deep inequalities of power that selectively enable some voices to be heard and recognised as worthy of our solidarity and not others" (p. 279). While expressions of solidarity are always rooted in these power asymmetries, they can also serve a powerful inclusive function in online communities, as they might work toward "the imagination of a safe and fairer global order for every human being" (Chouliaraki, 2016b, p. 4). This act of imagining a more equitable global order requires new configurations between people, ideally that position oneself and others in reciprocal relationships. As a networked writing practice, expressing solidarity with others requires a careful negotiation of the power inequalities Chouliaraki warns about, as writers rhetorically signal openness and a willingness to listen, but also awareness of whose voices are positioned in the speaking and listening roles. Writers must guard against appropriation or paternalism as they work toward reciprocity.

Finally, we consider the rhetorical means by which networked writers engage in a critique of relations of power, recognizing their positions of relative privilege even as they work to decenter those positions. Scholarship by Campano and colleagues (e.g., Campano, Ghiso, & Sanchez, 2013) illustrates the importance of recognizing and valuing people's multiple epistemic positions, arguing that people from minoritized social locations have unique perspectives on issues of inequality that can challenge normative viewpoints (see also Moya, 2001). Networked writers often work to recognize and value these multiple positions by engaging in collaborative practices to build knowledge together for a shared world. For example, these efforts to co-construct knowledge, particularly from minoritized positions, can be seen in hashtag activism (Williams, 2015) as people join together on Twitter to collectively discuss a topic via a shared hashtag. One of the most salient hashtags in the US has been #BlackLivesMatter (BLM), a movement begun by three Women of Color after teen Trayvon Martin was killed in 2012 (Carney, 2016).

The hashtag gained momentum in the protests that erupted nationwide after the killing of Michael Brown in Ferguson, MO, sparking a movement that collectively challenges "racialized policing, the vulnerability of black bodies, and the problematic ways in which blackness is perceived as a constant threat" (Bonilla & Rosa, 2015, p. 8). While hashtag activism represents one way people have been using ethical rhetorical practices to recognize and legitimize different ways of knowing, young people are regularly using new tools and networks to "restory themselves" (Thomas & Stornaiuolo, 2016, p. 313)—that is, to write themselves into narratives and discourses that have historically excluded them (Gates, 1986). We suggest that these networked writing practices that name power and privilege and the systems that serve to dehumanize can be turned to ethical ends, as people individually and collectively "restory," challenge, and decenter privileged viewpoints.

**Implications for Educational Practice: Write4Change**

To illustrate the cosmopolitan potential of these three digital writing practices, we turn now to one context in which young people are engaged in writing as a form of social action, the Write4Change (W4C) online writing community (see Stornaiuolo & Jung, in press). Working collaboratively with a group of teachers, youth, and partners, we designed the W4C community to virtually link educators and adolescent students committed to multilingual, multicultural, and multimodal writing for social justice. In the online global community, adolescents from countries including Pakistan, India, South Korea, the UK, Canada, and the US (currently) engage in inquiry to action projects that aim to intervene in the world around them. Examples of networked writing projects that young people have designed include documentaries about domestic violence, essays about schools' overreliance on testing, blogs about Islamophobia, and digital posters about gender discrimination.

In the W4C community, youth create and share digital writing at various stages of completion. Using hashtags to organize their writing, youth post brainstormed ideas, in-progress work, inspirational or creative postings, and material they want to share beyond the network. W4C positions young people to write about social issues they would like to impact. Because they post their work in a global forum with peers who represent diverse linguistic and ideological experiences, critically reflecting on their own position in tandem with acknowledging others' perspectives and rights is at the forefront of students' networked participation. Many of the topics they have chosen directly or subtly question or challenge systems of power. While we acknowledge that stratification and "othering" can and does arise from these interactions, in the following sections, we offer examples of young people who turned these three networked writing practices toward ethical ends, opening possibilities for dialogue, and reflective action.

18 • Amy Stornaiuolo, Glynda Hull, and Matthew Hall

**Negotiating Visibility: Claiming Identities and Creating Space**

The first networked writing practice with cosmopolitan potential that we traced in W4C was autoethnographic, as young people made themselves visible, and vulnerable, in different ways. While sometimes this took the form of first-person accounts, similar to the young people in Beltrán's (2015) study who shared their own stories of marginalization to powerful effect, other times writers combined modes to "counternarrate inequality" (Duncan-Andrade, 2007) by making themselves (and the issues they were writing about) visible—often in a literal sense. We share one example of a young writer in the community who designed a project to make visible those with mental illness, creating a series of self-portraits that revealed the dehumanization and marginalization of those who suffer stigma with mental illness.

In four panels of original art accompanied by writing, Lexy (name used with permission) cast herself as a central figure, as someone grappling with mental health issues (Figure 1.1). In the rightmost panel of the artwork, Lexy represented herself as a young person with mental illness, asking in the caption, "Am I going insane?" To convey anguish, she juxtaposed a photograph of herself in a distressed position, clutching her head (visible in the top right of Figure 1.1) with an illustrated

**Figure 1.1** Lexy's project about mental health issues

representation of the image. Similar to the ways photography has been used in social work to document and humanize a variety of social issues (Huff, 1998), Lexy's post works to complicate and reposition the stigma of mental illness by making herself the face (and body) of schizophrenia across multiple representations. She discussed the act of making herself the subject of the photos and writing as a deliberate way of addressing the stigma of mental illness, literally putting her identity and body on the line and making herself visible, and vulnerable, to others in the community.

In her commentary, Lexy further made herself vulnerable, sharing that several members of her family struggled with mental illness: "Many family members of mine suffer from mental health issues and I wanted to really express this through my art. To show others what it's really like, that these things are real and these disorders are not just excuses." By narrating herself as a member of this stigmatized group through image and positioning, Lexy chose not to take a documentary stance, depicting others' experiences, but placed herself as the object of the reader's gaze. This act of humanizing, whereby she gave what could have been an abstract issue, mental illness, a face and name, grounded it in her personal experience to challenge the stigma (and silence) that often accompanies the topic. To negotiate visibility in the community, Lexy made explicit her commitments by claiming and enacting a particular identity and thus brought awareness to an issue important to her. Such an effort to use her voice (and image) to counternarrate dehumanizing discourses about mental illness—offering herself and her personal experiences as a ground to such an effort—made possible spaces for dialogue. That is, she signaled to others that she would be open to talking and thinking *with* others about the issue, one of the first steps we found was necessary in creating spaces for dialogue and understanding to flourish. The practice of rhetorically negotiating visibility offered potential for cosmopolitan action, particularly when young writers, like Lexy, used different writing strategies to expand opportunities for dialogue by positioning themselves as open, vulnerable, and willing to contribute their voices to illuminate causes of common concern.

**Expressing Solidarity: Imagining Equitable and Reciprocal Relationships**

The second networked writing practice we examine is the act of expressing solidarity, not, as Chouliaraki (2013) reminds us, as merely or only a spectator but as an empathetic attempt to imagine someone's reality and a more equitable social order. While young people regularly sought to put themselves in other's shoes (much as Lexy attempted in her artwork), such efforts to express solidarity were not easily managed. One of the central challenges involved how to express solidarity while not positioning others as vulnerable, objects of our mediated gaze, or in need of our (paternalistic) assistance. In other words, young people struggled to find and express reciprocal relationships with others. Nonetheless, we want to call attention to the ways young people persisted through the challenge and worked toward solidarity rhetorically.

We turn to one young man from the UK, Sam (real name used with permission), and his efforts to express solidarity—and his struggles to do so in reciprocal, sensitive ways. Sam regularly and thoughtfully posted about current events worldwide that he felt promoted justice and equity. In one particular post we examine here, he called attention to the BLM movement that had recently gained national prominence in the US (see Figure 1.2). As a young man outside of the US national context, he was removed from BLM, though certainly he was aware of the dehumanizing, racist discourses and practices that gave rise to the movement and were circulated through the international news media. Despite his outsider status, he was keen to call attention to the "Black Lives Matter organization" as an important movement to promote racial justice that was rooted in the US but spread worldwide. This post also served as an early introduction to a writing project Sam planned to take on. Paired with the image in Figure 1.2, he wrote: "I will be researching into some of the deaths of innocent black citizens who were killed by white police officers in the USA. I will be looking in detail as to what happened with specific deaths such as the death of Eric Garner and Michael Brown of which triggered the protests from people all over the world." Later, he continued by asking others to "Please tell me your own opinions of the tragic events in particular how you feel about it and whether or not you feel affected by it."

Like Lexy, Sam combined his text with image to create greater impact in the community. He included an image foregrounding two Black women holding protest signs, drawing specific attention through his text to the woman on the left holding a sign asking, "Is my son next?" Using image, specifically documentary photography, to explore the lived complexities of experiences has a long-standing history in social research and policy change (see Russell & Diaz, 2011; Szto, Furman, & Langer, 2005). In featuring this photo, Sam drew on the affordances of image to contextualize while also evoking emotion—working to humanize the protesters by identifying with them personally and situating those struggles historically. While potentially participating in "othering" a group of people through posting an image, by combining the image with text that explained his interest in researching the BLM movement, Sam attempted to interrupt such patterns by using the networked space to imagine how he could learn more and intervene.

**Figure 1.2** Sam's post about #BlackLivesMatter

An important dimension of expressing solidarity through networked writing involves positioning oneself in relation to others and the world discursively. While the photo alone might locate him as outside the movement looking in, his text linked these local BLM events to worldwide protests and acknowledged the need for interaction and communication about the topic by formally addressing his audience with requests for their reactions. In doing so, he positioned himself and his imagined audience in conversation with each other, acknowledging the varied viewpoints and perspectives that might be held on the topic but also expressing openness to discussing core issues of equity, race, and power.

**Critiquing Systems of Power: Naming Conditions of Injustice**

The final networked writing practice we examine involves young people using various rhetorical means to name conditions of injustice and foreground multiple voices and perspectives on issues. We found that the practice of critiquing systems of power involved young people regularly questioning their own positions in relation to others, as we highlight in the following example. In a collaborative writing project by a group of students in Korea, the PJPK team was a group of four students who all shared an interest in working in education in their future. In their project, they co-constructed knowledge about different ways that various countries structure educational opportunities for adolescents compared to the opportunities they had access to in Korea. They created a short newspaper offering a critique of the Korean education system, which included a description of the current system, comparisons to other countries, individual opinions of the four writers, and results of a survey conducted by the team to gather perceptions of education opportunities from peers (see Figure 1.3 for one page from the newspaper). Throughout the newspaper, the four students worked to reconcile their different opinions and positions about their education system by locating those viewpoints in relation to others (e.g., through surveys, research into different global opportunities with which they were familiar, comparison charts, and opinion pieces).

One of the students' central arguments revolved around the injustice of the Korean system, which they felt limited and narrowed students' potential career options. They described the current process that required Korean teenagers to choose liberal arts or natural sciences as a career focus early in their studies, which then dictated the kinds of classes and career paths available to the student. Each of the writers included an opinion piece about the effects of such a system toward the end of the newspaper, with one student writing, for example: "I think it is too early for students to choose their path during high school years. Even Confucius, the great saint of China, set up his aim at the age of 30." Each of the students shared personal experiences to support their opinions, suggesting that they had suffered, and known others who suffered, from narrow expectations and high pressure. Through their collaborative writing process, the students engaged in reflection about their individual and collective experiences as they worked to trace their positions and assert their opinions.

Throughout the newspaper, the students described the impact of the Korean education system and the power it asserts over teenagers by including charts, graphs, images, and texts to make their argument tangible. In the opening to the newspaper, PJPK specifically name how this structure, which forces teenagers to choose a career focus at an early stage in the process, "has caused some problems for students who are not convinced of their dream." The students' critique of the rigidity of this system involved them naming their own experiences and positions as students, with each of the four students describing different positions and perspectives and their efforts to negotiate those different stances. They further explore differentiating opinions through a survey of over 150 students, reminding readers of the ways this system of power fails to take into account the perspectives of the very youth they claim to serve. The newspaper can serve as an example of the ways collectively challenging privilege and power can be a humanizing act, by explicitly naming injustice and working to legitimize the underrepresented voices of the youth who experience education in this system.

### America's Education System

Most koreans think graduating university is the last process of fundamental education. However, in America, people consider highschool education as a stage of adult education.

So, besides curriculums for going to college, highschool in America provide various curriculums for fostering professional. For example, students who prepare for college concentrate on cultural studies or mathematics; Whereas, students who want career choose accounting, managing and industry field, etc. Highschools in America open these classes or provide it by connecting with other schools. The most notable differences are selection and concentration. There is variety of choice and students can concentrate on classes which they chose. Korean highschool students study about 15 subjects for 3 years. On the other hand, there are about 150 subjects in public school in Virginia, so students select 6 subjects and learn them for 3 years.

### Finland's Secondary Education

Finland's Secondary Education is same as Korean's highschool education. There are two areas; Vocational school and Upper secondary school. Vocational school incubates career education for finding employment. However, students who graduated vocational school can also get a college degree. Attending two kinds of school is allowed.

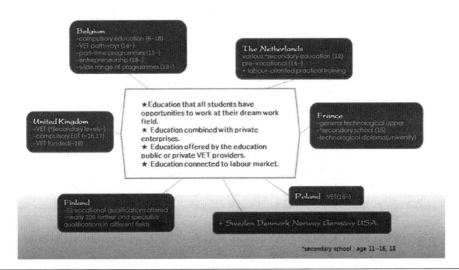

**Figure 1.3** One page of PJPK newspaper

## Future Directions

In her scholarship on the media representations of human suffering, Chouliaraki (2006, 2013) has called attention to the ways in which injustice is reproduced discursively. In her earlier work (2006), she examined how spectators in Western countries related to images produced on television of the suffering of distant others—in India, Somalia, and other countries remote from the West. She paid attention to the ways in which the news media shapes or mediates how we experience faraway misfortune, embedding in the selection of images and language particular values and mores that position viewers, or spectators as she calls them, to feel and act and engage in particular ways—to view some sufferers, for example, as worthy of attention and empathy and others as undeserving of these. She makes the point that whether viewers of media adopt cosmopolitan attitudes and actions depends on how the stories are told through the media. More recently, Chouliaraki (2013) has explored changes in media representations over the last four decades in how we express solidarity with others. She argues that images and multimedia displays of vulnerable others, in connection with related institutional and political shifts, have resulted in a different kind of moral self that she labels an "ironic spectator"—someone who is skeptical but open to action. Chouliaraki holds out hope, in fact, that the human capacity for imagination, to put ourselves in someone else's shoes, to experience in even a small or temporary way that person's suffering, can be harnessed in this new media age for ethical ends and actions.

We are hopeful, too, and see in the networked participation of youth in the W4C community the opportunity to foster dispositions that are alert to dehumanization and that are instead at the ready to humanize self and other through reflective action in the world. In some ways, the sharing of images and commentary by youth to take forward conversations about social justice, such as the photo of a suffering mother at a Black Lives Matter protest, could be seen as part and parcel of the larger media-driven discourse on human suffering that Chouliaraki so helpfully theorizes. But in other ways, this project and youth's writing potentially interrupts that discourse, positioning youth, not CNN or BuzzFeed, as authors, curators, and commentators. Rather than spectating, youth are participating in an educational project that explicitly asks them and organizes them to "write for change" and thereby to experiment with, try on for size, inhabit an ethic of caring and a sensibility for doing. This expectation sets apart the work of youth in W4C, potentially distinguishing their praxis from passive viewership or unreflective action, even as if perforce is influenced by the dominant "limit situations" (Freire, 1970) of our era.

The ethical dimensions of literacy practices we understand to be intertwined with aesthetic, creative, and rhetorical dimensions as people engage their capacities to question and challenge the status quo and to work toward human rights and equity (see Hull & Stornaiuolo, 2014). In our view, this intertwining—its description, range, and variation—has yet to be fully documented and theorized. Nor has its import for writers been articulated, especially those who desire to influence an audience to think and act differently via a constructed, shared sense of moral agency. In analyzing witnessing as a news genre, Chouliaraki (2013) comments on its "irreducible aesthetic dimension," going on to argue that, far from indexing an external reality, it is a "narrative performance with moral effects" (p. 152). She even offers the metaphor of theater to account for the rhetorical nature of news representations. In W4C, as in other networked communities that privilege the sharing of multimodal, translingual, and sometimes collaboratively composed texts, there is a treasure trove of artifacts waiting to be sorted, analyzed, appreciated, and understood for what they reveal about how the complex dimensionality of ethical engagement with global audiences for social good. There is also substantial work to be done in exploring how people develop the capacity to take another's perspective and acknowledge their rights and suffering as well as the role that writing and symbolization generally might play in that process.

## References

Appadurai, A. (1996). *Modernity at large: Cultural dimensions of globalization.* Minneapolis: University of Minnesota Press.
Appiah, K. A. (2006). *Cosmopolitanism: Ethics in a world of strangers.* New York, NY: W.W. Norton.
Beltrán, C. (2015). "Undocumented, unafraid, unapologetic": DREAM activists, immigrant politics, and the queering of democracy. In D. Allen & J. S. Light (Eds.), *From voice to influence: Understanding citizenship in a digital age* (pp. 80–104). Chicago, IL: University of Chicago Press.
Bezemer, J., & Kress, G. (2008). Writing in multimodal texts: A social semiotic account of designs for learning. *Written Communication, 25*(2), 166–195.

Bhabha, H. (1994). *The location of culture*. London, UK: Routledge.
Brandt, D. (2014). *The rise of writing: Redefining mass literacy*. Cambridge, UK: Cambridge University Press.
Bonilla, Y., & Rosa, J. (2015). #Ferguson: Digital protest, hashtag ethnography, and the racial politics of social media in the United States. *American Ethnologist*, *42*(1), 4–17.
Campano, G., & Ghiso, M. P. (2011). Immigrant students as cosmopolitan intellectuals. In S. A. Wolf, K. Coats, P. Enciso, & C. A. Jenkins (Eds.), *Handbook of research on children's and young adult literature* (pp. 164–176). New York, UK: Routledge.
Campano, G., Ghiso, M. P., & Sanchez, L. (2013). "Nobody knows the… amount of a person": Elementary students critiquing dehumanization through organic critical literacies. *Research in the Teaching of English*, *48*(1), 98–125.
Canagarajah, S. (2012). *Translingual practice: Global Englishes and cosmopolitan relations*. London, UK: Routledge.
Carney, N. (2016). All lives matter, but so does race: Black Lives Matter and the evolving role of social media. *Humanity & Society*, *40*(2), 1–20.
Chouliaraki, L. (2006). *The spectatorship of suffering*. London, UK: Sage.
Chouliaraki, L. (2013). Re-mediation, inter-mediation, trans-mediation. *Journalism Studies 14*(2), 267–283.
Chouliaraki, L. (2016a). Cosmopolitanism. In J. Gray & L. Ouelette (Eds.) *Media studies*. New York, NY: New York University Press.
Chouliaraki, L. (2016b). *The ironic spectator: Solidarity in the age of post-humanitarianism*. Hoboken, NY: Wiley. Kindle Edition.
Couldry, N. (2012). *Media, society, world*. Cambridge, UK: Polity Press.
Cruz, C. (2012). Making curriculum from scratch: "Testimonio" in an urban classroom. *Equity & Excellence in Education*, *45*(3), 460–471.
Delanty, G. (2012). The idea of critical cosmopolitanism. In G. Delanty (Ed.), *The Routledge handbook of cosmopolitanism studies* (pp. 38–46). London, UK: Routledge.
Del Carmen Salazar, M. (2013). A humanizing pedagogy: Reinventing the principles and practice of education as a journey toward liberation. *Review of Research in Education*, *37*(1), 121–148.
Duncan-Andrade, J. M. R. (2007). Urban youth and the counter-narration of inequality. *Transforming Anthropology*, *15*(1), 26–37.
Fine, R., & Boon, V. (2007). Cosmopolitanism: Between past and future. *European Journal of Social Theory*, *10*(1), 5–16.
Flower, L. (2008). *Community literacy and the rhetoric of public engagement*. Carbondale: Southern Illinois University Press.
Freedman, S., Hull, G., Higgs, J., & Booten, K. (2016). Teaching writing in a digital and global age: Toward access, learning, and development for all. In D. H. Gitomer & C. A. Bell (Eds.), *Handbook of research on teaching* (5th ed., pp. 1389–1449). Washington, DC: American Educational Research Association.
Freire, P. (1970). *Pedagogy of the oppressed*. 30th Anniversary Edition (2000) with an introduction by Donaldo Macedo (pp. 71–86). New York, NY: Continuum.
Freire, P. (1985). *The politics of education: Culture, power, and liberation*. New York, NY: Continuum Publishing.
Gates, H. L., Jr. (1986). 'Race' as the trope of the world. In H. L. Gates Jr. (Ed.) *"Race," writing, and difference* (pp. 590–597). Chicago, IL: University of Chicago Press.
Go, J. (2013). Fanon's postcolonial cosmopolitanism. *European Journal of Social Theory*, *16*(2), 208–225.
Gutiérrez, K. D. (2008). Developing a sociocritical literacy in the third space. *Reading Research Quarterly*, *43*(2), 148–164.
Hansen, D. T. (2010). Cosmopolitanism and education: A view from the ground. *Teachers College Record*, *112*(1), 1–30.
Haraway, D. J. (1991). *Simians, cyborgs, and women: The reinvention of nature*. London, UK: Free Association Books.
Harper, H., Bean, T. W., & Dunkerly, J. (2010). Cosmopolitanism, globalization and the field of adolescent literacy. *Canadian and International Education*, *39*(3), Article 2.
Hayles, K. N. (1999). *How we became posthuman: Virtual bodies in cybernetics, literature, and informatics*. Chicago, IL: University of Chicago Press.
Huff, D. D. (1998). Every picture tells a story. *Social Work*, *43*(6), 576–583.
Hull, G. A., & Hellmich, E. (in press). Locating the global. *Teachers College Record*.
Hull, G., & Stornaiuolo, A. (2014). Cosmopolitan literacies, social networks, and "proper distance": Striving to understand in a global world. *Curriculum Inquiry*, *44*(1), 15–44.
Hull, G. A., Stornaiuolo, A., & Sahni, U. (2010). Cultural citizenship and cosmopolitan practice: Global youth communicate online. *English Education*, *42*(4), 331–367.
Jenkins, H., Ford, S., & Green, J. (2013). *Spreadable media: Creating value and meaning in a networked culture*. New York, NY: New York University Press.
Juzwik, M. M., & McKenzie, C. (2015). Writing, religious faith, and rooted cosmopolitan dialogue: Portraits of two American evangelical men in a public school English classroom. *Written Communication*, *32*(2), 1–29.
Kleingeld, P., & Brown, E. (2013). Cosmopolitanism. In E. N. Zalta (Ed.), *The Stanford Encyclopedia of Philosophy*. Retrieved September 22, 2014, from http://plato.stanford.edu/archives/fall2014/entries/cosmopolitanism/.

Mignolo, W. D. (2002). The many faces of the cosmo-polis: Border thinking and critical cosmopolitanism. *Public Culture*, *12*(3), 721–748.

Moya, P. (2001). *Learning from experience: Minority identities, multicultural struggles.* Los Angeles: University of California Press.

Papastephanou, M. (2002). Arrows not yet fired: Cultivating cosmopolitanism through education. *Journal of Philosophy of Education*, *36*(1), 69–86.

Pin-Fat, V. (2013). Cosmopolitanism and the end of humanity: A grammatical reading of posthumanism. *International Political Sociology*, *7*(3), 241–257.

Pratt, M. L. (1999). Arts of the contact zone. In D. Bartholomae & A. Petrosky (Eds.), *Ways of reading* (5th ed., pp. 582–596). New York, NY: Bedford/St. Martin's Press.

Rheingold, H. (2008). Using participatory media and public voice to encourage civic engagement. In W. L. Bennett (Ed.), *Civic life online: Learning how digital media can engage youth* (pp. 97–118). Cambridge, MA: MIT Press.

Rizvi, F. (2009). Toward cosmopolitan learning. *Discourse: Studies in the Cultural Politics of Education*, *30*(3), 253–268.

Russell, A. C., & Diaz, N. D. (2011). Photography in social work research: Using visual image to humanize findings. *Qualitative Social Work*, *12*(4), 433–453.

Silverstone, R. (2007). *Media and morality: On the rise of the mediapolis.* Cambridge, UK: Polity.

Sobré-Denton, M. (2015). Virtual intercultural bridgework: Social media, virtual cosmopolitanism, and activist community-building. *New Media & Society*, *18*(8), 1715–1731.

Stornaiuolo, A. (2016). Teaching in global collaborations: Navigating challenging conversations through cosmopolitan activity. *Teaching and Teacher Education*, *59*, 503–513.

Stornaiuolo, A., & Jung, J. K. (in press). Public engagement and digital authoring: Korean adolescents write for/as action. In R. Naqvi & J. Rowsell (Eds.), *Literacy in Transcultural, Cosmopolitan Times*.

Stornaiuolo, A., & Thomas, E. E. (in press). Disrupting educational inequalities through youth digital activism. *Review of Research in Education*, *41*.

Szto, P., Furman, R., & Langer, C. (2005). Poetry and photography: An exploration into expressive/creative qualitative research. *Qualitative Social Work*, *4*(2), 135–156.

Thomas, E. E., & Stornaiuolo, A. (2016). Restorying the self: Bending toward textual justice. *Harvard Educational Review*, *86*(3), 313–338.

Vasudevan, L. (2014). Multimodal cosmopolitanism: Cultivating belonging in everyday moments with youth. *Curriculum Inquiry*, *44*(1), 45–67.

Werbner, P. (2008). Towards a new cosmopolitan anthropology. In P. Werbner (Ed.), *Anthropology and the new cosmopolitanism* (pp. 1–29). Oxford, UK: Berg Publishers.

Williams, S. (2015). Digital defense: Black feminists resist violence with hashtag activism. *Feminist Media Studies*, *15*(2), 341–344.

Zuckerman, E. (2014). New media, new civics? *Policy & Internet*, *6*(2), 151–168.

# 2
# Sensory Literacies, the Body, and Digital Media

Kathy A. Mills, Len Unsworth, and Beryl Exley

The human senses have always been vital to literacy practices but are seldom acknowledged within literacy studies in education. Historically, the senses have been central to the aesthetics of representation across cultures (Howes & Classen, 2014). The senses are essential to everyday communication practices, necessitated by an expanding range of new technologies that interact with a greater range of the sensorium. Devos (2014, p. 68) contends: "Sensory perception constitutes the primordial channel through which a person acquires knowledge about the material world." So too, the senses are primordial to channels of communication with the world and with others. What is needed in current understandings of literacy practices is systematic attention to the role of the full sensorium evoked in the process of meaning making.

In this chapter, we build up examples of the sensorial dimensions of reading, extending Mills' (2016) theory of sensory literacies to focus on the role of haptics and interpretive meaning-making possibilities with interactive tablet e-books. The theory of sensory literacies concerns the multisensory nature of literacy and communication practices that varies across cultures, practices, and technologies. This theory extends ongoing work located in sensory studies more broadly and draws on an anthropology of the senses. Some of the key principles include as follows: (a) the prioritization of the role of the human body in communication practices; (b) a recognition that the mind is not separate from the body, nor the role of the body taken for granted, but mind and body are seen as integral to literacy practices; and (c) a critique of Western hierarchies of knowledge, which privilege the visual over other forms of perception and expression, at the expense of researching the whole body in communication practices.

Of particular interest is the neglected realm of the nonvisual senses, including haptic communication (involving touch), olfaction (smell), taste, and locomotion (Mills, 2016). This has been demonstrated through sensory ethnographic research in which kinesis—movement of the body, limbs, hands, and feet—was central to the digital filmmaking of Indigenous and non-Indigenous children (Mills, Comber, & Kelly, 2013). The children filmed themselves as they glided down slides and balanced on walls, or used breath to blow dandelions. Walking feet and climbing bodies were salient in the children's films, essential to both the process and product of text making. It is timely for literacy educators to attend more consciously to the senses in the study of communication practices in everyday life and in education sites.

There has been an upsurge of agreement among philosophers, sociologists, ecologists, ethnographers, and sensory anthropologists that the role of the body must be taken into account seriously in theories of knowing, perceiving, and practising (Howes, 2003; Pink, 2009). The burgeoning sensorial turn in literacy studies has been foregrounded by a paradigm shift across the social sciences. This shift is a critique of ocularcentrism, which privileges what is seen with the eyes over other modes of perception. As Howes (1991, p. 3) argues, a central tenet of sensory studies is to recognize the "visual and textual biases of the Western episteme." It is only by beginning here that "we can hope to make sense of how life is lived in other cultural settings" (p. 3). Likewise, from the perspective of "sensory literacies," it is only by understanding the hegemony of sight that we can hope to make sense of how the full sensorium is intimately involved in communication (Mills, 2016).

Here, we focus on the role of the affordances of the touch screen and interactive e-book design in the process of navigating the text to make meaning. We also highlight examples of the sensorial dimensions of primary classroom literacy practices, including handwriting lessons and process drama. In doing so, we aim to expound a revitalized way of conceptualizing the multisensoriality of literacy practices in an era of new communications and new pedagogic possibilities.

**Dominance of the Visual**

The privileging of sight has blinded literacy theorists to the central role of the senses in communication, such as touch and kinesis (movement, including movement of the feet). Societies and cultures ascribe varying values and meanings to different sensory perceptions and experiences (Howes & Classen, 2014). An historical view of the senses affords an appreciation of why the senses matter to literacy practices, why they have been ignored for so long, and why they matter now. In Western society, there has been a long period of empiricism in which objective truth is determined by what can be observed through the eyes. The dominance of the visual mode over other forms of human perception has influenced many disciplines (Howes, 1991; Porteous, 1990). However, societies and cultures beyond the West have given attention to a range of multisensorial experiences, including sight, sound, touch, movement, smell, and taste. For example, Feld (1991, p. 81) elaborates the varieties of Kaluli drum sounds of the Southern Highlands of Papua New Guinea that actively "embody deeply felt sentiments" of the Kaluli—a symbolic system, based on a socially organized acoustic assemblage.

Yet even in early Western history, such as in ancient Rome (500 BC–500 CE), attention was given to the senses and to social identity, including cultural meanings that extended well beyond vision. There was a close connection between the senses and social status, and social outsiders were linked to unacceptable sights, smells, and sounds associated with manual labor and dirty work (Toner, 2014). In the second half of the Middle Ages (1000–1450), sculptures were often created to evoke emotions through the senses of touch and sight, such as through the practice of liturgical dramas for pilgrims (Palazzo, 2014).

During the period of the Enlightenment (1650–1800), the flow of printed materials from the presses increased impressively. This was a time of accelerated literacy rates and the role of vision gained prominence for accessing specialized knowledge. Yet the intensification of the role of vision did not occur in isolation from other senses, as talk was still vital for gaining news and information in the taverns. Listening and speaking practices, such as reading aloud and listening to sermons, were important forms of learning. Significant social meanings were attached to the sounds of bells to mark worships, births, deaths, and other announcements in townships (Rath, 2014).

In contemporary societies, sensorial and embodied actions in social life are performed everyday, such as in occupational (Green & Hopwood, 2015) and domestic duties of many kinds (Wall, 2010), in exercise and recreation (Headrick Taylor & Hall, 2013), and in the performance of the arts (e.g., Wilf, 2010). The role of the senses and the body has been acknowledged in literacy practices, such as in writing with technologies (Haas, 1995), digital video production (Potter, 2010), claymation figure making (Mills, 2010), filming places and playgrounds (Mills et al., 2013), and tablet technologies (Flewitt, Kucirkova, & Messer, 2014; Walsh & Simpson, 2014). The increased focus on the senses has been called a sensual revolution or paradigm shift that has sought to focus on the corporeality of social interaction (Howes, 2003).

**Touch across Cultures and Time**

Touch has only recently received attention in literacy studies and semiotics (e.g., Bezemer & Kress, 2014). This may be attributed in part to changes to the materiality of the book and associated changes to the sensorial engagement of the body in the interpretative practices of reading and literacies (Do Rozario, 2012; Mills, 2016). Irrespective of the dematerialization inherent in many historical accounts of literacy practices, touch has always been an important means of communication across many cultures and throughout history. In modern psychology of the West, touch is critical in a baby's first experiences of the world, particularly through sharing physical contact with a mother's body, which influences a child's thoughts and feelings throughout life (Ong, 1991). Touch is considered vital to the construction of a child's first utterances. This is not only true of Western society. A conspicuous example of touch in infant life is a Moroccan ritual in which a mother and her new baby are rubbed daily with a mixture of henna, mastic, oil, sugar, marjoram, mint, sugar, walnut bark, and kohl. The crying child is held above the smoke of burning incense, providing a rich sensory experience associated with protective touch and soothing aromas (Griffin, 1991).

Touch has been ascribed many complex and contradictory meanings throughout history, denoted by Aristotle as an elementary form of sense, functioning through direct contact, like taste, and essential for well-being. Yet touch is also deemed morally inferior to the other senses (Synnott, 1991). For Aristotle, touch and taste are animal senses. So too, in the 1900s, the visual work of paintings was always regarded more highly than the technical craftwork required to prepare the canvas or frame the artworks. Sight was regarded as more noble than touch, and the artist more visionary than the common craftsperson (Daley, 2014). The Greek or Cartesian dualistic separation of the mind and body has continued to influence many disciplines. Disembodied accounts of communication, learning, and reading reflect a centuries-old epistemology that places knowledge obtained through reason or cognition above knowledge that is derived through the senses. Such accounts render invisible the bodily dimensions of lived experiences (Green & Hopwood, 2015).

The advent of touch screen technologies, such as tablet and smartphone apps, have opened up a range of playful potentials for children's sensorial literacy learning with digital media, and these interpretive potentials differ from the kinds of touch that are involved in reading conventional printed books. Many video game technologies are now responsive to much more than pressing buttons on the game controls, including swiping, tapping, dragging, shaking, and tilting. This can be accompanied by human breath and voice activation. Motion sensing technologies in games are responsive to the users' whole body movements, including the movement of the hands and feet. As Mills (2016, p. 39) has argued, "It is not that the technologies of communication have made the senses matter for the first time to literacy practice." Rather, the context of increased affordances of multisensory response technologies has highlighted how "bodies…are central to the practical accomplishment of literacy" in its widened array of forms (Mills, 2016, p. 139). As the advent of the printing press afforded new status to the sense of vision in the hierarchy of the Western episteme, so too do digital technologies afford new status to the senses of touch and movement.

**Sensory Elements of Tablet Picture Book Apps**

Sensory literacies are readily appreciated through digital media and concomitant new bodily engagement with multimodal text and interpretative practices. An example of this is the exploration of picture book apps designed for touch devices such as tablet computers or smartphones. Many picture book apps are adaptations of existing picture books, although some have been developed independently of book versions (Sargeant, 2015). Picture book apps are stand-alone mobile applications as distinct from e-books or animated e-books, which require reading apps (Zhao & Unsworth, 2017).

A defining feature of picture book apps is their interactivity, entailing the bodily engagement of their readers, most significantly for sensory literacies, through physical interaction with the touch screen. The touch design involves touch-sensitive areas of the screen, in the form of buttons or hotspots, that can be activated through finger movements, such as tapping, swiping, and drawing the thumb and fingers together in a pinching movement on the screen. Conversely, haptic interaction can involve moving the thumb and fingers apart from a closed position, as well as by larger movements, such as shaking the mobile device. Recent research has begun to explore the meaning-making potential of this aspect of interactivity in negotiating the interpretive possibilities of picture book apps (Zhao & Unsworth, 2017). Here, we compare a picture book app with the paper version from which it was adapted to show how bodily engagement through the touch design of the app involves the reader in constructing interpretive possibilities for the narrative in ways that are distinctively different from those available through reading the book version.

Firstly, we outline the typology of "touch interactives" in picture book apps described by Zhao and Unsworth (2017). We illustrate these in the picture book app of *The Heart and the Bottle* adapted from the picture book of the same name by award-winning author, Oliver Jeffers (2009). We apply systemic functional semiotic (SFS) accounts that elaborate the metafunctions or dimensions of meaning in texts (Halliday & Matthiessen, 2004; O'Halloran & Lim, 2014).

Two kinds of touch design were identified by Zhao and Unsworth (2017). The first involves "extratext" interactivity. An example of this is a hotspot in the form of an icon of a microphone, which signifies its functionality in activating an audio recording. The second kind of touch design is "intratext" interactivity—interactivity that is not just a function of the technology, but a resource for making meaning within the narrative context of the picture book app. These hotspots are typically part of the images that are the characters or background in the visual portrayal of the narrative. For example, in *The Heart and the Bottle*, when the app user drags the little girl toward the top of the screen, she gradually turns into a grown-up, and a bottle appears around her neck. In this book, the "extratext" touch design includes a "hint" button, which when tapped produces a dotted line indicating the intratext hotspot and the type of touch gesture required for activation. While a detailed account of touch design in picture book apps is provided in Zhao and Unsworth (2017), in the discussion here, the focus will be on intratext touch design and the activation of sensory literacy experience. In intratext touch design, the interactivity is not simply a function of the technology but is also a resource for making meaning in the context of picture book apps. Physical tapping or swiping of the screen, for example, is also a semiotic or meaning-making action, and hence, integral to interpretive processes of sensory literacies.

The story of *The Heart and the Bottle* portrays a little girl's journey through grief as she grows to adulthood. In the orientation the reader is introduced to an unnamed white girl "whose head was filled with all the curiosities of the world." She was close to a paternal figure depicted in the drawings—perhaps her father or grandfather—with whom she shared her rich intellectual and emotional life. Then the little girl finds an empty chair where he used to sit, symbolizing his death. Unsure how to deal with the grief, the girl put her heart in a bottle. The girl is then depicted as a fully grown woman with a heart in a bottle hung from her neck, who "was no longer filled with all the curiosities of the world." She tries and fails repeatedly to get the heart out of the bottle. Eventually, she meets another curious little girl who takes the heart out of the bottle for her. The ending of the story shows the woman able to enjoy a rich inner life again.

The intratext bodily interactivity in the app augments the visual experience of the static images in the book in a number of ways. First, gratuitous additional action occurs when touch initiates peripheral actions not shown in the book. Second, revelation involves touch-activated appearance of image elements present in the book version. Third, elaboration activation occurs when touch makes static depictions of processes dynamic. Fourth, elaboration explication involves the dynamic depiction of a process that is implied but not explicitly portrayed in the book. Fifth, extension refers to the touch-activated appearance of characters and/or processes additional to their portrayal in the book. Finally, changing ambience occurs when touch changes the color of the app images.

The actions of touching, swiping, and shaking the screen result in intratext interactivity augmenting the static images in these various ways to construct three different kinds of meanings. SFS accounts of the meaning-making resources of language and images propose that all instances of language use and all images simultaneously communicate three dimensions of meaning: ideational, interpersonal, and textual. Ideational meaning refers to material and mental processes, the characters who engaged in the processes, and the circumstances in which the processes occur (Halliday & Matthiessen, 2004; Kress & van Leeuwen, 2006). Interpersonal meaning concerns the nature of the relationships among the characters in terms of their interactive roles, their relative power and status, and the evaluative positions characters assume in relation to what is being communicated. Textual meanings deal with the relative emphasis or prominence of visual or verbal elements and the ways in which the text is constructed as a cohesive whole.

In most of the *elaboration* and all of the *extension* instances analyzed in the app, the touch action of the reader initiates the visual communication of a process in which the main character, the girl, is doing, seeing, thinking, or feeling. This physical participation of the app user in the semiotic representation of the story may increase the reader's involvement and identification with the main character. For example, an image is shown where the girl tries the saw, drill, and several other tools to break the bottle. The app user is physically involved in depicting these ideational meanings through touch initiation of the sawing and drilling processes (i.e., elaboration as explication). But this bodily participation also invokes interpersonal attitudinal meaning through a sensory involvement in the determination and growing frustration of the character.

In the example of *extension*, the user, through touch, accesses many more processes in which the main character is involved and is hence vicariously participatory in those processes. For example, if the reader successfully traces the pattern in the stars indicated in the speech balloon of the paternal figure, as the two stare at the night sky, a realistic image of what the star pattern represents appears in the child's thought/speech balloon. Several such opportunities occur. It is as if the reader is participating in the activity as the girl with her loved one.

As the reader shakes the tablet, the character shakes the bottle, so again the user engages bodily in the construction of ideational meaning through vicariously participating in the process with the character. This pseudo participation in events as the character also tends to more strongly invoke interpersonal meaning in terms of affect. Examples of this include the satisfaction the reader can experience in achieving the recognition of star patterns or the determination and frustration of the reader when trying to shake the heart out of the bottle. This seems to be a kind of kinesthetic focalization that positions the reader's point of view as being aligned with that of the main character.

This kinesthetic focalization is also emphasized in the role of the reader in changing the ambience or color of the images through touch in several places of the book. For example, the reader's role is to rub his or her fingers over the screen to cast a shadowy, muted, and dark overlay onto the image of the room with the empty chair.

This positions the reader in a form of vicarious experience of the sadness that has come over the girl's view of this room. After painting over this scene, there is only a fraction of the former light, with only the warm red, pink, and brown colors on the top part of the empty chair resisting the shadowy effect. Similarly, the ability of the reader to erase the entire image of the stars and sea becomes a metaphorical expression of these phenomena being virtually wiped from the young girl's consciousness.

There is also at least one very stark instance in the app of difference in compositional meaning from that of the book. This follows after the girl had tried the saw, drill, and mallet to break the bottle, and the narration indicates that "…nothing seemed to work." On turning the tablet "page," the reader is then confronted by the girl standing on the edge of a very high wall.

Unlike the book, the bottle is nowhere in sight in this first tablet image. This seems to invoke the possibility of a suicide attempt. It is not until the "hint" (touching the girl) is enacted by the app user that she produces and drops the bottle. This, of course, is very different from the book, which conveys this sequence by juxtaposing two images of the girl standing on the same wall: The first showing her holding the bottle, and the second showing her outstretched arm and the bottle hitting the ground.

While the interpretive possibilities of the book and the app of *The Heart and the Bottle* are not discrepant, they are also not isomorphic. However, the sensory literacy practices in exploring these possibilities are certainly very different in experiencing the book and the app versions.

The new sensory potentials of e-books and other technologies have also prompted changes to the design of printed books. A novel example is the children's board book *Press Here*, by Hervé Tullet (2010). The book mimics the features of tablet e-books by instructing the reader to "press here" on a simple yellow dot framed by an expansive white page. The reader turns the page to reveal two identical yellow dots. The written text offers praise, such as "*well done,*" as if pressing has resulted in the duplication of the dots. Tullet's (2010) book continues to invite different forms of tactile engagement—"*rub the dot on the left…gently*" (p. 4), "*try shaking the book*" (p. 9), "try *blowing on them*" (p. 18), and "*…clap your hands…*" (p. 21). With each new page, the dots are dispersed as if shaken, gathered to one side as if tilted, and so on.

Accordingly, the book becomes a pastiche of children's contemporary haptic engagement with a tablet, mimicking simple "cause-effect" physics to expand conventional tactile relations between the user and the book. Sensory engagement with children's reading materials is not exclusive to touch screen technologies, but digital texts evoke different kinds of sensorial and haptic affordances, and there are certainly possibilities for the interplay between digital and nondigital textual formats. There are also limits to the varieties of sensory literacy experiences that are possible in educational institutions, and these are discussed below in relation to the regulation of the senses.

**The Regulation of the Senses for Literacy Learning**

Technologies mediate the sensoriality of language practices in highly politicized, regulated, and institutionalized learning environments. In the nineteenth-century schools, like armies, factories, prisons, and modern museums, "the sense of touch was disciplined, the sense of taste controlled…" (Classen, 2014, p. 16). The uniform seating of children or prisoners in rows has been likened to the rows of letters and words on the printed pages from the printing presses of the era (Classen, 2014, p. 16). Even today, schools continue to be an apparatus that regulates how the senses are proscribed and prescribed for literacy learning. In the context of schooling, the body of the young child as a reader and writer is shaped by the social and institutional forming of the schooled subject as the student learns to sit still, listen, and "perform" reading or writing. For example, Luke (1992) described and theorized the literate bodies of Year 1 students (ages 5–6 years) during a whole-class book reading on the mat demonstrating how literacy practices are inscribed in and on the bodily habitus. Teachers observe the children's bodily engagement with the text and "inscribe and read the student body as the surface of the mind" (p. 118).

As another example of the multiplicity of sensorial practices and the dominance of particular actions over all others, we turn to a handwriting lesson—lower case letter to upper case letter transcription—observed in a low-socioeconomic, multilingual, multicultural classroom in France.

Observational data were collected and translated into English by French researcher Richard-Bossez and analyzed by Exley and Richard-Bossez (2013). The researchers were interested in these transcripts for the way seemingly routine lessons not only employ multiple sensorial practices but also make complex demands of young children as they participate in writing lessons within the institute of schooling.

Visual identification of congruence between lower and upper case letters is often a focus of literacy teaching and learning tasks in the early years where the Latin alphabetic script is the medium of instruction. Aside from the focus on visual senses, during the teachers' instructional discourse on learning the alphabet, five-year-old multilingual, multicultural Francophone children from the *école maternelle* (nursery school) were required to listen to a story book being read by the teacher that contained the target vocabulary. Children were then required to individually complete a worksheet about lower and upper case letters used in the story book. The teacher provided the following instruction (Exley & Richard-Bossez, 2013, p. 350), asking the children to write the upper case letters in the word Yumi, which was written in lower case letters on a worksheet:

> …The alphabet, you've got it underneath in lower case and in upper case. So, if, for example, the [lower case] 'y', you don't know how to do it in upper case, you look for the [lower case] 'y' at the bottom, and underneath, it's in upper case. So, you look at the bottom if you don't know how to do the letter, OK?

However, the teacher's instructions did not stand-alone as text to be heard. Wall posters became part of the pedagogic discourse when a young boy questioned the teacher, literally asking in the original translation, "Upper case, how is it?" The children were required to internalize the visual cues of letter learning as the teacher pointed to a salt dough alphabet hung on the wall, "The upper case, it's the letters which are up there, in salt dough, up there" (Exley & Richard-Bossez, 2013, p. 350). During the independent transcription task, one child said the names of the letters and tried to sound them out. He then chatted to another friend about the French word "éventail" [fan], noting that no sound corresponded to the letter "n." He explained that it is a "dumb [silent] letter" but still must be written (Exley & Richard-Bossez, 2013, p. 351). Another girl asked, "How did you do the [upper case] 'I'?" and her friend responded, "Just a line." The little girl subsequently wrote a vertical line on her worksheet. A little boy began the writing task, commencing from the right end of the word, and working toward the left. The literal translation of the teacher's feedback was, "That is not the good way. Please begin to write from the left side" (Exley & Richard-Bossez, 2013, p. 351). Finally, another little boy sat with his thumb in his mouth. The teacher approached him with the instruction, "Get your thumb out of your mouth" (Exley & Richard-Bossez, 2013, p. 351).

In theoretical terms, through a pastiche of teacher instructions and resources, the teacher explicated both the conduct, character and manner required of the children's visual senses and embodied actions for regulative discourse, as well as the way the children's senses are put to work for mastery of the instructional discourse of letter formation. The role of visual senses, touching of learning materials, and unsanctioned self-soothing are regulated to meet the learning objectives. Children are also inducted into societal norms for the appropriate use of eyes, hands, mouth, and manipulation of materials. Accordingly, mastering the regulation of sensorial habits is interconnected in conflicting ways with the children's acquisition of knowledge and skills in the earliest years of school.

## The Affordances of Sensorial Engagement with Literacy Learning

In contrast to the aforementioned practices, the importance of children's spontaneous tactile interactions with developmental toys and learning objects has been prominent in early learning and child development theories (e.g., Montessori, 1991; Vygotsky, 1978). Until recently, the privileging of sight has blinded literacy theorists to the central role of the senses in communication, such as touch and kinesis (movement), including locomotion of the feet. The active participation of whole bodies—the eyes, the ears, the feet, the hands, and other organs—as well as active minds, are involved in communicating through many kinds of multimodal texts. The senses are essential to representing perceptions and knowledge of the world.

Another oft-used pedagogical strategy that capitalizes on bodily literacies for enhancing literacy learning is process drama. Process drama is a form of applied theater in which the children, together with the teacher, take on the role of characters to "constitute the theatrical ensemble and engage in drama to make meaning for themselves" (Bowell & Heap, 2005, p. 59). As shown in classroom lessons recorded by Exley and Dooley (2015), young children are not involved with rehearsing and performing lines from a prewritten play; instead, in process drama, the children are both the theatrical ensemble who creates the drama and the audience who views it. In a fairy tales unit with 4.5–5.5-year-old children, a classroom teacher introduced a series of reinterpreted fairy tale picture books. A reinterpreted fairy tale somehow "twists" a time-honored fairy tale to make aspects of a familiar story unfamiliar.

One picture book was the focus of the lesson, *Beware of the Bears* (MacDonald, 2004). This book begins where the modern-day version of *Goldilocks and the Three Bears* usually closes. The three bears return from an outing to find their home ransacked during Goldilocks' unauthorized visit. The bears decide to seek revenge. After finding out where she lives, they make an unauthorized visit to her home, wreaking a similar sort of havoc. Goldilocks enters the home, nonchalantly exclaiming that she's not the homeowner but trespassing yet again. A double page, wordless spread shows the bear family sneaking out the rear door while an unwitting wolf enters the front door. The wolf's reaction is captured in another wordless, double page spread. As is typical of the staging features of narratives in postmodern picture books, the reader must actively compose the ending from an amalgam of visual clues and knowledge of other texts. The children responded well to the humor in this postmodern picture book, spontaneously erupting with discussion about the choice of words and visual images (Exley & Dooley, 2015).

In the process drama activities that followed, the teacher asked the children to describe each character with an adjective, and to act out the adjective as they presented their character to the remainder of the class. For example, one child nominated "a happy Goldilocks," while showing a happy expression and skipping on the spot (Exley & Dooley, 2015). Embodied action became intertwined with spoken language as the key mechanism for "unmaking or unpicking" (Janks, 1993, p. iii) the ideological choices of the author and illustrator.

In another activity, the children worked in groups of three to "sculpt" each other from a "lump of clay" into a character statue. Touch and vision, either in unison or in syncopation, are the two dominant senses for a sculptor. However, in a point of departure, the teacher instructed the children to give one another oral instructions and descriptions about how they were being sculpted, rather than using their hands to "sculpt" their peers into different forms. In the regulatory context of the classroom, child-on-child touch was proscribed due to matters concerning personal safety and litigation when personal safety is breached. The verbal instructions to the children in role as "statues" substituted the sense of touch that otherwise would have been made available to the child sculptor, as well as the tactile perception that would have been made available to the child who was being sculpted. The dominant sensorial experiences became oral as instructions were translated into bodily forms, embodied as each child twisted and contorted their own bodies to better appreciate or demonstrate the pose. It also became visual as poses were watched and judgments were made. Digital photography was also used as a mechanism for documenting the artifact of the children's pseudo-haptic communication.

In another activity, the children returned to a scene from the picture book. They collaboratively used their own bodies to recreate a freeze frame of that scene. Again, no child-on-child touching ensued as each child took responsibility for their own pose. Once poses were judged and approved by the group members, each group of children presented their freeze frame to the class. The teacher used the process drama "tap-in" technique to bring one individual character to "life." Under this circumstance, the teacher was permitted to physically touch each child with a "tap," which served as the cue for the character to keep moving or to share an utterance that the character would make, until the teacher tapped the child a second time to indicate that the character had to return to the original freeze frame position. All characters were tapped into and out of life. Digital photos were taken of the freeze frames, uploaded to a software program, and edited so the character's spoken words were recorded as printed text. In this activity, bodies provided the communication for inferential comprehension of a picture book, touch provided the teacher with control of the action and dialogue, and digital media provided the resource to archive the children's embodied and oral demonstrations of inferential comprehension.

In total, when process drama was employed as a mechanism for children to respond to a shared picture book, the multiple sensorial literacies of sight, sound, touch, and movement permitted the participating children to enter characters' different subject positions and explore the possibilities of meaning making behind each character's action, thoughts, and reactions. Such activities enhance children's inferencing skills, moving beyond listening to a story or reading a story to becoming "with and in" the story.

The examples explored in this chapter suggest that what is needed in current understandings of literacy practices is systematic attention to the role of the full sensorium evoked in the process of meaning making. Of particular interest is the hitherto neglected realm of the nonvisual senses and their role in children's literacy learning.

## Conclusion: A Democracy of the Senses in Literacy Learning

Reading, writing and process drama are embodied practices. Tactility and other sensorial and material dimensions of reading, writing, and drama have been neglected in literacy research (Paterson, 2007). This chapter has demonstrated how the sensorial engagement of the body is intertwined in meaning making with different material presentations of digital and print copies of a picture book and in handwriting and process drama lessons. The e-book version of the *Heart and the Bottle* and process drama activities that draw on *Beware of the Bears* invite the reader to participate with the body in sense-making through haptic affordances that open up a rich set of possibilities for vicarious sensory engagement with the feelings and perspectives of the characters. Similarly, the letter formation lessons demonstrate the sensory dimensions of handwriting, which can extend to the sanctioned and unsanctioned performances of the regulated body in writing classrooms. Haas (1995) has argued in relation to writing that "the body is the mechanism through which the mediation of the mental and the material occurs" (p. 226).

This principle is equally applicable to the reading and comprehension tasks when engaging with interactive e-books and process drama activities. In particular, the movements of the eyes and the hands are essential to reading practices. Reading can be more fully understood by attending to the materiality of the text and the related sensorial meanings and engagement of the literate body. Such accounts of literacy experiences can potentially free theory from a hegemony of sight to move toward a democracy of the senses (Berendt, 1992). There is scope for literacy research to attend more consciously to the forgotten role of the body and the senses, whether of touch, taste, smell, or locomotion, particularly in the digital context of use where new sensory possibilities are likely to emerge in the future.

## References

Berendt, J. (1992). *The third ear: On listening to the world.* New York, NY: Holt.
Bezemer, J., & Kress, G. (2014). Touch a resource for making meaning. *Australian Journal of Language and Literacy, 37*(2), 77–85.
Bowell, P., & Heap, B. (2005). Drama on the run: A prelude to mapping the practice of process drama. *Journal of Aesthetic Education, 39*(4), 58–69.
Classen, C. (2014). Introduction: The transformation of perception. In C. Classen (Ed.), *A cultural history of the senses in the age of the empire* (pp. 1–24). London, UK: Bloomsbury.
Daley, N. (2014). The senses in literature: Industry and empire. In C. Classen (Ed.), *A cultural history of the senses in the age of the empire* (pp. 161–184). London, UK: Bloomsbury.
Devos, P. (2014). Touched by surrealism: Reflections on a new sensory approach to literature. *Relief, 8*(2), 62–77.
Do Rozario, R. C. (2012). Consuming books: Synergies of materiality and narrative in picture books. *Children's Literature, 40*(1), 151–166.
Exley, B., & Dooley, K. (2015). Critical linguistics in the early years: Exploring functions of language through sophisticated picture books and process drama strategies. In K. Winograd (Ed.), *Doing critical literacy with young children* (pp. 128–144). New York, UK: Routledge.
Exley, B., & Richard-Bossez, A. (2013). The ABCs of teaching alphabet knowledge: Challenges and affordances of weaving visible and invisible pedagogies. *Contemporary Issues in Early Childhood, 14*(4), 345–356.
Feld, S. (1991). Sound as symbolic system: The Kaluli drum. In D. Howes (Ed.), *The varieties of sensory experience: A sourcebook in the anthropology of the senses* (pp. 79–99). Toronto, ON: University of Toronto Press.
Flewitt, R., Kucirkova, N., & Messer, D. (2014). Touching the virtual, touching the real: iPads and enabling literacy for students experiencing disability. *Australian Journal of Language & Literacy, 37*(2), 107–116.
Green, B., & Hopwood, N. (2015). *The body in professional practice, learning and education.* London, UK: Springer.
Griffin, K. (1991). The ritual of silent wishes: Notes on the Moroccan sensorium. In D. Howes (Ed.), *The varieties of sensory experience* (pp. 210–220). Toronto, ON: University of Toronto Press.
Haas, C. (1995). *Writing technology: Studies on the materiality of literacy.* Hillsdale, NJ: Laurence Erlbaum Associates.
Halliday, M. A. K., & Matthiessen, C. (2004). *An introduction to functional grammar* (3rd ed.). London, UK: Arnold.
Headrick Taylor, K., & Hall, R. (2013). Counter-mapping the neighbourhood on bicycles: Mobilizing youth to reimagine the city. *Technology, Knowledge and Learning, 18*(1–2), 65–93.
Howes, D. (Ed.) (1991). *The varieties of sensory experience: A sourcebook in the anthropology of the senses.* Toronto, ON: University of Toronto Press.
Howes, D. (2003). *Sensual relations: Engaging the senses in culture and social theory.* Ann Arbor: The University of Michigan Press.
Howes, D., & Classen, C. (2014). *Ways of sensing: Understanding the senses in society.* London, UK: Routledge.
Janks, H. (1993). *Language, identity and power.* Johannesburg: Witwatersrand University and Hodder and Stoughton.
Jeffers, O. (2009). *Heart and the bottle.* Hammersmith, UK: Harper Collins.
Kress, G., & van Leeuwen, T. (2006). *Reading images: The grammar of visual design* (2nd ed.). London, UK: Routledge.
Luke, A. (1992). The body literate. *Linguistics and Education, 4,* 107–129.
MacDonald, A. (2004). *Beware of the bears.* London, UK: Little Tiger Press.
Mills, K. A. (2010). Filming in progress: New spaces for multimodal designing. *Linguistics and Education, 21*(1), 14–28.
Mills, K. A. (2016). *Literacy theories for the digital age: Social, critical, multimodal, spatial, material, and sensory lenses.* Bristol, UK: Multilingual Matters.
Mills, K. A., Comber, B., & Kelly, P. (2013). Sensing place: Embodiment, sensoriality, kinesis, and children behind the camera. *English Teaching: Practice and Critique, 12*(2), 11–27.
Montessori, M. (1991). *The advanced Montessori method I.* Oxford, UK: Clio Press.
O'Halloran, K., & Lim, V. (2014). Systemic functional multimodal discourse analysis. In S. Norris & C. Maier (Eds.), *Texts, images and interactions: A reader in multimodality* (pp. 137–154). Berlin, UK: Mouton de Gruyter.
Ong, W. (1991). The shifting sensorium. In D. Howes (Ed.), *The varieties of sensory experience* (pp. 25–30). Toronto, ON: University of Toronto Press.
Palazzo, E. (2014). Art and the senses: Art and liturgy in the Middle Ages. In G. Newhauser (Ed.), *A cultural history of the senses in the Middle Ages* (pp. 175–194). London, UK: Bloomsbury.
Paterson, M. (2007). *The senses of touch: Haptics, affects, and technologies.* Oxford, UK: Berg.
Pink, S. (2009). *Doing sensory ethnography.* London, UK: SAGE.
Porteous, D. (1990). *Landscapes of the mind: Worlds of sense and metaphor.* Toronto, ON: University of Toronto Press.
Potter, (2010). Embodied memory and curatorship in children's digital video production. *English Teaching: Practice and Critique, 9*(1), 22–35.

Rath, R. (2014). Sensory media: Communication and the Enlightenment in the Atlantic world. In A. C. Villa (Ed.), *A cultural history of the senses in the Age of Enlightenment* (pp. 203–224). London, UK: Bloomsbury.

Sargeant, B. (2015). What is an ebook? What is a book app? And why should we care? An analysis of contemporary digital picture books. *Children's Literature in Education, 46*(4), 454–466.

Synnott, A. (1991). Puzzling over the senses: From Plato to Marx. In D. Howes (Ed.), *The varieties of sensory experience* (pp. 61–78). Toronto, ON: University of Toronto Press.

Toner, J. (2014). Introduction: Sensing the ancient past. In J. Toner (Ed.), *A cultural history of the senses in antiquity* (pp. 1–22). London, UK: Bloomsbury.

Tullet, H. (2010). *Press here*. San Francisco, CA: Chronicle Books.

Vygotsky, L. S. (1978). *Mind in society: The development of higher psychological processes* (M. Cole, V. John-Steiner, S. Scribner, & E. Souberman, Eds. & Trans.). Cambridge, MA: Harvard University Press.

Wall, W. (2010). Literacy and the domestic arts. *The Huntington Library Quarterly, 73*(3), 383.

Walsh, M., & Simpson, A. (2014). Exploring literacies through touch pad technologies: The dynamic materiality of modal interactions. *Australian Journal of Language and Literacy, 37*(2), 96–106.

Wilf, E. (2010). Swinging within the iron cage: Modernity, creativity, and embodied practice in American postsecondary jazz education. *American Ethnologist, 37*(3), 563–582.

Zhao, S., & Unsworth, L. (2017). Touch design and narrative interpretation: A social semiotic approach to picture book apps. In N. Kucirkova & G. Falloon (Eds.), *Apps and pre and primary-school-aged children: International perspectives and empirical evidence*. (pp. 89–102) London, UK: Routledge.

# 3
# Experiencing Electracy
*Digital Writing and the Emerging Communicative Landscapes of Youth Composing Selves*

Anna Smith and Jon Wargo

The beginnings of this chapter happened quite serendipitously. Sitting alongside one another in a conference room in Bloomington, Indiana, US, we talked across connections between digital rhetorics and literacies studies. The 2015 Indiana Digital Rhetorics Symposium (#IDRS15) was a space where transdisciplinary dialogue emerged. From the algorithmic nature and rhetorical possibilities of code to the movement and vibrancy of choric compositions in what Ulmer (2003) calls *electracy*, we were excited to examine the metaphorical twists and turns of the fiber that weaves digital rhetorics and literacies together. As writing researchers, our work has examined how seemingly mundane "everyday" literacies have large impacts concerning youth voices and identities (Smith, 2015; Wargo, 2015, 2016). We have witnessed how as youth traverse across transmediated contexts, understandings of how, why, and where they write selves are blurred. Though binaries such as digital/analog, online/offline, and virtual/real persist in research and pedagogy, youth are architecting coherent selves on the move, in new contexts, and through new means.

Traveling toward experience, this chapter examines the nexus of digital rhetorics and literacies in education. Writing in an era of electracy, we argue, heightens attention toward *experience*—to the ephemerally emergent, not just retrospectively rational. We open the chapter by detailing distinctions in and between digital rhetorics and literacies, charting what each contributes to understandings of digital writing experience. Then, drawing on data from two longitudinal studies of youth writing, we chart new forays in educational inquiry by attending to how multimodality, techne, praxis, and mobilities resonate as youth write with place, trope, and culture across new(er) communicative landscapes—focusing on the ways digital writing mattered in the lives of the young people with whom we have worked. This chapter closes by highlighting future research possibilities, meditating on how the particulars of our cases are not generative in the sense that they speak to a broad pattern of digital writing, practice, and mattering, but rather how they illustrate the tensions and possibilities of analyzing and articulating digital writing experience.

## Piecing Apart the Fiber: Locating Digital Rhetorics and Literacies

To understand young people's everyday composing ecologies, we each began developing a transdisciplinary lens informed by the nexus of digital rhetorics and literacies. Thus, our goal in this chapter is not to reproduce static representations of these fields. Rather, we follow Sullivan and Porter's (1993) lead to "locate" the interstices of these evolving fields as they inform our current understandings.

Prior to nuancing these particulars, however, we find it worthwhile to lay groundwork by articulating how we think about the "digital" and what we mean by "writing."

At its theoretical core, the kinds of compositions we refer to as *digital* did not emerge with electronics; rather threads of encoding, multimedia, and hypertext have served multimodal rhetorical purposes for centuries. Arguing that all writing is digital, Haas (2007) describes the rhetorical purposes of multimediated artifacts, such as the uses of wampum belts in American Indian communities, which—with their "interconnected, nonlinear designs and associative storage and retrieval methods" (p. 77)—have long served as hypertextual technologies. With humans' long social histories layering semiotics to make and communicate meaning, it is not surprising that many architects of early computing put binary coding to communicative purposes early in its development (e.g., Wiener, 1954). With recent developments in wearable technologies, depth and facial recognition sensors, and experience architecture, evolving digital technologies are woven ever more seamlessly, reaffirming the adage that "even in the age of the technosocial subject, life is lived through bodies" (Stone, 1991, p. 113). The digital, in this sense, becomes a thread that sutures (mis)characterizations of online and offline experience and other false binaries. Rather than a distinct form of experience, we angle to see the digital as an imbricated component of our sociophysical worlds through which we make sense of that world and with which we write into the same (Freire & Macedo, 1987).

*Writing*, for us, is an activity that is always already situated, mediated, and social (Prior & Hengst, 2010; Wertsch, 1991). In line with the resurgence of do-it-yourself maker culture (Halverson & Sheridan, 2014), we value seeing composition as more than recognizable finished products, and further still, more than a staged recursive process (Andrews & Smith, 2011). We favor developing a rhetorical sensitivity and affective material engagement that has the potential to be applied across mediums, genres, situations, and contexts. Writing is making (Shipka, 2011). Digital writing, as we see it, is a postprocess theory (Arroyo, 2005). A postprocess stance shifts the goal away from turning theory into practice and instead highlights practicing theory as it emerges. A postprocess theory is indeed a postprocess pedagogy.

**Tracing Perspectives on Digital Literacies**

In many arenas, "digital *literacy*" is characterized by its utilitarian value (Bruce, 1997). However, ability represents only a portion of a larger picture painted by those in literacy studies who draw attention to the situated, contingent, and ideologically rooted nature of meaning making across languages, modes, contexts, media, things, and people. Theoretical concepts such as "events, practices, activities, ideologies, discourses, and identities" have been used and developed in literacy studies to discuss the situated nature of literate activity as entangled in the physical and social worlds in individuals' lives, or as Hull and Schultz (2002) describe, "literacies come stitched tight with activities, identities, and discourses" (p. 27). Digital literacies, in such perspectives, refer to "the practices of communicating, relating, thinking, and 'being' associated with digital media" (Jones & Hafner, 2012, p. 13). In such usage "digital" is a modifier that accentuates practices and culturally located conditions within an array of media technologies that overlaps and intersects with literacy as a sociohistorically situated practice.

Suggesting that common text-centric analytic frameworks tend to domesticate literacy's indeterminacy and thus obscure literacy activity, Leander and Boldt (2013) challenged literacies scholars to leave space for movement, unruliness, emotional investments (Lewis & Tierney, 2013), and affective intensities (Ehret & Hollett, 2014). Stornaiuolo, Smith, and Phillips (2017) further argue that focusing on the emerging, connecting, and mobile nature of a digitally enabled communicative landscape can "foreground how people and things are mobilized and paralyzed, facilitated and restricted, in different measure and in relation to institutions and systems with long histories" (p. 5).

Though conceptualizations of literacy are developing in these critical and expansive ways, there are those who maintain that the term itself, with its long history related to schooling, is too conceptually stifling for the types of participatory composition and social action seen in the current era (Ulmer, 2003). To this end, theoretical apparatuses like *electracy* have surfaced. Originally cited as a paradigmatic shift that emerged in response to the choric invention of the Internet (Arroyo, 2013), electracy has more recently developed as a perspective on (non)representational understandings of delivery, collaboration, social action, and everyday practice (Inman, 2004). Electracy illuminates multiplicities of meanings, augments imagination, embodies parody, and supports invention. Morey (2016) argues,

> Metaphorically, electracy breaks from 'digital literacy,' as the latter term retrofits a prior logic (literacy) onto a new technology, a logic that was designed for an older technology (alphabetic writing). Thus, a concept of digital literacy closes off possible lines of inquiry that a new, native term and concept would allow to emerge.
>
> (p. 2)

Framed as postprocess pedagogy, Arroyo (2005) suggests electracy as an entry point into theory making and praxis only rendered intelligible through its action, suggesting alternative perspectives on process and practice. Consequently, and as a result of our hyper-mediated contemporary condition, *experience* is taking precedence over explanation and description, or ekphrasis.

## Reading Digital Literacies through Rhetorical Perspectives

Davis and Shadle (2007) argue,

> [I]n a technological age, rhetoric emerges as a conditional method for humanizing the effect of machines and helping humans to direct them…Rhetoric is a syncretic and generative practice that creates new knowledge by posing questions differently and uncovering connections that have gone unseen.
>
> (p. 103)

Digital rhetorics, hence, refracts the communicative frameworks in which individual acts of "digital" reading, writing, and being take place. In contexts of evolving writing and literacies, such as those prevalent with youth and youth communities, digital rhetorics of practice and purpose influence how people use, learn, and value the possibilities of text. Thinking about digital rhetorics (frameworks and purposes), as entwined and distinct from digital literacies (practices and processes), provides us a locating mechanism to nuance the curves of emerging (digital) communicative contexts.

We locate our work alongside of Eyman's (2015) insofar as it is "most simply defined as the application of rhetorical theory (as analytic method or heuristic for production) to digital texts and performances" (p. 44). Digital writing, thus, not only communicates meaning through the genres we write in and/or the modal messages we compose through, but also the experiences we architect. This form of writing, as Duffy (2004) suggests, sees literacies as rhetorical. It considers "the influence of particular rhetoric on what writers choose to say…the words and phrases they use…and the audience they imagine while writing" (p. 227). To see digital literacies from a rhetorical perspective is to consider the dynamism of practice. A digital rhetorics perspective foregrounds race, ethnicity, language, history, and "difference," foci that often fall to the periphery when solely considering the sociotechnical and rote knowledge of enacting the digital with the machine.

Engaging digital literacies through a rhetorical lens examines the possibilities of understanding composition through ekphrasis (explanation and description), while simultaneously being affected by it as an experience (Conrey, 2016; Farman, 2012). Digital rhetorics helps us to consider what strategies are employed in the production of digital texts, analyze the modal affordances of new media, nuance how digital identities are formed and social communities maintained, theorize the function of ideology and culture in digital work, and inquire about the development of technology in writing research and education.

**Twisting the Knot: Interlocking Digital Rhetorics and Digital Literacies**

Although many would argue that digital rhetorics and digital literacies are separate fields, distinct by their logics of (re)presentation and purpose (Eyman, 2015), we twist these interlocking strands to illustrate how the emerging apparatus "electracy" centers *experience* in digital writing. In an age of mobile media and locative literacies, as composing shifts from the page and toward the network, work on and with digital writing demands such a key change. Thinking with electracy, we see four concepts mutually informing a rhetorical/literacies perspective on digital writing: *multimodality*, *techne*, *praxis*, and *mobility*.

*Multimodality*

Modal tools, despite their purpose and intent, bring with them different kinds of textual and processual affordances and constraints always already imbued with power. We see multimodal digital writing and its semiotic mobilities (Stroud & Prinsloo, 2015), thus, as a call and response to the ethics of (re)presentation and storytelling of selves. Recent scholarship (e.g., Thomas & Stornaiuolo, 2016; Vasudevan, 2006) draws our senses to multimodality as a construct concerning ethics in exemplary analyses exploring the visual and somatic modes of (re)authoring and restorying narratives of place and self. Taking difference as a resource for (re)making and mediating meaning, multimodal writing is becoming an increasingly important tenet for what Shipka (2016) calls a "compositional fluency," a fluency that drives toward ways of being, knowing, and being known differently.

In the era of wearable technologies and a mobile Internet of Things, however, multimodality is not merely about the textual product of the "there" (e.g., classroom) but also the "here," the material realities woven into our everyday. As digital interfaces become more "embedded, embodied, and everyday" (Hine, 2015), so too do the materialities of multimodality. "More and more of our overall cultural experiences," as Markham (2017) contends, "are mediated by digital technologies…The Internet is so ubiquitous we don't think much about it at all, we just think through it" (p. 650). Whether worn, read, written, felt, or experienced, the nexus of multimodal techne is realized in the movement of bodies, texts, and forms.

*Techne*

If multimodality is the means by which communicative landscapes are realized, then techne are the paths of navigation by which digital writing twist, turn, and ebb. As we illuminate through our cases of writing research, we think of digital composition as a lived knowledge. Thus, techne (often reduced to "art," "craft," or "technological knowledge or skill") is a dimension interested in participation, making, and the acknowledgment of experience (corporeally and digitally). Rhodes and Alexander (2015) detail two broad parameters of this layered approach to the construct: "(1) the acknowledgment and even embrace of the idea of spectacle, the alienating distance between bodily self and representation as a productive space for critique; and (2) the importance of lived experiences to the formation of an ethical stance" (n.p.). We consider techne within such an ethical framework—a digital delivery that can extend new identities and ways of being developing through technologies of participatory composition.

Techne manifests in the maker—in the assemblage of activity, genre, histories of participation, and anticipated futures. The craft knowledge that is heightened when exploring digital writing, rather than focused on the rote skill, knowledge, or competency is attuned to the experience of making (Kafai, Fields, & Searle, 2014). Techne, further, explores how participation is designed. With digital writing techne, we are interested in the following questions: How does the composer augment interactions with and through the digital? How is techne functioning for architecting experience (with place, the nonhuman, etc.)? Techne does more than examine the efficacy of tools, methods, and rhetorical approaches. It enhances and changes the way we live and learn.

### *Praxis*

In a world often described as "virtual," "posthuman," and "augmented," praxis recognizes the humanizing experience of writing. We think of writing ontologically as a way of being, of sensing ourselves and our world that emerges through and during the writing experience (Yagelski, 2011). Freire (1970) articulates this experience as the "dynamic present," moments of intensity in which the word, the self, and the world are created as remembered pasts and anticipated futures are enacted in literacy activity. In drawing from Emerson's (1844/2001) notion of finding or founding in his classic essay "Experience," Hansen (2010) describes the dialectical tension in praxis of recognizing self in relation to others in the act of establishing the self in the world. Researchers have documented myriad ways youth engage in the ontological self-work of critical literacy praxis through gameplay, remix, and participatory politics threaded across relationships with family (Ellison, 2014), community and institutions (Soep, 2014), and international peers (Smith & Hull, 2012). Zeroing in on the digital that sometimes modifies our ontological understanding of self in relation to the human—self and other—and more (e.g., nonhuman), we think of digital writing as a form of connecting by way of designing and architecting experience for others—to act and transform self and others—to read in a way that transforms self. As we attend to the tropes and realities created in semiotic engagement, praxis alerts us to the textures of the finding/founding compositional experience.

### *Mobility*

In literacies and rhetorics research, attention to the increased circulation and flows characteristic of the era (Appadurai, 1996) is not just focused on the *movement* of people, things, modes, and ideas, but on the power geometries and affective intensities of semiosis in these sociophysical crossings—to questions of access, turbulence, boundaries, hierarchies, and scales (Blommaert, 2010), and the qualities of life these *mobilities* engender (Stornaiuolo et al., 2017). Lemke's (2000) work with timescales similarly draws our attention to temporal mobility, to what and how writing practice "takes hold" (Gutiérrez, 2008, p. 150), resonates (Stornaiuolo & Hall, 2014), and becomes layered across time (Prior & Shipka, 2003). In recognizing and emphasizing the dynamism of language use, persons, and texts, scholars such as Canagarajah (2006) advocate for shifts in curricular focus from rules and conventions to building repertoires of semiotic codes and navigating strategies of communication. As Moje (2013) notes: "hybridity does not lie in the person but rather in the experience of navigating and struggling across different spaces, discourses, and demands" (p. 366). Digitally composing mobility, through practices such as geocomposing (e.g., Farman, 2012; Rivers, 2016), counter-mapping (Taylor & Hall, 2013), place-making (Phillips, 2014), and writing trade routes (Pennell, 2014), engages critical consciousness and techne in (re)mapping desired futures.

## Key Concepts in Motion

To illustrate how this transdisciplinary approach has shifted our focus from ekphrasis toward experience, we trace identity resonances across two longitudinal connective ethnographic (Hine, 2015) studies: First, looking across the developing compositional practices of young men as they navigate a city center, and then zooming in to the compositional experiences of one young man, Zeke. Attuned by electracy, we tell these stories sensitive to multimodality, techne, praxis, and mobility composed across their lives. Highlighting the contrastive stories of digital literacies amidst distributed learning ecologies, the young men's digital writing not only illuminates how learning lives are situated and informed by a number of social relations and locations, but with a rhetorical perspective on their literacy practices, are also instantiations of desire, being, and relation.

### *Feeling Tropes: Young Men on the Train*

"I go to Midvale High School…it's such a long train ride from where I am," explained Aaron, a sixteen-year-old African American young man I (Anna) met as part of an ethnographic study of young men's transcontextual writing development. The study crossed multiple contexts in an urban setting including school, community, and digital platforms, focusing on one out-of-school educational organization, Urban Word NYC (UDub), that the young men had in common (see also Smith, 2015). At that time, the city's complicated high school choice system left each of the young men I met with long daily commutes—often over an hour—across the five boroughs of New York City. Aaron continued,

> …I guess my reflection [in the window] inspired me to write. I could see myself from the other side—sitting down, on the train, and it's at Church Avenue, and now it's at Newkirk Avenue, and finally, it's at Flatbush, and everyone gets up, and we walk off.

As the primary form of transportation, the felt experience of using the subway—the jostling of strangers' bodies against each other, the repeated mechanical motions of starts and stops along a track, the quick rushes of wind wafting scents—not only thematically frequented the pieces Aaron and the other young men composed, the train as trope became more apparently influential to how they, and Aaron in particular, interpreted the world—the epistemological stances that resonated for him as he made sense of who he was as a Black young man in the city preparing to transition from high school.

With headphones and mp3 players, second generation iPods, and hand-me-down smartphones, the young men's commutes traversed across a digitally augmented landscape. Devices in hand, much of the young men's writing and studying of others' multimodal compositions of various sorts—music, poetry, videos—were done in transit. One of Aaron's pieces, "Asthma," began as he jotted down words he had in mind as he sat on the train, "I take frequent breaths with the city. With the city I breathe. On the platform as my train arrives. From the platform, I leave." To explain the metaphorical representation of the train routes repeated routine starts and stops as the city's breath, he mentioned that he felt his identity was "lost in it." I asked what he meant, and he explained taking long breaths, "Sort of like [*takes a breath*]. Everyone's doing what they're doing, and that's what gives life to a city. And so when I say 'lose identity,' it's because it's greater than me. [*pauses*] So, right now I'm [*takes four long breaths*]." He explained that these words served as placeholders for a companion digital composition that he was simultaneously composing to manifest the essence he could not capture in poem form:

> It's like, again, again, again…I just want[ed] to find something to express. I could see it sort of like on a screen, all the different slides… It can be this day, Monday, Tuesday, Wednesday,

Thursday. Different clothes, same, same attitude. Different clothes, same attitude. Same feeling, you know, different, different weather. That's why I think it's—that's why I feel that it's beyond, um. It's something that exists that I can't talk about.

Composing on the train was often this sort of dialogical, transliterate techne crossing devices, genres, and modalities. In the register of experience, Aaron's designs were not just to be decoded but to be felt and lived.

The train motif not only arose in the pieces Aaron composed, but ever more frequently in the way he explained how he was thinking about his future. He explained his future occupational choices as options along previously laid tracks for a newborn child,

You know, like be a lawyer, be a doctor, all these things, these paths that are laid out before him before he even existed, and in thirty years this child should already be doing one of those—something that is already created.

The digital writing praxis involved extended effort in working with and through this frame of reference in the pieces he composed: "There's always this train," he explained as he reflected on his composing processes, "and there's always the fear of coming of age right now, or growing, and there's always a train involved."

Patrick, a seventeen-year-old African American young man, was similarly engaged in an extended exploration he called, "a journey to manhood" (see Smith, Hall & Sousanis, 2015). He too tried on the train-as-established-sequence trope in his compositions for a time. While composing one piece inspired by watching a woman make her way down a train car taking donations for the poor, and imagining her at different stages of life as she weaved, he established a new writing process of drafting on a laptop, printing off a draft, and placing it in a folder designated for writing process stages learned in school: prewriting, drafting, revising, and editing. This lock-step digital then analog process differed greatly from a previous process he called "just living," which included composing in his mind and on a mobile device as he walked aimlessly through a park near his home. In extending the train metaphor as techne, his process grew increasingly regimented, and the frequency and variety of composition styles with which he wrote decreased. Finding this trope discordant, he returned to the "just living" approach and ceased using the train metaphor in his pieces, processes, and ways of thinking about being on a "journey to manhood."

Over an hour by transit from home, and at just 16, Aaron's mother became nervous about the extended commute to and from UDub after school for workshops, events, and interviews. Our research was taking place during an era marked by aggressive stop-and-frisk policing, a policy which raised particular fears of targeted racial profiling of Black and Latinx young men across the city (Haddix & Sealey-Ruiz, 2012). Aaron stopped attending workshops and only occasionally came to events, halting his participation in research activities in the process. While the other young men's physical mobility around the city, and their compositional approaches diversified as they leveraged relationships and opportunities in relation to UDub, Aaron's became more restricted (cf. Harper, 2013). In considering the role that this transportation played in their digital writing praxis, coming to understand the young men's practices necessitated more than setting the research site in motion but required responsive sensing of the intertwining finding/founding praxis of self, composed and resonating.

### *(Re)writing the Rhetorical Here and Now: Zeke's Lifestreaming*

Zeke (he/his), is an African American seventeen-year-old gay cisgender male student who participated in Jon's longitudinal empirical study examining how lesbian, gay, bisexual, transgender (LGBT)

youth of color navigated inequality through digital writing. Zeke was a student at an urban arts magnet high school in a medium-sized Midwestern city. A self-proclaimed artist, Zeke leveraged the resources of the school to write his way into more academic and school-sanctioned literacies. He also used the arts "to perform" (his words) Black masculinity. Zeke navigated the tensions of be(com)ing "masculine" and Black through a number of digital literacy practices and rhetorical acts. I (Jon) focus on one, digital lifestreaming, as it was the expressive means which most textured our time together.

Throughout the larger study, I navigated youth lifestreaming, the "ongoing sharing of personal information to a networked audience" (Marwick, 2013, p. 208), to explore how identities converged across contexts. Temporally, lifestreaming charted linear frames for understanding histories of participation, experience, and personal interest. As I argued elsewhere (Wargo, 2015), these youths' lifestreaming with new media operated to comment on identities and the politics of schooling, and to connect to queer culture. For Zeke, lifestreaming crystallized through multimodal expressions of electracy, the layerings of texts and technologies, and the experiential practices of queer rhetorics. Lifestreaming was not a rhetorical act of composing but rather a decomposing and recomposition of self. Zeke transformed his identity into a techne and praxis for tomorrow.

Zeke's digital writing, in comparison to the other youth I worked and learned alongside of, was primarily refracted through intersections of race and gender. It presented a multimodal counterstory to the cisgender masculine expression he displayed in the larger arts magnet community. "Feeling Black" (his words) for Zeke was an inexperience that forcefully invited itself into every facet of his life. Whether captured with his iPhone and mediated through Instagram or affectively felt through reblogs of the white male body (Zeke's "type"), desire was located online and stitched onto the body. "It's like you throw up that hoodie," Zeke explained to me, "and you look like everyone else here. Last thing I want people to see me for is a fag." "It's not like I'm homophobic," he continued. "I like dudes. It's just I can't show it. I go to church, I go to work, people know. It just isn't me. I'm not flashy like that." Curious, I asked him about the various sitings of queer literacies work done online, as I continuously noticed sexually explicit material lining his Tumblr dashboard throughout our dialogic selection of lifestreaming work. "Well yeah," Zeke went on, "but you can really be yourself there." Queer was performed across the techne and invention of writing. He located the elsewhere of desire in the more mundane here of performative masculinity. Zeke presented a false logic of identities.

Across three days, Zeke and I performed a content analysis of 128 mined posts (see Figure 3.1). The three days were chosen as focal units as they included common patterns of literate practice. Each day included a full-length two- to three-minute Snapstory, a video narrative that Zeke told in "confessional" style to detail the trials and tribulations of working during the holiday break. Similarly, the staccato patterns of text-based posts, photo reblogs, and personal shared histories marked this stream as one that was indicative of Zeke's larger practices across time. I include the full exchange below to highlight the paradox of reading that is inherent in Zeke's queer rhetorical work of electracy.

*Wargo:* So what's the story behind these posts?…Walk me through these three days.
*Zeke:* Well, I worked over twenty hours. I was forced to take the night shift because it was New Years.
*Wargo:* Is that what the Snapstory is about?
*Zeke:* I basically call them out for breaking child labor laws. Then, the last one I'm talking at the group about hanging out with those ratchet hoes at the movies.
*Wargo:* You worked a lot…What about that first post?
*Zeke:* I ended up leaving my mom's apartment. I couldn't tweet all of that message so I took a screenshot of what I said.
*Wargo:* OK, and what's with all the half-naked white guys?
*Zeke:* That's my type.

| | |
|---|---|
| Wargo: | What? |
| Zeke: | My type. They're like models. It's about the spectacle, about seeing it. |
| Wargo: | But they're all white. |
| Zeke: | So? |
| Wargo: | What's that dude in the wig? |
| Zeke: | I reblogged it because I thought it was funny. He's flaming. He is like "Hey, I'm gay and I'm working." |
| Wargo: | That's basically your Tumblr. |
| Zeke: | What? |
| Wargo: | "I'm gay, look at me." |
| Zeke: | Yeah, that's the point. You can be flaming. I mean, I am pretty sure everyone knows now. I took contemporary as my elective this semester. [*Points to last image in stream*]. |
| Wargo: | Is that what that is? |
| Zeke: | That song. Oh my god. That dance. It gave me life. |
| Wargo: | What do you mean? |
| Zeke: | It was like, there I was the only dude in the class and I'm gay. I'm acting like some kind of pimp. The dance was basically them trying to get at me. |
| Wargo: | But at the end (of the film)? |
| Zeke: | I know, that's why I'm laughing. I couldn't keep a straight face. |
| Wargo: | So why'd you share it on your Facebook, didn't you say your mom and auntie are on there? |
| Zeke: | I don't care. I thought it was funny. My ma, she probably thought her prayers been answered. "Thank god for giving my son a girlfriend." But really, she can keep praying. Everybody else be reading it the right way. |

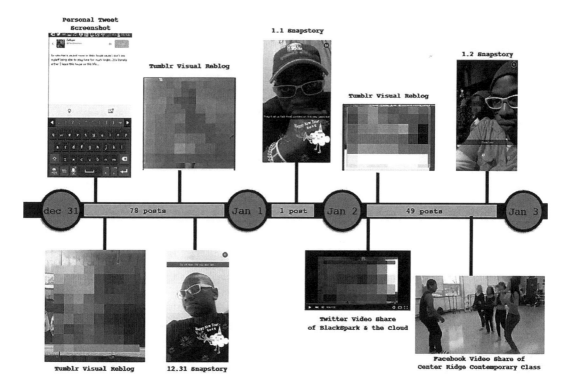

**Figure 3.1** Zeke's Lifestream 12.31.14–1.2.15 (blurred images due to copyright)

If we unpack these anchored artifacts that Zeke highlights, the rhetorical resistance and techne he deploys online becomes quite apparent. As Zeke mentioned, he used the affordances of streamed video to orchestrate a connection to his Snapchat community of followers. Zeke presented a confessional regarding his work and home life to break down the third wall and engage a dialogue between composer (Zeke) and audience (his Snap community). After working two ten-hour days, Zeke posted a third Snapstory that detailed to his followers that he was using an excursion to the movies as a reprieve from home, a sentiment that commenced the three-day stream. In the opening post, Zeke took a screenshot of an emotionally vulnerable text-based post that read, in part, "I don't see myself being able to stay here for much longer. It's literally either I leave this hour or this life." Through detailing the emotional struggle he had with home, Zeke streamed a softer side, one that was not often in sync with his high school identity or familial position as son/grandson. Zeke, however, did not use lifestreaming solely as a process of catharsis but to also stream and locate desire. The two videos that conclude Zeke's curated lifestream serve the greatest paradox for his archive. The first is a still frame shot from anonymous male filmmaker Black Spark. Most noted for hyper-sexualized scenes of male intimacy, Black Spark films are spectacles in every sense of the word. I did not prod Zeke to tell me the specifics about reblogging the Black Spark film, but rather asked him about it in relation to the other video that closed his three-day stream, a YouTube video documenting his contemporary dance class final project.

Dancing to Rihanna's "Hard," Zeke (alongside of five female peers) performed a mixed ensemble routine that riffed on a hyper-masculine man being "hard" and having his girls turn against him. "That video," in describing the dance final,

> is like just the complete opposite of the Black Spark video. In one, people would be like, 'Oh, he is *GAY* [vocal emphasis]!' but then you see me dancing 'hard' [uses air quotes] for those girls. We choreographed it like that…I fall between those two (films). I can wild out and be thirsty but I can also act like Rihanna said, 'hard,' and make it through the everyday here.

For Zeke, the logic in his multimodal counter-storytelling presented a dynamic sense of queer that was made mobile through the experiences of electracy. Like his lifestreaming work above, Zeke demanded to be decoded in different ways. He camouflaged his queer to be deciphered and "read" by a select few.

## Discussion

Aaron, Patrick, and Zeke illuminate how electracy, as a nexus of techne and invention in digital writing and rhetorics, is not so much about turning a theory into practice, but rather practicing theory as it is emerging. Through the young men's use of tropes and counter-storying across modalities, spaces, and devices they manifested identity resonances in the ongoing, living, negotiation of identity construction. For Aaron and Patrick, the felt experience of composing on trains served as epistemological proxy as they engaged in finding/founding praxis of what it meant to transition from adolescence to adulthood as Black young men in NYC. The curated imagery in Zeke's lifestream functioned as a mechanism of techne, a form of disidentification (Munoz, 1999). Disidentification, however, was not solely a working against logics of racial masculinity. For Zeke, it was also about the modal aesthetic. The rhetorical argument that desire was something he had, shared, and yearned to make visible. In these examples, youth are not always designing more just social futures, but rather composing to interface with the turmoil of today. With their digital composing came consequential issues of mobility, and visibility of self and message. This transdisciplinary perspective, newly accented by electracy, and attuned to multimodality, techne, praxis, and mobility, illuminates dimensions of the youths' writing experience—affective, emotive, and emergent.

In this chapter, we have considered distinct contributions of digital rhetorics and digital literacies, and mapped a resulting transdisciplinary lens in seeing anew the identity resonances of youth mobilities, techne, and multimodal praxis. This perspective asks us to engage as educators and researchers in practicing a theory as opposed to only studying or evaluating a practice in retrospect and relation to preexisting forms. It legitimizes the emergent, embodied activity as inherent of value, and in valuing this work, humanizes the activity of digital writing. In foregrounding experience, this chapter also serves as a call for the reflexive and responsive participation of the researcher as a digital writer herself—be it through methodological approaches, such as lifestreaming with participants, or in the digital composition of scholarship. Such approaches show promise in mitigating the tensions of the domesticating tendencies of description and explanation. Threaded through this chapter are pieces—primarily from the field of digital rhetorics—that engage in *experiencing* scholarship. We encourage this and other transdisciplinary scholarly efforts in digital writing praxis.

**References**

Andrews, R., & Smith, A. (2011). *Developing writers: Teaching and learning in the digital age*. London, UK: Open University Press.
Appadurai, A. (1996). *Modernity at large: Cultural dimensions of globalization*. Minneapolis: University of Minnesota Press.
Arroyo, S. (2005). Playing to the tune of electracy: From post-process to a pedagogy otherwise. *JAC, 25*(4), 683–715.
Arroyo, S. (2013). *Participatory composition: Video culture, writing, and electracy*. Carbondale, IL: SIU Press.
Blommaert, J. (2010). *The sociolinguistics of globalization*. Cambridge, UK: Cambridge University Press.
Bruce, B. (1997). Literacy technologies: What stance should we take? *Journal of Literacy Research, 29*(2), 289–309.
Canagarajah, S. (2006). After disinvention: possibilities for communication, community and competence. In S. Makoni & A. Pennycook (Eds.), *Disinventing and reconstituting languages* (pp. 233–239). Clevedon, UK: Multilingual Matters.
Conrey, S. (2016). Listening for phoné, a film. *Enculturation*. Retrieved from http://enculturation.net/listening-for-phone.
Davis, R., & Shadle, M. (2007). *Teaching multiwriting: Researching and composing with multiple genre, media, disciplines, and cultures*. Carbondale: Southern Illinois University Press.
Duffy, J. (2004). Letters from the fair city: A rhetorical conception of literacy. *College Composition and Communication, 56*(2), 223–250.
Ehret, C., & Hollett, T. (2014). Embodied composition in real virtualities: Adolescents' literacy practices and felt experiences moving with digital, mobile devices in school. *Research in the Teaching of English, 48*(4), 428–452.
Ellison, T. (2014). Digital ontologies of self: Two African American adolescents co-construct and negotiate identities through The Sims 2. *Digital Culture & Education, 6*(4), 334–357.
Emerson, R. (1844/2001) Experience. *Essays: Second Series*. Retrieved July 10, 2016, from www.emersoncentral.com/experience.htm.
Eyman, D. (2015). *Digital rhetoric: Theory, method, practice*. Ann Arbor: University of Michigan Press.
Farman, J. (2012). *Mobile interface theory: Embodied space and locative media*. New York, NY: Routledge.
Freire, P. (1970). *Pedagogy of the oppressed*. New York, NY: Herder & Herder.
Freire, P., & Macedo, D. (1987). *Literacy: Reading the word and the world*. Westport, CT: Bergin & Garvey.
Gutiérrez, K. (2008). Developing a sociocritical literacy in the third space. *Reading Research Quarterly, 43*(2), 148–164.
Haas, A. (2007). Wampum as hypertext: An American Indian intellectual tradition of multimedia theory and practice. *Studies in American Indian Literatures, 19*(4), 77–100.
Haddix, M., & Sealey-Ruiz, Y. (2012). Cultivating digital and popular literacies as empowering and emancipatory acts among urban youths. *Journal of Adolescent & Adult Literacy, 56*(3), 189–192.
Halverson, E., & Sheridan, K. (2014). The maker movement in education. *Harvard Educational Review, 84*(4), 495–504.
Hansen, D. (2010). A response to a new book about Maxine Greene's philosophy. *Journal of Educational Controversy, 5*. Retreived from www.wce.wwu.edu/Resources/CEP/eJournal/v005n001/a003.shtml.
Harper, S. (2013). *Succeeding in the city: A report from the New York City Black and Latino male high school achievement study*. Philadelphia: University of Pennsylvania Center for the Study of Race and Equity in Education.
Hine, C. (2015). *Ethnography for the internet: Embedded, embodied and everyday*. New York, NY: Bloomsbury Publishing.
Hull, G., & Schultz, K. (2001). *School's out: Bridging out-of-school literacies with classroom practice*. New York, NY: Teachers College Press.

Inman, J. (2004). Electracy for the ages: Collaboration with the past and future. In Inman, J., Reed, C., & P. Sands (Eds.), *Electronic collaboration in the humanities: Issues and options.* London, UK: Lawrence Erlbaum Associates.

Jones, R., & Hafner, C. (2012). *Understanding digital literacies: A practical introduction.* New York, NY: Routledge.

Kafai, Y., Fields, D., & Searle, K. (2014). Electronic textiles as disruptive designs: Supporting and challenging maker activities in schools. *Harvard Educational Review, 84*(4), 532–556.

Leander, K., & Boldt, G. (2013). Rereading "a pedagogy of multiliteracies": Bodies, texts, and emergence. *Journal of Literacy Research, 45*(1), 22–46.

Lemke, J. (2000). Across the scales of time: Artifacts, activities, and meanings in ecosocial systems. *Mind, Culture, and Activity, 7*(4), 273–290.

Lewis, C., & Tierney, J. (2013). Mobilizing emotion in an urban classroom: Producing identities and transforming signs in a race-related discussion. *Linguistics and Education, 24*(3), 289–304.

Markham, A. (2017). Ethnography in the digital internet era: From fields to flows, descriptions to interventions. In N. Denzin & Y. Lincoln (Eds.), *Sage handbook of qualitative research* (pp. 650–668). Thousand Oaks, CA: SAGE Publications.

Marwick, A. (2013). *Status update: Celebrity, publicity, and branding in the social media age.* New Haven, CT: Yale University Press.

Moje, E. (2013). Hybrid literacies in a post-hybrid world: Making a case for navigating. In K. Hall, T. Cremin, B. Comber, & L. C. Moll (Eds.), *International handbook of research on children's literacy, learning, and culture* (pp. 359–372). New York, NY: Wiley-Blackwell.

Morey, S. (2016). *Rhetorical delivery and digital technologies: Networks, affect, electracy.* New York, NY: Routledge.

Munoz, J. (1999). *Disidentifications: Queers of color and the performance of politics.* Minneapolis: University of Minnesota Press.

Pennell, M. (2014). (Re)placing the literacy narrative: Composing in google maps. *Literacy in Composition Studies, 2*(2), 44–65.

Phillips, N. (2014). Re-placing bodies across imaginative geographies in classroom activities with map argument performances. In J. L. Polman, E. A. Kyza, D. K. O'Neill, I. Tabak, W. R. Penuel, A. S. Jurow, K. O'Connor, T. Lee, & L. D'Amico (Eds.), *Learning and becoming in practice: The International Conference of the Learning Sciences (ICLS) 2014,* (pp. 1243–1246). Boulder, CO: International Society of the Learning Sciences.

Prior, P., & Hengst, J. (2010). Introduction: Exploring semiotic remediation. In P. Prior, & J. Hengst (Eds.), *Exploring semiotic remediation as discourse practice* (pp. 1–23). Houndmills, UK: Palgrave MacMillan.

Prior, P., & Shipka, J. (2003). Chronotopic lamination: Tracing the contours of literate activity. In C. Bazerman & D. Russell (Eds.), *Writing selves/writing societies: Research from the activity perspectives* (pp. 180–238). Fort Collins, CO: WAC Clearinghouse.

Rhodes, J., & Alexander, J. (2015). *Techne: Queer meditations on writing the self.* Logan, UT: Computers and Composition Digital Press/Utah State University Press. Retrieved from http://ccdigitalpress.org/techne.

Rivers, N. (2016). Geocomposition in public rhetoric and writing pedagogy. *College Composition and Communication, 67*(4), 576–606.

Shipka, J. (2011). *Toward a composition made whole.* Pittsburgh, PA: University of Pittsburgh Press.

Shipka, J. (2016). Transmodality in/and processes of making: Changing dispositions and practice. *College English, 78*(3), 250–257.

Smith, A. (2015). The serious work of writing. *English Journal, 105*(1), 81–84.

Smith, A., Hall, M., & Sousanis, N. (2015). Envisioning possibilities: Visualizing as inquiry in literacy studies. *Literacy, 48*(1), 3–11.

Smith, A., & Hull, G. (2012). Critical literacies and social media: Fostering ethical engagement with global youth. In J. Ávila & J. Zacher Pandya (Eds.), *Critical digital literacies as social praxis: Intersections and challenges* (pp. 63–84). New York, NY: Peter Lang.

Soep, E. (2014). *Participatory politics: Next-generation tactics to remake public spheres.* Cambridge: Massachusetts Institute of Technology.

Stone, A. (1991). Will the real body stand up?: Boundaries stories about virtual cultures. In M. Benedikt (Ed.), *Cyberspace: First steps* (pp. 81–118). Cambridge, MA: MIT Press.

Stornaiuolo, A., & Hall, M. (2014). Tracing resonance: Qualitative research in a networked world. In G. B. Gudmundsdottir & K. B. Vasbø (Eds.), *Methodological challenges when exploring digital learning spaces in education* (pp. 29–44). Rotterdam, Netherlands: Sense Publishers.

Stornaiuolo, A., Smith, A., & Phillips, N. (2017). Developing a transliteracies framework for a connected world. *Journal of Literacy Research, 49,* 68–91.

Stroud, C., & Prinsloo, M. (2015). *Language, literacy and diversity: Moving words.* New York, NY: Taylor & Francis.

Sullivan, P., & Porter, J. (1993). Remapping curricular geography: Professional writing in/and English. *Journal of Business and Technical Communication, 7*(4), 389–422.

Taylor, K., & Hall, R. (2013). Counter-mapping the neighborhood on bicycles: Mobilizing youth to reimagine the city. *Technology, Knowledge and Learning, 18*(1–2), 65–93.

Thomas, E., & Stornaiuolo, A. (2016). Restorying the self: Bending toward textual justice. *Harvard Educational Review, 86*(3), 313–338.

Ulmer, G. (2003). *Internet invention: From literacy to electracy.* New York, NY: Longman.

Vasudevan, L. (2006). Making known differently: Engaging visual modalities as spaces to author new selves. *E-Learning and Digital Media, 3*(2), 207–216.

Wargo, J. (2015). "Every selfie tells a story…" LGBTQ youth lifestreams and new media narratives as connective identity texts. *New Media and Society,* 1–19.

Wargo, J. (2016). Literacy sponsorscapes and mobile media: Lessons from youth on digital rhetoric. *Enculturation: A Journal of Rhetoric, Writing, and Culture.* Available at http://enculturation.net/literacy-sponsorscapes

Wertsch, J. (1991). *Voices of the mind: A sociocultural approach to mediated action.* Cambridge, MA: Harvard University Press.

Wiener, N. (1954). *The human use of human beings: Cybernetics and society.* Garden City, NY: Doubleday Anchor Books.

Yagelski, R. (2011). *Writing as a way of being: Writing instruction, nonduality, and the crisis of sustainability.* New York, NY: Hampton Press.

# 4
# Fostering Impossible Possibles through Critical Media Literacies

Jessica Zacher Pandya and Noah Asher Golden

In this chapter, we define *writing, literacies, and education in digital cultures* as a Bourdieusian field, fundamentally a field of struggles, and explore some of the ideological and practical ramifications of viewing the field as a "field." Such an undertaking requires understanding the power dynamics that allow only some of us to define fields, critique products, and name what Bourdieu called "impossible possibles" (2000). Our analysis of this particular field of cultural production—of authors, readers, and digital texts—affords understandings of how digital literacies are shifting and have shifted the possibilities of authorship and readership. Our survey of the field will show how we currently understand what it means to create spaces for "cognitive subversion" and then "political subversion" through a Bourdieusian framework (Bourdieu, 1991, pp. 127–128). By this, we mean space for questioning the "naturalization of...arbitrariness" (Bourdieu, 2008), or doxa, of what is considered to be critical, a space for moving the field forward via work that analyzes the conditions in the fields we as literacy researchers engage. If our larger goals are to build knowledge and work toward social justice in an unjust world, we must aim to convert our visions of the world. We must understand the ways the field in which we write and research shapes and is shaped by the larger field of power, or we may miss key moments of fluidity, key shifting points, places where power, and even reality, are fluid and might be cognitively, and then politically, subverted.

In his oeuvre, Bourdieu sought to map out the relationships between power, agency, structure, and capital; the concept of the *field* is both central to this work and often elided. Fields must be viewed first in relation to the field of power, which Bourdieu described conceptually as the "fundamental opposition" between economic and cultural capital (Swartz, 1997, p. 137). Seeking to understand the ways "agents and institutions constantly struggle, according to the regularities and rules constitutive of" a given field (Bourdieu & Wacquant, 1992, p. 102), Bourdieu analyzed the fields of higher education institutions (1988), literature (1983), and the juridical field (1987), among others. Fields interact with an agent's habitus—embodied cultural capital that is both shaped by past events and shapes future possibilities, a "history turned into nature" (Bourdieu, 2008, p. 78)—to foster possible subject positions and courses of action. Following Bourdieu's suggestions for studying fields in the beginning of this chapter, we define our particular field "vis-a-vis the field of power" (Bourdieu & Wacquant, 1992, p. 104); map out "the objective structure of the relations between the positions occupied by the agents" who compete for authority in the field, including readers and authors; and analyze "the habitus of agents" in the field (Bourdieu & Wacquant, 1992, p. 105). We then move on, in the second half of the chapter, to look closely at some of the recent work on critical media literacies, a subfield of the broader field of new literacy studies, trying to understand the field's current "possible" objects of study and make space for new, previously impossible possibles. Such revisionings of what is possible prefigure actual social change, we (and Bourdieu) argue.

**Defining the Field as a "Field"**

A field is a "network, or a configuration, of objective relations between positions" (Bourdieu & Wacquant, 1992, p. 97); it is "a separate social universe having its own laws of functioning independent of politics and the economy" (1993, p. 162). Holland, Lachicotte, Skinner, and Cain (1998) call a field a "structure-in-practice" (Bourdieu, 1985, as cited in Holland et al.), a "world of relationships, of social positions, defined only against one another" (p. 58). Dissensus—disagreement about the boundaries of a field and the positions and position-takings of agents within the field—is par for the course (Lane, 2000). There are always common premises held by agents in a field that allow for the struggles that define and delineate the field's contours. Fields only solidify, or become completely consensually defined, when they become top-down apparatuses, no longer sites of struggle.

We can view the field as a separate social universe, but it is also intertwined with and defined in part by "the field of power" (Bourdieu & Wacquant, 1992, p. 104) and the economic capital therein. Bourdieu defines the field of power as a function of broader class relations. Agents in the field of writing, literacies, and education in digital cultures, for example, may hold values which conflict with the values of the larger field of power. For instance, agents in this particular academic field value certain kinds of cultural capital (i.e., teaching, publishing, service to communities) over economic capital (viz. the relatively low pay of the professoriate). One of the consequences for agents in a field that values cultural over economic capital is that those with relatively high amounts of economic capital in the larger field of power tend to ignore some of that cultural capital. These power relations are visible in the neoliberal trends swirling all around the academy, such as the trend toward more and more contingent faculty (Shulman et al., 2016). For a more concrete example, one can look at the ways that the Common Core State Standards were written, adopted, and enacted, and how technology and digital texts are used within them, and how university faculty and professional organizations' input came very late in the game (cf. Moore, Zancanella, & Ávila, 2016). These are only a few of the many ways the field of power shapes this subfield.

In addition to attending to the relationship of this field to the field of power, we must map out "the objective structure of the relations between the positions occupied by the agents" who compete for authority in the field, and analyze "the habitus of agents" in the field (Bourdieu & Wacquant, 1992, p. 105). Bourdieu discusses the actual positions people in a field hold—as adjuncts, full professors, endowed chairs, classroom teachers, etc.—but he also analyzes the *prises de position*, the "structured set of manifestations of the social agents involved in the field—literary or artistic works, of course, but also political acts or pronouncements, manifestos or polemics" (1983, p. 312) that agents in the field take up. These distinctions and relationships are critical to the analysis of any field. For example, we may take positions (*prises de positions*) as social justice-oriented teachers and researchers, while holding *actual* positions of more or less power relative to others in our fields.

Echoing Bourdieu, we believe that researchers engaged in the production and dissemination of knowledge in relation to writing, literacies, and education in digital cultures should understand "the regularities and the rules" of this field (Bourdieu & Wacquant, 1992, p. 102), as well as know the fundamental roles of capital and structure their own struggles, and the struggles of others in this field. Agents in it struggle with competing, colliding values. Take, for example, the prizing of work on social justice. Fighting the good fight and being generally socially liberal are almost prerequisites for advancement in this field. We as researchers "should" have social justice goals, and our work "should" help in the larger struggle against oppressive class structures. In these ways, the struggle of agents in this field is against oppression, and working with teachers and students against oppression is valued. However, at the same time, agents in the field experience the commodification of their own and others' research. This commodification in turn influences the kinds of work agents undertake, get funded, and get published, as well as where it is published. Research may become a product that helps institutions climb (or descend) in rankings, and the production of knowledge may be reduced to the impact factors of an article (instead of the lives changed by the research, or the thinking and ideas fostered over time, etc.). Such collisions are closely tied to struggles in the larger field of power and suggest the intricacies of internal and external field power relations.

How do individual researchers; trainers of teachers and future education professors; and others in the field of writing, literacies, and education in digital cultures navigate the pressures created by these conflicting values? We believe the field is thriving, perhaps because it is forward thinking, shifting focus from mass media to the Internet, from paper and pencil to paper, pencil, tablet, web 2.0, etc. Indeed, we believe that agents in this field derive some cultural capital from being associated with a forward thinking, digitally oriented field, and from being forward thinking, digitally oriented scholars and agents. We are reminded by Bourdieu (and Bakhtin, 1981) that authorship and readership, literacy practices and position-takings we in this field often take for granted, are socially produced functions of particular fields. Bringing Foucault's description of the "author-function" (1986, p. 148) into his own theorizing, Bourdieu suggested that "the invention of the writer, in the modern sense of the term, is inseparable from the progressive intervention of a particular social game, which [he terms] the *literary field*" which is of course established "within the field of power" (1993, p. 163). Bourdieu's discussion of authors in the literary field resonates with our casting of literacy researchers as forward thinking, since some researchers in this field seek to explicitly redefine the "writer" or "author," to transform and enlarge "the set of people who have a legitimate voice in literary matters" (Bourdieu, 1983, p. 323). This expansion requires a cognitive and then political subversion of the definition of an author.

The function of author is important to Bourdieu precisely because it can work to legitimize a notion of the universal that masks access for some and reproduces inequality. Once created, this structuring structure, the discourse of the author, is difficult to see. It is challenging for those of us familiar with this sense of the author to imagine "the intellectual world with which and against which [s]he evolved and which, in return, [s]he profoundly transformed and indeed *revolutionized*, by helping us create the literary field, a radically new world…one that, for us, is self-evident" (Bourdieu, 1983, p. 86). What is evident, but rarely critically reflected upon, is that canonized authors are positioned within the literary field as being both outside of discourse, outside of time, and in a neutral space (the "classics"), yet also interpellated as "those closest to us—so contemporary and so close that we do not doubt for an instant the apparently immediate understanding (in reality mediated by our whole education) that we think we have of their work" (Bourdieu, 1983, p. 85). Bourdieu (2000) uses the example of Baudelaire to explore the "space of already made possibles, which, for [great authors] and them alone, designates in advance *a possible to be made*" (p. 92, emphasis in original). He labels this space "the impossible possible, both rejected and called for by the space which defines it, but as a void, a lack" (Bourdieu, 2000). Pushing this metaphor further, we see that some work in this field may push at the boundaries of existing social structures, toward new impossible possibles.

Indeed, a hallmark of this field is the drive to bring new forms of authorship into existence against structural resistance and exclusion, through new discourses and discursive practices. In many ways, agents in this field seek to disrupt old ways of seeing authorship (and readership), but to what effects, and why? Echoes of these fundamental questions span this handbook, which offers a particular framing of the field of writing, literacies, and education in digital cultures. Indeed, it is both a version of the field constituted by the field and a snapshot of some of its internal and external struggles. The editors and authors have chosen to focus on the digital, of course: digital futures, digital diversity, digital lives, digital spaces, and digital ethics. While the entire volume may be an attempt to transform the larger field of New Literacy Studies, it also highlights conservative and transformative trends in the smaller field. Some of the topics are instantiations of current dialogues, and indeed solidifications or sedimentations of ongoing work, of efforts to *conserve* key themes: cosmopolitan and global practices, networks, and flows; digital divides; writing selves; identities; critical race theory; materiality; real and virtual playful literacies; space and time; critical media literacies; reading images; aesthetics; and justice.

Other topics, woven throughout the chapters, are transformative and new or newer: social inclusion; locative literacies; sensory literacies; refugee displacement; imagination and making; mobilities/digital geographies; metroliteracies; big data; indigenous digital ethics; and ethics. We do not mean to suggest an old/new binary in operation in this handbook, but rather that the handbook's contents offer a sense of the warp and weft of the field at the moment. Within it, we wonder what constitutes "critical" scholarship and advocacy work, and how this work might connect with the "possible impossibles," the spaces of cognitive and political subversion Bourdieu describes, those that have the power to reorder social worlds in more equitable ways.

## A Critical Look at the Field of Critical Media Literacies

### *"Critical" as Naturalized Signifier*

We, and many others in this field, seek to expand who can be an author in the research sites and products that are partially constitutive of our field. At the same time, we authors (Pandya & Golden) are somewhat resistant to the hegemony of the critical in our own work (cf. Pandya & Ávila, 2014) and in the work of others. While it is important to empower youth to see through the messages of Nike ads and fake websites, as much early work on critical consumerism did do (e.g., Cortes, 1991), we would prefer to see children, youth, and adults as empowered critical consumers of media and advertisements. In other words, we shy away from Freirian and Marxist work that seeks to teach cultural dupes to become critical consumers (cf. Hall, 1980), and lean toward more sophisticated, nuanced ethnographic work that shows how people take up, make meaning of, and challenge the media and products that they consume (Johnson & Vasudevan, 2014; Lewis, Doerr-Stevens, Tierney, & Scharber, 2012). While we do not mean to make what Bourdieu would call an "heretical subversion" (Bourdieu, 1991, p. 128), we do want to question the ways in which "critical" as a signifier has become naturalized, often referencing work that falls within a particular political spectrum, instead of a generative questioning and process of critique. In this sense, we intend to render contingent a truth that many in our field consider to be a necessary one.

An exploration of all "critical" work in the field of writing, literacies, and education in digital cultures is beyond the scope of this chapter, so we look to the discourses of one subfield of research, theorizing, and praxis within it: critical media literacies. How might "critical media literacies," a subfield that includes both analysis and production, as well as the interplay between the two, resist the doxa of the critical? In what ways does work in the field allow for the cognitive and then political subversions that Bourdieu posits can lead to a revisioning of our social worlds?

Delving into this question requires that we name the struggles that shape the contours of the field and explore what is at stake. What assumptions and empirical work grounds agents' premises regarding the utility of critical media literacies? What are the field's recent currents? First, it must be noted that the "critical" in critical media literacies can serve as a marker of distinction and enact symbolic violence in its own right (Bourdieu, 1984). Buckingham (2007) has argued that labeling one's work as "critical" can serve as a privileging discourse, a signaling that one's work is of greater worth than other pedagogical or theoretical endeavors. Beyond this act of distinguishing, "critical" can serve to embed an author's politics in lieu of dominant readings, with little attention paid to new analyses of media texts, or to creating a space within which to engage a new reading (Gee, 2011; Luke, 2013).

Within Marxian and Freirian traditions that employ the term, the use of "critical" can suggest the aforementioned ability to resist being a cultural dupe (Hall, 1980), meaning that one can then step outside of discourse, shed false consciousness, and access a truer form of social reality. In the sense of replacing one regime of truth with another, "critical" work can serve as a continuation of current circulations of the cognitive and political representations of our social worlds, themselves impeding the "conversion of the vision of the world" (Bourdieu, 1991, p. 128). It is questions about and tension around this promise of critical media literacies that structure the current field of theoretical and empirical scholarly production, and shape conversations about the power derived from participation in digital and analytic literacy practices.

## *Emancipatory Literacies*

The promise of critical media literacies, and the generative digital literacies associated with them, is nothing short of more equitable uses of power in the public sphere, a more participatory democratic practice. Mirra, Morrell, Cain, Scorza, and Ford (2013) offer one example of work in this vein, describing interactive uses of digital media that help high school youth to "develop new forms of civic interaction" (p. 1). The use of digital tools and participation in new literacies is seen as a means of resisting dominant readings of participants' educational potential and school environment, and the authors and participants engage multimedia to offer a different reading of the context, one grounded in specific experiences and policy recommendations. The youth are described as shaping their voices while they position "themselves as powerful actors in the political process" (p. 5).

There are, of course, nuanced versions of this promise: One example is Polling for Justice, participatory data collection and analysis enacted by urban youth and adults focused on building knowledge about youth social justice work (Fine, Stoudt, Fox, & Santos, 2010). This project is grounded in critical youth engagement, investigating the conditions under which youth become civically engaged and challenge structural injustices (Fox et al., 2010). There is a growing body of work that seeks to complicate media representations of members of a particular group (e.g., a Critical Race Media Analysis of Latina/o youth, [Vélez, Huber, Lopez, de la Luz, & Solórzano, 2008]).

While this sort of investigative and descriptive work continues, there are currents within the field that presume emancipatory or liberatory aspects of a critical media analysis. This sort of analytical work is framed as either a precursor to, or the principal means of, liberating awareness, activism, and/or social change. Within recent empirical work investigating analysis specifically tied to media education, research on critical media literacies has been linked to positive effects ranging from combating discrimination to minimizing eating disorder risk factors. Recent empirical work on action research in seven European countries shows the potential of critical media education to support youth in challenging the "derogative and essentialist media representations of the other," while noting the challenges involved with analyzing media outside the interests of youth (Ranieri & Fabbro, 2016, p. 1). Media literacy, as measured by the Media Attitudes Questionnaire instrument, was related to lowered risk factors for eating disorders and negative body image (McLean, Paxton, & Wertheim, 2013).

While these studies note limitations, critical media literacies are associated with youth empowerment and greater possibilities for a more participatory democratic sphere. Authors often discuss the particular conditions necessary to create space for critical work (e.g., Morrell, 2015); on the whole, though, this work can be read in such a way that it suggests the practices of critical media literacies can combat the "cultural dupe-ness" that engenders social ills such as xenophobia and negative body image/eating disorders. It is seen as the cognitive and political subversion that engenders a more desirable or positive revisioning of the social world. We ask, though: To what extent does research and scholarship in this subfield warrant such readings?

*Questioning the Simplicity of Emancipatory Literacies*

We bring the promise of critical media literacies into question, not to deny their correlations and positive associations, but to complicate simplistic and reductive understandings of this subfield. We argue here that the field itself is structured by the tensions between the promises of emancipatory literacies—the doxa of the critical—and the complexities of the ways that people interact with, take up, negotiate, shift, and resist meanings (Bourdieu, 1983, 1984, 2000; Bourdieu & Wacquant, 1992). Popular psychological discourse suggests that digital literacies consume young people's attention in ways that detract from intrapersonal relationships (cf. Steiner-Adair & Barker, 2013), an argument that is as least as old as Socrates' argument that the new technology of writing will "create forgetfulness in the learners' souls, because they will not use their memories; they will trust to the external written characters and not remember of themselves" (Plato, 1952, p. 148). Similar arguments have followed every new technology that shifts literacy practice, from the typewriter to the latest digital media production tool. We wish to differentiate these from scholarship that questions the claims made regarding critical media literacies and emancipation.

In much the same way that some proponents of new educational technologies associate these tools with expanded access, opportunity, and potential for learning, grandiose claims are made for critical media literacies and its effects. Just as researchers of new literacies and digital tools have cautioned that there is no "silicon bullet" (Lynch, 2015, p. 1) to ameliorate all that ails educational institutions and processes, researchers and theorists in the field of critical media literacies have advised caution against grandiose and perhaps unwarranted claims. Indeed, some scholars have argued that we should "beware of the hyperbole… these tools that appear to offer so much democratic promise also permit forms of marketing and surveillance that are much more pervasive and intrusive" (Buckingham & Martinez-Rodriguez, 2013, p. 10). This marketing and surveillance reflects a broader "economization of education" (Spring, 2015), one that anticorporate and somewhat-reified framings of "critical" purport to challenge, yet the tools of critical media literacies are often profit-making technologies that are themselves marketed to educational institutions and networks. In other words, digital media production tools have been promoted because of the ways that media production fosters media literacy, yet the promotion of these tools has, at times, supplanted the importance of meaningful pedagogies (Philip & Garcia, 2013).

Given these histories and tendencies, it is necessary to temper claims made about critical media education in practice that have indeed been grandiose and "revolutionary" (Buckingham, 2015) at times. It is here that we must question whether new platforms and tools shift the positions of readers and writers, the authors, creators, and critics that Bourdieu conceives of as having "legitimate voice" (1993, p. 42). Media production and analysis have been seen as possessing revolutionary, transformative powers, qualities attributed to social media to an even greater degree. The "2.0" aspect of social media has led many scholars to posit that media have become democratized, yet "social media is far less social than we imagine, with a majority of people merely lurking on social media or simply using it to promote their own individualistic work" (Lynch, 2015, p. 13; see also Selwyn, 2014). While there are notable examples of interactive media shaping social change (e.g., in the Arab Spring, [Howard & Hussein, 2011; Lotan, Graeff, Anarry, Gaffney, & Pearce, 2011; Wolfson, Segev, & Sheafer, 2013]), people are far more likely to consume rather than produce media even with the many digital tools that are widely available in some communities.

Once we sift through the hyperbole surrounding digital literacies, social media, media production and analysis, and promises of emancipation, we are left with questions about how and why the shifts in literary production and reception afforded by digital literacies and platforms matter. New literacies can engender greater participation, an increased ability to write and be read, yet empirical work is needed to qualify grandiose claims. Important caveats include the fact that "the competencies that people need in order to take up those opportunities are not equally distributed, and they do not arise simply because people have access to technology" (Buckingham, 2015, p. 12). Further, in the instances when greater participation is a documented aspect of a new literacy practice, the notion that increased participation always leads to a more democratic participation is often left unexamined (Buckingham, 2015).

From a Bourdieusian perspective, exploring the fields of production of new literacy practices and investigating their relations to habitus can allow researchers to build knowledge on who can respond to the call of "author," and what counts as legitimized production with digital tools. A vital research agenda might thus investigate how certain forms of capital come to be valued or devalued, creating opportunities for shifts that can lead to recognition of a broader range of participation and creation, an agenda that follows the broader new literacy studies' investigations of valuing "out-of-school" literacies in formal learning spaces (e.g., Hull & Schultz, 2001; Moje, 2015). Finally, researchers in the field must ask: Whose literacy practices, digital and otherwise, are we studying? Scholars have posited that much of the field is focused "on the practices of young people in predominantly middle-class family backgrounds in well-resourced countries" (Prinsloo & Snyder, 2007; Todd, 2008; Walton, 2007, as cited in Mills, 2010). This critique bolsters other challenges within and to the field and serves to support a focus on local practices.

## *Local Conditions and Meaning-Making Processes*

Responding to critiques of simplistic versions of "cultural duping" at work, and resisting reductive understandings of how macro-level ideologies shape local or individual meaning-making processes, research in the current field of critical media literacies offers work framed in poststructuralist rather than structuralist terms. This work focuses on subjectivity, aesthetics, and pleasure as it documents how texts are taken up in local spaces, downplaying the power of text producers to control their meanings. As a subfield of new literacy studies, critical media literacies have increasingly focused on the ways that people take up practices as they build meanings in these local spaces. As Street (2003) reminds us, "it is the social construction of such technologies and their instantiation in specific social contexts that creates such 'impact' rather than literacy and its technologies in themselves" (p. 2825). For this reason, scholars have resisted promises of blanket emancipation or release from false consciousness, instead documenting specific instantiations of practices that might be considered "critical." Such a tight focus has, we argue, afforded spaces to generate impossible possibles, the cognitive and political subversions that precede the revisioning of social worlds.

The field has shifted away from documenting a one-size-fits-all media literacy vision to describing, analyzing, and questioning rich ecologies of practice, many of which might meet our criteria of proving fertile ground for "impossible possibles." As such, many in our broader field have begun to refer to "critical literacies" and "critical digital literacies" as opposed to "critical literacy" and "critical digital literacy" (e.g., Ávila & Pandya, 2012), and to speak of organic critical literacies to recognize criticality that precedes or grows alongside of and sometimes outside of formal educational contexts (Campano, Ghiso, & Sánchez, 2013). Within this poststructuralist variant of critical media literacies, which resists macro-level ideological framings and simplistic notions of emancipatory literacies, we are offered descriptive cases of how meanings are constructed in relation to media texts. Lewis et al. (2012) provide the exemplar of high school students negotiating competing narratives regarding media analysis, production, and overlaps between marketing and advocacy in their analysis of a secondary-level media project. Employing Pennycook's

(2010) notion of relocalization, which suggests that instantiations of global discourses, through language-in-use, construct time, space, local meanings, Lewis and colleagues argue that the adolescent scholar relocalized global discourses to create a school promotional video grounded in her own understandings of advocacy and identity positionings (as opposed to the class's focus on "marketing" the school).

This exemplar of a relocalizing practice and the lived and embodied critical literacy practices that young people often employ are not always recognized as complex literacies (Johnson & Vasudevan, 2014) signal the ways that descriptive work has represented the nuances at play in exploring "critical" interactions with media. Shifting from structuralist analyses of power and its relationship to ideology, critical literacies and media research has delved into the realm of axiology, exploring the roles aesthetics, ethics, location, and affect play in readings and productions of media texts (cf. Comber, Thompson, & Wells, 2001; Misson & Morgan, 2006). One central tension that structures the field of critical media literacies is how to recognize and document relocalizing, embodied, lived critical literacies as sites of resistance and complex meaning making while steering clear of hyperbolic framings that suggest liberation from ideology or discourse. Following the groundbreaking work of McLuhan and Fiore (1967), recent work in critical media literacies has moved to examine not only the messages of media but the media themselves. A critique of both emancipatory and more nuanced descriptive work on people's relationships with media texts can become mired in analysis of the content as opposed to the form (Mason, 2016). Multimodal analysis (e.g. Kress, 2009) focuses on these multiple forms, including exploration of how digital technologies, images, colors, and interactive qualities shift meaning and experience. Analysis of these forms adds further complexity to the traditional terrain of content in critical media literacies.

## Conclusion: Questions for the Field

We recognize that the meaning-making processes we term literacy events occur on the local level, and we must not forget that fields of cultural production exist in relationship to larger fields of power. As we have noted, our intellectual endeavors are often at odds with the economic structures that shape our lives in so many ways; we must temper discussions about emancipation happening through our critical work with this awareness, while recognizing important advances in authorship, readership, and other position-taking possibilities afforded through new technologies and critical media literacies work. Without awareness of the structuring forces of the field of power, we can slide along a slippery slope from recognition of local meaning makings to fetishizing the local, with the end result suggesting that recognitions of "impossible possibles" can circumvent existing power circulations. Our challenge is to acknowledge the "limits of the local" (Brandt & Clinton, 2002) with regard to these power structures, recognizing meaningful critical literacies in their embodied, lived, and intellectual forms without conflating them with emancipation from these durable structures, and without losing sight of the ways local literacies may be hindered or misrecognized within the larger field of power (Collins & Blot, 2003).

We have seen this done in analyses undertaken from a scale perspective. The metaphor of scale can offer fresh perspectives on the relationships and tensions between local practices and broader discursive circulations and ideological systems (Howitt, 1998; Marston, 2000). A vertical metaphor that locates situated meanings and practices within larger systems (cf. Smith, 1993), scale has been used in literacy research to contextualize questions of the ways literacies are valued and the relationship between local literacies and larger fields of power (Nespor, 2004; Pandya, 2011; Stornaiuolo & LeBlanc, 2016). Employing scale can allow scholars to value relocalizations and critical literacies, whether embodied, organic, lived, rational, etc., while recognizing their relationships with broader systems.

For us, the "critical" ought to reference anything that allows the cognitive and political break about which Bourdieu writes (1991). We would like to be able to continue to argue that children and youths' agency has increased as a result of their participation in critical media literacies, and that children and youth can now imagine more possible roles, possible futures, and possible selves (Holland et al., 1998) than ever before. What cognitive and political subversions have had to take place to make this state of affairs possible, we wonder, and what are the next subversions we need to undertake? To what extent is "our" vision of the world good enough, and where does it need work? How can critical media literacies approaches to *writing, literacies, and education in digital cultures* retain its currency, and what should we critically analyze next?

## References

Ávila, J., & Pandya, J. Z. (Eds.) (2012). Critical *digital literacies as social praxis: Intersections and challenges*. New York, NY: Peter Lang.

Bakhtin, M. (1981). *The dialogic imagination: Four essays*. M. E. Holquist (Ed.). Austin, TX: University of Texas Press.

Bourdieu, P. (1983). The field of cultural production, or the economic world reversed. *Poetics, 12*, 311–356.

Bourdieu, P. (1984). *Distinction: A social critique of the judgement of taste*. Cambridge, MA: Harvard University Press.

Bourdieu, P. (1985). The genesis of the concepts of "habitus" and "field." *Sociocriticism, 2*, 11–24.

Bourdieu, P. (1987). The force of law: Toward a sociology of the juridical field. *Hastings Journal of Law, 38*, 209–248.

Bourdieu, P. (1988). *Homo academicus*. Palo Alto, CA: Stanford University Press.

Bourdieu, P. (1991). *Language and symbolic power*. J. Thompson (Ed.) (G. Raymond & M. Adamson, Trans.). Cambridge, MA: Harvard University Press.

Bourdieu, P. (1993). *The field of cultural production: Essays on art and literature*. New York, NY: Columbia University Press.

Bourdieu, P. (2000). *Pascalian meditations*. Palo Alto, CA: Stanford University Press.

Bourdieu, P. (2008). *Outline of a theory of practice*. Cambridge, UK: Cambridge University Press.

Bourdieu, P. & Wacquant, L. D. (1992). *An invitation to reflexive sociology*. Chicago, IL: The University of Chicago Press.

Brandt, D., & Clinton, K. (2002). Limits of the local: Expanding perspectives on literacy as a social practice. *Journal of Literacy Research, 34*(3), 337–356.

Buckingham, D. (2007). Digital media literacies: Rethinking media education in the age of the Internet. *Research in Comparative and International Education, 2*, 43–55.

Buckingham, D. (2015). Do we really need media education 2.0? Teaching media in the age of participatory culture. In T. Lin, D. Chen, & C. Chai (Eds.), *New media and learning in the 21st century* (pp. 9–21). Singapore: Springer.

Buckingham, D., & Martínez-Rodríguez, J. B. (2013). Interactive youth: new citizenship between social networks and school settings. *Comunicar, 20*(40), 10–13.

Campano, G., Ghiso, M. P., & Sánchez, L. (2013). "Nobody knows the... amount of a person": Elementary students critiquing dehumanization through organic critical literacies. *Research in the Teaching of English, 48*, 98–125.

Collins, J., & Blot, R. K. (2003). *Literacy and literacies: Texts, power, and identity*. Cambridge, UK: Cambridge University Press.

Cortes, C. E. (1991). Empowerment through media literacy: A multicultural approach. *Empowerment through multicultural education*, 143–157.

Fine, M., Stoudt, B., Fox, M., & Santos, M. (2010). The uneven distribution of social suffering: Documenting the social health consequences of neo-liberal social policy on marginalized youth. *The European Health Psychologist, 12*(3), 30–35.

Fox, M., Mediratta, K., Ruglis, J., Stoudt, B., Shah, S., & Fine, M. (2010). Critical youth engagement: Participatory action research and organizing. In L. Sherrod, J. Torney-Puta & C. Flanagan (Eds.), *Handbook of research on civic engagement in youth* (621–650). Edison, NJ: Wiley.

Foucault, M. (1986). What is an author? In H. Adams & L. Searle (Eds.), *Critical theory since 1965*. Tallahassee, FL: University of Florida Press.

Gee, J. P. (2011). Discourse analysis: What makes it critical. In R. Rogers (Ed.), *An introduction to critical discourse analysis in education* (19–50). Mahwah, NJ: Lawrence Erlbaum.

Goodman, S. (2003). *Teaching youth media: A critical guide to literacy, video production & social change* (Vol. 36). New York, NY: Teachers College Press.

Hackforth, R. (1952). *Plato: Phaedrus* (No. 119). Cambridge, UK: Cambridge University Press.

Hall, S. (1980). Encoding/decoding. In S. Hall, D. Hobson, A. Lowe & P. Willis (Eds.), *Culture, media, language* (pp. 128–138). London, UK: Hutchinson.

Holland, D., Lachicotte, W., Skinner, D., & Cain, C. (1998). *Identity and agency in cultural worlds*. Cambridge, MA: Harvard University Press.

Howard, P. N., & Hussain, M. M. (2011). The upheavals in Egypt and Tunisia: The role of digital media. *Journal of Democracy*, *22*(3), 35–48.

Howitt, R. (1998). Scale as relation: Musical metaphors of geographical scale. *Area, 30*(1), 49–58.

Hull, G., & Schultz, K. (2001). Literacy and learning out of school: A review of theory and research. *Review of Educational Research*, *71*, 575–611.

Johnson, E., & Vasudevan, L. (2014). Looking and listening for critical literacy: Recognizing ways youth performing critical literacy in school. In J. Z. Pandya & J. Ávila (Eds.), *Moving critical literacies forward: A new look at praxis across contexts* (pp. 98–112). New York, NY: Routledge.

Kress, G. (2009). *Multimodality: A social semiotic approach to contemporary communication.* New York, NY: Routledge.

Lane, J. F. (2000). *Pierre Bourdieu: A critical introduction.* London, UK: Pluto Press.

Lewis, C., Doerr-Stevens, C., Tierney, J., & Scharber, C. (2012). Relocalization in the market economy: critical literacies and media production in an urban English classroom. In J. Ávila & J. Z. Zacher (Eds.), *Critical digital literacies as social praxis: Intersections and challenges* (pp. 179–196). New York, NY: Peter Lang.

Lotan, G., Graeff, E., Ananny, M., Gaffney, D., & Pearce, I. (2011). The Arab Spring the revolutions were tweeted: Information flows during the 2011 Tunisian and Egyptian revolutions. *International Journal of Communication*, *5*(31), 1375–1405.

Luke, A. (2013). Regrounding critical literacy. In M. Hawkins (Ed.), *Framing languages and literacies: Socially situated views and perspectives* (pp. 136–147). New York, NY: Routledge.

Lynch, T. L. (2015). *The hidden role of software in educational research: Policy to practice.* New York, NY: Routledge.

Marston, S. A. (2000). The social construction of scale. *Progress in Human Geography, 24*(2), 219–242.

Mason, L. (2016). McLuhan's challenge to critical media literacy: The city as classroom textbook. *Curriculum Inquiry, 46,* 79–97.

McLean, S. A., Paxton, S. J., & Wertheim, E. H. (2013). Mediators of the relationship between media literacy and body dissatisfaction in early adolescent girls: Implications for prevention. *Body Image, 10,* 282–289.

McLuhan, M., & Fiore, Q. (1967). The medium is the message. *New York, 123,* 126–128.

Mills, K. A. (2010). A review of the "digital turn" in the new literacy studies. *Review of Educational Research, 80*(2), 246–271.

Mirra, N., Morrell, E. D., Cain, E., Scorza, D. A., & Ford, A. (2013). Educating for a critical democracy: Civic participation reimagined in the Council of Youth Research. *Democracy and Education, 21*(1), 3.

Moje, E. B. (2015). Youth cultures, literacies, and identities in and out of school. In J. Flood, S. B. Heath, & D. Lapp (Eds.), *Handbook of research on teaching literacy through the communicative and visual arts*, Volume II: A Project of the International Reading Association (pp. 207–219). New York, NY: Routledge.

Moore, M., Zancanella, D., & Ávila, J. (2016). National standards in policy and practice. In D. Wyse, L. Hayward & J. Z. Pandya (Eds.), *The SAGE handbook of curriculum, pedagogy, and assessment* (pp. 984–996). London, UK: Sage.

Morrell, E. (2015). *Critical literacy and urban youth: Pedagogies of access, dissent, and liberation.* New York, NY: Routledge.

Nespor, J. (2004). Educational scale-making. *Pedagogy, Culture, & Society, 12*(3), 309–326.

Pandya, J. Z. (2012). A Scale Analysis of the Effects of US Federal Policy. *Pedagogies: An International Journal, 7*(2), 115–131. doi.org/10.1080/1554480X.2012.655886

Pandya, J. Z., & Ávila, J. (Eds.) (2014). *Moving critical literacies forward: A new look at praxis across contexts.* New York, NY: Routledge.

Pennycook, A. (2010). *Language as local practice.* New York, NY: Routledge.

Philip, T., & Garcia, A. (2013). The importance of still teaching the iGeneration: New technologies and the centrality of pedagogy. *Harvard Educational Review, 83*(2), 300–319.

Prinsloo, M., & Snyder, I. (2007). Young people's engagement with digital literacies in marginal contexts in a globalised world. *Language and Education, 21*(3), 171–179.

Ranieri, M., & Fabbro, F. (2016). Questioning discrimination through critical media literacy. Findings from seven European countries. *European Educational Research Journal, 15*(4), 1–18

Selwyn, N. (2014). *Digital technology and the contemporary university: Degrees of digitization.* New York, NY: Routledge.

Shulman, S., Hopkins, B., Kelchen, R., Mastracci, S., Yaya, M., Barnshaw, J. & Dunietz, S. (2016). Higher education at a crossroads: The economic value of tenure and the security of the profession. *Academe,* March–April, 9–23.

Smith, N. (1993). Homeless/global: Scaling spaces. In J. Bird, B. Curtis, T. Putnam & G. Rovertson (Eds.), *Mapping the futures: Local cultures, global change* (pp. 87–119). London, UK: Routledge.

Spring, J. (2015). *Economization of education: Human capital, global corporations, skills-based schooling.* New York, NY: Routledge.

Steiner-Adair, C., & Barker, T. (2013). *The big disconnect: Protecting childhood and family relationships in the digital age.* New York, NY: Harper.

Stornaiuolo, A., & LeBlanc, R. J. (2016). Scaling as a literacy activity: Mobility and educational inequality in an age of global connectivity. *Research in the Teaching of English, 50*(3), 263–287.

Street, B. (2003). The limits of the local – 'autonomous' or 'disembedding'? *International Journal of Learning, 10,* 2825–2830.

Swartz, D. (1997). *Culture and power: The sociology of Pierre Bourdieu.* Chicago, IL: The University of Chicago Press.

Todd, R. J. (2008). Youth and their virtual networked words: Research findings and implications for school libraries. *School Libraries Worldwide, 14*(2), 19–34.

Vélez, V., Huber, L. P., Lopez, C. B., de la Luz, A., & Solórzano, D. G. (2008). Battling for human rights and social justice: A Latina/o critical race media analysis of Latina/o student youth activism in the wake of 2006 anti-immigrant sentiment. *Social Justice, 35*(111), 7–27.

Walton, D. (2007). *Media argumentation: Dialectic, persuasion and rhetoric.* Cambridge, UK: Cambridge University Press.

Wolfson, G., Segev, E., & Sheafer, T. (2013). Social media and the Arab Spring: Politics comes first. *The International Journal of Press/Politics, 18*(2), 115–137.

# II
# Digital Diversity

Jessica Zacher Pandya

Chapters in this section do not aim for an exhaustive explication of all types of diversity but rather focus on specific angles and populations to highlight its complexities. For example, one chapter uses national data look at access broadly conceived, while another dives deep into the digitally literate lives of one African American woman. We believe that together, they offer the reader a sense of the myriad ways diversities are experienced and researched in digital cultures and education. We also hope that they will provoke dialogue around unanswered and evolving questions about digital diversity: How do we conceive of diversity in digital spaces? What axes of difference matter, and when, and to whom?

In the opening chapter of the section (Chapter 5), Warschauer and Tate set the stage with some considerations of how we define access to and inclusion in digital technologies. They describe unequal access to digital technologies and information at home and school. They deploy statistics to underscore digital inequality, arguing that binary constructions of access have evolved to obscure more nuanced, and necessary, discussions of device density, Internet speed, and relevant skills and social support. Instead of a focus on binaries, they argue, research is and should be moving toward examinations of which groups are using what kinds of digital media for distinct purposes.

In her chapter on necropolitics—the ways power over life and death is asserted by those in power, and, here, particularly against People of Color—Elizabeth Losh brings together current theorizing on and practices in digital literacies and digital rhetoric. Her analysis of rhetorical moves (digital and otherwise) in the Black Lives Matter and other social movements suggest that our identities constrain the kinds of rhetorical moves we make on- and offline. The distorted norms of the Internet contribute to racialized and sexualized violence, and we need, Losh suggests, an intersectional and ethical approach to talking and teaching about digital rhetorics in such an age.

Lewis Ellison's chapter on the agentive practices of Black feminist women, whom she terms "knowledgeable agents of the digital," offers a deep dive into the multiple frameworks through which researchers examine African American women's digital, literate lives. Drawing on her own life experiences, she argues for humanizing research on African American women's digital literacy practices in relation to other aspects of diversity (such as race, gender, class, sexual orientation). Lewis Ellison describes tensions in the lives of Black women in regards to digital technology use: She reviews her own and others' work on African American women's digital lives, narratives, and identity work. She ultimately suggests ways researchers and educators can maximize the voices and experiences of misrepresented actors, urging us to bring humanity back into our lenses and perspectives.

In Chapter 8, Vaidehi Ramanathan and Ariel Loring discuss literacy and media coverage concerns in an era of ongoing global refugee crises. They ask the important question: What is the role of language, and news media, in shaping how others see and interpret immigration patterns and refugee flows? Issues of resettlement and naturalization are linked to political and linguistic tensions. The authors examine both the actual and expected use of digital media by refugees and the news media's use of digital literacies and rhetoric in their coverage of refugee movements.

The final chapter in this section offers ideas about what critical race theory might contribute to research on technocultures. Authors Kathy Mills and Amanda Godley discuss how race and racism online, and in person, might be interrogated using critical race theory approaches. Complementing other approaches in the section, they argue that the prevalence of racism in digital spaces necessitates an engagement with anti-racist pedagogies and practices, as well as theories. Digital opportunities exist, they suggest, for coalition-building and anti-oppressive tactics and movements. Together, these chapters help us begin to answer questions about when diversity matters and for whom. The arguments in these chapters also push us to consider issues taken up in latter sections of the handbook about digital lives and ultimately digital ethics.

# 5
# Digital Divides and Social Inclusion

Mark Warschauer and Tamara Tate

This chapter will begin by looking at popular notions of a digital divide and the most current data on hardware and Internet access and use at home and in school. After looking at the current data, we discuss how the idea of a digital divide has evolved to conceptions of social inclusion, identify tensions and conflicting viewpoints surrounding the notion of a digital divide, and outline related current and emerging theories. Implications for educational practice are organized around a brief outline of related national policy initiatives and an exploration of practical implementation issues such as workability, complexity, and performativity. Finally, we conclude with some recommendations for education researchers and thoughts on the future of the digital divide.

## Relevance and Key Concepts

### Digital Divide

The term *digital divide* was used by the US National Telecommunications and Information Administration (NTIA) under the Clinton administration to refer to the gap between those who do and do not have access to computers and the Internet (Warschauer, 2003). It now more broadly refers to unequal access to digital technology and information. Census data show that while progress has been made providing computer and Internet access to low-income and minority households, access remains uneven. With the rapid growth of the Internet as a medium for both economic and social transactions, being part of this network has become essential to inclusion and participation (Horrigan, 2016).

### Current Statistics

The degree of access to digital technology by diverse demographic groups has been well documented in the US through reports issued by NTIA. These reports are based on the Current Population Surveys (CPS) of about 50,000 US households, conducted by the US Bureau of Labor Statistics and the US Census Bureau. Every month the CPS surveys collect general demographic data; extensive data are available online through the NTIA Data Explorer (NTIA.doc.gov). These reports provide high-quality, useful information, because of the large sample size, the quality of the sampling, the in-person surveying with a response rate of more than 90%, and the consistency of questions over the years (Warschauer & Matuchniak, 2010). Recently, the survey instrument was significantly revised to be more person-centered, rather than household-centered, and expand the data on the range of devices people use, the places they are used, and how they are used (Goldberg, 2016).

Another widely cited source of related information comes from the Pew Internet & American Life Project telephone surveys (www.PewInternet.org). These reports show increasing computer ownership and Internet access, with differences largely reflective of socioeconomic levels (in terms of both finances and education); a plateauing of home broadband (67%; a related increase in "smartphone only" adults (13%) with Internet access solely through these devices; and smartphone access equal to broadband (68%; Horrigan & Duggan, 2015). Pew reports that some of the most significant changes in the adoption patterns are seen among African Americans, those with relatively low household incomes, and those living in rural areas (Horrigan & Duggan, 2015). While overall Internet access seems to have plateaued in the last few years at about 80%, the switch from home broadband to smartphone access has practical implications on usage, with people having to be concerned about data limits and difficulties for prolonged research, writing, and academic content creation for students in these smartphone-only households (Horrigan & Duggan, 2015).

The digital divide is complex, with factors relating to hardware, Internet, and usage varying across context. Specifically, we discuss four digital differences that impact teaching and learning: school access to both hardware and the Internet, home access to both hardware and the Internet, school use of digital technology, and home use of digital technology (Warschauer, 2007; Warschauer & Matuchniak, 2010).

*School Access: Hardware*

School access refers to the availability of digital technology in schools. If public schools in the US can help compensate for unequal access to computers at home, they can provide an important means for promoting social inclusion and equality. Today, most students have some access to technology in school, but the quality and quantity vary widely. As of 2009, a self-reported 97% of teachers have a computer in the classroom every day; the daily ratio of students to computers in these classrooms was 5.3 to 1 according to the National Center for Education Statistics (2010).

*Home Access: Hardware*

Beyond schools, there are public access points for technology in libraries and other public spaces, but computer access in the home allows a degree of flexibility and autonomy difficult to replicate elsewhere. The hardware component of computer ownership continues to grow but at a more reduced rate than in prior periods. In 2012, 79% of households reported computers at home according to NTIA (NTIA Data Explorer). Over 90% of students in more recent NAEP assessments report having a computer at home (Zhang et al., 2016). Computer use tends to be higher in households with children (Horrigan & Duggan, 2015). Low-income households (less than $25,000/year) were less likely than higher earning ($100,000 or more/year) households to have a home computer according to the 2012 NTIA data. Educational levels also correlate with ownership; households with no high school graduates are far less likely than households with college graduates to own a computer in 2012 (NTIA, 2012). Similarly, Internet usage is higher for increased educational attainment (Snyder, de Brey, & Dillow, 2016). When other devices such as cell phones and smartphones are considered, connectivity to digital information increases to over 90% (Rainie, 2015). However, as noted below, usage of these devices is less correlated with educational attainment (Figure 5.1).

Children in lower-income families are significantly less likely than others to live in homes with digital technologies (Common Sense Media, 2015; see also Snyder, de Brey, & Dillow, 2016).

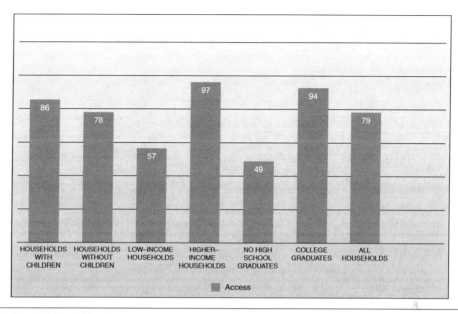

**Figure 5.1** Percent of Households with Access to Computers

*School Access: Internet*

Robust computer access requires more than simply owning a computer, it requires access to the Internet—preferably reliable, fast access. The quality of Internet access makes a difference in the true usefulness of both school and home computers. Using the application data from the Federal Communications Commission (FCC) Schools and Libraries Program (known as E-rate), which reflects data from over 6,700 public school districts, the nonprofit Education Superhighway's 2015 report showed that in the prior two years, an additional 20 million students were connected to broadband, but over 21 million students still were without access to broadband connectivity. Notably, 23% of school districts do not meet the minimum FCC Internet access goals (Education Superhighway, 2015). These differences no longer reflect differences in locale (urban, suburban, and rural schools are at 78%, 78%, and 85%, respectively) or percentage of free and reduced lunch (89% at *both* (a) less than 5% free and reduced lunch, and (b) for 75% and above free and reduced lunch) (Education Superhighway, 2015). The lessening of this part of the access divide likely reflects the $2.5 billion per year in federal funding through the E-rate program as well as improved broadband affordability (the cost of Internet access has declined 50% from 2013 to 2015; Education Superhighway, 2015; see also US Department of Education, 2016). However, a 2014 survey of districts by the Consortium of School Networking reported 45% of schools had insufficient capacity for a one-to-one initiative (Jones, Fox, & Neugent, 2015). Inequalities to material access persist (Huang, Cotten, & Rikard, 2016).

*Home Access: Internet*

Use of the Internet at home as of July 2015 was at 68% of the population, up from 22.3% in December 1998 (NTIA, 2014). The most notable difference in saturation is between families with less than $25,000 in income (46.5%) compared to those with higher levels, ranging from 62% at $25,000–$49,000 to 82% at $100,000 or more annual income (NTIA, 2014). Internet use by children has grown from 56% in 2013 to 66% in 2015 (Morris, 2016). Researchers have found that children with home Internet access are more likely to go online to look up information about things they are interested in (52% often do so) compared to those with mobile-only access (35%; Rideout & Katz, 2016).

The density of usage, or people per computer, affects the availability of that technology. For example, density of usage may affect the amount of time a computer is available for use by the school children of a household, rather than the adults, or for homework versus unstructured uses. One study suggests that there are dramatic differences in household members per computer by racial/ethnic group (Warschauer & Matuchniak, 2010). White families have roughly one household member per computer and Hispanic families have nearly four people per computer (Warschauer & Matuchniak, 2010). This disparity would certainly restrict computer time available to Hispanic children, particularly for nonschool-related exploration and creation. The age, quality, and specifications of the actual hardware owned also impact the quality of home computer access, but there is little data currently available (see discussion in Rideout & Katz, 2016).

*School Use*

Digital inequality is not limited to questions of hardware access but also usage patterns (Huang et al., 2016). As of 2015, over 40% of school-aged children used computers at school, up from less than 20% in 1998 (NTIA, 2016). In NAEP's 2014 Technology and Engineering Literacy assessment, a majority of students reported significant information and computer technology use in school (www.nationsreportcard.gov/tel_2014/). Levels of use appear to be leveling off in recent years (NTIA, 2014) and are slightly lower for families with incomes under $75,000 per year (NTIA, 2014) (Figure 5.2).

A number of studies provide evidence that student income and race correlated strongly with the type of use students make of computers in schools (Warschauer, 2007). Generally, students who are African American, Hispanic, or low income are more likely to use computers for drill and practice, compared to White and higher income students who are more likely to use them for authentic and enrichment activities (Becker, 2000; Cotten, Davison, Shank, & Ward, 2014; Schofield & Davidson,

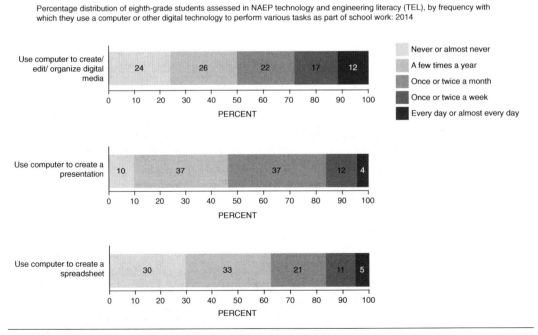

**Figure 5.2** NAEP Eighth Grade Students' Computer and Diigital Technology Use in School

2004). The National Education Plan states that "a digital use divide continues to exist between learners who are using technology in active, creative ways to support their learning and those who predominantly use technology for passive content consumption" (US Department of Education, 2016, p. 5). The different patterns of usage correlate with academic outcomes; for example, prior use of technology for academic writing significantly affects writing achievement scores (Tate, Warschauer, & Abedi, 2016). Students with access to devices in schools have been found to have increased attention, interest, and motivation; meanwhile, teachers in schools with access were found to use more learner-centered, individualized practices (Cavanaugh, Dawson, & Ritzhaupt, 2011; Warschauer, 2006; Zheng, Warschauer, Lin, & Chang, 2016). In addition, the knowledge that students in low-SES schools may have limited or poor access to digital technology and may lack basic computer skills leads teachers to avoid projects and homework that would need such access (Warschauer, 2007). Even one-to-one laptop programs have shown mixed results at decreasing the achievement gap (Zheng et al., 2016). Recent studies seek to untangle the broad and complicated relationships among access to hardware, usage patterns, and digital inequality (e.g., Huang et al., 2016, investigating the roles of affective and emotional factors in actual access constraints and unequal distribution of skills and usage).

*Home Use*

Social and contextual factors are also important in shaping the quality of home computer access (see discussion in Battle & Attewell, 1999). Family and friends influence the amount and type of computer usage by students (see discussion in Rideout & Katz, 2016). Indeed, home computers may generate another "Sesame Street effect" or "Matthew effect," where advantaged students gain more from the innovation than disadvantaged students (Battle & Attewell, 1999). For example, research suggests that students in lower socioeconomic areas tend to use computers more for content consumption (e.g., passively viewing text, images, and video created by others) and social uses (e.g., social media, texting) rather than for content creation (e.g., authoring their own text, images, video to express their own ideas) and interest-driven uses (e.g., learning more about a subject of interest, exploring personal passions; see Witte & Mannon, 2010; Zillien & Hargittai, 2009). In order for students to use their home computers successfully for more challenging, creative, and constructive purposes, they benefit from higher levels of technological resources (e.g., quality graphics, multimedia capacity, digital recorders) and rich social resources such as a community that values and enables the sharing of media knowledge and interests. Certainly, students in diverse communities engage in content creation with the available resources, but their context is generally less enriched and their resources (both personal and community-based) may not be visible as they move from one setting to another (Hull & Schultz, 2001). Thus, researchers have found that "how family members help each other learn with technology—both within and across generations—matters a great deal. Particularly for families with limited access to other digital learning supports, parents and children enabling each other's learning can be a critical compensating mechanism" (Rideout & Katz, 2016, p. 27). Family and friends also provide resources for troubleshooting as issues inevitably arise and support in developing important digital literacy skills (cf. Rideout & Katz, 2016).

*The Growing Relevance of Connectivity*

Digital devices are often a primary access point to online resources for news and other information, as well as social connections, particularly for people ages 18–34 (Rainie, 2015). Participation in online socially communicative environments has become widespread, and the participatory, collaborative nature of these environments provides a creative space for students to author content across a variety of modes (Stornaiuolo, Higgs, & Hull, 2013). Younger individuals report that their technology use is an important part of their personal identity and their generational identity (Rainie, 2015). Indeed, political and civic life reflects the increased information flow and personal empowerment that can be engendered through the digital information exchange facilitated by such widespread access (Rainie, 2015; Warschauer & Newhart, 2015). Even mandatory state summative testing is moving online, with the majority of testing administered online for the first time in the 2015–2016 school year (Levin, 2015).

Digital literacy is an essential skill, with writing for purposes of work, learning, citizenship, and leisure becoming common (Stornaiuolo et al., 2013). Increasingly, a lack of digital literacy seems likely to hold people back in the workplace (Kenworthy & Kielstra, 2015). In addition, most Americans feel that they are lifelong learners, gathering information as they need for professional purposes, to implement projects, for personal growth, or simply out of interest (Horrigan, 2016). The Internet has become an increasingly popular tool to facilitate this learning outside of traditional community resources (Horrigan, 2016). Horrigan (2016) notes broad patterns associated with personal and professional learning, with higher-educated adults in higher-income households more likely to participate in the digital educational ecosystem. Of course, access to digital devices and the Internet, particularly convenient and robust access, increases the likelihood of use for personal learning online (Horrigan, 2016).

Youth are even more digitally connected than adults today. The Common Sense Census was a large-scale, probability-based survey of more than 2,600 young people (both tweens 8–12 years and teens 13–18 years) conducted in 2015. The survey explored the use of screen-based media activities, documenting both the activities engaged in and the devices used, along with the amount of time spent. Key findings included that American teenagers average about 9 hours of entertainment media and tweens about 6 hours, but patterns of use vary widely (Common Sense Media, 2015). Six different types of media users were identified: social networkers, mobile gamers, video gamers (combined with mobile gamers and computer users into a single category for teens), heavy viewers, readers, and light users (Common Sense Media, 2015). Boys' and girls' usage was different, and all media consumption was highly mobile (Common Sense Media, 2015). The Common Sense Census found substantial differences in the amount of time young people spend with media based on family income, parent education, and race/ethnicity (Common Sense Media, 2015). In general, Black youth and children from lower socioeconomic groups tend to spend more time with media than Hispanic, White, or higher-SES youth do (Common Sense Media, 2015). Higher levels of parent education also show reduced average usage time (Common Sense Media, 2015). Given these heavy usage patterns, what does a digital divide mean for today's youth? If they do not have access to digital media, are they at a disadvantage? Do these disadvantages, if any, impact them socially, academically, or in other ways? These are all questions worth exploring in future studies in order to more fully understand, and perhaps address, the consequences of the digital divide.

**Tensions/Conflicting Viewpoints**

Some digital technology advocates believe that access alone can improve education and other social problems. Many of the early digital initiatives focused exclusively on creating low-cost devices to increase the affordability of device ownership (e.g., Brazil's Peoples Computer, India's Simputer, and the XO computer used by One Laptop per Child, www.laptop.org). This technocentric focus is exemplified by the "Hole-in-the-Wall" project in New Delhi in 2000, in which an outdoor computer kiosk was placed in one of the poorest slums without teachers or instruction. The idea was to allow children to teach themselves at their own pace and was hailed as groundbreaking by many (e.g., Mitra, 1999). Unfortunately, the results were less clear (Warschauer, 2003), with many researchers and parents concerned by the lack of supervision, instruction, collaboration, and educational value. Similar US projects with little curricular integration, teacher development, or communication among stakeholders such as the Birmingham, Alabama One Laptop per Child effort resulted in dismal results (Warschauer, 2011; Warschauer, Cotton, & Ames, 2011).

Critics claim that school technology initiatives are wasteful and provide little educational benefit. Scholars like Larry Cuban (2003, 2013) argue that the digital technology is adopted initially in strong implementations, but that subsequent implementations are haphazard without sufficient curricular ties and teacher support. The cycle of adoption runs its course and the technology, originally hailed as transformative, makes no significant inroads in long-term instruction (Cuban, 2013). Morgan Ames (2016) raises similar issues with the One Laptop Per Child implementation, noting that the money would be better spent building schools, training teachers, developing curricula, providing books and other materials, and subsidizing attendance.

Fairlie and Robinson (2013) illustrate a different concern: lack of efficacy. In their experiment, they randomly provided free home computers to families and found no effect on any educational outcomes (Fairlie & Robinson, 2013). Even more concerning, Vigdor, Ladd, and Martinez (2014) found evidence that home computers were associated with modest statistically significant and persistent negative impact on student math and reading scores. A recent OECD (2015) report comes to similar conclusions at an international level, finding that moderate school use of computers somewhat improves learning outcomes, but very frequent use predicts worse achievement in learning outcomes. The report also found no improvement in student achievement in reading, math, or science in countries with heavy technology investments, and that technology did not help bridge the skills divide between advantaged and disadvantaged students (OECD, 2015).

Substantial effort and funding are required to develop the necessary infrastructure, teacher development, and curriculum for laptops to be meaningful levers of change. Failure to adequately plan and engage all members of the community leads to costly and highly visible failures like the Los Angeles Unified School District iPad roll out (see, e.g., Blume, 2015, 2016). This is not an isolated or random example. The same types of problems occur over and over in technology projects around the world when the focus on hardware and software exceeds the focus on human and social systems needed for the technology to have a productive, positive impact on people.

**Current or Emerging Theory**

***Expanded Notions of the Digital Divide***

Over the years, we have seen that both the notion of a digital divide and its logical implication—that social problems can be addressed through providing computers and Internet accounts—have seemed increasingly problematic (Warschauer, 2003). Meaningful access to digital technology comprises far more than merely providing computers and Internet connections. Content and language, literacy and education, and community and institutional structures must all be taken into account if meaningful access to new technologies is to be provided (Warschauer, 2003). From a policy standpoint, the goal of using digital devices with marginalized groups is not to overcome a digital divide, but rather to further a process of social inclusion (Warschauer, 2003; Warschauer & Newhart, 2016).

Social inclusion refers to the extent that individuals, families, and communities are able to fully participate in society and control their own destinies, taking into account a variety of factors related to economic resources, employment, health, education, housing, recreation, culture, and civic engagement (Warschauer, 2003; Warschauer & Newhart, 2016). Social inclusion refers not only to an adequate share of resources but participation in life opportunities.

The ability to access, adapt, and create new knowledge using new information and communication technology is critical to social inclusion today. Today's information age calls for digital skills in order to be proficient at accessing resources and participating fully in relevant communities

(Economist, 2015; Rideout & Katz, 2016). The hypertextual organization of the Internet allows a horizontal, associative connection between sources of information (Warschauer, 2003). The creation of multimedia necessitates a complex array of semiotic, technical, and design skills and understanding, and differential access to these skills and knowledge will be one important divider between participants in today's society (Warschauer, 2003).

Models of access often focus on *device* ownership or physical access to a particular device. Of course, full access would also require Internet access as well as the skills and understanding how to use the computer and Internet in socially valued ways (Warschauer, 2003; Warschauer & Newhart, 2016). It accomplishes little to have a computer but not know how to use it.

Other models see access as a conduit, a supply line that provides information and requires periodic payments for continued access, similar to access to electricity. Like access to other utilities, access to information reflects broader issues of political, social, and economic power (Warschauer, 2003). Although the conduit model may be an improvement on the device ownership model, it fails to reflect the need for people to make use of devices for meaningful social practices.

We find the model of literacy to be a more compelling choice. There are many similarities between literacy and digital technology access. First, both are closely connected to advances in human communication and the means of knowledge production. Second, just as digital technology access is a prerequisite for full participation in the informational stage of capitalism, literacy was (and remains) a prerequisite for full participation in the earlier industrial stages of capitalism. Third, both necessitate a connection to a physical artifact (a book, computer), to sources of information that get expressed as content within or via that physical artifact, and to a skill level sufficient to process and make use of that information. Fourth, both involve not only receiving information but also producing it. Finally, they are both tied to somewhat controversial notions of societal divides: the great literacy divide and the digital divide (Warschauer, 2003).

The definition of literacy, like that of technology access, has expanded to encompass the literacy practice that takes place in historical, political, and sociocultural context (see, e.g., Gee, 1996). The concepts of digital literacy have evolved as well. Further, we note that literacy, much like digital technology proficiency, is unequally distributed and highly correlated with income and wealth (Warschauer, 2003). It is also almost always confounded with other variables, especially schooling.

As Scribner and Cole (1981) have shown—at least at the individual level—there is no single construct of literacy that divides people into two cognitive camps. Rather, there are gradations and types of literacies, with a range of benefits closely related to the specific function of literacy practices. Literacy, in a general sense, cannot be said to cause cognitive or social development; rather literacy and social development are intertwined and co-constituted, as are technologies and society in general.

Using the model of literacy to explore our model of digital information access leads us to start with the basic understanding that there is not just one type of access, but many types. The meaning and value of access vary in particular social contexts. Access exists in gradations rather than in a bipolar opposition. Computer and Internet use bring no automatic benefit outside of context-specific functions. Use is a social practice, involving access to physical artifacts, content, skills, and social support. And acquisition of access is a matter not only of education but also of power.

The range of resources required for true access is varied (see Carvin, 2000; US Department of Education, 2016; Warschauer, 2003) but generally comprises physical resources, digital resources, human resources, and social resources. Physical access refers to computer and Internet access. Digital resources refer to digital information that is made available online. Human resources encompass things like literacy and education. Finally, social resources refer to the community, institutional, and societal structures that support effective access and use. We note that these resources have an iterative relationship with use: While each resource contributes to effective use, it can also be a *result* of effective use of digital technology. Thus, these resources can be either a virtuous upward spiral or a vicious cycle of decreasing resources.

## Implications for Educational Practice

We have seen that access to digital resources and the ability to use digital resources are quickly becoming fundamental to participation in today's society. Because home access and support vary widely, we must look to public schools to provide a baseline of knowledge and skills. We need students to have access to the resources—hardware, Internet, and social support—to enable proficiency with digital technology. Policy initiatives, such as the E-rate program, initially focused on providing access to digital technology and later efforts have focused in Internet access, such as the National Broadband Plan released by the FCC in 2010.

Many believe that if schools do not harness technology, the achievement gap will grow between those with and without access (Economist, 2015; OECD, 2015; US Department of Education, 2016). Some also believe that distance learning has the potential to address some gaps in educational access (Economist, 2015; but see Horrigan, 2016, for an opposing viewpoint on the value of distance learning), but if students are not digitally literate, they cannot avail themselves of these opportunities. Similarly, personalization and individualization of curriculum and education may be enhanced through the use of digital technology (Economist, 2015; OECD, 2016), but without digital literacy may again be inaccessible to those students who need the most help. The OECD (2015, p. 4) contends that "technology is the only way to dramatically expand access to knowledge" and digital technology allows teachers and students to access specialized materials in multiple formats with few space and time constraints.

The US' National Education Technology Plan (NETP; US Department of Education, 2016) outlines a national vision and plan for learning enabled by technology, with a goal of providing greater access and accessibility. It articulates the potential of technology, when carefully designed and thoughtfully applied, to accelerate, amplify, and expand the impact of effective teaching practices (US Department of Education, 2016; cf., OECD, 2016). However, it acknowledges that in order to be transformative, educators need to have the knowledge and skills to take full advantage of technology-rich learning environments:

> On its own, access to connectivity and devices does not guarantee access to engaging educational experiences or a quality education. Without thoughtful intervention and attention to the way technology is used for learning, the digital use divide could grow even as access to technology in schools increases.
>
> (US Department of Education, 2016, p. 18)

Learning, teaching, and assessment enabled by technology require a robust infrastructure, including not only the devices but a comprehensive learning feature, which includes digital learning content and other resources as well as professional development for educators and education leaders (cf., OECD, 2016).

An additional complication of note for educators is that the digital divide encompasses all types of learners. This diversity drives the need for technology to include accessibility for all learners, including those with special needs. Universal design for learning (UDL) principles are now part of the Every Student Succeeds Act (2015), which replaced No Child Left Behind. The UDL framework emphasizes that there are no "average" learners in practice and that effective designs must take into account the fundamental differences that actually exist in any population of learners, especially to achieve equitable results with the most vulnerable and disenfranchised (Rappolt-Schlichtmann et al., 2013). Digital learning tools can offer more flexibility and learning supports than many traditional tools.

Digital technology can also bring the world into the classroom, both motivating and contextualizing literacy practices (Warschauer, 2007). Students have access to authentic, interesting, and self-selected information from multiple sources and viewpoints, enabling them to gather information on topics of interest. Then, digital technology can help them create and publish their work for a wider, authentic audience beyond their teacher and classmates, establishing their identity as digital global citizens (see Hull & Stornaiuolo, 2014).

Educators must remember, however, that sufficient amounts of scaffolding and support are required to help learners make sense of and learn from digital environments (Warschauer, 2007). In particular, the amount of scaffolding and support needed for effective learning is inversely proportional to the learners' prior expertise (Kalyuga, Ayres, Chandler, & Sweller, 2003). At-risk students, including English language learners, students with learning disabilities, and students reading behind grade level, are least able to cope with unstructured environments because the lack of structure places too heavy a cognitive load on the learner (Warschauer, 2007).

The digital divide(s) creates a daunting task for teachers, especially in low-income and linguistically diverse communities. Some of the problems and difficulties faced by educators include issues of workability, complexity, and performativity (Warschauer, Knobel, & Stone, 2004).

*Workability*

Workability refers to the everyday logistical challenges of coordinating access: keeping it running, scheduling shared use, and updating software and applications. Everyday logistical challenges must be met in a highly mobile community of teachers and children passing through schools for four to eight years, and, unsurprisingly, the highest turnover rate and mobility of students is found in the most challenging social environments.

*Complexity*

Even if all the digital technology works and is available, it is difficult to integrate quality usage into the (ever-evolving) curriculum. Students enter the classroom with different initial competencies (e.g., different levels of content knowledge, technology skills). The current environment places a great deal of importance on standardized test scores, many of which are not testing the type of skills best suited to digital technology and only recently are the assessments done digitally (thus requiring modality shifting by students who may become used to writing on computers, for example). Nonetheless, designing technology-enhanced lessons for culturally and linguistically diverse students can be done and can lead to meaningful learning (Cummins, Brown, & Sayers, 2007; Miller, 2015).

*Performativity*

Another difficulty often encountered is "performativity," meaning uses of digital technology for its own sake rather than to increase meaningful learning goals. Students may be able to design complicated PowerPoint presentations including sound and animation but fail to have simple understanding of the embedded content or meaningful communication skills. Comfort and fluency with hardware, software, and the Internet are not ends in themselves but are important components of broader learning goals and should be taught within that context.

**Recommendations and Forward Thinking**

If we are to overcome this digital divide, however we contextualize it, we must expand student access and quality use of digital technology at school and at home. We must use digital technology in pedagogically sound ways to support the curriculum and reflect the context of the community and student. The reasons for the disparities discussed above are varied and involve issues of economics, infrastructure, politics, education, and culture (Warschauer, 2003). Schools have been, and are likely to remain, a major focus of efforts to overcome the digital divide.

With use of the Internet becoming more widespread, it has also become stratified, with some using it principally as an entertainment and social communication device and others using it to seek and create new knowledge (Warschauer, 2003). Thus, digital inequality research is increasingly looking at the use of digital technology, moving beyond simple access to look at which groups are using the information online, for what purpose, and for what length of time. Zillien and Hargittai (2009) refer to this as the *Internet-in-practice*. Variations in use and outcomes for different subpopulations are also being explored. For example, the *digital production gap*—who is creating digital content—is one focus of current research (Schradie, 2011).

Future directions in school-based use focus on optimizing blended learning, which combines in class and online learning environments. Blended learning seems particularly well suited to providing opportunities for personalization of learning so that it meets the needs of a diverse range of students, particularly students who are low-performing, underrepresented minorities, and poor (e.g., Walkington, 2013). Promising advances are being made in adapting instruction based on the characteristics of individual learners, including their prior knowledge, preferences, goals, motivation-related beliefs, mind-sets, and interests (Wigfield et al., 2015). Digital technology offers the opportunity for educators and learners to interact with, customize, and control digital learning environments (Means, Bakia, & Murphy, 2014). Digital technologies used in conjunction with evidence-based practices offer unprecedented opportunities to support the mastery and interest in content areas in personalized ways. Digital media that are dynamic, individualized, and interactive can support motivation and skill acquisition across a diverse range of learners (Graham, Culatta, Pratt, & West, 2004). Integrating digital learning opportunities into ongoing classroom practices with adherence to UDL principles allows teachers and students to access content that is interesting, relevant to each student's life spaces and identities, within each student's zone of proximal development, and scaffolded to allow each student to reach higher levels of learning than otherwise possible (Means et al., 2014).

The concept of a digital divide has helped focus public attention on a critical social issue: The extent to which the diffusion of digital technology and the Internet fosters stratification and marginalization or development and equality (Warschauer, 1993). The policy challenge is not to overcome the divide, but instead to expand access and use for promoting inclusion.

## References

Ames, M. G. (2016). Learning consumption: Media, literacy, and the legacy of One Laptop per Child. *The Information Society, 32*(2), 1–13.

Battle, P., & Attewell, J. (1999). Home computers and school performance. *The Information Society, 15*(1), 1–10.

Becker, H. J. (2000). Who's wired and who's not: Children's access to and use of computer technology. *The Future of Children, 10*(2), 44–75.

Blume, H. (2015). New report finds ongoing iPad and technology problems at L.A. Unified. *LA Times*. Retrieved September 2, 2015, from www.latimes.com/local/lanow/la-me-ln-critical-lausd-tech-report-20150902-story.html.

Blume, H. (2016). L.A. Unified to get $6.4 million in settlement over iPad software. *LA Times*. Retrieved September 25, 2016, from www.latimes.com/local/lanow/la-me-ln-la-unified-ipad-settlement-20150925-story.html.

Carvin, A. (2000). Mind the gap: The digital divide as the civil rights issue of the new millennium. *Multimedia Schools, 7*(1) (January). Retrieved June 22, 2016, from www.infotoday.com/MMSchools/Jan00/carvin.htm.

Cavanaugh, C., Dawson, K., & Ritzhaupt, A. (2011). An evaluation of the conditions, processes, and consequences of laptop computing in K-12 classrooms. *Journal of Educational Computing Research, 45*(3), 359–378.

Common Sense Media, Inc. (2015). The common sense census: Media use by tweens and teens. Retrieved June 22, 2016, from www.commonsensemedia.org/sites/default/files/uploads/research/census_researchreport.pdf.

Cotten, S. R., Davison, E. L., Shank, D. B., & Ward, B. W. (2014). Gradations of disappearing digital divides among racially diverse middle school students. *Communication and Information Technologies Annual, 8,* 25–54.

Cuban, L. (2003). *Oversold and underused: Computers in the classroom*. Cambridge, MA: Harvard University Press.
Cuban, L. (2013). *Inside the black box of classroom practice: Change without reform in American education*. Cambridge, MA: Harvard University Press.
Cummins, J., Brown, K., & Sayers, D. (2007). *Literacy, technology, and diversity: Teaching for success in changing times*. Boston, MA: Pearson.
Education Superhighway (2015). State of the States: A report on the broadband connectivity in America's public schools. Retrieved June 22, 2016, from www.educationsuperhighway.org/stateofthestates.
Fairlie, R., & Robinson, J. (2013). Experimental evidence on the effects of home computers on academic achievement among schoolchildren. *American Economic Journal: Applied Economics, 5*(3), 211–240.
Goldberg, R., January 13, 2016, Data preview: What's new in the July 2015 CPS Computer and Internet Use Supplement. Retrieved from www.ntia.doc.gov/blog/2016/data-preview-what-s-new-july-2015-cps-computer-and-internet-use-supplement.
Graham, C., Culatta, R., Pratt, M., & West, R. (2004). Redesigning the teacher education technology course to emphasize integration. *Computers in the Schools, 21*(1–2), 127–148.
Horrigan, J. B., & Duggan, M. (2015). *Home Broadband 2015*. Pew Research Center. Retrieved June 6, 2016, from www.pewinternet.org/2015/12/21/home-broadband-2015/.
Horrigan, J. B. *Lifelong Learning and Technology*. Retrieved March 22, 2016, from www.pewinternet.org/2016/03/22/lifelong-learning-and-technology/.
Huang, K., Cotten, S. R., Rikard, R. V. (2016). Access is not enough: The impact of emotional costs and self-efficacy on the changes in African-American students' ICT use patterns. *Information, Communication & Society, 20*(4), 637–650.
Hull, G., & Schultz, K. (2001). Literacy and learning out of school: A review of theory and research. *Review of Educational Research, 71*(4), 575–611.
Hull, G. A., & Stornaiuolo, A. (2014). Cosmopolitan literacies, social networks, and "proper distance": Striving to understand in a global world. *Curriculum Inquiry, 44*(1), 15–44.
Kalyuga, S., Ayres, P., Chandler, P., & Sweller, J. (2003). The expertise reversal effect. *Educational Psychologist, 38*(1), 23–31.
Kenworthy, L., & Kielstra, P., The Economist Intelligence Unit, Inc. (2015). Driving the skills agenda: Preparing the students for the future. Retrieved from www.eiuperspectives.economist.com/sites/default/files/Drivingtheskillsagenda.pdf.
Levin, D. (2015). *Pencils Down: The Shift to Online & Computer-Based Testing*. Retrieved June 16, 2016, from www.edtechstrategies.com.
Means, B., Bakia, M., & Murphy, R. (2014). *Learning online: What research tells us about whether, when and how*. New York, NY: Routledge.
Meyer, A., Rose, D. H., & Gordon, D. (2014). *Universal design for learning: Theory and practice*. Wakefield, MA: CAST Professional Publishing. Retrieved from http://udltheorypractice.cast.org.
Miller, S. M. (2015). Teacher learning for new times: Repurposing new multimodal literacies and digital-video composing for schools. *Handbook of research on teaching literacy through the communicative and visual arts, volume II: A project of the International Reading Association*, 441.
Mitra, S. (1999). Minimally invasive education for mass computer literacy. *CSI Communications* (June), pp. 12–16.
Morris, J. (2016). *First Look: Internet Use in 2015*. Retrieved June 29, 2016, from www.ntia.doc.gov/blog/2016/first-look-internet-use-2015.
National Center for Education Statistics (NCES). (2010). *Teachers' Use of Educational Technology in U.S. Public Schools: 2009* (NCES 2010–040). Retrieved August 27, 2015, from https://nces.ed.gov/fastfacts/display.asp?id=46.
National Telecommunications & Information Administration (NTIA), United States Department of Commerce (2014). www.ntia.doc.gov. Retrieved from www.ntia.doc.gov/files/ntia/publications/exploring_the_digital_nation_embracing_the_mobile_internet_10162014.pdf.
National Telecommunications & Information Administration (NTIA) (2016). *Data Explorer*. Retrieved from www.ntia.doc.gov/other-publication/2016/digital-nation-data-explorer.
OECD. (2015). Students, Computers and Literacy: Making the Connection. PISA, OECD Publishing. http://dx.doi.org/10.17871978926423558.en.
Rainie, L., *The Changing Digital Landscape: Where things are heading*. Retrieved November 20, 2015, from Pew.org, http://www.pewinternet.org/2015/11/20/the-changing-digital-landscape-where-things-are-heading/.
Rampey, B. D., Finnegan, R., Goodman, M., Mohadjer, L., Krenzke, T., Hogan, J., & Provasnik, S. (2016). *Skills of U.S. Unemployed, Young, and Older Adults in Sharper Focus: Results from the Program for the International Assessment of Adult Competencies (PIAAC) 2012/2014: First Look* (NCES 2016–039). U.S. Department of Education. Washington, DC: National Center for Education Statistics. Retrieved from: http://nces.ed.gov/pubsearch.
Rappolt-Schlichtmann, G., Daley, S. G., Lim, S., Lapinski, S., Robinson, K. H., & Johnson, M. (2013). Universal design for learning and elementary school science: Exploring the efficacy, use, and perceptions of a web-based science notebook. *Journal of Educational Psychology, 105*(4), 1210.

Rideout, V. J. & Katz, V. S. (2016). *Opportunity for all? Technology and learning in lower-income families*. A report of the Families and Media Project. New York, NY: The Joan Ganz Cooney Center at Sesame Workshop.

Rose, D., & Meyer, A. (2002). *Teaching every student in the digital age: Universal design for learning*. Alexandria, VA: Association for Supervision and Curriculum Development.

Schofield, J. W., & Davidson, A. L. (2004). Achieving equality of student Internet access within schools: Theory, application, and practice. In A. H. Eagly, R. M. Baron, & V. L. Hamilton (Eds.), *The social psychology of group identity and social conflict* (pp. 97–109). Washington, DC: APA Books.

Schradie, J. (2011). The digital production gap: The digital divide and Web 2.0 collide. *Poetics, 39*(2), 145–168.

Scribner, S., & Cole, M. (1981). *The psychology of literacy*. Cambridge, MA: Harvard University Press.

Snyder, T. D., de Brey, C., & Dillow, S. A. (2016). *Digest of Education Statistics 2014 (NCES 2016–006)*. National Center for Education Statistics, Institute of Education Sciences, U.S. Department of Education. Washington, DC.

Stornaiuolo, A., Higgs, J., & Hull, G. (2013). Social media as authorship: Methods for studying literacies and communities online. In P. Albers, T. Holbrook, & A. S. Flint (Eds.), *New literacy research methods* (224–237). New York, NY: Routledge.

U.S. Department of Education (2016). Future Ready Learning: Reimagining the role of technology in Education. Office of Educational Technology. 2016 National Education Technology Plan. Retrieved from http://tech.ed.gov.

Vigdor, J. L., Ladd, H. F., & Martinez, E. (2014). Scaling the digital divide: home computer technology and student achievement. *Economic Inquiry, 52*(3), 1103–1119.

Walkington, C. A. (2013). Using adaptive learning technologies to personalize instruction to student interests: The impact of relevant contexts on performance and learning outcomes. *Journal of Educational Psychology, 105*(4), 932.

Warschauer, M. (2003). *Technology and social inclusion: Rethinking the digital divide*. Cambridge, MA: MIT Press.

Warschauer, M. (2006). *Laptops and literacy: Learning in the wireless classroom*. New York, NY: Teachers College Press.

Warschauer, M. (2007). A teacher's place in the digital divide. *Yearbook of the National Society for the Study of Education, 106*(2), 147–166.

Warschauer, M. (2011). *Learning in the cloud: How (and why) to transform schools with digital media*. New York, NY: Teachers College Press.

Warschauer, M., Cotten, S. R., & Ames, M. G. (2011). One laptop per child Birmingham: Case study of a radical experiment. *International Journal of Learning and Media, 3*(2), 61–76.

Warschauer, M., Knobel, M., & Stone, L. (2004). Technology and equity in schooling: Deconstructing the digital divide. *Educational Policy, 18*(4), 562–588.

Warschauer, M., & Matuchniak, T. (2010). New technology and digital worlds: Analyzing evidence of equity in access, use, and outcomes. *Review of Research in Education, 34*(1), 179–225.

Warschauer, M., & Newhart, V. A. (2015). Broadening our concepts of universal access. *Universal Access in the Information Society, 15*(2), 1–6.

Wigfield, A., Eccles, J. S., Fredricks, J. A., Simpkins, S., Roeser, R. W., & Schiefele, U. (2015). Development of achievement motivation and engagement. *Handbook of child psychology and developmental science* (pp. 657–700). New York, NY: John Wiley.

Witte, J. C., & Mannon, S. E. (2010). *The Internet and social inequalities*. New York, NY: Routledge.

Zhang, T., Xie, Q., Park, B. J., Kim, Y. Y., Broer, M., & Bohrnstedt, G. (2016). Computer Familiarity and Its Relationship to Performance in Three NAEP Digital-Based Assessments.

Zheng, B., Warschauer, M., Lin, C.-H., & Chang, C. (2016). Learning in one-to-one laptop environments: A meta-analysis and research synthesis. *Review of Educational Research, 86*(4), 1052–1084.

Zillien, N., & Hargittai, E. (2009). Digital distinction: Status-specific types of Internet usage. *Social Science Quarterly, 90*, 274–291.

# 6
# Beyond the Techno-Missionary Narrative
## Digital Literacy and Necropolitics

Elizabeth Losh

"Stay with me." These were the first words Diamond Reynolds uttered as she live-streamed video to the social network site Facebook that would eventually be seen by millions. The gruesome ten and a half minutes of footage displayed the bloody aftermath of the traffic stop in which her boyfriend, Philando Castile, had been mortally wounded by a police officer. He lay next to her in the driver's seat, which appeared onscreen to be the passenger's seat because the image had been digitally mirrored by software. Reynolds continued with remarkable stoicism as she narrated the circumstances of the shooting. She addressed the officer as "sir" when he interrupted her account of the events, which began with her questioning the fundamental issue of probable cause.

> We got pulled over for a busted taillight in the back. And the police just he's he's he's covered. They killed my boyfriend. He's licensed. He's carried to. He's licensed to carry. He was trying to get out his ID and his wallet out his pocket. And he let the officer know that he was, he had a firearm, and he was reaching for his wallet. And the officer just shot him in his arm. We're waiting for a back up.

Facebook Live was still a relatively new feature that users had been testing with fireworks displays and family reunions that summer, but the use of mobile phones to document apparent police abuses and post them to social media was already an established phenomenon in visual culture that gave support to the Black Lives Matter movement and to other campaigns against lethal police interactions with citizens of color. *New York Times* critic James Poniewozik described how Reynolds' phone video communicated both agency and a profound lack of agency in its rhetorical style: "The video puts you in the moment, but it disembodies you. You are this machine, picked up, dropped down, pulled back out. You are eyes and ears without arms and legs."

That same day Joan Donovan, a white postdoctoral researcher and member of the FemTechNet collective of feminist digital researchers, posted a blog entry about the phenomenon of "statactivism" in which statistics were used by news organizations and activist collectives to make visible pervasive patterns of inequality and abuse. According to Donovan, "statistics are the language of the state, yet, when produced in a rigorous and methodical way, data production can be a complementary tactic to street protests." Her blog post entitled "How Many Stolen Lives?" examined data from five sources about police killings of black suspects: two newspapers with a significant online presence (*The Guardian* and *The Washington Post*) and three activist websites (Killed by Police, Fatal Encounters, and

Mapping Police Violence). In pointing to discrepancies in the numbers reported between different sources, Donovan advocated for taking up the "weapons of the geek" that fostered data literacy in the interest of greater information access and transparency. However, such data visualizations also always conceal as much as they reveal by abstracting, simplifying, and disembodying information in order to make messages more legible to the user of a given data interface. Text-oriented delivery mechanisms, such as Donovan's blog, can provide context, background, and interpretive nuance, as well as foster dissemination of statistical evidence to the broadest possible publics.

As these two case studies demonstrate, digital literacies are being fundamentally reshaped by new practices involving increasingly ubiquitous technologies and the growing capacities of institutions, corporations, communities, and even individuals for the collection and display of big data (Joseph, 2016). With more students expressing solidarity with Black Lives Matter and other online social movements devoted to urban human rights, their repertoire of rhetorical tactics may also be shaped by the positions available for their identity work. Unlike the open and relatively unscripted playable experimentation imagined by James Paul Gee's vision of discourse as an "identity kit" (1998), race and gender are not categories of difference that can be easily removed, even in the supposedly disembodied territory of cyberspace (Nakamura & Chow-White, 2012).

Although affiliation with networked activist collectives may operate in physically remote locations, students' digital utterances often respond to real-time exigencies that are perceived as hyperpresent and site specific. Furthermore, the formulation of "life" as a value to be defended counters the rationalization of death by political institutions and provides an alternative theoretical framework to the dominant culture of necropolitics.

Despite the dire circumstances of a police shooting as a traumatic moment in time, when compelled to perform rhetorically in situations of crisis, students may appreciate being recognized by more experienced signal-boosting activists likely to retweet or repost their content. These digital mavens may welcome them into a "community of practice" (Wenger, 1998) or acknowledge their proficiency as composers through more formalized "literacy events" (Heath, 1982).

This essay argues that different kinds of rhetorical engagement necessitate different tactics and—just as they may for the composing self in academic settings (Canagarajah, 2002)—require the deployment of different identities, subjectivities, roles, and voices. Such new tactics include augmenting citizen journalism with live video streaming and self-broadcasting, designing information graphics that complement data journalism efforts, experimenting with the invisible algorithms of playable media to gamify activism, and appending metadata to political messages in hashtag campaigns. Although these new digital activities may present exciting opportunities for educators to engage students who are already deeply invested in the Black Lives Matter movement, they can be fraught with peril for instructors who may ignore their own entanglements with existing structures of power and privilege (Kim & Kim, 2014) and appropriate student discourse unethically if the need for community informed consent is ignored (Bailey, 2015).

## Defining Digital Literacy

In considering how digital literacy is defined, Reynolds' powerful use of live streaming technologies on her mobile phone would generally be considered a performance that did not require any special skills. There was no editing, compositing, coding, tagging, or fabricating requiring knowledge of arcane lexicons or procedures to communicate with her device. In fact news commentators frequently described her performance as "raw" and characterized it as unmediated and paraprofessional "citizen journalism."[1]

However, just as Susan Sontag has argued that "authentic" and "staged" do not operate as simple binaries in still photography, producing live footage inevitably involves practice and rehearsal to manage the complex networks of relationships that exist between human actors, remote audiences, and ubiquitous technologies. In *Updating to Remain the Same,* Wendy Chun (2016) has pointed out that "habitual new media" assumes conditions in which the mobile and embedded technologies for constantly recording and disseminating information are assumed to omnipresent, user-friendly, and universally accessible. Chun also posits that the channel to and from various networked publics is defined not by "an imagined and anonymous 'we'" but rather by the constant compulsive claims of "a relentlessly pointed yet empty, singular yet plural YOU" (p. 3). According to Chun, despite this movement of media to the position of an invisible background condition for an ever-performing self, "our media matter most when they seem not to matter at all" (p. 1). Chun's formula "Habit + Crisis = Update" theorizes a close and symbiotic relationship between banality and urgency in using the new media of daily life.

Certainly, Reynolds' use of Facebook Live should not be dismissed as unsophisticated. Her Facebook feed showed that she had been experimenting with Facebook Live for weeks, testing it out to take a variety of video selfies and even using it several times in a car in traffic. Some of the footage she had captured in the days before the traffic stop was dramatic and violent. For example, one of her earlier videos caught a fight between two men which was happening in real time outside of her car window. Her knowledge of digital signifying practices also stretched across several domains: she posted animated gifs, emojis, and videos with digital filters that transformed moving images of herself into cartoon characters, aged women, or other chimerical beings.

This is not to suggest that Reynolds' "Police" stream is somehow inauthentic, merely because she had been practicing with the technology and had knowledge of how to use it in a variety of rhetorical occasions to serve different purposes and audiences. Moreover, although the genre of the selfie is conventionally associated with vanity, exhibitionism, superficiality, and commodification of lifestyle, the selfie also facilitates many kinds of important identity work and political performance at a transnational scale (Senft & Baym, 2015). For example, acts of poiphotographic self-representation were central to black activists who used the #iftheygunnedmedown hashtag that highlighted differences between legitimated and subaltern imagery, and their combination of adopting common metadata naming conventions and performing gestures of political solidarity through online image-sharing practices attracted the attention of mainstream media outlets to concerns about police abuse. Furthermore, the subject's body isn't the only focus of attention in such images, which may also perform place-making activities or communicate information about the subject's relationship to technological apparatuses.

In other words, the self always exists in a context and that context is part of the complexity of composing and interpreting such multimodal messages. As Manuel Castells (2012) points out of the Arab Spring demonstrations in Cairo's Tahrir Square in 2011, the tasks of individuals "broadcasting live" and "recording history-making with their cell phones" entailed also maintaining connections between "Internet's social media, people's social networks, and mainstream media" as well as focusing "on developments in the public space" (p. 60) in which the physical constraints and affordances of the urban built environment allowed their signal for public protest to be amplified. Nicholas Mirzoeff (2015) observes that those who regularly participate in visual culture seek to understand how mobile photography may communicate information about power and status—including economic, social, and political status—in complicated ways and that seeing is invariably a learned activity that reflects the conditions of particular individuals, particular communities, and particular infrastructural conditions.

## Mediating Immediacy in Intersectional Frameworks

Jonathan Alexander and Elizabeth Losh (2010) have argued that there are often competing claims about the entities best suited to teach digital literacies and about the institutional settings that maximize inclusive forces and minimize exclusive ones. So what does the acute risk to the body faced by young Men of Color in urban communities mean for digital education efforts, particularly for feminists who assert that the personal is the political and benefit from the legacies of Take Back the Night and other social movements that developed out of their own outrage about violence experienced on the street?

Moreover, how do digital literacy practices that respond to the threat of police violence and asymmetrical power relations with law enforcement relate to the more conventional techno-missionary project of teaching computational literacy in urban areas to foster STEM education and diversify technology fields?

A number of digital literacy projects designed with and by white feminists have explored how urban young People of Color can engage with coding, hacking, glitch testing, circuitry, 3D printing, and physical computing. What are the lessons learned from these projects and how can potential blind spots about intersectional identity be acknowledged in these efforts?

Kimberlé Crenshaw, who is widely credited with coining the term "intersectionality," recently remarked that it functions primarily as "an analytic sensibility" or "a way of thinking about identity and its relationship to power," which was initially "articulated on behalf of black women" and the consequences of biases involving both race and gender. The term has come to be applied to other confluences of discrimination to challenge "the invisibility of many constituents within groups that claim them as members, but often fail to represent them." An intersectional understanding of digital literacy initiatives encourages those who enter communities of color not to appropriate the resources of those communities or to presume to represent the needs of the inhabitants.

As Jacqueline Wernimont and Elizabeth Losh (2016) have asserted, technology facilitates the formation of many kinds of hybrid identities, including "cyborgs," "intermediaries," "negotiators," "translators," and "go-betweens" (p. 43) but Whiteness often seems to function as a kind of default setting for technology educators. In this work, we build on the ideas of Jasmine Rault who has described how "white affects" block out contradictory information that might rebut white activists' fantasies of solidarity and universalism in shared struggles. Rault has used the trope of "white noise" to describe the constant co-presence of active interference and background state in activist interventions that lack critical reflection. In thinking about digital technology initiatives intended for underprivileged youth, Wernimont and Losh claim that this premise of Whiteness as a norm often extends to ways that hackerspaces, maker spaces, fab labs, and other environments for informal knowledge-sharing among members of affinity groups assume the norms of gentrification, slumming, squatting, doling out charity, and other practices of White privilege that are common in urban postindustrial environments (2017).

Certainly, ideas about the popularization of technical knowledge may be marked by particular preconceptions about age, gender, sexuality, class, ability, and race. When Ron Eglash (2008) recounts a story about graduate students in computational mathematics enthusing about strategies for community engagement and applying theory to practice, he is clearly dismayed by their unconscious frames of privilege. He describes a planned expertise transferal to teach computational literacy that is structured around the graduate students' allegiances as fans of the America's Cup. He is distressed by the confluence of "computing power and financial power" that allows yacht owners to make "their problem more attractive than poverty, racism, sexism, and other humanitarian problems" (p. 62), which he partially attributes to the advantages of "good problem definition" (p. 62).

S. Craig Watkins (2009) has asserted that young People of Color are often extremely astute and sophisticated users of computational media, particularly as users of mobile and ubiquitous computing technologies. Although these devices might not be designed with programming interfaces like the desktop or laptop machines conventionally associated with hackers, their affordances favoring a range of phatic interactions (channel checking, in common parlance) may foster rich conversations to sustain networks and build communities. Watkins argues that the stereotypical "digital divide" narrative that casts Black and Latina/o young people as in need of charity distorts how they actually exercise their agency while also being marked by race in online spaces. Watkins ends *The Young and the Digital* on a hopeful note by emphasizing how the election of Barack Obama might symbolize new forms of digital participation for underrepresented youth.

In contrast, Ernest Morrell's *Critical Media Pedagogy* (2013), which was published four years after Watkins' text, cautions that teachers of media skills might find themselves interacting with students who are more despairing than hopeful and more committed to extra-institutional social movements than to electoral politics. He suggests that the shooting of 22-year-old Oscar Grant, an unarmed black man who had been handcuffed by officers at the Fruitvale station, which was captured on cell phones by bystanders using the Bay Area Rapid Transit system, displays not only "skills" but "sensibilities" (p. 16). In addition to creating viral videos, he notes that hacktivists who wanted to spur more public outrage about Grant's killing also orchestrated denial of service attacks on the BART website (p. 21).

Developing media activism curricula to address police brutality in the United States has been a special concern of the international human rights organization WITNESS. From their New York offices, the website at Witness.org supplies lesson plans, assignments, and training materials to teach students about how to effectively document abuses of police power by the state. Although many of the materials on the site address the needs of activists in other countries, they have specifically designed materials for recording the actions of armed officers in the United States. Instructions include basic digital literacy guidelines for mobile devices about passwords, storage, and data backup, as well as advice about capturing salient details and seeking expert advice before posting to social networks. Elsewhere on the site, potential video witnesses are counseled about IP addresses and distinctive signatures left on digital files to protect the privacy and security of vulnerable sources, and software that masks the identity of witnesses is also discussed as a potential safety tool.

In an environment of constant digital surveillance, John Palfrey and Urs Gasser (2008) have warned that the data histories of youth may serve as comprehensive "digital dossiers" to be mined by third parties in ways that compromise their privacy. In their educational efforts, WITNESS cautions that these trails and traces can create risks to security and safety as well, particularly if would-be citizen journalists face retaliation and retribution for exposing abuses of power with mobile digital media. This understanding of digital literacy may challenge the dominant transparency paradigm that emphasizes how media expose and make visible and may suggest that masking identity can be an important aspect of learning about computational media as well.

**Resisting Digital Necropolitics**

Some argue that literacy in computational media involves not only making, viewing, and sharing digital files but also sometimes *refusing* to make, view, or share images of the mortality of People of Color, because such transmission may exploit trauma and normalize voyeurism. In her essay on "How Do I (Not) Look? Live Feed Video and Viral Black Death," Alexandra Juhasz (2016) discusses the power of Reynolds' video while also defending her choice not to view it. She expresses admiration for what she knows second-hand about the digital rhetoric of the video and its "clear, pointed and at times emotional voice over," "expert framing and camera movement," and "steady sequencing of emotions, information and reveals," but she also advises against uncritical consumption of the digital artifacts of black death. In explaining her decision not to watch Reynolds' Facebook Live video of the brutal death of her boyfriend in the driver's seat, Juhasz emphasizes how diverting one's gaze should "not be a closing of one's eyes to the actual and ongoing brutality against black people in our society and its ever-increasing video record" but rather a commitment "to also look carefully elsewhere—away from documents of the act of violence itself—to do the harder work of seeing the 'causality, responsibility, and impact' that often (or must) go unseen." Juhasz argues that focusing on discourses about the right to look (Mirzoeff, 2011) may obscure how playing and sharing such files promulgates revictimization and potential breaches of ethics in certain digital literacy practices.

Like Morrell, Juhasz references the cell phone videos of the death of Oscar Grant. However, drawing on the work of Jennifer Malkowski, Juhasz claims that the Grant videos were fundamentally different because they were circulated primarily among members of a regional audience in Bay Area communities of color as part of their efforts to effect policy change and foster affiliations with specific activist cohorts. In contrast, Reynolds' video was disseminated for general consumption to further the affective gratification of the viewer at the prurient spectacle of black death. According to Juhasz, the Grant videos also did not reproduce the familiar cinematic grammar of graphic violence deployed by Reynolds' video in which she presents herself as a "politically, personally, and aesthetically skilled" master of formal conventions.

In his work coining the term "necropolitics" or the biopolitical ideologies that routinize and rationalize the deaths of People of Color, Achille Mbembe (2003) claims that racism serves as both a "technology" and a "calculus" to maintain political control by a dominant racial group. Mbembe argues that "savage life" becomes perceived of as "animal life" and that "dehumanizing and industrializing death" has a long history for the slave or the colonial subject who is controlled by regimes of aerial surveillance and other forms of state oversight. The question for those involved in digital literacy education may be whether competing activist practices of "sousveillance" that captures footage documenting oppression from an on-the-ground perspective (Mann, Nolan, & Wellman, 2002) counter the dehumanizing and scopophilic tendencies of the necropolitical gaze.

The "statactivism" that Donovan advocates presents another alternative for promulgating digital literacy with an awareness of necropolitical biases. By teaching the young people most likely to be affected by death at the hands of the state how to appropriate the data catalogued by surveiling bureaucracies and compile it, it becomes possible present competing narratives about black male death resulting from interactions with the police. Teaching information visualization has probably received less national attention from STEM initiatives than activities more familiar to engineering subcultures like teaching programming languages or 3D printing, but these skills may also be closer to the conventional K-12 agenda for promoting digital, numerical, and multimodal literacy, although programs for so-called "data journalism" generally focus on postsecondary education.[2]

It is worth noting that necropolitical visualizations have a long predigital history. For example, information designer Edward Tufte (1997) is fond of citing John Snow's map of 13 community pump-wells and 83 deaths from an 1854 cholera epidemic in London as a classic example of best practices for representing data honestly. Tufte insists that a good information visualization should have four basic elements to facilitate responsible decision-making: (1) placing the data in an appropriate context for assessing cause and effect, (2) making quantitative comparisons, (3) considering alternative explanations and contrary cases, and (4) assessment of possible errors in the numbers reported in graphics. Tufte also lauds visualizations that show Charles Minard's map of troop losses from Napoleon's 1812 march on Moscow and other novel ways to communicate death statistics.

However, Ben Williamson (2014) emphasizes in a blog post for educators focusing on digital media and learning that information visualization should not claim to be completely neutral or objective:

> The visualization and diagrammatization of the world described here is a complex technical act involving a variety of actors and technologies that ultimately possess the persuasive power to shape people's engagement and interaction with the world itself. Data visualization acts as a kind of lens, shaping the gaze, through which the world beyond is made visible in order to be seen in particular ways, with a particular focus, framing, coloring, and direction.

Williamson's colleague Sarah Doyle asserts that visualizing data is always "a kind of translating, but like all translations, the work requires decisions about form and content" and those decisions about "what to code in and what to code out" are made by both human and nonhuman entities. Using digital humanities techniques, Lauren Klein has shown that many predigital data visualizations were also riddled with errors, because creating a legible visualization always involves normalizing and cleaning up data.

## Hashtag Syllabi

Another strategy for combining digital literacy efforts with attention to the problem of necropolitics involves the rapid production of crowd-sourced online syllabi, which are often developed by educators seeking to channel outpourings of outrage and grief about the violent deaths of People of Color into pedagogical activities and academic analysis. Using hashtags with the metadata of geographical place names such as #Ferguson (for the police shooting of Michael Brown), #Charleston (for the shooting of black parishioners by a white supremacist), and #Orlando (for the shootings of LGBT People of Color at a gay nightclub) allows educators to quickly compile resources for reading and viewing, such as critical essays, philosophical treatises, or sociological case studies. In addition to academic content created by the scholarly community, such syllabi also present lists of relevant novels, films, online videos, and blog postings. Often there is considerable second-order curation and collaborative authorship, as teams of educators organize materials on the syllabi on shared resource pages hosted on platforms such as Google Docs. In this way, educators created the #Ferguson syllabus, the #Charleston syllabus, and the #Orlando syllabus. Even the #Lemonade syllabus that responded to the launch of a popular Beyoncé music album and video offered an intersectional exploration of necropolitics, along with probing uncomfortable silences about infidelity, sexuality, spirituality, and the black family. The #Lemonade syllabus specifically included material about the segment of Beyoncé's *Lemonade* video devoted to the deaths of People of Color at the hands of the police by showing the mourning families holding pictures of their loved ones.

Such syllabi make explicit connections between affective responses on social media and formal literacy practices in scholarly and artistic communities by directing participants who might be overwhelmed by outpourings of feelings expressed on online social networks to literary, historical, philosophical, and other critical readings in the traditional print canon to promulgate interpretive activities from the scene of information overload and communal sense-making from the alienated reactions of seemingly autonomous individuals. In the case of the #CharlestonSyllabus, the collection of hashtagged materials eventually evolved into an anthology available as a print textbook.

## Race as Technology: Gaming Literacies

These online syllabi, information visualizations, and archives of citizen videos generally do not address how the categories of race and gender themselves can be read as technologies, as Beth Coleman, Wendy Chun, Lisa Nakamura, Anne Balsamo, Judy Wajcman, and many other scholars of computational media do. If whiteness and maleness are seen as the default skins for digital participation in the supposedly postracial environment of computational media, that norm in algorithmic expression is a product of a variety of design decisions and encoding of rule sets, many of which predate digital culture.

Fox Harrell argues in his work on "phantasmal media" that software functions as "expressive media" that performs identity work for "[s]elves, others, social ills, and everyday experiences" as well as "emotions, culture, beauty, gender, race, privilege, civilization, and power" (2013, p. 29). In Harrell's account, even software designed for utilitarian purposes creates "integrated epistemic spaces and images spaces" (p. 29). As a case in point he examines software designed to simulate the conditions of riots responding to grievances against the police, which can be visualized in digital models (pp. 28–29). Rather than merely address coding literacy, Harrell identifies "subjective computing," "cultural computing," and "critical computing" as key areas for inquiry (2009) and by extension digital literacy efforts. Borrowing from cognitive science, Harrell embraces subjective experiences that are often divorced from the supposed objectivity of STEM education, and he elevates the figure of the traveling African griot as a metaphor for the storytelling, entertainment, and play from which meaning and development emerge.

In his collaborations with Sneha Veeragoudar Harrell, Fox Harrell has focused on the computational identities of black male youth and how particular cultural constructions of digital avatars might be perceived by these audiences as either meeting or failing to meet the standard of an ideal "solid" persona. In describing one student's sense of how identity matches algorithmic output, members of the research team assert that by using the term "solid" to characterize desired black masculinity, as one boy in their case study, "does not mean something so simplistic as being provided with an avatar of appropriate skin tone," because "in addition to physical appearance, the avatar should be able to present the body language, gestures, facial expressions, fashions, discourse styles, and other attributes that would allow it to become a paragon for the values encapsulated by the term." For these young men, "solid" functions as "an epistemic form" that supersedes one-size-fits-all labels and is "grounded in marginalized urban, youth, northern Californian, self-identified person of color experiences" and a performance of intersectional identity that requires design of a system of computational media with an adequate set of affordances.

Ian Bogost (2007) claims that by examining the procedural rhetorics—rather than more obvious verbal or visual rhetorics—that govern videogame play, it is possible through experimentation with the mechanics of a game to deconstruct computational arguments that rely on unstated premises written into the code. For example, in his analysis of *Grand Theft Auto: San Andreas*, Bogost (2006) argues that because the game's inner city gangster protagonist CJ must eat "to maintain his stamina and strength" but only has easy access to fast food that causes weight gain that inhibits his abilities to "run or fight very effectively" (p. 176), the game also teaches a lesson about food deserts, structural racism, and how barriers to economic inclusion can be linked to obesity rates in urban areas of color. In Harrell's view, such procedural rhetorics also function at the level of avatar choice by linking particular gender and racial stereotypes together in the design process.

White feminist digital educators have also focused on responding to the perceived constructs of black masculinity. For example, Betsy DiSalvo and Amy Bruckman have studied Atlanta-area African-American teens involved in service learning projects arranged by their university with video game companies. Unlike computer camps or technology lab after-school programs that assume access to disposable income and leisure time, DiSalvo's "Glitch Game Testers" treated students as paid employees. Glitch Game Testers participants had part-time jobs during the school year and full-time jobs during the summer that provided economic as well as educational incentives to pursue careers in computer science and other STEM-related fields. By treating young Black men as valid economic actors, DiSalvo addresses the criticism that digital literacy initiatives often assume that children exist in a separate sphere from adult commerce. According to Sarah Banet-Weiser (2004), this misguided "sacralization of childhood" entails prohibitions on many forms of participation that display, exercise, or develop the technological competencies of young people because they must be excluded from adult realms of computational literacy, economic participation, and sexual agency.

The Glitch Game Testers program also made a long-term commitment to mentoring and economic support and tried to tailor services around stated needs. According to DiSalvo, other programs "parachute-in" with a rescue mentality that shows little respect for existing attitudes in African-American communities. Local mentors from Georgia Tech and historically black Morehouse College were also part of the Glitch Game Testers team and served as both coaches and role models. In keeping with her general philosophy of digital literacy education, DiSalvo appreciated how communities could be sites of knowledge production, just as universities or tech corporations might be.

At the very least, DiSalvo wished to avoid repeating mistakes made by other digital literacy initiatives, such as those lampooned by Lori Emerson. Emerson sees a long history of misguided technomissionary efforts that is epitomized by Nicholas Negroponte and the MIT Media Lab beginning with the Hessdorfer Experiment with three Black men in a "Boston ghetto" in the late sixties and later extending to the millennial ambitions of the One Laptop Per Child initiative to export computers to impoverished children in the developing world. In response to Negroponte's assertion that "the machine was not black, was not white, and certainly had no prejudices," Emerson (2016) laments that "the entire racist, deceptive undertaking… demonstrates what can happen when we believe so completely in the neutrality of the machine." Emerson even summarizes Negroponte's solutionism and reductionism in a mocking aphorism: "Got a race problem? Get a computer!"

By considering the situated experiences of her core group of clients, DiSalvo decided to focus on fostering STEM learning around sports video games. This choice was based on assessing the interests of participants and evaluating the software they used most frequently, although such games were usually not seen as particularly educational or intellectual and might play into the stereotypes about "solid" normativity questioned by Harrell. DiSalvo recruited students attending schools that were 99% African-American and where most students were well below the poverty line. Students adopted the professional roles of play testers doing quality assurance jobs for commercial video game companies and were tasked with searching for bugs in new games. With three years of funding from the National Science Foundation, DiSalvo paid students and offered job training and introductory courses in computer science.

DiSalvo was soon intrigued by the discovery that her clients often had contempt for common video game play practices such as "hacking, cheating, and modding," which other digital literacy educators had claimed provide powerful informal learning practices among self-described "geeks" destined for careers in technology. For example, James Paul Gee (2003) argued that it was necessary for players to disobey stated directives and experiment with consequences, Mia Consalvo (2007) argued that cheating was the rule rather than the exception in video game play, and Mimi Ito and Judd Antin (2010) argued that gossip and appropriation could be important venues for digital literacy. However, for many African-American urban youth, as DiSalvo said in an interview (2011), notions of masculinity seemed to be defined by codes of idealized sportsmanship and physical prowess rather than a so-called "hacker ethic" that emphasized exploiting vulnerabilities.

As DiSalvo explained in a video for the DML Summer Institute (2011), the trajectory of her somewhat unconventional career as a digital educator, activist, and researcher had begun with a focus on preparing middle school girls for technological careers, about half of whom were African American. Appealing to the female demographic had already been emphasized in dozens if not hundreds of digital literacy initiatives, including high profile efforts like Black Girls Code, Girls Who Code, and Made with Code. The surge of such digital inclusion efforts aimed at girls as designed to counter the predominant "brogrammer" culture of Silicon Valley and to retain underrepresented employees and students in the field. Nonetheless, critics charged that these "pinkification" projects would do little to address sexism, misogyny, microaggressions, and implicit bias (Brown, 2014). As a graduate student formulating research questions for her dissertation, DiSalvo realized that STEM efforts that used gaming to appeal to young African-American men were comparatively undertheorized, and she began to develop the Glitch Game Testers concept.

Rather than assume that her subjects only needed access to technology and mastery of content, DiSalvo seriously examined why, as rational actors, African-American male students might have "motivation to not learn" and expectations of "taking responsibility" that inhibited formal schooling. It could be said that in promoting computer science through sports gaming the body and questions of presence come to the forefront despite the transhuman rhetoric of many in technological fields. Ironically, many students soon found that the QA work of playing games was often detail-oriented and repetitive and thus preferred the supposedly less desirable computer science instruction that provided more variety and satisfaction.

Of course, the impetus to disseminate the knowledge of computer science as a discipline often means that programming is prioritized as a form of digital literacy. Annette Vee has argued that all such literacy efforts—especially those targeting disenfranchised populations—come with assumptions about positive character values, although "justifications for teaching programming as a generalized skill are often pronounced along civic lines, rather than the moral and religious forces behind textual literacy campaigns in the nineteenth century" (p. 54). In working with different computer languages and programming interfaces (Alice, Jython, and Java) with the Glitch Game Testers, DiSalvo discovered that students were resistant to composing code they perceived of as too "toy-like" and aspired to competence programming in environments associated with professionalism and maturity.

In writing for audiences in game studies, educational technology, and digital inclusion, DiSalvo does not provide much critical reflection about how her identity as a white female researcher who is considerably older than the black male students in her project might be better understood through intersectional frameworks or about how their mobile video practices with technologies of ubiquitous computing might also provide an avenue to participation in expert digital publics. The ritualized and stylized aggression in the virtual environments of sports video games is obviously also very different from a summary execution in the street.

**Online Violence and Police Violence**

Digital literacy efforts also must acknowledge that the distorted norms of internet communication itself—which grew out of practices developed decades ago on bulletin boards, online forums, and ranking sites—may contribute to racialized and sexualized violence. In seeking possible remedies to toxic online racism and misogyny, the Center for Solutions to Online Violence (CSOV) represents a novel experiment in online pedagogy. As a digital literacy resource center with a design philosophy informed by Woman of Color feminism, it presents numerous tutorials and lesson plans to combat online harassment, stalking, identity theft, defamation, humiliation, and virtual rape and lynching. Visitors to the site can choose one of four identities ("survivor," "educator," "journalist," and "do better" for contrite former offenders) to explore materials or get tips about locking down their digital identities. Because Reynolds was harassed by perpetrators of online violence after her video went viral, much of her public digital profile on Facebook has been deleted, so it is difficult for educational researchers to analyze how her online persona might have evolved and developed if it were able to do so in a misogynoir-free public online space.

One of the more radical practitioners involved in digital literacy efforts at the CSOV, micha cárdenas, has addressed the concerns of the #BlackLivesMatter movement even more directly by repurposing ideas about digital fabrication from the maker movement to the needs of People of Color for survival gear. As a transgender Woman of Color aspiring to be an "android goddess," her projects for potential victims of violence who are suspicious of police authority have included mesh network signaling systems and DIY wearables with bulletproof materials. Such approaches acknowledge necropolitical conditions for digital literacy efforts more directly and the need for intersectional awareness among educators who teach students to compose digital media for a variety of audiences and purposes.

As an educator, I tend to see myself as an advocate for "digital rhetoric" rather than "digital literacy." I worry that the term "literacy" fosters a false sense among administrators that such instruction is apolitical, although the digital literacy advocates that I have cited in this essay certainly know better. I also think that it is important to ensure that digital rights and responsibilities remain part of the discussion of digital performance in activist contexts. Engaging with other people online should always be informed by an ethics of care (Boellstorff, Nardi, Pearce, & Taylor, 2012) and an awareness of the problematic nature of our invariably intersectional identities. As a White straight cisgender woman thinking through what digital literacy means in the era of #BlackLivesMatter both for digital theorists of color and for urban populations of young men at risk of sudden death or bodily injury in communities in which people are armed with smartphones, I would counsel others to avoid the techno-missionary mistakes that are so easy to make out in the field.

**Notes**

1. A robust conception of "citizen journalism" that is enabled by access to digital devices and in which "every citizen is a reporter" is often traced to around the year 2000 with the launch of OhmyNews in South Korea. This millennial narrative might obfuscate the fact that many other online forums for the aggregation of independent or alternative media sources existed throughout the eighties and nineties. Many have argued that the term "citizen journalism" itself is flawed. For example, Sam Gregory of WITNESS.org claims that "witness journalism" may be a more accurate characterization of such activities to account for the possibility of legal reckoning and the requirements of processes of judgment. In 1999 Jay Rosen characterized journalism by those who are not paid professionals as "public or civic journalism."
2. "Data journalism" is another important term of art in these discussions to describe how numerical information supports particular advocacy positions or quests for transparency. Unlike citizen journalism, data journalism is assumed to be resource-intensive and to require a high level of technical expertise, because collaborations with designers, computer scientists, or statisticians may be required. See the Data Journalism Handbook at http://datajournalismhandbook.org/1.0/en/ for further reading.

**References**

Alexander, J., & Losh, E. (n.d.). Whose literacy is it anyway? Examining a first-year approach to gaming across curricula currents in electronic literacy. *Currents in Electronic Literacy*. Retrieved from http://currents.cwrl.utexas.edu/2010/alexander_losh_whose-literacy-is-it-anyway.

Andén-Papadopoulos, K. (2014). Citizen camera-witnessing: Embodied political dissent in the age of "mediated mass self-communication." *New Media & Society*, 16(5), 753–769.

Bailey, M. (2015). #transform(ing)DH writing and research: An autoethnography of digital humanities and feminist ethics. *Digital Humanities Quarterly*, 9(2). Retrieved from http://digitalhumanities.org/dhq/vol/9/2/000209/000209.html.

Banet-Weiser, S. (2004). Surfin' the net: Children, parental, obsolescence, and citizenship. In M. Sturken, D. Thomas, & S. Ball-Rokeach (Eds.), *Technological visions: the hopes and fears that shape new technologies* (pp. 270–292). Philadelphia, PA: Temple University Press.

Boellstorff, T., Nardi, B., Pearce, C., & Taylor, T. L. (2012). *Ethnography and virtual worlds: A handbook of method*. Princeton, NJ: Princeton University Press.

Bogost, I. (2006). Videogames and ideological frames. *Popular Communication*, 4(3), 165–183.

Bogost, I. (2007). *Persuasive games: The expressive power of videogames*. Cambridge, MA: MIT Press.

Brown, K. V. (2014, July 8). How not to attract women to coding: Make tech pink. *SF Gate*.

Canagarajah, A. S. (2002). *Critical academic writing and multilingual students*. Ann Arbor: University of Michigan Press.

Castells, M. (2012). *Networks of outrage and hope: Social movements in the Internet age*. Cambridge, UK; Malden, MA: Polity Press.

Center for Solutions to Online Violence – FemTechNet. (2016). Retrieved from http://femtechnet.org/csov/.

#Charlestonsyllabus. (n.d.). Retrieved from www.aaihs.org/resources/charlestonsyllabus/.

Chun, W. H. K. (2016). *Updating to remain the same: Habitual new media*. Cambridge, MA: MIT Press.

Consalvo, M. (2007). *Cheating: Gaining advantage in videogames*. Cambridge, MA: MIT Press.

Crenshaw, K. (2015, September 24). Why intersectionality can't wait. *The Washington Post*. Retrieved from www.washingtonpost.com/news/in-theory/wp/2015/09/24/why-intersectionality-cant-wait/.

DiSalvo, B. (2014). Graphical qualities of educational technology: Using drag-and-drop and text-based programs for introductory computer science. *IEEE Computer Graphics and Applications*, 34(6), 12–15.

DMLResearchHub. (n.d.). *Betsy DiSalvo-DML Summer Institute 2011*. Retrieved from www.youtube.com/watch?time_continue=19&v=XKcS7uRResw.

Donovan, J. (2016, July 6). *How many stolen lives?* Retrieved from http://occupythesocial.com/post/147020069698/how-many-stolen-lives.

Doyle, S. (2013, September 19). Data visualization as a socio-digital practice. Retrieved from https://codeactsineducation.wordpress.com/about/.

Eglash, R. (2008). Computing power. In M. Fuller (Ed.), *Software studies: a lexicon* (pp. 55–64). Cambridge, MA: MIT Press. Retrieved from www.books24x7.com/marc.asp?bookid=26536.

Emerson, L. (2016, February 17). *Selling the future at the MIT Media Lab*. Retrieved from https://loriemerson.net/2016/02/17/selling-the-future-at-the-mit-media-lab/.

Gee, J. P. (1998). What is literacy? In V. Zamel, & R. Spack (Eds.), *Negotiating academic literacies: Teaching and learning across languages and cultures* (pp. 51–59). Mahwah, NJ: Lawrence Erlbaum.

Gee, J. P. (2003). *What video games have to teach us about learning and literacy*. New York, NY: Palgrave Macmillan.

Harrell, D. F. (2009). Toward a theory of phantasmal media: An imaginative cognition-and computation-based approach to digital media. *Ctheory*.

Harrell, D. F. (2013). *Phantasmal media : An approach to imagination, computation, and expression*. Cambridge, MA: MIT Press.

Heath, S. B. (1982). Protean shapes in literacy events: Ever-shifting oral and literate traditions. In D. Tannen (Ed.), *Spoken and written language: Exploring orality and literacy* (pp. 91–117). Norwood, NJ: Ablex.

Ito, M., & Antin, J. 2010. *Hanging out, messing around, and geeking out kids living and learning with new media*. Cambridge, MA: MIT Press.

Joseph, B. (2016, July 14). *The secret sauce in Pokémon Go: Big data*. Retrieved from http://dmlcentral.net/secret-sauce-pokemon-go/.

Juhasz, A. (2016, July 20). *How do I (not) look? Live feed video and viral black death*. Retrieved from http://daily.jstor.org/how-do-i-not-look/.

Kim, D., & Kim, E. (2014, April 7). *The #TwitterEthics Manifesto*. Retrieved from http://modelviewculture.com/pieces/the-twitterethics-manifesto.

Lemonade Syllabus. (n.d.). Retrieved July 29, 2016, from www.candicebenbow.com/lemonadesyllabus/.

Losh, E. (2011a, February 17). *Young black males, learning, and video games*. Retrieved from http://dmlcentral.net/young-black-males-learning-and-video-games/.

Losh, E. (2011b, March 1). *Identity, avatars, virtual life-and advancing social equity in the "real" world*. Retrieved from http://dmlcentral.net/identity-avatars-virtual-life-and-advancing-social-equity-in-the-real-world/.

Mann, S., Nolan, J., & Wellman, B. (2002). Sousveillance: Inventing and using wearable computing devices for data collection in surveillance environments. *Surveillance & Society*, *1*(3), 331–355.

Mbembe, A. (2003). Necropolitics. *Public Culture*, *15*(1), 11–40.

Mirzoeff, N. (2011). *The right to look*. Durham, NC: Duke University Press.

Mirzoeff, N. (2015). *How to see the world*. London, UK: Pelican.

Morrell, E. (2013). *Critical media pedagogy: Teaching for achievement in city schools*. New York, NY: Teachers College Press.

Nakamura, L., & Chow-White, P. (2012). *Race after the Internet*. New York, NY: Routledge.

Palfrey, J. G., & Gasser, U. (2008). *Born digital: Understanding the first generation of digital natives*. New York, NY: Basic Books.

Poniewozik, J. (2016, July 7). A Killing. A Pointed Gun. And Two Black Lives, Witnessing. *The New York Times*. Retrieved from www.nytimes.com/2016/07/08/us/philando-castile-facebook-police-shooting-minnesota.html.

Rault, J. (forthcoming). White noise, white affects: Filtering the sameness of queer suffering. *Feminist Media Studies*.

Reynolds, L. (2016, July 6). *Police*. Retrieved from www.facebook.com/100007611243538/videos/1690073837922975/.

Senft, T. M., & Baym, N. K. (2015). Selfies Introduction ~ What Does the Selfie Say? Investigating a Global Phenomenon. *International Journal of Communication*, *9*, 19. Retrieved from http://ijoc.org/index.php/ijoc/article/view/4067/1387.

Sontag, S. (2003). *Regarding the pain of others*. New York, NY: Farrar, Straus and Giroux.

Teaching #FergusonResources. (n.d.). Retrieved July 29, 2016, from https://docs.google.com/document/d/1kwZl23Q9tgZ23dxSJWS-WpjZhOZ_mzVPtWL8-pWuLt8/edit?pli=1&usp=embed_facebook.

The #Orlando Syllabus. (2016, June 24). Retrieved from https://bullybloggers.wordpress.com/2016/06/24/the-orlando-syllabus/.

Tufte, E. R. (1997). *Visual explanations: Images and quantities, evidence and narrative*. Cheshire, CT: Graphics Press.

Vee, A. (2013). Understanding computer programming as a literacy. *Literacy in Composition Studies*, 1(2), 42–64.

Veeragoudar Harrell, S., & Harrell, D. F. (2009). Exploring the potential of computational self-representations for enabling learning: Examining at-risk youths' development of mathematical/computational agency. *Digital Arts and Culture 2009*. Retrieved from http://escholarship.org/uc/item/4b6913rb.

Watkins, S. C. (2009). *The young and the digital: What the migration to social-network sites, games, and anytime, anywhere media means for our future*. Boston, MA: Beacon Press.

Wenger, E. (1998). *Communities of practice: Learning, meaning, and identity*. Cambridge, UK; New York, NY: Cambridge University Press.

Wernimont, J., & Losh, E. (2016). Problems with White feminism: Intersectionality and digital humanities. In C. Crompton, R. J. Lane, & R. G. Siemens (Eds.), *Doing digital humanities: practice, training, research* (pp. 35–46). Routledge.

Wernimont, J., & Losh, E. (forthcoming). Breaking breadboards: Bringing feminism to the table. In *The Routledge Companion to Media Studies and Digital Humanities*. Routledge.

Williamson, B. (2014, June 26). *New centers of data visualization in education*. Retrieved from http://dmlcentral.net/new-centers-of-data-visualization-in-education/.

Witness.org. (2016, May 30). *Filming the police – USA*. Retrieved from https://library.witness.org/product/filming-the-police-usa/.

# 7
# Integrating and Humanizing Knowledgeable Agents of the Digital and Black Feminist Thought in Digital Literacy Research

Tisha Lewis Ellison

> Living life as an African American woman is a necessary prerequisite for producing Black feminist thought because within Black women's communities thought is validated and produced with reference to a particular set of historical, material, and epistemological conditions.
>
> (Collins, 1990, p. 230)

Throughout my discussions and research on African American[1] women,[2] mothers, and adolescent females from my dissertation and the *Dig-A-Fam: Families' Digital Storytelling Project*,[3] I observed how they created, composed, and dominated digital texts and tools in and out of the home. They spoke about the challenges they experienced that stimulated their love, attraction, and addiction to the digital in their lives. I observed the ways they used these tools to help them cope with life issues on social networking sites, interact with their children, and establish voice across multiple texts, all while creating a sense of agency[4] throughout various practices (Lewis, 2010, 2011, 2013, 2014; Lewis Ellison, 2016, 2017; Lewis Ellison & Kirkland, 2014).

Each woman was unique and literate in their own right and, whether they admitted it or not, they were brilliant, sharp, and resourceful. They also carried with them qualities that I call *knowledgeable agents of the digital*, as those who acquire powerful, agentive, and candid realities around their experiences with digital and non-digital texts that are reaffirming and salient. Within these *agents*, African American women self-define, empower, and advocate for themselves that disrupt oppression, sexism, and exploitation in digital spaces. For instance, African American women possess the multiple ways that they enact digital literacies (multiple and interactive practices mediated by technological tools) (Lewis, 2013) and digital (and non-digital texts) to make sense of their literate worlds. For example, these women made literate decisions in how they wished to be identified, created practices that expressed *the needs and desires of and with their children*, and characterized multiple modes of texts to produce the narratives they wanted to be and see. In essence, I argue that these African American women humanized themselves as knowledgeable agents through their involvement with the digital and in how it transformed them within these practices.

As an African American woman, I celebrated the fact that their practices around the digital were unique, salient, yet were lacking. However, I experienced that when a woman, in particularly an African American woman, exudes the knowledge she possesses in dominant spaces, society's perception of her is noted, but is often followed by bewilderment and disdain which, in turn, seeks to oppress and desensitize her abilities as powerful and relevant. In fact, based on the current political climate of the potential of having the first woman president of the United States, there are still barriers that refuse to acknowledge how wisdom and knowledge come in all shapes and hues. Yet, for African American women, the struggle is real and intense where our voices, ideas, and intellectualism are often muted, not known, or not believed in. These beliefs resemble an interplay between oppression and freedom (Collins, 1990, 2009).

Historically, Black women have been active knowledgeable agents in how they live, think, survive, and achieve in and out of the home. In fact, they are humanized as such. While uniquely complex, they have often been embodied by the emblems of how they are shaped, misshaped, and are read based on distorted narratives or stories that have been written to understand and exploit them and their epistemologies in the world (Bailey & Cuomo, 2008; LaVoulle & Lewis Ellison, under review; Lewis Ellison & Kirkland, 2014; Richardson, 2002). Black women have been known for their assertiveness and outspoken nature but their voices have been misconstrued and misunderstood. Yet their resiliency and resourcefulness rests on their ability to be creative and negotiate the selves they want and attempt to portray in their homes and in their world. Based on this belief, Orbe, Drummond, and Camara (2002) contend, "Black feminist thought constitutes a conceptual approach that reflects the special standpoints that African American women use to negotiate their positioning of self, family, and society" (p. 123).

African American women today stand on the shoulders of Black women agents who took on active roles to write and rewrite themselves in the spaces they inhabit. Because of activists like Sojourner Truth, whose oral text (1851), "Ain't I A Woman," became a sounding board for women against the deferential and sexist treatment of woman; or Harriet Tubman, a leading feminist abolitionist, who fought for freedom of the inequitable injustices perpetuated against Black women and men; or Anna Julia Cooper, a renowned educator and scholar, who later became the personification of Black feminist thought (BFT) because of her political achievements and activism toward the uplifting of Black women without neglect; or even Ida B. Wells, known for her journalistic abilities, who led an anti-lynching campaign and formed clubs for women's suffrage; my first encounter of this force in a woman came from my mother, whose quiet, yet profound stories, actions, and artifacts came offline.

My mother's notes in her Bible and church bulletins spoke about the kind of woman she wanted to be, and is, and she never hesitated to verbally and nonverbally support my ventures on a daily basis. As a successful small business owner for twenty-nine years and mother to me and my two older brothers, she thrived to be a knowledgeable agent and worked hard at her tailor shop in addition to holding down the home front when my father, a now retired police officer, was on his beat. My mother often felt guilty working on Saturdays. She recalled, in a selfless comment that suggests how she had to juggle between the family, work, life balance, and faith ethics that still speaks to the daily struggles and social norms of the African American woman:

> I felt that I was supposed to be at home with you all…I always felt guilty, and still do. In my mind, I should not put my work in front of my family. I thought it was my duty to put myself on hold and be a nurturer till you all were able to do for yourselves.

She wrote pieces of herself on scrap paper and slid them under my brothers' and my pillows each Saturday morning for years before she left for work. Each paper, composed of different positive and miscellaneous notes and artifacts, reaffirmed her presence until she arrived home that evening. Overtime, those scraps grew into letters, cards, text messages, and digital images that helped me understand how literacy practices, small, large, monomodal, or multimodal, were relevant and powerful within family relations. Most importantly, because of my mother's versatility, as a woman whom I perceived as agentive and knowledgeable, I sought more understanding of my narratives and the narratives of the powerful African American women, mothers, and adolescent females I studied and continue to study. I highlight how their views about themselves and their families around the digital and non-digital help explore these analytic connections within digital literacy scholarship and also, humanize their efforts in these spaces.

In this chapter, I outline both Knowledgeable Agents of the Digital and BFT as frameworks to examine the ways African American women, mothers, and adolescent females are portrayed and empowered within digital and non-digital texts and literacies. I argue for this examination and integration of frameworks because BFT became a catalyst for Knowledgeable Agents to exist. Due to the paucity of studies that reflect African American women's digital literacy practices among issues of race, gender, and class that reclaim their voices, I draw from studies with the above themes in mind to strengthen these claims. I examine the ways women have been acting as knowledgeable agents across multiple intersectional contexts and settings. In addition, I take on a new paradigm of BFT to articulate the importance of including, invoking, and recognizing the voices and perspectives of African American women as knowledgeable agents in their own right. As BFT seeks to acknowledge the perspectives of Black women, I question the ethical implications and obligations that the larger literacy field and policies have to fully humanize all people, in particular, Women of Color, which involves positioning them as knowledgeable agents. This stance comes during critical moments in educational, racial, and political history of the marginalization of the African American woman in various spheres in society. Thus, in light of systemic inequalities and unfair structures that create tensions around this population, research and practice need to embrace equitable responses throughout time and space.

## Tensions

Over twenty-six years ago, Patricia Hill Collins (1990) favored us with her book *Black Feminist Thought: Knowledge, Consciousness, and the Politics of Empowerment*. BFT is a term that carries contradictory and complex meanings. First, with this theory, Collins privileges the viewpoints of Black women. She argues that for Black women there is a Black feminist consciousness that is based on their experiences and ideas, and that Black women have to constantly struggle for equality as both women and African Americans. BFT is situated under Black women's emerging power as "agents of knowledge" (Collins, 1990, p. 256), stating it is impossible to understand African American women in practice without acknowledging their agentive, dominant, and knowledgeable selves. BFT attends to how African American women speak about themselves and the issues that affect them and the intersections between race, gender, and class. According to Collins, "African American women use their social locations as intersections of multiple systems of power to claim and not apologize for the vision provided by that space" (personal communication, 2014).

BFT was created based on the self-actualizations, self-affirmations, and self-valuing of African American women and their experiences in the world as relevant and meaningful, but Black women continue to occupy a space between oppression and freedom with the recurrent trajectories of adversity as they seek respect and recognition. The racial, gender, and class discrimination in and out of educational, workplace, and societal environments are prevalent, and with little attention focused on the challenges of the African American woman, there is a deficit in approaches that address a historical timeline about their stance in society.

For instance, in 1905, Fannie Barrier Williams, an African American educator and political and women's rights activist exclaimed, "the colored girl…is not known and hence not believed in; she belongs to a race that is best designated by the term 'problem,' and she lives beneath the shadow of that problem which envelops and obscures her" (Williams, 1987, p. 150). Similarly, in his 1962 speech, Malcolm X shared about men's accountability to respect and protect Black women, he argued how society viewed them as "the most disrespected woman…the most unprotected person…the most neglected person in America, is the Black woman" (see www.youtube.com/watch?v=XWfM9DOEJf0). These quotes carry the weight of how African American women are negatively stereotyped and perceived in today's society that stem, in one way, from the effects of slavery, segregation (see "The Doll Test" from the 1940s),[5] and sexual abuse of female slaves.

Throughout history and now, Black females, along with males as young as five- and six-year-olds, are perceived by society as threats to school and public safety and receive the highest levels of exclusionary discipline in educational settings, which led to the "school-to-prison pipeline." This term relates to the increasing patterns, implemented by educational institutions, where youth and young adults have contact with the juvenile and criminal system, which ultimately results in incarceration (Crenshaw, Ocen, & Nanda, 2015; Morris, 2012; Winn, 2011). Slavery, the Civil Rights movement, and now the Black Lives Matter movement, reflect centuries of racialized, hatred, and violent killings of African American women and men that continue to validate the claim of how this population is negatively portrayed, spoken about, and vilified by digital media and in society.

These racial threats and stereotypes slither throughout the school system and land in higher education, and African American women, even with the highest level of academic degrees, still receive more biased, unethical treatment than their White counterparts during the tenure and promotion processes. In addition, some African American women have to include subliminal texts (images, messages) about personal issues of race or advocacy in digital platforms for the fear of allowing their ideas and voices to cause judgment or the loss of employment. Furthermore, when African American women and men celebrities seek to project their voices toward activism by rewriting the narratives about this population and affirm the political Black Lives Matters movement, the media, for instance, continues to represent this spirit as disrespectful and unimportant (i.e., Beyoncé's Super Bowl 2016 halftime show and Colin Kaepernick).

Thus, these tensions represent why BFT was created: to be a voice in the dialogue of African American women who have been oppressed, silenced, and overlooked. It is important to understand their stance as knowledgeable agents who rewrite the narratives and histories, that we see and want to see in digital and non-digital texts, that portray a humanistic approach rather than an animalistic approach to and about this population (i.e., ex-Univision TV's host Rodney Figueroa's firing over racist comment about the comparison of First Lady Michelle Obama to characters from movie *Planet of the Apes*).

**Emerging Theory: Literature on BFT and Black Women**

While BFT has been explored to speak to the African American woman's "agents of knowledge," when it comes to the emerging theory about digital literacies, and extending to knowledgeable agents of the digital framework, this work is least researched. Within this age of new technologies, literacies, and practices, it matters to explore African American women's digital narratives and practices in research because it humanizes our stake in the world of who we are. Collins (1990, 2002) argues that there is much to learn from an African American woman's knowledge. Collins (1990) has acknowledged that "African American women not commonly certified as 'intellectuals' by academic institutions have long functioned as intellectuals by representing the interests of Black women as a group and fostering Black feminist thought" (p. 15). It is significant to examine African American women's empowering thoughts and agency in an effort to recognize how these lives matter and why. The integration of African American women's digital literacy practices in digital literacy studies can help situate this culture, gender, and population to determine how programs and policies can be implemented to make theoretical contributions to the field of education.

Headlining this important topic across several years of study (Lewis, 2009, 2011, 2014; Lewis Ellison, 2014, 2016; Lewis Ellison & Kirkland, 2014), my work describes the tenets of knowledgeable agents of the digital. I examined the digital literacy practices of an African American mother and her family. Data illustrated themes of agency, identity, and power through family relational practices that addressed how their engagement with digital tools helped them make meaning of their lived experiences (Lewis, 2011). Through extensions of this work, I focused on Larnee, a participant from my longitudinal study, who described her allegiance to digital literacies from a past of physical, emotional, psychological, and sexual abuse, and having been born with a rare skin disease, Epidermolysis Bullosa (EB). She viewed digital literacies and the accompanying digital tools as a way to help her cope with the trauma in her life. Even through her past, she was still noted as a knowledgeable agent of the digital because she explicitly became a sounding board for survival, one that echoes themes raised in BFT. For instance, she educated herself and her son to rely on digital tools for living, and to express their knowledgeable selves, both in and out of their digital worlds, and she became an activist for EB.

Overtime, I explored, along with co-author David Kirkland, in a critical piece how conceptions of language, literacy, and black femininity, via the agentive, powerful, and knowledgeable selves of African American women, were often missing from the scholarship on African American women, digital literacies, and their practices of self-definition. More specifically, we used BFT as a conceptual lens and a framework to illustrate how two African American women used figurative language alongside technological tools. We captured how they understood their experiences, histories, and relationships that carried meaning through scenes of struggle, abuse, and silence (Lewis Ellison & Kirkland, 2014). Both women created relationships with a computer motherboard and a microphone as extensions of self to articulate aspects of their identities and self-expressions—even labeling themselves: "I call myself the motherboard" and "I am the mic" (Kirkland, 2010; Lewis, 2011; Lewis Ellison & Kirkland, 2014, p. 392). The authors concluded that by using hardware as language to articulate metaphorical selves, these women embodied a much broader notion of literacy by reshaping Black female narratives where the technologies of the self-embodied the subject.

Our analysis spoke to how African American women made use of, reshaped, and/or remade themselves through a variety of literacy tools. This work contributes to the emergent perspectives of BFT in that it adds another dimension to how we understand Black female narratives of the self. What BFT offers is how Black females are agentive in reconstructing the Black feminine mystique (Collins, 1986; Robinson & Ward, 1995), and use technologies that have boldly transformed how voice is amplified, through complex and emerging Black female self (Knadler, 2001; Paris & Kirkland, 2011; Richardson, 2002).

Based on emerging literature about African American women in digital literacy research, three characteristics of the literature reveal how they have been examined. One characteristic explores how African American women are agentive in rewriting the histories and images of themselves in digital and non-digital spaces. Another characteristic develops the idea that Black women, and their family's relational practices, shape the digital and non-digital worlds in which they live. A third characteristic demonstrates how the utilization of online digital tools helps them cope with trauma (i.e., physical and sexual abuse and illnesses). These characteristics set a foundation for how this population contributes to digital learning and composition in and out of places and spaces of color, and can provide a critical analysis to learning and education. The above are descriptors of how knowledgeable agents are extended from BFT that are used as a point of departure to explore neglected concerns of Black women's culture.

There exists a body of scholarship around the consciousness, knowledge, and lineage of Black women within the terrain of knowledgeable agents and BFT (Collins, 1990; Cooper, 2015; du cille, 1994), within the academy (Griffin, 2012; Harris, 2007; hooks, 1996), childhood education (Pérez, Guerrero, & Mora, 2016; Pérez, Medellin, & Rideaux, 2016), queer theory (Story, 2015), hip-hop (Morgan, 1999; Pough, 2007; Richardson, 2013), and violence (Crenshaw, 1991). However, there are few studies that highlight how African American women enact agency into the digital worlds in which they live. Studying African American women and their on- and off-line literacies (i.e., digital and print) from a knowledgeable agents and BFT lens, are salient in understanding how they choose to (a) revise their identities to make sense of their lives as knowledgeable agents; (b) explore issues of race, gender, and class in families and community spaces; and (c) rewrite new narratives about how their emerging presence informs digital literacy research and literacy education. In the following sections, I highlight the interconnections between knowledgeable agents of the digital, BFT, and African American women's agentive practices with digital texts, and how African American adolescent females write their identities with digital and non-digital texts.

### *Black Women's Digital Narratives*

In creating knowledgeable agents of the digital, some scholarship examines the ways Black women create themselves and negotiate within digital tools for empowerment and agency. For instance, Hall (2011) chronicled how three young African American women positioned themselves as "knowledge producers" for their digital stories. The three women drew upon, created, and wrote narratives that spoke against the dominant discourses they perceived about body image and beauty as sources of pain for African American women. This work is relevant to this culture and their digital literacy practices because it positioned them and their voices as dominant readers, writers, and creators about something that was meaningful to them.

In addition, Kirkland (2010) penned *organic phemininst (/feminist/) framework* as an exploration of the stories and lives of females of influence, and shared the writings of his mother and a young Black woman's narratives on MySpace and YouTube. The narratives illustrated the delicate truths of being a Black female in an oppressive world through poetry and performance. Behind the tools of online social sites, such as MySpace, BlogSpot, and YouTube, these women rewrote and re-extended the ways they had been written about to create new counter-stories and digital identities as constructed in digital contexts. Findings illustrated how Black women use digital tools to tell their stories online which moves toward ways to fortify how Black female online narratives can provide a critical analysis to engage in digital literacies as a liberating space.

### *Writing Identities across an Ecology of Texts*

There are knowledgeable and agentive practices that cross texts and contexts among African American adolescent females. For instance, in two separate qualitative studies, Muhammad and Womack (2015) examined what Black adolescent females did with texts based on their representations of their worlds. The authors explored how these females used *pens* (writing pens) and *pins* (pinning images and objects on Pinterest boards) to shape their histories and identities about their girlhood in popular culture. Through collected writings from twelve Black females that represented forms of self through multiple modes (i.e., journaling, poetry, letters) and two 15–19-year-old Black females' autoethnographies that utilized digital tools (i.e., Pinterest and Prezi), they collected literacy artifacts from topics to (re)pin and (re)write images that represented Black girlhood. Findings illustrated that the females penned and pinned against representations connected to physical beauty, sexualizing, and education. This study is important because it allowed each female to self-identify texts and tools that made sense to her, something that is not often discussed in the literature around adolescent and adult females of color.

Moreover, the need for African American females to occupy spaces where trauma, poetry, and music become safe havens add to the belief and understanding about BFT, as in the case of Riley's (2009) autobiographical research that helped her express herself through digital texts and writing after her childhood friend committed suicide. Studies like Brock, Kvasny, and Hales (2010) frame BFT to understand how issues of technology and social inequalities displayed in three weblog discourses about Black women help them accumulate and activate cultural and technical capital. Similarly, Johnson and Nuñez (2015) used social and digital media platforms as a place to meet and vent personal stories about their traumatic, activist, abusive, and loving lives they have survived on blogs, tweets, and posts. Calling it a digital Black feminist community, they sought power from each other to build a community online. They used "notifications, status updates, timelines, dashboards, and reblogs" to create a bond online. What makes this study of theirs and other women's digital lives so relevant to today's knowledgeable agents is that it epitomizes BFT via the ways that these digital Black feminists expressed their oppressed selves to feel free and meaningful. Similar to Larnee, her survival through creating blogs for her son and me, as researcher, not only gave us the space to share our digital literacy experiences with one another but it also provided Larnee with the opportunity to explore parts of herself by writing poems, creating videos, and sharing very candid narratives online about her struggles with having EB where she would not be seen or judged (Lewis, 2014). These women all epitomized what a knowledgeable agent of the digital (and non-digital) embodied.

**Ethical Implications for Pedagogy**

The ideas and layers formulate how knowledgeable agents of the digital and BFT frameworks intersect that explore and identify the already-existing (digital) literacy practices, digital and non-digital texts, voices, and perspectives of African American women. The lineage of my research on the digital literacy practices of African American women and families, and the agentive identities and powerful stances within the narratives of this population, demonstrates the reason why this work on being a knowledgeable agent of the digital and BFT are needed in literacy research as well as for educators. For educators committed to understanding the plight of the African American women and mothers, this work is important to consider how one can engage in teaching about race, culture, social justice, and empowerment, without a deficit approach, but through methods that foresee the full and real realities of what a knowledgeable agent is. This information is important to understand how African American women situate themselves across various ecologies of texts within the digital.

Being able to communicate, interact, and create across digital and non-digital texts, helps them make meaning of their literate lives. It also brings attention to ways in which they matter in a field that wants to discover new experiences and knowledge about their educational and everyday literacies. As many reports are now studying the means and ways this population interacts with digital texts and on networking sites (The Nielsen Company, 2014; Smith, 2014), it is bourgeoning a new integration for knowledgeable agents of the digital and BFT.

For instance, honing in on Larnee's rich traditions of her literacy, experience, and self-actualization within the digital, I have been met with numerous disparaging comments about her life and her agentive practices. These comments asked, "what was wrong with her," how to "fix her," and her enactments of her digital literacy practices were often thought of as "dumb" or "dismissed," rather than seeing her through agentive lens. These observations told me how I had to speak back to my research about her in educational research, at conferences, and in everyday conversations. That is, without the BFT perspective, she is marginalized and placed in a space that is undermined, devalued, and disenfranchised that breaks her from her agency.

As an African American woman, I am privy to the ways that Larnee, and other women mentioned earlier, might be theorized within the conversations on literacy. For instance, these women would continue to remain irrelevant within the floods of deficit view models that would capitalize on the "things" she may not have instead of focusing on the strengths, competencies, and agencies that she does exemplify. Without examining stories like Larnee and other African American women knowledgeable agents, we first lose out, as members of the field, on the true intersections of their lives and identities that would have never examined race, class, gender. Without this understanding, such notable African American women advocates from our past (Anna Julia Cooper, Sojourner Truth, Harriet Tubman, Ida B. Wells, Fannie Barrier Williams) will no longer be regarded and remain silent.

In taking an ethical approach to understand the intersections between knowledgeable agents of the digital and BFT, instructional practice, literacy research, and policy need to provide ways to understand and account for the lived, digital, and racial experiences of African American women, mothers, and females as important factors to be included in curricular, research, and policy reports. With this in mind, African American women can no longer be reduced to objects or dominated by narratives to be stereotyped. Rather, we come from historical upbringings of strength, power, and expression. While honing in on the Black feminists of the past, Harriet Tubman, Anna Julia Cooper, and Coretta Scott King, primarily during Black History Month, let us also imagine, daily, up and coming African American women whose digital (and non-digital) narratives have yet to be explored.

Let education, research, and policies be held accountable to humanize African American women as knowledgeable agents who are unapologetic about who they are in the world today (Collins, 1990; Kirkland, 2010; Lewis Ellison & Kirkland, 2014; Richardson, 2002). In addition, African American mothers can be seen first, as teachers of their children's education, and can be acknowledged as owning unique educational skills and digital practices that they embody and mature at home with their children (Lewis, 2010, 2011, 2013, 2014; Lewis Ellison, 2016). Lastly, young African American females can position themselves and experiences in and out of digital spaces, to become advocates of their learning (Crenshaw et al., 2015; Hall, 2011, Muhammad & Haddix, 2016; Price-Dennis, 2016).

As a result, I designed seven key components that are needed to make the above claims about being a knowledgeable agent an impetus for teaching and researching digital literacy practices and creating policies (see Figure 7.1).

Each component of knowledgeable agents of the digital framework extends from BFT to include distinct ways that African American women should now be perceived about who they are and how

**Figure 7.1** Knowledgeable agents of the digital framework

they embody parts of the self through digital and non-digital tools that resemble themselves (Lewis Ellison & Kirkland, 2014; Muhammad & Womack, 2015). In addition, African American women disrupt oppressive, inequities, and injustices that have tried to historically damage the narratives of who they identify as. They possess power and are advocates for issues that they envision on digital and social media that attempts to oppress rather than empower (Richardson, 2002). They are constantly making meaning of their lived experiences whether on blogs, texting, or social groups with expression and candor (Lewis, 2013, 2014). Knowledge agents of the digital also create moments that challenge individuals to explore intersectional settings among race, gender, class whether they are comfortable with these factors or not, in and out of educational borders (Lewis Ellison & Kirkland, 2014). Similarly, knowledgeable agents of the digital are women who foster agency to re-identify and remake themselves across diverse social and geographic populations (Lewis, 2013, 2014, 2016, 2017; Price-Dennis, 2016). Lastly, knowledgeable agents of the digital always reaffirm and self-define the roles they play, work, write, and learn in (Lewis, 2013).

**Recommendations and Forward Thinking**

Since the digital will continue to be increasingly powered by individuals, corporations, and educational entities, I question, how might (digital) literacy researchers maximize the voices and perspectives of the misrepresented? Within this vein, (digital) literacy researchers can challenge researchers to maintain an ethically responsible approach for the research they conduct among African American families, women, mothers, and adolescent females. In this way, I argue for humanization of what these women experience and practice to make it more authentic and tangible to understand the nuances and complexities of what it means to be a knowledgeable agent of the digital in this racialized, gendered, and classed society. This means, more examinations of African American women's digital literacy practices and their roles as powerful, agentive women across spheres in and out of educational spaces need to be explored.

I recommend that educators and researchers first think about their own pedagogies and their roles as knowledgeable agents in their disciplines. Then explore how continued work on this topic matters for the African American community, in particular among African American women. In other words, this work has and is shaping how African American women have been seen and are portrayed today.

The seven components of the knowledgeable agents of the digital were structured for educators and researchers to consider: *How might I teach with this approach/framework? How can I use the (digital) narratives of African American women, mothers, and females with curricula? In what ways can I create a humanistic approach to integrate knowledgeable agents of the digital and BFT in my classroom, around my community, in my research?*

I challenge and place the onus on educators and researchers to answer for themselves these questions and why being a knowledgeable agent of the digital is relevant for their students and their parents and research participants, and why would we *want* to study this population. I argue that when these statements are explored and questions answered, and when we reaffirm what African American women do with digital and non-digital texts as worthy in pedagogies and communities, then the oppressive vandalisms, via speech, texts, artifacts, music, literature, that effect this population and the generations to come, can shut down. Rather, we began to integrate and to *bring humanity back* that positions African American women as knowledgeable agents of the digital as relevant.

**Notes**

1. The terms African American and Black are used interchangeably.
2. The terms women, woman, and females are used interchangeably.

3. The *Dig-A-Fam: Families' Digital Storytelling Project* was funded by the National Council of Teachers of English Research Foundation.
4. Agency and agentive are used interchangeably as a heuristic to describe one's understanding, the re-identifying, and remaking of self (see Bruner, 1994; Moje & Lewis, 2007) and the understanding of capacity to act upon one's world and give it personal significance (Holland, Lachicotte, Skinner, & Cain, 1998).
5. *The Doll Test* was a series of experiments conducted by African American psychologists Kenneth and Mamie Clark 14 years before the *Brown v. Board of Education*. NAACP Legal Defense and Educational Fund, Inc. *Brown at 60: The Doll Test*, www.naacpldf.org/brown-at-60-the-doll-test.

## References

Bailey, A., & Cuomo, C. (Eds.) (2008). *The feminist philosophy reader*. New York, NY: McGraw-Hill.
Brock, Kvasny, & Hales, K. (2010). Cultural appropriations of technical capital: Black women, weblogs, and the digital divide. *Information, Communication & Society, 7*(13), 1040–1059.
Collins, P. H. (1986). Learning from the outsider within: The sociological significance of Black feminist thought. *Social Problems, 33*(6), 514–532.
Collins, P. H. (1990). *Black feminist thought: Knowledge, consciousness, and the politics of empowerment* (Vol. 2). New York, NY: Routledge.
Collins, P. H. (2002).Contemporary Black feminist thought. In T. Lee Lott (Ed.), *African-American philosophy: Selected readings*. Prentice Hall.
Collins, P. H. (2009). *Black feminist thought in the matrix of domination*. Retrieved April 26, 2009, from www.hartford-hwp.com/archives/45a/252.html; www.turning-the tide.org/files/Feminist%20Thought%20and%20Matrix%20of%20Domination.pdf.
Collins, P. H. (2014). *We who believe in freedom cannot rest: Lessons from Black feminism*. Retrieved from www.youtube.com/watch?v=36Iq8XkfQ-0.
Cooper, B. C. (2015). Love no limit: Towards a Black feminist future (in theory). *The Black Scholar, 45*(4), 7–21.
Crenshaw, K. (1991). Mapping the margins: Intersectionality, identity politics, and violence against women of color. *Stanford Law Review 43*(6), 1241–1299.
Crenshaw, K., Ocen, P., & Nanda, J. (2015). *Black girls matter: Pushed out, overpoliced, and underprotected*. New York, NY: African American Policy Forum & Center for Intersectionality and Social Policy Studies.
du cille, A. (1994). The occult of true Black womanhood: Critical demeanor and Black feminist studies. *Signs: Journal of Women in Culture and Society, 19*(3), *591–629*.
Griffin, R. A. (2012). I am an angry Black woman: Black feminist autoethnography, voice, and resistance. *Women's Studies in Communication, 35*(2), 138–157.
Hall, T. (2011). Designing from their own social worlds: The digital story of three African American youth women. *English Teaching: Practice and Critique, 10*(1), 7–20.
Harris, T. (2007). Black feminist thought and cultural contracts: Understanding the intersection and negotiation of racial, gendered, and professional identities in the academy. *New Directions for Teaching and Learning, 110,* 55–64.
hooks, b. (1996). *Bone Black: Memories of girlhood*. New York, NY: Holt.
Johnson, J. M., & Nuñez, K. (2015) Alter egos and infinite literacies, Part III: How to build a real gyrl in 3 easy steps. *The Black Scholar, 45*(4), 47–61.
Kirkland, D. (2010). 4 colored girls who considered social networking when suicide wasn't enuf: Exploring the literate lives of young Black women in online social communities. In D. Alvermann (Ed.), *Adolescents' online literacies: Connecting classrooms, digital media, and popular culture* (pp. 71–90). New York, NY: Peter Lang.
Knadler, S. (2001). E-racing difference in e-space: Black female subjectivity and the web-based portfolio. *Computers and Composition, 18*(3), 235–255.
LaVoulle, C., & Lewis Ellison, T. (under review). Bad Bitch Barbie craze and Beyonce: African American women bodies as a commodity in hip-hop culture, images, and media.
Lewis, T. Y. (2010). Intergenerational meaning-making between a mother and son in digital spaces. In C. Compton-Lilly & S. Greene (Eds.), *Bedtime stories and book reports: Connecting parent involvement and family literacy* (pp. 85–93). New York, NY: Teachers College Press.
Lewis, T. Y. (2011). Family digital literacies: A case of awareness, agency, and apprenticeship of one African American family. In P. J. Dunston, L. B. Gambrell, K. Headley, S. K. Fullerton, P. M. Stecker, V. R. Gillis, & C. C. Bates (Eds.), *60th literacy research association yearbook* (pp. 432–446). Oak Creek, WI: Literacy Research Association.
Lewis, T. Y. (2013). "We txt 2 sty cnnectd:" An African American mother and son communicate: Digital literacies, meaning-making, and activity theory systems. *Journal of Education, 193*(2), 1–13.

Lewis, T. Y. (2014). Apprenticeships, affinity spaces, and agency: Exploring blogging engagements in family spaces. *Journal of Adolescent and Adult Literacy, 58*(1), 71–81.

Lewis Ellison, T. (2014). An African American mother's stories as T.M.I.: Ethics and vulnerability around traumatic narratives in digital literacy research. *International Journal of Qualitative Methods, 13*, 255–274.

Lewis Ellison, T. (2016). Artifacts as stories: Understanding families, digital literacies, and storied lives. *Journal of Adolescent & Adult Literacy, 59*(5), 511–513.

Lewis Ellison, T. (2017). Family stories, texts, meaning: A study of artifacts during a digital storytelling workshop. In C. Burnett, G. Merchant, B. Parry (Eds.), *Literacy, media and technology: Past, present and future*. Bloomsbury Press.

Lewis Ellison, T., & Kirkland, D. (2014). Motherboards, mics, and metaphors: Reexamining new literacies and Black feminist thought through technologies of self. *Journal of E-Learning and Digital Media, 11*(4), 390–405.

Lewis Ellison, T. (under review). Bringing humanity back: Conceptualizing race, police, and racism among families and communities of color.

Morgan, J. (1999). *When chickenheads come home to roost: My life as a hip-hop feminist*. New York, NY: Simon & Schuster.

Morris, M. (2012). *Race, gender and the school-to-prison pipeline: Expanding our discussion to include Black girls*. New York, NY: African American Policy Forum.

Muhammad, G. E., & Haddix, M. (2016). Centering Black girls' literacies: A review of literature on the multiple ways of knowing of Black girls. *English Education, 48*(4), 299–336.

Muhammad, G. E., & McArthur, S. A. (2015). "Styled by their perceptions": Adolescent girls' interpretations of Black girlhood in the media. *Multicultural Perspectives, 17*(3), 1–8.

Muhammad, G. E., & Womack, E. (2015). From pen to pin: The multimodality of Black girls (re)writing their lives. *Ubiquity: The Journal of Literature, Literacy and the Arts, 2*(2), 6–45.

The Nielsen Company. (2014). Powerful. Growing. Influential. The African American consumer 2014 report. Retrieved from www.thechicagourbanleague.org/cms/lib07/IL07000264/Centricity/Domain/76/nielen-essence-2014-african-american-consumer-report-Sept-2014.pdf.

Orbe, M. P., Drummond, D. K., & Camara, S. K. (2002). Phenomenology and Black feminist thought: Exploring African American women's everyday encounters as points of contention. In A. Davis & M. Houston (Eds.), *Centering ourselves: African American feminist and womanist studies of discourse* (pp. 123–144). Cresskill, NJ: Hampton Press.

Pérez, M. S., Guerrero, R., & Mora, E. (2016). Black feminist photovoice: Fostering critical awareness of diverse families and communities in early childhood teacher education. *Journal of Early Childhood Teacher Education, 37*(1), 41–60.

Paris, D., & Kirkland, D. E. (2011). The consciousness of the verbal artist: Understanding vernacular literacies in digital and embodied spaces. In V. Kinloch (Ed.), *Urban literacies: Critical perspectives on language, learning, and community* (pp. 177–194). New York, NY: Teachers College Press.

Pérez, M. S., Medellin, K., & Rideaux, K. (2016). Repositioning childhood experiences within adult contexts: A Black feminist analysis of childhood/s regulation in early childhood care and education. *Global Studies of Childhood, 6*(1), 67–79.

Pough, G. (2007). What it do, shorty?: Women, hip-hop and a feminist agenda. *Black Women, Gender & Families: Women's Studies and Black Studies Journal, 1*(2), 78–99.

Price-Dennis, D. (2016). Developing curriculum to support Black girls' literacies in digital spaces. *English Education, 48*(4), 337–367.

Richardson, E. B. (2002). *African American literacies*. New York, NY: Routledge.

Richardson, E. B. (2013). Developing critical hip hop feminist literacies: Centrality and subversion of sexuality in the lives of Black girls. *Equity & Excellence in Education, 46*(3), 327–341.

Riley, T. (2009). *From the academy to the streets: Documenting the healing power of Black feminist creative expression*. (Unpublished master's thesis). University of South Florida, Tampa, FL.

Robinson, T., & Ward, J. V. (1995). A belief in self far greater than anyone's disbelief: Cultivating resistance among African American female adolescents. In C. Gilligan, A. G. Rogers & D. L. Tolman (Eds.), *Women, girls, and psychotherapy: Reframing resistance* (pp. 89–91). Binghamton, NY: Hawthorn Press.

Smith, A. (2014, January 6). *African Americans and technology use: A demographic portrait*. Retrieved from the Pew Research Center website: www.pewinternet.org/2014/01/06/african-americans-and-technology-use/.

Story, K. (2015). (Re)presenting Shug Avery and Afrekete: The search for a Black, queer, and feminist pleasure praxis. *The Black Scholar, 45*(4), 22–35.

Truth, S. (1851, May 28–29). "Ain't I a Woman?" Women's Convention, Akron, OH.

Williams, F. B. (1987). The colored girl. In M. Washington (Ed.), *Invented lives: Narratives of Black women 1860–1960* (pp. 150–156). New York, NY: Doubleday. (Original work published 1905).

Winn, M. T. (2011). *Girl time: Literacy, justice, and the school-to-prison pipeline*. New York, NY: Teachers College Press.

# 8
# Global Refugee Crisis
*Literacy Concerns and Media Coverage*

**Ariel Loring and Vaidehi Ramanathan**

Movements of displaced people are not new phenomena: According to the United Nations High Commissioner for Refugees (UNHCR), there are currently 65.3 million forcibly displaced people worldwide (Global trends, 2016). However, in 2015 alone, 12.4 million people were newly displaced from conflict or persecution, of which over 1 million migrants and refugees, predominately from Syria, Afghanistan, and Iraq, sought asylum in Europe (Global trends, 2016; Migrant crisis, 2016), leading to the current moniker "global refugee crisis." To be labeled a refugee, one must be "outside the country of his nationality [and] unable or…unwilling to avail himself of the protection of that country" due to "a well-founded fear of being persecuted for reasons of race, religion, nationality or political opinion" (UN General Assembly, 1950). Legally speaking, a refugee is someone whose asylum claim has been approved; an asylum seeker is seeking refugee status but has not yet been granted such status (Mitchell, 2006). What distinguishes refugees from other migrants is threefold: their movement is not voluntary; having suffered from prior trauma, they often have physical and mental health issues and limited/interrupted education; and they hold special legal status granting them access to welfare and education, albeit limited (Feuerherm & Ramanathan, 2016). Economic migrants, another commonly employed term, would not be considered refugees if they are seeking employment opportunities without a fear of persecution.

Part of the "crisis" stems from the unprecedented numbers of displaced individuals, and part stems from Europe's political and humanitarian responses. Some countries have openly welcomed refugees, some have raised fences, and others have shuttled refugees into neighboring countries. These are some initial reactions to the arrival of migrants and refugees; subsequent decisions countries must make concern the duration and type of refugee assistance and policies for permanent residency and naturalization. Influencing and influenced by this political agenda is each country's news media and its linguistic treatment of refugees. In reporting on political events, media discourse often transmits political rhetoric to its constituents who then translate it to everyday conversations (van Leeuwen & Wodak, 1999). News media also offers a window into language attitudes of the general population because not only does the media affect public opinion (Bell, 1991; Gabrielatos & Baker, 2008; Garrett & Bell, 1998), but it also reflects the sentiments of its readers who often subscribe to newspapers that share their own world views (Crawley & Sriskandarajah, 2005).

Media in an increasingly digital era necessitates an increasingly savvy consumer. A media literate person has the ability to "decode, evaluate, analyze and produce both print and electronic media" (Koltay, 2011, p. 212). This overlaps with the term "digital literacy," which encapsulates access and knowledge of how to acquire information in ways made possible by technology

(Dobson & Willinsky, 2009). Often, these digital communications occur across geographic locales and languages, necessitating the competency and inclination to send and receive messages to those who are different (linguistically, culturally, economically, etc.) (Hull & Nelson, 2009). Such views of literacy follow those scholars within New Literacy Studies who view literacy as the socially determined ways to make and transmit meaning through written text or other modalities (Gee, 2015; Mills, 2010; The New London Group, 2000). These scholars break from traditional theorists who saw literacy as solely the ability to read and write (see Gee, 1987, 2015). As Gee (2015) remarks, even those who can read and write in their *primary discourse* may not be familiar with the socially prestigious *secondary discourse* learned through formal schooling or from being raised in a mainstream household. Thus, he defines literacy as the ability to use the necessary secondary discourses in socially and contextually appropriate ways—essentially, possessing the rules to participate in different linguistic domains. These more unacknowledged literacy demands can prove especially challenging for refugees and certain types of migrants who must first learn the *de facto* sociopragmatic requirements to partake in different discourse and policy procedures from their new country and later learn the country's national language(s) (if need be) and procedures for continual residency.

The purpose of this chapter is to bring attention to the media's treatment of the "global refugee crisis," situated within established research on discursive representations of migrants, refugees, and resettlement and reconceptualizations of citizenship in terms of access and inclusion (Loring & Ramanathan, 2016b; Ramanathan, 2013a, 2013b). Interwoven within this research is the topic of literacy, and digital literacies in particular, which have a twofold relationship: refugees' expected adeptness of (digital) literacies and the news media's use of (digital) literacies in representing refugeehood and resettlement. These connections have implications for linguistic gatekeeping and naturalization policies, pedagogical aspects of refugee education, and demonstrations of critical literacy/citizenship.

## Tensions for Refugees in the Resettlement Process

Literacy demands punctuate the many hurdles that refugees experience throughout their displacement and resettlement process, beginning with who is labeled a refugee and who is not and ending[1] with the decision to become a naturalized citizen. For the sake of simplicity, only one country's migration policies (the US) will be expounded upon as an example of how literacy concerns overlap with the resettlement process. Before 1980, the US only defined a refugee as one leaving a communist nation or the Middle East. A broader definition from UNHCR was quoted above: A refugee is unable or unwilling to return to his country of origin due to a fear of persecution. Under this definition, someone fleeing a natural disaster or global warming is not legally a refugee, which some policy makers would dispute (Ludwig, 2016). Those who remain in their country of naturalization while still being displaced from their home (e.g., victims of Hurricanes Katrina and Sandy in the US) are sometimes colloquially referred to as refugees but legally are not so (Ludwig, 2016). With these problematic discrepancies, it is not surprising that the general public does not always understand the legal differences between categories of migrants.

One early tension asylum seekers are met with is the need to demonstrate a history of persecution and a legitimate fear of returning to their home country. The US Immigration and Nationality Act specifies that "the burden of proof is on the *applicant* to establish that the applicant is a refugee" (INA Section 208, italics added for emphasis). Linguistic and literacy capabilities have been a component in assessing the veracity of an applicant's claims, for example by demonstrating the ability to speak the national language of the country of origin. Linguists have rightly pointed out the vast problems in using language proficiency as a barometric of nationality (Blommaert, 2009; Eades, 2009), which conceptually conflates language and nationhood as static and singular (Piller, 2011). When an asylum seeker's perceived eligibility rests on his linguistic repertoire matching outsiders' expectations of which language are exclusively spoken in which countries (Blommaert, 2009), we see the sweeping impact literacy judgments can have.

Once (and if) an asylum seeker legally becomes a refugee, he has a period of time to receive government support, including "cultural orientation, language and vocational training, as well as programs to promote access to education and employment" (Resettlement, n.d., para. 8). Literacy plays heavily into this stage of resettlement: Refugees are expected to use these services to develop greater linguistic competency in the national language(s), to learn sociopragmatic norms for interactions, and to determine the means by which to acquire unknown information, often digitally. In the US, these social services are supposed to be available for up to eight months (Bruno, 2011), but some US states' services differ and last for less than six months (Tyeklar, 2016). The overall objective of refugee resettlement is to ensure a refugee's economic and cultural self-sufficiency, but many question whether this is functionally achievable in such a short period (Bruno, 2011; Tyeklar, 2016).

In the US following resettlement, refugees apply for permanent resident status after one year of residence. This gives the refugee (and any immigrant) permanent legal authority to live and work in the US. National discourse portrays the decision to apply for naturalization as a symbolic demonstration of attachment and assimilation, but there are various reasons why permanent residents choose to become citizens. These reasons are shaped in part by language policies and ideologies, and they affect not only the attitudes of prospective citizens, but also the attitudes of the host country's population (Loring & Ramanathan, 2016a). Without becoming a naturalized citizen, permanent residents experience certain constraints such as restrictions on travel time abroad, the threat of deportation, and the reduction of social security benefits. However, the intricacies of the naturalization test often deter otherwise-qualified permanent residents from applying (Loring, 2013a, 2013b).

To become a naturalized citizen in the US, one must demonstrate three requirements through a naturalization application and oral interview: a knowledge of history and government; the ability to read, write, and speak English; and good moral character. The literacy component became a prerequisite for naturalization in 1917, but it wasn't until 1952 that literacy became required in *English* in particular (Orgad, 2011). It is debatable to what extent these stipulations for naturalization are actually achieved in practice, as the history and government test has a fixed number of memorizable questions, the English proficiency component can be practiced through published vocabulary lists and memorizing question responses, and the good moral character requirement is merely defined as an absence of certain undesirable traits (Kunnan, 2009; Loring, 2013a, 2015). However, there are unstated test requirements as well; reading and understanding the English application is not counted as part of the English requirement, and it includes specialized terminology (*procured, narcotics, alimony*) and complex morphology and syntax (Loring, 2013a). Additionally, because the language of the test itself is English, the entire test becomes a *de facto* policy of English literacy (McNamara & Shohamy, 2008).

Undergoing naturalization gives one citizenship in an adopted country. In this legal sense, citizenship is defined in terms of rights and responsibilities; political theorists additionally reference membership, community, and participation (Castles, 1998; Marshall, 1950; Touraine, 1997). However, citizenship has a wider range beyond its legal realm. The US news media often equates *citizenship* with desirable ethics, values, and principles (Loring, 2013a, 2016a). Recently, scholars have shifted to analyzing citizenship in terms of what it permits, namely access to fuller participation (Heller, 2013; Ramanathan, 2013a, 2013b; Wiley, 2013; Wodak, 2013). More than exclusively referring to civic or legal participation, *full participation* is the ability to access any or all societal resources constrained by language, literacy, and culture, such as health care (Ziegahn et al., 2013), professional jobs (Ricento, 2013), equal educational opportunities (Lillie, 2016), and language communities outside one's nation-state (McPherron, 2016). While not legally categorized as citizens, many inhabitants do already participate in their community and nation in ways that are unacknowledged in traditional citizenship policies (Leymarie, 2016).

## Current Media Studies of Migrant Groups

Throughout the resettlement process, a country's populace can decide how to interact with and think about its country's newcomers. Helping to inform their choices and actions, the news media has the capability to frame the discussion of current events and set a dominant narrative. The rhetoric used to report on minorities and foreigners can incite xenophobia and racism in its readers and listeners, or profess a humanitarian connection between people of difference. Even though a news article may be a factual report, its choice of quotes, quote placement, visuals, metaphors, caricatures, and catchphrases can show the political leaning of its author and institution (Nelson, Clawson, & Oxley, 1997). A choice of a particular frame renders some facts more salient than others, giving them more weight when the audience forms attitudes. This section outlines some key scholarship in the analysis of news media's coverage of immigrants, migrants, and refugees, also summarized in Loring (2016b).

Wodak (2007) analyzed Austrian anti-Semitic post-war discourse to unearth instances of everyday racism, which she called *syncretic racism*. This type of oblique racism occurs when the discourse of exclusion is de-referentialized so that the audience can *infer* discriminatory understandings through shared knowledge and collective memories. In other work on anti-Semitism in post-war Austria, Wodak (2003) examined stereotypes, labels, allusions, minimizations, and quotations in oral and written news accounts to demonstrate how racist rhetoric is coded in discourse. Austrian discourse was also investigated in van Leeuwen and Wodak's (1999) study of official rejection notices concerning immigrant families' reunion applications. The discursive strategies of legitimation and justification create rejection letters based on "objective" reasons that would seem justifiable while simultaneously appearing sensitive to human rights issues. Legitimation was additionally analyzed in Martín Rojo and van Dijk's (1997) study of political discourse of the Spanish Secretary of the Interior in a speech on the military expulsion of "illegal" African migrants.

In the UK, several studies have analyzed the discursive representation of refugees, immigrants, and asylum seekers through critical discourse analysis, corpus analysis, or both. Baker and McEnery (2005) compared concordances of *refugee(s)* and *asylum seeker(s)* in articles from British newspapers and the UNHCR Office. The researchers found that refugees tended to be described in terms of their country of origin and current country of residence. Notably, they unearthed several common metaphors used to depict refugees, in overarching discourses of victimhood, natural disasters, tragedy, crime, and nuisance (Baker & McEnery, 2005).

Gabrielatos and Baker (2008) reported on a ten-year data sample of nineteen UK newspapers concerning refugees, asylum seekers, immigrants, and migrants (RASIM). Analysis revealed that the vast majority of themes commonly associated with RASIM were negative and included references to destinations, numbers, economic problems, residence, repatriation, legality, and plight. The researchers concluded that in doing so, the British press created and sustained what can be described as a moral panic (Hill, 2008) around RASIM (Baker et al., 2008; Gabrielatos & Baker, 2008).

Turning to the US, Santa Ana (2013) analyzed all television network stories reported on the four largest national networks in 2004 to discover what type of Latino news stories were covered and what percentage of these stories concerned immigration. He found that through the story framing, networks portrayed immigrants and refugees from Cuba, the Dominican Republic, and Mexico in a different light: Mexican migrants were depicted as irresponsible parents and criminals, while Cuban migrants were described with admiration and positive regard (Santa Ana, 2013).

Loring (2016a, 2016b) used a corpus and critical discourse analysis of articles and blogs in 2011 from the *New York Times* to investigate the treatment of the words *citizenship*, *refugee*, *alien*, and *immigrant*.[2] A ten-word concordance strand of *citizenship* revealed that the word was commonly coupled with a specific nationality (similar to Baker and McEnery's [2005] finding), especially when a person did not reside in his or her original country of origin. European and Middle Eastern stories that referenced *citizenship* thematically concerned conflict and strife while American stories addressed immigration (often *illegal immigration*) and the birther movement (Loring, 2016a). The word *refugee* commonly collocated with a geographic locale, such as "refugee from Eritrea," "Haitian refugees," and "refugees coming into Peshawar, Pakistan." Four metaphors were regularly employed in refugee discourse: quantification, tragedy, veracity, and crime and nuisance (Loring, 2016b); the first three have been encountered in other studies of public news corpora (Baker & McEnery, 2005; Gabrielatos & Baker, 2008; Santa Ana, 2002), and the fourth metaphor is an iteration of US government policy discourse. Use of the word *immigrant* also metaphorically referenced quantification and tragedy but uniquely addressed the themes of legality and movement. Also significant was the considerable preference for the phrase *illegal immigrant* (95 instances) instead of *undocumented immigrant* (three instances) (Loring, 2016b).

### *Digital Media Reporting on Migrant Groups*

To investigate the "global refugee crisis" that began in 2015 through the lens of digital literacy, we analyzed the first three webpages returned from a Google search of the phrase "refugee crisis" in May 2016[3]: "Refugee crisis: When is a tragedy a massacre?", an editorial from Richard Seymour at *Al Jazeera* from April 2016; "Migrant crisis: Migration to Europe explained in seven charts" from the *BBC* in March 2016; and "The global refugee crisis" from *The Atlantic*, a collection of 12 expandable articles written in September and October 2015. We looked at general trends and prototypical discursive strategies in the media's reporting and consumers' responses to this issue to lend credibility to our theoretical claims.

The three webpages analyzed are more digitally complex than print articles: they include images, Instagram photos, Twitter handles, hyperlinks, advertisements (some from external sources and some self-promotional), charts, large quotes of the article's key phrases, options to expand a synopsis to a full article, and opportunities to add comments as a user. Thus, fully understanding the webpages requires more than English comprehension; it also necessitates the navigation of a digital document and an awareness of avenues for follow-up readings. For example, the first sentence in the first article of *The Atlantic*'s page is "David noted yesterday the tendency of presidential candidates to make Holocaust analogies, but Godwin's Law isn't an American monopoly, and in some cases the comparison may be historically apt" (Calamur, 2015, para. 1). The words "noted yesterday" appear in blue, which the reader needs to know signals a hyperlink, taking the reader to an article written the previous day in *The Atlantic* by David Graham. The article ends with three icons (for Facebook, Twitter, and email), which a savvy user understands are clickable links to share the article across various platforms. Even before understanding the content of each article, it is clear that users must know how to access the available digital tools, or even know what are appropriate "guesses" in the sense of what to click on and look for.

The following subsections use these three articles to illustrate prevalent themes from media reporting of refugees and migrants, many of which have been confirmed in the literature. The final subsection (Anti-migrant sentiments) is a collection of overtly discriminatory anti-refugee themes found in the *Al Jazeera* article's comment section.

> **Dangerous water.** All three articles characterize refugees' presence as "dangerous water," to use Santa Ana's (2002) metaphor (what Baker and McEnery [2005] call "refugees as movement"). This is seen in the phrases "small trickle relative to total migration," "latest surge," "stemmed the flow," "stop the flow," "largest flow," "unregulated flow," the quote "stemming the flow of African migrants" and the quote of other media coverage itself: "Waves of asylum seekers

flowing into European countries in a 'relentless stream.'" Reducing people to flowing bodies of water prompts readers to see refugees and migrants as a natural disaster (a flood) and constant pressure. This is a commonly found representation in media discourse of immigration and migration, and its effects are that individuals are likened to a faceless, homogenous mass (Baker & McEnery, 2005; Loring, 2016b).

**Large numbers.** Similar to this theme is the constant framing of refugees and migrants in terms of their large numbers: "more than a million," "huge numbers," "massive scale," "thousands of migrants." Sometimes the numbers are vague, as seen above, and sometimes the numbers are precise: "60 million people" and "70,000 refugees." This theme is called "quantification" by Baker and McEnery (2005) and often suggests a core sentiment of apprehension or distress. In a similar vein, magazine covers use "infinityline" and "mass of heads" metaphors to visually depict large numbers of migrants (Chavez, 2001). An underlying assumption behind this discourse is that a greater number of immigrants threatens the status quo. It also reduces the immigrant experience to a mere description of numbers, indicating that their quantity is more important than their backgrounds or personalities.

**Tragedy.** The tragedy metaphor is seen in discourse that uses words such as *despair, stricken, dying*, and *tragedy* itself. It constructs refugees (as well as other minority groups) as powerless and unfortunate (Baker & McEnery, 2005). Loring (2016b) found this metaphor more commonly used in *immigrant* discourse than *refugee* discourse, "imply[ing] that immigrants are down on their luck and in unfortunate situations. In Kim's (2012) study of Korean editorials, overly sympathetic discourse similarly painted migrants as "helpless victims." Discourse describing the global refugee crisis uses many instances of "drowning," "death," "dying," and "fatalities," as well as more evocative constructions such as "massacre," "brutal detainment," "harassment at sea," "tragic consequences," and "throes of conflict." Thus, these authors frame migrants as powerless and rarely as empowered.

**Problems.** Under the broad theme of refugees and migrants "as a problem" are mentions of high costs of processing and resettlement (*The Atlantic* even calculates a figure—$15,714 per person, from Syria to the US). Referencing high costs can give readers who struggle with their own finances a visceral negative reaction. Mentions of refugees in terms of crime and nuisance (Baker & McEnery, 2005) and burden on society (Kim, 2012) would also be included under this theme. Labeling refugees as an "economic burden" (Loring, 2016b) and "disproportionate burden" paints them as a problem. General mentions of "tensions," "dimensions of the problem," and "scale of the problem" from the global refugee crisis webpages are not overtly discriminatory but do frame the crisis by its challenges.

**Borders.** When a country's borders are seen as representative of political, linguistic, and cultural divisions, its inhabitants feel a sense of unity (Shohamy, 2006). They are seen as an authentic and legitimate way of making sense of political and nationalist divisions. Therefore, crossing into a foreign country is symbolic for entering a neighbor's house. This is seen in the expression "Germany had opened its doors" (*The Atlantic*), which compares the border to a front door (Santa Ana, 2002). Also employed are less metaphorical expressions: "closed its borders" and "cross into Hungary." Although more literal, these expressions still rely on an interpretation of borders as a veritable and legitimate division.

**Transaction.** A recently-used theme in the global refugee crisis discourse describes the relationship between refugees and the countries they are moving into as a transaction or commodity. Oft-repeated is the phrase "take in [particular number of] refugees." This language objectifies refugees as a commodity or transactional item to be passed from one country to another (Kim, 2012). Other similar phrases such as "will be allowed to stay" and "accepted more refugees" also highlight the hierarchical relationship between the powerless refugees and the authoritative host countries and governments.

Table 8.1 Anti-migrant Sentiments Expressed through Online Readers' Comments

| Theme | Example phrase |
|---|---|
| Blame | "Refugee crisis is the result their own mistakes…" |
| Pass the buck | "Let the refugees migrate to another Muslim country…" |
| Stay and fight | "…Why are these people not staying to fight Issad and ISIS????" |
| Resistance to (cultural) integration | "Europe doesn't want these Muslims. Once established in their ghettos they… attempt to force their practices and customs on them." |
| Slippery slope | "What is the alternative that is being proposed? Opening the boarders and allowing everyone through?" |
| Priority of Europe's problems | "But please continue dragging Europeans through the dirt. Countries that are themselves failing on a mass scale." |
| Fairness | "Why can't *I* get processed for free??" |
| Exhausted charity | "I don't blame them at ALL for doing what they do. But it DOES NOT MEAN they have some guaranteed, transcendental right of acceptance on the part of their host country." |
| Choice | "The Europeans didn't put those fools on a boat and send them to Europe; they did, and they got what they deserved for being stupid." |

**Coping.** Two of the three articles reference "coping," another theme newly in use. This word is seen in the phrases "unable to cope with the flow," "Europe cannot cope," "to show the country can cope with migrants," and "countries struggle to cope with the influx." This theme relates to the problem and transaction themes: All three position migrants and refugees as a burden that higher status countries can choose to assist. The word "cope" signals the imbalance of power and global inconvenience of mass displacements of people.

**Anti-migrant sentiments.** The *Al Jazeera* webpage was the only one of the three to allow readers to post comments, receiving 34 posts by 28 unique users. The majority of these comments demonstrate popular tropes of refugees as viewed by the anti-refugee community. Table 8.1 presents the nine themes referenced more than once in the comments section with an example phrase for each.[4] Common within the example sentences above are the referential labels used to describe the migrants and refugees; there are many instances of "these people," "these Muslims," "they," and "them," along with "these economic migrants." The positioning of "us"/"them" language is not new, but what is interesting are the many occurrences of "*these* people/migrants/Muslims" that not only emphasize the "other-ness" of the group but also lump them together stereotypically. Possibly, these fearful, self-preservation responses are triggered by the number of migrants in Europe exceeding a tacit threshold.

## Implications for Educational Practice

Issues such as the above force us to consider what we can alter in our current respective pedagogic domains to raise awareness about media coverage regarding refugees. For clarity's sake, we list them below:

1. Engaging in simple discourse analysis: For a start, we can engage students in the kind of simple discourse analysis shown here. Alerting them to how online journalism tends to overgeneralize by speaking of refugees as singularities is a necessary first step.
2. Realizing the differences between newcomers: Raising awareness among students and educators about differences between various groups of "newcomers"—refugees, immigrants, voluntary migrants—each of whom has very different histories and starting points seems crucial.

3. Understanding the special needs of refugees: Educators should be sensitized to the special needs of refugees that stem from an interrupted education, past history of trauma and instability, and probable repercussions for mental and physical health (Feuerherm & Ramanathan, 2016). While many refugees may lack formal education and literacy in their native language(s) (Camps, 2016), others possess strong speaking skills in the target language which, while valuable, may mask the need for cultural competency education (Feuerherm, 2016). These differences speak to the divergent needs of refugee groups and the deficiencies of a one-size-fits-all approach to refugee education.
4. Developing sites for participatory research: Creating contexts whereby refugees themselves can shape the direction of their program through voicing their own educational objectives (Feuerherm, 2016) would be empowering. Once the curricular outcomes have been agreed to, educators of refugees and permanent residents can lead their students to develop familiarity with necessary school-based literacy practices ("classroom literacy") (Loring, 2013a, 2013c). Having the instructor demonstrate and exemplify the academic practices necessary to completing certain handouts would ensure that students have equal access to classroom participation.
5. Promoting inclusion: To promote inclusion, scholars recommend including a tutoring component in the program (Feuerherm, 2016) or organizing frequent collaborations with target language speakers and community members (Elmeroth, 2003). Additionally, such participatory curriculum would help prepare refugees for the diverse set of literacies expected of them upon resettlement: "navigating the job market, creating resumes, understanding the job search process,…computer literacy,…banking,…using credit, navigating the US healthcare system,…tenant's rights,…understanding the school system, [and] grocery shopping" (Tyeklar, 2016, p. 169–170).
6. Rethinking "Survival English" to additionally value home languages: Often, refugee literacy education in the US is geared toward finding and keeping an entry-level job and is subsumed under the label of "survival English." Survival English problematically treats language instruction as "a means to an economic end" and as "a remedy for a perceived deficiency" (Camps, 2016, p. 63). This framing oversimplifies the ubiquity of English in the nation as a whole and the individual workplace in particular, and it ignores the multilingual interplays that English affords *in addition to* whichever first languages are already spoken. Additionally, teaching English with a survivalist mentality can more readily lead to teaching English, citizenship, and literacy in a minimalist and cursory way. Instead, ESL/citizenship classes for refugees could not only teach basic English but also recognize the linguistic capital (Bourdieu, 1991) of students' native languages and commemorate their multilingualism and multiculturalism. Furthermore, these classes could endeavor to promote refugee students' critical literacy and citizenship: thinking critically, questioning prescribed responses, making comparisons with one's home country, and identifying societal inequalities (Loring, 2013a)—components that the next section will elucidate.

**Recommendations and Forward Thinking**

The goal of this chapter is to explore media representations of refugees and possible implications for literacy practices regarding refugee education. In focusing on the initial displacement and migration of refugees during the "global refugee crisis," the media tends to frame the issue largely in terms of the population impact on European countries. Frequent exposure to discourse that focuses on refugees' and migrants' large numbers, difficulties, and economic and demographic effects on the host country may result in a tendency to think about refugees as a homogenous mass in a negative light.

Consequently, dehumanizing language can lead to political and social actions that treat immigrants and refugees as a problem—one more challenge refugees face in their displacement and resettlement. Many commenters reacting to the news cycle fixate on the decisions leading to and the aftermaths of border-crossings in ways that recycle xenophobic and discriminatory discourse more overtly. By presenting displacement as a "choice," the discourse places the onus on the refugee to account for "mistakes" and "stay and fight" for one's native country. A similar discursive construction appears in asylum and naturalization policy, where the burden of proof is on the applicant to prove his qualifications before being granted rights and privileges of protection (Blommaert, 2009; Loring, 2013a).

What these discourse patterns ignore are the ongoing resettlement processes and the difficulties in resettling from *the refugees'*, not the host country's, perspective. As mentioned, after less than a year of financial and linguistic assistance, it is assumed that refugees can live self-sufficiently (speaking the national language(s), having employment, knowing their rights, and being culturally adjusted). Not only are these feats difficult, if not impossible, to accomplish in eight months, they are also more gradable than they appear: *Having* an entry-level minimum-wage job is one obstacle, but working in a position matched to the strengths and qualifications of the applicant is far more difficult to manage. One compounding factor is the fact that not all educational degrees or credentials are internationally transferable (Feuerherm, 2016; Tyeklar, 2016). As Tyeklar (2016) muses, "should not truly supportive resettlement ultimately include the development of those particular literacies necessary beyond just survival?" (p. 161).

By "particular literacies," Tyeklar is acknowledging the meaning-making activities that compose a person's day-to-day life (navigating to and from locations in one's community; participating in transactions of goods and services; asking/responding to questions, requests, favors, and complaints; accessing (digital) information; understanding legal, local, bureaucratic, and *de facto* policies; interacting with friends and strangers in socioculturally appropriate ways, etc.). These types of knowledge are multiple, broad, and domain specific, and must be learned to be "read" (Gee, 2003). These literacies are often unacknowledged but arguably present the most comprehensive challenge for resettlers. As we have argued elsewhere, there is often a mismatch between *legal* citizenship and *de facto* citizenship, where de facto citizenship entails a knowledge of how to navigate government websites and offices to obtain information and access documents, how to act within government buildings, and inclusion and participation in one's community (Loring, 2017; Loring & Ramanathan, 2016; Ramanathan, 2013a, 2013b). Likewise, comfort in such literacies is a measure of de facto access and integration.

Many scholars have called attention to the literacy needs for an active citizenry (Banks, 2008; DeJaeghere, 2008; Loring, 2013a, 2013b; Mulcahy, 2011), where questioning judgments, ideologies, and dominant discourses transforms normative structures and informs curricular development (Luke, 2014; Mulcahy, 2011). In a pedagogic model of critical literacy, teachers and students together use "new literacies to change relations of power, both people's everyday social relations and larger geopolitical and economic relations" (Luke, 2014, p. 28). This entails a critique of both the consumption and production of discourse (Janks, 2014). A critical citizen demonstrating critical literacy is one who becomes a critical evaluator of how one's own and others' language can be used for gatekeeping and marginalization.[5] By bringing attention to these issues, this chapter reminds researchers and educators of the consequences of power-laden political discourse and the opportunities they have in interacting with refugees and migrants.

### Notes

1. We use "ending" to represent the final legal status change, but we acknowledge that (literacy) hurdles do not end with naturalized citizenship.
2. The 2016b study drew on the full corpus of 270 articles and blogs that had at least one mention of the word *citizenship*. Data used in the 2016a study came from a three-month subsection of the corpus, which totaled 171 articles and blogs.

3. This excluded the Wikipedia page and the section "In the News" with the most recent articles posted a few hours before the search.
4. The quotes are displayed verbatim, including misspellings, original punctuation, and capitalized words.
5. For instance, when media discourse tends to reproduce dominant discourses and ideologies of those who are different, a critical citizen questions assumptions and consequences that these views instigate (Loring, 2013a).

# References

Baker, P., Gabrielatos, C., Khosravinik, M., Krzyzanowski, M., McEnery, T., & Wodak, R. (2008). A useful methodological synergy? Combining critical discourse analysis and corpus linguistics to examine discourses of refugees and asylum seekers in the UK press. *Discourse & Society, 19*(3), 273–306.

Baker, P., & McEnery, T. (2005). A corpus-based approach to discourses of refugees and asylum seekers in UN and newspaper texts. *Journal of Language and Politics, 4*(2), 197–226.

Banks, J. (2008). Diversity, group identity, and citizenship education in a global age. *Educational Researcher, 37*(3), 129–139.

Bell, A. (1991). *The language of news media.* Cambridge, MA: Blackwell.

Blommaert, J. (2009). Language, asylum, and the national order. *Current Anthropology, 50*(4), 415–441.

Bourdieu, P. (1991). *Language and symbolic power.* Cambridge, MA: Harvard University Press.

Bruno, A. (2011). *U.S. refugee resettlement assistance* (Congressional Research Service report). Retrieved from www.fas.org/sgp/crs/row/R41570.pdf

Calamur, K. (2015, October 14). Goodwin's law comes to the refugee crisis. *The Atlantic.* Retrieved from www.theatlantic.com/notes/all/2015/08/the-global-refugee-crisis/402718/. Accessed on 28 May, 2016.

Camps, D. M. J. (2016). Restraining English instruction for refugee adults in the United States. In E. M. Feuerherm & V. Ramanathan (Eds.), *Refugee resettlement in the United States: Language, policy, pedagogy* (pp. 54–72). Tonawanda, NY: Multilingual Matters.

Castles, S. (1998). Globalization and the ambiguities of national citizenship. In R. Baubock and J. Rundell (Eds.), *Blurred boundaries: Migration, ethnicity, and citizenship* (pp. 223–244). Brookfield, VT: Ashgate.

Chavez, L.R. (2001). *Covering immigration: Popular images and the politics of the nation.* Berkeley: University of California Press.

Crawley, H., & Sriskandarajah, D. (2005). Preface. In R. Greenslade (Ed.), *Seeking scapegoats: The coverage of asylum in the UK press* (pp. 1–40). London, UK: Institute for Public Policy Research.

DeJaeghere, J. (2008). Citizenship as privilege and power: Australian educators' lived experiences as citizens. *Comparative Education Review, 52*(3), 357–380.

Dobson, T. M., & Willinsky, J. (2009). Digital literacies. In D. R. Olson and N. Torrance (Eds.), *The Cambridge handbook of literacy* (pp. 286–312). New York, NY: Cambridge University Press.

Eades, D. (2009). Testing the claims of asylum seekers: The role of language analysis. *Language Assessment Quarterly, 6*(1), 30–40.

Elmeroth, E. (2003). From refugee camp to solitary confinement: Illiterate adults learn Swedish as a second language. *Scandinavian Journal of Educational Research, 47*(4), 431–449.

Feuerherm, E. M. (2016). Building a participatory program for Iraqi refugee women and families: Negotiating policies and pedagogies. In E. M. Feuerherm & V. Ramanathan (Eds.), *Refugee resettlement in the United States: Language, policy, pedagogy* (pp. 75–95). Tonawanda, NY: Multilingual Matters.

Feuerherm, E. M., & Ramanathan, V. (Eds.) (2016). *Refugee resettlement in the United States: Language, policy, pedagogy.* Tonawanda, NY: Multilingual Matters.

Gabrielatos, C., & Baker, P. (2008). Fleeing, sneaking, flooding: A corpus analysis of discursive constructions of refugees and asylum seekers in the UK Press, 1996–2005. *Journal of English Linguistics, 36*(1), 5–38.

Garrett, P., & Bell, A. (1998). Media and discourse: A critical overview. In A. Bell & P. Garrett (Eds.), *Approaches to media discourse* (pp. 1–20). Malden, MA: Blackwell.

Gee, J. P. (1987). What is literacy? *Teaching and Learning, 2*(1), 3–11.

Gee, J. P. (2003). *What video games have to teach us about learning and literacy.* New York, NY: Palgrave Macmillan.

Gee, J. P. (2015). *Social linguistics and literacies: Ideologies in discourses* (5th ed.). New York, NY: Routledge.

Global trends: Forced displacement in 2015. (2016). *UNHCR.* Retrieved from http://www.unhcr.org/576408cd7.pdf

Heller, M. (2013). Language and dis-citizenship in Canada. *Journal of Language, Identity, and Education, 12*(3), 189–192.

Hull, G. A., & Nelson, M. E. (2009). Literacy, media, and morality: Making the case for an aesthetic turn. In M. Baynham and M. Prinsloo (Eds.), *The future of literacy studies* (pp. 199–227). New York, NY: Palgrave Macmillan.

Immigration and Nationality Act, 8 U.S.C. § 208.

Janks, H. (2014). The importance of critical literacy. In J. Z. Pandya & J. Ávila (Eds.), *Moving critical literacies forward: A new look at praxis across contexts* (pp. 32–44). New York, NY: Routledge.

Kim, S. (2012). Racism in the global era: Analysis of Korean media discourse around migrants, 1990–2009. *Discourse & Society*, *23*(6), 657–678.

Koltay, T. (2011). The media and the literacies: Media literacy, information literacy, digital literacy. *Media, Culture & Society*, *33*(2), 211–221.

Kunnan, A. (2009). Politics and legislation in citizenship testing in the United States. *Annual Review of Applied Linguistics*, *29*, 37–48.

Leymarie, C. D. (2016). Language as a fund of knowledge: The case of Mama Rita and implications for refugee policy. In E. M. Feuerherm & V. Ramanathan (Eds.), *Refugee resettlement in the United States: Language, policy, pedagogy* (pp. 172–190). Tonawanda, NY: Multilingual Matters.

Lillie, K. E. (2016). "The ELD classes are… too much and we need to take other classes to graduated": Arizona's restrictive language policy and the dis-citizenship of ELs. In A. Loring & V. Ramanathan (Eds.), *Language, immigration, and naturalization: Legal and linguistic issues* (pp. 79–100). Tonawanda, NY: Multilingual Matters.

Loring, A. (2013a). *Language & U.S. Citizenship: Meanings, ideologies, & policies* (Doctoral dissertation). Retrieved from ProQuest Dissertations and Theses. (Accession Order No. 3596915).

Loring, A. (2013b). The meaning of 'citizenship': Tests, policy, and English proficiency. *The CATESOL Journal*, *24*(1), 198–219.

Loring, A. (2013c). Classroom meanings and enactments of citizenship: An ethnographic study. In V. Ramanathan (Ed.), *Language policies, language pedagogies: Rights, access, citizenship* (pp. 188–208). Tonawanda, NY: Multilingual Matters.

Loring, A. (2015). Citizenship policy from the bottom-up: The linguistic and semiotic landscape of a naturalization field office. *Critical Inquiry in Language Studies*, *12*(3), 161–183.

Loring, A. (2016a). Ideologies and collocations of "citizenship" in media discourse: A corpus-based critical discourse analysis. In A. Loring & V. Ramanathan (Eds.), *Language, immigration, and naturalization: Legal and linguistic issues* (pp. 184–206). Tonawanda, NY: Multilingual Matters.

Loring, A. (2016b). Positionings of refugees, aliens, and immigrants in the media. In E. M. Feuerherm & V. Ramanathan (Eds.), *Refugee resettlement in the United States: Language, policy, pedagogy* (pp. 21–34). Tonawanda, NY: Multilingual Matters.

Loring, A. (2017). Literacy in citizenship preparatory classes. *Journal of Language, Identity, and Education*, *16*(3), 172–188.

Loring, A., & Ramanathan, V. (2016a). Introduction: Language, immigration, and naturalization: Legal and linguistic issues. In A. Loring & V. Ramanathan (Eds.), *Language, immigration, and naturalization: Legal and linguistic issues* (pp. 1–24). Tonawanda, NY: Multilingual Matters.

Loring, A., & Ramanathan, V. (Eds.) (2016b). *Language, immigration, and naturalization: Legal and linguistic issues*. Tonawanda, NY: Multilingual Matters.

Ludwig, B. (2016). The different meanings of the word *refugee*. In E. M. Feuerherm & V. Ramanathan (Eds.), *Refugee resettlement in the United States: Language, policy, pedagogy* (pp. 35–53). Tonawanda, NY: Multilingual Matters.

Luke, A. (2014). Defining Critical Literacy. In J. Z. Pandya & J. Ávila (Eds.), *Moving critical literacies forward: A new look at praxis across contexts* (pp. 19–31). New York, NY: Routledge.

Marshall, T. (1950). *Citizenship and social class and other essays*. London, UK: Pluto.

Martín Rojo, L., & van Dijk, T. A. (1997). "There was a problem, and it was solved!": Legitimating the expulsion of 'illegal' migrants in Spanish parliamentary discourse. *Discourse & Society*, *8*(4), 523–566.

McNamara, T., & Shohamy, E. (2008). Viewpoint: Language tests and human rights. *International Journal of Applied Linguistics*, *18*(1), 89–95.

McPherron, P. (2016). Local, foreign, and in-between: English teachers and students creating community and becoming global "citizens" at a Chinese university. In A. Loring & V. Ramanathan (Eds.), *Language, immigration, and naturalization: Legal and linguistic issues* (pp. 101–120). Tonawanda, NY: Multilingual Matters.

Migrant crisis: Migration to Europe explained in seven charts. (2016, March 4) *BBC*. Retrieved from www.bbc.com/news/world-europe-34191911. Accessed on 28 May, 2016.

Mills, K. A. (2010). A review of the "digital turn" in the New Literacy Studies. *Review of Educational Research*, *80*(2), 246–271.

Mitchell, H. (2006, January 24). The difference between asylum seekers and refugees. *Migration Watch UK*. Retrieved from www.migrationwatchuk.org/briefing-paper/70.

Mulcahy, C. M. (2011). The tangled web we weave: Critical literacy and critical thinking. In J. L. DeVitis (Ed.), *Critical civic literacy: A Reader* (pp. 1–10). New York, NY: Peter Lang Education List.

Nelson, T. E., Clawson, R. A., & Oxley, Z. M. (1997). Media framing of a civil liberties conflict and its effect on tolerance. *American Political Science Review*, *91*(3), 567–583.

Orgad, L. (2011). Creating new Americans: The essence of Americanism under the citizenship test. *Houston Law Review*, *47*(5), 1–46.

Piller, I. (2011). *Intercultural communication: A critical introduction*. Edinburgh: Edinburgh University Press.

Ramanathan, V. (2013a). *Language policy and (dis)citizenship: Rights, access, pedagogies.* Clevedon: Multilingual Matters.

Ramanathan, V. (2013b). Language policies and (dis)citizenship: Who belongs? Who is a guest? Who is deported? [special issue]. *Journal of Language, Identity, and Education, 12*(3): 162–166.

Resettlement. (n.d.). *UNHCR.* Retrieved from www.unhcr.org/en-us/resettlement.html.

Santa Ana, O. (2002). *Brown tide rising: Metaphors of Latinos in contemporary American public discourse.* Austin, TX: University of Texas Press.

Santa Ana, O. (2013). *Juan in a hundred: The representation of Latinos on network news.* Austin, TX: University of Texas Press.

Seymour, R. (2016, April 28). Refugee crisis: When is a tragedy a massacre? *Al Jazeera.* Retrieved from www.aljazeera.com/indepth/opinion/2016/04/refugee-crisis-tragedy-massacre-160426110904507.html. Accessed on 28 May, 2016.

Shohamy, E. (2006). *Language policy: Hidden agendas and new approaches.* London, UK: Routledge.

The global refugee crisis. (2015). *The Atlantic.* Retrieved from www.theatlantic.com/notes/all/2015/08/the-global-refugee-crisis/402718/. Accessed on 28 May, 2016.

The New London Group. (2000). A pedagogy of multiliteracies designing social features. In B. Cope & M. Kalantzis (Eds.), *Multiliteracies: Literacy learning and the design of social features* (pp. 9–37). New York, NY: Routledge.

Touraine, A. (1997). *What is democracy?* Boulder, CO: Westview Press.

Tyeklar, N. (2016). The US refugee resettlement process: A path to self-sufficiency or marginalization? In E. M. Feuerherm & V. Ramanathan (Eds.), *Refugee resettlement in the United States: Language, policy, pedagogy* (pp. 152–171). Tonawanda, NY: Multilingual Matters.

UN General Assembly. (1950, December 14). *Draft Convention relating to the Status of Refugees*, A/RES/429, available at www.refworld.org/docid/3b00f08a27.html.

van Leeuwen, T., & Wodak, R. (1999). Legitimizing immigration control: A discourse-historical analysis. *Discourse Studies, 1*(1), 83–118.

Wiley, T. (2013). Constructing and deconstructing "illegal" children. *Journal of Language, Identity, and Education, 12*(3), 167–172.

Wodak, R. (2003). Discourse of silence: Anti-semitic discourse in post-war Austria. In L. Thiesmeyer (Ed.), *Discourse and silencing* (pp. 179–210). Philadelphia, PA: John Benjamins.

Wodak, R. (2007). Pragmatics and critical discourse analysis: A cross-disciplinary inquiry. *Journal of Pragmatics and Cognition, 15*(1), 203–227.

Wodak, R. (2013). Dis-citizenship and migration: A critical discourse-analytical perspective. *Journal of Language, Identity, and Education, 12*(3), 173–178.

Ziegahn, L., Ibrahim, S., Al-Ansari, B., Mahmood, M., Tawffeq, R., Mughir, M. … Xiong, G. (2013). *The mental and physical health of recent Iraqi refugees in Sacramento, California.* UC Davis Clinical and Translational Science Center. Sacramento, CA: UC Davis.

# 9
# Race and Racism in Digital Media
*What Can Critical Race Theory Contribute to Research on Techno-Cultures?*

Kathy A. Mills and Amanda Godley

The world has become a place of ubiquitous human engagement in digital media using an expanding array of mobile devices and other technologies. With the rapid production and circulation of digital texts new questions must be asked about the social construction of racialized identities, discourses, and interactions. While some theorists have pointed to the potential of the Internet to usher in a digital "global village" (Negroponte, 1995)—a place where visual indicators of race are concealed—others counter that race is also constructed discursively online and in the media (Glaser, Dixit, & Green, 2002; Tynes, Reynolds, & Greenfield, 2004). A central concern is the extent to which networked digital media have become a platform for transforming social action, maintaining the status quo, or reproducing racism and colonization.

The aim of this chapter is to examine the contemporary contributions of critical race theory (CRT) for interpreting representations of race and racism in multimodal and digital literacy research and practice. The term multimodal refers to texts that combine two or more modes, including words, images, audio, and other elements (Mills, 2016). Multimodal and digital literacies include the use of social media, digital film and television, video games, digital storytelling, and the sharing of music videos and podcasts. There has been a rise in the production and circulation of digital texts about race and racialized dialogue through social media and other forms of digital encoding and sharing.

Race is a highly contested concept. Following Haney-Lopez (1994), we define race in this chapter as a social construct, the ongoing and contradictory process of social grouping by phenotype, ancestry, and other historically contingent and socio-political struggles. Race is always constructed in relation to other racial groups, particularly on the basis of ethnicity, physical characteristics, culture, or mannerisms. Racialized ideologies function to naturalize the idea of the superiority of one race over another (Lorde, 1992).

We define racism as the beliefs, practices, or structural systems that function to oppress racial groups in society. Racism is endemic in most societies across the globe and in the digital spaces that youth inhabit. A recent example from Australia is a controversial and widely publicized racist attack against Adam Goodes, an elite Indigenous Australian footballer and 2014 Australian of the Year. Goodes was publicly booed by a 13-year-old girl, who shouted the derogatory term "ape" during a televised game (Crawford, 2013). Anti-racist and racist commentaries of the event became viral. Conversely, social media has been used to produce a groundswell of anti-racist counter-movements, such as the #BlackLivesMatter movement, which began in 2012 as George Zimmerman was acquitted of the murder of Trayvon Martin (Barza, Tometi, & Cullors, 2013; Timeline: The Black Lives Matter Movement, 2016).

Techno-culture is a term used in this chapter to refer to technologically mediated communication cultures that are constituted in certain epistemologies and views about the world (Brock, 2012). For example, Dinerstein (2006) argued that American techno-culture is based on beliefs about scientific progress, modernity, Whiteness, masculinity, and the future. Similarly, digitally-mediated communication is not a form of value-free information transfer, but rather mediates racial and cultural identities like the technologies that preceded it. It has been argued that the digital communications environment has enabled the extension of ideologies located in Western culture, and that the new affordances of digital media need to be evaluated critically with attention to equity and colonization (Carey, 2009). Thus, in this chapter, we examine current techno-cultures and their associated discourses, practices, and identities through the lens of three tenets of CRT: Whiteness as property, colorblind racism, and counter-stories. We first provide an overview of CRT, including the tenets above, and then describe the application of each principle to research on digital, multimodal literacies, and techno-cultures. We both review existing CRT research and also suggest places where the addition of CRT could illuminate current and future research on digital literacies.

## CRT and Race in Digital Spaces

CRT is a theory of race and racism that emerged from critical legal studies in the US in the 1970s. Drawing on historical and legal evidence, CRT contends that racism against African Americans and concomitant White supremacy are inextricably tied to the history of chattel slavery in the US. Racism continues to be endemic to US society, its culture, and its legal systems (Bell, 1992; Delgado & Stefancic, 2001). Racism is not simply an individual belief or a psychological state; rather, it is a hegemonic ideology and a system of material inequities that are ubiquitous in society (Bell, 1980; Crenshaw, 1988; Delgado, 1990; Matsuda, 1989).

In educational research, CRT scholars such as Ladson-Billings (1998, 2013) and Tate (1997) have argued that despite prevalent views that education is "the great equalizer" and despite educational policies such as desegregation, racism against Students of Color remains endemic in US schools. Racism in schools is perpetuated by discriminatory policies such as disproportionate suspensions of Students of Color and in-school ability grouping, and by the belief that such policies are colorblind (Howard & Navarro, 2016). We use the terms "People of Color" and "Students of Color" deliberately and politically to refer to groups of people who are often positioned in opposition to the category of "White." These terms imply that race is a social construct and that the definition of "White" is socially, historically, and culturally embedded as well as continually changing.

CRT views racism as interwoven in all aspects of society, including seemingly benign and neutral literacy policies, such as use of technology in schools and online access. Three key tenets of CRT are particularly applicable to scholarship on race and racism in digital literacies, and illuminate the ways in which racism continues to be both systematic and endemic in digital spaces and techno-cultures: Whiteness as property, colorblindness, and counter-stories.

First, Whiteness as property posits that property has historically been defined and defended only when it relates to the material, economic, cultural, and social capital enjoyed by White citizens (Delgado & Stefancic, 2001). For instance, ability grouping, unequal school funding, standardized testing, banning the use of Indigenous language (e.g., Vass, 2014), and cultural norms about appropriate student talk in classrooms (e.g., Shapiro, 2014), all serve to maintain access to high-quality education as the property of White citizens, even when legal and governmental policies suggest otherwise.

Second, CRT scholars have shown how racial "colorblindness"—the belief that race is insignificant and that racism does not exist—has led to laws and policies that profess to serve all citizens, but that support racism through ignorance of White racial privilege and structural and ideological racism (Reese, 2008; Yosso, Parker, Solorzano, & Lynn, 2004). Examples include the "stand your ground" law that was used to acquit George Zimmerman of the murder of Trayvon Martin, and calls for the end of affirmative action for historically oppressed peoples.

Third, CRT can help to critically analyze digital texts—both racialized texts, and those that provide anti-racist counter-stories. Since its founding in legal studies, CRT has argued for the use of counter-stories, or accounts that represent the perspectives and experiences of People of Color, as legitimate and valuable legal and scientific evidence (Richardson, 2009). CRT scholars have argued that in the absence of such counter-stories, dominant "master narratives," that often ignore or disparage the perspectives of People of Color, come to be seen as factual and normative. In online spaces, master narratives about Indigenous cultures and People of Color can be seen in many online games, media, and blogs (Nakamura, 2013). Conversely, virtual worlds can create character choices that obscure race, anti-racist movements can flourish on social media sites (e.g., Twitter), and online forums open dialogue about racial issues (Byrne, 2008).

Although CRT began with a focus on racism against African Americans, CRT scholarship and theory has been extended to include Latinos, Asians, Pacific Americans, American Indians and other oppressed people, Indigenous peoples, and People of Color beyond the US (Buenavista, 2010; Hylton, 2012; Marable, 1992). For instance, LatCrit or Latino CRT, which shares many tenets and methods with CRT scholarship, focuses on issues of language, immigration, and identity that influence the oppression of Latinos. At the same time, LatCrit strongly emphasizes intersectionality as it seeks to acknowledge differences among Latinos' experiences and to address the intersections of racism, sexism, classism, and other forms of oppression (Solorzano & Bernal, 2001).

## Whiteness as Property in Digital and Online Literacies

Given both the cost of Internet access and the control of social media and search engines by companies owned by White men, the Internet has historically been a space that has been "owned" and controlled by Whites (Daniels, 2013). The CRT tenet of Whiteness as property raises the question of who controls access to and circulation of digital texts, and how such control is protected as White property or, conversely, extended to People of Color.

Twenty years ago, research on race and digital literacy in the US focused heavily on "the digital divide"—the racial disparities between access to and use of the Internet—with White Americans twice as likely to have access to the Internet as Black Americans (Perrin & Duggan, 2015). However, in recent years, access and use of the Internet among Black and White Americans has become nearly equal, particularly among people younger than 30 (Perrin & Duggan, 2015; Tynes, Umana-Taylor, Rose, Lin, & Anderson, 2012). In a 2015 Pew Research Center survey, 97% of Asian Americans, 85% of Whites, 79% of Latinos, and 78% of Black adults over 18 reported using the Internet (Perrin & Duggan, 2015). Although racial disparities in access to Internet access are decreasing in the US, global access and use of the Internet varies widely by region, and issues of access remain among Indigenous peoples and People of Color (UNESCO, 2011). Internet use by race is also explored further by Warschauer and Tate (2017), Chapter 5 of this volume.

Some social media sites are used more by People of Color than by White Internet users. Approximately twice the proportion of Black Internet users use Twitter when compared with White Internet users, and Black and Latino Internet users are 50% more likely to use Instagram than White Internet users (Perrin & Duggan, 2015). Media consumption of television among Latino, Asian, and African American youth, ages 8 to 18 years, is high—four hours more per day than Whites (Rideout, Lauricella, & Wartella, 2011). However, characters of color are severely underrepresented in television and film (Hunt & Ramón, 2015). The rise in Internet access and use has been partially attributed to the rise in inexpensive smartphones, raising questions about differences in the quality of Internet access across racially defined groups. Additionally, questions remain about how social media and other Internet sites are owned and controlled by White interests.

A related issue in digital spaces is the prominence of video games and the analysis of White control over the representation of race. Researchers of race beyond CRT have called for strengthened understandings of the social construction of race in video games and related fan-sites and online discussions, and implications for broader civic participation (McKernan, 2015). Many video games invite users to try on the bodies of others, and to indulge in the other, such as through avatar or character selection. Games such as Grand Theft Auto III and others employ virtual tourism to explore representations of inner cities communities, exotic lands, and illicit places where ethnicity is depicted as a taste of something different, offering a "virtual ethnic sampling" and "dark bodies" (Leonard, 2003, p. 5). The underside of White property and White privilege is the fascination with the "other," with what is non-White, and its characterization of the exotic (Picart, 2013). Such games are a continuation of the Western historic project of securing pleasure through the other and as virtual relations of power and domination (Leonard, 2003).

Illustrating the potential of video games that are owned and controlled by People of Color, the Digital Songlines Project is creating software for the rapid prototyping of natural and developed Aboriginal Australian heritage in a three-dimensional, virtual environment (Leavy, 2014). The project has assisted Indigenous Australian communities to preserve and document their cultural heritage in specific geospatially defined regions of Australia, including culturally significant landforms, flora, fauna, ancestral histories, and the historically contested terrain of White colonization. It has been used to record knowledge in real time to support Indigenous language and cultural heritage management against a history of White oppression and dispossession of Aboriginal people, the traditional owners of the land. Conducted in consultation with Indigenous elders, the study utilizes the new affordances of virtual worlds for preservation of Indigenous knowledge. However, the use of technologies that ultimately reproduce White notions of high fidelity virtual prototyping has also created epistemic tensions through the White representation of Indigenous sacred places in simulations that rupture notions of sacredness. The researchers and designers of Digital Songlines have recognized inescapable design constraints that originate in Western techno-cultures, White property, and game design, leading to the White transgression of sacred places by the uninitiated designers of simulated Indigenous realities.

More research is needed within school settings to document ways that the valued knowledge, practices, and ways of communicating in Indigenous communities are embedded in digital and multimodal literacies, and the ways that Eurocentric notions of digital and multimodal literacy as White property are decolonized. One of the key issues with notions of literacy achievement, whether digitally mediated or not, is that it is defined and measured against performatively constituted identities implicated in Whiteness (Mills, Davis-Warra, Sewell, & Anderson, 2016). Reports of literacy achievement continue to position Whiteness as the measure, bringing benefits to those who possess Whiteness.

A recent study with an Indigenous school community in Australia demonstrated how Indigenous teachers developed the multimodal literacy learning of their students by embedding the valued knowledge and beliefs of their ancestral history in the English curriculum (Mills et al., 2016). Transgenerational and Indigenous ways of multimodal literacy practices emerged as the children digitally retold stories from the Elders and from the Dreamtime. Digital literacies highlighted the importance of connections and belonging to the land, and of standing together against racial oppression. Indigenous modes of knowledge sharing included traditional dance, storytelling, arts, and music which were written, filmed, and shared digitally. Collective knowledge of Indigenous people, self-determination, fighting back, and pride in their histories were vital themes woven throughout their digital practices at school.

These examples of the digital construction of race bring to light the ways in which Whiteness as property and its subordination of People of Color can be maintained or transformed. CRT has aimed to challenge and transform racial marginalization in the social order (Pane & Salmon, 2009), while online spaces produce new configurations of knowledge that evoke modified forms of Whiteness as property. CRT suggests that countering Whiteness as property and its related privileges online involves more than superficial changes to production and design of digital spaces. It requires a recognition of the enormity of the endemic nature of White control of online social orders and a belief that People's of Color ownership and circulation of online and digital texts is essential for creating more equitable and anti-racist techno-cultures

**Colorblind Racism on the Social Web**

Critical race theorists posit that colorblindness—"the view that race does not matter"—upholds racist systems and institutions (Neville, Lilly, Lee, Duran, & Browne, 2000, p. 60). Since the 1960s Civil Rights Movement, European Whites have often been socialized to think that seeing race is wrong (Yosso et al., 2004). This may appear to be a noble ideal in terms of not excluding other racial groups, and avoiding discrimination on the basis of skin color. However, colorblindness is associated with several assumptions: (a) race is an invisible characteristic, (b) race is a taboo topic, and (c) social outcomes are based on individual circumstances, not on systems of privilege and discrimination, including White privilege and racial discrimination (Schofield, 1986).

Racism is endemic to human societies, and the Internet is not exempt from experiences of racial discrimination, including those linked to racial colorblindness. It is often assumed that the Internet is a colorblind social space where social interactions and techno-cultures transcend racism because interpersonal communication often occurs without knowledge of others' racial identities. However, in the rise of the social web, colorblindness has been shown to lead to low multicultural competence, minimization of the role of race in racist events, and resistance to discussing racial differences in order to appear to be nonbiased (Tynes & Markoe, 2010).

In a noteworthy study of colorblind racism conducted by Tynes, Giang, Williams, & Thompson (2008), the researchers studied reactions to racially themed party images on a social networking site. Racially themed parties involve the guests dressing, acting, and utilizing stereotypes of racial others. The participant responses to racial theme party images varied from "not bothered" to "bothered." A multinomial logistic regression revealed that participants differed in their reactions to the images based on their racial group and colorblind racial ideology. European Americans and participants who scored high in racial colorblindness were more likely to provide a "not bothered" response. In addition, the racial colorblind group were more likely to condone and encourage the racial theme party practice with laughter and other inappropriate suggestions. Contrastingly, the group who scored low in colorblindness vocally opposed the racist images.

Colorblind racism is also well documented in the technology industry and among massively multiplayer online game players (Daniels, 2015; McKernan, 2015). The unique modality of digital, online literacies—most notably in spaces such as multiplayer games and massive open online courses—provides opportunities for individuals to represent themselves both through image and print in various raced (and gendered) ways through avatars and other representations of the self. As Nakamura (2013) notes:

> [These spaces] are also theatrical and discursive spaces where identity is performed, swapped, bought, and sold in both textual and graphic media. When users create characters to deploy in these spaces, they are electing to perform versions of themselves as raced and gendered beings.
> (p. v)

The ability of White users to present themselves as non-White in online spaces has the potential to lead to the development of empathy for the racism experienced by People of Color (Behm-Morawitz, Pennell, & Speno, 2016). However, such experiences also allow White users to appropriate the culture of Indigenous and People of Color and to gain from "virtual blackface" and being temporary "tourists" into racist experiences without working to change them in their lived worlds. Furthermore, White dominance in some online social media and games has been shown to have negative effects on racial identity construction (Nishi, Matias, & Montova, 2015).

In her study of avatar-based diversity representation, Lee (2014) found that Adolescents of Color who created avatars in White-dominated virtual reality worlds were more likely than adolescents in diverse virtual reality worlds to lighten the skin tone of their avatars and to refuse to share their offline racial identities with other users. Other studies have traced the connections between minstrelsy, film, and literature, and the projection of Whiteness embedded in the design of online personae through White avatars. For example, Nishi and colleagues (2015) describe how White avatar creation in popular virtual gaming scenarios served to reproduce the hegemonic race relations, reifying racism and racial marginalization in virtual worlds.

Some massively multiplayer online games, such as Second Life, offer opportunities for users to represent themselves as non-human and without representing race or gender. Mahiri (2011) describes how African American youth used the multi-user virtual environment, Teen Second Life, to interacted and create dialogue with avatars that depicted both human and non-human physical features, including metal robots, animals, and characters with green skin. They were able to create for themselves imagined identities and access an array of virtual (European) possessions in the game, such as art galleries, houses, cars, helicopters, and music stages. While the remixing of identities is possible in such digital spaces, Internet users are also more likely to engage in forms of discrimination online than offline because their identity is often unknown (Glaser, Dixit, & Green, 2002). Ultimately, the design and features of the game may be used to reproduce racism, to maintain the status quo, or to open up spaces for the construction of diverse representations of racial identity.

The racist environments underpinnings of colorblindness and the normalcy of White identities in games and online are robust, collectively reproduced, and widespread. Virtual worlds that include alternative bodies do not afford colorblind utopian spaces where race is invisible. Rather, research demonstrates that these spaces often reinforce colorblind racial attitudes where White privilege is not uncovered and where racial differences are not discussed (in order to appear non-racist). Together, these studies suggest that the widely held assumption that online digital literacies are "post racial" is incorrect, and that colorblindness in techno-cultures and virtual worlds reinforces racism, as it does in the physical world. Additional studies are needed to investigate the design of virtual experiences, such as those described by Behm-Morawitz, Pennell, and Speno (2016), in which experiencing social interactions as a member of another racial group leads to empathy, acknowledgment of White privilege, and anti-racist allyship.

**Counter-Narratives of Race and Racism in Digital Literacies**

CRT defines counter-stories as historical and personal accounts of race and racism that center on the lived experiences of those who are "othered" within oppressive social structures. Texts such as narratives, poems, and oral histories are seen as central to maintaining a collective history of marginalized racial groups, as observed through the lens of the oppressed, and as a contrast to dominant narratives constructed by those in power (García, 2008). Counter-narratives powerfully and directly challenge racist assumptions and ideologies, allowing alternative or previously unobserved racial understandings to become relocated as official knowledge (Godley & Loretto, 2013). Counter-storytelling can provide vital heuristics that help to enlighten educational experiences and outcomes of racial groups, while disrupting hegemonic conceptions of meritocracy based on White values in society (Chang, 2013).

There are many studies of CRT counter-narrative construction in non-digital spaces, which have been autobiographical (e.g., Montoya, 1994; Schroeter & James, 2015), biographical (e.g., Fernandez, 2002), and composite (e.g., Yosso, 2006). However, there are currently few examples in digital spaces. In one study of counter-narrative production through digital media, Mills and Exley (2015) studied Indigenous Australian students creating digital stories using the iPad application Tellagami to create counter-narrative historical poetry about the White colonial invaders who displaced Indigenous people from their lands. The students created avatars that were digital versions of themselves, and photographed vivid Aboriginal paintings, such as ancestral spirits in the Australian bushland, as the background. The audio recordings of their poetry decolonized White accounts of conquest and power to reframe and understand their own racial identities and ancestry. Such counter-stories have the potential to be produced and widely shared digitally through the multimodal combination of words, images, and audio (Turner, Hayes, & Way, 2013).

Online social media, such as Twitter and Facebook, can also be powerful and fast avenues of dissemination for counter-narratives. Beyond CRT, researchers have examined the wide circulation of anti-racist messages and movements on Twitter. The term "Black Twitter" has been used to describe the social network of African American users on Twitter who focus on issues important to Black Americans, including racism. Theorists have attributed the success of the Black Twittersphere to the use of Twitter's hashtag function and domination of Twitter's trending topics as a social public (Brock, 2012).

Other research on youth in the Netherlands suggests that social media can facilitate positive interracial and interethnic interactions, leading to the creation and dissemination of counter-narratives that reduce stereotypes and discrimination. Though such interactions were rarely deliberately sought by the youth, common interests and affinity groups facilitated positive interactions across interracial groups that rarely interacted offline (Dekker, Belabas, & Scholten, 2015). Likewise, Ito and her colleagues (2015) draw upon multiple examples of "connected civics," that is, digitally-mediated participatory politics that develop through online "affinity groups"—groups that share activities, interests, and goals—that often cross racial, national, and gender categories. Such groups have been shown to collaboratively construct counter-narratives that support social justice causes (Ito et al., 2015).

Similarly, Mahiri (2015) has continued to argue for the growth in counter-narratives about race through affinity groups in digital spaces. He contends that digital literacies afford adolescents the opportunity to "remix" their identities and to produce complex counter-narratives of identity and affinity that challenge the reductive and essentializing racial categories, like Asian or Latino, that serve to uphold White supremacy. Mahiri, following Gee (2008), argued that digital literacies and affinity groups "honor the fluid, micro-cultural identity connections of today's youth that are driven by affinities that subvert traditional, static associations with ethno-racial or national cultural formations" (Mahiri, 2015, p. 22). In an example of this principle, Lam (2009) studied the online communication between transnational youth of Asian descent and documented how they shared their interests in gaming, music, and socializing through a hybrid of languages, including African American English, Chinese, and Standardized English.

Hull and Stornaiuolo (2014) and Jocson (2013) demonstrated how the circulation of digital counter-narratives across geographic boundaries can lead to coalition building and new understandings of cosmopolitanism, that is, the understanding of humanity as a community that transcends national borders and local geography. Studying multimedia digital texts exchanged by adolescents in the US and India using a closed social networking space, Hull and Stornaiuolo (2014) document how youth-produced films about issues such as domestic violence and poverty led to cross-cultural conversations that provoked new understandings, agency, and collective action on social issues. In her study, Jocson describes how US youth involved in spoken word poetry and film groups communicated and circulated their art and their critical representations of race, gender, and media through online video performances that were shown at regional film festivals and on global websites, such as YouTube.

As Jocson (2013), Hull and Stornaiuolo (2014), and other studies reviewed here demonstrate, the potential of digital counter-narratives to provoke social change lies not just in their content, but also in their circulation across traditionally isolated geographic and cultural contexts. Counter-storytelling has the potential to make voices heard on a global scale via the World Wide Web. Critical Race scholars have conventionally drawn on methods such as storytelling because it affords "subaltern" portraiture of race and racism, challenging dominant or grand meta-narratives, while grounded in the strength of experiential knowledge (Ladson-Billings, 1995). These studies suggest that digital, online literacies—despite being largely dictated by White interests—can provide a space to co-construct and widely circulate counter-narratives that challenge racism in the physical world.

**Conclusion: New Challenges for Critical Race Theory in a Global Circulation of Texts**

Early scholars of online literacies often suggested that the Internet would become a space that was free of racism and in which race would no longer matter (Daniels, 2013). However, as demonstrated in this chapter, multiple studies have shown that interactions in such digital spaces often reinscribe the racist behaviors that exist in the offline world (Eastwick & Gardner, 2008; Gamberini, Chittaro, Spagnolli, & Carlesso, 2015). In the increasingly globalized and transnational context of digital literacies, we call for CRT, LatCrit, and similar critical theories of race and racism to account for the multiple forms of racism, oppression, and colonization that exist in and beyond the US. Future CRT studies of digital literacies would also benefit from increased attention to critical Indigenous studies and Indigenous sovereignty (Moreton-Robinson, 2016).

As we wrote this chapter, the people of the UK voted to leave the European Union in the "Brexit" referendum. In the months leading up to the vote, those in favor of leaving were circulating increasingly racist and anti-immigration digital texts via the #leave hashtag and the "Breaking Point" campaign, which included images of dark-haired and olive-skinned refugees waiting in line to enter the EU (Lowe, 2016; see also Chapter 8 of this volume). Such digital and social media campaigns are a strong reminder that the defense of White property—visually and textually represented in the "Breaking Point" campaign as residing at the intersection of race, nationality, and religion—is a transnational phenomenon. The #leave and "Breaking Point" texts are also a reminder of the relevance of CRT to scholarship on digital literacies since, like our real worlds, neither digital nor virtual worlds are "post-racial."

There is a burgeoning field of digital media research in education that attempts to take up issues of race and diversity, yet much of this work is not explicitly advanced from a CRT perspective—including many studies reviewed here. This chapter has applied CRT principles to demonstrate the potentials of CRT to formally engage in research of techno-cultures. In framing this chapter, we have demonstrated how the key principles of CRT have untapped potentials for examining race in digital cultures. As we look to the future of scholarship on race, racism, and digital literacies, we see three important ways in which CRT can uncover racism and work toward social justice in digital spaces.

First, there is an increasing need for the application of anti-racist approaches to multimodal and digital text analysis, production, and circulation within the academy in order to build socially just techno-cultures. Visual representations of race, such as avatars in online games, or the photographs of refugees in the "Breaking Point" campaign, tell us much about how race is represented. Through attending to race in digital practices using the principles of institutional racism, Whiteness as property, and racial colorblindness, researchers, educators, and students can recognize how racism operates systemically and discursively in various international contexts to construct anti-racist and unoppressive digital representations.

Second, in the current context of globalized techno-cultures and the transnational circulation of digital texts, we see that the CRT concept of intersectionality is vitally important to framing race and racism in digital literacies research and educational practice. Intersectionality calls into question the traditional binary understanding of identity and systems of oppression (Black/White, native/immigrant, wealthy/poor), and instead posits that oppression and people's lived realities are based on interrelated forms of discrimination and inequity, including racism, nationalism, classism, homophobia, sexism, and ableism (Haney-Lopez, 1994). Relatedly, CRT critiques essentialism—the notion that all people in a particular racial group think, act, and experience life in the same ways (Delgado & Stefancic, 2001). Essentialism masks the reality of diverse and multi-layered identities and does not account for the ways in which the intersection of multiple forms of oppression and identities shape people's lived experiences and the oppression they face. Acknowledging intersectionality in scholarship on digital literacies is essential for understanding the increasingly complex dimensions of racism and oppression in online and multimodal communication and representation.

Third, CRT studies of counter-narratives in digital spaces are needed to voice the lived experiences of Indigenous people and People of Color through powerful coalition-building and new agentive identities (Brock, 2012; Byrne, 2008). A better understanding of how such counter-narratives circulate across space and time, and how they affect both creators and users, can contribute to anti-racist literacy pedagogies in which students gain awareness of intertwining modes of oppression (Florini, 2015; Gabriel, 2016; Hull & Stornaiuolo, 2014). Similarly, through literacy pedagogies that encourage anti-racist engagement in interactive digital texts—through retweets, public comments on news sites, and other media—youth can consider how to participate in techno-cultures and dialogues in ways that affect social change.

Digital spaces and techno-cultures, like the tangible spaces and cultures that we participate in, are not neutral, post-racial environments. They have the potential to reproduce racism and oppressive representations of race or to create liberatory alternatives. To create anti-racist techno-cultures, researchers, educators, students, and youth need conceptual tools, such as offered by CRT, to challenge their own racial biases. We need to continually dissemble oppressive representations of racism to produce and circulate powerful counter-narratives that speak to self-determination, social justice, and agency across global contexts. White scholars of digital literacies can apply CRT principles to uncover "White bound" thinking and practices (Hughey, 2012). Research and pedagogy informed by CRT can help break the bonds that serve to maintain White privilege and property in digital sites, in scholarship, and in our digital lives.

## References

Barza, A., Tometi, O., & Cullors, P. (2013). *About Black Lives Matter.* Retrieved June 13, 2016, from http://Blacklivesmatter.com/about/.

Behm-Morawitz, E., Pennell, H., & Speno, A. G. (2016). The effects of virtual racial embodiment in a gaming app on reducing prejudice. *Communication Monographs, 83*(3), 396–418.

Bell, D. (1980). Brown and the interest convergence dilemma. In D. Bell (Ed.), *Shades of Brown: New perspectives on school desegregation* (pp. 90–106). New York, NY: Teachers College Press.

Bell, D. (1992). *Faces at the bottom of the well: The permanence of racism.* New York, NY: Basic Books.

Brock, A. (2012). From the blackhand side: Twitter as a cultural conversation. *Journal of Broadcasting and Electronic Media, 56*(4), 529–549.

Buenavista, T. L. (2010). Issues affecting US Filipino student access to postsecondary education: A critical race theory perspective. *Journal of Education for Students Placed at Risk, 15*(1–2), 114–126.

Byrne, D. N. (2008). The future of (the) 'race': Identity, discourse, and the rise of computer-mediated public spheres. In A. Everett (Ed.), *Learning race and ethnicity: Youth and digital media.* The John D. and Catherine T. MacArthur Foundation Series on Digital Media and Learning (pp. 15–38). Cambridge, MA: The MIT Press.

Carey, J. (2009). *Communication as culture: Essays on media and society.* New York, NY: Routledge.

Chang, B. (2013). Voice of the voiceless? Multiethnic student voices in critical approaches to race, pedagogy, literacy and agency. *Linguistics and Education, 24*(3), 348–360.

Crawford, A. (2013). Swan Goodes 'gutted' but places no blame. Retrieved June 13, 2016, from www.abc.net.au/news/2013–05–25/goodes-gutted-but-places-no-blame/4712772.

Crenshaw, K. (1988). Race, reform and retrenchment: Tranformation and legitimation in anti-discrimination law. *Harvard Law Review, 101*, 1331–1387.

Daniels, J. (2013). Race and racism in Internet studies: A review and critique. *New Media & Society, 15*(5), 695–719.

Daniels, J. (2015). "My brain database doesn't see skin color" colorblind racism in the technology industry and in theorizing the web. *American Behavioral Scientist, 59*(11), 1377–1393.

Dekker, R., Belabas, W., & Scholten, P. (2015). Interethnic contact online: Contextualising the implications of social media use by second-generation migrant youth. *Journal of Intercultural Studies, 36*(4), 450–467.

Delgado, R. (1990). When a story is just a story: Does voice really matter? *Virginia Law Review, 76*, 95–111.

Delgado, R., & Stefancic, J. (2001). *Critical race theory: An introduction.* New York, NY: NYU Press.

Dinerstein, J. (2006). Technology and its discontents: On the verge of the posthuman. *American Quarterly, 50*(3), 569–595.

Eastwick, P. W., & Gardner, W. L. (2008). Is it a game? Evidence for social influence in the virtual world. *Social Influence, 4*(1), 18–32.

Fernandez, L. (2002). Telling stories about school: Using critical race and Latino critical theories to document Latina/Latino education and resistance. *Qualitative Inquiry, 8*, 45–65.

Florini, S. (2015). The podcast "Chitlin' Circuit": Black podcasters, alternative media, and audio enclaves. *Journal of Radio & Audio Media, 22*(2), 209–219.

Gabriel, D. (2016). Blogging while black, British and female: a critical study on discursive activism. *Information, Communication & Society, 19*(11), 1622–1635.

Gamberini, L., Chittaro, L., Spagnolli, A., & Carlesso, C. (2015). Psychological response to an emergency in virtual reality: Effects of victim ethnicity and emergency type on helping behavior and navigation. *Computers in Human Behavior, 48*, 104–113.

García, D. G. (2008). Culture clash invades Miami: Oral histories and ethnography center stage. *Qualitative Inquiry, 14*, 865–895.

Gee, J. (2008). *What video games have to teach us about literacy and learning.* Basingstoke: Palgrave and Macmillan.

Glaser, J., Dixit, J., & Green, D. P. (2002). Studying hate crime with the Internet: What makes racists advocate racial violence? *Journal of Social Issues, 58*(1), 177–193.

Godley, A. J., & Loretto, A. (2013). Fostering counter-narratives of race, language, and identity in an urban English classroom. *Linguistics and Education, 24*, 316–327.

Haney-Lopez, I. (1994). The social construction of race: Some observations on the illusion, fabrication, and choice. *Harvard Civil Rights-Civil Liberties Law Review, 29*, 1–63.

Howard, T. C., & Navarro, O. (2016). Critical race theory 20 years later: Where do we go from here? *Urban Education, 51*(3), 253–273.

Hughey, M. (2012). *Whitebound: Nationalists, antiracists, and the shared meanings of race.* Stanford, CA: Stanford University Press.

Hull, G. A., & Stornaiuolo, A. (2014). Cosmopolitan literacies, social networks, and "proper distance": Striving to understand in a global world. *Curriculum Inquiry, 44*(1), 15–44.

Hunt, D., & Ramón, A. C. (2015). *2015 Hollywood diversity report: Flipping the Script.* Los Angeles, CA: Ralph J. Bunche Center for African American Studies at UCLA.

Hylton, K. (2012). Talk the talk, walk the walk: defining critical race theory in research. *Race Ethnicity and Education, 15*(1), 23–41.

Ito, M., Soep, E., Kligler-Vilenchik, N., Shresthova, S., Gamber-Thompson, L., & Zimmerman, A. (2015). Learning connected civics: Narratives, practices, infrastructures. *Curriculum Inquiry, 45*(1), 10–29.

Jocson, K. (2013). Remix revisited: Critical solidartity in youth media arts. *E-Learning and Digital Media, 10*(3), 68–82.

Ladson-Billings, G. (1995). New directions in multicultural education: Complexities, boundaries, and critical race theory. In J. A. Banks & C. A. McGee Banks (Eds.), *Handbook of research on multicultural education* (2nd ed., pp. 50–65). San Francisco, CA: Jossey-Bass.

Ladson-Billings, G. (1998). Just what is critical race theory, and what's it doing in a nice field like education? *International Journal of Qualitative Studies in Education, 11*, 7–24.

Ladson-Billings, G. (2013). Critical race theory—what it is not! In M. Lynn & A. D. Dixson (Eds.), *Handbook of Critical Race Theory in Education* (pp. 34–47). Mahwah, NJ: Routledge.

Lam, W. S. E. (2009). Multiliteracies on instant messaging in negotiating local, translocal, and transnational affiliations: A case of an adolescent immigrant. *Reading Research Quarterly, 44*(4), 377–397.

Leavy, B. (2014) *Australian aboriginal virtual heritage* (Master's Thesis). Queensland University of Technology, Brisbane, Australia. Retrieved from http://eprints.qut.edu.au/72790/1/Brett_Leavy_Thesis.pdf.

Lee, J. E. R. (2014). Does virtual diversity matter? Effects of avatar-based diversity representation on willingness to express offline racial identity and avatar customization. *Computers in Human Behavior, 36*, 190–197.

Leonard, D. (2003). "Live in your world, play in ours": Race, video games, and consuming the other. *Studies in Media & Information Literacy Education, 3*(4), 1–9.

Lorde, A. (1992). Age, race, class and sex: Women redefining difference. In M. Anderson & P. H. Collins (Eds.), *Race, class, and gender: An anthology* (pp. 495–502). Belmont, CA: Wadsworth.

Lowe, J. (2016). *Brexit: UKIP launches 'Breaking Point' immigration poster*. Retrieved from www.newsweek.com/brexit-eu-immigration-ukip-poster-breaking-point-471081.

Mahiri, J. (2011). *Digital tools in urban schools: Mediating a remix of learning*. Ann Arbor, MI: University of Michigan Press.

Mahiri, J. (2015). Micro-cultures: Deconstructing race/expanding multiculturalism. *Multicultural Education Review, 7*, 185–196.

Marable, M. (1992). Blueprint for black studies and multiculturalism. *The Black Scholar, 22*(3), 30–35.

Matsuda, M. (1989). Public response to racist speech: Considering the victim's story. *Mitchigan Law Review, 87*, 2320–2381.

McKernan, B. (2015). The meaning of a game: Stereotypes, video game commentary and color-blind racism. *American Journal of Cultural Sociology, 3*(2), 224–253.

Mills, K. A. (2016). *Literacy theories for the digital age: Social, critical, multimodal, spatial, material, and sensory lenses*. Bristol: Multilingual Matters.

Mills, K. A., & Exley, B. (2015). *Decolonizing digital heritage practices for indigenous literacy: A multimodal analysis of iPad Tellagami videos*. Paper presented at the 2015 AERA Annual Meeting. Chicago, IL. Retrieved from www.aera.net/Publications/OnlinePaperRepository/AERAOnlinePaperRepository/tabid/12720/Default.aspx.

Mills, K. A., Davis-Warra, J., Sewell, M., & Anderson, M. (2016) Indigenous ways with literacies: Transgenerational, multi-modal, placed, and collective. *Language and Education, 30*(1), pp. 1–21.

Montoya, M. (1994). Mascaras, trenzas, y grenas: Un/masking the self while un/braiding Latina stories and legal discourse. *Chicano-Latino Law Review, 15*, 1–37.

Moreton-Robinson, A. (2016). *Critical indigenous studies: Engagements in first world locations*. Tuscan: The University of Arizona Press.

Nakamura, L. (2013). *Cybertypes: Race, ethnicity, and identity on the Internet*. London, UK: Routledge.

Negroponte, N. (1995). *Being digital*. New York, NY: Knopf.

Neville, H. A., Lilly, R. L., Lee, R. M., Duran, G., & Browne, L. (2000). Construction and initial validation of the color-blind racial attitudes scale (CoBRAS). *Journal of Counseling Psychology, 47*, 59–70.

Nishi, N. W., Matias C. E., & Montova, R. (2015). Exposing the white avatar: projections, justifications, and the ever-evolving American racism. *Social Identities: Journal for the Study of Race, Nation and Culture, 21*(5), 459–473.

Pane, D. M., & Salmon, A. (2009). The experience of isolation in alternative education: A heuristic research study. *Western Journal of Black Studies, 33*(4), 282–292.

Perrin, A., & Duggan, M. (2015). *Americans' Internet Access: 2000–2015*. Washington, DC: Pew Research Center. www.pewInternet.org/2015/06/26/americans-Internet-access-2000-2015/#Internet-usage-by-raceethnicity.

Picart, C. J. (2013). *Critical race theory and copyright in American dance: Whiteness as status*. New York, NY: Palgrave Macmillan.

Reese, D. (2008). Indigenizing children's literature. *Journal of Language and Literacy Education, 4*, 59–72.

Richardson, E. (2009). My ill literacy narrative: growing up Black, po and a girl, in the hood. *Gender and Education, 2*, 753–767.

Rideout, V., Lauricella, A., & Wartella, E. (2011). *Children, media, and race: Media use among White, Black, Hispanic, and Asian American children*. Evanston, IL: Northwestern University.

Schofield, J. (1986). Causes and consequences of the colorblind perspective. In J. Dovidio & S. Gaertner (Eds.), *Prejudice, discrimination, and racism* (pp. 231–253). San Diego, CA: Academic Press.

Schroeter, S., & James, C. E. (2015). 'We're here because we're Black': The schooling experiences of French-speaking African-Canadian students with refugee backgrounds. *Race, Ethnicity, and Education, 18*, 20–39.

Shapiro, S. (2014). 'Words that you said got bigger': English language learners' lived experiences of deficit discourse. *Research in the Teaching of English, 48*, 386–406.

Solorzano, D. G., & Bernal, D. (2001). Examining transformational resistance through a critical race and Latcrit theory framework Chicana and Chicano students in an urban context. *Urban Education, 36*, 308–342.

Tate, W. (1997). Critical race theory and education: History, theory, and implications. *Review of Research in Education, 22*, 195–247.

Timeline: The Black Lives Matter Movement. (2016, July 22). Retrieved from www.abc.net.au/news/2016-07-14/black-lives-matter-timeline/7585856.

Turner, K. N., Hayes, N. V., & Way, K. (2013). Critical multimodal hip hop production: A social justice approach to African American language and literacy practices. *Equity and Excellence in Education, 46*, 342–354.

Tynes, B., & Markoe, S. (2010). The role of colorblind racial attitudes in reactions to racial discrimination on social network sites. *Journal of Diversity in Higher Education, 3*, 1–13.

Tynes, B., Reynolds, L., & Greenfield, P. (2004). Adolescence, race, and ethnicity on the Internet: A comparison of discourse in monitored vs. unmonitored chat rooms. *Applied Developmental Psychology, 25*, 667–684.

Tynes, B., Giang, M., Williams, D., & Thompson, B. (2008). Online racial discrimination and psychological adjustment among adolescents. *Journal of Adolescent Health, 43*, 565–569.

Tynes, B., Umana-Taylor, A., Rose, C., Lin J., & Anderson, C. (2012). Online racial discrimination and the protective function of ethnic identity and self-esteem for African American adolescents. *Developmental Psychology, 48*, 343–355.

UNESCO (2011). *ICT's and Indigenous People: Policy Brief*. Moscow: Russia.

Vass, G. (2014). The racialised educational landscape in Australia: Listening to the whispering elephant. *Race, Ethnicity, and Education, 17*, 176–201.

Yosso, T. J. (2006). *Critical race counterstories along the Chicana/Chicano educational pipeline.* New York, NY: Routledge.

Yosso, T. J., Parker, L., Solorzano, D. G., & Lynn, M. (2004). From Jim Crow to affirmative action and back again: A critical race discussion of racialized rationales and access to higher education. *Review of Research in Education, 28*, 1–25.

# III
# Digital Lives

Anna Smith

In this section, scholars consider the embodied and affective dimensions of everyday writing and literacies across the life course. Foregrounding the imbrication of the digital, material, and human within contemporary writing ecologies, these scholars challenge us to recognize the innovation, surprise, desire, and commitment arising in and expressed through literacy practices, propelling writing and learning across contexts.

In Chapter 10, Christina Haas and Megan McGrath provide a transdisciplinary review of research and theory on how the embodied act of writing, focusing on visual and motor haptics of writing-by-hand, is intimately linked to the material world through tools. Considering research regarding writing tools and letter recognition, production fluency, and memory, they highlight the complexity of seemingly fundamental writing processes and suggest the need for further scholarship that extends across fields.

In Chapter 11, Karen Wohlwend, Beth Buchholz, and Carmen Liliana Medina examine imaginative play and innovative making through material, embodied, and digital media production in contemporary childhoods. Redefining play and making as literacy practices, even where there is an absence of print text, they theorize the nexus of play, imagination, and making as sites of cultural production by way of collective meaning making. This, they argue, suggests the need for a repositioning of children in schools and curricula from passive learners to inherent makers and doers.

Ty Hollett, Nathan Phillips, and Kevin Leander trace the technological, social, embodied, and literate production of digital geographies in Chapter 12. They theorize writing and literacies as fundamentally mobile, and as simultaneously digital and physical as people, material, media, and information are perpetually on the move, interpreting, producing, and acting on each other in everyday literacy activity. They suggest, moving forward, the need to consider critical place-making, such as digitally layering and augmenting landscapes through writing to respond and remake physical place and social space.

In Chapter 13, Donna Alvermann and Bradley Robinson explore the centrifugal power of digital media composition and communication in youths' contemporary writing ecologies. With examples of consequential writing in the lives of many youth, they suggest sensitivity to intersectionality, disruption of reader and writer binary, and attentiveness to youths' global interconnectivity as pressing needs. This is not just when researching youths' digital writing but also in terms of curricula and pedagogical approaches in the classroom.

With the rise of fandoms, and fan-based literacy practices, in Chapter 14, Jayne Lammers, Alecia Marie Magnifico, and Jen Scott Curwood highlight how young writers' literate identities shape and are shaped by the interconnectivity in contexts in which they participate. Drawing from qualitative research across a variety of online affinity spaces, they illustrate the ways in which fan-based affinity spaces allow young adults to explore interest-driven literacy practices and identities. They conclude by considering the epistemological tensions between fan-based literacy practice and the assessment regimes and typical practices of English education in schools.

In focusing on the lives, bodies, interests, and mobilities of digital writers, the chapters in this section emphasize people's lived, everyday practices as central to culture making in digital ecologies. This section also highlights the need for agile, responsive, interdisciplinary methodologies attuned to affect and intersectionality.

# 10
# Embodiment and Literacy in a Digital Age
*The Case of Handwriting*

**Christina Haas and Megan McGrath**

> How…should the education system accommodate the fact that the hand is not merely a metaphor or an icon for humanness, but often the real-life focal point—the lever or the launching pad— of a successful and genuinely fulfilling life?
>
> Frank Wilson, *The Hand* (1998; 14)

The tools and technologies of literacy in contemporary culture are myriad (as the chapters in this book attest), with a seemingly unprecedented expansion of digital technologies for creating and disseminating the written word. Of course, writing itself is a technology (Bolter, 2001; Haas, 1996), a technology tied to the bodily senses of touch (Schmandt-Besserat, 1992) and of vision (Ong, 1981). Our focus in this chapter is on the original writing tool, *the human hand*, an embodied instrument that, as we hope to illustrate below, remains powerful and relevant in our digital age.

Intriguing examples of the cultural power of handwriting abound: the historically and culturally overdetermined signature, for example (Derrida, 1988; Harris, 1995); the almost mystical power of original artistic manuscripts (Chen, 2012; Gioia, 1997); and the resistance to power inscribed by scribes in the marginalia of medieval manuscripts (Camille, 1992). Hensher (2012) presents a series of narratives about both the demise and the resilience of handwriting in Western culture—including an interesting tidbit about how the Latin script imposed by the Nazis was recast after the war by both East and West Germany. Hensher notes that the idea of a national script retained its power, although particular scripts were adopted or dropped as political power changed. Another example of cultural power at work is the disciplining of handwriting and the writing hand in the Renaissance (Goldberg, 1990). We will return to this idea, cultural disciplining of writing hands, in our discussion.

Rather, our modest goal in this chapter is to review important recent research on the embodied practice of writing by hand from the neurosciences, educational psychology, and writing/literacy studies. Specifically, we analyze (1) the importance of writing by hand in letter recognition (a critical skill in reading acquisition), (2) issues of fluency and production in writing by hand and in keyboarding, and (3) the relation of writing by hand to memory and retention.[1] In each case, we contrast writing by hand with keyboarding with a QWERTY keyboard. Before proceeding to our main argument, however, we briefly discuss (1) the human hand in cognition and culture generally and in writing, specifically, (2) theories of embodiment, and (3) literacy and haptics.

## The Writing Hand

Neurologist Frank Wilson (1998) documents the evolution of the human hand, its role in social and cultural life, and its relation to language, skill, and thought. His central claim is stark, almost strident: "No serious account of human life can ignore the central importance of the human hand" (p. 7). Aristotle (trans. Lennox, 2001), it seems, might have agreed. In *On the Parts of Animals*, he describes the hand as "the instrument for instruments." Aristotle's characterization of the hand suggests its versatility, and its import: "For the hand becomes a talon, claw, horn, spear, sword, and any other weapon or instrument—it will be all these thanks to its ability and grasp and hold them all" (p. 99).

For the architect Juhani Pallasmaa (2009), the hand and the sense of touch it conveys have not only been underestimated (per Wilson), but also misunderstood: "the hand is not a faithful, passive executor of the intentions of the brain; rather, the hand has its own intentionality, knowledge, and skills" (p. 21). Pallasmaa (2005) identifies a contemporary cultural bias toward vision and a resultant suppression of other senses, particularly touch; he goes so far as to identify a "hegemony of vision" (p. 11) in our experiences and knowledge of the world, a hegemony of the ocular that has been exacerbated in contemporary culture "by a multitude of technological inventions"—presumably, including keyboards of every kind—"and the endless…production of images" (p. 21). Pallasmaa's point echoes Ong's (1981) linkage of writing systems and the visual in ancient Greece, although Ong does not explore the sense of touch in writing or speech.

Cultural linguist Jurgen Streeck (2009), drawing extensively on the work of John Napier (1980), documents the human hand's multiple degrees of freedom and the resultant kinds of grasping (or gripping) of which the hand is capable. At the broadest level, there is a distinction between a power grip and a precision grip, but features like thumb opposition, extremely sensitive fatty pads on fingers and hands, and the bone and muscle structure of the hand allow for shape-adaptive grips. Streeck illustrates how the hand differentially anticipates grasping a demitasse cup, a coffee mug, and a wine glass (p. 50). Insights about the hands' morphology, functionality, and evolution are important for writing because handwriting makes use of many more of the degrees of freedom and functionalities of the human hand than does keyboarding. There are few differences in finger and wrist movements in keyboarding, with keystrokes performed in highly stereotypical and repetitive ways (Jones, 1998).

We acknowledge that differences in typing comfort and speed may arise from changes in keyboard dimensionality and shape, as research in ergonomics has shown (Crump & Logan, 2010; Rempel, Barr, Brafman, & Young, 2007; Sears, Revis, Swatski, Crittenden, & Shneiderman, 1993; Swanson, Galinsky, Cole, Pan, & Sauter, 1997), and we do not mean to suggest that the findings gathered from typing on a laptop keyboard would apply seamlessly to typing on a tablet's soft keyboard. Despite these differences, however, we argue along with Norman and Fisher (1982) that the QWERTY setup that has persisted through the progression from manual typewriter, to electric typewriter, to desktop keyboard, to laptop keyboard, to soft keyboard demands a similar ergonomic interaction between person and keyboard, since QWERTY's persistence has culturally disciplined Western hands (Goldberg, 1990) to a certain machine-orientation and range of motion. Therefore, the studies we review focus on the QWERTY keyboard on desktop and laptop computers because of these devices' continued ubiquity in classrooms and in contemporary Western culture.

## Theories of Embodiment

Scholarly interest in the human hand is, arguably, part of a larger cultural phenomenon: an explicit interrogation of materiality and embodiment (often cast as a response to Descartes' bifurcation of mind and body) in the conduct of human activity. For example, Gibbs (a cognitive scientist) argues that human cognition is fundamentally shaped by embodied experience, that this experience is phenomenological, and that cognitive science has overlooked the ways in which perception, cognition, and language are shaped by embodied experience. Gibbs posits the concept of *embodied mind*, a term that acknowledges thinking, selfhood, and experiences as rooted in kinesthetic activity. Embodied practices of writing are one such activity.

Anthropologist Thomas Csordas (1994) extends this argument, noting that despite a spirited interest in the body by scholars in the humanities and social sciences since the 1970s, much research and theory still treat the body as an analytic theme or object. Csordas insists on expanding understandings of body-as-cultural-construct to encompass embodiment as a kind of being-in-the-world. That is, the body is not a bounded object of analysis; it is ubiquitously embodied and experienced.

Philosophers Clark and Chalmers (1998) explore the related question of where the mind's boundaries begin and end, and offer *active externalism*, a view by which cognition occurs in a dynamic system that engages the human and external entities—such as literacy technologies and written texts—in a reciprocal relationship. Such a view joins cognition to the complex interplay of body and environment, which in turn undergirds how information is perceived and processed. Hutchins (2005) makes a similar point, using the term *material anchors* for the close association of material artifacts in the environment and conceptual cognitive structures.

## Literacy and Haptics

Our broad-brush interpretation of this scholarship on the human hand and on embodiment is that the body (as phenomenologically experienced and embodied) serves as both a metaphoric and functional *interface* between the mind and the material world. This interface relies on visual and aural input, but—more directly to our purposes here—it is also inherently haptic. Haptic perception includes the tactile dimension, the sense of touch, and the kinesthetic or proprioceptive sense—the sense of place, position, and movement of the body.

Mangen and her colleagues (Mangen, 2008; Mangen & van der Weel, 2016; Mangen & Velay, 2010) have contributed foundational work to literacy and haptics. Mangen (2008) argues that haptic perception and manual dexterity are vitally important in reading but have been neglected in research heretofore. Maintaining that "materiality matters," Mangen argues that unlike print—where readers are physically, phenomenologically, and literally *in touch with* a text—digital readers are at an indeterminate distance from the actual text.

More directly relevant to our purposes here is Mangen and Velay (2010), where the authors note that research in embodied cognition, from fields like psychology, neuroscience, and philosophy, has shown that perception and motor action are interdependent. Indeed, writers' sensorimotor interactions with physical writing tools affect cognitive processing, and different brain regions are activated when handwriting letters versus typing them. Movement and manipulation, then, are critical to Mangen and Velay's conception of literacy. And, far from being transparent or incidental, technological shifts profoundly alter the embodied experience and practice of writing.

Writing, itself, is a technology, dependent on supporting technologies, and Mangen and Velay show how technologies' differing haptics influences writers' engagement with the world at cognitive, affective, cultural, bodily, and phenomenological levels. It is to phenomenological accounts of writing by hand that we now turn.

## Phenomenological Accounts of Writing by Hand

Powerful phenomenological accounts of writing by hand are provided by phenomenologists Merleau-Ponty and Heidegger, as well as by contemporary writers such as Sudnow and Hensher.

In each of these cases, the typewriter, whose QWERTY keyboard persisted with desktop and laptop keyboards, provides the foil for the human hand. In describing the important concept *habit*, Merleau-Ponty uses the example of the typewriter to note that "the acquisition of a habit is indeed the grasping of significance, but it is the motor grasping of a motor significance…It is a knowledge in the hands" (1945/1962, p. 143). Heidegger laments that the mechanical typewriter separates body and word: "the word no longer passes through the hand as it writes and acts authentically… The typewriter snatches script from the essential realm of the hand…The word becomes something 'typed'" (1942/1982, p. 118).

In what he calls his production account of learning to play jazz piano, sociologist David Sudnow contrasts the ways he perceives his hands playing jazz (as intimately familiar, known, and trusted) to how they appear to him while typing: "I don't recognize their movements…[I]t's as though I were watching an interior part of my body do its business (2001, p. 1).

More prosaically, writing researchers have documented phenomenology aspects of writing with different technologies. Haas and Hayes (1986) interviewed college writers, and noted that many of these writers report a vague lack of *text sense*—"There's a problem getting a feel for the piece"—when using word processing rather than handwriting (p. 24). The researchers postulate that visual/spatial factors may erode locational recall and reordering a text while revising, but they acknowledge that these factors may not fully account for problems with text sense. Over twenty-five years later, the language writers use to describe composing remains intriguingly elusive: Ehret and Hollett (2014), in the conclusion of their research on students using mobile technologies to compose, pose the rhetorical question: in a world where all writing is mobile and multiple, what would literacy "feel like?" (450).

## Empirical Studies of Language by Hand

Educational psychologist Virginia Berninger aptly calls writing *language by hand* to counter popular perceptions that writing is merely a motor skill (Berninger, Richards, & Abbott, 2009; Berninger et al., 2006). Building on Liberman's (1999) claim that language has no sensory organ of its own, Berninger and her colleagues posit a framework that includes Language by Ear (listening to aural language), Language by Mouth (producing oral language), Language by Eye (reading written language), and—relevant to this chapter—Language by Hand (producing written language). In the sections below, we review recent research on language by hand and its relationship to letter recognition, fluency, and learning and retention.

### *Letter Recognition*

Letter recognition, reading, and writing are interrelated activities (Longcamp, Anton, Roth, & Velay, 2003; Vinter & Chartrel, 2008). The act of handwriting conditions people to form and recognize letters, and proficient letter recognition precedes proficient reading. Research has established a relationship between sensory modalities and creating neural systems that build critical literacy foundations and foster future literacy connections (James & Gauthier, 2006; Kato et al., 1999; Matsuo et al., 2001).

Longcamp et al. (2003) explore the relationship between visual representations of language and motor activation. They found that writing movements spark motor activation in the brain, regardless of whether an individual actually provides motor responses. Their study suggests that the sensory modalities of vision and proprioception, in particular, are hallmarks of handwriting that are inextricable from letter recognition, and the act of writing by hand brings these modalities together in space and time through a specific type of motor manipulation.

Japanese scholars (Kato et al., 1999; Matsuo et al., 2003) have also studied the relationship between movement and letter recognition. Although these researchers were not studying technological differences (i.e., between handwriting and keyboarding), we find their research relevant for our discussion of handwriting and embodiment because it establishes that visual/spatial/motor connections are not the exclusive property of alphabetic systems.

Japanese uses two types of characters, ideograms, or *kanji* (many borrowed and adapted from the Chinese), and phonetic syllabaries, *hana*. Research has suggested that the two types of characters are processed differently by readers, so Kato et al. examined whether these differences were also evident in writing. Functional MRI showed that writing *kanji* activated pre-motor centers of the brain, showing a strong connection between writing and the motor center used for movement. As the researchers note, *kanji* have a complicated structure and are performed in a certain stroke order. Research by Matsuo and colleagues (2001) found slightly different results, suggesting that the relationship between activation of the motor and language areas in writing is varied and complicated.

Given handwriting's role in letter recognition, many researchers have also explored what happens when handwriting is altered by tools or removed from the equation altogether, following keyboards' and other digital tools' dominance in learning environments today. Longcamp, Zerbato-Poudou, and Velay's (2005) study compared letter recognition in preschoolers when writing twelve uppercase letters by hand versus typing them. The specific movements engendered by the handwriting experience catalyze memorization of letter forms; "in short, handwriting provides on-line signals from several sources, including vision, motor commands, and kinesthetic feedback, which are closely linked and simultaneously distributed in time" (p. 77).

Vinter and Chartrel (2008) examined the time that elapses between learning letter shape and learning to create the actual trajectory of movements that form letter shape. In studying children ages three to five, they found that visual recognition of cursive letters proliferates between these ages, with proprioceptive recognition peaking between the ages of four and six. Their observations supported Lurçat's (1974) finding that mastering the movements used to form letters must be preceded by having learned letters' shapes, and that proficiencies in proprioceptive processing foster the ability to write by hand. Thus, Vinter and Chartrel recommend that cursive handwriting instruction begin at age six.

James and Engelhardt (2012) extend this work by looking at how handwriting and typing prompt activation in certain areas of the brain, and how these brain-activation differences impact pre-literate children's abilities to produce and recognize letters. James and Engelhardt analyzed keyboarding on how well pre-literate, native English-speaking children were able to distinguish between letters' critical and incidental features, arguing that the act of creating letters by hand is important in the feature-distinguishing process critical to reading. James and Engelhardt also found that creating letters through free-form printing has a unique sensorimotor element, one that leads to letter recognition and, hence, to reading. However, not just any motor engagement catalyzes letter recognition; brain activity in the *fusiform gyrus*, an area integral to letter processing, was stronger when letters were printed by hand, line by line, than when letters were typed, traced, or just perceived.

Mangen and Velay (2010) also showed that different brain areas are activated when handwriting versus keyboarding. In their review of experiments in neuroscience and experimental psychology, these researchers explore what roles bodily movements, as well as tool and text manipulability, play in letter recognition, language development, and learning. Specifically, these experiments study the effects that bodily, sensorimotor haptics have on writing and low-level reading skills. When comparing writing by hand with keyboarding, the authors found that, on the letter level, handwriting leads to better letter recognition, because when a writer shifts from pen and paper to keyboard, they move from a slower, more exacting, unimanual process of handwriting to a faster, bimanual process of typing. Handwriting is slower and more exacting because the hand forms each letter graphomotorically as the writer reproduces standard letter shapes. This graphomotoric letter formation is removed when people keyboard, since they select ready-made letters (often from a QWERTY keyboard), rather than forming the letters themselves. Keyboards, then, inspire a comparatively disembodied writing experience by providing levels of remove between the writer and their writing tools. Seamless letter recognition and formation set the stage for another critical literacy milestone: fluency of text production.

## *Fluency/Production*

In the previous section, we evaluated handwriting's effects on enabling letter formation and recognition. In this section, we turn to handwriting's impact on producing extended text. Text is typically produced in bursts dependent on a writer's fluency, which results from a writer's ability combined with experience (Chenoweth & Hayes, 2001, 2003; Hayes & Chenoweth, 2007; Kaufer, Hayes, & Flower, 1986). With regard to written expression, fluency is an evaluative term that assesses how adeptly students can recognize and process content well enough to translate it into verbal and written text.

But fluency is more than a demonstration; it is also a process of transformation made possible through transcription. Connelly, Gee, and Walsh (2007) note that children develop transcription processes which directly allow the writer to convert ideas and language into a written form on the page. For most children at school, transcription development is partly gaining proficiency in fluent and accurate letter formation and a rudimentary knowledge of spelling. Therefore, as Graham and Weintraub (1996) and Jones and Christensen (1999) argue, transcription is more than a rote or mechanical skill; it is an executive-order, fundamental, cognitive translation process for symbolic expression (Berninger, Abbott, Abbott, Graham, & Richards, 2002). In the studies we have reviewed, handwriting fluency is determined largely by evaluating the speed at and ease with which writers can produce, with particular interest in how the writing instrument employed influences speed and ease. Connelly et al. (2007), for example, found that students who wrote with pens produced longer essays with superior idea development, organization, coherence, sentence structure, grammar, and punctuation.

Due to its translational function, handwriting fluency is a catalyst to creating high-quality compositions, and often serves as a vital stepping stone to text generation. The studies we review position fluent writing as the type of handwriting achieved after a person has mastered spelling, as well as an important facilitator of memory. Hayes and Berninger (2009) argue that causal relationships exist between transcription (i.e., primarily handwriting and spelling), and composition length and/or quality. For students in grades two through six, idea expression could be impeded by transcription problems. Therefore, handwriting provides a pivotal intermediary between being able to *recognize* letters, words, and sentences, *form* them, and *use* them to learn and retain information.

Berninger, Abbott, Augsburger, and Garcia (2009) also studied handwriting and fluent text generation. In their study, fourth through sixth graders generated longer essays—containing more complete sentences and expressing more ideas—when writing with pens. Despite their apparent ease, keyboards did not alleviate mechanical setbacks in students with or without learning disabilities. Together, these findings suggest that handwriting speed and ease do, indeed, forecast students' skills at composing lengthy and quality text, suggesting that transcription by hand—by serving a sensorimotor, translational function—helps students to produce extended, quality text (Berninger, 2008; Berninger et al., 1992; Graham, Berninger, Abbott, Abbott, & Whitaker, 1997).

This section and the previous one have examined how writing by hand enables students to recognize and produce text, suggesting handwriting's potential to lead to higher order processes. One of the key higher order processes engaged is memory, operationalized in the studies we review below as retention. In the next section, we look at how writing by hand and keyboarding may, to different degrees, help students transform given information into personalized knowledge, knowledge that may be available later through memory (i.e., retention).

## *Retention and Learning*

Note-taking is an established form of capturing information in print. A significant body of scholarship has shown that the mere capture of information, alone, will not foster learning; students must return to and engage with this information, as well. Igo, Bruning, and McCrudden (2005) review research that suggests that when students read from Internet sources, most use a verbatim copy-and-paste (CP) strategy. Other research suggests that students do not recall noted information very well unless they review or study it. Some note-making strategies may allow students to learn information in the actual process of note-making.

Igo, Bruning, and McCrudden found that restrictions placed on note-taking (either by the students themselves or in research contexts) may help students learn material, even without further review. In this study, some students used CP without any limits, while others were instructed to only use CP for main ideas and important points. Students then performed cued recall, were prompted for factual and conceptual learning, and asked to write about the material they had read. In each case, the students who had been instructed to limit or restrict their note-taking to important or main ideas performed better. Follow-up interviews helped the researchers to see that the restrictions on note-taking by CP lead to deeper levels of processing. While Igo, Bruning, and McCrudden focus only on keyboard note-taking, their study is relevant to our chapter because it reinforces the usefulness of strategies used in note-taking by hand, such as selectivity and decision-making, and how these may lead to deeper processing and, thus, to better learning and retention.

The distinction between reproducing and reconstructing text is at the heart of Mueller and Oppenheimer's (2014) studies comparing college students' note-taking by hand with note-taking on laptops. In the first study, students took notes on TED Talks, were subsequently distracted, and then answered questions requiring recall of the TED Talk content and conceptual application of content. Their review found that keyboards' interfaces may allow students to take more notes, but that *more* does not necessarily translate to *better* when it comes to producing notes that allow students to process information. Although laptops led to more notes being taken, notes taken on laptops tended to contain more verbatim language from the TED Talks. In contrast, notes written by hand contained fewer words and less verbatim recording of the TED Talks, and led to better results on the conceptual application questions.

The second study attempted to control for verbatim recording by replicating the first study, but students were explicitly advised not to use their laptops to transcribe the TED Talks verbatim. Again, students writing by hand produced notes with fewer words and less verbatim language, suggesting that the mandate to not transcribe verbatim by laptops was ineffective at eliminating verbatim recording and at improving memory on the questions following the lecture. In a third study, Mueller and Oppenheimer examined whether taking *more* notes might help strengthen retention. This time, students took notes by hand or by laptop on passages read from a teleprompter. They were allowed ten minutes to study their notes before being tested. Once again, students writing by hand generated fewer words with less verbatim recording. Furthermore, the students who took notes by hand and subsequently reviewed their notes outperformed their peers using laptops, ruling out the hypothesis that more content might provide a more comprehensive archive for review. Fundamentally, Mueller and Oppenheimer found that note-taking on laptops led to simple verbatim recording of content, foreclosing the activities of summary and synthesis that foster retention and learning.

Activities such as summary and synthesis foster retention and learning because they promote deep processing. Two studies conducted by Diemand-Yauman, Oppenheimer, and Vaughan (2011) raised questions regarding the extent to which struggle, or disfluency, is productive at facilitating deep processing. In the first study, university students were presented material on foreign (i.e., alien) species to promote taxonomic learning. Students were divided into disfluent and fluent groups, with disfluent groups receiving font-manipulated content in Comic Sans MS or Bodoni MT font, and fluent groups receiving unmanipulated font. The students were then asked to memorize the content, distracted, and tested for memory retrieval. Students in the disfluent group were correct 86.5% of the time, while students in the fluent group were correct 72.8% of the time.

To test these findings on younger students, Diemand-Yauman, Oppenheimer, and Vaughan conducted a second study. In this study, some high school students were given regular worksheets and PowerPoint slides, while the others received worksheets and slides were made disfluent through an editing process that either changed the font to Haettenschweiler, Monotype Corsiva, or Comic Sans Italicized or moved the paper while it was being copied. As with the first study, students in the disfluent group achieved higher scores than students in the fluent group. Students were also surveyed about whether the disfluency efforts impacted motivation. While no noticeable motivational differences were found between disfluent and fluent groups, responses did indicate personal preferences based on levels of confusion and propensities for certain subjects.

Finally, the potential for using keyboards and laptops to divert attention from learning and encourage multitasking while writing is important to analyze, due to the compromise such diversion and multitasking pose to the type of focus that handwriting typically affords. Mangen and Velay (2010) reiterate that, since visual attention is more focused when writing by hand, typing provides a level of remove from the haptic input and takes place in two separate spaces: the motor space and the visual space. Space and time converge when writing by hand. "Hence, attention is continuously oscillating between these two spatiotemporally distinct spaces which are, by contrast, conjoined in handwriting" (p. 396). Notes are ultimately representations of knowledge, and—as we have illustrated above—knowledge representations have sensorimotor origins and implications. Research that continually updates understandings of how technological innovations engage and influence these sensorimotor components of knowledge construction remains imperative.

**Discussion**

In the preface to his edited collection, *The Psychobiology of the Hand*, Connelly (1998) quotes Jacob Bronowski's (1973) *The Ascent of Man*: "The hand is the cutting edge of the mind" (x). Bronowski's statement was prescient, because research conducted forty years later confirms the power of his metaphor. Connelly, himself—a psychobiologist, not a literacy researcher—uses the example of writing as one of the "everyday activities [that] point to the remarkable properties and astonishing capacities of the hand" (ix). The studies we have reviewed here just begin to suggest these astonishing capacities of the writing hand.

Letter recognition, text production, and retention and learning interanimate each other. As such, successes or weaknesses in one activity will, respectively, fuel or inhibit successes or failures when working toward the other literacy milestones. When attempting to establish the type of neural system required to process and recognize letters—seen as a gateway to reading, writing, and future learning—writing by hand seems to serve an important foundational purpose, since spelling and handwriting speed and ease forecast students' skills at composing lengthy and quality text (James & Engelhardt, 2012).

When attempting to write for memory, writing by hand is more likely to generate text that solidifies memory of not just the content in question, but of the spatio-temporal relationships that create and depict the content, as well. Furthermore, the ability to return to and review this information is also important. In other words, documentation is not enough; the information must be revisited and re-engaged for reinforcement.

The ability to alter or distinguish content in some way also helps to facilitate its recognition and retention. Whether in the form of personalized, internalized notes or font changes, text that has been manipulated—either by, or prior to, the reader in question—is more likely to spark memory due to the way that it unsettles the types of subconscious expectations that shape literacy practices. Although mastery is used as an important benchmark in establishing fluency, Diemand-Yauman et al.'s (2011) work suggests that mastery can also invite a certain level of complacency that can undermine deep processing. In other words, while speed and ease are often prized and used as benchmarks, they can discourage mindfulness when producing text for retention and learning.

Due to what this research suggests about how digital tools influence multitasking, and how these tools can bifurcate the motor and visual spaces, it would behoove teachers and researchers to consider the particular attentional needs demanded of certain tasks and assignments when deciding which kinds of literacy tools might best serve particular pedagogical goals. Meeting pedagogical goals while navigating the practical realities that bind the classroom is a reminder that teaching is fraught with tensions. One tension emerges in discussions of how to teach handwriting, which—with its emphasis on technique—can evoke retrograde models of mechanistic training. We recognize that all classroom recommendations inevitably reflect and are shaped by capital and ideology, and that efforts to improve pedagogical practices have potential to resurrect or perpetuate counterproductive power structures (Luke, 1992). We are also cognizant of the difficult choices teachers make about how to allocate precious classroom time. But, we believe that some amount of habitual training is necessary to move from a rudimentary to even elementary level in creative fields. Witness the musician's virtuoso performance which is undergirded by months, if not years, of practicing chords and scales.

Given the complexity of the anatomical hand (Connelly, 1998; Lederman & Klatzky, 1998; Page, 1998), the evolving cultural hand (Wilson, 1999), and the hand-in-use—Aristotle's *instrument of instruments* which takes on the power of whatever instruments it grasps—it is not surprising that the hand's role in literacy is complex and varied. We have reviewed only three of what may be myriad roles of the hand in writing, and we hope that our admittedly brief foray into literacy and embodiment via the human hand can lay the groundwork for future synthetic work that brings research from other fields—from evolutionary biology to philosophy of mind to neuroscience—to bear on enriched understanding of the material practices of literacy.

## Note

1. A significant amount of research on handwriting (including some of the pieces we review) is set within the context of disability studies. In our view, the topic of disability in a digital age is vast and diverse, ripe for further study and certainly beyond the scope of this chapter.

## References

Aristotle. (2001). *On the parts of animals, Books 1–4* (J. G. Lennox, Trans.). Oxford: Oxford University Press (Original work published 350 BCE).

Berninger, V. W. (2008). Written language instruction during early and middle childhood. In R. J. Morris & N. Mather (Eds.), *Evidence-based interventions for students with learning and behavioral challenges* (pp. 215–235). New York, NY: Routledge.

Berninger, V. W., Abbott, R. D., Abbott, S. P., Graham, S., & Richards, T. (2002). Writing and reading connections between language by hand and language by eye. *Journal of Learning Disabilities, 35*, 39–56.

Berninger, V. W., Abbott, R. D., Augsburger, A., & Garcia, N. (2009). Comparison of pen and keyboard transcription modes in children with and without learning disabilities. *Learning Disability Quarterly, 32*(3), 123–141.

Berninger, V. W., Abbott, R. D., Jones, J., Wolf, B., Gould, L, Anderson-Youngstom, M., ... Apel, K. (2006). Early development of language by hand: Composing, reading, listening and speaking connections; three letter-writing modes; and fast mapping in spelling. *Developmental Neuropsychology*, *29*, 61–92.

Berninger, V. W., Richards, T., & Abbott, R. (2009). The role of the hand in written idea expression. In D. Alamargot, J. Bouchand, E. Lambert, V. Millogo, & C. Beaudet (Eds.), *Proceedings of the International Conference de la France au Québec: l'Ecriture dans tous ses états*. Poitiers, France.

Berninger, V. W., Yates, C., Cartwright, A., Rutberg, J., Remy, E., & Abbott, R. (1992). Lower level developmental skills in beginning writing. *Reading and Writing*, *4*(3), 257–280.

Bolter, J. D. (2001). *Writing space: Computers, hypertext, and the remediation of print* (2nd ed.). Mahweh, NJ: LEA.

Camille, M. (1992). *Image on the edge: The margins of medieval art*. London, UK: Reaktion Books, Ltd.

Chen, A. (2012). In one's own hand: Seeing manuscripts in a digital age. *Digital Humanities Quarterly*, *6*.

Chenoweth, N. A., & Hayes, J. R. (2001). Fluency in writing generating text in L1 and L2. *Written Communication*, *1*, 80–98.

Chenoweth, N. A., & Hayes, J. R. (2003). The inner voice in writing. *Written Communication*, *20*, 99–118.

Clark, A., & Chalmers, D. (1998). The extended mind. *Analysis*, *58*(1), 7–19.

Connelly, K. J. (1998). *The psychobiology of the hand*. London, UK: Mac Keith Press.

Connelly, V., Dockrell, J., Walter, K., & Critten, S. (2012). Predicting the quality of composition and written language bursts from oral language, spelling, and handwriting skills in children with and without specific language impairment. *Written Communication*, *29*, 278–302.

Connelly, V., Gee, D., & Walsh, E. (2007). A comparison of keyboarded and handwritten compositions and the relationship with transcription speed. *British Journal of Educational Psychology*, *77*, 479–492.

Crump, M. J., & Logan, G. D. (2010). Warning: This keyboard will deconstruct—The role of the keyboard in skilled typewriting. *Psychonomic Bulletin & Review*, *17*(3), 394–399.

Csordas, T. J. (1994). Introduction: the body as representation and being-in-the-world. In T. J. Csordas (Ed.), *Embodiment and experience: The existential ground of culture and self* (pp. 1–24). Cambridge: Cambridge University Press.

Derrida, J. (1988). Signature event context. In *Limited Inc* (S. Weber and J. Mehlman, Trans.). Evanston, IL: Northwestern University Press.

Diemand-Yauman, C., Oppenheimer, D. M., & Vaughan, E. B. (2011). Fortune favors the bold (and the italicized): Effects of disfluency on educational outcomes. *Cognition*, *118*, 111–115.

Ehret, C., & Hollett, T. (2014). Embodied composition in real virtualities: Adolescents' literacy practices and felt experiences moving with digital, mobile devices in school. *Research in the Teaching of English*, *48*, 428–452.

Gioia, D. (1997). The magical value of manuscripts. In R. Phillips (Ed.), *The hand of the poet: Poems and papers in manuscript*. New York, NY: Rizzoli.

Goldberg, J. (1990). *Writing matter: From the hand of the English Renaissance*. Stanford, CA: Stanford University Press

Graham, S., Berninger, V. W., Abbott, R. D., Abbott, S. P., & Whitaker, D. (1997). Role of mechanics in composing of elementary school students: A new methodological approach. *Journal of Educational Psychology*, *89*, 170.

Graham, S., & Weintraub, N. (1996). A review of handwriting research: Progress and prospects from 1980 to 1994. *Educational Psychology Review*, *8*, 7–87.

Haas, C. (1996). *Writing technology: Studies in the materiality of literacy*. Mahweh, NJ: LEA.

Haas, C., & Hayes, J. R. (1986). 'What did I just say?' Reading problems in writing with the machine. *Research in the Teaching of English*, *22*, 22–35.

Harris, R. (1995). *Signs of writing*. New York, NY: Routledge.

Hayes, J. R., & Chenoweth, N. A. (2007). Working memory in an editing task. *Written Communication*, *24*, 283–294.

Hensher, P. (2012). *The missing ink: The lost art of handwriting*. New York, NY: Faber & Faber.

Hutchins, E. (2005). Material anchors for conceptual blends. *Journal of Pragmatics*, *37*, 1555–1577.

Igo, L. B., Bruning, R., & McCrudden, M. T. (2005). Exploring differences in students' copy-and-paste decision making and processing: A mixed-methods study. *Journal of Educational Psychology*, *97*, 103.

James, K. H., & Engelhardt, L. (2012). The effects of handwriting experience on functional brain development in pre-literate children. *Trends in Neuroscience Education*, *1*, 32–42.

James, K. H., & Gauthier, I. (2006). Letter processing automatically recruits a sensory-motor brain network. *Neuropsychologia*, *44*, 2937–2949.

Jones, L. (1998). Manual dexterity. In K. Connolly (Ed.), *The psychobiology of the hand* (pp. 47–63). London, UK: Mac Keith Press.

Jones, D., & Christensen, C. A. (1999). Relationship between automaticity in handwriting and students' abilities to generate written text. *Journal of Educational Psychology*, *91*, 44–49.

Kato, C., Isoda, H., Takehara, Y., Matsuo, K., Moriya, T., & Nakai, T. (1999). Involvement of motor cortices I retrieval of *kanji* studies by functional MRI. *NeuroReport*, *10*, 1335–1339.

Kaufer, D. S., Hayes, J. R., & Flower, L. (1986). Composing written sentences. *Research in the Teaching of English*, *20*(2), 121–140.

Lederman, S. J., & Klatzky, R. (1998). The hand as a perceptual system. In K. Connolly (Ed.), *The psychobiology of the hand* (pp. 16–35). London, UK: Mac Keith Press.

Liberman, A. (1999). The reading researcher and the reading teacher need the right theory of speech. *Scientific Studies of Reading, 3*, 95–111.

Longcamp, M., Anton, J. L., Roth, M., & Velay, J. L. (2003). Visual presentation of single letters activates a premotor area involved in writing. *Neuroimage, 19*, 1492–1500.

Longcamp, M., Anton, J. L., Roth, M., and Velay, J. L. (2005) Premotor activations in response to visually presented single letters depend on the hand used to write: A study of left-handers. *Neuropsychologia, 43*, 1801–1809.

Luke, A. (1992). The body literate: Discourse and inscription in early literacy training. *Linguistics and Education, 4*(1), 107–129.

Lurçat, L. (1974). *Etudes de l'acte graphique*. Paris: Mouton.

Mangen, A. (2008). Hypertext fiction reading: Haptics and immersion. *Journal of Research on Reading, 31*, 404–419.

Mangen, A., & van der Weel, A. (2016). The evolution of reading in the age of digitization (E-READ): An integrative framework for reading research. In E. Bearne and R. Kennedy (Eds.), *Literacy and community: developing a primary curriculum through partnerships* (pp. 116–124). Leicester: United Kingdom Literacy Association.

Mangen, A., & Velay, J. L. (2010). *Digitizing literacy: reflections on the haptics of writing*. INTECH Open Access Publisher.

Matsuo, K., Kato, C., Okada, T., Morita, T., Glover, G., & Nakai, T. (2003). Finger movements lighten neural loads in the recognition of ideographic characters. *Cognitive Brain Research, 17*, 263–272.

Merleau-Ponty, M. (1945/1962). *Phenomenology of perception* (C. Smith, Trans.). London, UK: Routledge & Kegan Paul.

Mueller, P. A., & Oppenheimer, D. (2014). The pen is mightier than the keyboard: Advantages of longhand over laptop note taking. *Psychological Science, 25*, 1159–1168.

Norman, D. A., & Fisher, D. (1982). Why alphabetic keyboards are not easy to use: Keyboard layout doesn't much matter. *Human Factors: The Journal of the Human Factors and Ergonomics Society, 24*(5), 509–519.

Ong, W. (1981). *Orality and literacy: The technologizing of the word*. London, UK: Metheun.

Page, R. E. (1998). The structure of the hand. In K. Connolly (Ed.), *The psychobiology of the hand* (pp. 1–15). London, UK: Mac Keith Press.

Pallasmaa, J. (2005). *The eyes of the skin: Architecture and the senses*. West Sussex: John Wiley.

Pallasmaa, J. (2009). *The thinking hand: Existential and embodied wisdom in architecture*. West Sussex: John Wiley.

Rempel, D., Barr, A., Brafman, D., & Young, E. (2007). The effect of six keyboard designs on wrist and forearm postures. *Applied Ergonomics, 38*(3), 293–298.

Schmandt-Besserat, D. (1992). *Before writing, vol. I: From counting to cuneiform* (Vol. 1). Austin: University of Texas Press.

Sears, A., Revis, D., Swatski, J., Crittenden, R., & Shneiderman, B. (1993). Investigating touchscreen typing: the effect of keyboard size on typing speed. *Behaviour & Information Technology, 12*(1), 17–22.

Streeck, J. (2009). *Gesturecraft: The manufacture of meaning*. Amsterdam: Johns Benjamins.

Sudnow, D. (2001). *Ways of the hand: A rewritten account*. Cambridge, MA: MIT Press.

Swanson, N. G., Galinsky, T. L., Cole, L. L., Pan, C. S., & Sauter, S. L. (1997). The impact of keyboard design on comfort and productivity in a text-entry task. *Applied Ergonomics, 28*(1), 9–16.

Vinter, A., & Chartrel, E. (2008). Visual and proprioceptive recognition of cursive letters in young children. *Acta Psychologica, 129*, 147–156.

Wilson, F. (1999). *The hand*. New York, NY: Random House.

# 11
# Playful Literacies and Practices of Making in Children's Imaginaries

Karen E. Wohlwend, Beth A. Buchholz, and Carmen Liliana Medina

In this chapter, we examine literacy research that looks beyond print to recognize the action texts in young children's media production and to better understand the mutually constitutive relationships among play and making in contemporary childhoods. How do these areas merge in children's classroom productions in digital puppetry, toymaking, drama, animation, filmmaking, and crafting of artifacts? Our focus is on shared imaginative production in classroom cultures to understand play and making as powerful literacies with value in their own right, producing unapologetically printless texts assembled with physical actions and materials that move and recruit across digital networks. We draw upon contemporary research on imagination and literacies as social action, looking at the nexus of play and making as a site of collective meaning-making and cultural production, that both contests and reinscribes boundaries in digital cultures, resonates and ruptures dominant discourses, and mobilizes youth and materials. Play and making are literacies that run on peer culture passions, often centered on electronic games and digital play with popular media. But it is also important to note that it is not necessary for children to be online or to be using new technologies to be deeply entangled in imaginative labor as young participants in global flows and digital cultures. In the following sections, we survey emerging theories and research that show the impact on children's learning and participation in classrooms of playful literacies and practices of making within the collective imaginaries that circulate in and through childhoods.

## Playful Literacies

This term describes a range of semiotic practices for collaborative imagining that enact meanings with bodies or that animate toys, props, and other materials to virtually inhabit a shared pretend context. Defining play is difficult; it slips through attempts at definition but sociocultural research suggests a few criteria with relevance.

- Play is ambiguous (Sutton-Smith, 1997), masking its meanings through pretense so that meanings in a here-and-now reality are exchanged for imagined ones. For example, even very young children become adept at coordinating pretend and real action during mock fights, landing and dodging pretend blows by tempering their physical actions to avoid actually hurting one another (Fleer, 2014).
- Play is contingent, maintained by co-players' agreeing upon a set of "as if" conditions: Their actions are "only play" and have a different meaning inside the play frame (Bateson, 1955), and the

meanings in play scenarios expire at the end of the session. In this way, play is "made fresh daily" (Wohlwend, Buchholz, Wessel Powell, Coggin, & Husbye, 2013), as each play session opens the possibilities for new players, characters, and meanings to be negotiated and agreed upon.
- Play is voluntary and fun. Play is only play when players choose when to start and when to stop (King, 1992) and who can and cannot play (Paley, 1992). Play that is teacher-assigned, or otherwise co-opted, is not play.
- Play is a modally rich. The meanings in play need to be easily recognizable so that other players can instantly respond in the emerging pretense. Play meanings are constructed with physical actions, sound effects, character voices, invented dialogue, and movements of bodies and things across space.

We define *playful literacies* as meaning-making and participatory practices for pretense that players voluntarily engage in for their own purposes, in complex interactions situated in home, peer, school, media, and digital cultures (Wohlwend, 2013).

**Practices of Making**

Everyday interactions with children highlight that *making* has always been a central component of childhood. From beaded necklaces to reconfigured cardboard boxes to paper airplanes, children utilize materials found in their everyday lives to produce artifacts and identities. But making has become "Making" in recent years with the emergence of the Maker Movement, moving the practice of artifact production into the national spotlight and into society's popular imagination (Dougherty, 2012; Peppler, Halverson, & Kafai, 2016a, 2016b).

In this chapter, we rely on Halverson and Sheridan's (2014) definition, broadly referring to the Maker Movement as a "growing number of people who are engaged in the creative production of artifacts in their daily lives and who find physical and digital forums to share their processes and products with others" (p. 496). One only needs to visit websites like Etsy, Instructables, and Pinterest to see the spirit of making and sharing alive in the world outside of Silicon Valley. What began with an emphasis on technological innovation and tools has grown to encompass a broader do-it-yourself ethos that is inclusive of digital technologies as well as hands-on making. Of particular importance to the Maker Movement is "makers" *participating* in communities of practice by *sharing* with and *learning* from other members (Hatch, 2013). Digital tools now allow these communities to emerge across contexts and times. Constructing making as a site of collective cultural production reflects notions of participatory culture, shifting the "focus of literacy [or making] from one of individual expression to community involvement" (Jenkins et al., 2009, p. 4).

The field of education is beginning to explore the potential of making as a productive learning engagement across grade levels, content areas, spaces, and materials, reaching across the "divide between formal and informal learning" (Halverson & Sheridan, 2014, p. 498). Drawing on the work of Papert (1980; Harel & Papert, 1991) and Dewey (1938/1963), the move to consider the role of the Maker Movement in education is undergirded by an approach to learning that places artifact production and sharing at the core of how people learn. Makerspaces for children and young people can now be found in schools, museums, libraries, churches, homes, and after-school spaces as well as virtual communities online. While the connection between writing, artifact production (making), and identity work has been of interest to literacy researchers for years (e.g., Leander, 2002; Rowsell & Pahl, 2007), global interest in the Maker Movement opens up new spaces for exploring the relationship between writing and making in the twenty-first century. This national enthusiasm for making is juxtaposed on a landscape of school surveillance and accountability. In this environment, making and play become a perquisite of after-school programs, museums, or affluent schools not on "low performance" state watch lists. It's crucial to understand what children are learning in these spaces, and what others are missing when play and making are relegated to enrichment, nice-if-there-is-time supplements to the literacy curriculum.

## Making Beast Quest

To illustrate the theories, research, tensions, and possibilities in the nexus of playful literacies and making, we unpack an excerpt of primary school filmmaking and set construction from one of our research studies (Wohlwend et al., 2013).

\*\*\*

Sliding both of his hands underneath, six-year-old Monroe carefully lifts up what looks to be a piece of paper almost as long as he is tall. The paper is white with a slim strip of green paper attached to the bottom left corner. He balances the paper while taking cautious steps across the crowded classroom. With his eyes moving back and forth between the paper and the wider classroom, he locates some space near the back where this large piece of paper can fit on the floor. As he bends down to place the paper on the floor, his nearby friend Liam leans over to get a better look, "Oh! Are we allowed to work on that now?" Monroe promises that as soon as Liam is done working on his current project, "you can help me." Liam reluctantly returns to his own writing.

Monroe looks over the large paper project, referring to it as a "setup," and begins to work (and/or play and/or write and/or make, depending upon the perspective of the observer). Grabbing a blue marker, he adds color to the white paper, squiggly lines soon filling the space around the green strip. Evan, another friend, comes by to check out Monroe's setup. He stands over the paper while Monroe continues to color. "I'm not close to being done," Monroe says, with clear excitement rather than annoyance, "When I'm done, this is probably going to be as big as the library!" Evan continues to observe. Sensing his interest, Monroe puts a lid on the blue marker to offer his friend a short tour of his creation so far.

Upon closer view, this is much more than a large blank piece of paper decorated with squiggly blue lines; this is an oceanscape (thus the need for a blue marker) with three-dimensional elements scattered about made from paper, tape, and popsicle sticks. Monroe points at the slim strip of green paper in the corner, "That's Sepron; he's a sea serpent." Grabbing one end of the green strip, he moves the paper around, creating the sense that the serpent is thrashing his head back and forth. "And that," grabbing a tangle of popsicle sticks sticking up vertically from the paper, "is a six-headed sea monster." Though it is stuck to the paper, Monroe tilts it to highlight the six heads. "It's from *Beast Quest*. I've read almost all the books in the series. I've seen the movies too, but now I'm more of a book person."

\*\*\*

This scene unfolded in a kindergarten and first grade (K/1) mixed age classroom. As the teachers in this classroom explored the possibilities of creating digital media with young children, writing workshop became a kind of filmmaking playshop. Notebooks and folders were pushed aside to have space for puppetmaking, setmaking, and digital filmmaking. Children were encouraged to work with friends to draw film plans on storyboards and construct paper toys/puppets, scenery, and props in order to tell stories. Monroe initiated his Beast Quest project by constructing a large piece of paper. What looked like a single large piece of paper was actually nine sheets of letter-sized white paper (most rescued from the recycling bin) connected together with masking tape on each seam, creating a nearly two-foot by four-foot canvas. Instead of drawing scenery on a flat backdrop and then taping it to the wall, Monroe's plan was to keep the large paper on the floor and add three-dimensional elements to create an interactive setting. His inventive approach reflected elements of play mats or play rugs often found on the floor of children's bedrooms as well as plastic play sets (e.g., Fisher-Price Little People, Playmobil, Melissa & Doug) that line the shelves of preschools and playrooms. Such play sets offer an open-ended context in which children add toys or everyday objects to enact different scenes.

Monroe referred to his three-dimensional creation as a "setup" instead of using terms like "backdrop," "setting," or "scene," which were used more regularly by the other children and teachers in the classroom. Rather than a backdrop where the action all happens in front of or apart from the two-dimensional paper or canvas scene, a setup implies a *set* of three-dimensional materials (or equipment) that human actors interact *with* when engaging in an activity or practice. The term "setup" is also used specifically within the world of theatrical and cinematic productions. Monroe's use of the term "setup" offers insight into how he positioned his making and storying as practices that stood apart from the schooled version of a puppet show. He was thinking (and talking) like a producer of a theatrical or cinematic production rather than a writer in a primary classroom writing workshop.

The details and intentionality of Monroe's creation can be easily overlooked by observers who see only wrinkled paper, scribbled markings, torn masking tape, and awkwardly positioned popsicle sticks. But for Monroe and his friends, these three-dimensional assemblages attached to the oceanscape base were forms of creative cultural production, bringing popular culture and children's collective imaginaries into the classroom. This wasn't just *any* ocean; this was the ocean from *Beast Quest,* a popular series of fantasy books for middle grade readers originally published in the UK and later picked up in the US. Described as "Narnia meets Pokemon via Potter," the books in the series are among the most borrowed from libraries in the UK (Flett, 2009). Though most of the Beast Quest book storylines are set on land, Monroe chose to remix or perhaps even tinker with the official set of storylines by selecting sea-living beasts from three different books and placing them in a single oceanscape.

### *From Tensions and Determinisms to Messiness and Blurring*

We situate Monroe's work/play in a filmmaking playshop on the uncomfortable edge of the possible and the problematic. This child's playful design work clearly situates him as a creative meaning-maker, but most educational interpretations of this classroom activity would likely ask, "Where's the writing?" As teachers invite making and play into classrooms as tools for imaginative meaning production, they are caught in the space between multiple practical tensions: making curricula relevant to modern childhoods, preparing children to pass high-stakes tests in school, and keeping children engaged as play migrates to digital playgrounds outside school. It is also important to note here that in the example provided Monroe was a strong "writer" and reader according to traditional K/1 school literacy standards. These labels imbue children with certain privileges in formal classroom spaces that likely contributed to the amount of space, time, and freedom that Monroe was given to create his oceanscape when no visible signs of writing were present.

We suggest that most literacy pedagogies position play and making as subordinate to writing. A range of educational approaches advocate play or making to provide instructional strategies for writing: to motivate children to write (Ray & Cleaveland, 2004), to offer experiential background in preparation for writing (Rowe, Fitch, & Bass, 2003), or as creative response to literature (Paley, 1997). These perspectives generally position Monroe's play and digital filmmaking as what happens *before* and/or *after* he engages in an actual literacy event (e.g., writing a script, reading a book, creating a storyboard). As literature response, the Beast Quest setup is reduced to an artistic reader response strategy that supports children in visualizing and comprehending a text that they've read. As a motivational or experiential activity, his making is framed by a prewriting brainstorming strategy: an engaging way for children to produce and evaluate writing ideas before capturing one of them with paper and pencil (Lysaker, Wheat, & Benson, 2010). In these approaches, some kind of authorizing print must be generated in order to justify play or making in the curriculum. In other words, "Where's the print?" serves as a litmus test for determining whether creative and productive digital meaning-making practices rise to the level of literacy.

The National Writing Project's (NWP) initial approach to bring making and writing together reflected this hierarchical divide. In their early summer workshops for teachers with MAKE Magazine, writing and making were treated as separate processes: Participants engaged in playfully *making* something (often with the use of technological tools) and *then* they engaged in *writing about* the make, often in the form of an informational/procedural text (Reed, 2011). A strength of this approach was that it offered writers an authentic purpose for sharing as a way to pass on expertise and knowledge within a larger community of makers. While this separation between writing and making certainly persists in research and in classrooms, in part because it offers a view of writing that is aligned with the Common Core State Standards, a growing group of NWP leaders and teachers is arguing for a more entangled approach, proposing a paradigm shift from writing *and* making to "writing/making" (Cantrill & Oh, 2016, p. 119). We see a similar shift in literacy research perspectives that view "writing as play" or "textual toys" (Dyson, 2003, p. 43) to reveal the depth of imaginative work in children's play and writing. Using this as a point of departure, we wonder: If Monroe never produced any print prewriting or written response to his Beast Quest setup, which theories and research support analysis of a young child's meaning-laden practices (coloring, cutting, taping, digital filming) as robust literacy practices?

### *Exploring Emerging Theories and Methods in Recent Literacy Research*

In the Beast Quest example, Monroe constructed a play world—a collective imaginary—for other players to inhabit. Although this scene was built of paper, tape, and popsicle sticks, its foundation was digital. In early childhood classrooms, where children cannot access the mobile phones or video game technologies they want to play, they make them with paper, crayons, and tape (Wohlwend, 2009). To characterize children's pretend digital props—their paper cell phones, cardboard box laptops, or in this case, Monroe's Beast Quest sea world—as *text* is too static and too flat a description for literacy practices that mold and mobilize materials, bodies, and artifacts. It is probably more accurate to describe the embodied scenes, material artifacts, and other meaning-products of play and making as *contexts,* rather than texts.

Monroe's ocean context was similar to a sandbox video game, a genre of open-ended games where players wander and explore a landscape. Sandboxes are interactive contexts rather than texts, digital environments with spatialized storylines for players to inhabit and navigate. By creating the Beast Quest sandbox, Monroe designed an imaginary, anticipating how others would explore and play in the constructed world. This is similar to the world-making in Minecraft, a highly popular sandbox construction game where children can build their own digital landscape for others to explore.

It is important to note that this production of an imaginary context was collaborative on multiple levels/times (Burnett & Bailey, 2015), in the immediate collaboration among multiple children sprawled on the floor drawing and coloring a very large set and in the imagined collaboration between these here-and-now makers who designed the ocean world and the anticipated players who would animate it during future play and filmmaking. Children also collaborated in a film crew, working together to handle digital cameras and animate particular portions of the paper landscape during the filming of a walkthrough narrated by Monroe.

In expanding the meaning-product from text to context, we broaden the territory for analysis. Interactions among bodies, artifacts, and the physical environment are suddenly foregrounded for consideration as literary elements. This aligns with a material turn in literacy studies that has renewed attention to the ways actions and things mean. Several literacy theories offer useful tools for unpacking the material meanings in children's making of play worlds. In this section, we sketch a few examples of theories that forefront materiality, with core constructs and promising directions in emerging research.

**Mediated Discourse, Nexus of Practice, and Collective Cultural Imaginaries**

Mediated discourse analysis (MDA) theory (Scollon, 2001) examines the cultural production in collaborative imagining, play, and making. We use Medina and Wohlwend's (2014) model of *multisited collective imaginaries* to understand how players draw on popular media flows as they imagine otherwise with peers, negotiating and performing the imaginaries they share. During play, children both reproduce and rupture an imaginary's often tacit, cultural expectations for who can be a proper fan, player, or maker and how they should behave. These ways of belonging are enacted as social practices and identities in a nexus of practice (Scollon, 2001), a mesh of shared social practices and identity performances that mark actors as members who recognize one another through their actions-in-common (e.g., That's just how we do things here). In digital cultures, insider status enables and is marked by greater opportunities, such as knowledge of shortcuts, access to restricted locations, avatar tokens or badges, or increased number of followers. Such digital artifacts indicate membership status and allow other members to quickly see who belongs or who is liking, following, or otherwise demonstrating affiliation with a particular imaginary.

Critically, mediated discourse theory recognizes children's collective cultural imaginaries as sites of both engagement and contestation, where the agentic meets the problematic. Imaginaries depend upon widespread participation, moving through online distribution channels and offline contributions of imaginative labor and cultural production. Increasingly, young children engage imaginaries through the video games, action figures, films, and merchandise they view, buy, enact, and design. In this framing, Beast Quest is a book franchise and a children's imaginary, similar to films, video games, or toy franchises circulating through media imaginaries with a foundational set of characters and connecting narratives. Media imaginaries circulate identity expectations for players and characters, often with well-worn patterns of gender, racial, and ethnic inequity and income disparity that are both challenged and reproduced in children's play and making (Medina & Wohlwend, 2014).

Recent MDA research includes longitudinal ethnographic work that documented the complex nexus of making, playing, and writing produced in relation to a classroom playground game that existed as part of the community's cultural and historical imaginary (Buchholz, 2015a). When one community member decided to write down the rules in a shared Google Doc (after a decade of play governed by unwritten rules), the community entered contentious negotiations over how digital *writing* impacted the *playing* of the game.

**Spatialized Literacies, Assemblage, and Place-Making**

Theories of spatialized literacies (Leander & Sheehy, 2004) enable analysis of the complexity of socio-material construction of space that laminates a there-and-then fantasy world onto a here-and-now classroom place, folding together layers of experienced and imagined space-times, as wrinkled as the paper Beast Quest map that carpeted the classroom floor. Just as paper is folded and tilted to add dimension to the waves to make the sea serpent appear to be rising out of the ocean, landscapes can pull in and layer previous space-times to authorize power relations among makers and their practices. In this framing, an assemblage of paper/tape/sticks/humans—while materially situated in a classroom—is a collaboratively produced site that anchors a social space and tethers space-times that are not fixed but fluid trajectories that can pulled in, smoothed out, or folded in on one another in children's play and making. The physical Beast Quest map is an anchoring "identity artifact" that can be wielded to recruit other makers and players into co-construction of physical artifact, its meanings, the identities of its makers, and a cohesive social space (Leander, 2002). The paper landscape grounds the children's identities as fans, filmmakers, and friends but also power relations among leaders and followers and trajectories across timespaces in the claim of a movie fan who has evolved into "more of a book person."

Recent spatial research on play and making in this area explores place-making as constructions of human-material-spatio-temporal assemblages that move along digital networks, in projects with virtual worlds (Burnett & Merchant, 2013) or stop-motion animation (Mills, 2010). Comber (2011) moves beyond "safe assignments" bounded by notebook pages and classroom walls to work with teachers and children to produce "culturally significant artifacts" and public spaces. This critical literacies work is conceptually and literally grounded in public sites in students' neighborhoods so that children engage in making that matters: "designing belonging spaces, advocating for their rights, producing community art works, researching the histories of their school community, and researching and planting sustainable gardens" (p. 346). Hollett (2015) uses spatialized literacies to understand the interactions among space, play, and making in a video game with a vast digital network and passionate fandom. Spatial analysis of teens' play with Minecraft, a sandbox construction video game, tracks how trajectories of affect, mobility, and place converge in players' place-making. Hollett's spatio-temporal mapping of teens' trajectories shows the value of recognizing a wandering, "wayfaring" model of learning where the end goal is place-making, rather than an accumulation of knowledge or a final destination point. In a study of after-school Minecraft play among preteens, Burnett and Bailey (2015) found collaborations to be fluid and fractional, as children negotiated overlapping texts, friendships, and communities across online and offline spaces.

**Embodiment, Messiness, and Random Acts of Play**

Theories of embodiment acknowledge bodies as "whole experiential beings in motion, both inscribed and inscribing subjectivities," positing that they are "both a representation of self (a 'text') as well as a mode of creation in progress (a 'tool')" (Perry & Medina, 2011, p. 63). Rather than positioning the body as biological (naturalistic) and/or body as sign (semiotics), literacy scholars explore the experiential, relational, and sensational body as well as embodiment as cultural practice (Jones, 2013; Leander & Boldt, 2013; Perry & Medina, 2015). Research on the role of emotion/affect in relation to educational practice and research (Kuby, 2013; Lewis & Tierney, 2013; Zembylas & Schutz, 2016) moves analysis from mental states within an individual's mind and body to interactions between individuals through embodied changes that are physical and visceral. Leander and Rowe (2006) described these affective intensities as the "forces between bodies through their contact or collision rather than an expression of their qualities as things" (p. 433).

In the Beast Quest example, an embodiment perspective draws the researcher's gaze from a three-dimensional paper set and/or a transcript of the boys' talk to the moment-by-moment emergence of their bodies in relation to affect, sensation, and interrelation. Medina and Perry's (2014) emergent model for analyzing performative experiences in education, moves us from asking questions of the data based on representation (e.g., What is meant by the boys?) to asking: How are cultural norms, histories, and knowledge inscribed or disrupted as they work together on the Beast Quest set? What relationships and dynamics (affects and forces) can be observed between the boys' bodies, positions, material and immaterial contexts, instruction, and action (i.e., interrelations)? What and how are changes, events, and creations occurring? The transition from focusing on representations to interrelations and sensations situates the boys' bodies and Beast Quest play as meaningful in its own right. Popular cultural and media texts like Beast Quest also signify powerful emotional attachments for children (Marsh, 2005; Pugh, 2009). Recent work in the field has recognized play as an embodied approach that engages children in critical meaning making (Campano, Ngo, Low, & Jacobs, 2016; Thiel, 2015), as well as the possibilities of children using digital technologies to visually document moments of improvisational, dramatic play in the classroom (Buchholz, 2015b). In these examples, researchers and teachers situate children's bodies as tools for producing knowledge and thinking critically, reflecting a willingness to analytically engage in the messiness of moving bodies rather than allowing them to "fall to the cutting room floor" (Leander & Boldt, 2013, p. 32).

*Implications for Educational Practice*

The question "Where's the print?" highlights a widening gulf between children's digitally mediated lives and the literacy experiences we offer in schools. To address this, we have moved from ethnographic stance to a more participatory one in our individual and collective work that moves toward social action with teachers and children. In doing this, we also respect the complexities of teaching tightropes stretched across school realities, recognizing teachers as already-active mediators. Productive pathways are neither either/or choices nor careful sidesteps around issues. Recognizing that play moves, we make a conscious decision to attend to the productive affordances of blurring and muddying, understanding that mess often becomes learning in the chaotic relationships among play, making, and children's collective imaginaries, and that collaboration is not merely harmonious cooperation but also uncomfortable disruptions and contestations.

The frustrating reality is that technological innovation is outpacing literacy research as well as classroom practice. Young children grow up swiping apps on phones, chatting virtually via computer games, building online virtual worlds, texting emoji-filled messages to family members, navigating complex websites, and recording and editing videos. Yet classroom writing instruction largely looks the same as it did decades ago. We may now see children on iPads and laptops during classroom writing instruction, but these devices are often used only for their word processing capabilities, simply alternative tools for producing alphabetic text on [virtual] paper, or even in more limiting ways as digital worksheets. The essential question then becomes how do we take the innovative and emergent research synthesized in this chapter, research that brings together strands of creative possibility in making, playing, and imagining, and ensure that children across diverse educational settings have access to a curriculum that positions them as makers and doers. If we begin to consider equitable access to play and making as social justice issues rather than extracurricular activities (see Campano et al.'s (2016) recent argument about "critical play"), then we, as researchers and educators, are challenged to consider how to move from theory-filled handbook chapters to the messiness of educational spaces filled with people and policies but also possibilities for participatory action.

*Recommendations and Forward Thinking*

While much of the research on making so far has occurred in unofficial, outside of school environments (summer camps, after school programs, weekend workshops/events, etc.), moving forward there is a need to explore how these maker practices and spaces might inform official school pedagogies and curricula. In terms of classroom research, we see two productive pathways: (1) preservice teacher education classes and (2) in-service teacher study groups, with both pathways recognizing teachers as makers of artifacts as well as makers of curriculum.

Classroom research necessitates positioning teachers (pre- and in-service) as knowledgeable, passionate, reflective professionals who bring expertise to reconceptualizing what it could look like for children to make, play, and imagine in official school spaces. In terms of the first pathway, working with preservice teachers, recent research in the field (e.g., Wohlwend, Scott, Yi, Deliman, & Kargin, in press) documented the transformative experience of university students whose literacy methods coursework included a Literacy Playshop (Wohlwend et al., 2013) on "toyhacking" and filmmaking. Crucially, preservice teachers, who had opportunities to *use* makerspace materials (e.g., art tools, saws, drills, glue guns) rather than just *reading about* the literacy potential of makerspaces, were surprised by the depth of their own learning and the engaging literacy resources in their remixes of toys, games, music, and viral videos. Making space for tinkering and making in teacher education coursework—and specifically in literacy methods courses—offers a productive direction for future practice and research.

The second pathway involves researchers partnering with in-service educators to explore questions of pedagogy, theory, and curriculum. Using a teacher study group model, researchers and practitioners can engage in action research, developing emergent curricula situated and responsive to the realities of classroom. In the Beast Quest example, Monroe's teachers participated in a study group that developed an emergent filmmaking curriculum for primary grades (Wohlwend et al., 2013). Though these teachers worked at a public charter school that arguably enjoyed more flexibility and professional support than many nearby neighborhood schools—especially those labeled as "low performing," state standards and high stakes testing were still very real pressures. As part of this group, teachers discussed a range of questions from the theoretical (Should children have to write something down for it to be considered writing?) to the practical (In a classroom where space was limited, how do we organize and keep track of children's three-dimensional creations?). Teacher study groups offer one model with clear benefits to teachers and researchers from building local face-to-face relationships. Another model for working with in-service teachers leverages online tools and platforms to build an extensive community of practice across time and space. NWP's involvement in the annual summer Connected Learning Massive Online Open Collaboration (CLMOCC) (Smith, West-Puckett, Cantrill, & Zamora, 2016) merges making and writing with the aim of remixing and reinventing core Writing Project practices through a Connected Learning perspective (see http://clmoocmb.educatorinnovator.org). Organized around iterative "Make Cycles," the CLMOOC invites educators of all kinds to make/compose, collaborate, and distribute multimediated artifacts as members of a participatory online community while collectively considering what this means for their work with children and youth.

The goal across both pathways should be to create ongoing support structures that provide opportunities for teachers to build community and to critically examine the possibilities and dilemmas of making in the classroom. Pooling collective resources, teachers "teach past contradictory institutional policies and free [themselves] from these 'stuck places'" (Boldt, Salvio, & Taubman, 2009, p. 15). Here, we push further, suggesting that teachers might also teach toward the messiness of an emergent curriculum, working with children in the nexus of play and making as a site of collective meaning-making and cultural production.

We suggest using the term "maker literacies" moving forward, describing collaborative, play-based, communicative practices that move beyond writing. Maker literacies include digital puppetry and e-textile puppetmaking (Buchholz, Shively, Peppler, & Wohlwend, 2014); mask-making, drama, animation, arts, digital filmmaking with child-produced props and artifacts (Honeyford & Boyd, 2015; Husbye & Vander Zanden, 2015; Wohlwend et al., 2013); stop-motion and cartoon animation

(Mills, 2010; Simpson, Walsh, & Rowsell, 2013); toymaking and "toyhacking" (Wohlwend, Scott, Yi, Deliman, & Kargin, in press); costume-making, mask-making, and set construction (Doerr-Stevens Lewis, Ingram, & Asp, 2015; Kuby & Rucker, 2016); video editing and game development (Tekinbas, Gresalfi, Peppler, & Santo, 2014); coding/programing (Burke & Kafai, 2012); remixing (Honeyford & Boyd, 2015; Knobel & Lankshear, 2008); curation (Mihailidis & Cohen, 2013); and critical play (Campano et al., 2016; Comber, 2011; Doerr-Stevens et al., 2015). These are just a few examples to provide a glimpse of possibilities. We hope that research and practice will vigorously extend and expand this list of maker literacies and contribute to curricula that cuts across grade levels, content areas, and school spaces.

## References

Anderson, B. (1991). *Imagined communities: Reflections on the origin of nationalism* (2nd ed.). New York, NY: Verso.

Bateson, G. (1955). A theory of play and fantasy. In G. Bateson (Ed.), *Steps to an ecology of mind* (pp. 177–193). San Francisco, CA: Chandler.

Boldt, G. M. (2006). Resistance, loss, and love in learning to read: A psychoanalytic inquiry. *Research in the Teaching of English*, *40*(3), 272–309.

Boldt, G. M., Salvio, P. M., & Taubman, P. M. (2009). Classroom life in the age of accountability. Occasional Paper Series 22. *Bank Street College of Education*.

Buchholz, B. A. (2015a). *Authoring time in the classroom: Multiage writers compose communities, relationships, and identities across timescales*. Unpublished doctoral dissertation. Indiana University, Bloomington, IN.

Buchholz, B. A. (2015b). Drama as serious (and not so serious) business: Critical play, generative conflicts, and moving bodies in a 1:1 classroom. *Language Arts*, *93*(1), 7–24.

Buchholz, B., Shively, K., Peppler, K., & Wohlwend, K. (2014). Hands on, hands off: Gendered access in crafting and electronics practices. *Mind, Culture, and Activity*, *21*(4), 278–297.

Burke, Q., & Kafai, Y. B. (2012, February). The writers' workshop for youth programmers: Digital storytelling with scratch in middle school classrooms. In *Proceedings of the 43rd ACM technical symposium on Computer Science Education* (pp. 433–438). New York, NY: ACM.

Burnett, C., & Bailey, C. (2014). *Conceptualizing collaboration in hybrid sites: Playing Minecraft together and apart in a primary classroom*. C. Burnett, G. Merchant, J. Rowsell, & J. Davies (Eds.), *New Literacies around the Globe: Policy and Pedagogy* (pp. 72–87).

Burnett, C., & Merchant, G. (2013). Points of view: Reconceptualising literacies through an exploration of adult and child interactions in a virtual world. *Journal of Research in Reading*, online first version.

Campano, G., Ngo, L., Low, D. E., & Jacobs, K. B. (2016). Young children demystifying and remaking the university through critical play. *Journal of Early Childhood Literacy*, *16*(2), 199–227.

Cantrill, C., & Oh, P. (2016). The composition of making. In K. A. Peppler, E. R. Halverson, & Y. B. Kafai (Eds.), *Makeology: Makerspaces as learning environments* (pp. 107–120). New York, NY: Routledge.

Comber, B. (2011). Making space for place-making pedagogies: Stretching normative mandated literacy curriculum. *Contemporary Issues in Early Childhood*, *12*(4), 343–348.

Dewey, J. (1938/1963). *Experience and education*. New York, NY: Collier MacMillan.

Doerr-Stevens, C., Lewis, C., Ingram, D., & Asp, M. (2015). Making the body visible through dramatic and creative play: Critical literacy in neighborhood bridges *Methodologies of embodiment: Inscribing bodies in qualitative research* (pp. 28–52). New York, NY: Routledge.

Dougherty, D. (2012). The maker movement. *Innovations*, *7*(3), 11–14.

Dyson, A. H. (2003). *The brothers and sisters learn to write: Popular literacies in childhood and school cultures*. New York, NY: Teachers College Press.

Fleer, M. (2014). The demands and motives afforded through digital play in early childhood activity settings. *Learning, Culture, and Social Interaction*, *3*(3), 202–209.

Flett, K. (2009). Boys into books: Dragons, wizards and a mother in search of a glass of red… at last, a boys' own bedtime story they actually want to read. *The Guardian*. Retrieved from www.theguardian.com/lifeandstyle/2009/dec/06/kathryn-flett-boys-into-books-dragons.

Halverson, E. R., & Sheridan, K. M. (2014). The maker movement in education. *Harvard Education Review*, *84*(4), 495–504.

Harel, I. E., & Papert, S. E. (1991). *Constructionism*. Norwood, NJ: Ablex.

Hatch, M. (2013). *The maker movement manifesto: Rules for innovation in the new world of crafters, hackers, and tinkerers*. New York, NY: McGraw-Hill.

Hollett, T. (2015). *Remapping learning geographies for youth within and beyond the public library.* Unpublished doctoral dissertation. Vanderbilt University, Nashville, TN.

Honeyford, M. A., & Boyd, K. (2015). Learning through play: Portraits, Photoshop, and visual literacy practices. *Journal of Adolescent and Adult Literacy, 59*(1), 63–73.

Hughes-Decatur, H. (2011). Embodied literacies: Learning to first acknowledge and then read the body in education. *English Teaching: Practice and Critique, 10*(3), 72–89.

Husbye, N. E., & Vander Zanden, S. (2015). Composing film: multimodality and production in elementary classrooms. *Theory into Practice.*

Jenkins, H., Purushotma, R., Clinton, K., Robison, A. J., & Weigel, M. (2009). *Confronting the challenges of participatory culture: Media education for the 21st Century.* Cambridge, MA: MIT Press.

Jones, S. (2013). Literacies in the body. *Journal of Adolescent & Adult Literacy, 56*, 525–529.

King, N. R. (1992). The impact of context on the play of young children. In S. Kessler & B. B. Swadener (Eds.), *Reconceptualizing the early childhood curriculum: Beginning the dialogue* (pp. 43–61). New York, NY: Teachers College Press.

Knobel, M., & Lankshear, C. (2008). Remix: The art and craft of endless hybridization. *Journal of Adolescent & Adult Literacy, 52*(1), 22–33.

Kress, G. (2009). *Multimodality: A social semiotic approach to contemporary communication.* London, UK: Routledge.

Kuby, C. R. (2013). Evoking emotions and unpacking layered histories through young children's illustrations of racial bus segregation. *Journal of Early Childhood Literacy, 13*(2), 271–300.

Kuby, C. R., & Rucker, T. G. (2016). *'Go be a writer': Expanding the curricular boundaries of literacy learning with children.* New York, NY: Teachers College Press.

Leander, K. M. (2002). Locating Latanya: The situated production of identity artifacts in classroom interaction. *Research in the Teaching of English, 37*(2), 198–250.

Leander, K. M., & Boldt, G. M. (2013). Rereading "A pedagogy of multiliteracies": Bodies, texts, and emergence. *Journal of Literacy Research, 45*(1), 22–46.

Leander, K. M., & Rowe, D. W. (2006). Mapping literacy spaces in motion: A rhizomatic analysis of a classroom literacy performance. *Reading Research Quarterly, 41*(4), 428–460.

Leander, K. M., & Sheehy, M. (Eds.). (2004). *Spatializing literacy research and practice.* New York, NY: Peter Lang.

Lewis, C., & Tierney, J.D. (2013). Mobilizing emotion in an urban classroom: Producing identities and transforming signs in a race-related discussion. *Linguistics and Education, 24*(3), 289–304.

Lysaker, J. T., Wheat, J., & Benson, E. (2010). Children's spontaneous play in Writer's Workshop. *Journal of Early Childhood Literacy, 10*(2), 209–229.

Marsh, J. (2005). Ritual, performance and identity construction. In J. Marsh (Ed.), *Popular culture, new media, and digital literacy in early childhood* (pp. 28–50). New York, NY: RoutledgeFalmer.

Medina, C. L., & Perry, M. (2014). Texts, affects, and relations in cultural performance: An embodied analysis of dramatic inquiry. In P. Albers, T. Holbrook, & A. Seely Flint (Eds.), *New methods in literacy research* (pp. 115–132). New York, NY: Routledge.

Medina, C. L., & Wohlwend, K. E. (2014). *Literacy, play, and globalization: Converging imaginaries in children's critical and cultural performances.* New York, NY: Routledge.

Mihailidis, P., & Cohen, J. (2013). Exploring curation as a core competency in digital and media literacy education. *Journal of Interactive Media in Education, 2013*(1).

Mills, K.A. (2010) Filming in progress: New spaces for multimodal designing. *Linguistics and Education, 21*(1), 14–28.

Paley, V. G. (1992). *You can't say you can't play.* Cambridge, MA: Harvard University Press.

Paley, V. G. (1997). *The girl with the brown crayon.* Cambridge, MA: Harvard University Press.

Papert, S. (1980). *Mindstorms.* New York, NY: Basic Books.

Peppler, K. A., Halverson, E. R., & Kafai, Y. B. (Eds.). (2016a). *Makeology: Makerspaces as learning environments* (Vol. 1). New York, NY: Routledge.

Peppler, K. A., Halverson, E. R., & Kafai, Y. B. (Eds.). (2016b). *Makeology: Makers as learners* (Vol. 2). New York, NY: Routledge.

Perry, M., & Medina, C. (2011). Embodiment and performance in pedagogy research: Investigating the possibility of the body in curriculum experience. *Journal of Curriculum Theorizing, 27*(3), 62–75.

Perry, M., & Medina, C. L. (Eds.). (2015). *Methodologies of embodiment: Inscribing bodies in qualitative research.* New York, NY: Routledge.

Pugh, A. J. (2009). *Longing and belonging: Parents, children, and consumer culture.* Berkley: University of California Press.

Ray, K. W., & Cleaveland, L. B. (2004). *About the authors: Writing workshop with our youngest writers.* Portsmouth, NH: Heinemann.

Reed, S. (2011, January 18). DIY movement: Teachers and students as makers. *The Notebook.* Retrieved from http://thenotebook.org/articles/2011/01/18/diy-movement-teachers-and-students-as-makers.

Rowe, D. W., Fitch, J. D., & Bass, A. S. (2003). Toy stories as opportunities for imagination and reflection in writers' workshop. *Language Arts*, *80*(5), 363–74.

Rowsell, J., & Pahl, K. (2007). Sedimented identities in texts: Instances of practice. *Reading Research Quarterly*, *42*(3), 388–404.

Scollon, R. (2001). *Mediated discourse: The nexus of practice*. London, UK: Routledge.

Simpson, A., Walsh, M., & Rowsell, J. (2013). The digital reading path: Researching modes and multidirectionality with iPads. *Literacy*, *47*(3), 123–130.

Smith, A., West-Puckett, S., Cantrill, C., & Zamora, M. (2016). Remix as professional learning: Educators' iterative literacy practice in CLMOOC. *Education Sciences*, *6*(1): 12.

Sutton-Smith, B. (1997). *The ambiguity of play*. Cambridge, MA: Harvard University Press.

Tekinbas, K., Gresalfi, M., Peppler, K., Santo, R. (2014). *Gaming the system: Designing with Gamestar Mechanic*. Cambridge, MA: MIT Press.

Thiel, J. J. (2015). "Bumblebee's in trouble!" Embodied literacies during imaginative superhero play. *Language Arts*, *93*(1), 38.

Wessel Powell, C., Kargin, T., & Wohlwend, K. E. (2016). Enriching and assessing young children's multimodal storytelling. *The Reading Teacher*, *70*(2), 167–178.

Wohlwend, K. E. (2009). Early adopters: Playing new literacies and pretending new technologies in print-centric classrooms. *Journal of Early Childhood Literacy*, *9*(2), 119–143.

Wohlwend, K. E. (2013). Play, literacy, and the converging cultures of childhood. In J. Larson & J. Marsh (Eds.), *The SAGE handbook of early childhood literacy* (2nd ed., pp. 80–95). London, UK: Sage.

Wohlwend, K. E. (2015). Making, remaking, and reimagining the everyday: Play, creativity, and popular media. In J. Rowsell & K. Pahl (Eds.), *Routledge handbook of literacy studies*. London, UK: Routledge.

Wohlwend, K. E., Buchholz, B. A., Wessel-Powell, C., Coggin, L. S., & Husbye, N. E. (2013). *Literacy playshop: New literacies, popular media, and play in the early childhood classroom*. New York, NY: Teachers College Press.

Wohlwend, K. E., Scott, J. A., Yi, J. H., Deliman, A., & Kargin, T. (in press). Hacking toys and remixing media: Integrating maker literacies into early childhood teacher education. In S. Danby, M. Fleer, C. Davidson, & M. Hatzigianni (Eds.), *Digital childhoods: Technologies in children's everyday lives*. Sydney: Springer.

Zembylas, M., & Schutz, P. (2016). *Methodological advances in research on emotion and education*. Switzerland: Springer International Publishing.

# 12
# Digital Geographies

Ty Hollett, Nathan C. Phillips, and Kevin M. Leander

## Relevance

In this chapter, we theorize and explore the production of digital geographies as essential everyday literacies with import for learning. In doing so, we conceptualize literacies as fundamentally social meaning-making practices that include the reading and writing of all kinds of texts, and we see these practices as inevitably mobile. As Leander, Phillips, and Taylor (2010) note in their brief analysis of Heath's (1983) seminal ethnography of literacy and learning in two communities in the Piedmont Carolinas, even literacy practices that we might think of as "local" are run through with crisscrossing cultures, histories, people, texts, practices, and things on the move—and always have been.

While we understand literacies to have always been mobile, more recent developments and technologies have untethered digital literacies in new and emerging ways. What is different about contemporary meaning making and writing practices and what is developing differently through emerging mobile technologies is the possibility for the virtual intertwining with the physical world and with everyday life as people interpret the world and write in the world. Examples of these intertwinings as people interpret the world include (a) geographic information overlayed on city streets through a Global Positioning System (GPS) device or smartphone to support decision-making related to traveling in the world, or (b) geofences that enable notifications on travelers' mobile devices of nearby friends or of historically important buildings while walking through a city. And examples of these intertwinings while writing in the world include (a) recording video and audio of police interactions with citizens, or (b) creating and remixing media on-the-go to be shared with social networks (see Leander & Vasudevan, 2009). We argue that these imbrications of virtual and physical in the reading and writing of the world can be productively theorized as digital geographies and that conceptualizing digital geographies as emerging and essential literacies on the move impacts educators, designers, and researchers in investigating and designing everyday teaching and learning.

Our conceptualization of digital geographies complements contemporary efforts in literacies studies to attend to meaning making on the move and draws from ongoing scholarship in geography, literacy, mobility studies, and media and communication studies. Our intention is to bring these interdisciplinary approaches into conversation to inform digital writing and literacies research and teaching to both support ongoing work and to point to new possibilities. In doing so, we are particularly interested in articulating how digital geographies research can respond to the ways that learners and learning are often constrained to cordoned-off spaces of formal learning in schools.

We first articulate key concepts from across these disciplines as they have informed our research and teaching, turn to examples from current and emerging theory of digital geographies, highlight specific exemplars of writing within digital geographies, and offer a way forward for research, namely through the relationship between writing and place-making.

**Key Concepts: Mobilities and Digital Geographies**

*Mobilities*

We begin with an overarching focus on mobilities, building toward the relationship between mobility and digital geographies. Digital geographies, we will argue, are fundamentally mobile. This mobility, however, depends on moving bodies that sense and feel as they move, especially with various things. In conceptualizing bodies on the move as mobilities, we are not abstracting bodies (Seiler, 2009). Instead, we intend bodies to be understood as human bodies engaged in interactions in the world in which identities including race, gender, sexuality, age, and dis/ability are consequentially read and produced in everyday human interactions that involve feeling, sensing, touching, and moving. We further articulate components of mobilities below.

Emerging approaches to mobility stem from recent shifts in human and cultural geography toward the "new mobilities paradigm" (Hannam, Sheller, & Urry, 2006). Naïve approaches to mobilities assert that everything is on the move and that contemporary culture is one of rapidity and speed. But this mobility occurs at different paces and intensities for different people, having varying impacts and consequences. Within the mobile turn, mobility is "acknowledged as part of the energetic buzz of the everyday (even while banal, or humdrum, or even stilled) and seen as a set of highly meaningful social practices that make up social, cultural, and political life" (Adey, Bissell, Hannam, Merriman, & Sheller, 2014, p. 3). In studying social life as mobilities, geographers, historians, and anthropologist shifted from fixing their work on "the field" to following their work along "routes" and tracing sets of relations across sites. Thus the mobilities paradigm emphasizes that all places are tied together in, at least, thin networks of connections. In the end, the new mobilities paradigm challenges social science research that is a-mobile and abstracted from moving, feeling, racialized bodies—both theoretically and methodologically. It seeks out fluidity as opposed to fixed, contained territories.

Mobilities also underscore the phenomenological experience of the moving, sensing human body. This entails attention to the corporeal engagement with other bodies and technologies, practices of movement (e.g., biking, walking), events of movement (e.g., commuting, sitting in traffic), and implications for movement (e.g., racialized practices of mobility; Nicholson & Sheller, 2016). A number of studies have sought to understand how bodies engage with and actively move through their surroundings, ranging from kinesthetic sensation produced by human-bike-road (Spinney, 2006) to the "micro-mobilities" of dancers, rock climbers, and walkers (Fincham, McGuinness, & Murray, 2010).

The new mobilities paradigm has undergone recent refinement. Cresswell (2010), for instance, calls out the name itself, recognizing that it builds up false dichotomies (new/old, mobile/immobile). In further differentiating mobility from movement, he provides additional nuance to mobility, arguing that "mobility involves a fragile entanglement of physical movement, representations, and practices" (p. 19). Physical movement, he clarifies, denotes the physical act of moving from one location to another; representations of movement give that movement a shared meaning (e.g., threatening, adventure); practices signal the embodied act of mobility that it can feel different from one day, or even one hour, to the next. Importantly, mobilities are produced by, and productive of, power (Cresswell, 2016).

## Digital Geographies

Mobility studies have informed interdisciplinary studies of interpenetrating digital and physical spheres. In the following, we review some of these studies, in order to develop a more holistic understanding of the imbricated—simultaneously digital and physical—nature of digital geographies and implications for reading and writing across digital geographies. Importantly, many of these studies challenge how cyberspace was originally formulated as an alternative to the physical world, a "consensual hallucination" that existed in the mind (Gibson, 1984, p. 69). This early conception, from Gibson's (1984) novel *Neuromancer*, has fed the public tendency to divorce the digital from the physical and to remove it from the material world as something into which one can escape. To enter cyberspace, Case, the novel's protagonist, "jacks into" a computer via neural implants, leaving his body and entering the world of information. This "hallucination," in part, stems from the invisible nature of the infrastructure, which supports the so-called cyberspace: the fiber-optic lines in ceilings, the hidden server centers, the underwater cables. This kind of invisibility has led to the "erroneous assumption that cyberspace is somehow immaterial, aspatial, and nongeographic" (Zook, Dodge, Aoyama, & Townsend, 2004, p. 158).

There is an evolving history of scholarship and theory, however, that views cyberspace as an "additional layer of function and access that maps onto physical space" (Zook & Graham, 2007, p. 467). Wakeford (1999), for instance, described the "overlapping set of material and imaginary geographies which include, but are not restricted to, online experiences" (p. 180). Mitchell (1995), in describing his "city of bits," envisioned code, the digital, to be just as important to physical spaces as bricks and mortar, as road and sidewalks. Both Wakeford and Mitchell, among others, provide early arguments for the inextricable nature of the digital and physical. Cyberspace and place are "intricately connected in a dynamic and mutually constitutive process" (Zook & Graham, 2007, p. 468).

A more recent line of thought focuses on the digital palimpsesting of physical locations (Graham & Zook, 2011). It considers how the digital adds a new layer to an understanding of place. As opposed to emphasizing how people make place online, it details how they use online activity to layer digital material over the physical world. By doing so, these digital representations of physical places shape not only how we interpret but also how we interact and write with the world.

Those early years of the Internet—concerned with the making of physical locations for people to "jack in" to digital arenas—have given way to or augmented realities. Graham, Zook, and Boulton (2013) move beyond describing how the digital mediates our interactions with space and toward how geographically referenced, or geo-located, content (images, text, video) shape our relationships with lived geographies. For them, the "visual, interactive, real-time nature of digital augmentations offer a fundamentally new way of interacting with, moving through, and enacting place" (p. 2). Geospatial content, though, is decentralized: User-generated data—Wikipedia articles, Twitter posts, YouTube videos—contribute to representations of place. In the following, we build from this line of thought, bringing together this focus on digital augmentations of the world with how people read and write it—especially with mobile bodies and mobile technologies.

### Digital Geographies, Literacies, and Writing

In an era of primarily sedentary technologies, Leander (2008) nudged literacy research toward the study of digital geographies, arguing that "the time for thinking about the Internet and digital literacies as revolutionary has passed" (p. 33). He questioned how literacy scholars think about the everyday, calling for an end to the bifurcation of digital and physical activity. Overall, Leander (2008) questioned the employment of traditional ethnographic methods in online spaces, aiming to build a methodological approach that assumes "that people routinely build connections to Internet-related practices and sites and myriad offline practices and sites" (p. 36), that moved "ethnography from a place-bound practice to a moving, traveling practice" (Leander & McKim, 2003, p. 237). Still, this conceptualization occurred in a technological era in which users built those connections from sedentary positions: from an Internet café or from home, for instance. Interpreting, engaging, and writing on the Internet, in this case, was certainly built across space-time, but that digital physical binary was still present. This, we argue, is the difference between networking literacy across digital-physical space-time and experiencing literacies and writing within digital geographies.

Literacy research has explored hybrid digital and physical spaces in diverse ways. Across multiple analyses, Vasudevan (e.g., Leander & Vasudevan, 2009; Vasudevan, 2010) has explored the literacies, learning, and digitally mediated lives of "court-involved" youth, focusing on the "landscape of multimodal literacies and digital practices involved in composing of meaning and diverse texts for a variety of purposes" (Vasudevan, 2010, p. 62). Vasudevan explicitly theorizes the productions of these multimodal textual landscapes, produced by young people moving throughout their lives "through the confluence of new communicative practices and available media technologies" (p. 62) as digital geographies. For Vasudevan, digital geographies conceptually highlight textual production and literacies practices that cross online and physical spaces.

Digital geographies signal an important shift from *crossing* to *imbrication*. Burnett and Merchant (2014), for example, drew attention to the relationship between the on- and offline in a classroom, specifically describing literacies that occur from within and outside of a virtual world. They employed a connective ethnographic approach to explore the youth literacy interaction that takes place within the virtual world, seeking multiple perspectives of literacy events (although they trouble that term), telling stories from inside the classroom as well as from inside the virtual world. To do so, they reflected on understandings of "fractional objects" to understand these layered activities. As Law (2004) details, fractional objects are "phenomena that occupy more than one dimension but less than two" (Burnett & Merchant, 2014, p. 43). Burnett and Merchant (2014) build from this language: "Incidents, individuals, objects or places are not completely in either the material or virtual world, and nor do they jump between" (p. 43). Instead, they argue, scholars can understand digital literacy events "in terms of a multiplicity that 'implies that different realities overlap and interface with one another. Their relations, partially co-ordinated, are complex and messy' (Law, 2004, p. 61)" (Burnett & Merchant, 2014, p. 43).

Moreover, research within the literacy community has explicitly explored the digital geographies affiliated with the pervasive computing paradigm. Vasudevan (2010) highlighted the compositional capabilities of mobile devices that youth embrace as they move through their worlds. She detailed the use of a PlayStation Portable (PSP) by one youth, Joey, as he created a multimedia narrative. Vasudevan attended, in particular, to how Joey's multimedia narrative took shape as he moved with the device. He was able to compose whenever—and wherever—he wanted: "while riding the subway, at the park, at home, attending the digital media elective" (p. 71). The portability of the device—the fact that it moved with Joey—allowed him to present a self that was variegated, one that was dynamic and that changed from place-to-place.

Buck's (2012) inquiry into Ronnie's digital literacy practices on social networking sites was also rife with mobility. Ronnie used his mobile device to document—and share—artifacts across time and space. Of Ronnie's movement with his mobile device, Buck writes: "On his walk to class, Ronnie takes a picture of some graffiti in front of a local restaurant and sends it to Twitter" (p. 9). Later, Ronnie used his device to film a twelve-second video of a squirt gun fight with friends and posted it to multiple social networks. Ronnie often composed on the move, frequently tweeting his "thoughts and musings on his way to class" (p. 16). When writing on the move via social media, he painted a temporal and spatial portrait of his day for his followers, making his audience aware of his location as he moved from place-to-place.

Similarly, Ehret and Hollett (2013) described Yvette and Adela's experiences of moving—and writing—with mobile devices in a school setting. They detailed how movement affected Yvette and Adela's meaning making as well as their experiences of and connections to people, places, and things in their school. Specifically, they focused on how Yvette and Adela (re-)placed school through the countermobilities, or how they moved against the typical mobility scripts associated with school.

### Exemplars of Writing within Digital Geographies: Layering and Augmenting Place

The following sections expand this focus on writing—with mobile bodies—by describing two exemplars of the experience of writing within digital geographies. The first focuses on the emergence of digital representations of physical places—new ways of, quite literally, "reading and writing aspects of the world that are important to participants" (Knobel & Lankshear, 2003/2011, p. 262) in these digital-physical activities. This section describes what we refer to as layering place as it explores digital mapping practices within online communities and how they are emblematic of writing within digital geographies. The second section focuses on the reading—or augmentation—of those physical locations through digital means and the writing that follows. It focuses on augmented reality installations and activities. We refer to this as augmenting place.

### Layering Place

The digital layering of place stems from three successive moments in the development of Internet practices and technologies as described by Graham et al. (2013, pp. 465–466): (a) the move toward mobile devices and the mobile web, (b) the growth of authorship via Web 2.0, and (c) the emergence of the geospatial web, or the geo-coding of web content to specific parts of the Earth. The shift from Web 1.0 to Web 2.0 allowed users to begin to reimagine, or even reexperience, physical places with digital material. Two ways in which this (re)imagining occurs today are through the practice of neogeography and volunteered geographic information (VGI). The following subsections, then, detail new emerging participatory practices that are influencing the relationship between people and places through digital/physical interaction. They act as exemplars of literacies and writing experiences within digital geographies, how digital interpretation and production practices are intricately tied with physical locations, interlocking the physical and the digital in place.

#### NEOGEOGRAPHY

Neogeography refers to techniques, practices, and tools typically reserved for geographers but employed by nonprofessionals (Turner, 2006). Hudson-Smith and Crooks (2008) describe neogeography as:

> a diverse set of practices that operate outside of or alongside…the practice of professional geographers. Rather than making claims on scientific standards, methodologies of neogeography tend toward the intuitive, expressive, personal, absurd, and/or artistic, but may just be idiosyncratic applications of 'real' geographic techniques.
>
> (p. 3)

Neogeography blurs "the distinctions between producer, communicator, and consumer of geographic information" (Goodchild, 2009, p. 82). The practice of neogeography, as Dodge and Kitchin (2013) label it, is an act of prosumption. Prosumption is a form of consumption/production in which users take part in both the creation and subsequent use of service. People, for instance, no longer purchase premade maps; rather, they "prosume"—they produce and consume their own maps. They access free mapping tools and customize maps for their own purposes: They shape the "representational 'look' of the map interface, undertake elements of spatial analysis, and, crucially, add to and edit the actual base cartographic information" (p. 35). While cartographic prosumption, though, necessitates a variety of complex literacy practices—setting the frame of their map, changing the scale, content, legend, orientation, and color scheme—it also hints at the embodied, sensed account of literacy that we affiliate with writing within digital geographies.

One of the creators of an early mapping website, Platial.com, illustrates the impetus for taking part in such mapping practices. In this instance, she describes making maps for guests visiting in Amsterdam:

> We made them maps, like everyone does, of the basic neighborhood amenities. If our guests wanted to go do some errands, it's handy to have a map with more than just museums and shopping malls on it. There was the grocery store, the post office, the good bakery and the locals' lunch spot, plus the place to watch the barges come around the canal, the place where the blue heron hangs out on the parked cars and the place not to lock up the bikes…we ended up with a kitchen drawer stuff full of these notes. It was our collection of Places…
>
> (Graham, 2010, p. 425)

In this case, the map producer has performed various forms of embodied meaning making in order to develop her map for a consumer: She plots based on, perhaps, the taste and aesthetic of the bakery, the views of barges that are most pleasing, what she considers to be safe areas for bikes. As such, the map itself depends upon her body-based accounts and her reading of the world and translation of it into visual representation.

But neogeographic practices are not solely contained to casual map-making. More recently, neogeographic practices have been applied to create mash-ups of data and maps, particularly during times of crisis (Liu & Palen, 2010). Crisis mash-ups aggregate real-time news from social media sites, like Twitter, and index them to their originating geographic location on a map. Often, the original source for this information is a user with a mobile device, experiencing an event in real time (e.g., a natural disaster). Crisis maps depend upon bodies-in-world. They depend upon sensed, felt places, which become represented via, for example, tweets and geographic coordinates. Those sensed-movements are then distributed to a geographically distant actor who manages the data, wrestling with the information as it pours in, creating the map that further shapes how others move through and interact within a physical space.

The greatest contributing factor to the development of neogeographic practices has been the significant adoption of GPS by consumers. GPS has enabled nonprofessional geographers to create spatial data. The portability of GPS technology, now embedded in mobile devices, has encouraged forms of mapping that are unique to individuals; it has transformed "everyday movements into creative expressions" (Parks, 2001, p. 220) that users can now share with others. Those who provide this place-based information volunteer their geographic information, making it available for others to visualize, use, and mash-up.

### VOLUNTEERED GEOGRAPHIC INFORMATION

If the term neogeography denotes how interactive mapping software makes cartographic production practices (i.e., map writing) available to new actors, then VGI denotes the data itself, how data are generated and used by producers and consumers as part of everyday practices of digital writing. As Elwood (2008) writes of VGI: "New forms of digital spatial data are created through a growing proportion of our daily activities, such as using electronic payment cards to board a bus whose location is tracked by the public transit agency, or using GPS-enabled cell phones that trace our location and movements throughout the day" (p. 133). The use of new technologies—ranging from Google Maps to Wikimapia to our own GPS-enabled smartphones—has led to new volunteered digital spatial data that detail the observations, geographic knowledge, physical location of people, and more.

Mobile bodies feel and sense their surroundings, generating and subsequently mapping data as they move. Wikimapia, for example, and the data added to it is an exemplar of VGI (Figure 12.1). Wikimapia allows users to click any portion of the Earth's service, evidenced below in Nashville, Tennessee, in the US, and provides a description of it. Other users can edit entries; volunteer reviewers moderate entries, checking for accuracy and authenticity. Entries range in details—some including hyperlinks to more information, others, like a description of the water treatment facility in Nashville, noting that the area "smells bad"—an account dictated by the sensed, embodied, even affective, experience in a specific physical location.

Another form of VGI, OpenStreetMap (OSM; Figure 12.2), a collaborative mapping project, allows users to add, edit, and correct geographic data. Contributors to OpenStreetMap "use aerial imagery, GPS devices, and low-tech field maps to verify that OSM is accurate and up to date" (OpenStreetMap, para. 1). The image below depicts a prominent building in Nashville and its surrounding area. A user could conceivably add any of the features on the left side to the map—regardless of their veracity.

As an exemplar of writing within digital geographies, the layering of place is intricately bound within both new technologies and new activities. Unlike current conceptions of new literacies (i.e., participatory, distributed, cyberspatial), these practices are intricately tied to the physical world, to one's locality. Operations like OSM and Wikimapia—as an extension of current conception of new literacies—call for "interesting new constellations or 'batteries' of ways of reading and writing in order to achieve one's purposes" (Knobel & Lankshear, 2003/2011, p. 264) as a neogeographer. For example, OpenStreetMap users not only sense the world around them, recognizing new roads,

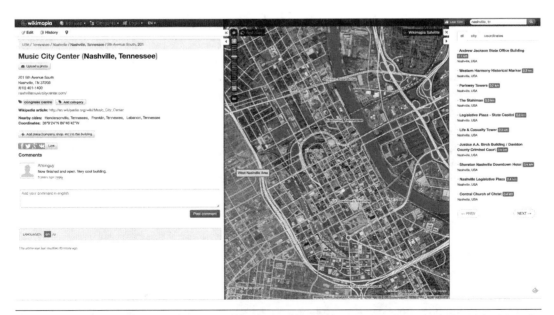

**Figure 12.1** An example of Wikimapia. Registered users can edit the map, adding comments, resizing areas, and add and delete information over time

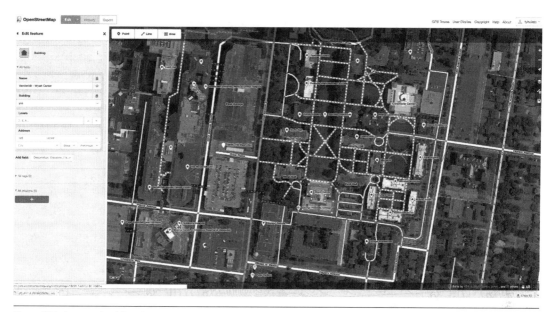

**Figure 12.2** An example of OpenStreetMap, an ongoing project to provide the most accurate, usable maps rather than comments about locations

one-way streets, and hazardous areas but also upload that data—either from on-the-ground experience or GPS track data—to the OSM server. Members of the community, then, might defend changes they made to the map in a forum or describe them in a blog post. For instance, one contributor, with the handle "numbfew," described his recent edits to the map in an OSM-affiliated blog post (numbfew, 2013). He detailed the changes made, many of which depended upon his sense-movement through the physical/digital world, including the following:

- Added footpaths in local suburb and surroundings (Weston Creek);
- Added some green spaces;
- Minor fixes of redaction things when it happened.
- Parliamentary Triangle. Including memorials in Kings Park/Commonwealth Park.

Numbfew's edits are based upon his embodied, felt-experience—and subsequent construction—of place. At the same time, numbfew's edits further contributed to the experience of place for others. By layering digital information onto the map, he shaped how other users would navigate—and sense—their surrounding environment. The digital and physical recursively shape one another. OSM and other mapping environments demand new forms of reading and writing the world—a new ethos that goes beyond the digital media space afforded by previous, sedentary technologies. Within digital geographies, digital literacy practices are never solely digital—they are a complex interaction between the digital and the physical.

*Augmenting Place*

In this section, we detail literacies and writing practices affiliated with digital geographies that stem from locative media initiatives. With continually evolving advances in mobile technology, location, as Gordon and de Souza e Silva (2011) argue, sets the "conditions for interaction and provides the context from which information is interpreted and used" (p. 12). Location-based technologies (e.g., WiFi, GPS, bluetooth) and locative media—mobile devices with the ability to recognize location—help users shape, better understand, and describe experiences of place. Aside from consumer-based applications like Four Square and Yelp, users take can part in location-based narratives, games, and art pieces that depend upon digital interaction with urban spaces. In the following, we survey locative media experiences as exemplars of literacies and writing practices in digital geographies.

Locative media have also allowed users to take part in forms of urban annotation or public authoring. *34 North, 118 West* (http://34n118w.net) was billed as the first locative media project to fuse location and mobile computing. Given a GPS-enabled tablet computer and headphones, participants maneuvered themselves through an area pre-configured with location-driven digital artifacts. As in other augmented reality experiences (e.g. Facer, Furlong, Furlong, & Sutherland, 2004), walking over hotspots would trigger pieces of the narrative—in this case, the history of the railroad industry in Los Angeles. Actors spoke and described events that occurred during that time relating to the physical location. By participants' movement through the urban landscape, "lost versions" of the city were recovered (Hight, 2003).

Similarly, Berry and Goodwin's (2013) "Poetry 4 U Project" links location and verse. Using GPS and other location-based technologies, participants pinned digital poems to physical locations using their mobile devices. Seeking new relationships between the "virtual imagined city and the geographic city" (p. 916), the project questioned how digital poetry could become a part of the cityscape. Acknowledging literature that argues that mobile devices "push a specific place into the background of perceptions" (p. 914), the project sought to further enhance a reader—and poet's—sense of place. The creators aligned this project with other professional communities of practice for writers (e.g., peer reviewed outlets for poets) in hopes that it would encourage writing that was both a part of the "space of social flows as well as a geographical place" (p. 927).

Mobile storytelling exploration seeks to establish community in public spaces, rather than the isolation often attached to mobile devices. One project, called *[Murmur]* (n.d.), seeks to retell community histories based on certain locations. [Murmur] locations are designated by green, ear-shaped signs that have a specific phone number on them. Passers-by can then call the number to hear the recorded stories. Through their recordings, community members contribute to "site-specific histories of the cities" (Farman, 2012, p. 117). A final example, Vozmob (n.d.), is a "platform for immigrant and/or low-wage workers in Los Angeles to create stories about their lives and communities directly from cell phones" (Vozmob, n.d., para. 1). The intention of Vozmob is to mobilize the highly mobile, to give them a voice and a space for it to be heard. Posts range from pictures and text about the police, to cultural events, to demonstrations and street performances.

Locative media, neogeography, and VGI are closely related. Where neogeographic practices leverage VGI for mapping purposes, locative media projects leverage that information for narrative purposes. Locative media, like neogeography, calls for new reading and writing practices. They are projects that depend upon the interaction of the digital and the physical. Furthermore, for participants, locative media projects necessitate not only the reading of the word but also the reading of the physical world. They depend on mobility through the world, on users' simultaneous navigation of representations of the world through maps as well as their own embodied experience of the world. In this section, the "new technical stuff" of mobile devices engender "new ethos stuff" of locative media (Lankshear & Knobel, 2007, pp. 7–9). The reading and writing of texts in place, however, are fully dependent upon the context in which they are experienced. Such experiences, then, are much less like the literacy events with which literacy scholars are most familiar, and more akin to place-events (Massey, 2005), or "intensities of activity and presence, as experienced by embodied human subjects, from specific subjectivities" (Pink, 2011, p. 349).

**Forward Thinking: Place, Writing, and Digital Geographies**

In thinking about the relationships among place, digital geographies, and writing, we are most drawn to studies of place-making as a way forward. The digital lives of contemporary youth exist in neither physical nor digital space; rather, youth are mobile—and mobilized—within digital geographies. We are particularly drawn to Massey's (2005) take on place as being "throwntogether," as consisting of diverse stories or "bundles." Arriving in a new place, she writes, means:

> joining up with, somehow linking into, the collection of interwoven stories of which that place is made. Arriving at the office, collecting the post, picking up the thread of discussions, remembering to ask how that meeting went last night, noting gratefully that your room's been cleared. Picking up the threads and weaving them into a more coherent feeling of being 'here,' 'now.'
> (p. 119)

This "joining up with," this "linking into," describes the agentive act of place-making. People "bundle" disparate space-times—those near and far—and integrate them into place. They make place. In doing so, they reference and (re)configure "the many places that they participate in; the place-bundles are socially negotiated, constantly changing and contingent" (Pierce, Martin, & Murphy, 2011, p. 58). Pierce et al. (2011) particularly emphasize place-making as "bundling." Bundling, they write, occurs through both conscious and unconscious acts. People select, or choose, the "raw materials, or elements, which comprise places in their experiences" (p. 58). If Massey describes place as a "constellation of on-going trajectories" (2005, p. 92), then this act of choice is "akin to identifying constellations among the stars of the night sky" (Pierce et al., 2011, p. 59).

De Certeau (1984) also offers useful insights into how people make place. He details the "procedures of everyday creativity" (p. xiv) people perform, especially as they move across the grid of the city. De Certeau emphasizes people's "ways of operating" in order to acknowledge, and even conform to power, "only in order to evade it." People subvert these powerful structures—and their strategic forms of control—through "tactics." Tactics, he writes, "make use of the cracks that particular conjunctions open in the surveillance of the proprietary powers. It poaches them. It creates surprises in them. It can be where it is least expected" (p. 37). People deploy these tactics "to suit their own interests and their own rules" (p. xiv).

Mobility—either across space, time, or scale—is critical to place-making. For a number of theorists, the physical, embodied movement of the human body through space begins to produce place: "Their intertwined paths," de Certeau (1984) writes, "give their shape to spaces" (p. 97). And it is through the movement from one space to another that people "weave places together." This weaving, he notes, is akin to storytelling, part of the "rhetoric of walking," which leads to place-making. Through "skips" and "leaps," the walker carves out "gaps in the spatial continuum," amplifying the meaningful places among the space of the ordered grid: a "less," de Certeau writes, is created from more; the "whole" is miniaturized.

In terms of literacies, we wonder how writers place-make through the imbrication of the digital and physical. How do writers make place as they move through it? In what way do traces of writing, digitally sedimented in place, impact how others are mobilized? Who becomes integrated into ones' experience of place? In what ways do writers speak back to or subvert powerful authorities? How might they embed data into place for others to access?

We are especially interested in place-making as a response to structural and institutional racism that has perpetuated what Martin (2011) has called "white institutional space" in schools and elsewhere. While digital geographies, like geographies of all kinds, can and do perpetuate structural and institutional racism, place-making has the potential to empower learners to respond and remake place. We are interested in how writers' mobilities across digital geographies are impeded and constrained by aspects of identities including age, race, gender, sexuality, and dis/ability and how writers might speak back, push back, move back against these constraints.

However, in considering the possibilities of pushing back against constraints, we want to also recognize that for racialized bodies on the move in the world, negotiating digital geographies involves not necessarily possibilities for movements against constraints but the realities of those constraints as dangerous, terrifying, and potentially life threatening. As an example, consider not only how people can read and write the world on the move while engaging in a widely popular augmented reality application like *Pokémon Go*, but also how the very bodies of people/players/learners on the move are read and written by others. The mobile game *Pokémon Go*, which demands one's movement through space with mobile device in hand, encourages players to move through their local surrounds in order to increasingly capture more Pokémon—virtual creatures that can be found while moving through the physical landscape. Blogger Omari Akil, an African American man, wrote about his experience of playing *Pokémon Go*—and moving—as a Black male in the US in 2016:

> I spent less than 20 minutes outside. Five of those minutes were spent enjoying the game. One of those minutes I spent trying to look as pleasant and nonthreatening as possible as I walked past a somewhat visibly disturbed white woman on her way to the bus stop. I spent the other 14 minutes being distracted from the game by thoughts of the countless Black Men who have had the police called on them because they looked "suspicious" or wondering what a second amendment exercising individual might do if I walked past their window a 3rd or 4th time in search of a Jigglypuff.
>
> (Akil, 2016, n.p.)

While place-making certainly provides opportunities for writers to empower learners to respond and remake place, the opportunity to do so for all writers is systemically constrained. Echoing Akil's experience, Black mobilities "in the context of the United States need to be interpreted contextually" (Cresswell, 2016, p. 21). Whiteness, Cresswell continues, has primarily depended on the privilege of mobility. The pathologization of, especially, Black male bodies "underlines forms of white privilege as white bodies remain (relatively) less likely to be stopped, penalized, rerouted, slowed down, or moved on" (p. 22). This privilege of White mobility runs in stark contrast to deep history of mobilities—and immobilities—that have been forced upon Black bodies.

In the end, and to bring these questions into contact with Massey and de Certeau, respectively, we wonder how youths' literacies and writing practices enable them to "make a here, now" for themselves, how they make a smaller "less," from, what can be, an overwhelming "whole." And we wonder how we as teachers, researchers, and designers can support, empower, guide, mentor, teach, and love in ways that recognize and respond both to the promise of contemporary digital geographies and to long-standing inequities that restrict who can move, where they can move, how they can move, at what speed they can move, with what things they can move, and at what time they can move across digital geographies.

## References

Adey, P., Bissell, D., Hannam, K., Merriman, P., & Sheller, M. (2013). Introduction. In P. Adey, D. Bissel, K. Hannam, P. Merriman, & M. Sheller (Eds.), *The Routledge handbook of mobilities* (pp. 1–20). New York, NY: Routledge.

Akil, O. (2016). Warning: Pokemon GO is a Death Sentence if you are a Black Man. Mobile Lifestyle. *Medium*. Retrieved from https://medium.com/mobile-lifestyle/warning-pokemon-go-is-a-death-sentence-if-you-are-a-black-man-acacb4bdae7f#.9gb2i1j3b.

Berry, M., & Goodwin, O. (2013). Poetry 4 U: Pinning poems under/over/through the streets. *New Media & Society, 15*(6), 909–929.
Buck, A. (2012). Examining digital literacy practices on social network sites. *Research in the Teaching of English, 47*(1), 9–38.
Burnett, C., & Merchant, G. (2014). Points of view: Reconceptualising literacies through an exploration of adult and child interactions in a virtual world. *Journal of Research in Reading, 37*(1), 36–50.
Cresswell, T. (2010). Towards a politics of mobility. *Environment and Planning D: Society and Space, 28*(1), 17–31.
Cresswell, T. (2016). Black moves: Moments in the history of African-American masculine mobilities. *Transfers, 6*(1), 12–25.
Dodge, M., & Kitchin, R. (2013). Crowdsourced cartography: Mapping experience and knowledge. *Environment and Planning A, 45*(1), 19–36.
de Certeau, M. (1984). *The practice of everyday life* (S. F. Rendall, Trans.). Los Angeles: University of California Press.
Ehret, C., & Hollett, T. (2013). (Re)placing school: Middle school students' countermobilities while composing with iPods. *Journal of Adolescent & Adult Literacy, 57*(2), 110–119.
Elwood, S. (2008). Volunteered geographic information: Key questions, concepts and methods to guide emerging research and practice. *GeoJournal, 72*, 133–135.
Facer, K., Furlong, J., Furlong, R., & Sutherland, R. (2003). *Screenplay: Children and computing in the home.* New York, NY: Routledge.
Farman, J. (2012). *Mobile interface theory: Embodied space and locative media.* New York, NY: Routledge.
Fincham, B., McGuinness, M., & Murray, L. (2010). *Mobile methodologies.* Farnham, UK: Ashgate.
Gibson, W. (1984). *Neuromancer.* New York, NY: Ace Trade.
Goodchild, M. (2009). NeoGeography and the nature of geographic expertise. *Journal of Location Based Services, 3*(2), 82–96.
Gordon, E., & de Souza e Silva, A. (2011). *Net locality: Why location matters in a networked world.* Malden, MA: Wiley-Blackwell.
Graham, M. (2010). Neogeography and the palimpsests of place: Web 2.0 and the construction of a virtual earth. *Tijdschrift voor economische en sociale geografie, 101*(4), 422–436.
Graham, M. (2013). Geography/internet: Ethereal alternate dimensions of cyberspace or grounded augmented realities? *The Geographical Journal, 179*(2), 177–182.
Graham, M., & Zook, M. (2011). Visualizing global cyberscapes: Mapping user-generated placemarks. *Journal of Urban Technology, 18*(1), 115–132.
Graham, M., & Zook, M. (2013). Augmented realities and uneven geographies: exploring the geolinguistic contours of the web. *Environment and Planning A, 45*(1), 77–99.
Graham, M., Zook, M., & Boulton, A. (2013). Augmented reality in urban places: Contested content and the duplicity of code. *Transactions of the Institute of British Geographers, 38*(3), 464–479.
Hannam, K., Sheller, M., & Urry, J. (2006). Editorial: Mobilities, immobilities and moorings. *Mobilities, 1*(1), 1–22.
Heath, S. B. (1983). *Ways with words: Language, life, and work in communities and classrooms.* New York, NY: Cambridge University Press.
Hight, J. (2003). Narrative archaeology. Retrieved from www.neme.org/texts/narrative-archaeology.
Hudson-Smith, A., & Crooks, A. (2008). The renaissance of geographic information: Neogeography, gaming and second life. *Centre for Advanced Spatial Analysis: Working Papers Series.* Retrieved from http://discovery.ucl.ac.uk/178942/1/PDF_142.pdf.
Knobel, M., & Lankshear, C. (2003/2011). The ratings game: From eBay to plastic. In *Literacies: Social cultural and historical perspectives* (pp. 261–284). New York, NY: Peter Lang.
Lankshear, C., & Knobel, M. (2007). Sampling "the new" in new literacies. In M. Knobel & C. Lankshear (Eds.), *A new literacies sampler* (pp. 1–24). New York, NY: Peter Lang.
Law, J. (2004). *After method: Mess in social science research.* London, UK: Routledge.
Leander, K. (2008). Toward a connective ethnography of online/offline literacy networks. In J. Coiro, M. Knobel, C. Lankshear, & D. Leu (Eds.), *Handbook of research on new literacies* (pp. 33–65). New York, NY: Lawrence Erlbaum Associates.
Leander, K. M., & McKim, K. K. (2003). Tracing the everyday 'sitings' of adolescents on the internet: A strategic adaptation of ethnography across online and offline spaces. *Education, Communication & Information, 3*(2), 211–240.
Leander, K. M., Phillips, N. C., & Taylor, K. H. (2010). The changing social spaces of learning: Mapping new mobilities. *Review of Research in Education, 34*(1), 329–394. Retrieved from http://rre.sagepub.com/content/34/1/329.short.
Leander, K. M., & Vasudevan, L. (2009). Multimodality and mobile culture. In C. Jewitt (Ed.), *The Routledge handbook of multimodal analysis* (pp. 127–139). New York, NY: Routledge.
Liu, S. B., & Palen, L. (2010). The new cartographers: Crisis map mashups and the emergence of neogeographic practice. *Cartography and Geographic Information Science, 37*(1), 69–90.
Martin, D. B. (2011). What does quality mean in the context of white institutional space? In B. Atweh, M. Graven, W. Secada, & P. Valero (Eds.), *Mapping equity and quality in mathematics education* (pp. 437–450). London, UK: Springer.
Massey, D. (2005). *For space.* Thousand Oaks, CA: SAGE.
Mitchell, W. (1995). *City of bits: Space, place, and the infobahn.* Cambridge, MA: MIT Press.

[Murmur]. (n.d.). About [murmur]. Retrieved from http://murmurtoronto.ca/about.php.

Nicholson, J. A., & Sheller, M. (2016). Race and the politics of mobility: Introduction. *Transfers, 6*(1), 4–11.

numbfew. (2013, May 14). Incomplete list of edits [Web log post]. Retrieved from http://89-16-162-21.no-reverse-dns-set.bytemark.co.uk/user/numbfew/diary/19240.

OpenStreetMap. (n.d.). About. Retrieved from www.openstreetmap.org/about.

Parks, L. (2001). Plotting the personal: Global positioning satellites and interactive media. *Ecumene, 8*(2), 209–222.

Pierce, J., Martin, D. G., & Murphy, J. T. (2011). Relational place-making: the networked politics of place. *Transactions of the Institute of Geographers, 36*(1), 54–70.

Pink, S. (2011). From embodiment to emplacement: Re-thinking competing bodies, senses and spatialities. *Sport, Education and Society, 16*(3), 343–355.

Seiler, C. (2009). Mobilizing race, racializing mobility: Writing race into mobility studies. In G. Mom, G. Pirie, & L. Tissot (Eds.), *Mobility in history: The state of the art in the history of transport, traffic and mobility* (pp. 229–233). Neuchâtel, Switzerland: Éditions Alphil–Presses.

Spinney, J. (2006). A place of sense: A kinaesthetic ethnography of cyclists on Mont Ventoux. *Environment and Planning D: Society and Space, 24*, 709–732.

Turner, A. J. (2006). *Introduction to neogeography*. Sebastopol, CA: O'Reilly Media.

Vasudevan, L. (2010). Education remix: New media, literacies, and the emerging digital geographies. *Digital Culture & Education, 2*(1), 62–82.

Vozmob. (n.d.). About vozmob. Retrieved from http://vozmob.net/.

Wakeford, S. (1999). Gender and the landscapes of computing in an Internet café. In M. Crang, P. Crang, & J. May (Eds.), *Virtual geographies: bodies, spaces, and relations* (pp. 178–201). London, NY: Routledge.

Zook, M., Dodge, M., Aoyama, Y., & Townsend, A. (2004). New digital geographies: Information, communication, and place. In S. D. Brunn, S. L. Cutter, & J. W. Harrington, Jr. (Eds.), *Geography and technology* (pp. 155–176). New York, NY: Kluwer.

Zook, M. A., & Graham, M. (2007). Mapping DigiPlace: Geocoded Internet data and the representation of place. *Environment and Planning B: Planning and Design, 34*(3), 466–482.

# 13
# Youths' Global Engagement in Digital Writing Ecologies

Donna E. Alvermann and Bradley Robinson

Although educators often express a general belief that there has been a decline in young people's engagement with reading and writing (Carr, 2010), this claim remains unsubstantiated. In this chapter, we stress the need for taking into account the many complex writing practices that youth between the ages of 12 and 18 exhibit when given access to digital media and sufficient bauds for communicating on the Internet. Inspired by Williams's (2012) and Bakhtin's (1981) play with centrifugal and centripetal forces, we examine the concepts of centripetal and centrifugal *cultural* forces in relation to *ecologies of writing* as a theoretical framework for interpreting and responding to adolescents' global engagement with digital writing and media.

To build this argument, we draw on what Brandt (2014, 2015) calls *deep writing* in her seven-year research project on mass literacy. As she forcefully argues,

> When it comes to what is new about literacy these days, digital technology tends to capture the attention...but this attention glosses over what may be a more radical—if quieter—transformation, namely, the turn to *writing* as a mass daily experience.
> (Brandt, 2015, p. 3, emphasis added)

She also presents an appealing counter-narrative to Carr's (2010) book on the decline of literacy in the twenty-first century:

> Whatever the fate of deep reading, we are just now entering an era of deep writing, in which more and more people write for prolonged periods of time from inside deeply interactive networks and immersive cognitive states, driven not merely by the orchestration of memory, muscle, language and task but by the effects that writing can have on others and the self.
> (Brandt, 2015, p. 160)

Deep writing resonates with our interest in ecologies of writing. In addition to signaling the interdependence of youth, digital writing, and media worldwide, it has a subversive ring to it that we find interesting. Beyond that, however, it supports our aim, following Dobrin (2012), to disrupt several dominant narratives surrounding traditional composing processes in an effort to make visible some of the tensions and conflicting viewpoints that young people's deep writing can amplify.

Such disruption is necessary, especially given that the field of education and literacy researchers in particular have yet to define comprehensive and sufficiently flexible theories for studying digital writing at its fullest. That said, the situation is not as bleak as one might imagine. By substantively extending Dobrin's (2012) call for a theory of writing ecologies, Saes (2012) has moved the field one step closer to its goal, urging us to rid ourselves of the need to assume writerly intentionality—and thus control of what happens to a written text once it is separated from its author(s). In point of fact, Saes's bid for uncertainty is the watchword in the second of two research studies we highlight in the following section.

**Two Cases of Global Writing Ecologies**

Both Stewart (2014a, 2014b) and Johnson, Bass, and Hicks (2014) underscore respect for diversity in a way that includes and transcends social justice among immigrant youth, and demonstrate the intersectionality and self-positioning of young people engaged in expanding global writing ecologies. In a cross-case analysis of four newly arrived Latino/as in the US, Stewart (2014a, 2014b) documented how they maintained ties with their homeland while simultaneously acclimating to life in a new country. An important part of the acclimation process involved writing. For instance, they wrote back home to let relatives and friends know about the music they were listening to and the videos and television shows they found engaging. Stewart also pointed to examples of writing as a means of translating for newcomers who were not yet sufficiently proficient in English to navigate social media sites, such as Facebook with all its discursive vagaries. Not surprisingly, Alvermann (2011) found in her review of the literature that young people's literate identities, as evidenced by the varied and rich multimodal digital texts they produced and distributed in out-of-school spaces, remained largely unknown to their teachers. Similarly, it could be argued that the majority of student activist projects accomplished by undocumented youths in the Immigrant Rights Movement (Zimmerman, 2012) were but footprints in the sand. Without teachers or other caring adults to guide and respond to newcomers' writings within digitally interactive networks, the writing-based mass literacy that Brandt (2015) envisions will likely not become part of immigrant youths' daily experiences.

In the second example, a notable exception to the literature just cited is an in-school case study conducted by Johnson et al. (2014). It revolved around Mr Hicks, an experienced eleventh-grade English teacher and his students, many of whom were Latino/as who identified as either undocumented or living in mixed-status families. As Mr Hicks and his two coauthors knew all too well, the students and their families had no choice but to learn how to navigate constantly changing state and national policies on immigration. It was, and remains, a situation that created a culture of uncertainty, especially among the undocumented youth who lived in isolated mobile home communities on the outskirts of a small Southern town that housed both the Title I high school they attended and a major research university. Then, and now, the students' undocumented or mixed status has resulted in their being denied access to the hometown university along with the other top two research institutions in the state. Added to these difficulties is the fear of being separated from their families, particularly on days when returning home from school might mean discovering that a parent or substitute adult caretaker had been moved to a temporary holding point for future deportation.

It was within this context and the uncertainties surrounding what happens to an author's intentionality via a written text that Mr Hicks encouraged his students to make use of online social media networks for locating and distributing information on how to apply to colleges and secure financial aid outside their adopted state. In doing so, the Latino/a youth in Mr Hick's classroom used information communication technologies to craft their written messages, including digital storytelling, for the express purpose of becoming activists and advocates of their own educational futures as well as those of others who would follow in the next wave of newcomers.

**Writing Ecologies as Emerging Theory**

Derived from the Greek word οἶκος meaning *home* or *dwelling*, the word *ecology* is particularly well suited for considering the ways in which young people, both in their homes and in their home countries, use digital writing as a means to interact with global issues and global others. A *home* is just that because it is the place to which one returns after moving through the world outside it, suggesting that the very notion of a *home*, and by extension an *ecology*, is shaped by that which lies outside. In other words, one can only know one's home by moving in and around and through the spaces circumscribing it and vice versa. Internet communication technologies have complicated the distinction between home and away from home largely because digital media allow users to explore the world from their homes with a simple tap, click, or touch. Indeed, thanks to Information Communications Technologies (ICTs), one could argue that it is easier to see the inside of the Taj Mahal than the inside of a neighbor's house. Moreover, social media platforms allow users to create virtual homes—how many people have Facebook set as their homepage?—which are of course circumscribed by the virtual spaces lying outside them. The complex proliferation of social media platforms within which individuals, especially young people, interact with each other through deep writing represents a sophisticated network of writing ecologies, of virtual homes and virtual worlds where users explore their relationships with and obligations towards themselves and others.

An ecological theory of writing as defined in this chapter focuses attention on interdependencies among youth, digital media, and writing. Although these linked variables have constituted a recurrent theme in the field of education for the past three decades or slightly more (Barton, 2007; Barton, Hamilton, & Ivanic, 2000; Gee, 1990; Heath, 1983; Kress, 1997; Luke & Freebody, 1997; Scribner & Cole, 1981; Street, 1984, 1995; Tierney & Shanahan, 1991), it would be a stretch to claim that a Kuhnian paradigm shift (Kuhn, 1970) has occurred in the way writing is conceived, taught, and tested in schools today, especially in the North American context.

Writing prior to Brandt's (2015) well-argued claim of the rise of writing, Boggs and Alvermann (2012) proposed elsewhere that the field's sustained interest in ecologies of literacy might be supported to some degree by Johnson's (2010) concept of "private paradigm shifts" (p. 59). With that as a possibility, Boggs and Alvermann explained how a series of private shifts could potentially have occurred, which the field is only now noticing. Almost as if a critical mass of literacy educators, some working alone but more often in groups found openings in the paradigm, inched their way through, effectively upended the presuppositions, unexamined assumptions, and personal interests that had kept the older paradigm in play. Using ecology as a framework for thinking about writing invites a brand of so-called theoretical anarchism (Feyerabend, 1975) that seems well suited to Dobrin's (2012) and Saes's (2012) calls for questioning worn out assumptions about writing and then moving on.

The possibility of writing ecologies targeting certain aspects of deep writing by mediating young people's digital media practices is promising in that it allows for flexibility in theorizing. It also adds credence to a brand of theoretical anarchism that "adjusts to ecological relations among literacy practices [and] ensures that what becomes dominant is not one particular scale setting, but ideas that gain consensus, whether in the form of a private paradigm shift or humoring one another" (Boggs & Alvermann, 2012, p. 206). In short, the goal becomes one of finding ways to negotiate settings in which deep writing—as viewed by Brandt (2015) in her analysis of sixty workaday adult writers and thirty writing-intensive young people (ranging in age from 15 to 25)—can add a fresh twist in interpreting the latest shifts in mass literacy, the discourses supporting that shift, and its upshots for researchers and teachers of writing.

## Methodological Considerations

As explained elsewhere (Alvermann & Rubinstein-Ávila, in press), research agendas focusing on the influence of digital writing and media in immigrant youths' developing literacies need to account for *intersectionality*—a concept that originated within Critical Race Feminist legal scholarship, according to Núñez (2014). Intersectionality was later adapted and applied in educational settings for the purpose of exploring "how individuals experience privilege, marginalization, or both, according to various combinations of social categories" (pp. 85–86).

In fact, it was Núñez's critique of the emphasis placed on individuals—ignoring the systemic forces at play on their lives—that first caught our attention relative to framing this chapter around the writing ecologies young people inhabit. Previously, by failing to take intersectionality into account at the design phase of inquiry, it was common for researchers to overlook (intentionally or unintentionally) the systemic oppression of particular groups—a failure that made it fairly easy for policy makers to point to individuals as somehow representing the larger group. Núñez effectively reversed opportunities for such oversights to occur by stressing the need to situate the micro within the macro power dynamic:

> Power relations in an intersectional manner must involve interrogating how certain social categories are constituted as inferior in comparison to others, how people are framed as part of a larger economic project rather than encouraged to actualize their own self-defined potential, and how resources are distributed in uneven ways to limit the life chances of certain individuals in specific social categories.
>
> (p. 86)

This methodological repositioning offers researchers a viable framework in which to accomplish greater analytical precision. It also helps to ensure greater attention to education inequities in studies involving writing within digital environments.

We argue here that the three levels of analysis Núñez (2014) proposed align well with our focus on young people's involvement as global citizens who use digital writing and media to engage with sociocultural, political, and economic issues that might otherwise go unnoticed. For instance, the first level—defining and examining relations among social categories that are relevant to one's topic of inquiry—draws attention to the potential individuality (or not) of a study's participants. The second level of analysis—identifying potential arenas of influence in which independent and interdependent structures are at work—points to what Núñez describes as "(a) organizational (e.g., positions in structures of society such as work, family, and education), (b) representational (e.g., discursive processes), (c) intersubjective (e.g., relationships between individuals and members of groups), and (d) experiential (e.g., narrative sense making)" (p. 88). It is, however, her third level of analysis—historicity—that best captures our interest in looking beyond the local to broader institutional systems, such as: "economic, legal, political, media, and social power and classification that evolve over time in specific places, as well as social movements to challenge these systems" (p. 89).

Despite the fact these categories are socially constructed and highly confounded, and given that individuals are likely to define themselves in multiple ways, social categories still play a role in shaping societal inequities (Núñez, 2014). Therefore, we agree with Núñez's claim that "within-and between-group comparisons" (p. 87) are essential—especially among Latino/a youth—a vastly heterogeneous group with diverse and intertwined characteristics that include "race, phenotype, nation of origin, im/migration status, language, history of colonization, and citizenship status…" (p. 87). We also agree that employing intersectionality as a methodological lens may be useful in research that focuses on different generations of Latino/a youth, especially given the variation in social, cultural, economic, and political contexts that different generations have experienced in the past (Núñez, 2014).

**Implications for Educational Practice and Policy**

As the writing ecologies young people inhabit continue to proliferate in number and modality, how can literacy educators create opportunities for students to inhabit them as global citizens? This question takes on added complexity when one considers the rather complicated position literacy educators occupy in relation to their students' engagement as global citizens. In the US, for example, the Common Core State Standards (CCSS) for English Language Arts (ELA) charge teachers to prepare students who are "college and career ready" in a "twenty-first century, globally competitive society" (National Governors Association Center for Best Practices, p. 3). Underlying the idea of a "globally competitive society" is a neoliberal conception of the global other, one that views global youth principally as competitors for increasingly scarce global resources. The CCSS for ELA, then, frames global citizenship fundamentally as an economic imperative, and this framing shapes the kinds of reading and writing assignments teachers in the US bring to their classrooms. Here is a typical example: Students are asked to read a news article, something like NBC News's "Study: International Students Outpace Americans in STEM Degrees" (2015), which alerts its US audience that young people in Asia—particularly those in China, India, and South Korea—are performing significantly better than American students in STEM fields. Their teacher will then follow this sort of reading with reflective or research-based writing assignments in which students interrogate the causes and long-term effects of Asian STEM superiority on their future job opportunities.

The tendency to frame the connection between new literacies and global engagement as a means to compete for capital is not an exclusively American phenomenon, and literacy researchers themselves sometimes operate under the same assumption, as we see in Mills's (2010) persuasive observation that "sophisticated technological knowledge is now a highly demanded credential for cosmopolitan recognition in globalised networks" (pp. 234–235). Mills goes on to point out that young people "engage in the transformation of existing multimedia designs, creating globally oriented funds of knowledge that are easily expanded and adapted to meet changing criteria for success in the new times" (p. 235). Note the way in which words like "cosmopolitan" and "globalised" combine with words like "credential," "funds," and "success." While there is no doubt that Mills is correct—technological competence is an essential prerequisite in the global marketplace—such associations between globalism, new literacies, and the acquisition of capital run the risk of eliding a more cosmopolitan conception of the ways in which technology and young people's literacy practices intersect.

In the US, though, the CCSS for ELA effectively limit teachers' attention to global issues to the reading standards for literature in grades 9 and 10: "Analyze a particular point of view or cultural experience reflected in a work of literature from outside the United States, drawing on a wide reading of world literature" (p. 38). While it would be reasonable to expect some reference to global perspectives in the Common Core standards for reading informational texts and writing, the world outside the US is conspicuously absent from those particular standards. It is, of course, important that students read literature from around the world as they develop global citizenry; however, with the exception of classics and mythology, it is difficult and expensive to access published world literature in translation. Which is not to suggest that students cannot develop a more global perspective by reading old literature from around the world, but such work seems unlikely to shed much light on being a contemporary global citizen, which we suggest requires authentic engagement with the world rather than simple knowledge of it. While important, reading literature and informational texts from around the world—both the old world and new—misses an element crucial to young people's growth as global citizens: namely, interaction.

To nurture meaningful interactions between young people and their global counterparts, literacy educators must find ways to take advantage of the complex networks of writing ecologies already inhabited by young people online, particularly via social media platforms. Because these ecologies often exist on or outside the margins of institutional sanction—for example, school networks often block students from accessing popular social media—educators committed to forging opportunities for global connections for their students must also commit to a radical, even subversive, form of writing instruction that introduces youth to diverse writing ecologies. Williams's (2012) concept of "centrifugal schooling," although oriented more toward policy than practice, offers educators some helpful guidance. For Williams,

> centrifugal schooling [is] an assemblage of polycentric governance in policy networks, educational marketing and mediatisation, new public-private relationships and the intermediary role of the third sector, which together constitute a technocratic policy vision of a post-bureaucratic, open source, connected curriculum ecology.
>
> (p. 793)

Williams's use of the word *ecology* here resonates well with the anarchistic qualities of the writing ecologies framework, particularly to the extent that they share an impulse to subvert the centralized, the conventional, and the controlled. To Williams's decentered, centrifugal approach to policy, curriculum, and pedagogy, we add the concepts of *centrifugal* and *centripetal cultural forces* in the literacy classroom.

Earth's orbit around the sun is a result of a careful balance between centripetal and centrifugal movement. The sun exerts a gravitational pull on Earth—a centripetal force that would eventually incinerate the planet if it were not countered by the centrifugal force pulling on the sun that keeps Earth in a steady orbit. Inward and outward forces are existing in a state of perfect equipoise. The interplay between such centripetal and centrifugal movements is a useful way of understanding the orbital relationship between the literacy classroom and the wider world, particularly when it comes to developing young global citizens through educational technology and digital literacy. Without some form of interaction with the global other built into their lessons, teachers' efforts to nurture their students' global dispositions can often function only as centripetal cultural forces, which is to say teachers may gather texts from outside the US and redirect them inward, often using them primarily as points of comparison for their students' own national experiences. In doing so, teachers can miss opportunities to create *centrifugal* cultural forces, those that create outward movement by which students can engage with the world as citizens of it. The point is not that educators should eschew creating centripetal cultural forces in favor of creating centrifugal cultural forces, but rather that educators need to establish a careful balance between the two, such that young people understand their sociocultural positioning in relation to their global peers. Young people need a balanced understanding of their roles as global citizens—one that acknowledges and honors their local identities while seeking to harmonize them with more global ones.

Bean's (2016) concept of Cosmopolitan Critical Literacy represents a more centrifugal expansion upon the limitations of the CCSS in that it "moves youth conversations into a larger sphere where they may find common ground centered on basic human rights" (p. 52). Through Cosmopolitan Critical Literacy, young people come to view their global peers as valuable cultural resources with whom they can engage as they hew their identities from the signals and noise of twenty-first-century global consumer culture. Digital writing is an excellent vehicle for centrifugal cultural movement because it can allow young people to "communicate cross national and international boundaries via the Internet…to find common ground around human rights issues and collaborate to generate solutions to problems" (p. 53). Bean points to the Space2Cre8 project (Hull & Stornaiuolo, 2010,

2014; Stornaiuolo, Hull, & Sahni, 2011) as a useful illustration of how young people can use digital writing to develop Cosmopolitan Critical Literacy. An online social network that connects young people to their global peers, Space2Cre8 has successfully demonstrated that digital writing via social networking platforms can cultivate in young people a cosmopolitan orientation toward their global peers (Stornaiuolo et al., 2011). At this point, however, Space2Cre8 remains a relatively small-scale platform exclusive to current participants and those who may be invited to join in the future. While literacy educators and researchers wait hopefully for uniquely robust projects like Space2Cre8 to scale up, how can they work to create centrifugal cultural forces in their classrooms on a more immediate basis?

There are, in fact, a number of web-based tools currently available to teachers as they work to create centrifugal cultural forces in their classrooms by connecting global youth via digital writing. Here is an example from the classroom of the chapter's second author. In the fall of 2015, amidst the international response to Syrians fleeing their homeland in search of safety from both ISIS and the Assad regime, the American and European media debated the meanings of the words "refugee" and "migrant": using one over the other suggested a particular way of understanding the Syrian diaspora that had real consequences on the legal status of Syrians in their respective sheltering countries. As part of a lesson on denotation and connotation, students were asked to research the meanings of the words "refugee" and "migrant" as the global media used them in the Syrian context, and then to post a blog entry in which they used text and images—pics, gifs, and/or embedded video—to make a case for whether the Syrians should be treated as "refugees" or as "migrants." Students then visited each other's blogs and left comments in which they agreed, disagreed, or qualified their peers' arguments.

At this point, the assignment has remained a centripetal cultural force to the extent that students have gained knowledge about the world and recontextualized it in their own experiences while gaining a greater understanding of how the denotations and connotations of words can have dramatic consequences on people's lives. An immensely valuable assignment in its own right, but the project only became a centrifugal cultural force when students were directed to find an article about the Syrian crisis on the English version of a global news outlet—*Al Jazeera, Der Spiegel International, The Guardian*, etc.—and post the text from their blog entries in the comments section. (Alternatively, they could post their comments to a relevant image on a news outlet's Instagram account. At the time, *National Geographic* published a number of powerful photos of Syrian refugees to the NatGeo Instagram.) To be sure, such interaction is qualitatively different from the wonderfully personal interaction facilitated by Space2Cre8. Nevertheless, when students added their voices to the millions of global voices weighing in on the "refugee"/"migrant" debate, they were not simply being taught how to be global citizens. They were using digital writing to *be* global citizens.

Reading about the world through literary or informational texts is a centripetal cultural force—an important and necessary one, to be sure—but if young people are to engage as global citizens in classroom contexts, educators would do well to explore the centrifugal power of writing, digital writing specifically. Digital writing on its own, however, is insufficient; it must be directed toward media and interaction. Mills and Chandra (2011) have shown "how meaningful contexts for literacy practice can be created through secure and free microblogging platforms designed for educational communities" (p. 35). Looking specifically at a secure platform built with schools in mind, Mills and Chandra found that microblogging changed the shape of students writing practices as well as the classroom community (p. 38). Ultimately, however, the secure nature of school-sanctioned social networks may very well work against their potential to create a centrifugal cultural force. Mills and Chandra argue that microblogging in the classroom via secure platforms "appropriate[s] digitally mediated literacies of youth in a social ecology of the classroom in ways that are meaningful and consistent with their uses in the world" (p. 44). While instructive, such thinking can perpetuate an unnecessary division between "the world" and "the social ecology of the classroom," a division researchers and educators must complicate in the service of young people's emergent cosmopolitan dispositions. Of course, there are reasonable explanations for this division, ones we should take seriously. For example, many young people's parents and guardians remain hesitant to allow their children to maintain social networking accounts, fearing they represent an unnecessary distraction at best, a life-threatening danger at worst (boyd, 2014). At the same time, younger children—particularly those in elementary school—may not be developmentally ready to navigate complex sociotechnological spaces such as Twitter and Facebook.

The growing popularity of Learning Management Systems (LMS) such as Moodle, Canvas, and Google Classroom risks reinforcing a similar division between the classroom and the world because the main function of an LMS is to serve as a self-contained ecosystem for delivering instruction, assessing student work, and facilitating student-to-student and student-to-teacher communications. Unfortunately, as writing ecologies, such platforms can become walled gardens where students develop innovative literacy practices and meaningful relationships with classmates without ever looking beyond the walls to the world outside. While it is clear that administrators at both local and state levels will find the security of LMS and school-sanctioned social networks appealing—and therefore be more inclined to fund them—researchers and educators must be conscious that such mechanisms can work against efforts to develop young people's global citizenship through digital writing and interaction. As researchers continue making a case for the importance of youth's global engagement in digital environments, educators must work within and around the constraints of programs such as the Schools and Libraries Program of the Universal Service Fund (often referred to as E-rate), which gives network administrators a great deal of power to censor what students can access on school networks. As the earlier example regarding the status of Syrian refugees demonstrates, teachers can supplement secure services and platforms by asking students to venture outside them in search of meaningful interactions with other global citizens. Even if the most popular social networks are blocked—Twitter, Facebook, Tumblr, and so on—teachers are able to direct their students toward online news outlets, where they can participate as global citizens through digital writing in real-world writing ecologies.

Because the development of global citizenry through digital writing demands the centrifugal cultural force created by social interactions with the global other, it is worth taking a moment to consider the sanctioning of the social in traditional classroom settings. Classrooms are fundamentally social spaces, but teachers are in the position to authorize and de-authorize various forms of interaction, sometimes allowing those that serve instructional aims while prohibiting those that allegedly hinder them. While teachers will often authorize students to collaborate in groups—understanding that their conversations will to some extent move in, around, and through the task at hand—teachers (and institutions) frequently de-authorize the use of social media platforms in the classroom, positioning them as unsanctioned forms of socializing, those more likely to distract than to edify. When combined with the walled gardens of secure social networks and most LMS's, the sanctioning of the social—even in the most digitally connected classrooms—can present a serious and complex obstacle to the creation of centrifugal cultural forces in the classroom.

The popular notion that today's young people cannot or will not write is fueled by a hierarchy that privileges specific modes of sanctioned academic writing while subordinating many of the vast and vibrant writing ecologies youth already inhabit. Yet comment sections are an unsanctioned ecology of writing in which young people frequently contribute to threaded discussions on platforms like Facebook, Instagram, and Reddit. This hierarchy of forms creates a dynamic similar to the one existing between the classroom and the world as it is codified in documents like the CCSS. Just as the centripetal acquisition of global knowledge is framed as an economic imperative in the CCSS, sanctioned forms of academic writing are often framed as a means for accessing higher education, which itself is privileged for its ability to provide economic security. (There is some irony, however, to the fact that more than a few young people have gained fame and fortune by their ability to leverage social media in establishing their own global brands, Justin Bieber being a prime example.) Due in part to their frequently anonymous nature and tendency for extremist speech, comment sections tend to register very low indeed on the traditional hierarchy of writing, a dynamic reinforced in the literacy classroom when educators neglect them. Of course, as anyone who has visited the comment section of blog or article knows, they can be rather poisonous spaces. A 2016 study sponsored by *The Guardian* demonstrates the extent to which the news site's own comment threads are rife with sexist and racist abuse:

> Although the majority of our regular opinion writers are white men, we found that those who experienced the highest levels of abuse and dismissive trolling were not. The 10 regular writers who got the most abuse were eight women (four white and four non-white) and two black men. Two of the women and one of the men were gay. And of the eight women in the "top 10," one was Muslim and one Jewish.
> And the 10 regular writers who got the least abuse? All men.
>
> (para. 3–4)

In short, comment sections are a polluted ecology of writing. Yet we wonder to what extent the pollution of comment threads is a consequence rather than a cause of their marginalization. Further, we suggest that literacy educators might help cleanse the toxic atmosphere of comment sections by embracing them in their classroom practice. After all, the continued marginalization of comment threads and similar ecologies in the literacy classroom does nothing to mitigate the abuse one witnesses in them—a real missed opportunity, it seems. On the other hand, if literacy educators were to resituate such ignored ecologies of writing, they could actively work against the continued abuse of marginalized identities while also cultivating young people's ability to interact in meaningful ways with their local, national, and global peers through the power of centrifugal cultural forces and deep writing.

**Ways Forward**

In their critique of the New London Group's "A Pedagogy of Multiliteracies: Designing Social Futures" (1996), Leander and Boldt (2012) caution against over-rationalizing literacies such that researchers and educators "[subtract] movement, indeterminacy, and emergent potential from the picture" (p. 24). Although constructs such as Bean's Cosmopolitan Critical Literacy offer useful frameworks for theorizing young people's diverse dispositions, we wonder if they too may be vulnerable to the kinds of subtractive tendencies Leander and Boldt observe in the New London Group's work. For Leander and Boldt, representational theories can freeze processes fraught with motion and uncertainty and thereby offer a tempting, yet ultimately misleading, impression of stability, clarity, and coherence. To avoid this kind of subtraction, researchers and educators might add to the Cosmopolitan Critical Literacies framework the "Deleuzo-Guattarian perspective [that] texts are not 'about' the world; rather, they are participants in the world" (p. 25). This consideration leads us to ask, how might young people's engagement as global citizens through digital writing and media benefit from a nonrepresentational approach to exploring the potential for developing youth's "everyday cosmopolitanism"? (see Stornaiuolo et al., 2011).

Conceptualizing texts as being "about the world" suggests a centripetal cultural force, whereas conceptualizing them as "participants in the world" creates a centrifugal cultural force. When literacy educators and researchers come to view digital writing as a centrifugal cultural force for young people's participation as global citizens, they must contend with the primacy of movement, dynamism, and emergence. This is particularly the case when it comes to the always-unfolding quality of such traditionally marginalized ecologies of digital writing as comment threads, Instagram feeds, Reddit posts, and so on. Indeed, for many online publications and social media platforms with active commenting communities, the users' contributions become a published extension of the content itself such that the content remains in a continuous state of emergence or uncertainty, not unlike Brandt's (2015) concept of deep writing. Indeed, deep writing is a given within an ecology of writing perspective— constantly amplified, clarified, and undermined by interactions in the virtual public sphere.

Or, as Smith and Hull (2012) would describe this phenomenon, "the reciprocal relationship between reading and writing becomes tighter in the digital sphere, making authorship more obviously tantamount to readership, and vice versa" (p. 63). This "reciprocal relationship" suggests that when readers add comments to online content, their relation to the text shifts such that they are readers-becoming-writers, or vice versa, and in the context of digital media related to global issues, they are readers-becoming-writers-becoming-global citizens. Stornaiuolo, Smith, and Phillips's (2016) articulation of the transliteracies framework offers a promising means for conceptualizing the disruption of the reader/writer binary at work in many digital writing ecologies: "A trans focus—explored in interdisciplinary scholarship through concepts like translanguaging, transmodalities, transmedia, trans* identities, and transnationalism—highlights the fluidity and indeterminacy of practice, leaving unspecified who or what moves and in what direction or fashion" (p. 2). This attention to ambiguity and movement in youths' literacy practices across space, time, and material suggests the transliteracies framework has a great deal to offer literacy researchers and educators committed to young people's emergent cosmopolitan dispositions.

Together, the anarchic freedom of nonrepresentational theories of literacy as well as the frameworks for writing ecologies and transliteracies appears to further complicate the notion that young people cannot or will not write. At best, this belief is based on a severely impoverished idea of writing—an important and focal language art (Brandt, 2015), which is better studied using theoretical frames that provide insight into the deep writing young people are already doing in marginalized writing ecologies and how such ecologies nurture global connections among global peers. As Masny (2013) cogently observed, "representation limits experience to the world as we know it, not as a world that could be" (p. 342). More than halfway through the second decade of the twenty-first century, some in the West as we know it express a strong desire to withdraw from the world, to close down borders, hearts, and minds in the face of economic uncertainty, mass migration, climate change, and the threat of violence. Literacy educators and researchers who push the boundaries of theory, methodology, and practice are helping to create the world as at it could be—one capable of informing (and being informed by) digitally literate young people whose writing practices intersect with new forms of media and technologies as they daily negotiate their positions in the world through active engagement with it.

## References

Alvermann, D. E. (2011). Moving on, keeping pace: Youth's literate identities and multimodal digital texts. In S. Abrams & J. Rowsell (Eds.), *Rethinking identity and literacy education in the 21st century. National Society for the Study of Education Yearbook* (vol. 110, part I, pp. 109–128). New York, NY: Columbia University, Teachers College.

Alvermann, D. E., & Rubinstein-Ávila E. (in press). A research agenda for Latin@ youth's new media use in the New South: ¿Common sense for the common good? In S. Salas & P. Portes (Eds.), *Latinization and K-12 communities: National perspectives on regional change*. Albany, NY: SUNY Press.

Bakhtin, M. (1981). Discourse in the novel. In M. Holquist (Ed.), *The dialogic imagination: Four essays by M.M. Bakhtin* (pp. 269–422). Austin: University of Texas Press.

Barton, D. (2007). *Literacy: An introduction to an ecology of written language* (2nd ed.). Hoboken, NJ: Wiley-Blackwell.

Barton, D., Hamilton, M., & Ivanic, R. (Eds.). (2000). *Situated literacies: Reading and writing in context*. London, UK: Routledge.

Beach, R. W. (2011). Issues in analyzing alignment of language arts common core standards with state standards? *Educational Researcher, 40*(4), 179–182.

Bean, T. W. (2016). Digital media and cosmopolitan critical literacy: Research and practice. In G. Barbara & L. Mellinee (Eds.), *Handbook of research on the societal impact of digital media* (pp. 46–68). Hershey, PA: IGI Global.

Boggs, G. L., & Alvermann, D. E. (2012). Introduction: Writing ecologies. *Pedagogies International, 7*(3), 203–208.

boyd, d. (2014). *It's complicated: the social lives of networked teens.* New Haven, CT: Yale University Press.

Brandt, D. (2014). Deep writing: New directions in mass literacy. In A.-C. Edlund, L.-E. Edlund, & S. Haugen (Eds.), *Vernacular literacies: Past, present, and future* (pp. 15–28). (Northern Studies Monographs 3 and Vardagligt Skrifbruk). Umeå, Sweden: Umeå University and Royal Skyttean Society.

Brandt, D. (2015). *The rise of writing: Redefining mass literacy.* Cambridge, UK: Cambridge University Press.

Carr, N. (2010). *The shallows: What the internet is doing to our brains.* New York, NY: W.W. Norton.

Dobrin, S. (Ed.). (2012). Introduction: Ecology, and a future of writing studies. In S. Dobrin (Ed.), *Ecology, writing theory, and new media* (pp. 1–23). London, UK: Routledge.

Feyerabend, P. (1975). *Against method.* London, UK: Verso.

Gardiner, B., Mansfield, M., Anderson, I., Holder, J., Louter, D., & Ulmanu, M. (2016, April 12). The dark side of Guardian comments. *The Guardian.* Retrieved from www.theguardian.com.

Gee, J. P. (1990). *Social linguistics and literacies: Ideology in discourses.* London, UK: Falmer.

Heath, S. B. (1983). *Ways with words: Language, life, and work in communities and classrooms.* New York, NY: Cambridge University Press.

Hull, G. A., & Stornaiuolo A. (2010). Literate arts in a global world: Reframing social networking as cosmopolitan practice. *Journal of Adolescent and Adult Literacy, 54*(2), 85–97.

Johnson, S. (2010). *Where good ideas come from: The natural history of innovation.* New York, NY: Riverhead Books/Penguin Group.

Johnson, L. L., Bass, T., & Hicks, M. (2014). Creating critical spaces for youth activists. In P. Paugh, T. Kress, & R. Lake (Eds.), *Teaching towards democracy with postmodern and popular culture texts* (pp. 37–58). Dordrecht, The Netherlands: Sense.

Kress, G. (1997). *Before writing: Rethinking the paths to literacy.* London, UK: Routledge.

Kress, G. (2009). What is mode? In C. Jewitt (Ed.), *The Routledge handbook of multimodal analysis* (pp. 54–67). London, UK: Routledge/Taylor & Francis Group.

Kuhn, T. S. (1970). *The structure of scientific revolutions* (2nd ed.). Chicago, IL: University of Chicago Press.

Lea, M. R., & Street, B. V. (1998). Student writing in higher education: An academic literacies approach. *Studies in Higher Education, 23*(2), 157–173.

Leander, K., & Boldt, G. (2012). Rereading "a pedagogy of multiliteracies": Bodies, texts, and emergence. *Journal of Literacy Research, 45*(1), 22–46.

Luke, A., & Freebody, P. (1997). The social practices of reading. In S. Muspratt, A. Luke, & P. Freebody (Eds.), *Constructing critical literacies* (pp. 185–225). Creskill, NJ: Hampton Press.

Masny, D. (2013). Rhizoanalytic pathways in qualitative research. *Qualitative Inquiry, 19*(5), 339–348.

Mills, K. A. (2010). What learners "know" through digital media production: Learning by design. *E-Learning and Digital Media, 7*(3), 223–236.

Mills, K. A., & Chandra, V. (2011). Microblogging as a literacy practice for educational communities. *Journal of Adolescent & Adult Literacy, 55*(1), 35–45.

National Governors Association Center for Best Practices, Council of Chief State School Officers. (2010). *Common core state standards for English language arts & literacy in history/social studies, science, and technical subjects.* Washington, DC: Authors.

New London Group. (1996). A pedagogy of multliteracies: Designing social futures. *Harvard Educational Review, 66*(1), 60–92.

Núñez, A. M. (2014). Employing multilevel intersectionality in educational research: Latino identities, contexts, and college access. *Educational Researcher, 43*(2), 85–92.

Saes, K. (2012). Writing ecologies, rhetorical epidemics. In S. Dobrin (Ed.), *Ecology, writing theory, and new media* (pp. 51–66). London, UK: Routledge.

Scribner, S., & Cole, M. (1981). *The psychology of literacy.* Cambridge, MA: Harvard University Press.

Smith, A., & Hull, G. A. (2012). Critical literacies and social media: Fostering ethical engagement with global youth. In J. Vila & J. Z. Pandya (Eds.), *Critical digital literacies as social praxis: Intersections and challenges* (pp. 63–86). New York, NY: Peter Lang.

Stewart, M. A. (2014a). "I don't want to write for them": An at-risk Latino youth's out-of-school literacy practices. *NABE Journal of Research and Practice, 5*(1). Retrieved from www2.nau.edu/nabejp/ojs/index.php/njrp/article/view/72.

Stewart, M. A. (2014b). Social networking, workplace, and entertainment literacies: The out-of-school literate lives of newcomer Latina/o adolescents. *Reading Research Quarterly, 53*(4), 347–371.

Stornaiuolo, A., Hull, G. A., & Sahni, U. (2011). Cosmopolitan imaginings of self and other: Youth and social networking in a global world. In J. Fisherkeller (Ed.), *International perspectives on youth media: Cultures of production and education* (pp. 263–280). New York, NY: Peter Lang.

Stornaiuolo, A., Smith, A., & Phillips, N. C. (2016). Transliteracies. In A. M. Peters (Ed.), *Encyclopedia of educational philosophy and theory* (pp. 1–6). Singapore: Springer Singapore.

Street, B. V. (1984). *Literacy in theory and practice*. New York, NY: Cambridge University Press.

Street, B. V. (1995). *Social literacies: Critical approaches to literacy in development, ethnography and education*. London, UK: Longman.

Tierney, R. J., & Shanahan, T. (1991). Research on the reading-writing relationship: Interactions, transactions, and outcomes. In R. Barr, M. L. Kamil, P. Mosenthal, & P. D. Pearson (Eds.), *Handbook of reading research, Volume II* (pp. 246–280). New York, NY: Longman.

Vygotsky, L. S. (1978). *Mind in society*. Cambridge, MA: Harvard University Press.

Wang, F. (2015, January 23). Study: International students outpace Americans in STEM degrees. *NBC News*. Retrieved from www.nbcnews.com.

Williams, B. (2012). Centrifugal schooling: Third sector policy networks and the reassembling of curriculum policy in England. *Journal of Education Policy, 27*(6), 775–794.

Zimmerman, A. M. (2012). *Documenting DREAMs: New media, undocumented youth and the immigrant rights movement*. San Diego, CA: University of Southern California, Annenberg School for Communication and Journalism. Retrieved from http://dmlhub.net/sites/default/files/Documenting%20DREAMs%20-%20Working%20Paper-MAPP%20-%20June%206%202012.pdf.

# 14
# Literate Identities in Fan-Based Online Affinity Spaces

Jayne C. Lammers, Alecia Marie Magnifico, and Jen Scott Curwood

As the Internet becomes increasingly interwoven into their lives, youth engage in new literacy practices to communicate, connect, and construct themselves through digital tools and online spaces. We know, for example, that 92% of American teens report going online daily and 76% use social media (Lenhart, 2015). Internet use among European children continues to rise as well (Holloway, Green, & Livingstone, 2013). Though there have been efforts to help teachers embed digital and multimodal writing into classrooms (e.g., Garcia, 2014; Hyler & Hicks, 2014), most technology use in writing instruction is teacher-directed and classroom-based, focused on word processing and editing, and disconnected from wider audiences (Applebee & Langer, 2011; Graham, Capizzi, Harris, Hebert, & Morphy, 2014). Therefore, it remains important to study adolescents' literacies "in the wild" (Curwood, Magnifico, & Lammers, 2013; Hutchins, 1995), where we see evidence of new interest-driven online practices. One particularly rich venue for such study has been fan-based online affinity spaces.

In this chapter, we review the extant research exploring young people's digital literacy practices as they participate in such spaces. Through this look back on what we have learned about the role these spaces play in adolescents' digital lives, we discuss how various theoretical perspectives have shaped (or might shape) our understanding of fan-based online affinity spaces, share educational and methodological implications, and offer insights into the productive tensions revealed by this review. We suggest directions to consider as we deepen our understanding of the impact of technology and connectivity on literate identities. To begin, we first define what we mean by literate identities in fan-based online affinity spaces.

## Defining Terms

*Literate identities.* Recognizing literacies as situated, social practices (e.g., Gee, 2004; Lankshear & Knobel, 2011; New London Group, 1996) begins with an understanding of literacies as "socially recognized ways in which people generate, communicate, and negotiate meanings, as members of Discourses, through the medium of encoded texts" (Lankshear & Knobel, 2011, p. 33). Discourses, with a capital D, are "integrate[d] ways of talking, listening, writing, reading, acting, interacting, believing, valuing, and feeling (and using various objects, symbols, images, tools, and technologies) in the service of enacting meaningful socially situated identities and activities" (Gee, 2001, p. 719). Thus, we use the term *literate identities* to acknowledge how literacies shape and are shaped by the identities people enact in social spaces, and we argue that adolescents' literate expressions within their fandoms are also expressions of themselves.

*Fan-based literacy practices.* Fans have long been writing their own versions of favorite storylines; some of the earliest fan art and fanzines—fan-created magazines—can be traced back to science fiction fans in the 1930s (Coppa, 2006). Transformative works—creative works about characters or settings created by fans of the original work—can take many forms, including fanfiction, fan art, musical works known as filk, and fanvids that remix clips from original sources. Fans also create websites, blogs, and social networking accounts based on media storylines or characters, participate in online discussion forums, and play text-based role-playing games that co-create storyworlds and narratives with other fans. We use *fan-based literacy practices* to broadly refer to the myriad literacies fans engage in to express their fandom of a particular media property.

*Online affinity spaces.* Affinity spaces are physical, virtual, or blended sites of informal learning, where "newbies and masters and everyone else" interact around a "common endeavor" (Gee, 2004, p. 85). A defining feature of affinity spaces is that they do not require everyone to participate in the same way but rather allow "different forms and routes to participation" (p. 87). As such, affinity spaces facilitate powerful learning experiences by encouraging multiple interest-driven trajectories, opportunities to learn with others, and paths toward becoming an authentic participant (Duncan & Hayes, 2012; Squire, 2011).

Now that much literate activity takes place online, affinity spaces often spread across many interconnected sites, with blogs, message boards, fandom websites, and social networking sites all serving as entry points—what Gee (2004) calls "portals"—to participating in and generating content for a given affinity space. Recognizing the increasing numbers of web-based portals, we argued that an update to Gee's theory was warranted and posited that *online affinity spaces* have the following defining features (Lammers, Curwood, & Magnifico, 2012):

1. A common endeavor is primary;
2. Participation is self-directed, multifaceted, and dynamic;
3. Portals are often multimodal;
4. Affinity spaces provide a passionate, public audience for content;
5. Socializing plays an important role in affinity space participation;
6. Leadership roles vary within and among portals;
7. Knowledge is distributed across the entire affinity space;
8. Many portals place a high value on cataloguing content and documenting practices; and
9. Affinity spaces encompass a variety of media-specific and social networking portals.

*Fan-based online affinity spaces.* In this chapter, we focus our discussion of adolescents' digital lives on the literate identities they enact in *fan-based online affinity spaces*. Thus, we limit the conversation here to online (and blended) affinity spaces wherein participants pursue a common endeavor related to fandom. Extant research in this area explores anime and manga series (e.g., Black, 2008; Chandler-Olcott & Mahar, 2003; Jwa, 2012), young adult literature and related movie franchises (e.g., Curwood, 2013), music groups (Korobkova & Black, 2014), videogames and virtual worlds (e.g., Grimes, 2015; Lammers, 2016; Magnifico, 2012), and Broadway musicals (Lammers & Marsh, 2015). Popular portals to fan-based online affinity spaces include Fanfiction.net—arguably the largest online archive for fanfiction, hosting stories based on media ranging from *Harry Potter* to *The Bible*, and more—and online writing repositories like Figment.com and Wattpad. These, along with fandom websites, like YouTube, Flickr, and DeviantArt, and social media tools, like Facebook, Twitter, and Tumblr, serve as portals to *many* fan-based online affinity spaces, whereas root websites, such as Mockingjay.net for *The Hunger Games*, offer a portal into *a specific fandom's* affinity space (Magnifico & Curwood, 2012).

**Reviewing the Research**

Early fandom scholarship largely focused on legitimizing fans' creations as products of literate practices. Media scholar Henry Jenkins (1992) established fans not as passive viewers but "as active producers and manipulators of meanings" (p. 23), whose transformative works blurred "any clear-cut distinction between media producer and media spectator, since any spectator may potentially participate in the creation of new artworks" (p. 247). As fandoms became more visible to outsiders through the proliferation of online fan communities, researchers sought to further understand fan-based practices from education perspectives (e.g., Black, 2008; Guzzetti & Gamboa, 2005). The work of Chandler-Olcott and Mahar (2003) argued that creating fanfiction and fan-based websites were "valid" literacy practices, while Thomas (2006) documented "remarkably sophisticated" (p. 229) reading, writing, and planning work in adolescents' online role-play.

With fandom practices established as literacies, researchers turned their attention to generating a concrete understanding of the designs and structures of online spaces themselves (e.g., Jwa, 2012; Lammers, 2012; Magnifico, 2017). This line of inquiry has pursued questions about how affinity spaces motivate writers to share their work (Curwood et al., 2013; Magnifico, 2012), how the designs of online spaces shape participation (Grimes & Fields, 2012), how corporate sponsorship influences virtual communities (Grimes, 2015; Grimes & Shade, 2005), and how participants teach each other (Lammers, 2013). In studying Fanfiction.net, Black (2007) used affinity space theory to examine how the site's structure organized content and facilitated interactions between readers and writers in ways that encouraged multiple routes to knowledge. Black then made comparisons between the design of online fan spaces and traditional school spaces (see also Korobkova & Black, 2014; Lammers, 2013; Lammers, Magnifico, & Curwood, 2014).

Additionally, many have drawn on the New London Group's (1996) multiliteracies framework to make sense of fans' literacies. From this work, we have greater understanding of fanfiction writing as a hybrid, intertextual practice that allows flexibility to draw from varied Discourses to craft creative stories based on favorite characters and settings. However, while fanfiction affords opportunities to take risks and play with writing (Lammers & Marsh, 2015; Thomas, 2006), applying a multiliteracies framework also reveals that, in order to receive recognition in an online affinity space, fanfiction writers often conform to that community's expectations (Lammers, 2016). Related work emphasizes the multimodal, multigenre nature of many fan-based literacy practices. Delving into the multiple genres welcomed by online affinity spaces, Tosenberger (2008) discussed the slash—fanfiction exploring same sex relationships between characters—that became popular in the *Harry Potter* fandom, while Padgett and Curwood (2016) focused on poetic writing shared in Figment.com.

Research on fan-based online affinity spaces additionally investigates the relationships between readers and writers, highlighting how audiences shape the writing shared in these spaces. Black's (2008) study of English language learners who shared anime-based stories on Fanfiction.net provides a rich example of how participation facilitates access to an audience who provides constructive feedback. In particular, Black highlighted the open, unbounded nature of online audiences who encourage authors to continue writing with comments about how they are eagerly awaiting the next chapter. Many have similarly argued that online audience motivates writers to persist in sharing their fan-based texts (e.g., Curwood et al., 2013; Lammers et al., 2014; Lammers & Marsh, 2015; Thomas, 2006).

Offering insights into the various audiences available in fan-based online affinity spaces, Magnifico's (2012) study of Neopets, a virtual pet site, found this online space provided writers with both a social audience who offered recognition to authors who shared their work and a gatekeeping, evaluative audience in the site's newspaper editor. What remains less clear in the literature are the direct effects online audiences have on writers' texts. Magnifico, Curwood, and Lammers (2015) begin to address this gap with their linguistic analysis of reader responses from Fanfiction.net and Figment.com. This study revealed that fanfiction readers typically provide general comments, often focused on their own reactions or dispensing "thin praise" (p. 165), rather than offering constructive feedback with specific strategies for improving the writing. Padgett and Curwood (2016) corroborated these findings, discussing a disconnect between writers' perceptions of reader feedback on Figment .com and the actual feedback content.

Throughout this scholarship, researchers often seek connections to classroom-valued literacy practices and pedagogies. In a rare example of fan-based literacies brought directly into an English classroom, McWilliams, Hickey, Hines, Conner, and Bishop (2011) designed and implemented a literature unit modeled after fanfiction practices. Secondary students first analyzed existing fanfiction and then wrote their own based on Arthur Miller's play *The Crucible*. The researchers argued that this activity illustrated how the characterization practices valued in Fanfiction.net aligned with the character analysis taught in English classrooms. Researchers more often draw parallels to classrooms based on studies of adolescents' out-of-school fan-based literacies. Curwood (2013, 2014), for example, showed how young people who role-play engage in literary analysis of texts and characters—much as students in literacy classrooms do. Some studies include data from both school-based and fan-based literacies in their analyses. Roozen (2009) illustrated the interconnection between one writer's disciplinary and fan-based literacies by examining both her writing in her English graduate program and her transformative works. Relatedly, Lammers and colleagues (2014) brought together studies of Fanfiction.net and an online tool for classroom-based writing and peer review to make claims about how these technology-mediated writing spaces similarly facilitated authors' receipt of and response to feedback. This analysis also revealed important differences in assessment of quality between the two spaces, primarily resulting from the influence of school-based norms and expectations.

A final theme in the literature explores the interconnected nature of fan-based literacies, adolescents' multiple identities, and the online affinity spaces in which they are enacted. Researchers have argued that participating in these spaces allows writers to play with their identities as they infuse elements of themselves into the creations they share online (Magnifico, 2012; Thomas, 2006) and provides marginalized youth access to empowering identities as successful writers (Black, 2008; Chandler-Olcott & Mahar, 2003).

In fan-based online affinity spaces, youth engage in identity work to position themselves as particular kinds of writers and fans (e.g., Jwa, 2012). Korobkova and Black (2014) examined how fans of One Direction (a British boy band) used transformative works they shared in Wattpad to "[lay] claim" (p. 624) to and negotiate such identities as "fangirl" (a particularly enthusiastic fan), "good fan," teenager, and writer. Similarly, Lammers and Marsh (in press) drew on a longitudinal case study of an adolescent writer to illustrate how she positioned herself and was positioned by others as she shared writing on Fanfiction.net. However, by recognizing the myriad contextual factors youth must navigate when they decide to participate in fan-based online affinity spaces, this particular literacy-and-identity analysis troubles celebratory notions of these spaces as sites where young writers can be agentic in their literacy and identity work.

## Current and Emerging Theories

### Current Predominant Theories

Many researchers exploring fan-based literacy practices adopt sociocultural orientations that focus on learning as a cultural experience, occurring in situ and in practice (Gerber, Abrams, Curwood, & Magnifico, 2017). Drawing on Vygotsky's (1978) work, this perspective favors an anthropological, cultural orientation to understanding learning, rather than seeing learning as a primarily cognitive, individual act. As such, these investigations emphasize how structure, language, tools, and interaction mediate learning in participatory, social situations. Lave and Wenger's (1991) communities of practice concept provides a theory of practice and apprenticeship with sociocultural origins that has been used to understand fan-based literacies. Adopting this theory led Guzzetti and Gamboa (2005) to note how adolescent participants formed social connections and relationships in service of their fan-based online activities.

New Literacy Studies (NLS) derives from this sociocultural perspective, adopting a similar situated, social orientation to studying literacies in context (e.g., Gee, 1996; New London Group, 1996; Street, 1997). Aligning with NLS means acknowledging the deictic, or rapidly changing and context-dependent, nature of literacies as new technologies and online spaces demand new social practices for full participation in civic life (Coiro, Knobel, Lankshear, & Leu, 2008). The affinity space theories (Gee, 2004; Lammers et al., 2012) often used to study fan-based literacy practices arise from this NLS orientation. In contrast to communities of practice, which implies membership and shared values among participants, taking an affinity space approach to studying fan-based literacies recognizes that such cohesion among contributors' values, actions, and goals may not exist even while people's shared practices contribute to the common endeavor (Hayes & Duncan, 2012). In problematizing notions of membership, an affinity space approach can shift the researcher's focus away from determining community membership status and toward an emphasis on mapping the interconnected portals and understanding practices within the space (e.g., Black, 2007; Curwood, 2013; Lammers, 2012; Magnifico, 2012).

### Related Audience Theories

Additional theories about online audiences have similarly been applied to fan-based literacy practices. Lunsford and Ede (2009) have argued that sharing writing in online spaces changes the rhetorical situation in ways "that make some writerly choices seem obvious and 'natural,' while others are 'unnatural' or entirely hidden from view" (p. 48) as the writer responds to the expectations of the online audience. Magnifico (2010) argues that two conceptualizations of audience shape a writer's writing: Considering audience in the abstract ("writing for readers") helps the writer internally plan her writing, whereas a social audience provides direct, external feedback on what gets shared online ("sharing writing with readers") (p. 176). Relatedly, boyd (2014) has theorized online audience as "networked publics," accounting for both the "space constructed through networked technologies" and "the imagined community that emerges as a result of the intersection of people, technology, and practice" (p. 8). Each of these theoretical perspectives honors how writers place themselves "among the audience" (Lunsford & Ede, 2009), and researchers have used these notions of audience to study writers who participate in fan-based online affinity spaces (e.g., Curwood et al., 2013; Lammers & Marsh, 2015; Magnifico, 2012).

### Emerging Theoretical Perspectives

In introducing affinity spaces, Gee (2004) explained that the necessity of membership in communities of practice is problematic because it led to "vexatious issues over which people are in and which are out of the group, how far they are in or out, and when they are in or out" (p. 78). He therefore focused on space, rather than membership and community. However, new research shows that community-building and socializing do seem to play an important role in affinity spaces (Bommarito, 2014; Lammers, 2012; Lammers et al., 2012). Abrams and Lammers (2017) proposed bridging affinity spaces and communities of practice by invoking Discourses (Gee, 1996) to illuminate the doing-being-valuing practices that guide young people's participation in ways that allow them to be recognized by others as belonging. By focusing on the features of belongingness in affinity spaces, inclusionary and exclusionary practices become more visible (Abrams & Lammers, 2017).

In another attempt to bridge existing theoretical perspectives, Ito and her colleagues (2013) proposed connected learning to make sense of participation and learning *across* media and educational spaces. Drawing on situated learning, socio-cognitive, and participatory culture frameworks, they argued that young people's digital lives and learning experiences combine academic pursuits, peer cultures, and interests. As such, a connected learning perspective honors how technologies have the potential to bring together interests, friendships, identities, and academic achievement to create equitable, social, engaging learning opportunities. Renninger and Hidi's work (2016) complements this view, theorizing the importance of interest development in motivation and persistence in learning.

Finally, in a recent critique of the New London Group's (1996) multiliteracies perspective, Leander and Boldt (2013) argue that theories of emergence better represent the literacy practices that involve a "moment-by-moment unfolding" (p. 34). This piece argues that too much purpose and rational design has been ascribed to youth literacies and identities. Others have taken up similar notions of emergence, movement, and temporality to examine literacy practices in online spaces (e.g., Stornaiuolo & Hall, 2014; Stornaiuolo, Higgs, & Hull, 2013). These perspectives, along with those that direct researchers' attention to global connectivity and mobility, such as transliteracies (Stornaiuolo, Smith & Phillips, 2017) and cosmopolitanism (Hull & Stornaiuolo, 2014), may yield more nuanced understanding of participation in fan-based online affinity spaces.

### *Linking Theory to Methodology*

In any study, researchers must first consider their "logic that links the data to be collected (and the conclusions to be drawn) to the initial questions of the study" (Yin, 1994, p. 18). Such a "logic of inquiry" (Gee & Green, 1998) demonstrates how their research questions, theory, methodology, and findings are inextricably linked together. When researchers are both reflective and forthcoming about their methodological choices and theoretical perspectives, others should be able to expand the line of inquiry from the original study. A number of different theories can inform research into literate identities and fan-based online affinity spaces; for researchers, the task is to both understand and be transparent about how theory shaped the design, implementation, and dissemination of their study (Trainor & Graue, 2014).

To date, much of the research into literacies and identities within online affinity spaces has been qualitative in nature, using ethnography and case study approaches. Fanfiction research has primarily focused on exceptional cases (Black, 2008; Magnifico et al., 2015) of young creators from around the world. Although these thick descriptions of writers' processes, products, and interactions within online affinity spaces have laid vital groundwork, further research must work to understand how literacy and identity shape the culture and the practices of the wider fan community. To accomplish this, a number of different theoretical lenses and methodological choices may be relevant. New studies might (1) focus an in-depth case study on tracing one writer's literacy practices across multiple affinity spaces; (2) construct a multiple-case study to examine interactions between writers and beta readers within a specific affinity space; (3) analyze written content and its evolution based on feedback, revision, and reflection; (4) explore diverse fan writers' experiences in online affinity spaces; and (5) draw on big data approaches to examine trends in participation across an entire online affinity space. Notably, each affords different perspectives on how adolescents' literate identities shape, and are shaped by, online affinity spaces.

## Tensions and Conflicting Viewpoints

When we compare the findings from literature reviewed earlier with studies that investigate digital literacy practices in English classrooms, we begin to see tensions among fandom literacies and typical school experiences. We find it productive to further explore such tensions so what we have learned from these informal literacies might have greater impact on formal learning environments. Notably, we think about how English teachers engage the digital literacies that students develop on their own, and how connections across students' literate identities might be strengthened.

Young people's digital lives and literate identities, after all, are enacted within many online and physical spaces. When students read novels in their classrooms, a few might be drafting fanfiction or doodling charts and maps to keep track of the action. These responses, common in the worlds of book fandom and fanfiction, could be generative possibilities for a wider array of students, too. In short, just because a reading or writing practice comes from an online fandom does not mean it should be ruled out as a classroom activity (although it does not guarantee success, either).

It is relatively rare for teachers and English education researchers to embrace fan-based genres, practices, tools, and spaces in their teaching and research. While research (including our own) often calls for school curricula to take up such ideas, we have found little literature about schools and teachers who have done so. Social and digital literacies challenge classroom teachers because engaging, meaningful practices must still be assessed in traditional ways. Citing Beach, Campano, Edmiston, and Borgmann (2009), McWilliams and colleagues (2011) explain that "meeting the accountability challenges of a testing system that continues to treat literacy as a set of discrete skills that can be measured without regard to context" is a complex negotiation (p. 239). Similarly, Stornaiuolo, Hull, and Nelson (2009) describe wondering how their social network participants' "literacy skills will be judged on more traditional assessments" (p. 382), even while their project had been designed to consider global young people's images of themselves and others—not skills-based literacies.

From a sociocultural standpoint, it may seem more obvious for educators to take up a multiliteracies perspective that engages with dominant pedagogies and ways of interacting digitally and contextually across modes with people around the world (e.g., Kalantzis & Cope, 2012). For education policy makers, however, and the schools and teachers who must demonstrate student progress under these systems, literacy must be taught—at least primarily—as a skills-based endeavor (e.g., Beach et al., 2009; Beach, Thein, & Webb, 2012). Perhaps this conflict is at the root of Hicks, Young, Kajder, and Hunt's (2012) observation that throughout the one hundred years in which *English Journal* has chronicled changes in English teaching and technology, "teacher-authors in *EJ* dare to look ahead toward bold changes in writing instruction and the integration of media and technology, yet quickly return to what is known" (pp. 69–70). Consequently, the tension between multiliteracies perspectives and English pedagogies is both a practical and an epistemic one.

Skills-driven epistemology, focused on the production of writing for the purpose of displaying knowledge, tends to dominate classroom instruction. In other words, despite massive changes in storytelling media, from microfilm to motion pictures to hypertext, English teachers often fall back on goals of helping students to think critically, to research positions, and to see themselves as writers (Hicks et al., 2012). All of these goals are achievable with a variety of technologies, both analog and digital, as Warschauer (2011) noted when he called for schools to think carefully about not just putting devices into the hands of students, but about how computers, tablets, and the like will be used in revised curricula.

When the focus remains on device acquisition, as is too often true (Warschauer, 2011), various technologies for writing, from multimedia to Twitter, become tools for improving test performance and student outcomes. As such, we see much of the research engaging with technology and education citing benefits to student knowledge production and retention. Collins and Halverson (2009), for instance, note that encouraging students to engage in online affinity spaces can help them develop research skills, content knowledge, and specialized vocabulary. Several pedagogical accounts support similar assertions, focusing on how digital tools can provide students with access to new forms and genres of writing and storytelling (e.g., Hodgson, 2009; Hicks, 2013), visions of themselves as communicative writers (Allison, 2009; Reed & Hicks, 2009), or as critical consumers of media (e.g., Janks, 2014).

At the same time, often such literacy skills and practices are ultimately assessed in concert with standardized curriculum outcomes, reinforcing this epistemic tension. Examining teachers' writing rubrics suggests that, regardless of the writing assignment, digital or otherwise, most teachers write evaluative rubrics and many use commercial or standards-based rubrics (e.g., the 6+1 Traits of Writing) that may not match individual composition tasks (Woodard, Magnifico, & McCarthey, 2013). While digital skills are certainly important to developing young people's sense of themselves as writers and citizens—literate identities that they will carry with them far beyond schools—they tend to be eclipsed by proximal assessments and the need to produce writing that is "good enough" to meet a standard. In short, when schoolwork is assessed one assignment at a time and focuses on the *writing* rather than the *writer*, teachers and students have difficulty transcending such expectations.

Whereas much schoolwork focuses on assessment, literate identities are informed by young people's interactions with peers, teachers, and others within their local and global communities. Prior research on fan-based online affinity spaces has demonstrated the importance of having a supportive audience, though the extent to which writers' identities and practices develop directly from the feedback received from readers remains less clear. As we previously argued, "Teachers' expertise is deeply needed in the difficult task of developing students' skills in writing, peer review, and critique. Few young readers and reviewers learn how to give constructive feedback without instruction, whether in classrooms or online environments" (Magnifico et al., 2015, p. 165). Teachers, in this sense, can help students learn how to give and receive feedback from their peers. Through modeling, teachers can also articulate the process involved in reading, responding to, interpreting, and reviewing creative work, from short stories to films.

In contrast to school contexts, participants in fan-based online affinity spaces choose their own technologies, and this autonomy changes the nature of the literate identities that they develop. Many studies of affinity spaces have traced adolescents' journeys into seeing themselves as authors, artists, or designers, and the ways in which those identities form as a result of creating and sharing a particular creation (Black, 2008; Ito et al., 2013; Jwa, 2012; Lammers, 2016). Even when young fanfiction writers do not receive productive feedback on their work, knowing that they have readers and fans pushes them to continue creating (e.g., Curwood et al., 2013; Lammers et al., 2014; Lammers & Marsh, 2015; Magnifico, 2012; Thomas, 2006). Their readers provide feedback and make suggestions, and, often, new drafts replace old ones. Furthermore, because many researchers in this area apply sociocultural frameworks and epistemologies that value learning about local Discourses and knowledge, and the ways in which such lore is built and maintained (e.g., Gee, 2001; Lankshear & Knobel, 2011), much affinity space research focuses on *writers* rather than *writing*.

We do not mean to suggest that bringing these two worlds together is impossible. Many teachers and researchers have certainly succeeded in using Internet tools (e.g., Google Drive, social media networks), building collaborative networks within classrooms, and studying the ways in which students develop new writing practices and literate identities as a result (e.g., Hull, Stornaiuolo, & Sterponi, 2013; Rish, 2015). We, do, though, see significant tension in calls for English teachers to teach the principles and practices of new literacies. While we have seen—in our own and other's work—young writers defining themselves in incredible ways and developing professional quality skills through their work in fandom spaces, we are concerned that the assessment regime under which schools have been defined would make it impossible for teachers to take up such work in meaningful ways. We do believe that fan-based online affinity spaces have improved the writing, critical thinking, and literary analysis methods of many young fans. But the deep epistemic gulf between these spaces and schools suggests that importing such practices into schools requires great care.

**Recommendations and Forward Thinking**

In this chapter, we illuminated key themes in the research on adolescents' literate identities in fan-based online affinity spaces. When we juxtaposed the findings and recommendations from this line of inquiry with the research on technology use and valued literacy skills in English education, an epistemological tension emerged. Teachers face challenges when they attempt to incorporate fan-based literacy practices, tools, and spaces into formal learning environments guided by standards-based, assessment-driven, skills-focused instruction. While the predominant theoretical frameworks typically employed in fan-based literacy practice research initially served to help researchers legitimize these practices, understand these spaces, and learn about their writers, emerging theories and methodologies may have greater potential to bridge the epistemic divide between fan-based online affinity spaces and literacy classrooms.

As we look ahead to how the field might move forward in this endeavor, we encourage researchers interested in young people's digital lives to consider the following:

- How might the theories and methods highlighted in this chapter yield new insights that could help ease this epistemological tension?
- What opportunities lie in designing literacy instruction and assessments with connected learning principles such as equity and interest in mind (Ito et al., 2013)?
- How might explorations of diverse identities among fan writers help us understand broader experiences of participation in online affinity spaces, as boyd (2011) has considered raced participation in MySpace and Facebook?
- What could be learned by shifting the researcher's gaze from a focus on the *writer* to one that investigates the *writing*?
- What if research "in the wild" shifted to engaging in collaborative digital literacies research in classrooms, with teachers and students as partners in the inquiry?

**References**

Abrams, S. S., & Lammers, J. C. (2017). Belonging in a videogame space: Bridging affinity spaces and communities of practice. *Teachers College Record, 119*(12).

Allison, P. (2009). Be a blogger: Social networking in the classroom. In A. Herrington, K. Hodgson, & C. Moran (Eds.), *Teaching the new writing: Technology, change, and assessment in the 21st century classroom* (pp. 75–91). New York, NY: Teachers College Press.

Applebee, A. N., & Langer, J. A. (2011). A snapshot of writing instruction in middle and high schools. *English Journal, 100*(6), 14–27.

Beach, R., Campano, G., Edmiston, B., & Borgmann, M. (2010). *Literacy tools in the classroom: Teaching through critical inquiry, grades 5–12*. New York, NY: Teachers College Press.

Beach, R., Thein, A. H., & Webb, A. (2012). *Teaching to exceed the English language arts common core state standards*. New York, NY: Routledge.

Black, R. W. (2007). Fanfiction writing and the construction of space. *E-Learning, 4*, 384–397.

Black, R. W. (2008). *Adolescents and online fan fiction*. New York, NY: Peter Lang.

Bommarito, D. (2014). Tending to change: Toward a situated model of affinity spaces. *E-Learning and Digital Media, 11*, 406–418.

boyd, d. (2011). White flight in networked publics? How race and class shaped American teen engagement with MySpace and Facebook. In L. Nakamura & P. Chow-White (Eds.), *Race after the internet* (pp. 203–222). New York, NY: Routledge.

boyd, d. (2014). *It's complicated: The social lives of networked teens.* New Haven, CT: Yale University Press.
Chandler-Olcott, K., & Mahar, D. (2003). Adolescents' anime-inspired "fanfictions": An exploration of multiliteracies. *Journal of Adolescent & Adult Literacy, 47*, 556–566.
Coiro, J., Knobel, M., Lankshear, C., & Leu, D. J. (2008). Central issues in new literacies and new literacies research. In J. Coiro, M. Knobel, C. Lankshear, & D. J. Leu (Eds.), *Handbook of research on new literacies* (pp. 1–21). New York, NY: Routledge.
Collins, A., & Halverson, R. (2009). *Rethinking education in the age of technology.* New York, NY: Teachers College Press.
Coppa, F. (2006). A brief history of media fandom. In K. Hellekson & K. Busse (Eds.), *Fan fiction and fan communities in the age of the Internet: New essays* (pp. 41–59). Jefferson, NC: McFarland.
Curwood, J. S. (2013). The Hunger Games: Literature, literacy, and online affinity spaces. *Language Arts, 90*, 417–427.
Curwood, J. S. (2014). Reader, writer, gamer: Online role playing games as literary response. In H. R. Gerber & S. S. Abrams (Eds.), *Bridging literacies with videogames* (pp. 53–66). Rotterdam, Netherlands: Sense Publishers.
Curwood, J. S., Magnifico, A. M., & Lammers, J. C. (2013). Writing in the wild: Writers' motivation in fan-based affinity spaces. *Journal of Adolescent & Adult Literacy, 56*, 677–685.
Duncan, S. C., & Hayes, E. (2012). Expanding the affinity space: An introduction. In E. R. Hayes & S. C. Duncan (Eds.), *Learning in video game affinity spaces* (pp. 1–22). New York, NY: Peter Lang.
Garcia, A. (Ed.). (2014). *Teaching in the connected learning classroom.* Irvine, CA: Digital Media and Learning Research Hub.
Gee, J. P. (1996). *Social linguistics and literacies: Ideology in discourses* (2nd ed.). London, UK: Taylor & Francis.
Gee, J. P. (2001). Reading as situated language: A sociocognitive perspective. *Journal of Adolescent & Adult Literacy, 44*, 714–725.
Gee, J. P. (2004). *Situated language and learning: A critique of traditional schooling.* New York, NY: Routledge.
Gee, J. P., & Green, J. L. (1998). Discourse analysis, learning, and social practice: A methodological study. *Review of Research in Education, 23*, 119–169.
Gerber, H. R., Abrams, S. S., Curwood, J. S., & Magnifico, A. M. (2017). *Conducting qualitative research of learning in online spaces.* Los Angeles, CA: SAGE.
Graham, S., Capizzi, A., Harris, K. R., Hebert, M., & Morphy, P. (2014). Teaching writing to middle school students: A national survey. *Reading and Writing, 27*, 1015–1042.
Grimes, S. M. (2015). Playing by the market rules: Promotional priorities and commercialization in children's virtual worlds. *Journal of Consumer Culture, 15*, 110–134.
Grimes, S. M., & Fields, D. A. (2012). *Kids online: A new research agenda for understanding social networking forums.* New York, NY: Joan Ganz Cooney Center.
Grimes, S. M., & Shade, L. R. (2005). Neopian economics of play: Children's cyberpets and online communities as immersive advertising in NeoPets.com. *International Journal of Media & Cultural Politics, 1*(2), 181–198.
Guzzetti, B., & Gamboa, M. (2005). Online journaling: The informal writings of two adolescent girls. *Research in the Teaching of English, 40*, 168–206.
Hayes, E. R., & Duncan, S. C. (2012). *Learning in video game affinity spaces.* New York, NY: Peter Lang.
Hicks, T. (2013). *Crafting digital writing: Composing texts across media and genres.* Portsmouth, NH: Heinemann.
Hicks, T., Young, C. A., Kajder, S., & Hunt, B. (2012). Same as it ever was: Enacting the promise of teaching, writing, and new media. *English Journal, 101*(3), 68–74.
Hodgson, K. (2009). Digital picture books: From Flatland to multimedia. In A. Herrington, K. Hodgson, & C. Moran (Eds.), *Teaching the new writing: Technology, change, and assessment in the 21st century classroom* (pp. 55–74). New York, NY: Teachers College Press.
Holloway, D., Green, L, & Livingstone, S. (2013). *Zero to eight: Young children and their Internet use.* London, UK: EU Kids Online. Retrieved from http://eprints.lse.ac.uk/52630/.
Hull, G., & Stornaiuolo, A. (2014). Cosmopolitan literacies, social networks, and "proper distance": Striving to understand in a global world. *Curriculum Inquiry, 44*, 15–44.
Hull, G., Stornaiuolo, A., & Sterponi, L. (2013). Imagined readers and hospitable texts: Global youth connect online. In Alvermann, D. E., Unrau, N. J., & Ruddell, R. B. (Eds.), *Theoretical models and processes of reading* (pp. 1208–1240). Newark, DE: International Reading Association.
Hutchins, E. (1995). *Cognition in the wild.* Cambridge, MA: MIT Press.
Hyler, J., & Hicks, T. (2014). *Create, compose, connect: Reading, writing, and learning with digital tools.* New York, NY: Routledge.
Ito, M., Gutiérrez, K., Livingstone, S., Penuel, B., Rhodes, J., Salen, K., ... Watkins, S. C. (2013). *Connected learning: An agenda for research and design.* Irvine, CA: Digital Media and Learning Research Hub.
Janks, H. (2014). *Doing critical literacy: Texts and activities for students and teachers.* New York, NY: Routledge.
Jenkins, H. (1992). *Textual poachers: Television fans and participatory culture.* New York, NY: Routledge.
Jwa, S. (2012). Modeling L2 writer voice: Discoursal positioning in fanfiction writing. *Computers and Composition, 29*, 323–340.
Kalantzis, M., & Cope, B. (2012). *Literacies.* New York, NY: Cambridge University Press.

Korobkova, K. A., & Black, R. W. (2014). Contrasting visions: Identity, literacy, and boundary work in a fan community. *E-Learning and Digital Media, 11*, 619–632.

Lammers, J. C. (2012). "Is the Hangout…The Hangout?" Exploring tensions in an online gaming-related fan site. In E. R. Hayes & S. C. Duncan (Eds.), *Learning in video game affinity spaces* (pp. 23–50). New York, NY: Peter Lang.

Lammers, J. C. (2013). Fangirls as teachers: Examining pedagogic discourse in an online fan site. *Learning, Media and Technology, 38*, 368–386.

Lammers, J. C. (2016). "*The Hangout* was serious business": Leveraging participation in an online space to Design *Sims* fanfiction. *Research in the Teaching of English, 50*, 309–332.

Lammers, J. C., Curwood, J. S., & Magnifico, A. M. (2012). Toward an affinity space methodology: Considerations for literacy research. *English Teaching: Practice and Critique, 11*(2), 44–58.

Lammers, J. C., Magnifico, A. M., & Curwood, J. S. (2014). Exploring tools, places, and ways of being: Audience matters for developing writers. In K. E. Pytash & R. E. Ferdig (Eds.), *Exploring technology for writing and writing instruction* (pp. 186–201). Hershey, PA: IGI Global.

Lammers, J. C., & Marsh, V. L. (2015). Going public: An adolescent's networked writing on Fanfiction.net. *Journal of Adolescent & Adult Literacy, 59*, 277–285.

Lammers, J. C., & Marsh, V. L. (in preparation). "A writer more than…a child": A longitudinal study exploring adolescent writer identity.

Lankshear, C., & Knobel, M. (2011). *New literacies: Everyday practices and social learning* (3rd ed.). New York, NY: Open University Press.

Lave, J., & Wenger, E. (1991). *Situated learning: Legitimate peripheral participation.* New York, NY: Cambridge University Press.

Leander, K., & Boldt, G. (2013). Rereading "a pedagogy of multiliteracies": Bodies, texts, and emergence. *Journal of Literacy Research, 45*, 22–46.

Lenhart, A. (2015). *Teens, social media, and technology overview 2015.* Washington, DC: Pew Research Center. Retrieved from www.pewinternet.org/2015/04/09/teens-social-media-technology-2015/.

Lunsford, A., & Ede, L. (2009). Among the audience: On audience in an age of new literacies. In M. E. Weisler, B. Felhler, & A. M. Gonzalez (Eds.), *Engaging audience: Writing in an age of new literacies* (pp. 42–72). Urbana, IL: National Council of Teachers of English.

Magnifico, A. M. (2010). Writing for whom? Cognition, motivation, and a writer's audience. *Educational Psychologist, 45*, 167–184.

Magnifico, A. M. (2012). The game of Neopian writing. In E. R. Hayes & S. C. Duncan (Eds.), *Learning in video game affinity spaces* (pp. 212–234). New York, NY: Peter Lang.

Magnifico, A. M. (2017). Theorizing context: A design-based analysis of an online affinity space. In M. Knobel & C. Lankshear (Eds.), *Researching new literacies: Design, theory, and data in sociocultural investigation* (pp. 59–80). New York, NY: Peter Lang.

Magnifico, A. M., & Curwood, J. S. (2012). Affinity space ethnography: Qualitative research in online spaces. Poster presented at the International Conference of the Learning Sciences, Sydney, Australia.

Magnifico, A. M., Curwood, J. S., & Lammers, J. C. (2015). Words on the screen: Broadening analyses of interactions between fanfiction writers and reviewers. *Literacy, 49*, 158–166.

McWilliams, J., Hickey, D. T., Hines, M B., Conner, J. M., & Bishop, S. C. (2011). Using collaborative writing tools for literary analysis: Twitter, fan fiction and the crucible in the secondary English classroom. *The Journal of Media Literacy Education, 2*, 238–245.

New London Group. (1996). A pedagogy of multiliteracies: Designing social futures. *Harvard Educational Review, 66*, 60–92.

Padgett, E., & Curwood, J. S. (2016). A figment of their imagination: Adolescent poetic literacy in an online affinity space. *Journal of Adolescent & Adult Literacy, 59*, 397–407.

Reed, D., & Hicks, T. (2009). From the front of the classroom to the ears of the world: Multimodal composing in speech class. In A. Herrington, K. Hodgson, & C. Moran (Eds.), *Teaching the new writing: Technology, change, and assessment in the 21st century classroom* (pp. 124–139). New York, NY: Teachers College Press.

Renninger, K. A., & Hidi, S. E. (2016). *The power of interest for motivation and engagement.* New York, NY: Routledge.

Rish, R. M. (2015). Researching writing events: Using mediated discourse analysis to explore how students write together. *Literacy, 12*(1), 12–19.

Roozen, K. (2009). "Fan fic-ing" English studies: A case study exploring the interplay of vernacular literacies and disciplinary engagement. *Research in the Teaching of English, 44*, 136–169.

Squire, K. (2011). *Video games and learning: Teaching and participatory culture in the digital age.* New York, NY: Teachers College Press.

Stornaiuolo, A., & Hall, M. (2014). Tracing resonance: Qualitative research in a networked world. In G. B. Gudmundsdottir & K. B. Vasbø (Eds.), *Methodological challenges when exploring digital learning spaces in education* (pp. 29–44). Rotterdam, Netherlands: Sense Publishers.

Stornaiuolo, A., Higgs, J., & Hull, G. A. (2013). Social media as authorship: Methods for studying literacies and communities online. In P. Albers, T. Holbrook, & A. S. Flint (Eds.), *New Literacy Research Methods* (pp. 224–237). New York, NY: Routledge.

Stornaiuolo, A., Hull, G. A., & Nelson, M. E. (2009). Mobile texts and migrant audiences: Rethinking literacy and assessment in a new media age. *Language Arts, 86*, 382–392.

Stornaiuolo, A., Smith, A. Phillips, N. C. (2017). Developing a transliteracies framework for a connected world. *Journal of Literacy Research, 49*, 68–91.

Street, B. (1997). The implications of the 'new literacy studies' for literacy education. *English in Education, 31*(3), 45–59.

Thomas, A. (2006). Fan fiction online: Engagement, critical response and affective play through writing. *Australian Journal of Language and Literacy, 29*, 226–239.

Tosenberger, C. (2008). "Oh my God, the fanfiction!": Dumbledore's outing and the online Harry Potter fandom. *Children's Literature Association Quarterly, 22*(2), 200–206.

Trainor, A. A., & Graue, E. (2014). Evaluating rigor in qualitative methodology and research dissemination. *Remedial and Special Education, 35*, 267–274.

Vygotsky, L. S. (1978). *Mind in society*. Cambridge, MA: Harvard University Press.

Warschauer, M. (2011). *Learning in the cloud: How (and why) to transform schools with technology*. New York, NY: Teachers College Press.

Woodard, R. L., Magnifico, A. M., & McCarthey, S. J. (2013). Supporting teacher metacognition about formative assessment in online writing environments. *E-Learning & Digital Media, 10*, 442–469.

Yin, R. K. (1994). *Case study research: Design and methods* (2nd ed.). Thousand Oaks, CA: Sage.

# IV
## Digital Spaces

Kathy A. Mills

This section narrates the vividly dynamic social spaces that discursively shape, and are shaped by, the writing and literacies practices of children and youth. From edgy theorizations of writing in virtual worlds and sandbox games like *Minecraft*, to analyzing the digital metroliteracy spaces of urban youth, the authors critically interweave concepts of digital gaming, assemblages, and image-text relations to explore inscribed worlds. In this volume, we see digital spaces for writing as socially produced. Digital spaces are not regarded as "containers" in which writing and literacy practices occur but constitute complex socio-material relations of space-time (Mills & Comber, 2015). These spaces allow both productive and transgressive forms of writing that are realized spatially, materially, and socially.

Chris Bailey, Cathy Burnett, and Guy Merchant, in Chapter 15, demonstrate how virtual worlds, in particular a multiplayer version of *Minecraft*, provided opportunities for new kinds of interaction and new forms of writing and textual practice. They develop a useful set of provisional categories—writing the world, writing in the world, and writing from the world—to differentiate the kinds of digital composition in and beyond virtual worlds. Similarly, they use Deleuze and Guattari's (1987) notion of the "assemblage" to explore the sometimes transgressive processes that were lived out in the Banterbury library of a *Minecraft* world.

Antero Garcia explores the role of writing and literacies within a range of game genres, including first-person shooters, alternate reality games, online roleplaying games, and digital sandboxes (Chapter 16). He expounds and interrogates new game concepts, from the "magic circle" to "gamification," "gamified," and "game-based" literacies, and the implications for communities of practice and for schooling. In doing so, Garcia highlights a key gap in existing conceptions of gaming and literacies, describing a layered ecology in which multiple frames of literacies overlap and are intertwined, with culturally mediated connections beyond the game.

Chapter 17, "Digital Metroliteracies," elaborates the parallel between writing and literacies that becomes manifest through physical urban space as metrolingualism, with social media practices such as Facebooking similarly contributing to the urban fabric. Sender Dovchin and Alastair Pennycook achieve this by theorizing the varied ways in which linguistic and cultural resources, spatial repertoires, and online activities are bound together to make meaning. They demonstrate how the mobility and mobilization of linguistic and other semiotic resources are distributed, recontextualized, and resemiotized in online spaces.

Peggy Albers, Vivian Vasquez, and Jerome Harste provide a rationale for critique of art in digital texts, and how image-text relations position readers (Chapter 18). Extending critical literacy to analyze artistic and design choices in digital composition, these authors bring knowledge of design principles of art to enable educators and students to interrogate their own and others' digital text production with a critical reading of the image.

In Chapter 19, Anna Smith, Bill Cope, and Mary Kalantzis critique the complexities of the techno-optimistic rendering of the "quantified writer" in education systems that have become digitally mediated and data-saturated learning and assessment contexts. The authors chart and evaluate the new opportunities for digital writing data and sources for learning. They argue that these data traces require an understanding of the underlying mechanisms that generate, archive, and make data accessible, opening up neoteric potentials for writing assessment.

The authors are united by a shared commitment to opening up productive spaces in the school curriculum for authentic and lively communicative practices that often occur in spontaneous and remarkable ways in digital worlds. The authors allow the stories, interactions, and texts of children and young people to speak for themselves. They survey a vibrant and conceptually rich collection of literacies in digital contexts of use that create very different kinds of material, textual, and discursive possibilities. They present new heuristics to reconfigure our conceptions of writing and literacies, and which resist old readings to inspire and critically challenge scholarship for the new times.

## References

Deleuze, G., & Guattari, F. (1987). *A thousand plateaus: Capitalism and schizophrenia* (B. Massumi, Trans.). Minneapolis and London, UK: University of Minnesota Press.

Mills, K. A., & Comber, B. (2015). Socio-spatial approaches to Literacy Studies: Rethinking the social constitution and politics of space. In K. Pahl & J. Rowsell (Eds.), *Handbook of literacy studies* (pp. 91–103). London, UK: Routledge.

# 15
# Assembling Literacies in Virtual Play

Chris Bailey, Cathy Burnett, and Guy Merchant

A group of nine children are playing *Minecraft* together during an after-school club. The Minecraft Club, set up by Chris at the request of the children, is a weekly event and it is in its twentieth week. When Chris is asked about Minecraft Club by adults, he tells them that the children are building a community, and to some extent this captures what they do. Anyone flying over Banterbury, as the children recently named it, would spot landmarks that signal a small- to medium-sized town—houses and flats, a library, a graveyard, shops, a theme park, and a zoo. Moreover, if you spoke to the children, what they'd say might sound like emerging folklore: the horse funeral, the mocking tower, the "Room of Doom." Together the children are conjuring up a new world—their world, one which is becoming ever more substantial. But this cumulative, linear description of what is happening in Minecraft Club belies the richness and complexity of their interactions. While they play in and with the shared virtual world, the boundaries and qualities of this world morph. Building is certainly going on, but there is an emergent, ephemeral nature to what they do, a way of being that can be lost in adult readings of what is produced. And what's more, the community they are building (and often disrupting) is not just being built on screen—their interactions *in the classroom*, with the people around them, and the stuff at hand seem just as important to their emergent and ongoing being-together as what they do *on screen*.

In many ways the story of *Minecraft* is a familiar one. Markus Persson, a Swedish programmer, creates a "sandbox videogame," which then goes viral. The game gets bought up, marketized, and subsequently developed to keep pace with a rapidly changing sociotechnical environment. Time goes by and *Minecraft* becomes a phenomenon with wide appeal (Wu, 2016). Then, in its most recent iteration, it boasts a version designed to work with a VR headset. Fans are enthusiastic. And so the story goes on…As we know, these sorts of playful practices in virtual spaces spread like wildfire, paying scant attention to the borders between nation states, languages, age groups, and so on. But divisions still exist; they don't reach all sectors of the population, and the notion that their spread is global is simply a myth. Nevertheless, in another era, such a phenomenon would be quickly dismissed as a fad, but now we take it more seriously. We get interested, Chris sets up his Minecraft Club, and studies *Minecraft* just as others do in different contexts (Hill, 2015; Hollett & Ehret, 2014). Perhaps we are obsessed by digital culture. In some ways we are in it together, but maybe we don't quite get it. And then again, at some level we worry about what it means for our children: Is it scary, is it normal, or is it rich with possibility—or is it all these things wrapped into one?

In some writing on the subject, digital culture appears like a feral beast, rattling the doors and windows of our classrooms. The trouble is, it is already in the classroom; it is already a part of children's everyday lives. How could it be otherwise? And so as a result the challenge for educators is what we do about it. Ignore it and it won't go away. In some ways that's why we keep agitating for a kind of schooling that addresses twenty-first-century literacies (Burnett & Merchant, 2015), and that's at least in part how the ephemeral practices of playing and building, like those that emerge in Chris's Minecraft Club, come to matter to us. But as we have already illustrated, playing and building is much more than screen-based activity in a virtual environment. It is always more than that, and in this chapter, we outline some ways of looking at what we are calling virtual play, how it combines and recombines with other things, with ideas, practices, and ways of being in the lives of a small group of children in the Minecraft Club based in a primary school serving a rural community in the north of England.

Virtual play is a generous description of engagement with *Minecraft*. It is borrowed from the work of Pearce and Artemesia (2010) and has been used to describe the ways "in which digital and networked media…support play and play-related activities and interactions" (Merchant, 2016, p. 301). It provides a way of talking about the sorts of affiliations and communities that grow up around a digital game like *Minecraft* (see Willet, 2016) and, indeed, in Chris's Minecraft Club. Virtual play is generous in the sense that it shows how there is far more at stake than just the game itself. In this way, the idea of virtual play cuts through some of the binaries that constrain discussions of digital culture—binaries like online/offline, on-screen/off-screen, human/nonhuman, and so on—and as such, it forms an animating concept for the empirical work we describe. But in what ways might virtual play relate to literacy and how might we begin to conceptualize writing in this context?

In what follows we suggest three provisional categories that trace different ways of thinking about current research in the field. Given all that we have said so far about the fluid nature of virtual play we acknowledge at the outset the overlap between these categories, but this does not detract from the differences in emphasis that they suggest. The first of these, *writing the world*, focuses on modifications to the screen-based world and implies a radical reworking of how writing itself is conceived, drawing heavily on an expanded notion of authoring. It encompasses activities such as content creation and the manipulation of in-world objects in which meanings are made using available semiotic resources, such as through the act of building in *Minecraft*. The second category, *writing in the world*, is concerned with more conventional communication conducted within a virtual space, and usually involves direct interaction with another player or players. This sort of writing often involves alphabetic literacy, such as in-world message exchange or synchronous chat, and where the game allows, creating texts such as signs, labels, books, and so on. Finally, *writing from the world* refers to the creation of texts that are related to, but not embedded within, the game or world. So this category includes producing paratexts related to a virtual environment, such as a message boards or blogs, as well as other forms of writing about online experiences, such as those that might be undertaken in classroom contexts.

**Writing the World**

With a sufficiently broad definition of writing, the ways in which in-world content is purposefully created or manipulated in order to communicate meaning to others is certainly worthy of attention. Studies that have addressed writing in this sense range from the organization of social events such as regattas or building structures in *Second Life* (Gillen, Ferguson, Peachey, & Twining, 2012, 2013), to game design using *Adventure Author* (Howells & Robinson, 2013) or similar tools (Burn, 2016). This category also includes working with commands that make things happen, such as those required to throw projectiles in *Whyville* (Fields & Kafai, 2010), or to manipulate objects in *Scratch* (Peppler, 2010).

Some more fundamental activity in virtual worlds and video games involves "playing the text" (Mackey, 2002) often through the use of keystrokes. Although we would argue that navigation in terms of moving through a virtual environment, shifting perspective or view, and changing between screens does not count as a communicative act, modifications of avatar design, clothing, and accessories introduce the notion of authoring the self online (Martey & Consalvo, 2011). Examples of this can be found in the work of Carrington and Hodgetts (2010), Marsh (2014), and Kafai, Fields, and Cook (2010). Research studies in this category often do not refer to these sorts of activity as writing, but they certainly do conceive of phenomena like avatar appearance as communicative codes, and therefore as a product of purposeful social action.

**Writing in the World**

This category is concerned with the use of the specific communication tools that are available to players in virtual environments. These studies regularly focus on messaging or in-world chat (Merchant, 2009, 2010) and have received considerable attention, particularly from educators advocating for the educational benefits of using virtual worlds in classrooms. In this vein, Marsh (2011, 2014) studied young children's communication in *Club Penguin* arguing that virtual play is a significant feature of contemporary childhood and early literacy development. Interestingly, in this context, young children will typically be using ready-made postcards or menu-based "safe chat" for communicating with other club members who are online (Marsh, 2014). Selecting an item from a menu and clicking send is, of course, a communicative act, but it certainly pushes on conventional views of what constitutes writing. Other examples of this sort of activity involving in-text messaging can be found in Dickey's work with older students in a variety of learning designs based in *Active Worlds* (Dickey, 2003, 2005).

**Writing from the World**

Situations in which writing activity comes about as a result of virtual interaction, but which is not directly dependent upon it for its production, have also received attention from researchers. Of particular note is the work of Beavis and colleagues (for example Apperley & Beavis, 2011; Beavis, 2014), which focuses on building connections between game texts and the curriculum; Dick's (2011) work on enriching literature study with virtual world play; and Berger and McDougall's (2013) study of video games in the English curriculum. These studies tend to focus on children and young people's experience of game texts and virtual worlds as a starting point for critical engagement. Another strand of work, which is directly concerned with the relationship between virtual play and literacy, draws attention to the "constellation of literacy practices" of informal gameplay. Here, Steinkuehler (2007) highlights not only the complexity of in-world communication, but also the considerable amount of writing that gets produced in both official and unofficial fandom.

**Tensions and Conflicting Viewpoints**

While these categories signal different ways of thinking about relationships between writing and virtual play, they do not sit easily with our complex take on virtual play outlined above, and indeed many of the authors cited would also challenge these distinctions. In some ways, Steinkuehler's work on constellations of literacy escapes our categories. By surveying the literacy practices that young gamers routinely engage in, she shows how these move in and out of interrelated virtual environments. Even if we can identify specific domains in which writing is produced, the meanings made always seem to exceed the immediate context, relating for instance, to shared experience, popular culture, real-world friendships, and events (Leppänen, Pitkänen-Huhta, Piirainen-Marsh, Nikula, & Peuronen,

2009). Although much has been written about immersive engagement, ideas like Fleer's notion of "flickering," in which players' attention constantly moves between concrete activity and imagination (Fleer, 2014), and that of "layered presence" (Martin et al., 2012), in which players are almost simultaneously attentive to multiple dimensions of online engagement, material, emplaced, and embodied experience, offer persuasive alternatives.

In Minecraft Club, for example, distinctions between writing the world and writing in/of the world are difficult to tease out. Children move fluidly between on/offline writing, and the scope of writing variously constricts and expands; off-screen interactions feel just as much part of writing the world as do on-screen activities. If we look, for example, at children's writing "in" and "of" the world, the children regularly produce notices, books, messages, and signs, just as young children in an early years setting do (Roskos & Christie, 2001). Most of these texts are made on-screen, but sometimes the children write on scraps of paper or in notebooks, creating lists of wished-for resources or making plans for future construction projects. These texts celebrate, mediate, or perform ways of being and doing in Banterbury, variously demarcating spaces, serving specific purposes, or providing an outlet for individuals' ideas or feelings. Some texts are rapidly discarded or erased while some have a longer life in the play. Others are ignored but survive in the world—testament to previous moments of significance, shared interest, enthusiasm, or outbursts of hilarity. And yet others gently tease, recycle in-jokes, and contribute to the ongoing banter of virtual play (Bailey, 2016).

In thinking about this blurring of on/off-screen activity, we can draw parallels, as others have done, with process drama (Dunn & O'Toole, 2009; O'Mara, 2012). Unlike the kind of rehearsed performance that typifies theatrical performance, process drama involves participants working together to produce a "dramatic elsewhere" or "dramatic world" in which events are unpredictable, driven by what people do and with no external audience (Dunn & O'Toole, 2009). This feels very much like what happens in Minecraft Club, as children improvise with what's available, and do things—e.g., build or make traps-in response to others' actions. As in process drama, the world is conjured through shared belief born of being and doing things together, of seizing opportunities, following possible directions, and accepting and building upon what others do or make either literally or figuratively. O'Mara has explored how video game play, like process drama, involves both being in and looking at the dramatic world. Just as process drama involves participating in a dramatic world and reflecting on that experience, so virtual play combines an immersive engagement in a fictitious world with the mechanics of navigating commands and toolbars, and managing interactions around or between screens.

But there are differences, too. In virtual play, the world is not just imagined or embodied but materializes as a shared text, enacted (or temporarily etched) on screen as avatars move through the world, entering new scenarios as they go. The traces of this play may live on in the ever-changing *Minecraft* text long after children's interest has moved on. And while process drama usually involves a collaborative engagement with a shared project, virtual play in Minecraft Club is as often divergent as convergent. Pairs and groups may temporarily collaborate on building projects, but individuals may just as often seek out new territory or combine in interest/friendship groups. And the direction of play is both enabled and constrained by the deep architecture of *Minecraft* as well as its iterative renewal through the ongoing introduction of various modifications (mods). Yet despite all this, Minecraft Club sustains a sense of ensemble. In many ways, it is built through a generative sense of being together, as children try things out, help one another, fall out, make themselves and each other laugh, and sing (Bailey, 2016; Burnett & Bailey, 2014).

As we reflect on this divergent, ebullient, and highly generative activity, it becomes difficult to define where writing begins and ends. In the next section, we propose a way of conceiving the relationship between virtual play and writing as an ongoing process of assembling. This perspective, we argue, allows us to see authorship as expansive, distributed, and fluid, and this in turn provides new directions for research and practice.

## Current or Emerging Theory: Assembling Virtual Play

Deleuze and Guattari use the word "assemblage," translated by Massumi from the French *agencement* (1987), to capture the way in which social, semiotic, and material flows converge and diverge from moment to moment. This notion has been used persuasively to explore how things of different "orders" —political, economic, organizational, subjective, affective, and so on—come together to generate and uphold certain ways of doing and being in educational contexts (Youdell, 2011). It is useful, for example, in thinking about how literacy gets constituted and sustained in particular ways. We could certainly explain some rather stultifying contemporary literacy provision in English schools in terms of an assemblage of, among other things, curriculum, assessment, school governance, teacher disaffection, international league tables, market forces, and a punitive accountability regime. However, our interest is in using assemblage to think about fluidity and possibility rather than intransigence. In this chapter, and in other work (e.g. Burnett & Merchant, 2017) we therefore follow John Law's lead, approaching assemblage as,

> …a process of bundling, or assembling, or better of recursive self-assembling in which the elements put together are not fixed in shape, do not belong to a larger pre-given list but are constructed at least in part as they are entangled together.
>
> (Law, 2004, p. 42)

From this perspective, things enact one another as they tangle together; things "make a difference to each other: they make each other be" (Law & Mol, 2008, p. 58). And these "things" include not just what is physically present, but what is folded into that presence. This focus on the *process* of assemblage is important to us, and something we like to foreground by using the gerund "assembling" rather than the seemingly more static "assemblage" (Burnett & Merchant, forthcoming a). As well as sensitizing us to how things assemble in "relatively stabilized ways" (Law & Mol, 2002, p. 2), it alerts us to *what else* gets produced in the moment of assembling, and to the potentialities generated as things assemble in multiple ways. This perspective has a number of implications for how we might think about relationships between virtual play and literacy, and about how we might usefully think about writing in this context. In order to introduce these points, we pause to consider a series of episodes that happened one day in Minecraft Club, before going on to reflect on how things assembled, and how these assemblings may be significant to our discussions about literacy.

### *Banterbury Library*

> …a lot of people think that *Minecraft* is just about building structures but you can build books and stories and stuff as well, which is quite good…it's a feature that is in *Minecraft* all the time, and it's part of real life…there's books in real life…

In one of Chris's group discussions with Minecraft Club members, the children talked about how it was possible to "build books." This phrase succinctly captures the uncanny way in which a textual form so deeply implicated in the history of print text resurfaces in the world of *Minecraft*. But after all books—the printed sort—were as much a part of the children's everyday life as *Minecraft* itself, and they had their place in Minecraft Club. In fact, print texts such as the *Redstone Handbook* (Farwell, 2015) were sometimes used for reference.

Chris's research notes chronicle his discovery of the first book, *Mia's Dead*. A screenshot of a chest in a windowless room, reminiscent of depictions of Carter's excavations of Tutankhamun's tomb, bears the caption: "This is the first book that I became aware of in the club, during week 20." To the side is a small facsimile of the text, looking just like a museum piece. It may not in fact have been the first book, and certainly there were rumors of other titles including *Mia's Twin Fish* and *Mia's Other Twin*, but Chris's discovery led him to conclude that "these books produced by Thomas form the basis of what became Banterbury Library…setting the tone of many of the books that followed."

History aside, books and library-play slowly became a feature of the club and in a later session, while laptops were being stowed away and Chris was reminding club members about chargers, one of the children could be heard singing "We got *Minecraft* books, We got *Minecraft* books" and a group of boys, now calling themselves the Banterbury Library Boys started making plans. The seed of an idea was beginning to germinate. Book production was to become a theme in subsequent sessions lasting for four or five weeks. In many ways, this typifies the fluid and emergent nature of the virtual play in Minecraft Club, as groups temporarily coalesced around an idea or interest which would then play itself out over time.

The texts produced for the library were playful and unfettered by the usual conventions of classroom writing. They could be described as transgressive and often involved ribald and scatological humor directed at other club members. In this way, they were imbricated with the gentle teasing and banter that contributed to the negotiation and renegotiation of social relationships within the club. Indicative titles collected by Chris include *The Sick Buk, Revenge, The Poop Buk, The Plastic Buk,* and *The Rap Buk*, and these titles often hinted at their content. But the books weren't just written and stored away in a chest in Banterbury Library, they were performed, read aloud, and shared on screens as they were composed. They lived as texts that wove in and out of the unfolding virtual play.

Although there was little attempt at controlling the subject matter, as this play evolved the Banterbury Library Boys entered into a power struggle. One boy produced *The Spam Book* comprised of a random string of text, while another was criticized for not producing a full page. A series of pronouncements were issued: *You can't put a book in if they aren't correct; and on the back page it has to be capital P "Property of" and then "Banterbury Library" and it has to be "the buk" B-U-K*. Here, lessons about authority and language were clearly being rehearsed. But even these were not immune from challenge. Firstly, an appeal was made to what you might call the social order of play: *Yeah, but me and you were the ones who came up with the idea in the first place* and then reference to the real world: *And how come books have to be exactly the same. In real libraries books aren't exactly the same!* But this was subsequently brushed off with the assertion that: *This is Minecraft and this is how we want to do it!*

### *Assembling Banterbury*

We are struck by various aspects of this play, and our first instinct, as seasoned analysts of children's classroom practices, is to frame them using various social-cultural constructs: the social shaping of gendered identity by the "Banterbury Boys;" the Banterbury Library Books as new genre; the transgressive nature of peer culture; and the power struggles arising from the push for conformity. Such interpretations articulate in interesting ways with our thinking about writing and virtual play, and echo other debates about writing in other contexts, linked for example to: writing as identity performance; the emergence of new genres in digital environments; the regulation of schooled writing; text production as always inflected by power relations, and so on. Another starting point for thinking about Banterbury Library is to use our three earlier categories to tease out some of the complex ways in which writing entangled with play. We could certainly identify writing "in world" (the books), and chart the negotiated—and contested—development of the library as an ongoing textual unfolding. We can even start to think about how we might adapt writing pedagogies to account for this kind of creative activity, providing opportunities for children to develop expressive, rhetorical, or critical dimensions of textual production for example. However, for us the drawback of both of these starting points is that—through sieving out writing from virtual play and holding it up against other social practices or writing events—we write out the messy complexity that seems central to what happens/gets generated; we neatly parcel it up, explain it, and sort it out. And yet just as we pull dimensions of the play apart, they all too easily snap together again, mingling with one another, acting on, being enacted by, and becoming each other.

An alternative approach might be to approach this example of virtual play by thinking about it as what Law and Singleton (2005) call a "fire object." Now of course Banterbury Library is a strange kind of object. It might more comfortably be described as a set of practices or a sequence of loosely associated actions, interactions, and texts. And yet it does seem to become a "thing" that has resonance for the children and around which various episodes revolve. For Law and Singleton, any "thing," whether concrete or abstract, comes into being through relationships between a set of absences and presences; it is generated through relationships with what's present as well as all the absent things folded into that presence.

If we think about Banterbury Library as a set of absences and presences, we might think about all the experiences, considerations, beliefs, and ways of knowing that assemble to generate what gets produced in the moment. So Banterbury Library has a certain visual presence in Minecraft Club (conjured through a combination of keys, pixels, screens, etc.), but all kinds of absences also make their presence felt in what it becomes: the programming of *Minecraft*, for example, the recent history of Minecraft Club, the children's previous experiences together and apart, and so on. Importantly, as the Library gets taken up by different children on different days it becomes different things as presences and absences assemble differently: a site of transgression, a focus for convergence, a point of contention, of belonging or exclusion, etc. And as it does so—and perhaps this is the important part for thinking about writing—it can generate, or set alight, new possibilities. As such it might be seen as a fire object. For Law and Singleton, fire objects are:

> …energetic, entities or processes that juxtapose, distinguish, make and transform absences and presences. […] The argument in part is that fires are energetic and transformative, and depend on difference—for instance between (absent) fuel or cinders and (present) flame. Fire objects, then, depend on otherness, and that otherness is generative.
>
> (Law & Singleton, 2005, pp. 343–344)

For us, thinking about clusters of activity as fire objects, such as the Banterbury Library example, disrupts our tendency to define and sort virtual play using habitual ways of thinking. This is not to devalue more established ways of describing literacy practices from a sociocultural perspective, in relation, for example, to gender, genre, or power. Much significant work has interrogated virtual play in relation to such themes (e.g. Beavis & Charles, 2007; Black & Reich, 2013; Carrington & Hodgetts, 2010; Walkerdine, 2007). It prompts us to focus on the stuff that escapes ordered tellings, and this in turn leads us to other ways of thinking about relationships between writing and virtual play.

First, it illustrates how it can be fruitful to think more expansively about writing. From this perspective, we might see writing as part of an ongoing flow of activity that generates affective intensities that in turn drive things forward. As such writing can't be researched as a bounded phenomenon, but must be approached as always entangled with multiple human and nonhuman activities. Writing unfolds moment to moment, and always in relation to a shifting assemblage of people, things, and available signs. It is both generated by and generative of an ongoing unfolding. Rather than focusing on what assembles to produce particular written artifacts or writing events, this perspective foregrounds how writing assembles with other things to generate a flow of activity.

Second, a focus on absence as well as presence foregrounds the multiple time-spaces folded into any moment, mediated by both human and non-human participants. Children bring to *Minecraft* their varied experience of playing *Minecraft* elsewhere (emerging from diverse human and non-human assemblages of *Minecraft* homes, families, friends, routines, preferences, and so so), not to mention their complex and varied experiences of being at school, of being together in this class, and their encounters with gameplay and artifacts produced by the wider *Minecraft* "community." These prior experiences and imaginings assemble with *Minecraft* to produce a particular kind of play. But Minecraft Club is not just enacted by the children; *Minecraft*, the screens, batteries, keyboard, Internet connection, etc., also enact Minecraft Club. Folded into the empty expanse of *Minecraft* are histories, precedents, and decisions that frame the possibilities enabled (or constrained) by screens and book pages of certain size and shape, keyboards, pixels, commands, available avatars, resources, and so forth. These resources are not just taken up by children but act upon them framing and prompting certain kinds of actions. The children and Chris (with all their histories, allegiances, preferences, imaginings, etc.) assemble with the stuff of *Minecraft*, the stuff of the classroom, stuff produced or given credence by other *Minecraft* players, and so on.

Third, in working with this complexity, we take from Law the idea of multiplicities—that multiple assemblings co-exist and work to disrupt and unsettle each other. Banterbury Library becomes different things within different assemblings, and writing therefore comes to do and mean different things, too. What is interesting is what happens as these different assemblings—of Minecraft Club, such as Banterbury Library, writing, gender, power, and transgression—co-exist and are held together in the moment, interrupting or entangling with one another. Of course, working with the idea of multiplicities means it is never possible to gain a "full picture" of what is happening in virtual play. Whatever we choose to focus upon, there is always something else assembling, and this has implications for how we think not just about educational practice but about research. To return to Law and Singleton:

> ...if objects are both present and absent, then we cannot know or tell them in all their otherness. Things will escape. If the world is messy we cannot know it by insisting it is clear.
> (Law & Singleton, 2005, pp. 349–350)

## Implications for Research and Educational Practice

There is plenty to know about virtual play, and there is plenty to know about play in and around specific games like *Minecraft*. So although this chapter focuses on children and *Minecraft* "in vivo" (self-consciously recognizing that an incomplete depiction is inevitable), researchers are challenged to illuminate its use with demographic studies (Minecraft-statistics.net (n.d.) is the only extant source), to explore particular pedagogic applications of *Minecraft* (e.g. Short, 2012), and to study *Minecraft* across home-school settings (Dezuanni, Beavis, & O'Mara, 2015). We also need to know how and under what circumstances games like *Minecraft* appeal to some and not others, and whether there are noticeable age, gender, or other social trends. Moreover, it's clear that there is much to be gained from fine-grained studies of interaction that trace such things as engagement and collaboration (as in Taylor, 2012, 2016). In short, the field is rich with possibilities. However, as Law and Singleton (2005) suggest, conventional research reports may struggle to account for the complexity explored in the previous section. If we are to work productively with the possibilities generated through virtual play, we need to be alert to *what is assembling*, to engage with multiple ways in which this is happening (to keep asking, "what else is going on?"), and to consider how we as researchers and educators *assemble with* what's happening. We end this chapter therefore with proposals for working with the notion of assembling in practice and in research.

**Recommendations and Forward Thinking**

We suggest that one way of sensitizing ourselves to multiple assemblings is to work with Bennett's idea of "enchantment," which mingles affective, sensory engagement with a disruption to taken-for-granted ways of understanding the world. As she writes,

> To be enchanted is to be both charmed and disturbed: charmed by a fascinating repetition of sounds or images, disturbed to find that, although your sense perception has become intensified, your background sense of order has flown out the door.
> (Bennett, 2001, p. 34)

We have attempted such an approach through our own work, juxtaposing multiple "stacking stories"—stories that trace divergent trajectories through particular moments, foregrounding our personal experiences. In doing so, we evoked not only what was felt as people and things assembled in certain ways, but also what might be felt or known if other stories had been told (Burnett & Merchant, 2014; 2016). Adopting a "mood of enchantment" helps us engage with the affective dimension of what children and young people are doing, opening us up to the vivid and felt dimensions of children's on and off-screen virtual play. It also, however, provides researchers and practitioners with a means of engaging differently with what is happening, of acknowledging some of the ephemeralities that escape ordered accounts of children's literacies. It may help us to look (and feel) beyond *what* children write to *the moment of writing* and all those moments that lead up to and from that moment, and to see those moments as fluid human and nonhuman assemblings. From this perspective, distinctions between writing the world, writing in the world, and writing of the world start to blur.

The disruptive wonder engendered through enchantment may also be generative for practitioners. Focusing on the moment brings us up close with what Massumi (2002) calls the "field of potentiality," the endless possibilities that are always immanent. It provides a counterpoint to the linear thinking that dominates the educational discourse in many jurisdictions (or in England at least), with its focus on outcomes led learning, evidence-based practice, and fixed criteria. Rather than looking in linear fashion at causal relationships, enchantment keeps us in the moment, with what's emerging, and with possibility. This invites us to consider what a writing pedagogy might look like if it were approached in a mood of enchantment.

A mood of enchantment might be generative in the way that Lenz Taguchi describes when she explores pedagogies aligned with an "ethics of immanence" that work and play with:

> …inter-connections and intra-actions in-between human and non-human organisms, matter and things, the contexts and subjectivities of students that emerge through the learning events.
> (Lenz Taguchi, 2010, p. xvi)

In previous work, we have noted how the struggle to grasp the complex, fluid, and hybrid nature of digital practices has led us to re-examine our conceptualizations of more established literacy practices (Burnett & Merchant, 2014). We suggest that the perspective on assembling we have sketched above may be generative in thinking about writing of different kinds, including the established literacy practices encountered in schools. Such an approach might undo some of the ennui engendered through the certainty and inevitability of schooled literacy in current times, and open up the possibility of disruption and new directions. This is not to underplay how certain powerful assemblages hold sway or to deny the challenges of resistance, but to allow other ways of knowing and being to seep in.

## References

Apperley, T., & Beavis, C. (2011). Literacy into action: Digital games as action and text in the English and literacy classroom. *Pedagogies: An International Journal*, 6(2), 130–143.

Bailey, C. (2016). Free the sheep: Improvised song and performance in and around a Minecraft community. *Literacy*, 50(2), 62–71.

Bennett, J. (2001). *The Enchantment of modern life: Attachments, crossings, and ethics*. Princeton, NJ: Princeton University Press.

Beavis, C. (2014). Games as text, games as action. *Journal of Adolescent & Adult Literacy*, 57(6), 433–439.

Beavis, C., & Charles, C. (2007). Would the 'real' girl gamer please stand up? Gender, LAN cafes and the reformulation of the 'girl' gamer. *Gender and Education*, 19(6), 691–705.

Berger, R., & McDougall, J. (2013). Reading videogames as (authorless) literature. *Literacy*, 47(3), 142–149.

Black, R., & Reich, S. (2013). A sociocultural approach to exploring virtual worlds. In G. Merchant, J. Gillen, J. Marsh, & J. Davies (Eds.), *Virtual literacies: Interactive spaces for children and young people* (pp. 27–40). London, UK: Routledge.

Burn, A. (2016). Making machinima: Animation, games, and multimodal participation in the media arts. *Learning, Media and Technology*, 41(2), 310–329.

Burnett, C., & Bailey, C. (2014). Conceptualising collaboration in hybrid sites: Playing Minecraft in the primary classroom. In C. Burnett, J. Davies, G. Merchant, & J. Rowsell (Eds.), *New literacies around the globe: Policy and pedagogy* (pp. 55–71). Abingdon, UK: Routledge.

Burnett, C., & Merchant, G. (2015). The challenge of 21st-century literacies. *Journal of Adolescent & Adult Literacy*, 59(3), 271–274.

Burnett, C., & Merchant, G. (2016). Boxes of poison: Baroque technique as antidote to simple views of literacy. *Journal of Literacy Research*, 48(3): 258–279.

Burnett, C., & Merchant, G. (2017). Assembling the virtual. In R. Parry, C. Burnett, & G. Merchant (Eds.), *Literacy, media, technology: Past, present and future*. London, UK: Bloomsbury.

Carrington, V., & Hodgetts, K. (2010). Literacy-lite in BarbieGirls™. *British Journal of Sociology of Education*, 31(6), 671–682.

Deleuze, G., & Guattari, F. (1987). *A thousand plateaus: Capitalism and schizophrenia* (B. Massumi, Trans.). London, UK: Continuum.

Dezuanni, M., Beavis, C., & O'Mara, J. (2015). 'Redstone is like electricity': Children's performative representations in and around Minecraft. *E-Learning and Digital Media*, 12(2), 147–163.

Dick, L. (2011). Riffing on the Pied Piper: Combining research and creativity. In A. Webb (Ed.), *Teaching literature in virtual worlds: Immersive learning in English studies* (pp. 97–107). Abingdon, UK: Routledge.

Dickey, M. D. (2003). Teaching in 3D: Pedagogical affordances and constraints of 3D virtual worlds for synchronous distance learning. *Distance Education*, 24(1), 105–121.

Dickey, M. D. (2005). Three-dimensional virtual worlds and distance learning: Two case studies of Active Worlds as a medium for distance education. *British Journal of Educational Technology*, 36(3), 439–451.

Dunn, J., & O'Toole, J. (2009). When worlds collude: Exploring the relationship between the actual, the dramatic and the virtual. In M. Anderson, J. Carroll, & D. Cameron (Eds.), *Drama education with digital technology* (pp. 20–37). London, UK: Continuum.

Farwell, N. (2015). *Minecraft redstone handbook*. New York, NY: Scholastic.

Fields, D. A., & Kafai, Y. B. (2010). Knowing and throwing mudballs, hearts, pies, and flowers: A connective ethnography of gaming practices. *Games and Culture*, 5(1), 88–115.

Fleer, M. (2014). The demands and motives afforded through digital play in early childhood activity settings. *Learning, Culture and Social Interaction*, 3(3), 202–209.

Gillen, J., Ferguson, R., Peachey, A., & Twining, P. (2012). Distributed cognition in a virtual world. *Language in Education*, 26(2), 151–167.

Gillen, J., Ferguson, R., Peachey, A., & Twining, P. (2013). Seeking planning permission to build a gothic cathedral on a virtual island. In G. Merchant, J. Gillen, J. Marsh, & J. Davies (Eds.), *Virtual literacies: Interactive spaces for children and young people* (pp. 190–207). Abingdon, UK: Routledge.

Hollett, T., & Ehret, C. (2014). Bean's world: (Mine)crafting affective atmospheres for gameplay, learning, and care in a children's hospital. *New Media and Society*, 17(11), 1849–1866.

Hill, V. (2015). Digital citizenship through game design in Minecraft. *New Library World*, 116(7/8), 369–382.

Kafai, Y. B., Fields, D. A., & Cook, M. S. (2010). Your second selves player-designed avatars. *Games and Culture*, 5(1), 23–42.

Law, J., & Mol, A. (Eds.). (2002). *Complexities*. Lancaster, PA: Duke Press.

Law, J. (2004). *After method: Mess in social science research*. Abingdon, UK: Routledge.

Law, J., & Mol, A. (2008). The actor-enacted: Cumbrian sheep in 2001. In C. Knappett & L. Malafouris (Eds.), *Material agency* (pp. 57–88). New York, NY: Springer.

Law, J., & Singleton, V. (2005). Object lessons. *Organization*, *12*(3), 331–355.
Lenz Taguchi, H. (2010). *Going beyond the theory/practice divide in early childhood education: Introducing an intra-active pedagogy*. Abingdon, UK: Routledge.
Leppänen, S., Pitkänen-Huhta, A., Piirainen-Marsh, A., Nikula, T., & Peuronen, S. (2009). Young people's translocal new media uses: A multiperspective analysis of language choice and heteroglossia. *Journal of Computer-Mediated Communication*, 14(4), 1080–1107.
Mackey, M. (2002). *Literacies across media: Playing the text*. London, UK: RoutledgeFalmer.
Marsh, J. (2011). Young children's literacy practices in a virtual world: Establishing an online interaction order. *Reading Research Quarterly*, *46*(2), 101–118.
Marsh, J. (2014). Purposes for literacy in children's use of the online virtual world Club Penguin. *Journal of Research in Reading*, *37*(2), 179–195.
Massumi, B. (2002). *Parables for the virtual: Movement, affect, sensation*. Durham, NC: Duke University Press.
Martey, R. M., & Consalvo, M. (2011). Performing the looking-glass self: Avatar appearance and group identity in Second Life. *Popular Communication*, *9*(3), 165–180.
Martin, C., Williams, C., Ochsner, A., Harris, S., King, E., Anton, G., ... Steinkuehler, C. (2012). Playing together separately: Mapping out literacy and social synchronicity. In G. Merchant, J. Gillen, J. Marsh, & J. Davies (Eds.), *Virtual literacies: Iinteractive spaces for children and young people* (pp. 226–243). New York, NY: Routledge.
Merchant, G. (2009). Literacy in virtual worlds. *Journal of Research in Reading*, *32*(1), 38–56.
Merchant, G. (2010). 3D virtual worlds as environments for literacy learning. *Educational Research*, *52* (2), 135–150.
Merchant, G. (2016). Virtual worlds and online videogames for children and young people: Promises and challenges. In M. Lesley & B. Guzzetti (Eds.), *The handbook of research on the societal impact of social media* (pp. 291–316). New York, NY: IGI Global.
Minecraft-statistics.net (n.d). *Players Minecraft online*. Retrieved from https://minecraft-statistic.net/en/players_list/.
O'Mara, J. (2012). Process drama and digital games as text and action in virtual worlds: Developing new literacies in school. *Research in Drama in Education*, *17*(4), 517–534.
Pearce, C., & Artemesia. (2010). *Communities of play: Emergent cultures in multiplayer games and virtual worlds*. Cambridge, MA: MIT Press.
Peppler, K. (2010). Media arts: Arts education for a digital age. *Teachers College Record*, *112*(8), 2118–2153.
Roskos, K., & Christie, J. (2001). Examining the play-literacy interface: A critical review and future directions. *Journal of Early Childhood Literacy*, *1*(1), 59–89.
Short, D. (2012). Teaching scientific concepts using a virtual world—Minecraft. *Teaching Science*, *58*(3), 55–58.
Steinkuehler, C. (2007). Massively multiplayer online gaming as a constellation of literacy practices. *E-Learning and Digital Media*, *4*(3), 297–318.
Taylor, R. (2012). Messing about with metaphor: Multimodal aspects to children's creative meaning making. *Literacy*, *46*(3), 156–166.
Taylor, R. (2016). The multimodal texture of engagement: Prosodic language, gaze and posture in engaged, creative classroom interaction. *Thinking Skills and Creativity*, *20*, 83–96.
Walkerdine, V., (2007). *Children, gender, video games: Towards a relational approach to multimedia*. London, UK: Palgrave Macmillan.
Willett, R. (2016). Online gaming practices of preteens: independent entertainment time and transmedia game play. *Children and Society*, *30*(6), 467–477.
Wu, H. (2016). Video game prosumers: Case study of a Minecraft affinity space. *Visual Arts Research*, *42*(1), 22–37.
Youdell, D. (2011). *School trouble*. London, UK: Routledge.

# 16
## Space, Time, and Production
*Games and the New Frontier of Digital Literacies*

**Antero Garcia**

And could Henry sit idly by and watch the kid get powdered, lose hope of becoming an Ace? He had to. Oh sure, he was free to throw away the dice, run the game by whim, but then what would be the point of it? Who would Damon Rutherford really be then? Nobody, an empty name, a play actor. Even though he'd set his own rules, his own limits, and though he could change them whenever he wished, nevertheless he and his players were committed to the turns of the mindless and unpredictable—one might even say, irresponsible—dice. That was how it was. He had to accept it, or quit the game altogether.

Robert Coover (1968). *The Universal Baseball Association, Inc., J. Henry Waugh Prop* (p. 40), New York, NY: Random House

Coover's comic novel details a purely analog game played with dice and a healthy dose of player-driven record keeping. For the protagonist, Henry Waugh, there is the world of his imagined baseball team and little else. He removes himself from the rest of the world, begs off work frequently, and *lives* within the imagined world of his fantasy sluggers.

In his novel, Coover captures the kind of scrutiny that literacies and educational researchers have pressed upon digital games long before video games were accessible or widely played by consumers. And while this intense focus on a player and her or his experience with a game has driven significant understanding of why games are powerful today, it is no longer enough. Understanding games and literacies in the twenty-first century is about much more than what happens with moving pixels and pawns on screens and devices.

This chapter attempts to clarify a literacies perspective of gaming. In particular, as parallel developments of spatial literacies and contexts for reading and writing within games proliferated over the past two decades, games now offer a means of better understanding what *digital* literacies means in an era when nearly every device can be connected to the Internet (Rose, 2014). While there continues to be an ongoing, historic enchantment of educational scholars about the possibilities of digital technologies, including video games (Cuban, 1986), gaming offers a unique lens for understanding production and writing today. On the one hand, video games have been continuously praised for their educational potential. At the same time, these tools for powerful learning also guide cultural oppression as illustrated by recent movements like Gamergate (noted below).

These two contrasting aspects of how games shape learning and identity highlight a key gap in how gaming literacies have so far been taken up. As such, I offer a contemporary definition of *gaming literacies* that broadens this space of research as a layered ecology in which different frames of literacies overlap and speak across one another. Through this layered understanding of gaming literacies, I focus on an intersection of space, production, and identity within games. Further, this chapter highlights how games are not confined within a metaphorical snow globe; society culturally mediates these games. Gaming literacies are about the broader ecology in which games are played: Individuals navigate the spaces within games and perform identities inside of games, while at the same time, these actions are paralleled *around* the games as well. Gaming literacies require reading the communities around us.

Reviewing the lineage of literacies research and educational gaming contexts that have been explored over the past two decades, this chapter highlights how gaming is a collection of layered activities and how gaming literacies must look at contexts of production and consumption within and across these layers of participation. Further, the general lack of acknowledgment of how negative cultural forces like Gamergate shape how games are played and by whom is a key tension in literacies gaming research. I emphasize how a broader "metagame" (Garfield, 2000) incorporates what game literacies have traditionally focused on, as well as what they have ignored.

Though this chapter is obviously built on a foundation of research about video games and video game communities (Gee, 2004, 2007; Hsu & Wang, 2010; Salen, 2007), this work speaks to non-digital contexts of gaming as well. More importantly, this chapter challenges what theories of digital literacies often assume about the elevating role of new technologies for learning. Like other forms of educational technology—from televisions to computers to SMARTboards (Cuban, 1986)—video games have been held up as another shiny context for "fixing" schools (Toppo, 2015). By looking at the nuanced layers of gaming literacies, and by emphasizing innovation, learning, and deep literacy, meaning making is found more so within peer-to-peer relationships and cultural analysis, than in the digitized worlds that drive capitalist marketplaces.

**The Magic Circle of Games**

I rely on Salen and Zimmerman's (2004) definition of a game as "a system in which players engage in an artificial conflict, defined by rules, that results in quantifiable outcomes" (2004, p. 80). While much of the emphasis in literacies research about games and gaming focus on *video* games, Salen and Zimmerman's definition functions equally well for non-digital contexts as well.

Looking at the many contexts in which games are played today, it is useful to consider Huizinga's (1955) understanding that play is "a free activity standing quite consciously outside 'ordinary' life as being 'not serious,' but at the same time absorbing the player utensil and utterly" (p. 13). Huizinga explains that games are played within a "magic circle" that temporarily casts aside traditional norms and cultural values. Transgressive behavior, such as simulated violence, becomes permissible because it is *outside* the space of traditional social norms when being conducted from within the magic circle of a game. Salen and Zimmerman describe this as "a special place in time and space created by a game" (2004, p. 95).

Considering the possibilities of the magic circle, a game becomes a venue for safe experimentation, failure, and identity development that is separate from the physical world. This "virtual" space is one that allows individuals to temporarily become someone other than themselves, adopting new skill sets, relationships, and moral stances within the contexts of play. In light of these opportunities for embodiment and exploration, it is no surprise that educational research continues to explore the learning benefits of play (Gee, 2004; Papert, 1980; Salen, 2007; Shaffer, 2006; Squire, 2011). What's more, the complex layers of multimodal reading and writing within gameplay and participation have made games an important space for better understanding digital literacies in the twenty-first century.

## Setting the Stakes of Gaming Literacies in the Twenty-First Century

As social media and technological advances shape researcher understandings of multiliteracies (New London Group, 1996) over the past two decades, it is necessary to spell out the historical turn that has led to a new definition of gaming literacies. In reviewing the shifts of the literacy field, Gee (2010) explains how new literacy studies (NLS) argued that "written language is a technology for giving and getting meaning" (p. 31). Gee notes a direct link between NLS and the kinds of new literacies that emerged at the turn of the twentieth century. Seeing that there are myriad litera*cies*, "new literacies studies is about studying new types of literacy beyond print literacy, especially digital literacies and literacy practices embedded in popular culture" (p. 31). Within this context, games can have overlapping meanings, interpretations, and cultural values dependent on the individuals interacting with them.

Games function as both digital texts and cultural domains in which texts are analyzed, constructed, and ascribed new meanings; they are the new technologies that expand the possibilities of digital literacies and they are a cultural domain in which "less new" literacies thrive. Literacies researchers have been unpacking the complicated and continually evolving relationship between games and literacies (Beavis, 2014; Gee, 2004; Snyder & Beavis, 2004), as well as how youth participate with and around games and literacy-based activities (Black & Reich, 2011; Hollett & Ehret, 2015; Wohlwend, 2011).

Gee's description of affinity spaces, in which participants share expertise, collaborate, and socialize, is a useful aspect of how gaming informs other literacies research. These gaming communities mirror sociocultural research that explores how "communities of practice" shape, mediate, and apprentice players (Lave & Wenger, 1991). Game-focused research on player communities and affinity spaces guides the fields of both education (Gee, 2004; Shaffer, 2006; Squire, 2011) and game studies (Pearce & Artemisia, 2011; Wardrip-Fruin & Harrigan, 2004).

Finally, spatial literacies (Compton-Lilly & Halverson, 2014; Leander & Sheehy, 2004) alongside fieldwork in digital virtual worlds (Boellstorff, 2008; Chen, 2011) have helped digital literacies theorists to understand how exploration, time, and narrative shape the construction of digital texts. Literacies are not simply about interpreting and making multimodal compositions, they are also about meaning making through movement and interaction with the broader world. This notion, ultimately, brings digital literacies back to Freirean notions of reading the world (Freire & Macedo, 1987).

The past research on digital literacies informs how researchers and educators understand games today. Salen (2007) describes gaming literacies as "specific to gaming and domains of media produced by games and supported through attitudes brought to bear on their play" (307). While this is a useful starting place for gaming literacies, the decade since Salen's definition requires a broader understanding of gaming literacies. For the remainder of this chapter, I argue that gaming literacies must explore multiple layers in which games are played and extrapolated. This includes the following:

- spatialized understanding of in-game worlds;
- recognition of collaboration and communication outside of games;
- fluency with the platforms on which games are played and mediated to a player base;
- reflection on how broader cultural influences shape games and their meaning;
- the intertextual exchanges that happen across these different layers of literacies.

Ultimately, gaming literacies cannot be tied to specific frames of play, but must actively look at how one frame of understanding is mediated by additional cultural layers and audiences. When researching or teaching with games, educators and researchers must acknowledge and work within the broader sociocultural ecologies of which games and gaming are a part.

## Tensions and Conflicting Viewpoints

### Gaming's Blind Spot

In reviewing the research on gaming, education, and literacies, there is a fundamental blind spot that is too often not acknowledged. Though games and the affinity groups around them can offer useful models for understanding digital literacies, these largely ignore some of the cultural dimensions of exclusion, bullying, and violence that permeate gaming culture today.

In the past few years, there has been an increase in how gaming communities misrepresent and attack women, minorities, and LGBTQ communities (Sullentrop, 2014). As Hurley (2016) explains, the recent Gamergate movement is "an online mob ostensibly about 'ethics in gaming journalism' that primarily targeted women for harassment" (Hurley, 2016, p. 15). These efforts directly affect who plays, produces, and socializes around games as "these targeted campaigns of hate and abuse have…driven some women of all races, men of color, and queer, trans, and other non-binary people from online spaces" (Hurley, p. 15).

Particularly in light of the ongoing effects of Gamergate, the role of gender in defining participation and identity in games and gaming communities must not be ignored. As Spain (1992) explains, "Gendered spaces themselves shape, and are shaped by, daily activities. Once in place, they become taken for granted, unexamined, and seemingly immutable. What *is* becomes what *ought* to be, which contributes to the maintenance of prevailing status differences" (pp. 28–29). Just as critical and sociocultural literacies take into account the broader contexts in which individuals read, write, and communicate (Gutièrrez, 2008), gaming literacies cannot ignore the fact that robust literacy practices in and around games are also innately tied to broader cultural systems.

Games are not played within a silo. Though digital games are often confined to the experiences and sounds produced by a discrete screen and set of speakers, they were also created as part of the broader sociocultural world and are, as such, an artifact that is part of this world. Games are mediated by the world and also mediate one's understanding of the world.

It is no longer enough to simply study gaming and literacies separate from the sociocultural world they are informed by and continue to shape. While initial gaming literacies have been successful in teasing out learning principles by holding gaming within an isolated "snow globe" of participation, the fact of the matter is that games exist as part of the broader world. To refer back to critical literacy traditions, "reading the world always precedes reading the word, and reading the world implies continually reading the world" (Freire & Macedo, 1987, p. 35); to play a game is to gather an understanding of the world in which it was developed.

### Acknowledging the Metagame

As noted above, games are to be understood as part of the broader social world, inclusive of any negative aspects of this world, such as the current harassment that female gaming critics suffer vis-à-vis Gamergate. In this sense, game designer Richard Garfield's (2000) definition of a "metagame"—"how a game interfaces outside itself"—is a useful understanding of broader gaming ecosystems (p. 16). Within the literacies community, Gee and Hayes (2012) have taken up this notion as well. Building on Gee's distinction between discourse and "big D" Discourse (Gee, 1990), Gee and Hayes see the *"big G" Game* as the combination of both a game and its metagame. They distinguish the "game" as "just the software that sets up game play, that is, what comes 'in the box' or, increasingly, is downloaded from the game distributor's website" and the metagame as "the social practices the happen inside and/or outside the game" (130).

The metagame or "big G" Game have largely been seen as a means of connecting player affinity spaces to the games that they play within educational contexts. However, gaming literacies acknowledge that a metagame is inclusive of the broader cultural values that imprint influence on games, game designs, and the player communities that interact with them. Be these the game specific trends, such as Gamergate, or previewed content discussed online, a "big G Game" must telescope to look at broader cultural shifts and political changes that funnel into gaming discourse.

If, more than twenty years ago the New London Group (1996) proposed multiliteracies partly as a means of understanding literacies within an increasingly globalized context, similar such efforts must be taken up as part of how we understand and interact with gaming literacies: They must incorporate how games reflect upon the "flattened" (Friedman, 2005) world in which games are produced, exchanged, and extrapolated.

It is easy to image why the cultural aspects of a broader metagame are not often taken into account within gaming literacies. On the one hand, the cultural ramifications of online harassment, such as that seen within Gamergate, have been largely occluded from view, except when researchers were also deeply immersed within gaming culture. At the same time, as a burgeoning medium, only a few decades in existence, digital gaming literacies are still primordially being constructed from the evolutionary soup of the bits, bytes, and tweets that make up their content. With this in mind, I offer below a way to take into account this key tension as part of the layers of gaming literacies in which digital scholars read and produce today.

**Emerging Theory: The Layers of Gaming Literacies**

As noted above, when games are discussed and analyzed, the focus is often solely on the digital experience *within* a broader gaming landscape. Discussions of learning and literacies within games like *Little Big Planet* (Rafalow & Tekinbas, 2014), *Deus Ex* (Gee, 2004), or the *World of Warcraft* (Chen, 2011) frequently disregard the platform on which the game is played, the interactions between players and the game, a broader gaming community, and the ever-changing sociocultural contexts in which all of this interacts. This Matroyshka doll-like structure of the layers of gaming literacies are represented in Figure 16.1. Beginning with a macro-level reading of Gaming, gaming literacies must include the following:

- the broader sociocultural context in which games are produced, discussed, and played,
- smaller affinity spaces and player communities focused around specific genres, franchises, and platforms for gaming,
- an individual's own interpretation and participation with a game,
- the platform and its specific designs for interpreting and interacting with the game, and
- a game's specific world, goals, and narrative structures.

Gaming literacies include reading and writing within the myriad layers that are a part of a broader "metagame" including the macro-view of a sociocultural world, all the way down to the individual actions and choices players can make within a singular game. Below is a detail of the scope of gaming literacies at each of the segments of the gaming ecology depicted above.

*The ("Little g") Game*

A distillation of the constructed narrative, actions, and virtual world depicted within a game is the smaller lens for considering gaming literacies. To be clear, significant research can focus on solely the protagonist within a game, its settings, and the kinds of player-to-player interactions within multi-player games and worlds.

Space, Time, and Production • 203

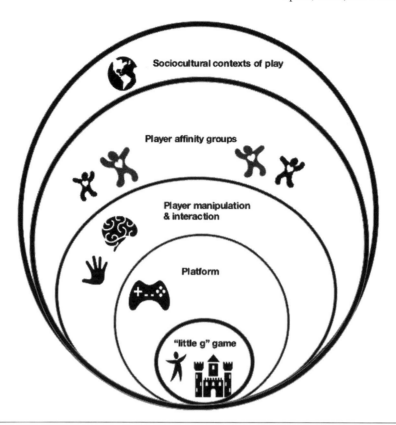

**Figure 16.1** A socio-cultural view of gaming literacies

(Source: Figure created by A. Garcia using images from game-icons.net under CC BY 3.0 license)

## *The Platform*

A game does not manifest itself wholesale from nothing. It must be loaded, set up, and often calibrated in order for someone to experience it. How a game is communicated and interacted with shapes and limits one's experiences, literacy production, and spatial exploration. Just as one can today play a classic word game, like *Scrabble*, on a board, on a computer, and on the mobile device kept in a pocket, the platform on which a game is executed matters. Since 2009, MIT Press, for example, has been steadily publishing books as part of gaming studies researchers, Nick Montfort and Ian Bogost's, "Platform Studies" series (Montfort & Bogost, 2009). Though that series focuses on specific gaming platforms, this layer of mediated experience is one that must be acknowledged in how literacies are constructed and interpreted.

## *Player Manipulation and Interaction*

Even once a game is loaded on a specific platform, it is not inherently played in and of itself. Though largely driven by the platform limitations, how a player manipulates a game, her emotional relationship to the world, its characters, and the aesthetic designs shape what the reading of a game means. Likewise, Figure 16.1 depicts this layer as represented by a hand and brain; this layer is indicative of the physical manipulation of a game, the ways the game is sensorily interpreted (see Chapter 2, this volume), and how an individual makes sense of the game. Of course, and as is noted below, this is also culturally bound by the experiences one has within larger social constructs.

## Player Affinity Groups

Aside from the "little g" game, this is perhaps the area that has received the most educational scrutiny. Player communities continue to be robustly described as a focus of connected learning (Garcia, 2014; Ito et al., 2013) and contemporary situated learning communities. As noted in much existing literature, textual production and communication are often at the heart of these analyses—participants often communicate in online spaces utilizing multimodal tools to collaborate and critique.

## Sociocultural Contexts of Play

Finally, this broadest of levels captures both gaming-specific cultures and histories that shape the landscape of play (e.g., Gamergate as recent example), as well as the broad sociopolitical context of playing games within Westernized, capitalist culture. Games and the cultural discussions and affinity spaces they instantiate do not (often) rely on large market forces of exchange, played on expensive platforms, and rely on data plans or broadband access frequently not available in all areas of the world. To ignore these aspects is to disregard large swaths of how games are read, by whom, and within what cultural lenses.

Looking at the telescoping nature of reading and writing across these different levels of gaming ecologies, it is useful to look at where the education and literacy gazes have focused. Largely, researchers focus on either the interactions that players have when making moment-to-moment decisions within games or on the collaborative practices of affinity space. However, by blurring a player's actions with its consequences within a game, such approaches often disregard the ways players' gestural fluency with handheld devices, game rules, and restrictions show a familiar and functional literacy with the individual platforms of play. To successfully defeat a boss, a player must intuitively manipulate a proprietary device that mediates an individual's relationship with the animated pixels on a screen. This is not a semantic argument, but one that acknowledges that gaming literacies are layered.

Similarly, a large focus of educational research looks at the affinity spaces and fan communities that coalesce and "hang out, mess around, and geek out" around specific titles and genres (Ito et al., 2009). Research on spaces like war gaming communities (Harrigan & Kirschenbaum, 2016), level designers (Rafalow & Tekinbas, 2014), and virtual world guilds (Chen, 2011) have looked at how players exchange knowledge, share fan-related media, and govern online servers. At the same time—just like the blind spots of research that ignore the mediation of player and game by platforms—the contexts of robust player affinity spaces often ignore the sociocultural world that more broadly informs the discourse, player styles, and demographic makeup of player communities.

The cultural frailty and symbolic violence often placed on women, People of Color, and the LGBTQ community is largely ignored when heralding the value of video games as tools for learning and literacy support. The lens of what *values* are exchanged within player communities alongside strategic discussions of play and fan-based multimodal composition must be reevaluated. How often, for instance, are misogynistic language and taunts shared by player communities? How are the body images and clothing choices within games discussed and analyzed? And while these are likely not the kinds of questions that player groups always choose to engage with, they are necessary for bridging understanding of how these layers interact.

Finally, in looking at these layers of reading within gaming, it is important to acknowledge that such layers are not uni-linear in terms of how content is consumed or interpreted. Transmedia artifacts that tell stories across games and films, like the Wachowski sisters' *Matrix* franchise (Jenkins, 2006), highlight how intertextual connections within games and across gaming layers play out. Intertextuality plays a fundamental role in our understanding of the fluid nature of language today

(Fairclough, 1992). As Fairclough explains, "Intertextuality is basically the property texts have of being full of snatches of other texts, which may be explicitly demarcated or merged in, and which the text may assimilate, contradict, ironically echo, and so forth" (p. 84). Based on the complex intertextual exchanges and informed dialogue *across* layers of gaming, digital literacies are not confined to singular frames of understanding. For every multimodal text that is read, so too must researchers consider the platforms on which they are read, and the cultural realm in which they are produced and influence.

**Where Is the Game?**

Looking at the layers at play within a contemporary understanding of gaming literacies, gamers and researchers alike must ask a simply question: *Where* is the game? Answers can be traced from various stances within Figure 16.1.

- It is the content flashed on the screen.
- It is the box that carries the platform or (increasingly now in the past) cartridges that are loaded in digital contexts.
- It is where one's thumbs connect with the gaming controller.
- It is in the conversation that happens around or in preparation for the next in-game conquest.
- It is in following the broader metagame cultural discourse around harassment, inclusion, and representation.

Pinpointing *where* one frames an understanding of a game better illustrates what is read, experienced, and produced from that perspective. Considering literacies from a critical stance, the frame helps to illustrate what words and worlds are read. Though we can easily make connections to reading the virtual worlds constructed within games and mediated on digital platforms, understanding what layer of gaming is being referenced is equally important to where a game takes place, and what possibilities emerge from this space.

Likewise, the literacy construction of playing a "small g" game may be ancillary to the actual play and world-reading that occurs after the game is played. As one video analysis of the recent game *Firewatch* (Satchbag's Goods, 2016) explained, the most fulfilling part of playing the game is "in the conversations had after the game is done, they thrive on the viscerally grey in the world and outside of it." The comment suggests that playing a game is merely in preparation for larger acts of gaming literacies, inscribing meaning and identity through what is played, how it is played, and in what context. These elements are all a part of how gaming literacies are both about outward production and inward acculturation to games, and "big G" Games.

In looking at where games take place, it is useful to consider the kinds of reading practices that most frequently occur. Assuming that reading is not simply restricted to print-based texts, and that it includes the sociocultural reading of virtual and physical worlds, as well as the spatial exploration within imagined spaced, here are five initial kinds of readings that are part of gaming literacies for researchers to consider:

- *Reading within:* reading the spaces, cues, and narratives that emerge within a game;
- *Reading about*: reading analysis, reviews, walkthroughs, and other discourse about a game or game series;
- *Reading across*: exploring tropes, references, and transmedia information that expands a gaming experience beyond a singular game. This intertextuality can inform the play experience by extending it, or it can be the broader discussions of genres, franchises, and histories of gaming;

- *Reading alongside*: reading with a broader community of gamers and gaming participants. This can be text that expands the world of gaming, the mechanics of play, or the cultural discussions relating to a game or gaming community;
- *Reading for context*: reading texts that may not be specifically about gaming. This includes the role of news, media, and cultural dialogue that shapes the broader world within which gaming is only one dimension.

This is not a comprehensive list, but it offers a means to look at where and why players are engaged in reading practices as gamers, and as participants in gaming communities. More importantly, the reading that happens here allows researchers to better understanding what is *produced* within these spaces as well, as noted below.

**Writing and Production**

Writing within game worlds—either as part of affinity-space fan production or as exploration within the "little g" game—is a process of embodiment and extrapolation. For digital literacies, this means that writing happens in tandem with playing. Further, it means that playing and writing are usually intertwined with narrative, space, and time.

Games, like books, films, and other media forms that extend across specific platforms, are too diverse to be generalized. However, the narratives told within and throughout a game are often broadly about individuals, groups of people, or cultures. Aside from abstract games, like *Tetris*, players guide, observe, motivate, or instruct individuals within a virtual world toward a specific game's goal. As such, *playing* a game is often about embodiment within a game. Moving Mario across the side-scrolling classic of the 1980s *Super Mario Bros* by controlling his actions with one's thumbs is conceptually about *being* Mario for a few minutes of play. Moving a pixelated "you" across a screen is an abstracted, literacy act. Further, it is one in which a player, whether emotionally connected to this character or not, inscribes meaning and action within a game. She or he co-constructs a narrative and its outcome alongside the narrative authority of a game. This is digital writing.

When playing within a game, a player is writing. Play is a productive process. While some games are built around actual construction in virtual worlds (e.g., You might construct a home or castle in the *Sims* or in *Minecraft*), games are productive, regardless of their intended purposes.

Further, given the affordances of socialization within such games, platforms for play, such as *Second Life*, while not necessarily classified as objective-based games, offer similar forms of interaction and "big G" Gaming, as the other games described. In all of these game-based forms of play and participation, production is at the core of interaction that players engage in. It is worth acknowledging that in-game labor and production are held to the same capitalistic rules of exchange as are found in the physical world. Though not a focus of this chapter, one consequence of intertextual exchange across the layers of gaming literacies is the exploitation of cheap labor within games. The *New York Times* report of Chinese gold farming in the *World of Warcraft* (Dibbell, 2007), as well as fictionalized accounts of this exchange in both adult (Stephenson, 2011) and young adult literature (Doctorow & Wang, 2014), illustrates this blurred challenge of gaming production and exchange.

As the gold farming example highlights, literacies research must continually refer to the layers of gaming literacies illustrated in Figure 16.1. Writing and production happen *across* and *within* each layer that comprises aspects of gaming literacies. Though "little g" games may have intertextual references encoded, such literacy practices occur from multiple kinds of layers of gaming participation. Further, remembering that "games and game modification are currently key entry points for many young people into digital literacy, social communities, and tech-savvy identities" (Salen, 2007, p. 302), the production of games is specifically tied to educational implications of gaming literacies.

## Implications for Research and Education

The education community stands at a cultural precipice when it comes to the classroom use of games, and it is one that literacies researchers can help safely navigate. On the one hand, researchers, policies, and school districts can continue to invest solely in the virtues of "little g" games and repeat Cuban's (1986) warning that researchers continue to look to and heavily invest in technologies to "fix" schools. On the other hand, gaming literacies can reiterate the need to focus on "the context not the tool" of technology (Philip & Garcia, 2013), and provide guidance for better understanding the reading and composition practices that emerge within and across the layers of cultural play. Bluntly, research on games can no longer simply extol the virtues of the "little g" game without looking critically at the metagame in which these texts are enacted.

In light of these implications of how much broader gaming research must focus, literacy researchers must guide more intentional language for otherwise slipshod phrases that drive funding and professional development decisions in schools today. Words like "gamification," "gamified," and "game-based," suggest that the educational research community has a suffix problem when it comes to discussing and understanding what games are for, and how they are developed and utilized within learning environments.

Likewise, if ours is a profession that sees gaming culture as potentially positive and "pervasive" (Montola et al., 2009), the literacies community must grapple with the methodologies that explore both the gaming communities and the in-game learning and socialization that occur. While there continues to be studies and methodological guidance on looking at these two separate spaces, there have been few efforts to actually bring closer together the lived experiences of gaming literacies as they occur *across* the layers of "big G" Games participation. Twenty years past the formative work of the New London Group (1996), we no longer need to focus on the piecemeal analysis of individual layers of gaming literacies. Instead, we must look at how our tools of sociocultural analysis and multimodal literacies commingle into new methodological vernacular. And while I've relied in this chapter on gaming contexts, this is also a concern regarding the lens of scrutiny for digital literacies more broadly.

## Recommendations

In the passage that opens this chapter, a fantasy baseball enthusiast dutifully adheres to the rules and systems of an imagined and game-driven world, while these rules slowly overwrite the rules of his day-to-day "real" life. Henry Waugh is slave to the mandates of a system that are governed by the roll (and role) of dice. And while there is a useful parallel between Waugh's drive to improve from within the game and research on games, motivation, and identity (McGonigal, 2011), it also depicts a past paradigm of gaming research.

Rather than focusing on the singular player and his or her relationship with a gaming virtual world, gaming literacies have taken a productive turn. At once they recognize that in-game literacies are both productive and consumptive; players navigate and explore the virtual spaces of games in ways that enfold narrative, identity, and space (see Chapter 15, this volume). Further, literacies explode beyond a game and its platform to include the possibilities of collaboration, cultural response, and intertextuality across layers of meaning making.

### *An Analog Turn*

As much as this is a volume dedicated to contemporary understandings of digital literacies, I would be remiss not to acknowledge that the practices described throughout this chapter apply to analog gaming as well. The fact of the matter is, the spatialized literacies that are constructed in digital spaces can be relatively easily unplugged. The $25 billion video game industry highlights why an increased scrutiny on the role of digital games and their academic potential is so important. However, there is little that a pad of paper and an imagination can't accomplish (as the passage about Henry Waugh suggests). Further, when looking at the learning affordances of world construction, expression, and player agency in non-digital roleplaying games like *Dungeons and Dragons*, one can imagine how developing and communicating in an imaginary world is a revolutionary act of literacy (Garcia, 2016); it is about *writing* the world before others can read it.

A need that literacies scholars must face is differentiating the value of *gaming* literacies and the value of *digital* literacies. Are the learning affordances of games inherently about using expensive computers for play, or are these affordances merely "sussed out" in digital contexts because gaming literacies have not been fully excavated in non-digital contexts?

## *On Agency and Transfer*

In both analog and digital contexts of games, there is a need to broaden the scope at the center of where learning and literacy production takes place. In looking at gaming literacies within these layers, we have the opportunity to more critically understand the nature of youth identity and meaning making within a broader context. Whereas some digital media scholars proverbially wring their hands about the plight of youth too absorbed in online spaces, gaming literacies helps draw out how identity is performed and embodied in many different layers of one fan-driven ecosystem. Acknowledging that not all youth are self-proclaimed gamers, these literacy practices help illustrate how textual production, peer relationships, and other "connected learning" spaces respond to broader cultural contexts as well as are mediated by their own platform-specific limitations (video bloggers—"vloggers"—for example must adhere to the specific video editing and online video sharing restrictions).

In looking at this new framework for literacies, one recommendation is to look at how skills and individual agency are transferred across layers. Can in-game agency manifest as organizing around broader sociocultural issues of social justice? Does hacking one digital platform to run the gaming software of another connect to civic agency?

In discussing the challenging nature of the *Dark Souls* video game franchise in an online essay, Cantor (2016) discusses the role of agency and responsibility within the game:

> *Dark Souls* is perceived as harder because it makes the player *responsible* for more than most games. Most games, you can turn off a certain analytical part of your brain and enjoy some mindless entertainment. [...] With responsibility comes *agency*. Progressing in a Souls game feels sublime because, quantifiably, you have *accomplished* more than you would with the same time investment in another game.

If we are to consider games as "professional practice simulations" (Salen, 2007), we must consider what practices are instilling agency, how these practices speak across the layers of gaming literacies, and what kinds of responsibilities young people face both within and around gaming contexts.

## References

Beavis, C. (2014). Games as text, games as action: Videogames in the English classroom. *Journal of Adult and Adolescent Literacy*, 57(6), 433–439.

Black, R. W., & Reich, S. M. (2011). Affordances and constraints of scaffolded learning in a virtual world for young children. *International Journal of Game-Based Learning*, 1(2), 52–64.

Boellstorff, T. (2008). *Coming of age in second life: An anthropologist explores the virtually human.* Princeton, NJ: Princeton University Press.

Cantor, M. (2016). Everyone is bad at Dark Souls, and you should be, too. *Medium.* Accessed at https://medium.com/@mcantor/everyone-is-bad-at-dark-souls-and-you-should-be-too-6f74dde29fa1#.ges1q8jr7.

Chen, M. (2011). *Leet noobs: The life and death of an expert player group in World of Warcraft.* New York, NY: Peter Lang.

Compton-Lilly, C., & Halverson, E. (Eds.). (2014). *Time and space in literacy research.* New York, NY: Routledge.

Coover, R. (1968). *The universal baseball association, Inc., J. Henry Waugh Prop.* New York, NY: Penguin.

Cuban, L. (1986). *Teachers and machines: The classroom use of technology since 1920.* New York, NY: Teachers College Press.

Dibbell, J. (2007). The life of the Chinese gold farmer. *The New York Times.* Accessed at http://www.nytimes.com/2007/06/17/magazine/17lootfarmers-t.html.

Doctorow, C., & Wang, J. (2014). *In real life.* New York, NY: First Second Publishing.

Fairclough, N. (1992). *Discourse and social change.* Cambridge, UK: Polity Press.

Friedman, T. L. (2005). *The world is flat: A brief history of the twenty-first century.* New York, NY: Picador.

Freire, P. and Macedo, D. (1987). *Literacy: Reading the word and the world.* Westport, CT: Bergin & Garvey.

Garcia, A. (Ed.). (2014). *Teaching in the connected learning classroom.* Irvine, CA: Digital Media and Learning Research Hub.

Garcia, A. (2016). Teacher as Dungeon Master: Connected learning, democratic classrooms, and rolling for initiative. In A. Byers & F. Crocco (Eds.), *The role-playing society: Essays on the cultural influence of RPGs* (pp. 164–183). New York, NY: McFarland.

Garfield, R. (2000). Metagames. In J. Dietz (Ed.), *Horsemen of the apocalypse: Essays on roleplaying* (pp. 14–21). Charleston, IL: Jolly Rogers Games.

Gee, J. P. (1990). *Social linguistics and literacies: Ideology in discourses.* London, UK: Taylor & Francis.

Gee, J. P. (2004). *Situated language and learning: A critique of traditional schooling.* New York, NY: Routledge.

Gee, J. P. (2007). *What video games have to teach us about learning and literacy.* New York, NY: Palgrave.

Gee, J. P. (2010). *New digital media and learning as an emerging area and "worked examples" as one way forward.* Cambridge, MA: MIT Press.

Gee, J. P. & Hayes, E. R. (2012). *Language and learning in the digital age.* New York, NY: Routledge.

Gutièrrez, K. (2008). Developing a sociocritical literacy in the third space. *Reading Research Quarterly, 43*(2): 148–164.

Harrigan, P., & Kirschenbaum, M.G. (Eds.). (2016). *Zones of control: Perspectives on wargaming.* Cambridge, MA: MIT Press.

Hollett, T., & Ehret, C. (2015). Bean's world: (Mine)crafting affective atmospheres for gameplay, learning and care in a children's hospital. *New Media & Society, 17*(11), 1849–1866.

Hsu, H. & Wang, S. (2010). Using gaming literacies to cultivate new literacies. *Simulation & Gaming, 41*(3), 400–417.

Huizinga, J. (1955). *Homo ludens: A study of the play-element in culture.* Boston, MA: Beacon Press.

Hurley, K. (2016). *The geek feminist revolution.* New York, NY: Tor Books.

Ito, M., Baumer, S., Bittanti, M., boyd, d., Cody, R., Stephenson, B. H., …, Yardi, S. (2009). *Hanging out, messing around, and geeking out: Kids living and learning with new media.* Cambridge, MA: MIT Press.

Ito, M., Gutiérrez, K., Livingstone, S., Penuel, B., Rhodes, J., Salen, K., …, Watkins, S. C. (2013). *Connected learning: An agenda for research and design.* Irvine, CA: Digital Media and Learning Research Hub.

Jenkins, H. (2006). *Convergence culture: Where old and new media collide.* New York, NY: New York University Press.

Lave, J., & Wenger, E. (1991). *Situated learning: Legitimate peripheral participation.* Cambridge, UK: Cambridge University Press.

Leander, K. M., & M. Sheehy (Eds.). (2004). *Spatializing literacy research and practice.* New York, NY: Peter Lang.

McGonigal, J. (2011). *Reality is broken: Why games make us better and how they can change the world.* New York, NY: Penguin.

Montfort, N., & Boost, I. (2009). *Racing the beam: The Atari video computer system.* Cambridge, MA: MIT Press.

Montola, M., Stenros, J., & Waern, A. (2009). *Pervasive games: Theory and design.* New York, NY: Morgon Kaufmann.

New London Group. (1996). A pedagogy of multiliteracies: Designing social futures. *Harvard Education Review, 66*(1) 60–92.

Papert, S. (1980). *Mindstorms: Children, computers, and powerful ideas.* New York, NY: Basic Books.

Pearce, C., & Artemisia. (2011). *Communities of play: Emergent cultures in multiplayer games and virtual worlds.* Cambridge, MA: MIT Press.

Philip, T. M., & Garcia, A. (2013). The importance of still teaching the iGeneration: New technologies and the centrality of pedagogy. *Harvard Educational Review, 83*(2), 300–319.

Rafalow, M.H., & Tekinbas, K.S. (2014). *Welcome to Sackboy planet: Connected learning among LittleBigPlanet 2 players.* Irvine, CA: Digital Media and Learning Research Hub.

Rose, D. (2014). *Enchanted objects: Innovation, design, and the future of technology.* New York, NY: Scribner.

Salen, K. (2007). Gaming literacies: A game design study in action. *Journal of Educational Multimedia and Hypermedia, 16*(3), 301–322.

Salen, K., & Zimmerman, E. (2004). *Rules of play: Game design fundamentals.* Cambridge, MA: MIT Press.

Satchbag's Goods. (2016). *Firewatch is Mine.* Retrieved from https://www.youtube.com/watch?v=Z74nUBkMdSg.

Shaffer, D. (2006). *How computer games help children learn.* New York, NY: Palgrave Macmillan.
Snyder, I., & Beavis, C. (Eds.). (2004). *Doing literacy online: Teaching, learning and playing in an electronic world.* Cresskill, NJ: Hampton Press.
Spain, D. (1992). *Gendered spaces.* Chapel Hill: University of North Carolina Press.
Squire, K. (2011). *Video games and learning: Teaching and participatory culture in the digital age.* New York, NY: Teachers College Press.
Stephenson, N. (2011). *Reamde.* New York, NY: Harper Collins.
Sullentrop, C. (2014, October, 25). Can video games survive? The Disheartening GamerGate Campaign. *The New York Times.*
Toppo, G. (2015). *The game believes in you: How digital play can make our kids smarter.* New York, NY: St. Martin's Press.
Wardrip-Fruin, N., & Harrigan, P. (Eds.). (2004). *First person: New media as story, performance, and game.* Cambridge, MA: MIT Press.
Wohlwend, K. (2011). *Playing their way into literacies: Reading, writing, and belonging in the early childhood classroom.* New York, NY: Teachers College Press.

# 17
# Digital Metroliteracies
## Space, Diversity, and Identity

Sender Dovchin and Alastair Pennycook

Facebook now plays a significant role in the everyday digital literacy practices of people around the world (de Bres, 2015). Desperately trying to keep up with the proliferation of online semiotic practices, scholarship on online digital literacy has emphasized linguistic diversity and semiotic heterogeneity as some of the crucial literacy characteristics of Facebook (Leppänen, Møller, Nørreby, Stæhr, & Kytölä, 2015). The combination of diverse linguistic resources, repertoires, modes, codes, genres, and styles in online and Facebook environments emphasizes the growing need to problematize more traditional concepts, such as bi/multilingualism and codeswitching (Sharma, 2012; Sultana et al., 2013, 2015), a process that has become a major focus of contemporary sociolinguistics (Pennycook, 2016). When Androutsopoulos (2007) refers to linguistic and literacy diversity on the Internet, he directly associates it with creativity saturated with different semiotic resources rather than mixed language systems.

As Velghe (2015, p. 27) notes, "Language and literacy are always the means to (obtain) voice ('to let one be heard and understood')." Facebook messages, from this point of view, can be viewed not so much as "linguistic objects" or "carriers of denotational meanings," but rather "as *indexical* objects that are meant to be used to 'socialize' with others." These phatic Facebook exchanges are therefore better measured by "the standards of the indexical order of conviviality, instead of by the standards of language only." While questioning the separability of language from other modes of communication on Facebook, Sharma (2012) also notes that the Facebook environment is a transmodal space, in which users redefine the role of English and other languages in relation to their existing online social relationships, innovatively transcending the meaning of English not only by mixing it with local language but also by using other multimodal texts drawing on both local and global media content.

Digital literacy practices on Facebook often involve semiotic/linguistic creativity, with users re-entextualizating and relocalizing varied available signs and linguistic resources to create their own versions of digital literacy (Thorne, 2013). As Leppänen et al. (2015, p. 4) point out, superdiversity in social media is realized by "the mobility and mobilization of linguistic and other semiotic resources that are distributed, recontextualized and resemiotized in various ways in countless and rhizomatic digital media practices mushrooming on the internet." "Sharing" an update, for example, is a classic case of "re-entextualization" or "re-semiotization" (Varis & Blommaert, 2015, p. 36). Re-entextualization on Facebook can be understood as the process by which a text (broadly understood) is "extracted from its original context-of-use and re-inserted into an entirely different one, involving different participation frameworks, a different kind of textuality" (a text might be condensed as a quote; an image used to suggest a place), producing "very different meaning outcomes."

Re-semiotization, by contrast, refers to the "process by means of which every 'repetition' of a sign involves an entirely new set of contextualization conditions and thus results in an entirely 'new' semiotic process, allowing new semiotic modes and resources to be involved in the repetition process" (Varis & Blommaert, 2015, p. 36). As Dovchin, Sultana, and Pennycook (2015, p. 8) point out, Facebook users make meaning "not only through how they borrow, repeat and mimic certain linguistic resources available to them, but also through the ways they make new linguistic meanings within this complex relocalizing process" (cf. Dovchin, 2016a,b).

Many recent Facebook studies have tended to concentrate on the relocalization/re-semiotization processes of multimodal resources in creating superdiverse literacy practices. Phyak (2015) cautions, however, that digital literacy practices of Facebook are not only about heterogeneity and fluidity, but also about homogenous and fixed identifications. As Otsuji and Pennycook (2010) have argued in the context of everyday urban multilingual practices, it is important to focus not only on the fluidity of linguistic practices but also on their fixity. Indeed, it is in the dynamic relation between fixity and fluidity that diversity needs to be understood. Facebook can be a discursive space that provides a critical and agentive place for people to reproduce their dominant offline identification and discourses (Phyak, 2015). It is important, therefore, for Facebook researchers not to overlook crucial aspects of how and in what ways Facebook-based digital literacy practices can be connected to offline worlds and offline identity practices.

It is not yet very clear how Facebook users' offline literacy and identity practices are filtered and leaked through their online literacy activities. As Sherman and Švelch (2015, p. 332) remind us, "Future research should pose the question of who the Facebook language managers actually are, consider their motivations, and examine their behavior-toward-language offline." Thorne (2013, p. 211) highlights that as literacy educators we should focus on the point where the forms of Internet-mediated activity are "demonstrably embedded in, and functionally disassociable from, many offline communicative contexts and social networks." The high frequency of interplay, as Thorne (2013, p. 211) adds, "between on- and off-line activity has the potential to make developmentally and instructionally oriented use of mediated communication more relevant and meaningful due to its articulation with students' broader amalgam of integrated on- and off-line lifeworld." It is also important in this context not to fall into the trap of seeing offline environments as somehow more "real" than "virtual" online environments. Once we start to think in terms of networks of texts, artifacts, practices, and technologies (Gourlay, Hamilton, & Lea, 2013), the distinction between being online and offline, between real and virtual, and between paper text and screen text, becomes much less important than an understanding of the relations among parts of diverse literacy assemblages.

This chapter thus seeks to expand the horizons of these emerging studies of Facebook literacy by examining not only the extent to which diverse linguistic and semiotic resources are relocalized, but also what kinds of offline identity meanings are intricately intertwined and leaked into the tapestry of daily online Facebooking practices. The focus of this chapter is particularly on examples of everyday Facebook literacy practices in the context of young urban Mongolians located in the capital city of Mongolia, Ulaanbaatar. Mongolia adds further dimensions to this chapter due to its geographic, and political, economic position in the Asian periphery, which has to date received little attention in the digital literacy literature.

Before 1990, Mongolia was a socialist country and a satellite of the USSR, with Russian being the only important foreign language. The communist authorities replaced the classic Mongolian Uyghur script with the Cyrillic alphabet in 1941, and Cyrillic Mongolian remains the official orthography. Following the fall of the Soviet Union, Mongolia transformed from a socialist regime to a democracy, embracing a free market economy in 1990 (Rossabi, 2005). Mongolia opened itself up to the rest of the world, and linguistic and cultural flows from outside started circulating quickly across the nation. In particular, Ulaanbaatar, the capital city of Mongolia, has witnessed major changes in urban lifestyle. Russian was replaced by English and other international languages.

Young urban Mongolians have been eager to learn English and other languages in institutional and non-institutional settings while also engaging with the various transcultural flows circulating across the country via the modes of new media, Internet, and technology. The figure of 1.5 million Internet users in Mongolia (Internet World Stats, 2016) is relatively high (almost 50%), given the small and dispersed population and level of socioeconomic development (compare Pakistan 18%; Cambodia 26%; Philippines 53%; Malaysia, 68%; Japan 91%). Social media platforms, such as Facebook, have soared in popularity, with data in June 2016 showing equal numbers (1.5 million; 50%) of Facebook and Internet users (Pakistan 14%, Cambodia 26%, Philippines 53%, Malaysia 62%, Japan 21%). As a result, many young Mongolians are engaging with a range of linguistic, cultural, and literacy practices, with implications for Mongolian language and culture, new post-socialist identities, and diverse literacy practices (Dovchin, 2011, 2015).

**Conceptual Framework: Online Metrolingual Identities**

To understand young urban adults' Facebook-based multimodal and multilingual digital literacy practices, we employ the conceptual framework of *metrolingualism* (Pennycook & Otsuji, 2015) and, in combination with digital (online) literacies, what we are here calling *digital metroliteracies*, or metrolingual practices in the online environment. An increasing number of recent studies have critiqued widespread notions such as bi/multilingualism and code-switching for falling short in addressing the contemporary mixed linguistic repertoires that are a product of transnational flows of linguistic and cultural resources (Dovchin, 2016a; Dovchin et al., 2016; Pennycook, 2016). Such studies suggest it may be more useful to talk, for example, in terms of *translanguaging*:

> an approach to the use of language, bilingualism and the education of bilinguals that considers the language practices of bilinguals not as two autonomous language systems as has been traditionally the case, but as one linguistic repertoire with features that have been societally constructed as belonging to two separate languages
>
> (García & Wei, 2014, p. 2)

Studies of urban youth in Denmark have likewise suggested that the ways in which young people draw on different linguistic resources to form various registers of youth talk can best be described in terms of *polylanguaging* rather than as mixed codes (Jørgensen et al., 2011). These ways of speaking also need to be seen in relation to style—they are part of a range of intentional social moves—becoming "integrated forms of stylization" (Sultana et al., 2013, p. 700). Canagarajah (2013) has argued along similar lines for a need to look at *translingual practices* where communication transcends both "individual languages" and words, thus involving "diverse semiotic resources and ecological affordances" (p. 6). To these reframings of mixed language use as translingual practices, Pennycook and Otsuji's (2015) *metrolingualism* adds a stronger focus on the urban environment. The focus is not so much on language systems, mixed language resources, or the linguistic repertoires of individuals, as on the ways in which multilingualism from below operates in urban workplaces—the availability of diverse semiotic resources in a particular place, which we have elsewhere termed the *spatial repertoires* that people draw on as they engage in everyday social and work activities (Pennycook & Otsuji, 2014, 2015).

While metrolingualism draws attention to the possibilities of flexible language crossing and identifications, it also acknowledges the salience of fixed identity markers: While speakers are engaged in fluid conversations drawing on a variety of linguistic resources, they may also mobilize ascriptions of fixed identities (Otsuji & Pennycook, 2010). What we in fact have to grasp here is the relation between the language practices in everyday contexts of urban work and interaction, the language ideologies of these participants in their ordinary articulations of language use, and the language ideologies at play in the broader social context, where more normative and fixed ascriptions of language are common (Pennycook and Otsuji, 2016).

Whereas the initial development of the term *metrolingualism* was dependent on a notion of physical offline urban space, we here expand *metrolingualism* in the context of online digital literacy practices (digital metroliteracies), where Facebook users articulate a range of more stable identities—sexual, ethnic, and class-based, for example—that cut across online and offline settings of the metrolingual fabric. While aspects of the urban environment may be absent from such interactions (the noise and bustle of the city, the movement of people, the physical presence of the built environment), texts as either digital or material artifacts can be understood as "devices through which realities are framed and shared so that material effects travel through and with them" (Hamilton, 2015, p. 8). Texts from this point of view "are not inert beings but have real effects when they are activated through networks" (p. 8). Digital literacies, or "semiotic activity mediated by electronic media" (Thorne, 2013, p. 192) —referring therefore to textual practices in online environments rather than particular technological skills (see Gourlay et al., 2013) —can thus be seen as real, spatial, and interlinked with the networks of daily offline life.

Daily offline metrolingual practices become part of everyday online literacy practices since "online identity is still embedded in, and influenced by, an offline, embodied, self" (Buck, 2012, pp. 14–15) just as an offline self is equally influenced by an online, networked self. As Buck (2012, p. 35) explains, "The online activity that individuals engage in on social network sites does not just stay online; students integrate social network sites into their daily literacy practices." Stæhr concludes (2015, p. 44) that "[…] everyday language use on Facebook indicates that the normative orientations and value ascriptions to particular language forms correspond to those found in [offline] speech." It would not make much sense to see the speakers' online interaction as a separate context detached from their other spheres of life since so many young people are active on and around Facebook (Nørreby & Møller, 2015).

Facebook provides these speakers with a significant social and communicative context where they can negotiate and organize both fixed and fluid offline identity categories. As Dovchin (2015) suggests, it is sometimes possible to understand particular individuals' offline "authentic/real" identities through their online mixed linguistic practices.

Facebook's non-anonymous nature is important here, since as Grasmuck et al. (2009) point out that people tend to "play-act" at being someone else in anonymous settings and be more realistic and honest in non-anonymous environments. As they explain, "online social dynamics in the anonymous environment of Facebook are reflective of offline social practices" and "identity claims regarding the extensiveness of social networks appear to be grounded in offline realities" (2009, p. 180). It is not only the case, therefore, that "Facebook identities are clearly real in the sense that they have real consequences for the lives of the individuals who constructed them" (Zhao et al., 2008, p. 1832), but also that these Facebook identities may also be closely related to the reality of offline identities— however constructed these too may be.

**Research Framework: Linguistic Netnography**

Following this framework, this chapter looks at the online metrolingual practices of young urban people in Mongolia from the perspective that their online digital literacy practices are closely related to their offline practices and identities. The relocalization of English and other linguistic and semiotic resources produces online metrolingualism, which simultaneously becomes part of the speakers' multiple offline identities and identifications (Sultana et al., 2015). The data used in this chapter derive from a larger netnography research project that looked into the online literacy practices of university students in Ulaanbaatar, conducted from July 2010 to November 2014. Overall, forty students from various social backgrounds aged between 17 and 28 from the National University of Mongolia (NUM) volunteered to participate in the research. Their socioeconomic and regional backgrounds before they gained admission to the universities were diverse, varying from affluent to poor and from rural to urban. Meanwhile, the participants were also immediately added to our own Facebook accounts as soon as they decided to become part of the research project. When students leave the classroom, the first thing many of them do is to switch their computers or mobile phones on (assuming they were off to start with) and open their Facebook.

This gave us unobtrusive access to observe the participants' language practices using "netnography" (Kozinets, 2002), and "Internet/online ethnography" (Androutsopoulos, 2006; Stæhr, 2015) to look at the digital literacy practices of Facebook users. We were able to learn about the students' offline practices through the online linguistic and cultural resources they draw upon. It provided a convenient space for self-reflection and self-identification for many students, which can be expressed through the array of textual and linguistic resources (Barton & Lee, 2013). We also hung out with students as participant-observers on multiple occasions during the students' leisurely get-togethers to learn more about the students' offline (and online) linguistic behaviors. Finally, the research participants were invited for interviews and casual discussions in terms of their own metalinguistic interpretations. They also provided some insights about their sociolinguistic biographies, social and cultural backgrounds, issues and tensions about their language use, and self-identifications. This research therefore combines aspects of linguistic and online ethnography, which we term *linguistic nethnography*, to explore the *digital metroliteracies* of our participants.

In the next section, we look at various online texts authored by our research participants to understand the ways in which online metrolingual practices (digital literacies) create affordances for enacting and enhancing aspects of their sexual, ethnic, and class-based offline identities. All three participants for the present study were students at the National University of Mongolia (NUM). All study English as a foreign language as a compulsory subject at NUM. Five data extracts have been selected to introduce ways in which digital metroliteracies are used to enact various identities. The names of both individuals and institutions in these extracts are pseudonyms to protect anonymity. All Mongolian data texts, including the interview accounts used in the data examples of this paper, have been translated from Mongolian into English by the researchers.

## Metrolingual Identities and Facebook Literacies

### Enacting Sexual Identity

In this section, we look at the online metrolingual practices of Baatar (NUM student majoring in math), showing how multimodal resources are relocalized in the metrolingual practices of this speaker in relation to his sexual identity.

Table 17.1

| Facebook text | Translation |
|---|---|
| 1. Suvd: …hehe end bgamu?<br>17 February 2012 at 11:56 · Like | 1. Suvd: …hehe are you here? |
| 2. Suvd: nz**ushka**<br>17 February 2012 at 11:56 · Like | 2. Suvd: my dear friend |
| 3. Baatar: *hey honey*, endee bgaa shd. Za chi min sain uu Suvd? *so sa*?<br>17 February 2012 at 11:57 · Like | 3. Baatar: hey honey, I'm here. How are you my dear Suvd? What's new? |

Language guide: regular font = Mongolian; *italics* = English; **bold** = Russian

Baatar has over 200 Facebook friends, and he updates his Facebook almost everyday, from uploading varied photos and albums to music videos and hyperlinks. In Table 17.1, Baatar uploads a photo of himself with his two friends sitting behind the table with full bottles of red wine. One of his female Facebook friends, Suvd, leaves a comment on this photo, combining Russian and English oriented linguistic resources and other paralinguistic symbols in her Mongolian dominated Facebook discourse (lines 1, 2). Suvd uses the transliterated Roman Mongolian script instead of official Cyrillic Mongolian, the common online orthographic choice of young urban Mongolians. Some may have no access to Cyrillic Mongolian font on their computers, while others simply prefer Roman Mongolian due to its convenience (they avoid the hassle of transliterating English names into Cyrillic Mongolian) (Dovchin, 2015).

In line 1, Suvd asks Baatar whether he is in Ulaanbaatar or not, presenting her situational mood as happy by integrating the paralinguistic symbol "he he" (a gentle laugh) perhaps playfully teasing Baatar's photo. In line 2, she adds the Russian-influenced Mongolian noun "nzushka" ("my dear friend") to draw Baatar's attention again. "Nzushka" is a shortened version of Mongolian/Russian "naizushka": The Russian morpheme "-ushka" is relocalized in combination with the Mongolian stem "nz"—an abbreviated form of the Mongolian noun "naiz" ("friend"). The Russian suffix "-ushka" is often used in integration with Mongolian nouns to create an affectionate tone, though this also usually carries connotations of "cute" femininity. This is perhaps related to the fact that the Russian suffix "-ushka" is often added at the end of the Russian female personal names ("Masha+ka= Mashka") to show affection (cf. Dovchin et al., 2015). Suvd thus refers to her male friend in language commonly denoting femininity.

In line 3, Baatar confirms that he is in Ulaanbaatar. The English phrase "hey honey" is incorporated in response to Suvd's question. Baatar uses English phrases such as "hun" (referring to "honey"), "my darling," "dear," "sweetheart," "sweetie," etc. extensively in his offline (non-Facebook) interactions with friends. His spoken style with these friends often includes tones and terms considered affectionate and feminine, such as coy giggles, or a child-like tone of voice. Using terms of affection such as "honey" occurs much more commonly among female friends in Mongolia, and is much less likely between men or between men and women unless the speakers are involved in a romantic relationship. Here, however, Baatar integrates these phrases platonically into his Facebook interactions with female friends, making salient his gay sexual identity. Following one of those "linguistic homonormativities" established within the transnational gay community (Leap, 2010)—it is relatively common for gay men to use such terms as "honey," "darling," and "dear" among themselves (Dovchin et al., 2015)—Baatar draws on this metrolingual resource as he maintains the tone of the interaction instigated by the affectionate "nzushka" (and the style of interaction when they interact offline).

Baatar's gay identity is also suggested through his use of Mongolian "chi mini" ("my dear") (line 3). The Mongolian phrase "chi mini" is predominantly used amongst women. It is considered a feminine way of expressing one's fondness and affection towards one another and is often avoided by men because of its association with femininity. Baatar commonly uses Mongolian terms such as "hongoroo" ("my dear") and "huurhunuu" ("hey beautiful") in both offline and online contexts, and his use here of "chi mini" when he interacts with his female friends is an extension of the particular ways in which he performs a gay identity in daily interactions. Baatar's use of the phrase "so sa" ("what's new?")—an abbreviated version of Mongolian "sonin saikhan?" ("what's new?")—in line 3 also reinforces this feminized gay identity since women often use this expression as an initiation of what is perceived as "female gossip." Baatar's gay identity is further enacted in the Facebook wall post below (Table 17.2).

In line 1, Baatar posts on his Facebook wall that he is feeling very sad, integrating the Cyrillic Mongolian "учиргүй гансрах" ("to be really sad") with the emoticon sad face to show his contextual

Table 17.2

| Facebook text | Translation |
|---|---|
| 1. Baatar: feeling учиргүй гансрах. <br> 8 August 2014 · Ulaanbaatar, Mongolia | 1. Baatar: feeling really sad |
| 2. Erdene: Get a wife hahahah <br> 8 August 2014 at 05:02 · Like | |
| 3. Baatar: hahaha, bullshit! u know i can't bastard :P <br> 8 August 2014 at 05:03 · Like | |

mood and Facebook default language "feeling" (Facebook users have the option of choosing certain situated moods by pressing the button "What are you doing?" under the section of "What's on your mind?"). In line 2, his male Facebook friend Erdene teases Baatar to "get a wife" in English. Erdene signals his ironic intent (whether a "wife" refers to a male or female partner) through the common re-semiotization of online onomatopoeic loud laughter "hahahah" (he knows his friend is gay). In line 3, Baatar appears to confirm he takes this as a joke (he repeats "hahaha" and adds a "sticking the tongue out" emoticon) but uses a more commonly masculine style of response (swearing) with his use of the English "bullshit! u know i can't bastard." Here he reaffirms his gay identity through a different mode of interaction—informal male banter—with a male friend.

Baatar's metrolingual practices deploy a mixture of linguistic, paralinguistic, and semiotic resources, including posts of various romantic pop songs by boy bands or female divas such as Beyonce and Rihanna. The use of a range of feminized English, Russian, and Mongolian oriented linguistic resources ("hun," "hairaa," "nzushka") can be understood as a "gender-bending" (Danet, 1998) practice, where the male gender uses female-oriented words in daily linguistic practice to perform an alternative sexual identity. Baatar thus draws on a range of digital metrolingual resources to enact a gay online identity by dissociating himself from the language practices of masculine "manly" heterosexual Mongolian men. Yet he also draws on a more masculine style (using English) as he reconfirms his sexuality with a male friend.

### *Enacting Ethnic Identity*

In this section, we look at how Timur's (male, NUM student majoring in international relations) ethnic minority identity is enacted through his online metrolingual practices (Table 17.3).

Timur predominantly hosts his Facebook in Mongolian. However, his Faceboook literacy employs the relocalization of varied linguistic and semiotic resources. He integrates transliterated Roman Mongolian script instead of Cyrillic Mongolian throughout the whole Facebook interaction. In line 1, Timur posts holiday greeting in English, "Happy Nauruz everyone!!!! (tomorrow)" to acknowledge New Year's Eve—one of the most important traditional holidays for Mongolian Kazakhs. In line 3 the term "clip" referring to the music video within the Mongolian sentence "Goe clip uzelde ain"—is best understood as derived from Russian "клип" ("klip") rather than English.

More striking than these uses of English and Roman script, however, is his use of much less widely used resources from Kazakh. In line 1, Timur integrates Kazakh resources in his English holiday greeting, "Happy Nauruz everyone!!!! (tomorrow)" using the transliterated Roman Kazakh, "Nauruz" ("Наурыз") to mark the first day of spring and the beginning of the New Year in the Persian calendar, often celebrated in mid-March. Timur's English holiday greeting is then accompanied by the YouTube hyperlink of a Kazakh music video portraying and celebrating the "Nauruz." The title and explanation of the YouTube hyperlink itself includes some Kazakh resources including varied names of Kazakh singers and music groups.

Table 17.3

| Facebook text | Translation |
|---|---|
| 1. Timur: *Happy* **Nauruz** *everyone*!!!! (*tomorrow*) **НАУРЫЗ - Клип 2014 HD !! ВИДЕОҒА ЛАЙК & АЛ КАНАЛҒА ЖАЗЫЛАМЫЗ !! Клипта: Тимур Омаров, Роза Мұқатаева, Ринго тобы, Ұлытау тобы, Таңшолпан жұлдыздары, Арнау, Лейлә Сұлтанқызы, ...** M.YOUTUBE.COM Like Comment Share | 1. Timur: Happy Nauruz everyone!!!! (tomorrow) |
| 2. Davaa: Битүүнээ тэмдэглээд байна уу 20 March 2014 at 11:02 · Like | 2. Davaa: Are you celebrating your New Years' Eve? |
| 3. Timur: Goe *clip* uzelde ain 20 March 2014 at 11:02 · Like | 3. Timur: Why don't you watch the nice clip, hey? |
| 4. Davaa: Мань ойлгохгүйшт 20 March 2014 at 11:03 · Like | 4. Davaa: I will not understand it, bro |
| 5. Timur: Oilgodog yumaa l uzej sonsdimu | 5. Timur: Do you only watch or listen to things that you understand? |
| 6. Davaa: заа үзээ андаа 20 March 2014 at 11:06 · Like | 6. Davaa: Ok, I will watch then, mate |

Language guide: regular font = Mongolian; *italics* = English; **bold** = Kazakh

Overall, Timur's relocalization of Kazakh-oriented resources in his metrolingual Facebook practices enacts Timur's ethnic identity as a Mongolian Kazakh—the largest ethnic minority group in Mongolia. His performance of Kazakh identity is achieved through the relocalization of both linguistic and nonlinguistic Kazakh symbolic strategies that take different shapes. While the majority of the Mongolian population are Khalkh Mongols, Kazakhs constitute 5% of the population and mostly reside in the far west of the country. They started migrating to Mongolia from the 1860s, mainly from the Xinjiang region of China. The majority of Khalkh Mongolians are Tibetan Buddhists, while Islam is the dominant religion among ethnic Kazakhs in Mongolia. The relationship between Mongolians and Kazakhs in Mongolia has been largely amicable and Mongolian Kazakhs have enjoyed a comparatively high status in the Mongolian society. Nonetheless Kazakhs have been strongly encouraged to learn Mongolian in order to be accepted into Mongolian society while very few Mongolians speak Kazakh or engage with Kazakh cultural practices.

Timur's parents are Mongol Kazakhs, his father being a renowned medical consultant in the largest cancer centre in Mongolia. Timur went to one of the most prestigious high schools in Mongolia alongside other pupils from affluent backgrounds. He is a multilingual user of Mongolian, Kazakh, and English, and his multilingual identity is very clear on his Facebook interactions. Yet Timur is also very proud of his Kazakh heritage, as suggested in this Facebook extract, when one of his Facebook Mongolian friends (Davaa) seems to be uninterested in watching the Kazakh music video because of the Kazakh language barrier (line 4). Timur, however, insists his Mongolian Facebook friend watch the music video, criticizing him for watching only the things that he understands (line 5). Here, Timur clearly shows his desire that his fellow Mongolian friends should appreciate and take the Kazakh music video seriously.

While engaging in cosmopolitan relationships through his use of English and Mongolian in his online metrolingual practices, Timur also emphasizes his ethnic identity and language. He redefines his Kazakh identity and language by relocalizing them with English and Mongolian and other multimodal resources. Given the rarity of Kazakh linguistic and cultural resources in urban and online Mongolian contexts, it does not take much to index his alternative identity affiliation, yet by doing so alongside other linguistic and cultural resources as part of his metrodigital literacy practices, he affirms his status as a young, cosmopolitan urban metrolingual.

### Enacting Elitist Identity

Bayar's (male, NUM student, majoring in international relations) online metrolingual practices on his Facebook site mainly concern the relocalization of Russian, English, and other semiotic resources integrated within Mongolian. His literacy practices also point to class-based aspects of his identity.

Bayar's presence on Facebook is intense and his feed is largely composed of multimodal and multisemiotic resources, including photos of his hobbies, such as exclusive vegetarian meals that he has cooked, photos of him doing his favourite sports activities such as fencing and marathon running, and hyperlinks to his preferred Russian and Western music videos. His status updates include information about his overseas travel experiences (a spectator at the World Cup in Brazil, selfies in front of the Eifel Tower, holidays on beaches in Thailand, etc.) and candid Facebook conversations with friends and relatives living all over the world.

Table 17.4 shows one of his typical Facebook activities, updating his wall posts using Russian linguistic resources. In line 1, in his Facebook status update, Bayar uses "musical speaking," in which he relocalizes lyrics and lines from songs (Dovchin, 2015), using Cyrillic Russian. He recycles the chorus lines from the Russian song "Komarova" (the name of a municipal district in Saint Petersburg, Russia) by Igor Sklyar, one of the popular Russian pop songs from the early 80s. Such knowledge of 1980s Russian songs is not common among young urban Mongolians, most preferring modern Russian popular music. By contrast, relocalizing the lyrics from this "vintage-feel" type of old Russian song, Bayar shows his intense knowledge of popular Russian music.

Meanwhile, in line 2, his Facebook friend Tuul identifies the lyrics straight away as "Huurhun duu" (cute song), using transliterated Roman Mongolian orthography. This instant recognition of an old type of Russian song by Bayar's friend suggests not only Bayar's, but also his interlocutor's deeper engagement with Russian popular culture. In fact, not only Bayar, but also some of his Facebook friends tend to post varied hyperlinks using predominantly Russian on Bayar's Facebook wall.

In Table 17.5, Bayar's friend Naran shares a photo to Bayar's timeline, with a long message written exclusively in Russian about how the planet Mars is going to travel in close proximity to the Earth (line 1). One of Bayar's main hobbies is galaxy and star constellations, and he often shares photos of different stars taken by his long range Celestron telescope. Bayar's friend is obviously aware of his exclusive hobby and shares the news about planet Mars with Bayar. In line 2, Bayar declines the news as false using Cyrillic Russian. The conversation around this topic with his Facebook friend requires advanced competency in the Russian language. Bayar and his friend seem to be at ease whilst interacting in Russian, signaling similar skill levels of Russian language and culture.

Table 17.4

| Facebook text | Translation |
| --- | --- |
| 1. Bayar: **На недельку до второго я уеду в Комарово** Like Comment Share | 1. Bayar: In the week before the second I will leave for Komarovo |
| 2. Tuul: Huurhun duu 27 October 2010 at 00:19 · Like | 2. Tuul: Cute song |

Language guide: regular font = Mongolian; *italics* = English; **bold** = Russian

Table 17.5

| Facebook text | Translation |
|---|---|
| 1. Naran shared a photo to Bayar's Timeline. 24 June<br><br>РЕБЯЯЯТ, НАДО НЕ ЗАБЫТЬ!)))<br>27 августа в 00:30, подними глаза и посмотри на ночное небо. В эту ночь планета Марс, пройдет всего лишь в 34,65 тыс. милях от земли. Невооруженным глазом планета будет видна как полная луна. Это будет выглядеть как две луны над землей! Следующий раз когда Марс будет так близко к Земле будет только в 2287 году. Поделись этой новостью со своими друзьями так как никто из живущих на Земле еще такого не видел!<br><br>20 August 2014 · Edited · Like Comment Share | 1. Naran shared a photo to Bayar's Timeline.<br><br>Guys! Don't forget! At 00:30, August 27, open your eyes and look at the night sky. This night, planet Mars will pass by Earth with only 34,65 thousand miles proximity. With bare eyes, planet Mars will look like a full moon. This will look like as if there are two moons on Earth. Next time when Mars travels this close to Earth will be only in 2287. Share this news with your friends as no living inhabitants on Earth has never seen this kind of thing before. |
| 2. **Bayar:** От Земли до Марса 34 милл. миля. Не 34 тыс. Так что, это не возможно и не правда<br>Like · Reply · 25 June at 07:18 | 2. Bayar: From Earth to Mars it is 34 million miles. Not 34 thousand. That's why this is impossible and this is not true. |

Beyond Facebook, Bayar and his friends also often tend to heavily integrate Russian resources within their daily offline literacy practices. The relocalization of Russian can be indexical of an affluent and elitist background in Mongolia. Bayar went to one of the most prestigious Russian secondary schools in Ulaanbaatar before starting his university degree. In socialist Mongolia, children who attended the prestigious Russian high schools were often considered the "elite" because their parents were usually high-ranking politicians or other elite officials. This tradition is still alive in current Mongolia, as the Russian high schools are still perceived among the most prestigious educational institutions. People who attended Russian high schools often integrate higher levels of Russian linguistic resources within their daily linguistic practices, which in turn becomes a common indicator of an elite background (Dovchin et al., 2015). In his elite Russian high school, Bayar also started mingling with students of the same background (that link between social, cultural, and economic capital identified by Bourdieu, 1991), some of whom are now interacting on his Facebook using Russian resources. Bayar thus enacts his elite background through the relocalization of Russian embedded within his daily multimodal literacy practices.

## Conclusion: Digital Metroliteracy Practices

This chapter has explored how the online engagement in everyday digital literacy practices through social media such as Facebook are, on the one hand, a product of the multilingual and multimodal affordances of the online environment. The examples above have shown how the *digital metroliteracy practices* of these urban Facebook users deploy an array of interconnected linguistic (English, Russian, Kazakh, Mongolian), semiotic, and cultural resources (posting multimodal hyperlinks, illustrations and images, aphorisms and paralinguistic symbols). On the other hand, we have also shown how the online identities of these participants are also deeply linked with their offline lives, histories, and cultural and linguistic repertoires. The online and offline spaces in which these young adults interact are complexly conjoined, with meanings, resources, and identities crossing over from one space to the other. The distinction between being online and offline, between real and virtual, is less important than an understanding of how these diverse literacy assemblages are part of their continuing metrolingual practices.

By showing these everyday creative online digital literacy practices, the notion of metrolingualism is extended beyond the notion of physical urban space, as Facebook users perform a range of identities (sexual, ethnic, and class-based) that are both part of but also adjacent to the offline metrolingual fabric. There are several implications of this observation. From the point of view of research, we should be cautious about trying to understand the cultural and linguistic lives and literacy practices of young adults without investigating both their online and offline practices: If we explore their online worlds without looking at the everyday offline lives, we fail to see how one may be grounded in the other; but if we focus on their offline lives, we fail to see how their online lives seep into their everyday practices. As Buck (2012, p. 35) concludes, online users integrate their online selves into their everyday activities "to the point that it is not possible to draw sharp distinctions between online and offline identities and activities."

From a more pedagogical perspective, it is also important to see the interweaving of these two modes of interaction. Online digital metroliteracies may provide richer multilingual and multimodal resources than offline lives, and the tendency to assume that Facebook is superficial entertainment, or to be online is to leave the real world behind, is to misunderstand contemporary modes of engagement. Students in our classes, in the coffee shop, on the bus are simultaneously on-and offline, and as literacy educators, it is important that we can grasp the workings of these worlds that are not parallel or separate but intertwined. Each metrolingual practice has its own sociolinguistic history, culture, and background. Facebook-based metrolingual practices are intricately woven into the tapestry of daily literacy practices, playing a significant role in how Facebook users present their varied selves. Offline metrolingual identities are filtered through their online literacy activities. It is thus important to consider social network sites as part of broader systems of metrolingual activities, which in turn can be a useful way to understand how online/offline identities are interrelated.

## References

Androutsopoulos, J. (2006). Introduction: Sociolinguistics and computer-mediated communication. *Journal of Sociolinguistics, 10*(4), 419–438.

Androutsopoulos, J. (2007). Bilingualism in the mass media and on the Internet. In M. Heller (Ed.), *Bilingualism: A social approach* (pp. 207–232). New York, NY: Palgrave Macmillan.

Barton, D., & Lee, C. (2013). *Language online: Investigating digital texts and practices*. New York, NY: Routledge.

Bourdieu, P. (1991). *Language and symbolic power*. Oxford, UK: Polity Press.

Buck, A. (2012). Examining digital literacy practices on social network sites. *Research in the Teaching of English, 47*(1), 9–38.

Canagarajah, S. (2013). *Translingual practice: Global Englishes and cosmopolitan relations*. New York, NY: Routledge.

Danet, B. (1998). Text as mask: Gender, play, and performance on the Internet. *Cybersociety, 2*, 129–158.

de Bres, J. (2015). Introduction: Language policies on social network sites. *Language Policy, 14*(4), 309–314.

Dovchin, S. (2011). Performing identity through language: The local practices of urban youth populations in post-socialist Mongolia. *Inner Asia, 13*(2), 315–333.

Dovchin, S. (2015). Language, multiple authenticities and social media: The online language practices of university students in Mongolia. *Journal of Sociolinguistics, 19*(4), 437–459.

Dovchin, S. (2016a). The ordinariness of youth linguascapes in Mongolia. *International Journal of Multilingualism, 14*(2), 144–159. Retrieved from http://www.tandfonline.com/doi/full/10.1080/14790718.2016.1155592.

Dovchin, S. (2016b). The translocal English in the linguascape of popular music in Mongolia. *World Englishes, 36*(1), 2–19. Retrieved from http://onlinelibrary.wiley.com/doi/ 10.1111/weng.12189/full.

Dovchin, S., Sultana, S., & Pennycook, A. (2015). Relocalizing the translingual practices of young adults in Mongolia and Bangladesh. *Translation and Translanguaging in Multilingual Contexts, 1*(1), 4–26.

Dovchin, S., Sultana, S., & Pennycook, A. (2016). Unequal translingual Englishes in the Asian peripheries. *Asian Englishes, 18*(2), 92–108.

García, O., & Li, W. (2014). *Translanguaging: Language, bilingualism and education*. Basingstoke, UK: Palgrave Macmillan.

Gourlay, L., Hamilton, M., & Lea, M. R. (2013). Textual practices in the new media digital landscape: Messing with digital literacies. *Research in Learning Technology, 21*, 1–13.

Grasmuck, S., Martin, J., & Zhao, S. (2009). Ethno-racial identity displays on Facebook. *Journal of Computer-Mediated Communication*, *15*(1), 158–188.

Hamilton, M. (2015). Imagining literacy: A sociomaterial approach. In K. Yasukawa and S. Black (Eds.), *Beyond economic interests: Critical perspectives on adult literacy and numeracy in a globalised world* (pp. 3–18). Rotterdam, The Netherlands: Sense Publishers.

Internet World Stats (2016) http://www.internetworldstats.com/asia.htm#mn. Last accessed September 30, 2016.

Jørgensen, J. N., Karrebæk, M. S., Madsen, L. M., & Møller, J. S. (2011). Polylanguaging in superdiversity. *Diversities*, *13*(2), 23–38.

Kozinets, R. (2002). The field behind the screen: Using netnography for marketing research in online communities. *Journal of Marketing Research*, *39*(1), 61–72.

Leap, W. (2010). Globalization and gay language. In N. Coupland (Ed.), *The handbook of language and globalization* (pp. 555–574). Colchester, UK: Wiley-Blackwell.

Leppänen, S., Møller, J. S., Nørreby, T. R., Stæhr, A., & Kytöla, S. (2015). Authenticity, normativity and social media. *Discourse, Context & Media*, *8*, 1–5.

Nørreby, T. R., & Møller, J. S. (2015). Ethnicity and social categorization in on- and offline interaction among Copenhagen adolescents. *Discourse, Context & Media*, *8*, 46–54.

Otsuji, E., & Pennycook, A. (2010). Metrolingualism: Fixity, fluidity and language in flux. *International Journal of Multilingualism*, *7*(3), 240–254.

Pennycook, A. (2016). Mobile times, mobile terms: The trans-super-poly-metro movement. In N. Coupland (Ed.), *Sociolinguistics: Theoretical debates* (pp. 201–216). Cambridge, UK: Cambridge University Press.

Pennycook, A., & Otsuji, E. (2014). Metrolingual multitasking and spatial repertoires: 'Pizza mo two minutes coming'. *Journal of Sociolinguistics*, *18*(2), 161–184.

Pennycook, A., & Otsuji, E. (2015). *Metrolingualism: Language in the city*. Oxon, UK: Routledge.

Pennycook, A., & Otsuji E. (2016). Lingoing, language labels and metrolingual practices. *Applied Linguistics Review*, *7*(3), 259–277.

Phyak, P. (2015). (En)Countering language ideologies: language policing in the ideospace of Facebook. *Language Policy*, *14*(4), 377–395.

Rossabi, M. (2005). *Modern Mongolia: From Khans to commissars to capitalists*. Berkeley: University of California Press.

Sharma, B. K. (2012). Beyond social networking: Performing global Englishes in Facebook by college youth in Nepal. *Journal of Sociolinguistics*, *16*(4), 483–509.

Sherman, T., & Švelch, J. (2015). "Grammar Nazis never sleep": Facebook humor and the management of standard written language. *Language Policy*, *14*(4), 315–334.

Stæhr, A. (2015). Reflexivity in Facebook interaction–enregisterment across written and spoken language practices. *Discourse, Context & Media*, *8*, 30–45.

Sultana, S., Dovchin, S., & Pennycook, A. (2013). Styling the periphery: Linguistic and cultural takeup in Bangladesh and Mongolia. *Journal of Sociolinguistics*, *17*(5), 687–671.

Sultana, S., Dovchin, S., & Pennycook, A. (2015). Transglossic language practices of young adults in Bangladesh and Mongolia. *International Journal of Multilingualism*, *12*(1), 93–108.

Thorne, S. (2013). Digital literacies. In M.R. Hawkins (Ed.), *Framing languages and literacies: Socially situated views and perspectives* (pp. 193–218). New York, NY: Routledge.

Varis, P., & Blommaert, J. (2015). Conviviality and collectives on social media: Virality, memes, and new social structures. *Multilingual Margins: A Journal of Multilingualism from the Periphery*, *2*(1), 31–46.

Velghe, F. (2015). "Hallo hoe gaandit, wat maak jy?": Phatic communication, the mobile phone and coping strategies in a South African context. *Multilingual Margins: A Journal of Multilingualism from the Periphery*, *2*(1), 10–31.

Zhao, S., Grasmuck, S., & Martin, J. (2008). Identity construction on Facebook: Digital empowerment in anchored relationships. *Computers in Human Behavior*, *24*(5), 1816–1836.

# 18
# Critically Reading Image in Digital Spaces and Digital Times

Peggy Albers, Vivian M. Vasquez, and Jerome C. Harste

Images play a significant role in our digital world. Billions of images are uploaded, downloaded, and shared every minute of every day. These images are far from neutral and, like written texts, may impose ideologies on viewers (Albers, 2011; Albers, Harste, & Vasquez, 2011a; Harste & Albers, 2013; Vasquez, 2004; Vasquez, Albers, & Harste, 2011). Further, these ideologies are often internalized and reproduced leading us to ask, "To what extent are images—digital or otherwise—discussed critically?" In this chapter, we attempt to lay out why such a discussion is central to preparing citizens for the twenty-first century, and what more can be done to further such a discussion. This work, we argue, is especially important when it comes to educating students to be critically literate in the digital era of the twenty-first century.

Statistics on Domo.com increasingly remind us of the plethora of information on the Internet and how much data are uploaded or accessed *per minute*: YouTube users share 100 hours of new video, Snapchat viewers watch 9,644,444 videos, Buzzfeed users view 159,380 pieces of content, Netflix viewers stream 86,805 hours of video, Instagram users like 2,430,555 posts, and Facebook users share 216,302 photos (James, 2016) (Figure 18.1).

Multiplying these numbers by 1,440 minutes per day produces staggering numbers that have led us to realize the importance of critical reading of images. While there has been attention to critical use of image and visual information in classrooms (see Burnaford, 2007), less has been written about the significance of this critical practice in digital spaces and in today's digital times.

## Relevance and Defining Key Concepts

Image plays an important and foundational role in how children learn to read the world through immersion in the visual world, through image in literature, digital texts, picture books, and among others. We define image as still or moving, digitized, illustrated, photographed, and/or imagined (or remixes of all). Our work across time has defined reading image as studying image from disciplinary knowledge (art principles, principles of design), structural and theoretical approaches (how the image is designed, laid out, object size, etc., multimodal analysis, mediated discourse analysis), and critical perspectives (cultural models, D/discourses, situated meanings, social languages) (Gee, 1999). While each of these areas signifies the range and complexity of image analysis, we also encourage different approaches to reading image in digital spaces, one includes an ideology of visibility (Comolli, 1985) and engages us in regimes of visibility (Dahlgren, 2011) in which visual language is marked with ideologies, beliefs, and practices around which it is used, read, and applied.

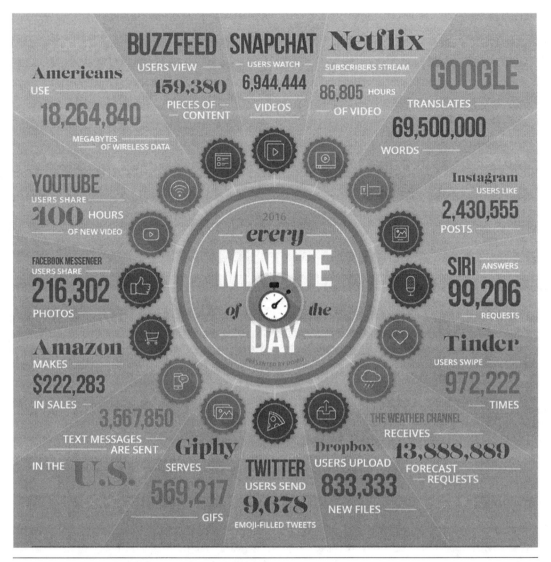

**Figure 18.1** Data that is generated or accessed per minute, June 28, 2016

(Source: © Domo 2016. Used by Permission)

Building knowledge about how to read images and learning how image works in digital spaces is of vital importance for several reasons. First, young children through adults regularly use digital devices for a range of purposes. For example, studies by Kabali et al. (2015) and the Pew Research Center (2016) found that use of digital devices was "almost universal" (Kabali et al., 2015). Kabali et al. found that three- to four-year olds in lower economic and minority communities could navigate smartphones without help. Further, 97% of this group of children used mobile devices and by age two used such a device daily with YouTube and Netflix being their most popular TV viewing. By ages three and four, most were able to multi-task on devices.

Activity in digital spaces, especially accessed through mobile phones, increases people's access to digital images, and the constant interruption of texts like advertisements, pop-up texts, and videos. The Pew Research Center found that 24% of teens are online "almost constantly," most likely through smartphones. Facebook is the site most visited by teens. Ninety-two percent of adults own a smartphone, devices that have impacted every facet of personal and workplace practices (www.pewinternet.org/2015/10/29/technology-device-ownership-2015/). We present these statistics to demonstrate the "almost universal" access to image, especially through social networking sites and Internet searches.

Second, for us, image in texts (picture books, videos, apps, video games) continues to play an essential part in how children are introduced to and learn to make sense of both fiction and nonfiction texts. Children learn cultural norms, for example, at least in part through their immersion into and talk around images in a range of texts, such as media texts and posters. Wohlwend's (2012) study of children's global media franchises Disney and Mattel suggests that popular media characters—through dolls, costumes, movies, and toys—"circulate identity texts, embedded storylines that communicate idealized ways of 'doing [for example] boy' or 'doing girl'" (p. 4). Through play, and especially through dolls, children are invited to enact gendered identities. In her work with pre-school children, Vasquez (2004) engaged children in a discussion of gender after they studied a poster that featured a Royal Canadian Mounted Officer. One girl noticed that there were no female Mounties, to which a boy responded that girls could not be Mounties. This initiated an inquiry into how females and males were positioned in texts like posters, especially in public spaces like schools.

Third, we suggest that the viewing of still images (e.g. stories, paintings, picture books, advertisements, and billboards) is always active. In interacting with these images, we actively construct or imagine ourselves in these spaces. In our study of teachers and their viewing of advertisements (Harste & Albers, 2013), teachers critically studied the images in advertisements from such companies as McDonald's, Ralph Lauren, Home Depot, and Disney. That is, they discussed the design of the ad in terms of art elements and object placement as well as social markers of identity (e.g., gender, class, race, and sexual orientation). Through redesign (Janks, 2013), teachers remade their own ads to problematize the messages in the original ads. We found that teachers did develop a language of critique for visual and written messages of consumerism, and found that knowing how to analyze visual texts enabled them to understand how to integrate this work into their own critical literacy curriculum.

Like Shannon (2011), we wish to argue that the vast amounts of visual data presented to us moment by moment inform how we are to act, think, and behave. Said another way, Shannon argues that visual information that we encounter has an underpinning pedagogy that teaches us to act. For example, a large department store in the US has an ad, "This Week Only!!" a phrase commonly used across companies to teach consumers to purchase immediately. A McDonald's billboard in Toronto has a picture of a coffee cup with the written text "Paying 4 Bucks is Stupid," teaching people that they do not have to pay for high-priced coffee in coffee shops like Starbucks. Common road signs in the South of the US have Christian religious messages like "Are you ready?", teaching people that they need to behave and believe if they want to go to heaven. Viewing an image is no longer a passive act, but rather one that affects personal and social practices.

**Tensions and Conflicting Viewpoints**

Over a decade ago, Kalantzis, Cope, and Harvey (2003) described key attributes of successful learners to imagine an effective model of curriculum and assessment. They suggested that "excellent learners" are "autonomous and self-directed—designers of their own learning experiences" (p. 17), collaborative, flexible problem-solvers, possess multiple strategies for tackling a task, and must be intelligent in more than one way. That is, learners must be able to engage with text in multiple ways, and create and produce texts that are comprised of multiple modes. Children today are increasingly exposed to, interacting with, and generating digital texts, and building and adapting to new literacies practices (Vasquez & Felderman, 2012).

From very early on, children are creating and remixing modes to create more complex, multimodal, digital texts, to express ideas and/or learning (Marsh, 2015; Vasquez, 2010). Very young children are learning new practices around literacy from technical use (stretching, pushing, tapping screens), interacting with digital texts, and shortening the distance between real and imagined. For example, *PokémonGo* uses GPS technology to let users roam around in their real-time locations to capture creatures in this popular game that blends together augmented reality with real-world sites, and allows players to photograph themselves with the *PokémonGo* characters. This app was released on July 6, 2016, and three weeks later, recorded 30 million downloads and $35 million in revenue.

Analyzing still images across texts has been taken up by a number of scholars who have drawn upon a range of perspectives to report on findings about gender, identity, ideology, and critical literacy. In our work, we drew from both critical literacy and social semiotics to study to what extent ideologies become visible in student- and teacher-generated texts (Albers, Vasquez, & Harste, 2011b; Harste & Albers, 2013; Vasquez, Albers, & Harste, 2013). Significantly, our studies demonstrate how student-generated texts make visible the appropriation of existing ideologies that reaffirmed or reified not-so-favorable perspectives around social markers of identity (e.g., race, gender, class, and beauty). In one study (Albers et al., 2011b), we asked teachers to talk back to issues of identity that they found operating in children's literature in writing, discussion, and image. We found that teachers could talk and write critically about ideologies; however, when asked to represent ideologies visually, they moved back into more traditional representations of identity (diversity=multicolored hands; friendship=hearts). We concluded that teachers have less experience and knowledge with representing ideas visually than they do through talking and writing. As a result, they moved into comfortable spaces to reify markers of identity.

In another study (Harste & Albers, 2013), we invited teachers to create counter-ads and advertisements that would talk back to the underpinning messages about gender, beauty, and health, among other issues. We found that the majority of teachers were unable to disrupt traditional discourses, but rather reproduced them in their own ads. Other scholars (Magno & Kirk, 2008; Serafini, Kachorsky, & Aguilera, 2015) have also studied still images in digital and print-based texts. Studying print and digital versions of the same children's picture book, Serafini, Kachorsky, and Aguilera (2015) found that readers' experiences and discussion shifted across platforms. They argue that understanding the potential of each platform enables multiple narratives to emerge rather than a single narrative, thus expanding meaning making of the reader.

Drawing from Sonneson's schematic analysis (1988), Albers, Frederick, and Cowan (2009) found that traces of identity were made visible through analysis of the objects, colors, and composition of children's visual responses to gender. Through analysis of images selected by developmental agencies about girls' education, Magno and Kirk (2008) argued that naïve image selection promoted particular ideologies around girls and girls' education. Through use of methods of visual analysis with photographs, they found that image selection by these agencies may not have been intentional, but due more to a lack of understanding of the multiplicity of potential readings.

Scholars have taken up different approaches to analyzing still and moving image through a lens of multimodality, and have signified the importance of multimodal/digital texts in literacy learning. Rowsell and Pahl (2007) discussed the role of process and materiality in multimodal texts as sedimented identities that gesture to the previous identities of the text maker. That is, traces of the text maker's social practices are visible in the text, and the materiality of the text highlights those traces. Norris's (2004) multimodal interaction analysis (MMIA) allows for a close-up perspective on how modes take on different relevance in moving image. Her work centralizes how modes operate together to convey meaning and how modes have different levels of significance in an overall message.

Tomlin's (2013) autoethnographic dissertation studied his role as an administrator who used MMIA to study video interactions that he had with teachers, students, and parents. He found how physical actions actually communicated more than verbal/written messages, communicative modes assumed to be the most important for administrators. Pahl (2007) studied children's texts as multimodal artifacts and identified "*traces* of practice, and as instantiations of identities" (p. 87). Across this work, scholars have examined the relationship between art elements, composition, and structure and critical readings of texts including advertisements, videos, information texts, and photography.

Texts created by digital/technology tools and their influence on social markers of identity and social practices have also been explored by a number of scholars. In 2009, Wohlwend critically analyzed children's play around Disney princesses to note the fusion between girls' identification as princesses with the corporate marketing of characters and stories. Most recently, Wohlwend (2015) explored tweens and identity through Monster High dolls, looking specifically at tweens' engagement with and enactment of these dolls in online and video spaces. These fashion dolls are inspired by monster, sci-fi, and thriller movies. Digital texts and critical readings/interpretations are central in Vasquez and Felderman's (2012) work, in which children not only create and analyze digital texts, but also use digital tools for social action. In another study, working with podcasting and grade two children, Vasquez (2015) found that children were able to address social issues (e.g., language and global warming) through their inquiry and development of podcast shows. Further, podcasting opened up participation for children in curriculum that "seemed inaccessible," and they were able "to take on different identities in the podcasting world that created space for them to participate in ways they hadn't previously" (p. 152).

Studies of children's text making through iPads have offered insights into critical image analysis. Mills, Comber, and Pippa's (2013) work suggests that critical attention to the senses must be part of children's digital media production or filmmaking. They argue that filmmaking not only supported children's formation and representation of knowledge, but it also showed that this knowledge is reliant on "embodiment, sensoriality, co-presence, and kinesis" (p. 25). Kerwin's work involved using apps on an iPad with sixteen young children (newborn to age eight) in six families. She found that digital play encouraged literacy development and expanded their experience with digital resources.

Our work (Albers, 2011; Albers et al., 2011a) argued for a need for critically analyzing the digital texts that teachers and students produce in classroom settings. Through projects such as public service announcements, which involves selection of images, visual transitions, music, and texts, we found that in-service and pre-service teachers often reified commonly assumed images of types (e.g., gang members, teenagers, and parents) through their projects. This work suggests that engaging children in critical discussions around how modes operate within texts is essential to teaching for a democratic citizenry. Further, critically reading and analyzing images is crucial because images position not only the viewers to read in a particular way, but also the subject of the image in particular ways.

In *Doing Critical Literacy*, Janks (2014) presents classroom strategies focused on images to show how these images work to re/produce discourses/ideologies. Studying image through her model of critical literacy (2010) creates a space for readers to "start to question things that you took for granted before…notice things that you used to ignore…" (Janks, 2014, p. 1). Significant to this work is Janks' analysis of a range of texts, including informational, such as world maps, that might be considered benign or neutral. She asks, how and why continents are represented (or not), why does it matter, and to whom does it matter? Such questions become opportunities for critical analyses and conversation around design that may have gone unnoticed (Antarctica is rarely represented; the Mountains of Kong never really even existed), and to acknowledge that "where we stand affects what we see" (p. 16). Across these approaches, scholars have focused on a range of methods to consider how viewing matters in print-based, digital, and video texts, methods that address structural, social, critical, and embodied aspects of how to view and interact with visual texts. Some approaches value the structural and grammatical aspects of viewing texts, others locate viewing and analysis within the situated and cultural aspects of viewing, while others see corporate marketing as central to how viewing and enactment materialize. Within what might be considered tensions arise multiple perspectives on viewing image—and specifically on how these viewings potentially inform and shape identities—that contribute to a larger critical perspective on how image is viewed across print-based, digital, and cyberspace texts.

**Current or Emerging Theory**

Elements of critical literacy, intra-action, and participation inform our work on the analysis of images and reading in digital times and digital spaces. First, critical literacy is a dominant framework for arguing in favor of analyzing image as part of developing a critical perspective on modes of expression often left out in instruction. Critical literacy, as both a theory and practice of literacy as social practice, aims to uncover inequitable economic, cultural, political, and institutional structures (Janks, 2010) through exploring notions of power. Janks (2014) identifies five interdependent elements that need to work in sync from a critical literacy perspective: dominance, diversity, access, design, and redesign. Where one is situated, in terms of power, informs: how and what s/he sees, who has the right to speak and act in different situations, what or whether they have access, how they speak and what they can or cannot speak to, whose perspective is valued (or not), and how we become, through language and power.

Other scholars' also have systematically taken up critical literacy to discuss curriculum, pedagogy, and learning (Comber, 2014; Lewison, Leland, & Harste, 2013; Luke & Freebody, 1999; Vasquez, 2004). Harste's (2003) work summarizes critical points in this scholarship. He argues that curriculum must entail a perspective in which we "want critically literate beings who know how language works and can use it to make meaning and reposition themselves in the world in a more democratically thoughtful and socially just manner" (p. 11). Freire (1970) understood the work of critical literacy as "reflection and action upon the world in order to transform it" (p. 36) within a cultural context that "mark [human beings] and which they also mark" (p. 90). This process, we suggest, results in becoming "more" by critically reflecting upon existence and by critically acting upon one's existence through intra-action (Barad, 2000). Importantly, this work redefines literacy as reading and changing the world as a central part of what it means to be truly literate.

Aspects of "more" may be explained by Barad's (2000) theory of agential realism, a framework that takes into account the discursive and material nature of social practices in the production of knowledge through intra-actions (Barad, 2012), an inseparable dynamic between human and non-human, material and discursive, and natural and cultural factors. For Barad (2012), agency, the ability to act, is not something afforded to someone; rather, it emerges from the intra-action that occurs between the individual and her/his interaction with objects, concepts, and texts, while maintaining their independence. From this perspective, everything is "entangled" with everything else (Barad, 2012).

Individuals do not exist, but materialize through intra-action with space, time, context, and material. Explained in another way, response to image(s) is not an interaction—as if the viewer and the image are separate entities. The viewer materializes as a transaction through intra-action with, in, and alongside the image viewed. Take for example, the use of slow motion (slo-mo) as a special effect, commonly used in film, sports, reality shows, videos, and still images in presentation software, to manipulate time to see details, for dramatic effect, for aesthetic purposes, and/or to elicit emotion (among other purposes).

Before slo-mo, particular actions in real time were unnoticeable, for example, the flight of a bullet. The intra-action between the viewer and the viewing of this flight in real time and slo-mo materializes a different viewing experience. *The Matrix*, for example, changed the way we view action through its use of slo-mo and the highly choreographed slow dance between characters dodging flights of bullets. We suggest that reality shows like *Forged in Fire* use techniques such as slo-mo to engage viewers aesthetically into actions that in real time are dangerous. In this show, bladesmiths are challenged to create blades which are then tested by judges for sharpness, handling, durability, and their ability to inflict harm. Particular actions are slowed way down to show, for example, how a blade cuts through a pig carcass; viewers see in detail the depth including the curve of the slice. Or viewers watch as a blade in slow-mo cuts through a sand-filled burlap bag causing the bright blue sand to cascade slowly down and onto the floor for the sole purpose of heightening aesthetic response. Even more graphic, a judge thrusts a blade into a synthetic human torso that in slow-mo oozes green synthetic liquid. If the blade fulfills "its purpose," the judge nods in affirmation, and smiles and says, "It will cut" or "It will kill." The slowing down of the slicing, piercing, and thrusting of blades lessens, we suggest, the graphic and horrific, and instead invokes the aesthetic. Unlike combat and action in shows like *Game of Thrones*, weapons slice, pierce, and thrust in real time to represent as closely as possible the realism of medieval warfare. However, in *Forged in Fire*, slo-mo engages the viewer, making the violent aesthetic, and the moment of impale extended.

This manipulation of time allows for what Greene (2001) calls "direct apprehension of some complex totality as it is given and presented to our viewing" (p. 12) in which viewers become aware of the many facets of a work, such as medium, textures, light, and color. We suggest that this sustained and conscious awareness engages a different intra-action of the viewer with the objects. Frame-by-frame actions allow for image sequences to build into narratives. A real-time violent sequence of actions now becomes a slowed down story in which the viewer notices and intra-acts with objects and their details aesthetically through color, texture, light, and mediums. Viewers become "more" as the viewing is slowed down; they engage aesthetically in the narrative around weaponry that "will cut" and "will kill."

Another aspect of becoming "more" may be viewed through the concept of participation in digital spaces. Participation is an action that is often viewed as beneficial and democratic. However, it cannot be guaranteed that everyone can participate. Who then can or cannot participate? Who has access (in terms of who is invited, committed, or empowered) to participate? Dahlgren (2011) writes that the Internet is not just a place where people "visit." Rather, as Jenkins writes, the Internet has led to a new participatory culture (Jenkins, n.d.) in which people "tak[e] media into their hands, to share, to express themselves, through every possible media channel" (http://video.mit.edu/watch/what-is-participatory-culture-3027/) and social networking site. Media and social networking tools allow Internet users to archive, appropriate, remix, and recirculate media content for creative expression. "Around those tools have grown a set of practices, institutions, ways of doing things…" (http://video.mit.edu/watch/what-is-participatory-culture-3027/).

Framing participation in this way, in which people are viewed as agentive, "taking into their hands….," has been critiqued by Fuchs (2016). He argues that Jenkins ignores the role of capitalism in participation, especially in online spaces like Google in which 90% of its revenue is driven by advertising. Google ranked first in Internet companies, earned $74.54 billion in 2015, with 67.39 billion US dollars generated by advertising, and with a market value of 373 billion US dollars (www.statista.com/statistics/266206/googles-annual-global-revenue/).

While users may perceive that they have control over media, Fuchs says that capitalism engenders a "colonization of societies and human spaces to open up new spaces of commodification and capital accumulation" (Fuchs, 2016, p. 62). In other words, viewing in digital spaces has become a commodity driven by capitalism where participation is not always voluntary. Consider how access is parceled out. How many pop-ups, ads, and commercials does one have to navigate to gain access to information and viewing? If someone wants to view information, what must this viewing cost them (e.g., in terms of time, what images/texts must be viewed)?

In our recent CNN search on the tragic Orlando night club massacre, it took us five hyperlinks to get to a visual timeline, and we had to watch a thirty-second ad before we could watch a news clip. So, to view this information, we had to spend time viewing other matter; thus, participation in online spaces may not be as democratic as one may think in a new participatory culture. Carpentier and Dahlgren (2011) argue that while participation in digital spaces may be possible, access may not be, especially when considering the costs associated with devices and data costs. So, participation, Dahlberg suggests, comes with privilege and creates an ideology of visibility: We know we are in digital arenas (think Facebook, Instagram, and Pinterest) where people can see and respond to us. While we might consider postings as "taking media into our hands" (we control when, what, and how we post), we also need to consider how this visibility also opens up new spaces for capital accumulation through social media surveillance (Fuchs & Trottier, 2105): "As we spend more and more time online on social media, a lot of our everyday activities in different roles during a lot of our working and free time become accessible, traceable, analyzable in real time to institutions with whom we do not necessarily have a relationship of trust" (p. 130).

Google offers a succinct demonstration of an online space through which critical literacy, intra-action, and participation can be viewed (see Dahlgren, 2011). As a powerful stakeholder regarding knowledge and information, Google, the most widely used search engine, controls how knowledge and texts are organized and how this information is designed and shown to us on the screen. Further, through its powerful analytics system software, Google oversees and keeps watch of our searches so that images/ads pop up and are traced back to previous searches. This prompts us to consider issues that need critical unpacking. Google's design networks track, archive, and analyze traces of our searches, which then manifest into pop-up ads to encourage us to shop from particular companies or sites that offer products that could be associated with our search. Viewing in digital spaces has become a commodity with companies competing for visibility by interrupting searches.

Our recent search of South African safaris has now become a common banner across multiple searches that entices us to click on South Africa First Class. As Fuchs suggests, our searches are tracked (surveilled) and shared with companies synchronously, and linked to pop-up ads that show up immediately in subsequent searches. These ads then are shared in our social network sites as products we endorse ([name] likes ProFlowers Facebook ads), a network of sharing around which we have no control, and positions in ways we may well find offensive. That Google can predict, organize, and prioritize our subsequent searches leads us to wonder, to what extent do we have control over what we view and read, and how we are constructed as viewers and consumers? What are we willing to look at or watch (put up with) in order to access our desired information ("You can skip this ad in…")?

**Implications for Practice**

So, what does all of this have to do with critically analyzing image in digital spaces and times? Google processes 40,000 search queries every second on average, 3.5 billion searches per day, and 1.2 trillion searches per year (yes, done through a Google search) (www.internetlivestats.com/google-search-statistics/). We want to suggest that within digital spaces, through intra-action and participation, we materialize differently as viewers, viewers that do not "take media into their own hands," and whose viewing is controlled by the information the search engines archive from our searches, which then push ads into our viewing spaces. While we have choice in what we type in our searches, we do not have choice in what we view in the sidebars, and where and how pop-up windows appear. As such, in these digital spaces, "digital identities" are constructed. Such identities predict who we are, what we desire, and who or what we might "like."

Critical issues around the inter-relatedness of power, dominance, and agency prompt us to argue for a more systematic, critical, and complex analysis of images in digital spaces. Viewed in relation, the new participatory culture, capitalism, and consumerism implicate viewers not by choice but by force. That 90% of Google's revenue is generated by advertising leads us to question how viewing impacts how we view and what we are becoming through this viewing. Our identities, we argue, become digitally sedimented, where traces of our searches manifest over and over again in products and information as search engines predict our desires.

To study how identities are digitally sedimented, we suggest that teacher educators and educators invite their students to do multiple searches on a topic of their choice, and take screen captures that show which pop-up windows, sidebars, images, and videos are generated by search engines. Invite them to analyze the content and design of these pop-ups, and study why these pop-ups may have been generated by their search engine. They might consider, "What do these pop-ups assume about me as viewer? As a consumer?" These screen captures can be printed out and studied across searches to understand how and what search engines construct around social markers of identity and occupation (e.g., race, class, teachers, and students).

Students could also be invited to study how many clicks or hyperlinks it takes to get to information they desire. While searching for a well-known shoe museum in Toronto we entered the words "shoe museum in Toronto, Ontario" in the search box. The first link led us to the Must-Visit Museum site for guided tours in the US. The second link led us to the Royal Ontario Museum, a museum of natural history, not shoes. The third link led us to the visitacity.com website which described the Bata Shoe Museum. The link on that site, which we assumed would take us to the shoe museum website, actually led us to a map of where the museum is located along with places to eat and other places to visit while in the city. It took a total of seven clicks or hyperlinks before we finally landed on the Bata Shoe Museum website. While doing a search like this, students could be asked to consider, how many hyperlinks it took get to their desired site, what the (dis)connections were between the hyperlinks encountered during their search, and the website they desired in the first place. Students could also identify any patterns, commonalities, and differences between the sites and what search engines assumed about them (as viewers and consumers). Further, students could consider if a different combination of words might have resulted in finding the museum site more readily and how different combinations of words produce different search results. This could also be an opportunity for students to explore the effects on them of pop-ups during their searches. Do they bypass the pop-ups or are they enticed to click on the links?

This study on one's reading navigation and practices can be done by capturing screenshots of the Internet pages accessed in a search using software like Movavi and Camtasia (trial versions are available for new users). From there, students systematically analyze how and why this set of texts was generated around their searches to understand the inter-relatedness of advertising and searching. We also suggest that educators actively draw upon visually heavy spaces such as Facebook, Instagram, and Pinterest among other visually heavy spaces as sites to develop critical engagements. Students can systematically study their posts over time, what they view on other posts, and which advertisements/texts appear in these posts, and how the information they desire is interrupted visually through moving and still ads. What are the objects that they notice immediately? How do they intra-act with these objects?

By engaging in such activities, we suggest that educators and students alike begin to critically study how our way of viewing and reading processes change in digital spaces through such things as hyperlinks, pop-ups, and sidebars. Such engagements allow for systematic study of how search engines operate, organize and present information, and create spaces of intra-action that generate digital identities. Critical discussions around who takes control in this new participatory culture, and how we can work against the power that search engines wield, are key to more democratic participation in digital spaces.

## Recommendations and Forward Thinking

We continue to argue for more systematic and complex analysis of visual image, not just in terms of content, but how that content is mediated and materialized. We value the research and work done with children and technology; however, we also encourage interrogation of how students' texts came to be and who they are becoming from the making of these texts. We offer several points to consider when discussing viewing in digital spaces.

First, as viewers of information and images, we must be aware that we are also viewed by search engines, most often re-materializing as consumers given the digital spaces that we inhabit daily. Dahlgren (2011) argues that we need to unpack this intra-active viewing as "regimes of visibility." In *Discipline and Punish*, Foucault (1991) suggests that discipline creates patterns in behavior and thought, while power and surveillance engender desired ways to socialize—and be socialized. We use search engines like Google as daily practice—a regime of sorts now—for accessing Internet sites for immediate and accessible desired information. We are disciplined to accept the practice of viewing images, pop-ups, and banners—it is part of the terrain of the Internet that we inhabit. Additionally, through these digital practices, viewers know that they are publicly visible in digital arenas (Facebook, Instagram, Google docs, etc.), with a presumption of agency and choice (typing in searches, posting). Thus, it is easy to believe that a new participatory culture suggests democratic participation and visibility; however, we ask, "At what cost do we participate, and what are we willing to access to get at the information we desire?" We do not suggest that accessing and viewing information on the Internet is bad, we do suggest that critical conscious awareness of how and what we view and critical understanding of what digital texts are trying to do to us, has the potential to shape how we are positioned as viewers (Harste & Albers, 2012), through critical pedagogies in these digital spaces (Shannon, 2011).

Second, intra-action, as we have attempted to describe it, is the "more" of critical literacy, a materialization of self with image/texts in digital spaces, which may or not be democratic but more disciplined through power (search engines). How we search (descriptors), which images are populated to represent people, places, objects, etc., and which digital texts are then downloaded become an inseparable dynamic between human and nonhuman, material and discursive, and natural and cultural factors. We suggest that this intra-action is at the crux of Janks' (2014) call for interrogation of power in language. Yet, with Internet access as a regime, to what extent can we "opt out" or should we? It is not our argument to stop using the Internet as a resource; rather, we pose questions to initiate more complex discussions around participation and viewing in digital spaces: How are we socialized (disciplined) or *not* to interrogate the tools and the technology in favor of capturing a dramatic image, moment, or event? How do we interrogate the very source of the information that we download, integrate, and reproduce? Intra-action enables us to study the forces of power in visual language, and we see who we have become or are becoming, made visible by the images/texts that populate around our searches. Conscious awareness of how our identities become digitally sedimented can then be critically disentangled through a number of different perspectives, several of which we outlined earlier.

Third, we also want to suggest that critical study of digital tools used to manipulate image and texts (e.g., time-lapse, slow motion, morphing) be discussed, studied, and interrogated to understand the textmaker's aesthetic, intellectual, technical, and social purpose. Just as lighting and music mediate the still or moving image story for viewers, so to do special effects involving time (see Albers, 2011). Redesigning texts through time and image has the potential to create narratives that change the viewing of horrific or violent events into stories of beauty. Viewers relive the event frame by frame, engaging more consciously and deeply with details, now removed from real-time action. Critical points of discussion might revolve around Janks' dimensions of critical literacy as simultaneously addressing: dominance, access, diversity, and design/redesign. How are real-time narratives redesigned in slow motion to capture different stories of guns, bullets, explosions, hammers, and medieval blades? How does intra-action of slowed down details shift our viewing of what might be considered actions of violence (bullets piercing watermelons or colored water in glass bottles, or gun powder-laced targets)? How do viewers mediate between the aesthetic and the horrific when digital tools are used to manipulate texts? How does real-time, time-lapse, and slow motion act on our viewing and shape how we become in digital spaces? Text created through software (iMovie, Moviemaker) and a variety of phone apps (Tracker Video Analysis, Plotly SloPro, Videocraft) need to be studied and interrogated in terms of both purpose and observed response.

We suggest several overarching concerns for further inquiry, research, and revisioning of literacy and language arts education. First, even more so now that information is immediately and easily accessible, viewing and interpreting images—still, moving, time-altered—is critical to understand how power and language operate. We argue for curriculum that not only values digital technologies, but consciously fuses critical stances within the making and evaluation of these texts. We argue for additional research on the reading of image, and unpacking the sources from which interpretations are articulated. Further, we want to suggest that analysis of image be situated within a pedagogy of digital spaces to understand how the digital—as a daily practice and regime—inform who we are, what we select, and how the forces outside of our actions intra-act. It is only in this way that we can socialize students—and ourselves—to notice, interrogate, and speak to and against the viewing of image in digital spaces.

## Conclusion

While our published work in analyzing visual imagery lay primarily in critical and structural approaches to reading image (see work cited in this chapter), we also recognize the importance of critical perspectives in understanding viewing in digital spaces. The research across the past two decades in still image has presented strong frameworks for analysis. Yet, we suggest that viewing and analyzing image, especially in digital spaces, requires now a more complex study of how image is viewed and analyzed through social media and digital spaces and the digital practices that emerge from participation in these spaces. The new participatory culture has the appearance as one of empowerment, but it is also an ideology of the visible (Comolli, 1985), in which the production of an image (moving, still, digital) is ideologically informed, not just in terms of what is shown, but viewers' intra-action with how they are shown (light, slo-mo, space, pop-ups). Viewers and viewing become sedimented by the very social media/digital sites that track and trace our searches, predict our beliefs through the action of these searches, and teach us to think about the images that are populated by the digital spaces that we inhabit daily. In this way, as viewers, we are socialized unconsciously in digital practices that prevent us from critically interrogating how we are implicated as consumers in the very searches we do many times daily.

## References

Albers, P. (2011). Double exposure: A critical study of preservice teachers' multimodal public service announcements. *Multimodal Communication, 1*(1), 47–64.

Albers, P., Harste, J. C., & Vasquez, V. (2011a). Making trouble and interrupting certainty: Teachers' critical and visual responses to children's literature. In P. J. Dunston, L. B. Gambrell, S. K. Fullerton, V. R. Gillis, K. Headley, & P. M. Stecker, (Eds.), *60th yearbook of the literacy research association* (pp. 68–83). Oak Creek, WI: LRA.

Albers, P., Vasquez, V., & Harste, J. C. (2011b). Making visual analysis critical. In D. Lapp & D. Fisher (Eds.), *The handbook of research on teaching the English language arts* (3rd ed.) (pp. 195–201). New York, NY: Routledge.

Barad, K. (2000). Agential realism. In L. Code (Ed.), *Encyclopedia of feminist theories* (pp. 15–16). New York, NY: Taylor & Francis.

Barad, K. (2012). Intra-actions. *Mousse*, (34), 76–81. Accessed from https://ucsc.academia.edu/KarenBarad.

Carpentier, N., & Dahlgren, P. (2011). Introduction: Interrogating audiences—theoretical horizons of participation. *Communication Management Quarterly, 4*(21), 7–12.

Comber, B. (2014). Literacy, poverty and schooling: What matters in young people's education? *Literacy, 48*(3), 115–123.

Comolli, J. (1985). Technique and ideology: Camera, perception, and depth of field (D. Matias, Trans.). In B. Nichols (Ed.), *Movies and methods* (Vol. 2, pp. 40–57). Berkeley, CA: University of California Press.

Dahlgren, P. (2011). Parameters of online participation: Conceptualising civic contingencies. *Communication Management Quarterly, 21*, 87–110.
Foucault, M. (1991). *Discipline and punish: The birth of a prison*. London, UK: Penguin.
Freire, P. (1970). *Pedagogy of the oppressed*. New York, NY: Herder and Herder.
Fuchs, C. (2016). *Social media: An introduction*. Thousand Oaks, CA: Sage Publications, Inc.
Fuchs, C., & Trottier, D. (2015). Towards a theoretical model of social media surveillance in contemporary society. *Communications: The European Journal of Communication Research, 40*(1), 113–135.
Gee, J. P. (2001). Reading as situated language: A sociocognitive perspective. *Journal of Adolescent & Adult Literacy, 44*(8), 714–725.
Harste, J. C. (2003). What do we mean by literacy now? *Voices from the Middle, 10*(3), 8–12.
Harste, J. C., & Albers, P. (2013). 'I'm Riskin' It': Teachers take on consumerism. *Journal of Adolescent & Adult Literacy, 56*(5), 381–390.
James, J. (2016). *Data never sleeps 4.0*. Retrieved from www.domo.com/blog/2016/06/data-never-sleeps-4-0/.
Janks, H. (2010). *Literacy and power*. New York, NY: Routledge.
Janks, H. (2013). Critical literacy in teaching and research. *Education Inquiry, 4*(2), 225–242.
Janks, H. (2014). *Doing critical literacy*. New York, NY: Routledge.
Jenkins, H. (n.d.). *Participatory culture*. Retrieved from http://video.mit.edu/watch/what-is-participatory-culture-3027/.
Kabali, H. K., Irigoyen, M. M., Nunez-Davis, R., Budacki, J. G., Mohanty, S. H., Leister, K. P., Bonner, R. L., Jr. (2015). *Exposure and use of mobile media devices by young children*. Retrieved from http://pediatrics.aappublications.org/content/early/2015/10/28/peds.2015-2151.
Kalantzis, M., Cope, B., & Harvey, A. (2003). Assessing multiliteracies and the new basics. *Assessment in Education: Principles, Policy & Practice, 10*(1), 15–26.
Kervin, L. (2016). Powerful and playful literacy learning with digital technologies. *Australian Journal of Language & Literacy, 39*(1), 64–73.
Lewison, M., Leland, C., & Harste, J. C. (2013). *Creating critical classrooms: Reading and writing with an edge*. New York, NY: Routledge.
Luke, A., & Freebody, P. (1999). *Further notes on the four resources model*. Retrieved from www.readingonline.org/research/lukefreebody.html.
Magno, C., & Kirk, J. (2008). Imaging girls: Visual methodologies and messages for girls' education, *Compare, 38*(3), 349–362.
Marsh, J. (2015, February 8). *Young children's online practices: Past, present and future* [Webinar]. In Global Conversations in Literacy Research Web Seminar Series. Retrieved from http://youtu.be/Gw9WOZ93okA.
Mills, K., Comber, B., & Kelly, P. (2013). Sensing place: Embodiment, sensoriality, kinesis, and children behind the camera. *English Teaching: Practice and Critique, 12*(2), 11–27.
Norris, S. (2004). *Analyzing multimodal interaction: A methodological framework*. New York, NY: Routledge.
Pahl, K. (2007). Creativity in events and practices: A lens for understanding children's multimodal texts. *Literacy, 41*(2), 86–92.
Pew Internet Project (2016). *Lifelong learning and technology*. Retrieved from www.pewinternet.org/2016/03/22/lifelong-learning-and-technology/.
Rowsell, J., & Pahl, K. (2007). Sedimented identities in texts: Instances of practice. *Reading Research Quarterly, 42*(3), 388–404.
Serafini, F., Kachorsky, D., & Aguilera, E. (2015). Picturebooks 2.0: Transmedial features across narrative platforms. *Journal of Children's Literature, 41*(2), 16–24.
Shannon, P. (2011). *Reading wide awake: Politics, pedagogies, and possibilities*. New York, NY: Teachers College Press.
Tomlin, D. D. (2013). *All the school's a stage: A multimodal interaction analysis of a school administrator's literate life as dramaturgical metaphor*. Unpublished dissertation, Georgia State University, Atlanta, GA.
Vasquez, V. M. (2004). *Negotiating critical literacies with young children*. Mahwah, NJ: Routledge.
Vasquez, V. (2010). *Getting beyond I like the book: Creating spaces for critical literacy in K-6 classrooms*. Newark, DE: International Reading Association Press.
Vasquez, V. M. (2015). Podcasting as transformative work. *Theory into Practice, 54*(2), 147–153.
Vasquez, V., Albers, P., & Harste, J. C. (2013). Digital media, critical literacy, and the everyday. In R. Meyer, R. & K. Whitmore (Eds.), *Reclaiming writing in the post NCLB world* (pp. 214–223). Mahwah, NJ: Lawrence Erlbaum Associates, Inc.
Vasquez, V. M., & Felderman, C. (2012). *Technology and critical literacy in early childhood*. New York, NY: Routledge.
Wohlwend, K. E. (2009). Damsels in discourse: Girls consuming and producing gendered identity texts through Disney Princess play. *Reading Research Quarterly, 44*(1), 57–83.
Wohlwend, K. E. (2012). 'Are You Guys Girls?': Boys, identity texts, and Disney princess play. *Journal of Early Childhood Literacy, 12*(3), 3–23.
Wohlwend, K. E. (2015). Ghouls, dolls, and girlhoods: Fashion and horror at Monster High. In V. Carrington, J. Rowsell, E. Priyadharshini, & R. Westrup (Eds.), *Generation Z: Zombies, popular culture, and educating youth*. New York, NY: Springer. Retrieved from http://karenwohlwend.com/papers/2016Ghoulsgirlhoods.pdf.

# 19
# The Quantified Writer
*Data Traces in Education*

Anna Smith, Bill Cope, and Mary Kalantzis

Though the electronic pulses that transmit data packets across the Atlantic in milliseconds can make digital writing seem ephemeral, writers composing with digital devices and within digitally networked environments leave traces. Through new media's social practices and algorithmic designs, these traces can be fed back and used, making them long lasting, seemingly indelible marks. User metrics and analytics—though still early emerging socio-technological phenomena—have quickly become foregrounded in big business, policing, and governmental decision-making. At the same time, they have also become backgrounded in social life—an everyday, "unseen" aspect of the social ecologies of daily life (Baym, 2013). In this chapter, we focus on a slice of social ecologies, to digital writing practices and processes. In doing so, we draw attention to critical questions that arise regarding what is recorded digitally as we write—how traces are generated and recorded, and why those mechanisms matter with particular focus on data traces in education.

This chapter borrows its name from the techno-optimistic "quantified self" discourse that proliferates media. This discourse, argue Ruckenstein and Pantzar (2015), rests on underlying beliefs that through the feedback of quantified information about the self, "reality" is made transparent and can be optimized. Such optimistic hopes, however, often fail to deliver. The "quantified writer"—like the "quantified self"—is always partial, offering a slant perspective on the realities of a writing life. This chapter explores the complexities of the techno-optimistic view of "quantified writer" in an era mediated by digital, networked capacities and computer-mediated instruction and assessment. We map data sources that have the potential to generate unprecedented amounts of trace data regarding writing. We make the case that these data traces necessitate an understanding of underlying mechanisms that generate, store, and provide data, and that these mechanisms have important potential for shifting traditional writing assessment approaches.

## What Are Digital Traces of Writing?

In the excitement of new composing technologies, the complexity of writing practices is newly accentuated; however, writing is and has always been a complex, technological phenomenon in dialogic relationship with social, cultural, and historical practices (Haas, 1996). From diary entries to scribbled marginalia (e.g., Camille, 1992), writers have always left socio-technological traces of developing ideas, relationships, and composing processes. Writers and scholars alike have been fascinated by what these traces *may* mean, such as by seeking to draw connections between the idiosyncratic habits of writers and their productivity (e.g., Popova, Accurat, & MacNaughton, 2013). This brings us to wonder: When compositional traces are born or captured *digitally*, what's new?

Describing the current participatory era of digital composition, Jenkins, Clinton, Purushotma, Robinson, and Weigel (2006) explain that "new literacies almost all involve social skills developed through collaboration and networking" (p. 4). We would add the modifier "online" to this argument to emphasize that in regard to writing, collaboration and networking are not new. Rather, digitally mediated collaboration affords new rhetorical dimensions, such as providing a greater potential reach to interactive audiences, making possible new relational and ethical dynamics when composing with those far distant geographically and socially (e.g. Smith & Hull, 2013; Stornaiuolo, Hull, & Sahni, 2011). In addition to collaboration and networking, Kalantzis, Cope, and Harvey (2003) highlight other "new basics" that schools could focus on as they support developing writers: autonomy, flexibility, problem-solving, creativity, and ability to work productively with linguistic, cultural, and context diversity. Andrews and Smith (2011) suggest that in addition to new rhetorical dimensions, and multimodal capacities of new technologies, educators must begin to support writers in developing an understanding of the mobilities and malleability of texts, modes, and meaning, particularly regarding how they are flexibly framing digital compositions. Understanding writing in the present era involves attending to evolving networked social practices, "new basics," and socio-technological mobilities.

With increased means to compose, writers are using data generated with mobile technologies—such as location markers, timestamps, and multimodal media—to compose. In geocomposing (Farman, 2012), for instance, the GPS data generated as the authors move across a city landscape videotaping and taking photographs become material and means by which writers compose multimedia products, such as "counter-maps" drawn to critically interrogate the built environment (Taylor & Hall, 2013). Composers use and learn from feedback quantifications to revise and develop distribution plans (Smith, McCarthey, & Magnifico, 2017). Using mobile apps such as Snapchat, YouTube, and Instagram, composers construct and deconstruct narrative lifestreams of video, image, and text snippets as they engage with interactive audiences (Saul, 2014; Wargo, 2015). Organizations, such as the Electronic Literature Organization (ELO; available at http://eliterature.org/), highlight literature composed with hypertext and interactive programming, bots, and other computer-generated literature (e.g. see Figure 19.1; Boluk, Flores, Garbe, & Salter, 2016).

## Data Trace Mechanisms

Emerging sources of trace data have the potential to generate unprecedented amounts of data, both unstructured, automatically collected data, and structured data embedded in composing activity through platform design. As complex activity fundamental, yet difficult to quantitatively model, writing and its traces push the boundaries of new measurement technologies and processes. This has inspired special sessions at educational conferences like the Learning Analytics and Knowledge Summit (LAK) of the Society of Learning Analytics Research (SoLAR) to run a workshop series expressly concerned with the limits and promise of collecting and analyzing writing's data traces. Indeed, to understand what writers' trace data may mean, we need to understand the mechanisms that produce these data.

### Shedding Light on Unstructured Data

By unstructured, we mean that much of the data captured in digital composing platforms that show periods of engagement, navigation paths, and social interaction, such as timestamps, keystrokes, and clickstreams, have not been framed by pre-determined statistical modeling and software programming. Increasing amounts of unstructured data are captured with technologies such as wearables,

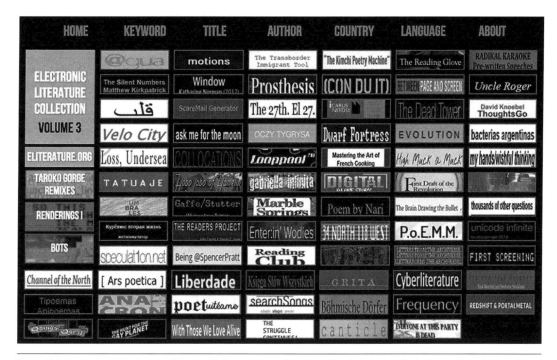

**Figure 19.1** Screenshot of *The Electronic Literature Collection, Volume 3* interactive interface (CC BY-NC-ND 4.0)

video capture, and RFID chips (Lindgren & Johnson-Glenberg, 2013). Behavioral actions captured by these technologies are incidental, yet constitutive of composing. Some behaviors are particular to the use of digital devices, but many are intrinsic to composing, but previously outside the purview of analysis. So much unstructured information is generated and collected, researchers warn of "data exhaust" (DiCerbo & Behrens, 2014). Lazer et al. (2009) argue that these data are so complex and "noisy" that only small parts may be rendered knowable and useful.

Unstructured data are not immediately legible or meaningful to users, researchers, or educators. Rather, they require aggregation and contextualization to be made legible, as well as interpretation to be made meaningful as traces of digital writing. In this sense, what might be considered "raw data" is not "raw"; rather, all data require some form of data mining or culling. Whether by hand, computerized aggregation, scraping macros, or statistical pattern recognition software, methods of data retrieval are built or trained by human inference. For example, now that social interaction dimensions of composition can be recorded, many scholars are considering ways to curate these previously ephemeral interactions for predictive forecasting of writing behaviors (e.g. Wise, Zhao, & Hausknecht, 2013). Interpreted from these interactions using natural language processing methods, affective states and sentiment (Fancsali, Ritter, Stamper, & Berman, 2014) that impact learning outcomes may be detectable (Baker, D'Mello, Rodrigo, & Graesser, 2010; Dowell & Graesser, 2014; Winne & Baker, 2013).

The edit history of a wiki or blog can tell a story of textual development of a single document, or the relative contributions in collaborative online writing environments (McNely, Gestwicki, Hill, Parli-Horne, & Johnson, 2012), but without additional analysis, the patterns of collaborative drafting, peer interaction, and revision are unintelligible. For these reasons, much of the work in the field of educational data mining is focused on making sense of large, noisy unstructured data sets. A challenge for the field is to keep in mind that even unstructured data points were generated through programmatic design and then made legible by algorithmic mechanisms, which influence what is looked to and looked for in composing process and practices.

## Structured Data in Writing Environments

In practice, structured and unstructured data are often generated simultaneously. By structured data, we mean data collection, analysis, and distribution "designed in" (Ho, 2015) to the programming of platforms and environments, such as intelligent tutors, games, simulations, and rubric-based peer review (Mislevy, Behrens, Dicerbo, & Levy, 2012; Pea & Jacks, 2014). Such programs use automated feedback loops (VanLehn, 2006) and complex decision trees (Xu, Chang, Yuan, & Mostow, 2014) that anticipate a range of learning paths, guiding the computer program and learner alike. In these systems, data, such as the answer to a question about writing conventions or a criterion rating in a rubric, are produced and recorded as semantically legible to writers and teachers. Data garnering programs can be modeled for simplistic aspects of writing, such as rule-bound conventions (used in intelligent tutoring or gaming), and also for more complex evidence- and argument-based structures (used in rubrics). At the most complicated end of the structured data spectrum are distributed machine learning processes, semantic tagging, and visualization technologies.

With advances in software and hardware, in technology-mediated learning environments such as learning management systems, discussion boards, and peer-reviewed writing spaces, writing environments can now be created that collate learning process data (Knight, Shum, & Littleton, 2014), and capture not just traces, but also trace patterns in learning events (Winne, 2014). Researchers have found that computerized writing tutors—though they can only "tutor" the most basic aspects of writing—can effectively include strategically placed game activities at different stages in the writing process (Roscoe & McNamara, 2013). In such systems, the workings of the technological interface—in responding to and delivering structured data—are similar to unstructured data, in that they are not neutral. Rather, they are built from pedagogical and theoretical models of writing and learning to write. McLeod, Hart-Davidson, and Grabill (2013) emphasize this in discussing the design and use of their peer review management system, Eli Review—that they are offering more than a learning management program, but rather a pedagogical approach to writing.

In developing an online learning environment called Scholar[1] (available at http://CGScholar.com) as a team led by Bill Cope and Mary Kalantzis, design decisions have been guided by principles of reflexive pedagogy (Cope & Kalantzis, 2016b) for the multiliteracies of contemporary digital writing (Cope & Kalantzis, 2009; Kalantzis & Cope, 2015; Kalantzis, Cope, Chan, & Dalley-Trim, 2016). Several iterative field-based trials and rounds of programming resulted in an infrastructure designed to support interdisciplinary, multimodal writing, and community-wide feedback through revision cycles. Scholar has been used effectively in classrooms at all levels from elementary through college (Kline, Letofsky, & Woodard, 2013; Magnifico, McCarthey, & Kline, 2014; McCarthey, Magnifico, Woodard, & Kline, 2014). It currently consists of five main components: (1) Creator (see Figure 19.2), a composing, revising, and editing space where students can review and annotate each others' multimodal compositions; (2) an Annotation tool allowing peer reviewers to highlight specific areas of text, prompt specific changes or additions using a dropdown menu of rubric criteria, and/or begin a comment thread with the author; (3) Publisher, a space where teachers design and manage multimodal projects and accompanying rubrics to guide learners; (4) Analytics, a dashboard providing multiple machine-enabled data displays of quantified aspects of written products including length, syntax complexity, ratings, composing stage, academic language level, etc.; and (5) Community, a social networking space including profiles, status updates, publication notifications, and interaction feed. Here, we provide one short example of an infrastructure decision made in the design of Scholar to utilize the capacities of semantic tagging and visualizing technologies to support writers in their composing processes (for further examples, see Cope & Kalantzis, 2017).

Acknowledging the capacities of digital writing to represent and communicate knowledge through multimodal composing, Scholar's Creator space (see Figure 19.2) is a "semantic editor"

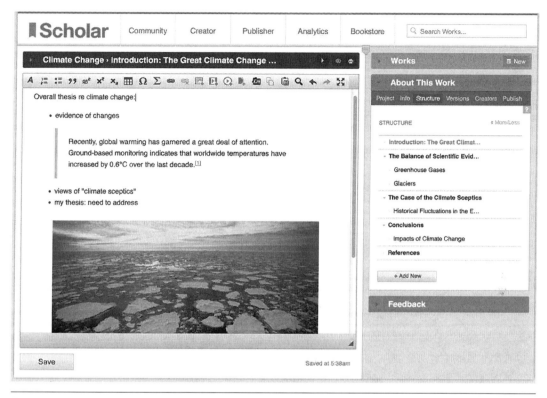

**Figure 19.2** Scholar's Creator. Writing drafted in the multimodal semantic editor (left); planning and navigating its demarcated structure (right)

(Cope, Kalantzis, & Magee, 2011), which allows the authors to include imported audio, video, and images in line with written text. Utilizing semantic tagging or markup, the Creator space supports writers in being explicit in their compositional decisions—while generating data regarding composing practices that can be analyzed for patterns and displayed in visual representations in Analytics. In semantic tagging, sections of written language that would otherwise not be legible to the computer are labeled by the author—as a block quote, sub-section, or title, etc. These labels are then executed differently depending on the publication medium, be it to the web or a PDF. Additional tags, such as marking the word "today" with the date, and structural demarcations are also possible. In layering multimodal compositions with structural markup and semantic tags, writers are prompted to consider the form and function of their developing text, and also have a flexible, markup version of the final product for rendering versions suited to various platforms and media.

Semantic tags can also be rendered visually in concept or structure maps (Rekers & Schürr, 1997). Maps of an argument, for instance, would use sections tagged as *claims, evidence, rebuttal*, etc. to make visible the underlying thinking in a text (Lynch, 2014). A browser-based visual mark-up add-on tool in Scholar called InfoWriter provides students an opportunity to re-mediate linear, written texts as concept maps. Using the tool, students apply node categories via semantic tags that correspond to features of informational writing. InfoWriter converts the coded texts into interactive nodes that students manipulate to visualize the content and organization of the text. In observing, interviewing, and analyzing drafts with 246 students using InfoWriter, Olmanson et al. (2016) found:

> In creating a menu of node types made up of the expected elements found in informational writing, student rereading is focused not on issues of editing but at the intersection of content

understanding and genre awareness. The color-coded student-generated nodes forefront the ideas, concepts, and evidence present and missing in their texts as well as how these are hierarchically linked and organized.

(p. 118)

In these ways, the deployment of semantic tagging and visualizations in Scholar's InfoWriter supported complex revision processes. Looking across visualizations, such as these, reveals instructionally significant variation between students' renderings of their disciplinary argument structures and guide instructors' decision-making.

**Studying Writing Trace Data for Educational Purposes**

Together, sources of trace data, both structured and unstructured, have the potential to generate unprecedented amounts of data regarding writing practices, processes, and products—bringing "big data" to school. In this section, we briefly outline the ways that big data is more than an issue of volume, but rather a socio-technical phenomenon with particular affordances and tensions regarding its use and uptake. We then turn to two approaches to understanding data traces in an era characterized by big data that show promise for addressing these tensions.

*Big Data*

Though the activities of composing are neither larger nor more complex than they ever were, the amount of data that can be recorded, stored, and used digitally has increased tremendously. Cope and Kalantzis (2016a) highlight that the volume of traces left in digital environments is "unprecedented in large part because the data points are smaller and the recording is continuous" (p. 2). Analyzing small data points, such as catalogued clickstreams and timestamps, brings the minute actions of composition into focus (Castro, Vellido, Nebot, & Mugica, 2007). The incidental recording of digital writing, which produces varied, finely grained data points, only becomes possible as automation technologies for recording, storing, accessing, and analyzing massive amounts of varied data points advance. As boyd and Crawford (2014) argue, "Big data is less about data that is big than it is about a capacity to search, aggregate, and cross-reference large data sets" (p. 663).

In addition to the technological and analytical advancements that make big data possible, boyd and Crawford (2014) also identify epistemological "mythologies" of big data to be at play in making the socio-technological phenomenon, particularly the "widespread belief that large data sets offer a higher form of intelligence and knowledge that can generate insights that were previously impossible, with the aura of truth, objectivity, and accuracy" (p. 663). As data sets have grown in volume and technologies have advanced that allow for their visualization and cross-referencing, the conflation between lived experience and its trace has become more common. This is particularly problematic in education in an era marked by invasive teacher accountability regimes and policies fixated on quantified representations of learning as the primary form of knowledge about educational progress. Impressive piles of data can distract from questioning the quality of the computer-enabled trace—whether it is incomplete, accurate, or representative (Rogers, 2013). This is exacerbated when data are seen as self-explanatory. Stephansen and Couldry (2014) remind, "Although network analysis can reveal connections and patterns, it has little to say about their meaning and context" (p. 4). Culled data, particularly as large data sets are layered in analysis, are decontextualized and require re-contextualization and interpretation to be made meaningful.

## Education Data Science

Two subdisciplines have developed in recent years to study learning's digital trace data—educational data mining and learning analytics (Baker & Siemens, 2014). Cope and Kalantzis (2016a) characterize *educational data mining* as mainly focused on analyzing and interpreting large unstructured data sets. In contrast, *learning analytics* is more concerned with understanding structured data, or "the measurement, collection, analysis and reporting of data about learners and their contexts, for the purposes of understanding and optimizing learning and the environments in which it occurs" (Long & Siemens, 2011, p. 34). In practice, the fields overlap considerably, "draw[ing] on and integrat[ing] research and methodology related to data mining, social network analysis, data visualization, machine learning, learning sciences, psychology, semantics, artificial intelligence, e-learning, and educational theory and practice" (Dawson & Siemens, 2014, pp. 290–291). Both approaches, with their close analysis of trace data, argue Bienkowski, Feng, and Means (2012), "have the potential to make visible data that have heretofore gone unseen, unnoticed, and therefore unactionable" (p. xi). Thus, following Pea and Jacks (2014), we construe the field as a whole as "education data science."

However, making data visible is not sufficient to understanding learning. Arguing that the social processes of literate activity are too complex to be assessed with simple metrics and surface-level analytics, Dawson and Siemens (2014) suggest that education data science be guided by a multiliteracies framework (New London Group, 1996). Focusing on the composing data traces of networking, negotiating, and transmedia navigation, they argue, would provide "deep and nuanced insight into the learning activities of students" (p. 298). Having a theoretically rich framework of composition to guide the design of complex quantitative data collection, analysis, and modeling, they suggest, addresses a critique leveled at educational data science for the field's limited degree of sophistication in its common analytical frameworks and research questions.

Many others have called for more sophisticated analytical goals for understanding data traces that merge multiple data types and analytical orientations (Crawford, 2013). Huc-Hepher (2015) suggests "small data" and small scale approaches typical of traditional qualitative methods in concert with quantitative metrics as a "strategy for overcoming the 'data deluge' inevitably triggered by non-selective, catch-all repositories" (p. 12). Approaches such as connective ethnography (Hine, 2015; Marsh, 2014), ethno-mining and thick data (Aipperspach et al., 2006; Wang, 2013), and transliteracies inquiry (Stornaiuolo, Smith, & Phillips, 2017) are flexible and responsive frameworks for "inquiry in contexts where flow is more relevant than object, physical presence is not necessarily connected to sociality, and time, as a malleable variable, is salient but difficult to isolate, much less comprehend" (Markham, 2017, p. 652).

## Software Studies

Lynch (2015) argues for critical attention in literacy education and research to the "software space" produced through the digital infrastructuring of algorithms, interfaces, networks, and information systems. Algorithms, for instance, are encoded protocols that govern the input and output of data in machines. Rather than neutral functional components, algorithms, like all writing, are socially—ideologically and ontologically—informed as they are composed, or scripted, by human programmers often in the service of business or governmental interests (Kitchin & Dodge, 2011). As Williamson (2014) reminds, an algorithm, as a "substrate" of software, "materializes particular ways of perceiving the world, as modeled and represented in the code that instructs it, which in turn can influence and shape how people act in and on that world" (p. 83).

These "invisible" substrate assemblages of algorithms, interfaces, and network infrastructures, or "software spaces" used in schools and classrooms, are often designed by outside companies or governing agencies, which may or may not share similar visions of the educational enterprise. This can hold true for programmers and educators working together to design and field-test writing platforms (Schwarz & de Groot, 2011). Further complicating the software space of digital writing in schools, each platform and device comes with differing terms of service, conditions of use, privacy provisions, and defaults. Feedback on dashboards, similarly, is not often negotiable and can skew perceptions or deceive the user through ambiguous display settings (Baym, 2013). Williamson (2014) argues that defaults and conditions of use have governing influence on what activities and forms of knowledge production are foregrounded. For these reasons, in addition to student privacy, critics also worry about the normative effects of quantitatively profiling learners in ways that could intensify didactic pedagogies in classrooms.

## Possibilities for Computerized Assessment of Writing

As an ideal medium for the representation of deep disciplinary knowledge, such as document analysis in history or argument in science, the computerized automation of writing assessment has been a growing interest in the past decade. In this section, we briefly introduce technological advancements in machine learning and natural language processing, which are facilitating computer-mediated assessments. We will then turn to considering ways of employing such technologies with an eye to shifting the traditional relationships between assessment and instruction from a didactic approach to a more reflexive framework.

### *Underlying Mechanisms of Computerized Assessment of Writing*

Natural language, in its ambiguities, context dependencies, and metaphorical overlays, is, for the most part, unreadable by computers. Natural language processing technologies offer two types of tools for writing assessment, often used together: machine learning through statistical corpus comparison and analytical text parsing (Cope, Kalantzis, McCarthey, Vojak, & Kline, 2011). Machine learning occurs through the identification and labeling of quantitative, or program-readable, patterns. These patterns are either provided in human-judged data sets or identified and clustered by computer programs and then made available for human judgment. In either case, the machine's "learning" relies on its interactions with humans—in its design and for interpretation of data. Then, and only then, can machines begin to predict results and "make" evaluations.

In the case of automated essay scoring (AES), such as TurnItIn's Revision Assistant, human readers rate hundreds of writing samples. These ratings, in combination with texts analyzed for structural and grammatical patterns, are used as training data sets for the computer program. The program is designed to compare new texts with patterns in the corpus, and grade new texts based on their statistical similarity with human-graded texts. As the corpus of human-graded texts grows, the tendency of the computer program to rate texts from the same prompts similarly to humans increases. Often, in tools like this, users are prompted to provide feedback to the program, such as if the feedback was helpful or if the issue was addressed. This feedback becomes further training data to improve the system's predictive capacity. Machine learning with natural language processing technologies has been shown to rate short-answer and essay-length texts reliably equivalent to human graders (Shermis, 2014; Warschauer & Grimes, 2008). A promise of such advances is the potential for instantaneous or "real-time" feedback (West, 2012). However, it is often the case that the automated feedback provided in such programs is general, and applicable to any text, such as the instruction to "increase cohesion" or "improve clarity."

In text parsing, used in WriteLab and other similar online tools, computers are programmed to search for language features, such as markers of textual cohesion, range and sophistication of vocabulary, and latent semantics based on word clustering and frequencies (Landauer, McNamara, Dennis, & Kintsch, 2007; McNamara, Graesser, McCarthy, & Cai, 2014). Vocabulary variety and text and sentence length have a significant impact on AES scores (Vojak, Kline, Cope, McCarthey, & Kalantzis, 2011). Text parsing is capable of giving specific feedback, including specific suggestions about simple and technical vocabulary (Cope & Kalantzis, 2013b). However, these discrete measures can also allow users to game the system by simply changing the length of sentences or increasing the variety of vocabulary. Emerging areas of development in this area include coh-metrics (McNamara & Graesser, 2012), conceptual topic modeling (Li & Girju, 2015), mapping argument structures (Ascaniis, 2012), and sentiment analysis (Shum et al., 2016; Wen, Yang, & Rose, 2014).

*Possibilities for Shifting Assessment Practices*

In our work with the digital writing environment, Scholar, we have applied natural language processing technologies, not for grading, but to provide formative feedback for learners and their instructors via the Checker and Analytics features of the platform. In this environment, writers and their teachers can see progress generalizations at different levels of granularity, and with hyperlinks and an interactive interface, can drill down to the semantically legible data points on which these generalizations are based. With such immediate interactive feedback from a variety of types and scales, assessment can be increasingly embedded in instruction, allowing long-held ambitions to offer richer formative assessment regarding writers' processes to be realized.

Machine-mediated feedback affords a collapse in the timeframe between instruction, practice, varied forms of feedback, reflection, and adjustments, resulting in tightened recursive learning sequences. Learners can gain access to a variety of actionable feedback from a variety of sources without waiting for individuated responses from a single instructor. As Behrens and DiCerbo (2013) argue, "As the activities, and contexts of our activities, become increasingly digital, the need for separate assessment activities should be brought increasingly into question" (p. 9). It is not only possible to imagine an end to separate, summative tests, but we can also see that a tightened imbrication of learning, instruction, and assessment is possible in digital environments wherein there is no learning activity without multiple forms of computer-mediated feedback.

Beyond mere changes in technology, there is potential in the deployment of these new sources of data to influence a shift in assessment practices from a "didactic" traditional instructional model to a more "reflexive" one (Cope & Kalantzis, 2015a). By this, we mean that there are ways of employing technologies to assess learning, while learners are engaged in cycles of active knowledge making with ideas, objects, and other learners—rather than assessing the replication of memorized, received "truths." However, as discussed throughout this chapter, new technologies themselves do not guarantee such a shift. Rather, depending on the aims of designers and users, these tools can be employed in ways that further decontextualize and dehumanize the learning process. However, as Cope and Kalantzis (2015b) assert, robust feedback plans, which include machine, instructor, and peer-generated prospective and constructive input throughout learning processes, assist in foregrounding feedback in the educational experience. As a result, feedback can be shifted from its typical retrospective and expert-judged role to one that is formative, multiperspectival, and instructional (Cope & Kalantzis, 2013a).

## Conclusion

The digital writer treads across an impressionable landscape. Structured and unstructured, quantified traces of composing actions and interactions are collected, tagged, fed back, and stored. Questions about the mechanisms for gathering the data, for who and what purposes, for how long, and how much are critical to consider, particularly in an era mediated by digital, networked capacities, and computer-mediated instruction and assessment. In this chapter, we have mapped a fraction of this landscape, considering trace data and mechanisms of its generation, approaches to studying trace data in educational spaces, and the potential impact of computerized writing evaluation on assessment frameworks.

We have found our experiences in interdisciplinary design research to be generative as teams of researchers, educators, and programmers articulate pedagogical assumptions and produce digital infrastructures that support reflexive and dialogic writing environments. The mechanisms that generate, gather, and display data traces can be designed in ways that counter didactic modes of instruction and assessment. However, to realize this potential, quantifications of writing in education need thoughtful consideration. We are encouraged by the increasingly robust and theoretically grounded methods called for in education data science. In turn, we encourage educators and educational researchers alike to consider the governing influences of digital device and software infrastructures, question program defaults and settings, and work to contextualize and humanize quantifications of writing, and their uses in educational settings.

## Note

1. Scholar was supported by a series of research grants—US Department of Education, Institute of Education Sciences: "The Assess-as-You-Go Writing Assistant" (R305A090394), "Assessing Complex Performance" (R305B110008), "u-Learn.net: An Anywhere/Anytime Formative Assessment and Learning Feedback Environment" (ED-IES-10-C-0018), "The Learning Element" (ED-IES-lO-C-0021), and "InfoWriter: A Student Feedback and Formative Assessment Environment" (ED-IES-13-C-0039). Bill and Melinda Gates Foundation: "Scholar Literacy Courseware."

## References

Aipperspach, R., Rattenbury, T., Woodruff, A., Anderson, K., Canny, J., & Aoki, P. (2006). *Ethno-mining: Integrating numbers and words from the ground up*. Technical Report No. UCB/EECS-2006-125, Electrical Engineering and Computer Sciences, University of California at Berkeley. Retrieved from www.eecs.berkeley.edu/Pubs/TechRpts/2006/EECS-2006-125.html.
Andrews, R., & Smith, A. (2011). *Developing writers: Teaching and learning in the digital age*. London, UK: Open University Press.
Ascaniis, S. (2012). Criteria for designing and evaluating argument diagramming tools from the point of view of argumentation theory. In N. Pinkwart & B. M. McLaren (Eds.), *Educational technologies for teaching argumentation skills*. Sharjah: Bentham Science Publishers.
Baker, R., D'Mello, S. K., Rodrigo, M., & Graesser, A. (2010). Better to be frustrated than bored: The incidence, persistence, and impact of learners' cognitive-affective states during interactions with three different computer-based learning environments. *International Journal of Human-Computer Studies, 68*, 223–241.
Baker, R., & Siemens, G. (2014). Educational data mining and learning analytics. In K. Sawyer (Ed.), *Cambridge handbook of the learning sciences*. New York, NY: Cambridge University Press.
Baym, N. (2013). Data not seen: The uses and shortcomings of social media metrics. *First Monday, 18*(10). doi:10.5210/fm.v18i10.4873
Behrens, J. T., & DiCerbo, K. E. (2013). Technological implications for assessment ecosystems. In E. W. Gordon (Ed.), *The Gordon Commission on the future of assessment in education: Technical report* (pp. 101–122). Princeton, NJ: The Gordon Commission.
Bienkowski, M., Feng, M., & Means, B. (2012). *Enhancing teaching and learning through educational data mining and learning analytics: An issue brief*. Washington, DC: Office of Educational Technology, U.S. Department of Education.
Boluk, S., Flores, L., Garbe, J., & Salter, A. (2016). *The electronic literature collection, Volume 3*. Cambridge, MA: Electronic Literature Organization. Available at http://collection.eliterature.org/3/index.html
boyd, d., & Crawford, K. (2012). Critical questions for big data. *Information, Communication & Society, 15*(5), 662–679.
Camille, M. (1992). *Image on the edge: The margins of medieval art*. London, UK: Reaktion Books.
Castro, F., Vellido, A., Nebot, À., & Mugica, F. (2007). Applying data mining techniques to e-learning problems. In J. Kacprzyk (Ed.), *Studies in computational intelligence* (Vol. 62, pp. 183–221). Berlin: Springer-Verlag.

Cope, B., & Kalantzis, M. (2009). 'Multiliteracies': New literacies, new learning. *Pedagogies: An International Journal, 4,* 164–195.

Cope, B., & Kalantzis, M. (2013a). Multiliteracies: New literacies, new learning. In M. R. Hawkins (Ed.), *Framing languages and literacies: Socially situated views and perspectives* (pp. 105–135). New York, NY: Routledge.

Cope, B., & Kalantzis, M. (2013b). Towards a new learning: The 'scholar' social knowledge workspace, in theory and practice. *e-Learning and Digital Media, 10,* 334–358.

Cope, B., & Kalantzis, M. (2015a). Assessment and pedagogy in the era of machine-mediated learning. In T. Dragonas, K. J. Gergen, S. McNamee, & E. Tseliou (Eds.), *Education as social construction: Contributions to theory, research, and practice* (pp. 350–374). Chagrin Falls, OH: Worldshare Books.

Cope, B., & Kalantzis, M. (2015b). Sources of evidence-of-learning: Learning and assessment in the era of big data. *Open Review of Educational Research, 2,* 194–217.

Cope, B., & Kalantzis, M. (2015c). Interpreting evidence-of-learning: Educational research in the era of big data. *Open Review of Educational Research, 2,* 218–239.

Cope, B., & Kalantzis, M. (2016a). Big data comes to school: Implications for learning, assessment and research. *AERA Open, 2,* 1–19.

Cope, B., & Kalantzis, M. (2017). Conceptualizing e-learning. In B. Cope & M. Kalantzis (Eds.), *e-Learning ecologies: Principles for new learning and assessment* (pp. 1–45). New York, NY: Routledge.

Cope, B., Kalantzis, M., & Magee, L. (2011). *Towards a semantic web: Connecting knowledge in academic research.* Cambridge, UK: Woodhead.

Cope, B., Kalantzis, M., McCarthey, S., Vojak, C., & Kline, S. (2011). Technology-mediated writing assessments: Paradigms and principles. *Computers and Composition, 28*(2), 79–96.

Crawford, K. (2013). The hidden biases in big data. *Harvard Business Review.* https://hbr.org/2013/04/the-hidden-biases-in-big-data.

Dawson, S., & Siemens, G. (2014). Analytics to literacies: The development of a learning analytics framework for multiliteracies assessment. *International Review of Research in Open and Distributed Learning, 25*(4).

DiCerbo, K., & Behrens, J. (2014). *Impacts of the digital ocean on education.* London, UK: Pearson.

Dowell, N., & Graesser, A. (2014). Modelling learners' cognitive, affective, and social processes through language and discourse. *Journal of Learning Analytics, 1*(3), 183–186.

Fancsali, S., Ritter, S., Stamper, J., & Berman, S. (2014). Personalization, non-cognitive factors, and grain-size for measurement and analysis in intelligent tutoring systems. *Proceedings of the 2nd Annual Generalized Intelligent Framework for Tutoring (GIFT) Users Symposium* (pp. 124–135). Pittsburgh, PA: US Army Research Laboratory.

Farman, J. (2012). *Mobile interface theory: Embodied space and locative media.* New York, NY: Routledge.

Haas, C. (1996). *Writing technology: Studies on the materiality of literacy.* Mahweh, NJ: Lawrence Erlbaum Associates.

Hine, C. (2015). *Ethnography for the internet: Embedded, embodied and everyday.* New York, NY: Bloomsbury Publishing.

Ho, A. (2015). Before "data collection" comes "data creation." In C. Dede (Ed.), *Data-intensive research in education: Current work and next steps* (pp. 34–36). Washington, DC: Computing Research Association.

Huc-Hepher, S. (2015). Big Web data, small focus: An ethnosemiotic approach to culturally themed selective Web archiving. *Big Data & Society, 2*(2).

Jenkins, H., Clinton, K., Purushotma, R., Robinson, A., & Weigel, M. (2006). *Confronting the challenges of participatory culture: Media education for the 21st century.* Chicago, IL: MacArthur Foundation.

Kalantzis, M., & Cope, B. (2015). Regimes of literacy. In M. Hamilton, R. Hayden, K. Hibbert, & R. Stoke (Eds.), *Negotiating spaces for literacy learning: Multimodality and governmentality* (pp. 15–24). London, UK: Bloomsbury.

Kalantzis, M., Cope, B., Chan, E., & Dalley-Trim, L. (2016). *Literacies.* Cambridge, UK: Cambridge University Press.

Kalantzis, M., Cope, B., & Harvey, A. (2003). Assessing multiliteracies and the new basics. *Assessment in Education: Principles, Policy & Practice, 10*(1), 15–26.

Kitchin, R., & Dodge, M. (2011). *Code/space: Software and everyday life.* Cambridge, MA: MIT Press.

Kline, S., Letofsky, K., & Woodard, B. (2013). Democratizing classroom discourse: The challenge for online writing environments. *e-Learning and Digital Media, 10*(4), 379–395.

Knight, S., Shum, S., & Littleton, K. (2014). Epistemology, assessment, pedagogy: Where learning meets analytics in the middle space. *Journal of Learning Analytics, 1*(2), 23–47.

Landauer, T., McNamara, D., Dennis, S., & Kintsch, W. (2007). *Handbook of latent semantic analysis.* New York, NY: Routledge.

Lazer, D., Pentland, A., Adamic, L., Aral, S., Barabá'si, A., Brewer, D., Christakis, N., Contractor, N., Fowler, J., Gutmann, M., Jebara, T., King, G., Macy, M., Roy, D. & Van Alstyne, M. (2009). Computational social science. *Science, 323*(5915), 721–723.

Li, C., & Girju, R. (2015, June). *Detecting causally embedded structures using an evolutionary algorithm.* Paper presented at the 3rd Workshop on Events: Definition, Detection, Conference, and Representation, Denver, CO.

Lindgren, R., & Johnson-Glenberg, M. (2013). Emboldened by embodiment: Six precepts for research on embodied learning and mixed reality. *Educational Researcher, 42*(8), 445–452.

Long, P., & Siemens, G. (2011). Penetrating the fog: Analytics in learning and education. *EDUCAUSE Review, 46*(5), 30–40.

Lynch, C. (2014, July). *Augmented graph grammars for complex heterogeneous data.* Paper presented at the 7th International Conference on Educational Data Mining, London, UK.

Lynch, T. (2015). *The hidden role of software in educational research: Policy to practice.* New York, NY: Routledge.

Magnifico, A., McCarthey, S., & Kline, S. (2014). *Reconsidering peer feedback in argumentative essays.* Paper presented at the annual meeting of the American Educational Research Association, Philadelphia, PA.

Markham, A. (2017). Ethnography in the digital internet era: From fields to flows, descriptions to interventions. In N. Denzin & Y. Lincoln (Eds.), *Sage handbook of qualitative research* (pp. 650–668). Thousand Oaks, CA: SAGE Publications.

Marsh, J. (2014). Researching young children's literacy practices in online virtual worlds: Cyber-ethnography and multi-method approaches. In P. Albers, T. Holbrook, & A. S. Flint (Eds.), *New literacy research methods* (pp. 195–209). Abington, MA: Routledge.

McCarthey, S., Magnifico, A., Woodard, R., & Kline, S. (2014). Situating technology—Facilitated feedback and revision: The case of Tom. In K. Pytash & R. Ferdig (Eds.), *Exploring technology for writing and writing instruction* (pp. 152–170). Hershey, PA: Information Science Reference.

McLeod, M., Hart-Davidson, W., & Grabill, J. (2013). Theorizing and building online writing environments: User-centered design beyond the interface. In G. Pullman & B. Gu (Eds.), *Designing web-based applications for 21st century writing classrooms.* New York, NY: Baywood.

McNamara, D., & Graesser, A. (2012). Coh-Metrix: An automated tool for theoretical and applied natural language processing. In P. M. McCarthy & C. Boonthum-Denecke (Eds.), *Applied natural language processing: Identification, investigation and resolution* (pp. 188–205). Hershey, PA: IGI Global.

McNamara, D., Graesser, A., McCarthy, P., & Cai, Z. (2014). *Automated evaluation of text and discourse with Coh-Metrix.* New York, NY: Cambridge University Press.

McNely, B., Gestwicki, P., Hill, J., Parli-Horne, P., & Johnson, E. (2012). *Learning analytics for collaborative writing: A prototype and case study.* Paper presented at the 2nd International Conference on Learning Analytics and Knowledge, Vancouver, BC.

Mislevy, R., Behrens, J., Dicerbo, K., & Levy, R. (2012). Design and discovery in educational assessment: Evidence-centered design, psychometrics, and educational data mining. *Journal of Educational Data Mining, 4,* 11–48.

New London Group. (1996). A pedagogy of multiliteracies: Designing social futures. *Harvard Educational Review, 66,* 60–92.

Olmanson, J., Kennett, K., Magnifico, A., McCarthey, S., Searsmith, D., Cope, B., & Kalantzis, M. (2016). Visualizing revision: Leveraging student-generated between-draft diagramming data in support of academic writing development. *Technology, Knowledge, & Learning, 21*(1), 99–123.

Pea, R., & Jacks, D. (2014). *The learning analytics workgroup: A report on building the field of learning analytics for personalized learning at scale.* Stanford, CA: Stanford University.

Popova, M., Accurat, & MacNaughton, W. (2013). *Famous writers' sleep habits vs. literary productivity, visualized.* Retrieved from www.brainpickings.org/2013/12/16/writers-wakeup-times-literary-productivity-visualization/.

Rekers, J., & Schürr, A. (1997). Defining and parsing visual languages with layered graph grammars. *Journal of Visual Languages & Computing, 8*(1), 27–55.

Roscoe, R., & McNamara, D. (2013). Writing Pal: Feasibility of an intelligent writing strategy tutor in the high school classroom. *Journal of Educational Psychology, 105*(4), 1010–1025.

Ruckenstein, M., & Pantzar, M. (2015). Beyond the quantified self: Thematic exploration of a dataistic paradigm. *New Media & Society,* 1–18.

Saul, R. (2014). Adolescence and the narrative complexities of online life: On the making and unmaking of YouTube's anonygirl1. *Digital Culture & Education, 6*(2), 66–81.

Schwarz, B., & de Groot, R. (2011). Breakdowns between teachers, educators and designers in elaborating new technologies as precursors of change in education to dialogic thinking. In S. Ludvigsen, A. Lund, I. Rasmussen, & R. Säljö (Eds.), *Learning across sites: New tools, infrastructures and practices* (pp. 261–277). New York, NY: Routledge.

Shermis, M. (2014). State-of-the-art automated essay scoring: Competition, results, and future directions from a United States demonstration. *Assessing Writing, 20,* 53–76.

Shum, S., Sándor, Á., Goldsmith, R., Wang, X., Bass, R., & McWilliams, M. (2016, April). *Reflecting on reflective writing analytics: Assessment challenges and iterative evaluation of a prototype tool.* Paper presented at the Sixth International Learning Analytics and Knowledge Conference, Edinburgh, UK.

Smith, A., & Hull, G. (2013). Critical literacies and social media: Fostering ethical engagement with global youth. In J. Ávila & J. Zacher Pandya (Eds.), *Critical digital literacies as social praxis: Intersections and challenges* (pp. 63–84). New York, NY: Peter Lang.

Smith, A., McCarthey, S., & Magnifico, A. (2017). Recursive feedback: Evaluative dimensions of e-learning. In B. Cope & M. Kalantzis (Eds.), *e-Learning ecologies: Principles for new learning and assessment* (pp. 118–142). New York, NY: Routledge.

Stephansen, H., & Couldry, N. (2014). Understanding micro-processes of community building and mutual learning on Twitter: A 'small data' approach. *Information, Communication & Society, 17*(10), 1212–1227.

Stornaiuolo, A., Hull, G., & Sahni, U. (2011). Cosmopolitan imaginings of self and other: Youth and social networking in a global world. In J. Fisherkeller (Ed.), *International perspectives on youth media: Cultures of production and education* (pp. 263–280). New York, NY: Peter Lang Publishers.

Stornaiuolo, A., Smith, A., & Phillips, N. (2017). Developing a transliteracies framework for a connected world. *Journal of Literacy Research, 49*(1), 61–84.

Taylor, K. H., & Hall, R. (2013). Counter-mapping the neighborhood on bicycles: Mobilizing youth to reimagine the city. *Tech Know Learn, 18*(1–2), 65–93.

VanLehn, K. (2006). The behavior of tutoring systems. *International Journal of Artificial Intelligence in Education, 16*(3), 227–265.

Vojak, C., Kline, S., Cope, B., McCarthey, S., & Kalantzis, M. (2011). New spaces and old places: An analysis of writing assessment software. *Computers and Composition, 28*(2), 97–111.

Wang, T. (2013). Big data needs thick data. *Ethnography Matters*. Retrieved July 25, 2016, from http://ethnographymatters.net/blog/2013/05/13/big-data-needs-thick-data/.

Wargo, J. (2015). "Every selfie tells a story…" LGBTQ youth lifestreams and new media narratives as connective identity texts. *New Media and Society*, 1–19.

Warschauer, M., & Grimes, D. (2008). Automated writing assessment in the classroom. *Pedagogies: An International Journal, 3*(1), 22–36.

Wen, M., Yang, D., & Rose, C. (2014, July). *Sentiment analysis in MOOC discussion forums: What does it tell us?* Paper presented at the 7th International Conference on Educational Data Mining (EDM 2014), London, UK.

West, D. (2012). *Big data for education: Data mining, data analytics, and web dashboards*. Washington, DC: Brookings Institution.

Williamson, B. (2014). Governing software: Networks, databases and algorithmic power in the digital governance of public education. *Learning, Media and Technology, 40*(1), 83–105.

Winne, P. (2014). Issues in researching self-regulated learning as patterns of events. *Metacognition and Learning, 9*(2), 229–237.

Winne, P., & Baker, R. (2013). The potentials of educational data mining for researching metacognition, motivation and self-regulated learning. *Journal of Educational Data Mining, 5*(1), 1–8.

Wise, A., Zhao, Y., & Hausknecht, S. (2013, April). *Learning analytics for online discussions: A pedagogical model for intervention with embedded and extracted analytics*. Paper presented at the Third Conference on Learning Analytics and Knowledge (LAK 2013), Leuven, Belgium.

Xu, Y., Chang, K., Yuan, Y., & Mostow, J. (2014, July). *Using EEG in knowledge tracing*. Paper presented at 7th International Conference on Educational Data Mining, London, UK.

# V
# Digital Ethics

Amy Stornaiuolo

This section opens up debate about a range of ethical issues associated with the risks, rights, possibilities, and social consequences of people's digital literacy practices. The chapters in this section take up critical, postcolonial, and sociocultural lenses to complicate prevailing discourses about the risks and possibilities of digital authorship, and in so doing highlight the ideological underpinnings of all technologies and digital literacy practices. In a "post-truth" era of fabricated news and eroding trust, the authors in this section each make a compelling case for centering ethics, which Luke and colleagues define as "the moral codes and norms of everyday life," in teaching and learning in digital cultures.

In Chapter 20, "Digital Ethics, Political Economy and the Curriculum: This Changes Everything," Allan Luke, Julian Sefton-Green, Phil Graham, Douglas Kellner, and James Ladwig critically interrogate how to teach current and future generations about rights and responsibilities, truth and lies, and freedom and privacy. Their chapter sets out a bold agenda, calling for educators to reorient teaching and learning around ethics in digital culture. In arguing for a critical approach to literacy curriculum and practice organized around social justice, the authors offer three foundational claims about the ideological, political, and economic dimensions of all digital literacy practices and the need for teaching and learning to offer models for digital citizenship that take those dimensions into central account.

In Chapter 21, "Digital Youth and Educational Justice," Lalitha Vasudevan, Kristine Rodriguez Kerr, and Cristina Salazar Gallardo propose a model of educational justice in which young people have control over the acts of crafting digital texts and making their narratives and images visible and accessible. The authors present two case studies that highlight the centrality of multimodal composing to enacting justice in young people's educational experiences. In both cases, they foreground young people's use of digital composing technologies in service of everyday forms of educational justice, through practices of pedagogical care, cultivating community, and fostering belonging. While these components of justice are largely missing in the schooling of court-involved or undocumented youth who are relegated to the institutional margins, the authors make the case for educators to take up a multimodal orientation toward digital youth as an important means of cultivating educational justice.

Kristin Arola, in Chapter 22, "Composing as Culturing: An American Indian Approach to Digital Ethics," proposes an ethical approach to authorship in a digital age that draws on American Indian epistemologies, particularly the making practices of the Anishinaabe peoples of the Upper Great Lakes. Such an ethic of composing makes central the process of culturing, which foregrounds the understanding that everything is related and that ethical composing practices honor those relations that have come before and will come after. The author negotiates the impasse between an open access remix culture on the one hand and copyright on the other, providing recommendations to approach digital production with care while acknowledging the ecologies of meaning within which we craft, compose, and circulate.

In Chapter 23, "Aesthetics and Text in the Digital Age," Theo van Leeuwen argues that aesthetic qualities are no longer found primarily in art and poetry, but also permeate formerly unadorned functional texts, such as invoices, company reports, and bureaucratic documents. After discussing the integration of functionality and aesthetics in such texts, and the role of contemporary writing software in this integration, the chapter presents the key elements of aesthetic literacy (composition, color, graphic form, parallelism, and provenance), listing the key parameters involved in each and outlining their aesthetic potential. The chapter ends by asserting the need to develop pedagogies for including aesthetics in the teaching of writing.

The chapters in this section all push forward contemporary thinking about how to shape ethical composing practices in a globally connected yet increasingly fractured—and fractious—world. The authors do not propose easy or uncomplicated directions for the field, yet their critical perspectives on how to make central the ethical dimensions of contemporary composing offer concrete and significant steps for educators and researchers. This section represents a fitting and compelling ending to this volume, as it draws together the various ethical threads appearing throughout the other chapters to suggest a clear path forward in centering digital ethics in literacy research.

# 20
# Digital Ethics, Political Economy, and the Curriculum
*This Changes Everything*

Allan Luke, Julian Sefton-Green, Phil Graham,
Douglas Kellner, and James Ladwig

The ethics of human communications are a core issue in Western philosophy. From Plato to Dewey, from Du Bois to Freire, and from Habermas to Benhabib, the powers and abuses of speech and writing have been considered focal in debates around the nature of truth and reality, civility and justice. The institution of modern European/AngloAmerican schooling has evolved for five centuries as a regulative technology in large measure dedicated to the teaching and learning of speech and writing, image and print. The history of language and literacy education offers a further important lesson that the teaching and learning of communication by definition entails ethical and ideological constraints and conventions, however explicit or implicit these may be to learners.

This chapter makes the case for a refocusing of teaching and learning across the curriculum on foundational questions about ethics in digital culture. We argue that to rethink current policy and curriculum strategies, *the educational challenge raised by digital culture for literacy is not one of skill or technological competence, but one of participation and ethics.*

Schools and education systems are caught in the headlights of the digital era. For over a quarter century, the field has lived through successive claims of paradigmatic and technological breakthroughs. From 1980s hypercards and CD Roms, to successive waves of packaged curricula for home and school on floppy disks, to digital whiteboards, pens, and other "tools," to tablet-based curriculum and online testing, and to wholly online face-to-face teaching, each successive technological innovation has been heralded as a revolution in teaching and learning, and then either superseded by the "next" wave of technology or simply forgotten (Buckingham, 2007; Nixon, 1998).[1]

The results are that schools and school districts have storage rooms packed with out-of-date technologies, teachers are perpetually grumpy at the latest in-service program for technologizing their work (and, increasingly, for mechanizing the regulatory compliance, surveillance, and accounting procedures that are the hallmarks of teaching as work in neoliberal schooling), and systems bureaucrats (and many researchers) continuously suffer from policy amnesia as they reinvent a perpetual tradition of the new (Selwyn, 2010). In schools and classrooms, researchers report local instances of innovation, of teacher and student digital creativity, and of the use of digital resources for community engagement and activism (e.g., Sanford, Rogers, & Kendrick, 2014), sitting alongside of compliance-level "adoption," next to digital versions of retrograde elements of face-to-face and print pedagogy (Cuban, 2001). The situation is further clouded by overlapping levels of commercialization and commodification: with major publishing companies in transition to the provision of digital classroom resources (e.g., Pearson), the major testing consortia moving quickly to provide online tests, digital portfolios and assessment tools, IT and infotainment companies cross-marketing educational commodities with toys, cinema, and TV programs, and a largely unregulated market of in-service consultants, technical advisors and firms.

At the same time, in response to increasing public moral panic about digital youth, students' digital practices increasingly are governed by ad hoc, idiosyncratic blends of prohibitions around pornography and bullying, privacy, safety, risk, and their future "digital footprint" (Selwyn, 2010). The results of the three-decade rise of educational technology are at best mixed, with systems' investments and aspirations failing to deliver improved learning, achievement, and equity (Warschauer & Matuchniak, 2010).

On the ground, the everyday issues faced by digital youth are *prima facie* ethical matters. How do today's young people deal with right and wrong, truth and falsehood, representation and misrepresentation in their everyday lives online? How do they anticipate and live with the real consequences of their online interactions with others? How do they navigate the complexities of their public exchanges and their private lives, and how do they engage with parental and institutional surveillance? Finally, how can they engage and participate as citizens, consumers, and workers in the public and political, cultural, and economic spheres of the Internet? These questions are examined in current empirical studies of young peoples' virtual and real everyday lives in educational institutions and homes (e.g., Livingstone & Sefton-Green, 2016; Quan-Haase, 2016).

We begin the chapter by outlining the limits of education with new technologies *sans* a foundational approach to ethics. We then turn to review, critique, and reframe debates over communicative ethics as they apply to the field of education. Our focus is on building a critical approach to digital media and culture organized around principles of social justice.

**The Problem**

There are now almost continuous public calls for heightened child protection and surveillance in response to widespread moral panic around digital childhood (e.g., Havey & Puccio, 2016). To refer to this as a moral panic is not to understate the very real difficulties that digital technology raises for families, schools, and teachers. It is, however, to acknowledge popular discourses and widespread generational frustration about the effects of digital technology on everyday life. These range from concerns about the displacement of embodied activity, physical play, and face-to-face verbal exchange by "compulsive" online messaging and gaming, to online harassment, bullying, real and symbolic violence, from sexual and commercial exploitation of young people and children, to exposure to violence, pornography, ideological indoctrination, and outright criminal behavior.[2]

In their power to generate fascinating new expressive forms and relationships, to reshape the arts and sciences notwithstanding, digital media are amplifiers of the best and the worst, the sublime and the mundane, the significant and the most trivial elements of behavior, knowledge, and interaction. How could it be any other way? It is all here online: statements, images, sounds, and acts of hatred and love, war and peace, bullying and courtship, truth and lies, violence and care, oppression and liberation—in ever-proliferating redundancy, cut through with noise and clutter.

How we can enlist and harness these media to learn to live together in diversity, mutual respect, and difference, addressing complex social, economic, and environmental problems, while building convivial and welcoming, just and life-sustaining communities and societies is the key educational problem facing this generation of young people and their teachers. This is an ethical vision and an ethical challenge.

Many school systems are in shock and denial over this turn of events, especially given the historic use of print textbooks as a practical and effective means for defining and controlling what might count as official knowledge for children and youth (Luke, DeCastell, & Luke, 1983). This disciplinary and epistemic function and all of its well-honed institutional machinery are now directly under threat by a digital access and archive that seems built to circumvent delimitation and undermine control—often with contradictory effects.

Consequently, schools—*in loco parentis*—have responded with a patchwork of rules governing what kids can and cannot do in their online exchanges and communications. These emerge in a reactionary and agglomerative way: often in response to incidents of abusive, illegal, or symbolically violent online acts, or to events whose origins are attributed to online actions—from suicides, to gun violence, to pedophilia. Schools work from a mix of regional and district-level policies that include constraints on hardware access, proprietary lock-out and surveillance systems, privacy and intellectual property regulations, school-level codes and class rules on everything from texting and screen time to plagiarism and copying from Internet sources. These sit alongside of home-based restrictions (or freedoms) on time, access, and use in those families that can afford mobile and online devices. This is complicated by increasing law enforcement efforts to prevent online recruitment, exploitation, and indoctrination of youth by terrorist groups, financial scammers, and criminal organizations. In this thicket of overlapping systems of surveillance, unmediated exchange by youth and children would appear to be the exception rather than the rule (boyd, 2015).

Taken together, the digital strategies of large public education systems in North America, the Asia Pacific and Europe (including the UK) appear to be at best post hoc and piecemeal—motivated by genuine concern and real problems, but typically lacking stated ethical foundations and working within prevailing neoliberal policy frameworks. In a policy context where education is defined as the competitive national production of human capital with technical expertise in STEM,[3] the kinds of social-ethical challenges we have identified here are not primary foci of educational policy or curriculum practice. This underlines what has become a significant (meta) ethical dilemma in itself that the policy push for teaching through and about educational technology presents itself as ethically and politically neutral.

Ethics refers to the codes, norms, and procedures that govern everyday life and interaction, civility, and exchange in institutions, societies, and cultures (Dewey, 2008). Our position is that *digital ethics*—the normative principles for action and interaction in digital environments—cannot be addressed through a listing of prohibitions for what kids can and cannot do online. For those young people who have everyday access to the Internet,[4] knowledge and learning, civic participation, work, leisure, and everyday social interaction with their peers and others occur online. Digital actions—whether clicking or tweeting, posting, sharing, or liking—are by definition, social actions (Burke, 1966; Isin and Ruppert 2015): as such, they are used for goal-seeking purposes with real pragmatic effects and consequences (Wilden, 1972).

Digital actions—even those of children and youth, students, and "average" citizens—*may* carry higher stakes and have amplified consequences that exceed the scope of their actions through speech, writing, and other modalities in everyday life. In real human experience and real geo/spatial and temporal contexts, digital actions can be used to launch drone strikes, they can pass on complex technical information for making weapons, they can draw the attention and approbation of millions to shame and humiliate. They can be used for play, to build community, to solve complex problems, to mobilize constructive and destructive social action. As is axiomatic in critical discourse theory, while much of what we know and experience in the world is represented through discourse—some discourse actions don't matter much, and others may kill or wound—and, indeed, some may enlighten and heal (Luke, 2004). Digital action is, indeed, discourse—semiotic and social action—through a "cognitive amplifier" (Bruner & Olson, 1977) that may have expansive and reflexive, durable and exponential effects across space and time.

In consequence, our case is that a digital ethics—an ethics of how to live just and sustainable lives in technologically saturated societies—is *the* core curriculum issue for schooling. This is a generational and pedagogic responsibility as we stand at a juncture where residual and emergent cultures meet, where Indigenous and non-Indigenous, historically colonized and colonizing, settler and migrant communities attempt to reconcile and negotiate new settlements, where traditional, modernist, and postmodern forms of life and technologies sit alongside each other, uneasily, often with increasing inequity and violence.[5] Our view is that this is a moment that requires more from researchers, scholars, and educators than descriptions of instances of local assemblage or voice. Following on from Naomi Klein's (2015) analysis of the effects of capitalism, technology, and modernity on the planetary ecosystem, our view is that this historical convergence of forces and events has the potential to "change everything."

Our response is to outline a definition of human ethics in relation to communications media. We describe foundational principles for a broader programmatic approach to digital ethics. In so doing, we make the case for *a critical literacy based on principles of social justice in relation to all forms of human communication*. Our case is that classroom practice—the everyday curriculum enacted through speaking and listening, print and digital reading, and writing, signing, and imaging—can be refocused to include rigorous debate, study, and analysis of digital communications in terms of: their real consequences as human actions; their ideological, scientific, and cultural codes, truth claims and meanings; and their everyday possibilities for community-based cultural and social action, for human conviviality and sustainable forms of life.

Part of the answer, from our perspective, lies in an ongoing engagement with Indigenous ethics of decolonization and reconciliation, care, and healing (Martin, 2008; Smith, 1999)—which are taken up at length in a major chapter in this volume—and which are imaginatively applied to the question of digital rights by Wittkower (2016). But also part of the answer, as argued by feminist philosophers Seyla Benhabib (2002) and Nancy Fraser (1996), is to pragmatically revisit and mobilize core democratic tenets of liberal thought and critical social theory, while acknowledging their Eurocentric and masculinist histories—as part of a larger agenda for social justice in pluralistic, democratic societies.

Our view is that a central aim of schooling now should be the interrogation of the forms and contents, practices, and consequences of digital communications, and this is now the ethical purpose of contemporary literacy education. The curriculum should engage with current issues regarding everyday actions and their consequences, corporate and state surveillance, privacy and transparency, political and economic control and ownership.

**Reframing Communicative Ethics**

To speak about ethics is to speak about the moral codes and norms of everyday life. Although the nominal foundations of Western ethics are attributed to Plato and Aristotle, *all* cultures—Indigenous, African, and Asian, historical and contemporary, and Eurocentric—depend upon normative rules, stated and unstated, regarding the rightness and appropriateness of actions and interactions (i.e., Dell Hymes' notion of "communicative competence" (cf. Cazden, 2018)). The conduct of daily practices, the coherence and cohesion of everyday communications, and the functional survival of communities depend upon shared (and, indeed, contested and dynamic) codes of conduct, epistemic standpoints, and world views. Without normative "cultural scripts" (Cole, 1996), everyday problem solving and learning are impossible. Ethical norms are presupposed in every instance of communication and exchange in social fields. Communicative ethics, then, are a kind of master cultural script that sets the interactional grounds and mediational means for building, critiquing, and using other scripts. Given the contentious political and cultural issues that schools and communities, teachers and children now face—even where we cannot presume ideological agreement or moral consensus, especially where we are not idealized, rational (White, male, heterosexual, urbane) speakers with equitable access to cultural codes, discourses, and knowledge (Benhabib, 1992): How could this *not* be the center of any literacy curriculum?

New communications technologies have the effect of destabilizing and reframing social and economic relations, and living cultures and planetary ecosystems. Such changes renew ethical dilemmas. At the macroeconomic and geopolitical levels, the reorganization and compression of space and time enabled by communications (and transportation) technologies have enabled new forms of monopoly, of profit, debt, and, indeed, of cultural and economic empire (Innis, 1949). The transitions from oral to literate culture, from manuscript to print culture, and, currently, from print and oral to digital exchange have destabilized and altered relations of power, authority, and control. This occurs on several levels: In terms of the actual everyday mediation of what will count as knowledge, action, utterance, and, indeed, in terms of whose collective cultural, economic, and political interests actually are served through these interactions. With the coming of the book (and newspaper, broadsheet, treatise, contract and legal brief, domestic manual, and romantic novel) and the emergence of nationalism and "print capitalism" (Anderson, 1983), the question of who owns, regulates, and controls, and indeed profits and dominates from control and use of the dominant modes of information comes center stage, shifting from religious authorities to the state and, ultimately, to the industrial and postindustrial, national and transnational corporation. Some regimes burn books, and others write, print, and mandate them; some governments censor the Internet, and all use it and monitor it; disputes over hate speech, libel, and what can and cannot be said in the media-based civic sphere are now daily news—alongside of revelations of the profit structures, labor practices, environmental consequences, and taxation schemes of profitable and dominant media and technology corporations. Note that this political economy of communications typically is *not* studied in schools—even as this corporate order competes for the *edubusiness* and how what counts as knowledge, is framed within these same schools (Picciano & Spring, 2012).

A first task, then, facing institutions is to reframe dialogue over ethics in relation to both changed human interaction, contexts for thought and action, and changed societal, cultural, and environmental ecologies. As is painfully clear in the current geopolitical and national debates over borders, terrorism, security, trade, and globalization—establishing criterial grounds for adjudicating "right" and "wrong," true and untrue, scientific and unscientific, civil and uncivil, humane and inhumane, private and public knowledge, and behavior is increasingly difficult for citizens, workers, consumers, voters, and audiences—let alone for young adults and children. We live in an era of post-truth, truthiness, factoids, and simulacrum where freedom of speech and expression is construed by many as meaning that all spoken or expressed statements or images are equally "true" or "right" or that statements, claims, and expressive actions have coequal effects, consequences (Kellner, 2012).

Almost all elements of conventional electoral politics and public discourse in democratic states have been put up for grabs as is evident from the recent UK Brexit referendum and the 2016 US Presidential election. Even the longstanding conduct and procedures for running autocratic and fascist states have had to accommodate and adapt to the capacity of social media. This includes the shift from television/broadcast and print-based campaigns to the use of social media for instant commentary and mobilization of constituencies. New social movements and coalitions across political and cultural spectra, and across social strata and regional location have been enabled through social media, including what was termed the "Arab Spring" of Middle East upheavals to the current Black Lives Matter movement (Jenkins, Shresthova, & Gamber-Thompson, 2016).

As the twentieth-century newspaper business and broadcast media struggle to survive, the procedural conventions of the fourth estate have been supplanted by online commentary reliant upon pastiche, forwarded tweets and images, tautological hotlinks, and Internet cross-reference for validation. News cycles are continuous, information proliferation, redundancy and appropriating unceasing, the accumulation and analysis of metadata by the state and the corporation omnipresent

(Davies, 2009). Further, the making "public" of what were considered governments', political parties', and individuals' proprietary face-to-face and online communications on putative grounds of transparency has confused matters even further. Literally nothing goes unreported, and verification, validation, and analytic refutation of claims are, at best, difficult without recourse to other online representation. Signs have been cut loose from the signified, from originary context and place, and the placement, attribution, and location of signs, signifiers, and signified is increasingly difficult. While the longstanding principles and strategies of political propaganda remain intact (Graham, 2017)—the cognate means for countering deliberate misinformation and untruth have become more difficult to disentangle in a fully mediatized world (Krotz, 2007).

There are, of course, longstanding criteria, standards, and conventions for the conduct of face-to-face verbal and embodied interactions, from how we read and interpret deictics, gesture, bodily disposition, and eye contact. These are vernacular and place-based: They are language and culture-specific, and vary by spatial locality and community, time of day, and age/color/gender/sexuality/kin of interlocutors. Nonetheless, there have been attempts from Plato to, notably, Austin (1962) and Habermas (1976) to establish forms of "universal pragmatics", that is, ethical procedures and criteria for judging both the truth (locutionary) of particular speakers and utterances, and the interactional consequences, intended and actual (illocutionary and perlocutionary) of utterances. These models have been forcefully criticized for their presupposition of an idealized (male, rational, White, Eurocentric) speaker with common and equitable access to discourse resources (Benhabib & Dallymar, 1990). Nonetheless, speech still matters—and we proceed each day to navigate through an array of speech acts and exchanges according to procedural norms, both *dejure* and *defacto*, stated and tacit, conscious and unconscious. Each vernacular community proceeds under assumptions about the maintenance of "face" in communications (Scollon & Scollon, 1981). Without shared assumptions about the intent of speakers and the consequences of speech acts in place, even the simplest verbal exchange between a parent and a child, or a classmate and teacher on the playground is problematic.

**Three Foundational Claims**

To begin to set a curriculum agenda for teaching and learning digital ethics, then, we outline three key foundational claims. These set the *curriculum contents* for digital ethics in the literacy field for teaching and learning.

Our first claim is that digital ethics must operate at two analytically distinct but practically interwoven levels: It must engage at once with now classical questions about ideology (Kellner, 1978) *and* with questions about social actions and relations. As we have argued, the core concerns of educators about student digital lives concern the ideational and semantic "stuff"—the ideologies, beliefs, and values that learners must navigate online. This raises key questions about the truth, veracity, verification, and belief, and, indeed, consequences of the information represented online. A recent article by a senior editor of *The Guardian* put it this way:

> For 500 years after Gutenberg, the dominant form of information was the printed page: knowledge was primarily delivered in a fixed format, one that encouraged readers to believe in stable and settled truths. Now, we are caught in a series of confusing battles between opposing forces: between truth and falsehood, fact and rumor, kindness and cruelty; between the few and the many, the connected and the alienated; between the open platform of the web as its architects envisioned it and the gated enclosures of Facebook and other social networks; between an informed public and a misguided mob. What is common to these struggles—and what makes their resolution an urgent matter—is that they all involve the diminishing status of truth.
> (Viner, 2016)

At the same time, truth claims and representations are themselves social actions—consequential assertions about what is. Hence, our simultaneous and equivalent ethical concern is with the interactional pragmatics of life online. In response to the aforementioned concerns of educators and the public, digital ethics must focus on the use of online social media as a primary site for everyday social relationships with peers and others. Hence, our first foundational claim:

1. *On ideology and social relations*: That digital ethics must address questions about ideological contents—the values, beliefs, ideas, images, narratives, and truths that we produce and access online—*and* questions about social relations that are lived and experienced online, specifically the interactional and material consequences of individual and collective actions.

This is a process already visible in critical literacy, as ideational contents (M.A.K. Halliday's (1978) "field") and the interactional relational protocols and consequences (Halliday's "tenor") may appear analytically distinct, but are always interwoven in practice. What we say, write, speak, signify, how we speak, write, gesture, sign, and to whom are ethical actions—no matter how conscious, unconscious, or self-conscious, explicit, tacit, or implicit the intentions and decisions of the human subject may be. In educational terms, then, digital ethics by definition, engages both the "classification" of knowledge *qua* ideational content (whether construed as disciplinary, thematic, artistic, or scientific) and the "framing" of knowledge via social relationships and actions (Bernstein, 1990).

Accordingly, our case is that schooling thus needs to introduce two interwoven strands of digital ethics:

- The teaching and learning of a performative ethics that enables the evaluation and anticipation of real and potential human and cultural, social and economic, bodily and environmental outcomes and consequences of digital actions and exchanges, their real and potential participants and communities;
- The teaching and learning of a critical literacy that enables the weighing and judging and critical analysis of truth claims *vis-à-vis* their forms, genres, themes, sources, interests, and silences.

Our second claim focuses on the political economy of communications (Graham & Luke, 2013), that is, the relationships between state regulation and control, corporate ownership of the modes of information, and their ideological and economic effects. Following the prototypical work of Stuart Hall (1974) on broadcast media, the field of cultural studies has focused variously on audience positioning and responses to media texts ("decoding"), on the actual economic ownership and control of dominant modes of information (political economy), and how these are manifest in ideological message systems ("encoding"). Of course, digital exchanges operate on radically different dimensions of scope and scale, speed and interactivity than the broadcast media studied by Hall and colleagues and have the revolutionary effect of altering the monologic and linear relationships of production/consumption, encoding/decoding established through broadcast radio, television, and cinema, leading to claims that social media enables new community, agency, and democratization (Jenkins et al., 2016).

For our present purposes, what remains powerful and relevant from Hall's groundbreaking work is the acknowledgment of the ideological interests at work in the production and reception of screen and image. Where it takes up the challenge of digital content, the tendency in schooling has been to focus principally on student and teacher responses and uses of media texts (through models of viewer and reader response), on the semantic content (through models of comprehension, literary, and, to an extent, political critique)—and, far less explicitly if ever, on *the relationships between ideological content, relationships of institutional control and power, and the corporate ownership of the modes of information.*

Consider this analogy. This would be very much if we were to teach—recalling Innis' prototypical analysis of the "bias of communications" (1951) in pre-industrial mercantilism and industrial capitalism—how to read newspapers or how to use the railroad, without raising questions about who owns the press and transportation infrastructure, whose interests these structures of ownership and control serve, who benefits, and who is exploited by these configurations of political economy.[6] As Innis' (1949) discussion of the relationships between "empire and communications" argues, all emergent communications media and transportation systems effectively reshaped human/machine *and* political economic *and* geographic ecosystemic relations as well.

The basis of economic rule (and plutocracy) has shifted from those of colonial trade documented by Innis (e.g., the Dutch East India Company, Hudson's Bay Company) to the owners of elements of the dominant transportation infrastructure (e.g., the railways, steel, oil, and auto industries), to the emergence of media empires (e.g., telephone, wireless, newspapers, television networks)—to the current situation, where the world's economy is dominated by digital hardware/software/information corporations (e.g., Apple, Facebook, Google/Alphabet, Oracle, Amazon, and Samsung), and producers of military and advanced technological hardware (e.g., Boeing, Airbus, arms manufacturers).

Hence, our second foundational claim:

2. *On the political economy of communications*: That in digital culture the political and economic are always personal, with every personal digital action an interlinked part of complex and often invisible economic exchanges that by definition, support particular corporate and class interests and by definition have material and ecosystemic consequences.

The educational lesson here is simple that the media that we use are not "neutral" or benign but are owned, shaped, enabled, and controlled, capitalized upon and managed in their own corporate interests (Pasquale, 2015). These interests, social scientists, ecological scientists, and community activists are increasingly realizing, have reshaped the transnational and domestic divisions of wealth, labor, and power, and have broad, heretofore unexamined, effects on the use and sustainability of finite planetary resources and ecosystems (cf. Klein, 2015). Thus, the literacy curriculum should entail both the study of the sources of information and their apparent distortions and ideological "biases"—but that such study can be extended to understanding the relationships between knowledge and global, planetary interests, including the corporate ownership, capitalization, and profit from dominant modes of information (including its relationship to carbon-based economy and resource utilization e.g., Bowers, 2014).

Our third claim is core to the establishment of any set of ethics. As argued, for many schools, digital policy and practice tends to be both prohibitive in reaction to "risks" posed by digital technologies and simultaneously silent about the reconstructive institutional uses of digital technology. Ethics is a *normative* field—predicated upon a vision of what should be, of how human beings can and should live together. The central message of Aristotle's *Nicomachean Ethics* (1999) is that everyday judgments about right and wrong are grounded on visions of what might count as the "good life." Ethical judgments are the prerequisite philosophic and practical grounds for civility and justice. Habermas (1996) refers to this as a "counterfactual ideal" that is presupposed in each speech exchange. Our third foundational claim is:

3. *On a normative model of digital culture*: That ethics cannot exist as a set of norms or procedures for everyday life in digital cultures without a shared normative vision of the good life.

In terms of digital ethics, this means that any set of ethical injunctions taught to youth and children by definitions presupposes a vision of "what should be": a lifeworld where digital communications are used for ethical purposes for "the good." Further, this version of "the good," following Benhabib (2002), must acknowledge the moral imperatives and challenges raised by diverse communities in pluralistic democratic societies, whether online or face-to-face. Our view, then, is that any school-based approach to digital ethics must move beyond silences, prohibitions, and negative injunctions (which, in-and-of themselves, rarely have salience with youth) to the reconstructive project of modeling and enacting digital citizenship, convivial social relations, and action for social justice in education, economy, and culture.

**What Is to Be Done?**

We have been here before. Dewey (1907/2012) surveyed the situation wrought by industrial technologies and new communications media, economic globalization, large-scale migration, and geopolitical conflict:

> The social change… that overshadows and controls all others is the industrial one—the application of science resulting in the great inventions that have utilized the forces of nature on a vast and inexpensive scale: the growth of a world-wide market as the object of production, of vast manufacturing centers to supply this market, of cheap and rapid means of communication. … One can hardly believe there has been a revolution in all history so rapid, so extensive, so complete. Through it the face of the earth is making over, even as to its physical forms; political boundaries are wiped out and moved about…; population is hurriedly gathered into cities from the ends of the earth; habits of living are altered with startling abruptness and thoroughness; the search for the truths of nature is infinitely stimulated…, and their application to life made not only practicable but commercially necessary…That this revolution should not affect education in some way is… inconceivable.
>
> (pp. 6–7)

In response to fundamental and profound changes in society, economy, and culture, education systems in the "hypercapitalist" (Graham, 2005) economies of North America, Europe, and the Asia-Pacific have attempted responses. Over the past three decades, they first viewed educational technology as a logical extension of school science and mathematics education, that is, as a matter of scientific technology and technique. This evolved into the current emphasis on finding a place for the naming of the digital in the formal curriculum, with the enumeration of digital skills and behaviors, competences and capacities—as a preparation for work, consumption, and citizenship in technocratic society. More recently, it has begun moving toward a begrudging embrace of gaming cultures and creative industries more generally, recognizing that the new pathways to competitiveness in the current multinational corporate economy may lie through exploitation of media and the popular cultures that previously were deemed counter-educational. These are, in part, attempts to "curricularise" the new, to domesticate it into the institution that, we noted, developed to ensure the intergenerational transmission of orality and literacy. These are, furthermore, predictable strategies for incorporation and appropriation of digital culture into a now teetering neoliberal project of social class-stratified, free-market schooling designed to serve (digital) transnational corporate capital.

There remains a persistent refusal by educational institutions to take on board larger ethical challenges. Finding a strategy that can cut through this refusal has not been proven easy. Whilst current versions of media literacy or media education are, fifty years after the era of the mass media, just about finding disciplinary respectability, as evidenced by the growth of various handbooks, courses, and accreditation,[7] there are very few examples of national or regional school systems making digital ethics central to their vision of literacy education.

The three foundational claims we have placed on the table here are neither startlingly original nor that different from earlier notions of critical self-consciousness that have been proposed by Dewey or Freire. One productive first step is to revisit and reinvent the longstanding work in critical literacies and media literacy (e.g., Buckingham & Sefton-Green, 1994; Share, 2009). In other words, the new kinds of social actions, political concerns, participatory dynamics made possible by the Internet have not erased but rather reframed classical debates around the relationship of truth to untruth, right, and wrong and what it means to be a citizen in democratic societies.

Here, we have offered a very different view of how and why digital cultures, capacities, and technologies might "fit" in schooling and in the literacy—to be at the heart of an engaged and relevant curriculum. What better way to educate youth about the powers and problems of digital communications than to make these same forces and problems (and indeed their digital representations) the object of study *across* the curriculum. We therefore return to the proposition that we began with: *the educational challenge raised by digital technology is not one of skill and technique or technology, but of participation and ethics.*

The territory is already being explored by teachers and students in the spaces left by what has become an increasingly narrow, test-oriented, and instrumental curriculum especially in community-based projects. Many of these are contemporary versions of Deweyian "projects" (1907/2012) using digital tools for community engagement and activism (e.g., Rogers, 2015; Sanford et al., 2014), in the use of digital resources for intergenerational and intercultural exchange (e.g., Poitras-Pratt, 2018), and in larger scale curriculum reform that focuses on the use of digital resources in purposive, real world "rich tasks" for students.[8] Several chapters in this volume highlight yet other cases where teachers and students are using digital technologies (1) for solving and addressing local political, social, and environmental problems; (2) for mobilizing cultural resources to connect with and engage with their Elders and younger generations, with peers, and with distant cultures that they might otherwise not have contact with; and (3) for the practice of active and engaged citizenship, participation in social movements and action.

At the heart of our argument is the need for schooling to realize what children and young people are demonstrating in their rapid creation of their own digital realities. On the one hand, the digital actions of our children represent a clear refusal to accept the twentieth-century artificial alienation of them from their full participation in "the real world." In many respects, the bubble of childhood and adolescences has been burst from within. It is no longer sufficient to construct curriculum in preparation for later life. It is no longer sufficient for children to learn about decisions adults make for the planet they will inherent. It is no longer sufficient to allow curriculum and assessment to remain subject to that "incubus of superstition" that educators can be guided by some fiction about the internal capacities of students which we somehow know (Dewey, 1916, p. 172). It is their world already.

At the same time, these newfound rights have unprecedented ethical consequences. One consequence we have placed on the table here is that the current digital corporate order—this political economy of transnational information and technology—runs the risk of a recolonization of everyday forms of life, both those of adulthood and childhood, work and play without the deliberative democratic dialogue and informed debate about what might constitute a just, ethical, and life sustaining world. Let's have this debate with teachers, children, young people, and students—and their parents, elders, and communities. Digital literacies, multiliteracies, and digital and creative arts are necessarily ethical, political, and cultural practices. They are not technical skills or capacities and schools and institutions cannot continue to cast digital technology as yet another, more efficient means for the production of a post-ethical human capital. This does indeed have the potential to change everything.

## Notes

1. http://hypecycle.umn.edu.
2. E.g., www.lse.ac.uk/media@lse/research/EUKidsOnline/Home.aspx.
3. STEM = Science, Technology, Engineering, and Mathematics is the newly founded school subject, with the production of graduate specialists requisite for increased GDP in traditional resource, manufacturing, and technology, and in the emergent military/digital/intelligence sector.
4. The common claim that the Internet is now universal is unfounded. While composite estimates are that 89% of North Americans and 73% of Europeans and Australians have Internet access, global access continues to be below 50%. Quan-Haase (2016) further describes the persistent stratification of Canadian and American access by social class, age, and social geography. See: www.internetworldstats.com/stats.htm.
5. The Yonglu Aboriginal peoples of Northwest Arnhem use the term *ganma* to describe cultural contact, blending, and, potentially, conflict: this refers to the point in river estuaries where fresh and salt water meets and blends. Its application to aboriginal "two-way education" is attributed to Mandaway Yunipinnu of Northwest Arnhem Land (see: http://livingknowledge.anu.edu.au/html/educators/07_bothways.htm). See also, Canadian economist Harold A. Innis' (1951) history of the river as a medium for intercultural exchange, communications, and transportation.
6. This is, ironically, exactly how traditional Canadian and American social studies and history textbooks have taught about the railroads, as a celebration of the domination of nature by monopoly capitalists. Until recently, there has been negligible reference to their impacts on Indigenous peoples and their utilization of Chinese labor.
7. http://eprints.lse.ac.uk/57103/1/Livingstone_media_information_literacy_2014_author.pdf.
8. Queensland's "New Basics" (1999–2005) reforms introduced curriculum "rich tasks" that required that students use digital tools to address community problems; current Finnish curriculum reforms are making comparable efforts.

## References

Anderson, B. (1992). *Imagined communities: Reflections on the origins and spread of nationalism.* London, UK: Verso.
Aristotle. (1999). *Nichomachean ethics* (2nd ed.) (T. Irwin, Trans.). London, UK: Hackett.
Austin, J. A. (1962). *How to do things with words: The William James lectures delivered at Harvard University in 1955.* Oxford: Clarendon Press.
Benhabib, S. (1996). *Critique, norm and Utopia.* New York, NY: Columbia University Press.
Benhabib, S. (2002). *The claims of culture.* Princeton, NJ: Princeton University Press.
Benhabib, S., & Dallmayr, F. R. (Eds.). (1990). *The communicative ethics controversy.* New York, NY: MIT Press.
Bernstein, B. (1990). *On pedagogic discourse.* London, UK: Routledge.
Bowers, C. (2014). *The false promises of the digital revolution: How computers transform education, work, and international development in ways that are ecologically unsustainable.* New York, NY: Peter Lang.
boyd, D. (2015). *It's complicated: The social lives of networked teens.* New Haven, CT: Yale University Press.
Bruner, J., & Olson, D. R. (1977). Symbols and texts as the tools of intellect. *Interchange, 8*(4), 1–15.
Buckingham, D. (2007). *Beyond technology: Children's learning in the age of digital culture.* Cambridge, UK: Polity Press.
Buckingham, D., & Sefton-Green, J. (1994). *Cultural studies goes to school: Reading and teaching popular media.* London, UK: Taylor and Francis.
Burke, K. (1966). *The philosophy of literary form.* Cambridge, UK: Cambridge University Press.
Cazden, C. B. (2018). *Communicative competence, classroom interaction, and educational equity: The selected works of Courtney B. Cazden.* New York, NY: Routledge.
Cuban, L. (2001). *Oversold and underused: Computers in the classroom.* Cambridge, MA: Harvard University Press.
Davies, N. (2009). *Flat earth news: An award-winning reporter exposes falsehood, distortion and propaganda in the global media.* New York, NY: Vintage.
Dewey, J. (1907/2012). *The school in society & the child in the curriculum.* New York, NY: Courier Press.
Dewey, J. (1916). *Democracy in education.* New York, NY: Macmillan.
Dewey, J. (1934). *Art as experience.* New York, NY: Anchor Press.
Dewey, J. (2008). J. Boydston (Ed.), *The later works of John Dewey, volume 7, 1925–1953: Ethics.* Carbondale, IL: Southern Illinois University Press.
Fraser, N. (1996). *Justice interruptus.* New York, NY: Routledge.
Freire, P. (1970). *Pedagogy of the oppressed* (M. Ramos, Trans.). New York, NY: Continuum.
Graham, P. (2005). *Hypercapitalism: New media, language and social perceptions of value.* New York, NY: Peter Lang.
Graham, P. (2017). *Strategic Communication, Corporatism, and Eternal Crisis: The Creel Century.* New York, NY: Routledge.

Graham, P., & Luke, A. (2013). Critical discourse analysis and political economy of communication: Understanding the new corporate order. In R. Wodak (Ed.), *Critical discourse analysis: Concepts, history, theory* (Vol. 1, pp. 103–130). London, UK: Sage.

Habermas, J. (1979). *Communications and the evolution of society.* (T. McCarthy, Trans.). Boston, MA: Beacon Press.

Hall, S. (1974). The television discourse: Encoding and decoding. *Education and Culture, 25,* 8–14.

Halliday, M. A. K. (1978). *Language as social semiotic.* London, UK: Edward Arnold.

Havey, D., & Puccio, D. (2016). *Sex, likes and social media.* London, UK: Vermilion.

Innis, H. A. (1949). *Empire and communications.* Toronto, ON: University of Toronto Press.

Innis, H. A. (1951). *The bias of communications.* Toronto, ON: University of Toronto Press.

Isin, E., & Ruppert, E. (2015). *Being digital citizens.* London, UK: Rowman & Littlefield.

Jenkins, H., Shresthova, S., & Gamber-Thompson, L. (2016). *By any media necessary: The new youth activism.* New York, NY: New York University Press.

Kellner, D. (1978). Ideology, Marxism and advanced capitalism. *Socialist Review, 42,* 37–65.

Kellner, D. (2012). *Media spectacle and insurrection, 2011: From the Arab uprising to occupy everywhere.* New York, NY: Continuum/Bloomsbury.

Klein, N. (2015). *This changes everything: Capitalism and the climate.* New York, NY: Simon and Schuster.

Krotz, F. (2007). The meta-process of 'mediatization' as a conceptual frame. *Global Media and Communication, 3,* 256–260.

Livingstone, S., & Sefton-Green, J. (2016). *The class.* New York, NY: New York University Press.

Luke, A. (2004). Notes on the future of critical discourse studies. *Critical Discourse Studies, 1*(1), 13–15.

Luke, C., De Castell, S. C., & Luke, A. (1983). Beyond criticism: The authority of the school text. *Curriculum Inquiry, 13*(2), 111–127.

Martin, K. (2008). *Please knock before you enter: Aboriginal regulation of outsiders and the implications for research and researchers.* Brisbane, QLD: PostPressed.

Nixon, H. (1998). Fun and games are serious business. In J. Sefton-Green (Ed.), *Digital diversions: Youth culture in the age of multimedia.* London, UK: Routledge.

Pasquale, F. (2015). *The black box society: The secret algorithms that control money and information.* Cambridge, MA: Harvard University Press.

Picciano, A., & Spring, J. (2012). *The great American education-industrial complex.* New York, NY: Routledge.

Poitras-Pratt, Y. (2018). *Educating with Digital Storytelling: A Decolonizing Journey for an Indigenous Community.* New York, NY: Routledge.

Quan-Haase, A. (2016). *Technology and society: Social networks, power, and inequality* (2nd ed.). Toronto, ON: Oxford University Press.

Rogers, T. (2015). *Youth, critical literacies and civic engagement.* New York, NY: Routledge.

Sanford, K., Rogers, T., & Kendrick, M. (Eds.). (2014). *Everyday youth literacies: Critical perspectives for new times.* Singapore: Springer.

Scollon, R., & Scollon, S. (1981). *Narrative, literacy and face in interethnic communication.* Norwood, NJ: Ablex.

Selwyn, N. (2010). *Schools and schooling in the digital age: A critical analysis.* London, UK: Routledge.

Share, J. (2009). *Media literacy is elementary* (2nd ed.). New York, NY: Peter Lang.

Smith, L. (1999). *Decolonizing methodologies.* London, UK: Zed Books.

Viner, K. (2016). How technology disrupted the truth. *The Guardian,* June 16, 2016. Retrieved from www.theguardian.com/media/2016/jul/12/how-technology-disrupted-the-truth.

Warschauer, M., & Matuchniak, T. (2010). New technology and digital worlds: Analyzing evidence of equity in access, use and outcomes. *Review of Research in Education, 34,* 179.

Wilden, A. (1972). *System and structure: Essays on communications and exchange.* London, UK: Tavistock.

Wittkower, D. (2016). Lurkers, creepers, and virtuous interactivity: From property rights to consent and care as a conceptual basis for privacy concerns and information ethics. *First Monday, 21*(10).

# 21
# Digital Youth and Educational Justice

Lalitha Vasudevan, Kristine Rodriguez Kerr, and Cristina Salazar Gallardo

In this chapter, we focus on the practices of adolescents who participate in American educational contexts, although the young people whose voices and experiences we draw on also share a wider, more global set of affiliations beyond their immediate geographical locations. As such, their insights and experiences with writing inside and outside of institutions have a reach beyond our national stage alone. For many of these young people, writing is a matter of justice. That is, access to writing, to authoring oneself, to seeking and finding audiences for one's stories is a pursuit of everyday justice, one that is not always realized. Even as adolescents across schools and other institutions of education are engaged in hundreds of interactions daily that contain numerous communication practices, they continue to experience miscommunications with various interlocutors—teachers, counselors, social workers, and the general public—that can negatively impact their lives.

A chasm of understanding between adults and adolescents has been well documented by researchers who underscore the disjuncture between the dominance of a developmental perspective of adolescence as a chronological artifact and the nature of youth culture as a shifting landscape of becoming (Bucholtz, 2002; Lesko, 2012; Maira & Soep, 2005). One consequence of this conceptual misunderstanding is the narrative about young people as literate beings that has emerged as one of deficit and in need of remediation. Recent curricula have reinforced an emphasis on basics, often to the exclusion of engaged and youth-focused pedagogical practice (Schultz, 2009; Zacher Pandya, 2011), even as there is ample evidence to suggest that the literate repertoires of youth have not only remained robust and, particularly in out of school spaces, have flourished in new and unpredictable ways.

The panicked clarion call of crisis at the perceived "loss" of writing has been somewhat quelled by a steady stream of research that purports the opposite: People, and young people in particular, are writing more—in more places, for more purposes, to and with more people, with more tools—than ever before (Lunsford, 2007). However, while there may be a reluctant acceptance of the influence of digital tools on writing, new standards for writing and literacy (NCTE, 2008/2013), along with the requirements for technology fluency embedded into curricular expectations, suggest that schools may be slowly embracing (however awkwardly) an expanded set of ideas about being literate in digital times. Digital youth are those who are immersed in digital landscapes of communication, socialization, and education in many if not all aspects of their lives. While others have pondered, with both lament and celebration, the seamless infusion of technology into our daily lives, our purpose here is to share our observations of this quotidian engagement with technologies in the lives of youth with whom we have worked. We pay special attention to the ordinariness of how youth access digital tools and spaces in service of enacting their agency, authoring themselves, and claiming narrative authority about what was being said, written, and known about them.

By doing so, we put forth two considerations for cultivating educational justice with digital youth that are presented using data from two different studies with youth. First, we argue for multimodal composing as central to the architecture of the enactment of justice in young people's everyday experiences with education. To illustrate this point, we focus on the experiences of a young man who has been involved with the juvenile justice system for several years and whose participation in an after-school alternative to detention program (ATDP) played an important role in shaping his adolescence. We examine the evolution of his writing practices across digital and non-digital spaces as a way of explicating the ways that new sites and audiences for writing, mediated largely through social media, provided opportunities to strengthen his renewed engagement with his in-school education trajectories.

A second proposition focuses on the affordances of collaborative composition practices for nurturing agency among youth. The experiences of a group of college-going, undocumented activist youth help to illustrate the importance of agency in experiencing educational justice. These young people self-identify as DREAMers, a moniker ascribed to immigrant youth who "meet the general requirements of the Development, Relief, and Education for Alien Minors (DREAM) Act" (American Immigration Council, 2012, p. 1). These youth organized themselves as activists focused on educating multiple publics about their educational experiences for the dual purposes of presenting counternarratives to the currently circulating discourses about undocumented youth. The texts they composed, as well as the rich range of activities and events, communicative opportunities and texts, and networks they continue to design and implement are examples of the ways that, through collaborative multimodal composing, these youth embody and enact new forms of citizenship that extend far outside their relationship to a single nation state. In both examples, young people's everyday and unstructured uses of technologies and digital composing platforms—ranging from media collages and cameras to the incorporation of mixed media, mobile technologies, and social media—created the contexts for micro-moments of justice through writing. (The sections are written in the voices of the authors who are closest to the data being shared; they are identified parenthetically.)

We hope to expound on their experiences to consider how educators and educational sites within and beyond schools can further support these efforts. We conclude our chapter by highlighting the significance of attending to small and local moments of educational justice, through practices of care, cultivating community, and fostering belonging, that are mediated through access to digital cultural forms, artifacts, and spaces.

## Educational Justice

In conceptualizing justice, we first draw from the writings of Rawls (1971), whose articulation of fairness amplified the non-universality of justice, and Sen (2009), who critiqued Rawls' embrace of "just institutions" with a recognition that institutions routinely fall short of their imagined and just ideals. A second meaning of justice derives from more contemporary conceptualizations of endeavors that are in service of broader social good and that apply concepts of sociality and spatiality to justice—for instance, social justice, spatial justice, and economic justice (Harvey, 1996; Soja, 2010). We do not mean to gloss across these discrete concepts, nor to suggest that they are wholly similar or mutually exclusive concepts. However, the infusion of spatial lenses into studies of justice has amplified the significance of social practices in constituting and maintaining differences, underscoring a view of justice as situated and context-dependent. And, a third influence in our use of justice comes from studies of institutions whose purported aim is to provide and maintain fairness and equitable access to social goods and societal flourishing, and yet whose institutions are some of the worst perpetrators of *in*justice against citizens. These institutions include the juvenile and criminal justice systems, the system of schooling, the child welfare system, and its contingent service agencies.

While "justice" is conceptually challenging and complex to define, the experience of justice or injustice is simple, local, and ordinary. People's lives and everyday actions and interactions are the sites—that is, the "when" not "where"—of justice. Like writing, justice is experienced and enacted in the space of interactions. For instance, a fleeting interaction can leave a long tail of consequence: a judge deciding between sentencing a young person to jail and an alternative to incarceration program, peers who do not cheer when a joke is told at a friend's expense, and a teacher responding to a child's unexpected behavior as a site of pedagogy rather than automatic punishment.

By locating this conceptual complexity within an educational context, we want to attempt a working definition of "educational justice." Thus, we understand education to not be tethered to schooling alone, but rather as a condition that may be found potentially in any settings, as suggested by an anthropological definition of education as "difficult collective deliberations" (Varenne, 2007, p. 1559), for example in the snapshots of interactions noted above. Any interaction has the potential to be educative and also a site of justice.

Thus, we also attend to the ways that labels and categorizations pertaining to young people's social practices shape, positively or negatively—recognizing, of course, that these are not binary phenomena—their educational experiences, within and outside of formal institutional settings. While categorization aids the efficiency goals of most institutions, persistent acts identifying, sorting, and placing on a scale from "valued" to "punishable" the everyday practices of youth can have challenging consequences for young people. Misinterpretations of digital youths' practices can be devastating for their flourishing; at the same time, nurturing and scaffolding digital youths' practices and inclinations can open up increasingly generative opportunities for education, exploration, and narrative authority.

## Digital Youth—Participation and Social Inclusion Through Literacies

We understand that not all youth are always digitally connected, nor are all youth immersed in digital landscapes to the same degree, yet we contend that most youth growing up today are doing so within a broad set of societal and cross-cultural expectations about digital competence, ability, and capacity for creativity. Many children and adolescents are growing up in a time that, regardless of their geographical location, presumes a new set of basics skills and knowledge for what they should know or be able to do (Bellanca, 2011).

Increased access to digital media is suggestive of increased opportunities for participation in educational and other spaces. Jenkins, Purushotma, Weigel, Clinton, and Robison (2009), in their now seminal work foregrounding participatory cultures, advocate for the increased use of technologies in educational settings precisely for the potential they hold for lowering barriers to participation in schooling. Jenkins argues that if schools reflected the participatory ethos of many of the spaces that youth inhabit in their out of school time, quite simply, young people may demonstrate more forms of engagement in their institutional practices.

In regions where there exists a relatively low barrier to accessing digital media, meanings about youth and youthfulness have become concepts that are, if not synonymous then at least concomitant with digital innovation, media savvy, and technological revolution. Youth are engaged not only as consumers of media products, but also as creators of media texts, designers of digital tools, and arbiters of taste in what they circulate, dismiss, or transform as evidenced by their frequency and nature of use. The narrative has not been entirely positive, however. With the rise of technological ubiquity, there has also emerged consistent concern about adolescents' over reliance on virtual communicative modes and spaces, that are illustrated by increased awareness and attention given to cyberbullying, claims of attention deficits, sexting, and other forms of digital practices identified as transgressive or dangerous (Ringrose, Gill, Livingstone, & Harvey, 2012).

And, while much has been made of multitasking as a metaphor for the digitization of youth culture, and while we appreciate the need to recognize the influence of everyday access to digital forms of communication in shaping youth practices, we are hesitant to characterize young people's engagements with technologies as occurring simultaneously. In contrast, we want to call attention to the ways that young people attend, with intentionality, to their digital forms of writing and composing meaning.

In this chapter, we unmoor a definition of writing from its sociohistorical roots as a practice involving the application of written script upon a canvas, be it digital or physical. Specifically, we engage a definition of writing that is situated in and stems from sociocultural understandings of literacy as a social practice and as rooted in evolving cultural milieus (Alvermann, 2010; Lankshear & Knobel, 2011). We also extend the calls made by Leander and Sheehy (2004) and others to recognize literacies as multi-spatial practices, that is, as existing and being practiced not in a singular location or context, but rather having the possibility of moving across and between locations—for example, a Google Doc being composed by multiple people in as many places and time zones that includes writing, hyperlinks, images, embedded files, and other contributions. Finally, we concur with similar advocacy made toward emphases on the multimodality of writing (Anderson, 2013; Jewitt, 2009). That is, writing is a practice that is multimodally enacted and practiced—using a variety of modes and across a wide range of literal and metaphorical canvases—as well as a form of text that emerges from within contexts whose routine materiality varies greatly. In our examples and discussion that follows, we strive to peek underneath the oft-interpreted layers of meaning and composition to consider the affordances of digital and multimodal spaces (including their ordinary materiality) for engendering more just spaces with and for youth. Thus, a multimodal *orientation* toward digital youth is of vital importance to the pursuit of understanding, enacting, and cultivating educational justice.

## Multimodal Composing and Educational Justice

Across his involvement with a summer internship, Walter, a sixteen-year-old focal participant in a larger study about court-involved youth and digital writing practice, took ownership of an existing workshop blog, volunteering to craft new sections of the blog for known and imagined potential audiences. In doing this, Walter was able to nurture multimodal composing practices to make himself known and to share and articulate his understanding of the world. His experience allows us to highlight the use of everyday technologies and the movement between traditional and digital writing practices in service of agency, self-representation, and educational justice.

Mediated through his access to a semi-public digital space for composing, Walter—a tall, slender, African American young man—was able to actively reshape his role in an ATDP, improve his strained engagement with the program staff, and express renewed confidence in his in-school educational trajectory. Focusing on seemingly small moments of an emerging multimodal composing practice, the following case seeks to highlight notions of educational justice that arise when digital youth are engaged as creators of digital texts and have control over how to make their own narratives visible.

### Contexts for Multimodal Composing

Within the context of Voices, an ATDP that serves youth twelve to fifteen years old as a court-mandated afterschool program, there are layered notions of justice and *in*justice enacted daily. ATDPs are designed to avoid the disruption and trauma that arise when young people are taken out of their schools and placed in detention away from their family and support networks. Located within New York, a state where sixteen-year-olds are tried as adults (CCCNY, 2010), Walter was only eligible to participate in Voices because of his previous involvement with the program. Walter had been court-mandated to attend Voices two previous times, beginning when he was thirteen years old.

In describing his relationship with Voices, Walter explains "To me, it's like, I regret ever getting caught up in [Voices] but then again, it's like, I'm like happy because…there's good people there that depend on me and are looking at me like 'you should really be on top of your game.' Cause I've been there for what, now, like three years? Ever since I was 13, so. Help was provided. And it's still here for me. And that's good for me. It's good to know and it's good for me" (Interview, August 2013). However, throughout his summer internship, Walter mentioned moments of tension that arose with staff and his frustration that they didn't always acknowledge how much he had changed over the years. In part, Voices staff approved Walter's and my (Kristine's) request for him to be a participant in the summer internship as a way to enhance his continued experience at Voices. In addition, Walter was selected for this internship because of his active participation in the creative writing and storytelling workshops that were offered at the time by the research team twice a week.

Throughout the internship, Walter was engaged in writing and revising pieces from workshops and posting and composing content on the blog. Walter was able to make himself known to his peers and to me, the workshop facilitator, as a curious, enthusiastic, humorous, young man who was both experienced and inexperienced in various aspects of life. He shared his views on multiple topics, his hobbies, his frustrations, and his successes. Walter used his passionate interest in rollerblading as a tool for self-expression and, perhaps, self-preservation—a way for him to find a new circle of friends and new areas of the city to explore. He wrote about the pain he felt at being judged by others he was close to for interests and ideas that may differ from theirs, he described his openness to sharing his opinions when he felt they were being valued, and he voiced his concern for starting high school in the upcoming year as a sixteen-year-old freshman.

Attending to the small, but intentional, moments of multimodal composing that Walter engaged in across his internship, also revealed glimpses of a relationship that formed over weeks of being together in the work of reflecting, composing, and working to fuse loyalty to the known with openness to the new (Hansen, 2010). As we spent time together, we listened, laughed, considered, challenged, shared, and reflected on the writing he produced in workshops and on the blog.

### *Multimodal Composing: Making the Self Known*

During our time together that summer, as Walter's familiarity with basic blog functions increased, he quickly lost interest in simply updating content on the existing site. He asked if he could create his own section of the blog to display, and possibly combine, his multiple interests:

> Like, a collage. Like pieces together. A collection of things I'm interested in…Like, I'm the type of person that asks a lot of questions about everything. I'm the type of guy that is interested in everything. Not all to the same level, but I think everything is interesting to know at least a little.
> (Interview, August 2013)

Walter's intentions regarding the design of his own blog space and the desire to post about his personal interests are both ways of being known and opportunities to showcase his knowledge of the world.

Walter created his own page on the blog, titled "Enter the World of Blading," and began posting original writing that related to his interest in rollerblading. Although Walter was not able to create the full "collage/blog" that he described during our interview—due to the length of his summer internship—he took several steps to customize his own section of online space and exercise an authorial stance (Vasudevan, Schultz, & Bateman, 2010). Opening up generative opportunities for exploration and narrative authority, Walter learned how to customize the blog to "change the look" of his pages and create an immediate visual distinction between his pages and the existing site.

In creating his own blog space, Walter was able to customize all the elements of his blog's design, including the font, images, layout, colors, and content. This form of multimodal composing allowed Walter to be very specific about the design decisions he made. He selected colors that matched his two favorite colors at the time: orange and blue. He chose to tile a background image advertising his favorite rollerblade company and purposefully did not include the company's name because he wanted his audience to "to know, to guess, or to ask." He identified and selected links to videos of professional rollerbladers to "make people excited." In all of his design decisions, Walter considered his audience to be the same as the workshop blog's intended audience—other youth participants at Voices. Describing blogging as a social and participatory practice, Lankshear and Knobel (2006) draw attention to the ways in which blogs invite "affiliation with the cultural logic of the insider" because of their means of participation (p. 13). Haffaker (2004) notes that blogs can promote both online collaboration and the development of online communities. Walter was motivated by the potential of the "social alliances" that could grow out of his postings about rollerblading (Blood, 2002). That is, Walter was hoping to find and connect with other Voices youth who shared his interest in rollerblading through the blog.

Contexts that are rich with multiple modalities provide digital youth with opportunities to develop and express their identities across the production of multiple kinds of texts that represent a variety of stories and use a range of modalities (Hull & Nelson, 2005). In making design and content decisions for his own blog space, Walter was composing using multiple modes to showcase his interests in, and expert knowledge of, rollerblade brands, skaters, and skills. In addition, Walter made plans to post his own videos to his blog.

After asking to borrow a camera to record videos, Walter came back with a clip to add to his blog. The video was of Walter rollerblading very quickly down the center of a city street. He was holding the camera while he was rollerblading and the video was shot from his perspective. In this video, the only sound that could be heard for over a full minute was the wind, followed by Walter's laughter. In wanting to add this video to his blog, Walter was not only using the multimodal affordances of his blog space to highlight his expert knowledge of rollerblading, but he was hoping to make himself known as a legitimate and skilled rollerblader.

In working to make himself known through the recording of this nonverbal artifact, Walter was newly invigorated by the potential for composing across the blog, and also saw new opportunities for how he could be (literally) seen and known differently by others. For Walter, the opportunity to share more than words was both motivating and connected to his developing digital literacy skills. Hull and Nelson (2005) argued that "multimodal composing might helpfully be viewed not as a threat to or impoverishment of the print-based canon or traditional means of composing, but rather as an opportunity to contribute to a newly invigorated literate tradition and to enrich our available means of signification" (p. 226). And yet, despite a rich history of new literacies research, which recognizes that literacy is no longer singular and print bound (Lankshear & Knobel, 2003) too often in formal learning settings, students need to succeed within traditional school-based literacies before they are allowed/rewarded with the opportunity to engage with nontraditional texts. For Walter, who was initially critical of his own written work, the opportunity to experiment with multimodal composing allowed for a broader range of expression and a deeper personal connection to his broader oeuvre of work that included photographs, design, and multimedia artifacts in addition to writing.

Potential new audiences and the possibility of developing a community of likeminded rollerbladers motivated Walter's composing practices. Particularly for a young man who expressed a great deal of anxiety in our time together over the summer with starting the upcoming school year "kind of old for a high school freshman," the opportunity to engage with digital experimentation and showcase expert knowledge and skill was significant.

Next, we focus on the practices of a group of young people, who, by collaborating in their advocacy work toward a comprehensive immigration reform develop opportunities for empowerment, mentorship, and agentive work.

**Agency and Collaborative Composition as Educational Justice**

Building from multimodal composing, a second consideration for cultivating educational justice in the lives of youth involves securing or creating opportunities for young people to compose collaboratively and for meaningful purposes. Soep and Chavez (2005) proposed "pedagogy of collegiality" as an approach to adults and youth working together to produce media, specifically radio broadcasts. While not explicitly focused on justice, the authors, who were also educators at Youth Radio, an afterschool broadcast-training program, sought to identify and document the collaborative process by which a radio broadcast moved from idea to transmission. Adults and youth were both invited to engage as teachers and learners in a collegial way of working in service of a shared goal: the radio broadcast. Collaboration and allowing participants to assume and move in and out of various roles was vital for the success of the program and its resultant media artifacts.

In a similar vein, the young people that I (Cristina) worked with were negotiating forms of digital and compositional collaboration in service of a shared goal: rewriting the inaccurate and often dangerously incomplete narratives about undocumented youth in service of impacting immigration policies. In focusing on how digital engagement shapes young people's *daily* lives, I discuss the practices that provided young people in circumstances of marginalization with opportunities to reframe their own self-representation. All of the youth in my research attend a college in the state of New York. By collaborating in their advocacy work toward a comprehensive immigration reform, they engaged in multimodal composing that allowed them to become activists in the political arena. In addition, the youth also developed opportunities for empowerment, mentorship, and collaboration.

Undocumented youth in the US have encountered an important space of engagement and collaboration in pro-immigration movements, such as DREAM Act organizations (Chavez, 2007; Suarez-Orozco, 2014). These groups take their name after the Development, Relief, and Education of Alien Minors (DREAM) Act, a federal legislation that would allow qualifying youth a pathway toward citizenship and higher education (Abrego, 2006, 2008; Gonzales, 2011). These organizations, while taking the name of the legislation, have advocated for a comprehensive immigration reform, through collaborative practices across states through digital networks, while at the same time, participating in local activism in their communities.

For the past three years, I have been engaged in a longitudinal study of one DREAM Act group (herein DREAMers) and have been studying patterns of activism that are embedded in and flourish from their multimodal and collaborative composing practices. These young people continue to demonstrate the impact this group has on their sense and experience of community and agency as members of a marginalized population, one that faces multiple challenges, both from legal and educational standpoints. I came to see how their work as activists benefitted from access to a wide range of composing tools, both digital and non-digital. Through their multimodal composing processes, the participants navigated their identity and institutional challenges as undocumented youth, in the form of shared and self-advocacy, acquiring and producing information, and creating contexts for sharing rewritten narratives.

In order to understand the practices of these young participants, I engaged Stornaiuolo's (2015) notion of worldmaking, which posits that multimodal literacy practices must be studied not only through the messages produced, but also by understanding the processes and spaces that foster the composition of multimodal messages that allow young people to engage in an exploration of the self and the world. Therefore, in the research with DREAMer youth, I aimed not only to study the messages that the participants crafted but also, and more importantly, sought to understand the embodied and spatial dimensions of their multimodal engagement. How and where these engagements unfolded hold significance for understanding how the youth enacted agentive practices in their collaboration with a global community.

### Context for Agentive and Collaborative Composing

Within a population of 11.3 million undocumented immigrants in the US (PEW, 2014), an estimated 2.5 million are young people who arrived to this country as children or adolescents and have spent the majority of their schooling years here. Multiple authors estimate that an average of 65,000 undocumented students graduate from American high schools every year (Abrego, 2008; Corrunker, 2012; Seif, 2011).

Their access to higher education is limited in comparison with their peers. According to multiple researchers, for undocumented youth, the trauma of growing up with a sense of illegality permeates in multiple aspects of their lives and has a tremendous psychological impact on them (Gonzales, Suárez-Orozco, & Dedios-Sanguineti, 2013). The challenges that these young people encounter only increase as they grow up, and they encounter what Chavez has denominated a "schizophrenic context" (Chavez, 2007). Their daily lives are replete with agency-stripping experiences that render these youth as a problem on the sole basis of their citizenship status. Our focus, therefore, on DREAMer youths' daily and ordinary experiences with agency further underscores the urgency to attend to the spaces of practices in between policy, reforms, and institutionalized procedures.

Seeking educational experiences and access, some of these young people display patterns of resilience and optimism that manifest through their civic engagement (Perez, Espinoza, Ramos, Coronado, & Cortes, 2009), including forms of activism surrounding issues of immigration reform, which can empower undocumented youth to productively navigate their struggles (Abrego, 2008; Seif, 2011). The activism that many of these young people have engaged in was focused on their support toward the DREAM Act, which has been modified in multiple occasions since 2001, when it was unsuccessfully introduced in the Senate (Abrego, 2006, 2008; Gonzales, 2011). The implications of the activities that these young people engage in can be analyzed on multiple levels: They have become active voices in the political debate around immigration and they have developed a digital network of support across states that share resources and support (Costanza-Chock, 2011).

### Spaces for Collaborative Composition

Harlow and Guo (2014) suggested that activists have a sense of audiences and are able to employ their "repertoire of contention" according to the context. This rang true with the DREAMers I spent time with, as they had multiple audiences for their composing practices. That is, working collaboratively, DREAMers crafted and remixed texts to appeal to different audiences and to serve multiple purposes. A recurrent space for mediating these practices was the group's weekly meeting, in which the activities were grounded on multiple instances of digital and non-digital artifact composing (Vasudevan et al., 2010).

During weekly meetings, youth participants engaged in organizing and planning events and other group related activities. There were also less structured moments where group members were encouraged by each other to collaborate in different types of compositions, including in the development of resources to navigate school (university). These unstructured moments were frequently flexible moments of informal mentorship, a feature of participatory cultures (Jenkins et al., 2009). These weekly meetings allowed multiple types of participation, and frequently included the practice of composing materials for the group's social media profiles. One semester, Josué, while leading the meeting, decided to start by sharing an audiovisual presentation that included posters and images he took from the group's Facebook page, and that he had edited in order to explicate the ethos of the group to other groups within the school. Josué's presentation, which was shared remotely by the members, was later adapted by two other members for a presentation for high school students about the experiences of being undocumented. Remixing and re-composition of digital resources was a common practice among the group members.

### *Public Events: Strategic Disclosure and Agency*

In keeping with a focus on multiple audiences, what emerged as a main purpose of the group's weekly meetings was to provide space for the participants to engage with each other, beyond the original goal of planning public advocacy events. Still, even engaging in the design of those public events allowed them to reflect deeply about their communicative practices as they pondered and collaboratively made decisions about which ones to choose. Their process is again reminiscent of a pedagogy of collegiality (Soep & Chavez, 2005) that recognizes that honoring plurality and multiplicity in digital composing is not synonymous with chaos, but in fact is a way to allow participants to assume various roles at various times. In other words, the timescale of collaborative composing was not necessarily simultaneous, but rather a shared and continued practice over time.

In all the events the DREAMer youth planned, the participants decided on the types of communicative resources to employ depending on the nature of audience, the location, and what they could assume about the audience's comfort level with the topic. Some group members were willing to talk about their undocumented status in public, for example, and answer questions. But the group leaders frequently emphasized that only those members who felt comfortable doing so should volunteer to do so. The rest of the members participated on different assignments such as designing posters and flyers, engaging in social media promotion, purchasing food, and posting flyers throughout the campus.

The act of "coming out" as undocumented in a public context is tremendously empowering but can also lead to anxiety for many of DREAMers. One of the founders of the group, Xochitl, once mentioned in an interview: "In a different group, they just gave me the mic and made me tell my story. I didn't want that to happen in [our] group." Her words echo the leadership style of the core members, who continuously encouraged participants through their own public disclosure to do it, but they never directly suggested to any member to do it. This flexibility allowed members to navigate their own identity negotiations in their own process. One of the group leaders, Sofia, told me in an interview: "I have always been very open about my status, but not everyone is like that, and that's ok."

In my time as a researcher in this group, I have seen several members navigate their initial hesitation to disclose their status and then make the decision to disclose it at some of the public events. These trajectories in their disclosure were not linear, as some of them only opted to disclose in specific contexts and others chose to do it as many times as possible. However, these instances do show how the leaders of the group fostered a sense of agency for the members of the team, by not imposing any type of disclosure. This group, therefore, was both the space and established a broader set of processes (Stornaiuolo, 2015) in which the collaborative composing occurred, giving rise to and emerging out of agentive acts.

*Public Events: Agency and Storytelling*

One strategy that the participants frequently employed was designing events in which documentaries were the first element in the event. The films were selected to provide general information about undocumented people in the US, and because they prepared the audience for the ensuing discussion with some members of the group. Sharing and discussing media was not all that transpired, however.

One time, when two of the group's members volunteered to field and answer questions from the audience, other members of the group spread out across four tables that had been set up for the event. Each table was covered with different flyers. Among the documents available for the audience were: a letter written by the group to the State's Governor requesting support for the State DREAM Act, a document offering links to websites with DREAM Act support, a guide for undocumented youth created by members of the team working remotely on a document, and five different event flyers designed by different group members. These artifacts are examples of the multiple opportunities that existed for group members to contribute meaningfully to the group's identity and public engagement, a common practice that was particularly useful for those young people who chose not to disclose their legal status.

In this particular event, after the documentary, the audience asked the two members of the group questions regarding their struggles and one of the audience members even disclosed that she had been undocumented as a young woman. The ability of the documentaries to offer an introduction and contextualization to the audience was tremendously helpful to the team members. The members of the group dedicated time to plan every one of these events, and they consistently displayed an understanding that different audiences demand different resources. They were able to engage in activities that allowed them not only to understand themselves, but also to "construct the world" (Stornaiuolo, 2015, p. 564), and to reimagine their agency.

## Toward Agentive and Just Spaces for Making Youth Known

As we have tried to illustrate, educational justice can be pursued and achieved—to varying degrees and purposes—through opportunities to compose and write multimodally, collaboratively, and in service of one's agency. More specifically, the acts of crafting new digital texts, media, public events were some of the ways that youth in our studies are writing—literally, multimodally, and figuratively.

By taking youth and youth practices seriously, adults in their lives—who are either institutionally or otherwise tethered to the young people—can begin to create conditions for everyday experiences of justice through and with writing. Too often the off-task or practices of youth that appear to exist on the margins of text production are delegitimized. A bent toward the digital has created an unfortunate distance from the physical and lived aspects of how young people enact and embody their digital writing selves.

Walter, whose literacies Kristine documented, made himself known multimodally through the texts he produced—contributing to the blog that Kristine had started, initiating his own blog, and video of his skating practice and new practices for communication he developed as a result. The DREAMers, who Cristina writes about, crafted spaces—weekly meetings, public events to provide education about the experience of being a DREAMer and undocumented, and collaboratively composed posters—in which to express and enact various forms of agency. Collectively, the writing lives of young people whom we discuss in this chapter can be characterized by the purposes that drive them, modes with which they are cultivated, and spaces in which they are practiced. For youth like Walter, Josué, Xochitl, and many others who share similar experiences, backgrounds, and trajectories—especially those youth whose daily lives are deeply embedded in broader systems of surveillance like juvenile justice and immigration enforcement and whose institutional affiliations push them to the margins of classrooms—glimpses of justice in their institutional experiences is vital. But glimpses, alone, are not enough.

As we have noted here, educational justice comes in the form of having control over how to make one's narrative or image visible and accessible and the contexts and conditions in which these practices can thrive. Practices need people, and visibility and narrative control, themselves, do not determine the sustainability of justice in one's life. Educators can alter the material conditions of their classrooms and pedagogical contexts in service of greater narrative authority and audience; and researchers can make methodological shifts to assume postures of noticing and documenting that exist beyond tangible, measureable, and observable impacts of practice to consider how experiences come into being. What is at stake is the foundation of assumptions about youth, their capacities, and their relationship to the digital on which pedagogical, methodological, and policy decisions are made. Centering inquiry and innovation in the ordinary and perhaps unexpected sites of practice of the same youth who experience institutional injustice is one important step toward remaking this foundation, one with a renewed embrace of justice toward youth as particular, as shared, as urgent, and as intentional.

## References

Abrego, L. J. (2006). "I can't go to college because I don't have papers": Incorporation patterns of Latino undocumented youth. *Latino Studies, 4*(3), 212–231.
Abrego, L. J. (2008). Legitimacy, social identity, and the mobilization of law: The effects of Assembly Bill 540 on undocumented students in California. *Law & Social Inquiry, 33*, 3, 709–734.
Alvermann, D. (Ed.) (2010). *Adolescents' online literacies: Connecting classrooms, digital media, & popular culture.* New York, NY: Peter Lang.
Bellanca, J. (2011). *21st century skills: Rethinking how students learn.* Bloomington, IN: Solution Tree Press.
Blood, R. (2002). Weblogs: A history and perspective. In Editors of Perseus Publishing (Eds.), *We've got blog: How weblogs are changing culture.* Cambridge, MA: Perseus Publishing.
Chavez, L. R. (1988). Settlers and sojourners: The case of Mexicans in the United States. *Human Organization, 47*(2), 95–108.
Chavez, L. R. (1991). Outside the imagined community: Undocumented settlers and experiences of incorporation. *American Ethnologist, 18*(2), 257–278.
Chavez, L. R. (2007). The condition of illegality. *International Migration, 45*(3), 192–196.
Citizens Crime Commission of New York City. CCCNY. (2010). Guide to Juvenile Justice in New York City. Retrieved on February 1, 2014 from www.nycrimecommission.org/pdfs/GuideToJuvenileJusticeInNYC.pdf.
Corrunker, L. (2012). "Coming out of the shadows": DREAM Act activism in the context of global anti-deportation activism. *Indiana Journal of Global Legal Studies, 19*(1), 143–168.
Costanza-Chock, S. (2011). Digital popular communication: Lessons on information and communication technologies for social change from the immigrant rights movement. *National Civic Review, 100*(3), 29–35.
Gonzales, R. G. (2011). Learning to be illegal undocumented youth and shifting legal contexts in the transition to adulthood. *American Sociological Review, 76*(4), 602–619.
Gonzales, R. G., Suárez-Orozco, C., & Dedios-Sanguineti, M. C. (2013). No place to belong: Contextualizing concepts of mental health among undocumented immigrant youth in the United States. *American Behavioral Scientist, 57*(8), 1174–1199.
Haffaker, D. (2004). The educated blogger: Using weblogs to promote literacy in the classroom. *First Monday, 9*(6), 25 pars.
Hansen, D. (2010). Cosmopolitanism and education: A view from the ground. *Teachers College Record, 112*(1), 1–30.
Harlow, S., & Guo, L. (2014). Will the revolution be Tweeted or Facebooked? Using digital communication tools in immigrant activism. *Journal of Computer-Mediated Communication, 19,* 463–478.
Harvey, D. (1996). *Justice, nature and the geography of difference.* New York, NY: Blackwell.
Hull, G., & Nelson, M. E. (2005). Locating the semiotic power of multimodality. *Written Communication, 22*(2), 224–261.
Jenkins, H., Purushotma, R., Weigel, M., Clinton, K., & Robison, A. J. (2009). *Confronting the challenges of participatory culture: Media education for the 21st century.* Cambridge, MA: MIT Press.
Lankshear, C., & Knobel, M. (2003). *New literacies: Changing knowledge and classroom learning.* New York, NY: Open University Press.
Lankshear, C., & Knobel, M. (2006). *Blogging as participation: The active sociality of a new literacy.* Paper presented to the American Educational Research Association, San Francisco, US, April 11, 2006.

Lesko, N. (2012). *Act your age!: A cultural construction of adolescence* (2nd ed.). New York, NY: Routledge.
Lunsford, A. (2007). *Writing matters: Rhetoric in public and private lives.* Athens, GA: University of Georgia Press.
Maira, S., & Soep, E. (2005). *Youthscapes: The popular, the national, the global.* Philadelphia: PENN/University of Pennsylvania Press.
Perez, W., Espinoza, R., Ramos, K., Coronado, H, & Cortes, R. (2009). Academic resilience among undocumented Latino students. *Hispanic Journal of Behavioral Sciences, 31,* 149–181.
Rawls, J. (1971). *A theory of justice.* Cambridge, MA: Belknap Press.
Ringrose, J., Gill, R., Livingstone, S., & Harvey, L. (2012). *A qualitative study of children, young people and 'sexting'.* London, UK: NSPCC
Schultz, K. (2009). *Rethinking classroom participation: Listening to silent voices.* New York, NY: Teachers College Press.
Seif, H. (2004). "Wise up!" Undocumented Latino youth, Mexican-American legislators, and the struggle for higher education access. *Latino Studies, 2*(2), 210–230.
Seif, H. (2009). The civic education and engagement of Latina/o immigrant youth: Challenging boundaries and creating safe spaces. Research Paper Series on Latino Immigrant Civic and Political Participation. Number 5. Woodrow Wilson International Center for Scholars.
Seif, H. (2011). "Unapologetic and unafraid": Immigrant youth come out from the shadows. *New Directions for Child and Adolescent Development, 2011,* 59–75.
Sen, A. (2011). *The idea of justice.* Cambridge, MA: Harvard University Press.
Soep, E., & Chavez, V. (2005). Youth radio and the pedagogy of collegiality. *Harvard Educational Review, 75*(4), 409–434.
Soja, E. (2010). *Seeking spatial justice.* Minneapolis: University of Minnesota Press.
Stornaiuolo, A. (2015). Literacy as worldmaking. In J. Rowsell & K. Pahl (Eds.), *The Routledge handbook of literacy studies* (pp. 561–573). New York, NY: Routledge.
Suarez-Orozco, C. (2004). Formulating identity in a globalized world. In M. M. Suarez-Orozco & D. B. Qin-Hilliard (Eds.), *Globalization: Culture and education in the new millennium* (pp. 173–202). Berkeley: University of California Press.
Suarez-Orozco, C. (Discussant) (2014, April 5). *Status and schooling in New Latino communities: Ethnographic perspectives on immigration status in K-12 contexts.* Lecture conducted from AERA 2014, Philadelphia.
Vasudevan, L, Schultz, K., & Bateman, J. (2010). Rethinking composing in a digital age: Authoring literate identities through multimodal storytelling. *Written Communication, 27*(4), 442–468.
Wissman, K., & Vasudevan, L. (2012). Re-writing the stock stories of urban adolescents. In D. Alvermann and K. Hinchman (Eds.), *Reconceptualizing the literacies in adolescents' lives: Bridging the everyday/academic divide* (pp. 160–180). New York, NY: Routledge.
Zacher Pandya, J. (2011). *Overtested: How high-stakes accountability fails English language learners.* New York, NY: Teachers College Press.

# 22
# Composing as Culturing
*An American Indian Approach to Digital Ethics*

Kristin L. Arola

While I've always known that there is a right way and wrong way when it comes to writing, particularly when it comes to issues of plagiarism, I can't say I ever thought much about the idea of cheating in craft. To me, if someone could show me a finished product—say a knitted scarf, beaded earrings, or a hand-sewn skirt—the finer points of how they actually constructed the text didn't occur, or matter much, to me. This all changed when I took part in a number of events surrounding the Spirit of the Harvest powwow—an autumn powwow sponsored by my alma mater and my mother's tribe, the Keweenaw Bay Indian Community. The two-day event includes a speaker series and workshops for the undergraduate students involved in the powwow. As part of this event, I attended a regalia making workshop where elders teach students involved in the American Indian student group methods for crafting powwow regalia. While my mother had been involved in the cultural life of her tribe for years, for a variety of complicated reasons it was something I hadn't yet paid much attention to.

Sitting around a big oak table in the basement of the multicultural center, I watched my mother use her 1970s Singer sewing machine to stitch together pieces of a pink shawl for a breast cancer awareness dance. Meanwhile, a college student worked on hand-sewing jingles onto her jingle dress, tediously stitching one jingle at a time in a pattern she had seen in a dream. Off to my left, Lori, the advisor for the student, was teaching Margarita how to sew fringe onto the bottom of a shawl.

"Like this" Lori says, as she winds a spool of white shawl fringe around a plastic binder. "You just keep doing it, but don't pull it too tight otherwise you'll have some that are kind of stretched uneven." After winding the fringe around a dozen or so times, she grabs a pair of scissors. "Then you just cut it. But don't do so many that you can't cut through them." After cutting through the fringe, creating a handful of even-lengthed pieces of fringe, she begins to illustrate the process of attaching the fringe to the bottom of a shawl. "You know, some people cheat and they use sew-on fringe. It is a piece of thin material where the fringe is already sewn on and you just sew that inside your shawl. Once it's on, you can't ever tell." Margarita pauses, cocks her head, and asks Lori, "Where do I find this?" The room erupts into laughter. Lori, through her giggles, says "I JUST said, that's cheating!" "But *why* is that cheating?" Margarita asks, already seeming to know the answer. "Well, it's that idea that you need to put yourself and your relations into what you're making, it should take some effort." Jill chimes in from being the sewing machine, "It's a labor of love."

Throughout my two days at the powwow, and in subsequent years of working with various American Indian women, I've come to understand more fully this distinction of making things the right way, of putting yourself into the objects you bring into the world so as to honor the relations that came before and will come after. And I have come to believe that the ways making is understood through American Indian epistemologies[1] has much to offer those of us concerned with digital writing and literacy. In this essay, I suggest a path for an ethical digital literacy, one that moves beyond a fascination with remix culture on the one hand, and an obsession with catching plagiarism on the other. Such an approach to digital literacy asks that we approach digital production with care, acknowledging the ecologies of meaning within which we craft, compose, and circulate.

**Plagiarism and Remix, Authenticity and the Product**

I begin here by describing how the narratives surrounding plagiarism are built upon false notions of authenticity and a focus on product over process. While plagiarism fears have always existed in the writing classroom, digital technologies have brought such concerns to the fore given the sheer amount of sources and paper mills easily accessible and downloadable. Pre-or post-digital writing, however, the concept of plagiarism remains the same and is largely founded on the idea that ideas can be original and can be owned. When we ask our students to include sources in their papers and to cite them properly, we are asking our students to give credit where credit is due. This is, on its face, not an unreasonable request. Yet the notion that our students (or even ourselves for that matter) can have completely original thoughts and make original arguments, even when those arguments bring in the source work of others, presumes an autonomous writer who writes to share authentic original thoughts.

Writing studies includes an abundance of scholarship that works to historically contextualize plagiarism and to disrupt such rigid notions of authenticity.[2] For example, as Johnson-Eilola and Selber (2007) write, "[Composition] has long attacked the idea of the lone genius in the attic slaving away on a piece of written work (see Porter, 1986; Selzer, 1993)" (p. 378). Such work attempts to complicate notions of plagiarism as simply an ethical breach, and understands that while blatantly stealing other's ideas is unethical, reusing and repurposing ideas is not so neatly definable. Consider that Ralph Waldo Emerson argued over a century ago that

> Our debt to tradition through reading and conversation is so massive, our protest so rare and insignificant—and this commonly on the ground of other reading or hearing—that in large sense, one would say there is no pure originality. All minds quote. Old and new make the warp and woof of every moment. There is no thread that is not a twist of these two strands.
>
> (para. 2)

While writing studies scholars may problematize authenticity and originality, as Johnson-Eilola and Selber point out, "as a practice composition still tends to hew pretty closely to this idea when teachers start dealing with issues of plagiarism" (p. 378). When dealing with issues of plagiarism in the classroom, the belief of individual authenticity holds sway. While not all composition instructors may buy into these beliefs, the institutional structures within which we teach are complicit with such narratives. This ideology becomes clearly apparent in our own universities' significant investment in plagiarism detection services, most of which look to detect a certain range of what is deemed "lifted" material by searching for matching strings of words in the document compared to texts in the detector's index. These services look for what their algorithms determine to be the absence of authenticity.

At present, there are ten commercially available plagiarism detection services, as well as a handful of free (and often less powerful) programs. Nearly all US universities invest in at least one of these software systems, and encourage instructors to make use of these thief-catching platforms. Take for example, that during my drafting of this essay, I received an email from our Provost titled "Academic Integrity Vital." The email begins with the claim that "According to research and surveys conducted between 2002 and 2015 from the International Center for Academic Integrity, 68% of college undergraduate students admitted to cheating in college" (para. 2). The email goes on to encourage all faculty to use Safe Assign, a plagiarism detection software built into Blackboard, and offers information about training sessions to use the software.

Perhaps the most popular plagiarism detection service is Turnitin, who, by their own count are "used by more than 26 million students at 15,000 institutions in 140 countries." Turnitin has, as Vie (2013) notes, "come under fire by many within rhetoric and composition for their reliance on a 'guilty until proven innocent' model of student academic integrity" (np), not to mention their questionable treatment of copyright and privacy. Additionally, as Carbone (2006) notes,

> Turnitin.com doesn't distinguish between cheating—intentionally cutting and pasting in elements from other electronic documents—from the inevitable mistakes in paraphrasing, summarizing, file management, note taking and so on. […] The service is not about teaching, it's about catching. In that, it's a pedagogic placebo.
>
> (para. 3)

Yet the fact that it remains so wildly popular amidst such concerns speaks to the academy's zealous obsession with plagiarism.

Writing scholars can critique plagiarism detection tools all we like, but at the end of the day these products sell, and our universities' investment in them indicates a serious dedication to perceived notions of academic authenticity. Such obsession focuses less on prevention and more on catching, less on the writing process and more on the writing product, and in doing so, it draws attention away from richer discussions we should be having about writing and digital literacy. As Chris Culter says in his discussion of plunderphonics (that is, the creative combining of two or more preexisting sound recordings to make a new one), when it comes to discussing new paradigms of composing, "The old values and paradigms of property and copyright, skill, originality,…and so forth are simply not adequate to the task" (p. 155). While Cutler is concerned primarily with sound composition, I would argue that the same old values and paradigms are no longer adequate to the task of discussing any composition in a digital age. These values focus not only on outdated notions of originality, they also focus on the fixed final product of the text itself. Plagiarism detection software does not, and cannot, detect the process a writer undergoes to compose a text. Instead, these services rely solely on the product itself. In choosing to use these services, we too are complicit with a system that values authenticity and product over process.[3]

As gestured to earlier, one avenue for rethinking plagiarism is remix culture and practice. In theory, remix culture affords the space to both disrupt rigid notions of authenticity as well as a product-based pedagogy. Ridolfo and DeVoss (2009) define remix as "the process of taking old pieces of text, images, sounds, and video and stitching them together to form a new product." Referencing Lessig's work on remix culture, Ridolfo and DeVoss suggest that "remix is perhaps the premier contemporary composing practice" (Remix section, para. 1). Given that we exist within a remix culture, they suggest an invention strategy, rhetorical velocity, that is deftly attuned to digital literacy and culture. They define rhetorical velocity as "the strategic theorizing for how a text might be recomposed (and *why* it might be recomposed) by third parties, and how this recomposing may be useful or not to the short- or long-term rhetorical objectives of the rhetorician" (Velocity section, para. 1). Rhetorical velocity is, then, a concern of invention and is acknowledges the new paradigms of composing that digital media have ushered forth.

That being said, remix culture isn't always necessarily focused on process nor does it necessarily, in spite of its best intentions, disrupt notions of authenticity. Take for example, Johnson-Eilola and Selber (2007) who propose the assemblage as a site for disrupting conceptions of originality. They define assemblages as "texts built primarily and explicitly from existing texts in order to solve a writing or communication problem in a new context" (p. 381). This remix ethos is also seen in those (Rice, 2003; Sirc, 2002, 2006; Williams, 2014) who advocate for a digital sampling approach to invention, one that draws from hip-hop's approach to composing whereby new texts are created through recontextualizing preexisting objects. In Paul D. Miller's, aka DJ Spooky that Subliminal Kid's, manifesto *Rhythm Science* he suggests there is no individual authenticity, instead composers now "create with found objects" and in doing so we "learn to speak in new forms" (p. 25). Miller proposes that the DJ mix serve as a model for composing in a digital age.

Interestingly, while such models appear on their face to embrace the process of composing, the creative value of the text remains focused on the product itself. That is, creativity is assessed, as Miller says, in "how you recontextualize the previous expression of others" (p. 33). Such a model still focuses on an individual in the world, one who acknowledges process and recognizes the power of recontextualization, but is still treated as the lone genius who selects and remixes the available resources to create an innovative product. Even for Selber and Johnson-Eilola's assemblage, which is founded not on hip-hop culture but on Deleuze and Guattari's notions of essence and repetition (a theory that is always about process), the litmus test for creativity is based on the product. In their case, the decision of whether or not an assemblage is effective or original hinges on how it helps to "solve a writing or communication problem in a new context" (Johnson-Eilola and Selber, 2007, p. 381).

While I appreciate the ways that remix culture attempts to disrupt outdated narratives of authenticity by acknowledging that texts are produced through the gathering of preexisting resources, and while I agree that writing studies should embrace a pedagogy that acknowledges the ways we are always borrowing and remixing ideas, texts, and concepts, remix still functions with the idea of a lone author. The lone author no longer comes up with *original ideas*, but does come up with *original ways* of remixing. This individual author gathers her resources and creates a new idea, albeit from previously existing texts.

So, on the one hand, we have the ideologies driving plagiarism discourses. In these discourses, writing spaces are presumed to involve a lone genius who generates original ideas on her own. Such a space encourages the investment in plagiarism detection services, focuses attention on the product of writing itself, and encourages a pedagogy that treats students as guilty before proven innocent. On the other hand are the ideologies driving remix culture discourses. In these discourses, writing spaces focus more on process; however, the author is still presumed to be a lone genius, but this time is able to reuse and remix preexisting ideas to her own ends. While remix disrupts notions of authenticity, it does not on its face disrupt the idea of the lone author. Additionally, in both plagiarism and remix discourses, the determination of whether a text was plagiarized or successfully remixed has less to do with the process of making and more to do with the judgment of the final product. For those in writing studies for whom a process-based approach to writing is how we approach pedagogy, this disjuncture seems peculiar at best. Turning to American Indian ways of making can help refocus our attention to process-based pedagogies and can help shift away from a lone author and instead to an author who composes in relation to the world around her.

## American Indian Rhetoric, American Indian Philosophy

Over the past decade, rhetoric and composition has seen a rise in American Indian writing studies scholarship (Crane-Bizarro, 2004; Cushman, 2008, 2011; Frost, 2011; Haas, 2005, 2007; King, Gubele, & Anderson, 2015; Lyons, 2000, 2010; Monroe, 2014; Powell, 2002, 2004, 2012). Broadly speaking, this work attempts to make visible American Indian writing practices and ways of being. In spite of this important work, the connections between digital writing practices and American Indian rhetorics have been few. Angela Haas (2005) stands as one exception, recommending that, "the promises are many for our scholarly communities to learn more about digital cultural rhetorics by including American Indians in the discourse surrounding information technologies." Haas (2007) has also argued seeing wampum as hypertext, thus placing the history of hypermedia far earlier than digital scholars might otherwise suggest. I take her suggestions seriously, and suggest we not relegate cultural rhetorics to their own corners of the field, but instead actively fold them into the warp and woof of our discipline.

To those ends, I propose, as I will describe in the next section, how American Indian epistemology can help us rethink how we treat authorship in a digital age. American Indian thought holds at its foundation the maxim that everything is related. While it's not entirely accurate to flatten all American Indian thought under one umbrella, strains of such thought, as Cordova (2007) argues, have more in common with one another than they do with the Western philosophical tradition. These commonalities are expressed by Deloria (1999) who suggests the following four premises hold true for American Indians: all things are alive, everything is related, all relationships are historical, and space and time determine the nature of relationships.

The adage that "everything is related" is an incredibly common thread throughout American Indian thought, one that Cordova (2007) describes as such:

> I suppose one could use the analogy of a stone thrown into a pond. Each 'thing'—stone, air, molecule, plant, animal, or vegetable—causes a ripple to form in the pond. The singular, particular being is not merely itself tossed into the pond. It is also the ripple, the wave, that is formed by our action. Our 'waves' overlap and extend beyond what we can foresee. Wisdom is knowing the effects of those 'overlaps.' This is how 'relatedness' enters the picture: A statement that 'all things are related' reminds us that we are not separate from all other things, that our actions have far-reaching consequences.
>
> (p. 30)

In Western thought, the analogy of a stone thrown into the pond is usually used to indicate how our individual actions have impacts beyond what we might originally intend. That is, we are a lone individual who acts. However, as Cordova describes it, the rock is never solitary. In American Indian thought, the ripple is just one piece of the overall picture. It is the stone thrown, the air through which the stone travels, the person throwing the stone, and where and how she's standing, it is all of these things and more. Acknowledging all of these pieces reminds us that we are not lone actors in the world. Instead all of our actions exist in a chain of connections and relations, some of which are known and some of which are unknown. We are never fully acting alone. As Deloria further describes (1999) "everything in the natural world has relationships with every other thing and the total set of relationships that make up the world as we experience it" (p. 34). There is no lone author. There is no lone remixer. Instead, "the world is constantly creating itself because everything is alive and making choices that determine the future" (p. 46).

In the case of my opening story of Margarita learning how to correctly sew fringe onto her powwow shawl, she is taught not to take a shortcut but to instead hand stitch the fringe so as to put herself into the text, to respect the craft. This practice also honors that Margarita isn't crafting an object separate from a series of relations. There were shawls before her, and people made them particular ways for particular reasons. It is her job to push forward her culture by reflectively honoring these methods. In this way, she is, as Lyons (2010) argues, culturing. Both Lyons and the stories I rely on in this essay come from the Ojibwe (also called Anishinaabe or Chippewa) people of the Upper Great Lakes. In the Ojibwemowin language, Lyons notes there is no real word for "culture," at least as a noun. But, there is a sense of culture-ing. That is, there is no static noun for *being* Ojibwe, but there is a sense of culture-ing *as* Ojibwe. By performing an act (making something, wearing something, living in a particular way) you are part of something larger in which others who also perform that act are also a part. All of the words Lyons interrogates in his hunt for a static easy-to-identify Ojibwe "culture"—izhitwaa (having a certain custom or practicing a certain ceremony), nitaa (behaving skillfully), and inaadizi (living in a certain way)—indicate a single overarching concern: the desire to produce *more life*. That is, by fishing in a particular way, or harvesting cedar in a particular way, or sewing regalia in a particular way, one not only *does* (that is, cultures as) Indian but also produces and sustains more life, more culture, more American Indian ways of being.

In all acts of production, then, there is the acknowledgment that you produce more life, opening up new possibilities and potentials for further acts of production and analysis. While specific to the Ojibwe language, this idea of culturing offers a framework for all acts of making. By making in a particular way, we honor a particular way of being while not foreclosing the possibilities and potentials for new ways of being. For American Indian thought, then, acknowledging the active and historical nature of all of our relations encourages we bring texts into the world in particular ways. This is a process-based approach to making, one that acknowledges that a writer never composes in isolation. There is no authentic self who produces original works, instead there are writers who exist in relation to one another, draw from one another, and produce within ecologies of meaning.

**Reflective Practitioners**

*In an Anishinaabe village long ago, there was a very sick young boy. A respected elder in the village, who had once been guided by the Seven Grandfathers in the sky, believed a healing lodge needed to be built where he could perform a ceremony to heal the sick boy. The old man gathered the village women— for women symbolize the life-giving force of the Earth—and asked them to build the lodge. First, they gathered maple saplings for the frame of the lodge, for maple is a life-giving being. Next, they gathered balsam, spruce, and fern and placed it along the sides of the lodges for these elements would help further draw upon the nourishment of the plant world. Soon, the lodge was completed. Yet, something still wasn't right—the Old Man knew something was missing.*

*After much meditation, he realized that the lodge needed a waterdrum like the one he saw in his childhood visit to the Seven Grandfathers. This drum represented all that was necessary for life. It embodied both the physical and the spiritual. The Old Man began to make the waterdrum from memory, so that it would resemble in every way the vessel that once sat in front of the Seven Grandfathers. He started with a hollowed-out log, for the log is symbolic of all our plant brothers and sisters with whom we must learn to live in a respectful way. He then made the head of the waterdrum from deerhide, for it represents and honors all of our four-legged brothers and sisters and brings with it the qualities and gifts of the deer, including speed and agility alongside a quality of peace and gentleness. Before he placed the head on the drum, the old man partially filled the wooden shell of the drum with water, for the water represents the life blood of Mother Earth. He used a hoop to attach the deerskin head to the Waterdrum, for the hoop represents the Sacred Circle in which all natural things move. It represents all seasons of the Earth. It represents the birth, growth, and death of all living things. It represents the movement of the waters on Mother Earth. The old man then carved a drumbeater out of a living root that he took from the Earth. He carved the head of the drumbeater with a curve to represent the neck of the crane and the loon. When all these preparations had been done, the old man took the Waterdrum and sounded its voice four times. The ceremony was about to begin.*

This story, told by Edward Benton-Bai (1988), is a retelling of an oral story passed down through generations of Ojibwe peoples. I share it here for the purposes of illustrating how existing objects (logs, deerhide, water) are used with great intention in order to create something new. This composing practice very carefully acknowledges the relations that existed before the composer entered the scene, while also acknowledging the relations the composer hopes to bring into existence. To be fair, students in our classrooms aren't making a medicinal lodge to heal a sick dying boy. Nor are they making a shawl to dance in a powwow with. But similar to drawing from hip-hop culture (our students also aren't performing DJ sets in the club), these ways of *composing* or *culturing* provide methods we can learn from. These ways of composing and culturing focus on a process of being in relation to and with the ideas, texts, and people that make up our rhetorical situation.

As such, these stories of making embody reflective action, what Robert Johnson (1998) refers to in his discussion of Aristotle's understanding of techne. Johnson points out that, for Aristotle, there is a distinction between a practitioner and a reflective practitioner, between someone who learns by doing only and someone who understands the "why and the cause of what is being done" (p. 132). A reflective practitioner is one who makes in active and conscious relation to the ecologies both past and present, and can describe as Johnson argues, the "why and the cause of what is being done" (p. 132). Reflective practitioners can move from what Giddens (1979) calls a practical consciousness, "tacit stocks of knowledge which actors draw upon in the constitution of social activity" to what he terms a discursive consciousness, that is, "knowledge which actors are able to express on the level of discourse" (p. 5). For Giddens, the move from practical to discursive allows actors to more fully see and critique the social systems of which they are a part.

For those who practice discursive consciousness through making, a composing practice that I'd argue both American Indian makers and those involved in hip-hop culture embrace, there is always an attunement to relationality, process, and community. Making is done not for or by the self, but for the good of furthering the community, or as Lyons calls it, culturing. Banks (2011) engages with this idea as seen in African American rhetorical practice, and challenges an ahistorical approach to remix culture, suggesting that those who drop "the practices of the DJ, MC, or hype-wo/man in Hip Hop…into our scholarship without thorough, searching attention to the discursive and rhetorical traditions from which they emerge" run the risk of appropriation. Such practice, he argues,

> risks becoming yet another in the long line of those who have 'taken our blues and gone,' as Langston Hughes would call it, if we somehow build our theorizing on individual practices without full recognition of the people, networks, and traditions that have made the practices their gift to the broader culture.
>
> (p. 13)

Seen through the lens of American Indian thought, a reflective practitioner would be one who recognizes, as Banks says, "the people, networks, and traditions" that make up acts of composing. Such a reflective practitioner would never assume all texts are there for the taking, nor would she assume all texts are there to bend to her individual will. Instead, she would see herself as part of a network in which all things (including texts) are alive and in process, everything is related, all relationships are historical, and space and time determine the nature of relationships (Deloria, 1999). In this space, no writer or remixer is a lone genius, but instead exists in space and time and creates texts that work to solve problems, extend ideas, and further culture.

Consider this story told by Anton Treuer, an Ojibwe Language Professor at Bemidji State and member of the Leech Lake Band of Ojibwe. In a presentation on language and cultural preservation, Treuer (2012) explained the importance of raising his own children with certain traditional Ojibwe cultural rituals or rites of passage. He talked about taking his own son on his first rabbit hunt, how he taught him to kill the rabbit, give thanks for the rabbit, and then clean the rabbit. He told him of ways to tan the hide, ways to use the fur, and ways of cutting and cooking the meat and organs. This rite of passage for his pre-teen son, said Treuer, was important because, "not only did it teach him a skill, it taught him a code of ethics for being in the world." As culturing does, it produced more life. And as such, his son can now talk about that code of ethics for being in the world much more richly than he could have had he not hunted with his father in the ways he did. This act of making created a space for Treuer's son to inhabit, one of a reflective practitioner, one who considers the why and cause of what is being done and who always composes in relation to her community.

**Composing as Culturing**

Approaching writing pedagogy with a focus on fostering reflective practice and treating composing as culturing is not necessarily an easy path. As teachers, it requires we let go of excessive plagiarism fears that trap us in the role of thief catcher. It also requires us to employ a process-based pedagogy, and imagine our students not as autonomous subjects but as always being in relation to ideas, texts, and communities. We should focus less on whether digital technologies are harming or hurting our students, or are making plagiarism more rampant or easier to catch, and instead turn our attention to more impactful writing outcomes, such as whether or not an author creatively problem solves by composing a text that helps further culture. This *composing as culturing* ethic also requires we don't uncritically glom onto remix culture as a panacea for rethinking individual authorship and authenticity. If we choose to ask students to remix preexisting texts, whether in the form of a mixtape, video, visual argument, or research paper, we need to mindfully encourage students to consider the web of relations from which preexisting texts emerge and are rearticulated. To these ends, I share three outcomes crucial for embracing an American Indian ethical approach in our classrooms.

First, reflective practitioners need to be critically aware of the risk of cultural appropriation in remix. Not everything is up for grabs, or as Adam Arola and I argue, "The world is not full of concepts just waiting to be plucked from their contexts" (p. 211). Colton (2016) offers a heuristic for helping students avoid such appropriation. In short, the heuristic asks students to question "Am I wounding and/or am I caring?" Relying on feminist theory, Colton suggests that while no author can know every relation and value of a community from which a text is drawn, "attempting to discover these values and discern whether my sampling and remixing are acts of caring or wounding necessitates great empathy on my part and an acknowledgment of the deficiency of my subject position" (p. 26). Not an easy task, but one I believe is worth striving for in our pedagogies, and one that helps sustain an approaching of composing as culturing.

Second, reflective practitioners need to be critically aware that authors and texts do not exist in isolation. All of our writing exists in context, or as American Indian thinkers would say, all of our writing exists in relation. Monroe (2014), relying on Lyons, argues that "we engage in rhetorical imperialism when we naturalize academic discourse as superior, stable, and definitive, instead of advancing an understanding of the values it embodies and the people it endows" (p. 173). We must engage our students in discussions of how any text embedded in a larger discourse, be it an academic essay or an N.W.A. track or a powwow shawl, embodies the values of a people. For example, we can interrogate a track such as N.W.A.'s "Fuck Tha Police," exploring how it had very particular resonances when it emerged in 1988 versus 2015, when the N.W.A. biopic "Straight Outta Compton" was released. Recognizing that texts that come from, and speak to, certain communities at certain times, and then asking students to consider what values are upheld through such practices over time, are important questions for instilling a discursive consciousness.

Third, reflective practitioners need to be attuned to the value of both process and product. If we don't articulate the values inherent in the process of composing itself, we are missing an opportunity for critical reflection. Take for example that while it's important to know how a shawl functions in the space of a powwow, it is also important to know how that shawl is made so as to honor the relations that came before. And while we should explore the reception of "Fuck Tha Police" at different times in different settings (an approach that pays attention to the product itself and its reception in different contexts), we can also explore the process that made the track, paying attention to both the parody court proceedings in the lyrics themselves, as well as the integration of various samples including Marva Whitney's "It's My Thing" and Wilson Pickett's "Get Me Back on Time, Engine #9." These processes matter, and asking students to pay attention to them allows students to see how all texts come from specific contexts with specific relations, all laden with specific values.

Authors and texts do not exist in isolation, and both the process and product, as well as the contextual impact based on time, space, and relations, matter. An American Indian approach to writing helps us acknowledge that authenticity never lies with an individual genius, but instead lies in the relations between us all. Such a code of ethics for being in the world is one worth fostering in our writing pedagogies and practices.

## Notes

1. The majority of my personal examples come from the Anishinaabe people of the upper Great Lakes region. While it's not entirely accurate to flatten all American Indian thought under one umbrella, strains of American Indian thought, as Cordova (2007) argues, have more in common with one another than they do with the Western philosophical tradition. I proceed with the understanding that American Indian tribes are unique, however most share a deep ethical commitment to relations and the land.
2. As Howard and Watson (2010) describe, "Most of [the] historical scholarship shares the common purpose of better understanding the extent of and reasons for plagiarism. These works usually offer teachers practical advice based in better policies, better pedagogy, or better policing" (p. 117). Additionally, those engaged in plagiarism studies tend to all agree "that plagiarism in a historically, legally, and culturally shaped textual and social phenomenon." (p. 120). This scholarly work on plagiarism rarely, if ever, echoes the ways that popular discourse both within and outside of the academy function. Such popular discourses, as Pflugfelder (2009) argues, include "'[s]imple ethical admonitions,' 'thief-catching,' and talk of 'plagiarism-proof' assignments" and "are vestiges of current-traditional methods still in wide acceptance in the academy" (para. 2).
3. Composition studies has a long history of valuing process-based (and subsequent post-process based) pedagogies. Such pedagogies concern themselves with the process of composing itself.

## References

Arola, K. L., & Arola, A. C. (2017). An ethic of assemblage: Creative repetition and the 'electric pow wow.' In K. B. Yancey and S. McElroy (Eds.), *Assembling composition*. Urbana, IL: NCTE.

Banai, E. B. (2010). *The mishomis book: The voice of the Ojibway*. Minneapolis: University of Minnesota Press.

Banks, A. J. (2011). *Digital griots: African American rhetoric in a multimedia age*. Carbondale and Edwardsville, IL: Southern Illinois University Press.

Carbone, N. (2006). *Carbone, Nick (2001). "Turnitin.com, a Pedagogic Placebo for Plagiarism."* Archived from the original on October 4, 2006. Retrieved from 28 January 2007, https://web.archive.org/web/20061004205113/http://bedfordstmartins.com:80/technotes/techtiparchive/ttip060501.htm.

Colton, J. S. (2016). Revising digital sampling rhetorics with an ethics of care. *Computers and Composition, 40*(1), 19–31.

Cordova, V. F. (2007). In K. D. Moore, K. Peters, T. Jojola, & A. Lacy (Eds.), *How it is: The native American philosophy of V.F. Cordova*. Tucson: University of Arizona Press.

Crane-Bizarro, R. (2004). Shooting our last arrow: Developing a rhetoric of identity for unenrolled American Indians. *College English, 67*(1), 61–74.

Cushman, E. (2008). Toward a rhetoric of self-preservation: Identity politics in Indian country and rhetoric and composition. *College Composition and Communication, 60*(2), 321–365.

Cushman, E. (2011). *The Cherokee syllabary: Writing the people's perserverance*. Norman: University of Oklahoma Press.

Cutler, C. (2010). Plunderphonia. In C. Cox & D. Warner (Eds.), *Audio culture: Readings in modern music* (pp. 138–156). New York, NY: Continuum International Publishing Group.

Deloria, V. Jr. (1999). *Spirit & reason*. Boulder, CO: Fulcrum Publishing.

Emerson, R. W. (1904). *Quotation and originality*. Retrieved from www.emersoncentral.com/quotations.htm.

Frost, A. (2011). Literacy stewardship: Dakelh women composing culture. *College Composition and Communication, 63*(1), 54–74.

Giddens, A. (1979). *Central problems in social theory: Action, structure and contradiction in social analysis*. Berkeley: University of California Press.

Haas, A. M. (2007). Wampum as hypertext: An American Indian intellectual tradition of multimedia theory and practice. *Studies in American Indian Literatures*, *19*(4), 77–100.

Haas, A. M. (2010). Making online spaces more native to American Indians: A digital diversity recommendation. *Computers and Composition Online*. Retrieved November 27, 2013 from www.bgsu.edu/departments/english/cconline/Haas/.

Howard, R. M., & Watson, M. (2010). The scholarship of plagiarism: Where we've been, where we are, what's needed next. *Writing Program Administration*, *33*(3), 116–124.

iThenticate. iThenticate: Software to verify the originality of written work. Retrieved from http://vpue.wsu.edu/iThenticate/.

Johnson-Eilola, J., & Selber, S. (2007). Plagiarism, originality, assemblage. *Computers and Composition*, *24*(4), 375–403.

Johnson, R. R. (1998). *User-centered technology: A rhetorical theory for computers and other mundane artifacts*. Albany: State University of New York Press.

King, L., Gubele, R., & Anderson, J. R. (2015). *Survivance, sovereignty, and story: Teaching American Indian rhetorics*. Boulder, CO: Utah State University Press.

Lyons, S. R. (2000). Rhetorical sovereignty: What do American Indians want from writing? *College Composition and Communication*, *51*(3), 447–468.

Lyons, S. R. (2010). *X-marks: Native signatures of assent*. Minneapolis: University of Minnesota Press.

Miller, P. E. (2004). *Rhythm science*. Cambridge, MA: MIT.

Monroe, B. (2014). *Plateau Indian ways with words: The rhetorical tradition of the tribes of the inland Pacific Northwest*. Pittsburgh, PA: University of Pittsburgh Press.

Pflugfelder, E. H. (2009). Review Essay of *Originality, imitation, and plagiarism: Teaching writing in the digital age*, Eds. C. Eisner & M. Vicinus, *Pluralizing plagiarism: Identities, contexts, pedagogies*, Eds. R. M. Howard & A. E. Robillard, and *Plagiarism: Alchemy and remedy in higher education*, Ed. B. Marsh. *Composition Forum*, *19*: n.pag. Web. 15 February 2016.

Powell, M. (2002). Rhetorics of survivance: How American Indians use writing. *College Composition and Communication*, *53*(3), 396–434.

Powell, M. (2004). Down by the river, or how Susan LaFlesche can teach us about alliance as a practice of survivance. *College English*, *67*(1), 38–60.

Powell, M. (2012). Stories take place: A performance in one act. *College Composition and Communication*, *64*(2), 383–406.

Rice, J. (2003). The 1963 hip-hop machine: Hip-hop pedagogy as composition. *College Composition and Communication*, *54*(3), 453–471.

Ridolfo, J, & Devoss, D. N. (2009). Composing for recomposition: Rhetorical velocity and delivery. *Kairos: A Journal of Rhetoric, Technology, and Pedagogy*, *13*(2): n.pag. Retrieved on 29 August 2015.

Sirc, G. (2002). *English composition as a happening*. Logan: Utah State University Press.

Sirc, G. (2006). Proust, death, and hip hop in first-year composition. *Teaching English in the Two-Year College*, *33*(4), 392–398.

Treuer, A. (2012, April 12). *Anishiinaabemowin mashkawendamang: Ojibwe language and cultural revitalization*. American Indian Society for Engineers and Scientists Region V Conference, Houghton, MI.

Turnitin.com. Retrieved from June 5, 2015, www.turnitin.com.

Vie, S. (2013). Turn it down, don't Turnitin: Resisting plagiarism detection services by talking about plagiarism rhetorically. *Computers and Composition Online*. Retrieved from www2.bgsu.edu/departments/english/cconline/spring2013_special_issue/Vie/history.html.

Williams, B. T. (2014). From screen to screen: Students' use of popular culture genres in multimodal writing assignments. *Computers and Composition*, *34*, 110–121.

# 23
# Aesthetics and Text in the Digital Age

Theo van Leeuwen

## The Return of Aesthetics

Medieval writing was richly decorated with initials, marginal elements, and miniature pictures and burnished with gold and silver, a source of aesthetic pleasure as well as an expression of the greater glory of God and the valor of knights and kings (cf. Eco, 2002). But from the sixteenth century onward, aesthetics and meaning began to part ways. The philosopher and rhetorician Peter Ramus (1511–1572) simplified Aristotelian rhetoric by separating meaning ("invention," "disposition," and "memory") from artful expression ("elocutio" and "delivery"), "a division whose implications remain with us to this day" (Hawkes, 1972, p. 22). The printed page became black and white. And Protestantism reacted against the Medieval love of colorful decoration by favoring plain clothes, plain churches, and plain language: "'Plaine delivery' of the word was the aim, 'painted eloquence' the enemy" (Hawkes, 1972, p. 28).

This separation of aesthetic pleasure and meaning left its traces in twentieth-century linguistics and semiotics. Mukarovsky influentially defined the aesthetic as foregrounding expression, causing expression to draw attention to itself, and thereby backgrounding content, creating "semantic emptiness" (Mukarovsky, 1964a [1932], p. 20). Jakobson similarly defined the "poetic function" of language as foregrounding form over meaning, though he did add that "it would be an unsound oversimplification to treat rhyme only from the standpoint of sound. Rhyme necessarily involves the semantic relationship between rhythmic units" (Jakobson, 1960, p. 368). And while the Prague school still had a place for the "aesthetic function," in Hallidayan functional linguistics (e.g., Halliday, 1994), the aesthetic disappears, and "form follows function." The human ability to play with language, to create rhymes and other parallelisms, no longer played a role here in understanding language and its uses, whether in relation to meaning or not.

The separation of aesthetic pleasure and meaning also left its traces on twentieth-century writing practices. Literary works were to be appreciated for their form and style, other forms of writing, such as journalism and bureaucratic language, for their functionality. Already in 1915, Reuters advocated "compressing news into minute globules" to condense news stories to their essential information-transferring function (Palmer, 1998, p. 184). A study of an English language Vietnamese newspaper showed how the Western subeditors who introduced this style to local journalists discouraged the wordplay and poetic flourishes which were prized by the Vietnamese journalists (Machin & van Leeuwen, 2007).

Yet, at the same time, advertising and branding had already begun to reintroduce aesthetics into everyday functional communication, to play with language in multimodal and creative ways, exploiting the affordances of typography and color, appealing to pleasure, and often transgressing linguistic norms (for instance, spelling rules) as well as social norms (for instance, through sexual allusions). Today, digital writing technologies such as Word and PowerPoint go to great length to encourage computer users to aestheticize their writing. Word templates for functional writing genres such as invitations, invoices, company brochures, and course assignments all focus on presentation, on visual style, on the use of illustrations, diagrams, layout, color, and typography, rather than on content and meaning. PowerPoint, similarly, offers a wide range of decorative designs to adorn a much more limited set of textual patterns such as "title plus list of bullet points"—from abstract patterns to tranquil seascapes and soft focus rust-colored autumn leaves, and from Bauhaus-inspired motifs in red and black to late nineteenth-century flower flourishes. We have come a long way from the uniformity of the typewriter and the densely-printed page. Aesthetics has returned.

For education this raises two issues. First, contemporary workplace literacy not only requires the ability to write good English and to master genres such as forms and applications, proposals and reports, but also the ability to write in a way that engages the reader affectively and expresses the values of the organization. It is true that today's young people are "digital natives" and thoroughly familiar with contemporary entertainment genres and styles. But with these workplace genres and their aesthetic requirements they will be less familiar, and the trajectory toward mastering them should perhaps begin well before they actually enter the workplace. A good start was made with the "Language of Administration," research that was part of the Disadvantaged Schools Project in Australia in the 1990s (Iedema, 1992), but this work now needs to be moved into the multimodal age.

Second, if education is to instill values as well as useful skills, it should foster a critical attitude toward these new forms of writing. Just as Medieval communication used aesthetics to communicate theological and chivalrous concepts and values, so contemporary digital communication integrates aesthetic pleasure with the values and interests of global corporate culture, whether in the form of personal lifestyle identities or in the form of corporate branding. Recognizing this is not a nostalgic rejection of digital technology, but can contribute to its discerning use, and toward the ability to be in charge of writing technologies for creating one's own designs as opposed to letting the technologies take charge.

## The New Writing

This section demonstrates some of the multimodal features of newer forms of aesthetic writing, which extends beyond a reliance on spacing and typography. Consistent with changes to the centrality of typography in books, websites, and other digital media, the multimodal texts examined here demonstrate how the prominence of language alone has receded, with important relations between the use of images and written language. Figure 23.1 shows a now yellowed page from the textbook from which I learned Latin in the Netherlands, in the early 1960s. The Latin textbook uses complex clauses to explain the grammar of "irrealis" moods: "The use of the imperfect in 2a, in Dutch as well as in Latin, may seem strange at first sight. Yet it is understandable. When one uses the past in a wish that relates to the present, one expresses, as it were, that it is too late for the wish to be fulfilled: the wish becomes 'irreal.'" The text is also multimodal. It does not rely on words alone, but also uses spacing and typography (italics and bolding)—to separate the headings from the text, the examples with which each section starts from their explanations, and so on. But it is not an aesthetic text, unless, perhaps, for typographers with a fine eye for the subtleties of different fonts.

2. niet meer voor vervulling vatbaar („irreële" (¹) wens).

In geval 1 gebruikt het Lat. de coniunct. **praesentis,** soms voorafgegaan door *utinam* „och!".

In geval 2 gebruikt het Lat. voor het **heden** de coniunct. **imperfecti,** voor het **verleden** de coniunct. **plusquamperfecti,** beide altijd voorafgegaan door **utinam.**

De ontkenning is **ne.**

N.B. 1. Het gebruik van het imperfectum in 2a, zowel in het Ned. als in het Lat., lijkt op het eerste gezicht vreemd. Toch is het begrijpelijk. Wanneer men in een wens, die betrekking heeft op het heden, een verleden tijd gebruikt, geeft men hiermee als het ware te kennen, dat het voor de vervulling te laat is: de wens wordt irreëel.

2. *Utinam* (= *ut*(*i*) + *nam*) betekent eigenlijk „hoe toch!"; *ut*(*i*) is nl. van oorsprong een adverbium van wijze: „hoe". Dus: *utinam veniat* eig. „hoe moge hij toch komen!", „hoe (wat) hoop ik toch, dat hij komt!".
*Ut* alleen leidt slechts zelden een wens in.

## Mogelijkheid

**110. (coniunctivus potentialis)**

1. *a.* **Aliquis dicat, dixerit**   Iemand zou kunnen zeggen
   *b.* **Diceres, crederes**   Men (*eig.*: je) had kunnen zeggen, geloven

Behalve in een werkelijke wens, wordt de (wens)coniunctivus ook gebruikt om een „mogelijkheid" uit te drukken: **coniunctivus potentialis** (vgl. *possum* = ik kan).

De Nederlandse vertaling gebruikt de hulpwerkwoorden „zullen" of (en) „kunnen".

Voor het **heden** (*a*) gebruikt het Lat. de coniunct. **praesentis** of **perfecti** (vgl. § 106, N.B.), voor het **verleden** (*b*) de coniunct. **imperfecti** (niet plusq. perf., zoals het Ned.!).

De ontkenning is **non.**

---

(¹) „irreëel" = onwerkelijk

Figure 23.1 Page from van der Heyde (1958, p. 79)

288 • Theo van Leeuwen

**ACCESSNSW**

**Event planning resource for Sydney and NSW**

- Professional, unbiased advice
- Time saving — we do the leg work for you
- FREE Service
- Events from 50 – 500 people
    o Conferences
    o Cocktail events
    o Breakfast/Lunch/Dinner
    o Seminars
    o Team Building

BUSINESS EVENTS SYDNEY

**Figure 23.2** Slide from a PowerPoint presentation

Turning to a more contemporary text, Figure 23.2 is a slide from a presentation by an event-organizing company associated with the City of Sydney. This text takes multimodality much further, integrating solid blocks of color and icons. The audience consisted of senior academics. With the exception of "We do the leg work for you," there are, again, no clauses, only nominal groups. The coherence that is normally created by verbs or verbal groups and by linguistic cohesion systems such as ellipsis, reference, and conjunction, is now achieved visually: the bullet points tells us that the bullet-pointed items form a list; the heading that it is a list of "event planning resources." The "white bullets" then form another list, and the frame around the whole, with the name of the company set against a reassuringly blue color with a faint outline of the Sydney Opera House, conveys that it is Access NSW which provides these resources.

Clauses combine ideational and interpersonal meaning. The clause "we do the leg work for you" not only informs the listener about the services of Access NSW, it also offers these services and relates the writer ("we") to the reader ("for you"). But the rest of the slide contains no clauses, and therefore no interpersonal meanings. The interpersonal has moved to the speech that accompanies the slide, which is replete with "we's" and "you's" and show the presenter's understanding of who the audience is ("professors and academics") and what their interests and concerns are ("those colleagues that are so important to you and your research"):

We are a joint venture between the State Government and our stakeholders and members in Sydney and what we aim to do is to bring business events to Sydney. So we...eighty % of what the organization does is bids for major international events and congresses that come into Sydney. So we have a whole lot of teams that work with your University. We come here to explain our services to some of the professors and academics. We're free. We can help you put together bids and information and bring the colleagues from overseas for all those meetings that are so important to your work and to your academic research.

In short, there is a division of labor between the semiotic modes involved: the mode of language provides bits of information; the visual mode unites these bits of information into a coherent whole; and the spoken word provides the interpersonal element. As a result the various semiotic modes can no longer stand on their own, nor can the slide as a whole, which, for its interpretation, needs to be embedded in a communicative practice, the presentation. More than 50 years ago, in a classic essay on text-image relations, Roland Barthes called this kind of relation as a "relay," a relation in which "text and image stand in a complementary relationship" (1977, p. 41), and he thought that it was mainly confined to comic strips, where the pictures show the speakers and the texts reveal what they say. Today, this kind of relation is much more common, and also extends to the relation between a text and the context in which it is used.

Figure 23.3 shows an Excel sheet. It was tabled at a university management meeting, as part of an agenda item aimed at determining the external research funding targets Faculty Deans should achieve. In the boxes we find, again, only nominal groups, and no clauses, and the "syntax" that makes these nominal groups cohere is, again, visual—the structure of the table, in which rows list related items and columns their attributes. If I attempt to "translate" the table into linear text, I might get something like this:

> The Key Performance Indicator 'Grant Application Success' is the responsibility of the PVC (Research). Success is measured as the percentage of national competitive grants received by a particular agency or scheme. To set a target, historical performance is taken into account, and the previous year's results are taken as a baseline. If, say, the percentage of ARC Discovery grants was 1.44 and the percentage of ARC linkage grants 3.89 in 2004, and if the percentages were 2.01 and 4.00 in 2005, then the 2006 threshold targets should tentatively be 2.00 and 4.00 respectively.

What did I have to *add* to make this "translation" work? Two things in particular: (1) the speech acts involved, the fact that KPIs are mandatory, something Deans *should* strive for, and (2) the logical relations: *(in order) to* (set a target), *if ... then*, and so on. In diagrams, logical relations become implicit. Before the rise of science, logical relations tended to be implicit in language as well: *and* was used as a kind of all-purpose link (Milic, 1970, p. 244). But from the sixteenth century on, new words were invented to make such links explicit, particularly in scientific writing. As John Locke said at the time, "To express methodical and rational thoughts, a man must have words to show what connexion, restriction, distinction, opposition, emphasis...he gives to each respective part of his discourse" (1972 [1706], p. 72). Should we start the same process with diagrams or do we no longer need or want explicit logical relations?

R3 | SAMPLE "BUSINESS AS USUAL" FACULTY TARGETS - BUSINESS FACULTY | (NOTE FINAL TARG

| A | B | C | D | E | F | L | M | N |
|---|---|---|---|---|---|---|---|---|
| SUMMARY REPORT | PERFORMANCE DOMAIN: RESEARCH | | | | | | | |
| | | UTS HISTORICAL PERFORMANCE | | | | | UTS FUTURE PERFORMANCE | |
| KPI REF NO. | KPI TITLE | KPI METRIC | SPONSOR | PREVIOUS RESULT (usually 2003) | BASELINE RESULT (usually 2004) | TARGET TYPE T=Threshold I=Improvement | 2005 TARGET | 2006 TARGET (TENTATIVE) |
| | | | | | | | | |
| R1 | Grant application success | % of national competitive grants received by agency and scheme | PVC (Research) | ARC DISCOVERY: 1.44% (2004) ARC LINKAGE: 3.89% (2004) | ARC DISCOVERY: 2.01% (2005) ARC LINKAGE: 4.00% (2005) | T | ARC DISCOVERY: 2.00% (ACTUAL) ARC LINKAGE: 4.00% (ACTUAL) | ARC DISCOVERY: 2.00% ARC LINKAGE: 4.00% |
| | | % of Category 1 Income from non-ARC funds | | 34% | 35% (TARGET) | I | 37% (21% NHMRC, 16% OTHER) | 39% (22% NHMRC, 17% OTHER) |
| R2 | Research commercialisation outcomes | No. of IP disclosures made & provisional patents filed | PVC (Research) | IP DISCLOSURES: 7 PROVISIONAL PATENTS: 1 | IP DISCLOSURES: 28 PROVISIONAL PATENTS: 7 | I (beyond 2005) | IP DISCLOSURES: 10 PROVISIONAL PATENTS: 10 STRETCH | IP DISCLOSURES: 11 PROVISIONAL PATENTS: 5 |
| | | $ commercial income (trade sales, start up dividends, royalties, licence fees, IP assignments, licensing and sales) - 3 yr moving average | | n/a | $75,879 | I | $91,055 | $109,266 |

**Figure 23.3** Detail of an Excel chart from a management meeting

Two further aspects of the "new writing" need to be mentioned. First, as new writing is so often embedded in interactive social practices, its meanings may be influenced by interactive dynamics and social pressure, by the need for social harmony, for "bonding." For this reason formerly impersonal, formal genres are everywhere becoming more personal and reactions more emotionally motivated, e.g., in political elections, where judgment is increasingly based on "likes" and "dislikes," just as in Facebook (which recently introduced five new reactions "to give you more ways to share your reaction to a post in a quick and easy way" (Facebook, 2016)—all of them emotive: "love," "haha," "wow," "sad," and "angry").

And, second, the new writing presents increasingly homogeneous functional structures, with increasingly varied styles which harness aesthetics to the purpose of expressing identity. In the case of PowerPoint, for instance, the "title plus bullet-pointed list" structure is ubiquitous and used for many different kinds of presentation, but it can be aesthetically dressed up in many different ways. A university finance director presented the year's financial results at a management meeting, using a calm sea with a blue sky as the background for his figures, and interlarding the figures from time to time with quotes from business gurus. Such stylistic choices signify identity—whether the identity of the presenter (who, in this case, perhaps wanted to present himself as both a good accountant and a visionary) or a corporate identity.

Another example is from a segment entitled "How to Erase Your Dating Mistake" (2004) in *Cosmopolitan* magazine in which the following advice appears within a solid-colored text box:

> Apologize ASAP. Own up to your gaffe by saying 'I was so nervous/temporarily brain dead, I ended up doing something out of character.' Your confession shows that you recognize your boobish behavior…

This initial advice, with the words "Apologize ASAP" emphasized in bold font, is followed by step two, abbreviated here:

> Make it up to him by showing your true colors. For example, if you barked his ear off the night before with a long list of personal problems, spend the next couple of dates subtly encouraging him to do most of the talking…

Again, the opening phrase "Make it up to him" is also highlighted in bold for clarity. Step three is called "Play it Cool":

> Wait a week, then assess where you stand. If your union is back on track…thumbs up. But if he seems iffy about hanging out…you might have to concede defeat and move on.

The basic structure of the text cited above is as follows:

Task (erasing a mistake)
↓
Problem (mistake)
↓
Solution (smooth over)
↓
Step 1 (apologize)
↓
Step 2 (make it up)
↓
Step 3 (play it cool)

This schema represents the text as a problem-solution advice genre, and as a template that can be applied to many other problems. In *Cosmopolitan,* it is also used for health problems, beauty problems, career problems, sexual problems, and so on, and to an even wider range of solutions. The same problem may have different solutions in the different versions of the magazine, for instance in North European versus East Asian versions (cf. Machin & van Leeuwen, 2007). The elements of this genre, and the structure in which they are brought together, are multimodally realized. The "task," the "problem," and its "solution," and the "steps" are spatially separated and have distinct fonts and colors. Machin and I (Machin & van Leeuwen, 2007) have called it the "hot tips" genre. It can be found in all the 42 versions of the magazine we looked at and always has the same basic structure. However, its multimodal realization shows many variations—in the color schemes and typography used, in the presence or absence of pictures (which are often used to represent the problem), and so on.

This is the logic of the new writing: Increasingly global and homogeneous functional structures combine with increasingly differentiated styles that creatively use the aesthetic affordances of layout, color, and graphic form to realize identity, whether personal or corporate (branding). Digital writing technologies such as Word and PowerPoint are designed to facilitate precisely this form of communication, both through their standardized templates and through the myriad of multimodal options they offer.

To summarize:

- The pages and screens of the new writing are multimodal.
- The lexicon may still be linguistic but syntax and textual coherence are realized visually.
- The interpersonal aspects of language diminish or disappear and logical relations become implicit.
- The resulting written texts can no longer be read aloud and must be embedded in social practices or simulations thereof, and are therefore mediated by group dynamics and the affects that attend it.
- New writing combines functional structures (genres) with aesthetic expressions of identity, with the former realizing use values and becoming increasingly global and standardized, and the latter realizing identities and becoming increasingly diversified and creative.

**The New Literacy**

Is the new literacy needed for the "new writing" built into the software, so that we do not need to learn it, just as we perhaps no longer need to learn to spell, to add up, to read a map, and so on? The answer is no. The software provides the resources but not the insight needed to use them effectively. Just as video editing software cannot tell where to place edits to make the story work, so writing software cannot tell us how to use multimodality to make our writing work. In this section I will focus on the aesthetic dimension and briefly review the key skills needed to make functional communication work aesthetically and aesthetic communication functional.

*Composition*

Composition involves the arrangement of the functional elements of the text on the page or the screen. In the 1958 Latin textbook (Figure 23.1), these elements were the section headings, the key examples, the distinct (numbered) explanations, and the footnotes. In the Cosmopolitan magazine dating advice discussed earlier in the chapter, these elements were the task, the problem and its solution, and the "steps." The spatial arrangement of such functional text elements involves three separate but integrated aspects: placement, framing, and salience, and it is especially the latter two which open up aesthetic possibilities.

- *Placement*

  Kress and van Leeuwen (2006) discuss the key dimensions of pages and screens: left and right, top and bottom, and center and margin. These locations, they claim, accord specific values to the text elements that are placed in them. If an element is placed on the left, it will be understood as the Given, as a familiar point of departure for the message; if it is placed on the right as the New, as something not yet familiar to the reader or viewer, and hence as important to pay attention to. If an element is placed on top, it will be understood as the Ideal, the generalized or idealized essence of the message; if at the bottom as the Real, as more specific or practical information. The central element of center-margin compositions, finally, will be understood as the core of the message, and the elements placed around it as complementary to that central element, or associated with it in some other sense.

- *Framing*

  The term "framing" denotes the degree to which the functional text elements are presented as visually connected or separate. Separation can be realized in many different ways, by actual frame lines, as in the case of text boxes, by spacing, as in the case of the Latin textbook, or by contrasts of color and typography. Connection can be suggested by similarities or color or typography ("visual rhymes"), as in the case of the "steps" in the dating advice, which appeared in within a solid color text box. The use of the term "rhyme" already suggests the aesthetic potential of framing, its ability to create parallelisms (see below). But, again, the effect will be functional as well as aesthetic. Different forms of framing will also create different meanings, as discussed in van Leeuwen (2005, p. 6ff).

- *Salience*

  Degrees of salience allow the functional text elements to draw attention to different degrees. This can, again, be done in many different ways, through size, boldness, foregrounding, sharper focus, eye-catching colors, and so on, opening up aesthetic possibilities and, at the same time, subtle differences in meaning. As digital writing technologies make it easy to play with these parameters, the effect of different types of salience can be discovered experimentally, by seeing what happens when they are applied, and reflecting on the results, both from the point of view of aesthetics and from the point of view of meaning.

Figure 23.4 shows the home page of the website of the University of York's Conference Centre. The name of the Centre is treated as Given and the Centre's mission ("Engage, Inspire, Innovate") is New. Yet, the Given is more salient, especially the word "hub." The design of the whole, in a vivid ochre, has yellow circles surrounding the "hub," and lines which converge to the center and create an ovoid shape, pointing to the right and framing the name of the Centre, thus visually representing it as "a melting pot for engagement" and "designed to encourage discussion." The name of the Centre is in fact placed slightly off-center, toward the left, pointing toward a future in which there is ample space for "engagement, inspiration and innovation." Color and abstract graphic shapes may at first appear mere decoration but in fact play a key role in communicating the identity of the Ron Cooke Hub.

## Color

The return of aesthetics was also a return of color, with the dreary colors of public transport and the black of motor cars (for a long time Henry Ford only produced black cars) making place for brighter

**Figure 23.4** Website of University of York Conference Centre

colors, and magazines, photographs, films, and newspapers one by one abandoning black and white and moving to color. In the digital age, color has replaced the austerity of type-written and densely printed documents with the visuality of the new writing, accessible to anyone with a computer. But color does not only make our world more bright and beautiful, it also opens up new meaning potentials. What can colors (and color schemes) communicate? Sometimes very precise meanings pertaining to a limited semantic domain, as with the colors of national flags or of maps of urban rail systems. Sometimes easily recognizable cultural references such the combination of purple and gold as an indicator of prestige and value, even on cheap chocolate boxes, or the green of organic products, even on the BP logo. But at other times color meanings are quite open and context-dependent. Take the color black, to which the French art historian Michel Pastoureau (2008) devoted a whole book. Depending on the context, it can mean seriousness and severity, death and misadventure ("a black day"), provocation, hate and aggression ("black shirts," "black flags"), sadness and depression ("a black mood"), fear (e.g., in "film noir"), and elegance or opulence ("the black tuxedo," "the little black dress," "the arthouse film"). Nevertheless, there is always a reason connecting the signifier with the signified. Yes, black can remind of darkness and the night, but it can also be interpreted as *not* being a color, as negating or suppressing the more extroverted emotionality of vivid color, and therefore as "restrained" or "modest." And its association with darkness can lead in different directions—to fearful things happening during the night or evil things that "cannot bear the light of day." The color of Figure 23.4 is a vivid ochre, becoming darker and somewhat browner toward the edges, and lighter and somewhat yellower toward the center. The circles are yellow and vary in intensity. The temperature and intensity of the colors signify energy, the "melting pot" idea, but it would be equally valid to see it as a sunrise, a beginning. There is an open, yet by no means unlimited range of possible associations, and context is fundamental—in Australia, the same colors might signify the red earth and be associated with the pigments of Aboriginal art.

To understand such meaning potentials, and to open them up for aesthetic expression, we need to pay attention, not only to hue, to whether the color is red or blue or green, for instance, but to a range of qualities that combine to define specific colors and color schemes, and all contribute to the aesthetic effect as well as the meaning. They will be briefly reviewed below (see van Leeuwen, 2011a, for a fuller discussion).

*Value*

Value is the scale from light to dark. The difference between light and dark is a fundamental human experience and can give rise to many associations, in which light often carries positive and dark negative values. But that can be reversed. White can also be the color of "bloodless" death and ghostly things and black the color of elegant dresses and luxury items.

*Saturation*

Saturation is the scale from intense to pale, from, for instance, the fullest red to a grey in which just a tinge of redness remains. Whatever meanings are built on this, saturation will always involve degrees of intensity. But a lessening of intensity need not be negative—it can also suggest modesty and restraint.

*Purity*

Purity is the scale from maximum purity to maximal "mixedness" or "hybridity." Impure colors are colors that belie description, colors we can only describe as, for instance, "a slightly reddish green," or a "bluish purple." Thus impurity, in context, can suggests a mixture of what these colors stand for, and also the idea of hybridity or ambiguity, and purity its opposite.

*Luminosity, Luster, and Luminescence*

Colors that have brilliance, that glow from within without emanating from an actual light source are said to be luminous. Whatever precise meaning this acquires in context, it will always bestow a quality of radiance or glowing, for whatever more precise reason—glowing with health, pride, glory, and so on, for instance. Closely related, but not quite the same, is luster, the scale from matte to shiny, which can also create radiance, and which, through the ages, has been associated with luxury and opulence. This again differs from luminescence, colors that are actually created by light sources. These have always existed, but are of increasing importance in our age of the vibrant colors of neon lights and television and computer screens.

*Modulation*

Modulation is the scale from flat, plain color to varied tints and shades. While plain color is even and unchanging, modulated color varies, usually irregularly, in brightness, saturation, purity, and so on. Depending on the context, this can be seen as subtle and nuanced, or as fussy, or smudgy, just as plain color can be seen as basic and unrealistic, or as bringing out the essence and spirit of a color. The colors in Figure 23.4 are modulated and this makes them less schematic and abstract, as though they have been affected by some kind of natural process.

*Temperature*

Temperature is the scale from warm to cold, as expressed by hue—the scale from red to blue. Our experience tells us that red can always be associated with energy—whether it is the red of passion or the red of danger or any other red, and blue with its opposite, with some form of relaxation or serenity.

*Differentiation*

Differentiation is the scale form monochrome to the use of a maximal varied range of different colors, which is therefore more a feature of color schemes than of individual colors (though all the color qualities I have discussed can characterize either individual colors or color schemes). And whatever differentiation can come to mean in a given context, it will always convey some kind of abundance—the context will then refine this.

Parameters of this kind have now become part of the color resources of digital writing software, making it easy to make colors lighter or darker, softer or more vivid, warmer or colder, more or less monochrome, and so on, and hence to manipulate the emotive effect of the new writing.

### *Typography and Graphic Design*

Digital technology also offers a wide choice of fonts and abstract graphic forms, whether in background patterns or in decorative items such as the lines that separate title and content on PowerPoint slides. To explore the aesthetic meaning potential of such resources it is, again, important to pay attention to their qualities. I will review them briefly below (see also van Leeuwen, 2006, 2011b).

#### *Weight*

Weight refers to the scale from bold, heavy lines to light lines. Both letter forms and abstract graphic shapes can be bold or light. Bold shapes can be assertive or daring, solid and substantial, light shapes more timid or insubstantial. But lightness can also be elegant or subtle, and boldness overbearing and domineering. It depends on the context, and on the way these meanings are valued in that context.

#### *Expansion*

Expansion refers to a scale that runs from maximally condensed to maximally expansive—from narrow, compressed shapes, closely huddled together, to expansive and widely spaced shapes or letterforms. Its meaning potential derives from our experience of space, and from the values we attach to different kinds of spaces. Maximally condensed forms make maximal use of limited space, packing the available space with content, so to speak. Expansion provides room to move, room to breathe, but can also become empty and alienating. The use of expansion may be related to the readers who are addressed. The covers of popular magazines, for instance, are packed with content and cheap restaurants pile the food on the plate, while the covers of elite magazines leave large areas blank and expensive restaurants serve small delicacies on large plates.

#### *Slope*

In typography, slope refers to the difference between cursive, "script"—like typefaces and upright typefaces. Even when a cursive typeface does not evoke a particular era, sloping scripts will remind of handwriting and upright scripts of printing, which can suggest the handmade versus the machine-made, the authentic and individual versus the mass-produced replica. Sloping shapes are also gravitationally unstable, which gives them a latent energy that can express some form of dynamism, as in many of the constructivist designs of the 1920s.

#### *Curvature*

Curvature refers to the degree to which a shape is angular or curved, rounded. Our understanding of his derives in part from our experience of trace making, of writing and drawing. We know that producing straight, angular forms requires brisk, decisive movements, and round forms a more gradual, fluid control of movement. But it can also be based on our experiential and cultural associations with essentially round or essentially angular objects. Human-made technological objects are often angular, and this may signify rationality, functionality, technological precision, and so on, while roundness can be smooth, soft, natural, organic, maternal, and so on (though we should not forget that sharp, spiky forms exist in nature as well). Clearly the field of possibilities is wide, but it is not limitless, and it will of course be narrowed down by the context in which curvature appears.

*Connectivity*

Connectivity refers to whether graphic shapes are connected or separate and self-contained. In typography it is associated with handwriting, and it shares much of its meaning potential with "slope." But it can also apply to abstract graphic shapes. External disconnection—disconnection between the different shapes in a design, forms—can suggest some form of atomization or fragmentation, and external connection wholeness or integration, belonging together. Internal disconnection, disconnection between the parts of a shape may look unfinished and sloppy—or easy-going. Internal connection may look neat and finished—or formal and buttoned up.

*Orientation*

Orientation refers to the degree to which graphic forms are either oriented toward the horizontal axis, by being comparatively flattened, or toward the vertical axis, stretching upwards and/or downwards. The meaning potential of this is ultimately based on our experience of gravity and of walking upright. Horizontal orientation can be solid and well grounded (no chance of toppling over), while vertical orientation can suggest upwards aspiration but also instability.

*Regularity*

Many forms have deliberate irregularities, such as ragged edges, distressed textures, or irregularities between repeated forms, e.g., between different occurrences of a given letter in the same text. This can be based on our experience of trace making, or on cultural connotation. Irregularity can signify the hand-made, hence the individual and the authentic, and regularity machine-like perfection. Again, irregularity can suggest a refusal or inability to produce neat, regular forms, hence rebellion, deviance, or disability, and regularity compliance, normality, and graphic skill. Irregularity can also suggest "out of the box thinking," playfulness and caprice. Its ubiquity, also in computer-generated designs, where, on closer inspection, irregularities may have their own regularities, shows the importance of these values in contemporary communication.

All these qualities will combine in different proportions in any letter form or graphic sign, so creating an endless range of aesthetic possibilities. The options created by digital writing technologies, on the other hand are not endless, and limited by what the software designers have decided to include.

The font in Figure 23.5 is not only colorful (maximal differentiation), but also bold, relatively expansive and somewhat irregular. It is therefore often used on invitations for children's birthday parties, the covers of books for young children, the logos of toy companies such as Toys "R" Us and so on, to express the exuberance and playfulness of childhood.

**Figure 23.5** "Childish" font

*Parallelism*

Parallelism, whether metrical, phonological or syntactical, is part of the stock in trade of literary stylistics. To borrow some examples from Leech (1969), in "Where wealth accumulates and men decay" (a quote from Oliver Goldsmith) there is syntactic similarity between "wealth accumulates" and "men decay" and in "I kissed thee 'ere I killed thee" (from *Othello*), there is syntactical as well as phonological similarity between "kissed" and "killed." The many forms of parallelism have been named and catalogued as rhetorical "schemes" and include rhyme and alliteration, anaphora (the repetition of a word or phrase at the beginning of subsequent portions of text), epistrophe (the repetition of a word or phrase at the end of particular portions of text), chiasmus (the juxtaposition of phrases which are each other's inverse, as in "never let a fool kiss you nor a kiss fool you"), antithesis (the putting together of opposite ideas, as in "speech is silver, silence is gold"), and so on.

But parallelism is rarely a matter of form alone. Formal identity or similarity signifies identity or similarity of content, and formal contrast signifies contrast of content. The meaning potential of parallelism is therefore based on three possible relations, identity, similarity, and contrast, often in complex ways, because similarity and difference may well go together to create more complex meanings. The same types of parallelism have been studied in poetics as a matter of form, and in rhetoric in relation to their communicative function of getting messages across in a concise and memorable form. It was again in advertising that these two strands came together, merging aesthetics with communicative functionality, and for this reason parallelism is a key aspect of the language of advertising and other forms of persuasive speech and writing, as noted by Cook (1992), who quotes, for instance, an advertisement for SHE magazine: "SHE is a woman and a lover/SHE is a worker and a mother/SHE is the magazine for women who juggle their lives."

Parallelism can also be visual. Durand (1970) systematically showed that all the rhetorical figures described by classical and Renaissance theorists have visual equivalents (see also Dyer, 1982, Chapter 8). An ad for a particular kind of long finger-like biscuit depicted the biscuit next to a finger—a visual rhyme; an ad for detergent showed a man dressed in pristine white on top of a heap of coal—a visual antithesis; and so on. All the aspects of color and of graphic form I have discussed can be repeated, compared, and contrasted. And symmetry in composition—giving different elements the same size, the same distance from each other, the same orientation to the vertical and horizontal axis, and so on—will not only create an aesthetic effect, but also signify that these elements belong to the same category, while dissymmetry and mirroring will have the opposite effect. In short, parallelism works regardless of whether the elements are words, abstract graphic forms, or pictorial elements. And only when visual parallelism is employed in tandem with the meaning potentials of composition, form, color, and texture, can the creative potential of aesthetics find its full expression.

Clearly this is, again, a key aspect of new writing literacy which can be experimented with exploring similarities and contrasts between the formal qualities of different modes, and reflecting on their aesthetic and rhetorical effect.

## *Provenance*

In Kress and van Leeuwen (2001, pp. 10, 12), we defined "provenance" as the introduction into a particular context, of signifiers from another context (another era, another social group, another culture), to signify the ideas and values associated with that other context by the context which "imports" the sign from the other context. Meaning is therefore based on provenance, on "where the signifier comes from." This can for instance play a role in the case of color. We can recognize the combination of purple and gold as a "royal" color combination—purple dyes were once a highly precious material in Ancient Persia and Rome as more than 10,000 murex shellfish had to be crushed to make a single gram. But even when we are not aware of this, we recognize the color scheme as a signifier of prestige. The same principle can be applied to typography and graphic form. The irregular and colorful font in Figure 23.5 can immediately be "placed," even when we encounter it in a context that does not relate to young children. The Google logo, for instance, uses the same range colors as Figure 23.5 (red, yellow, blue, and green) to suggest values that are often related to children and childhood—playfulness, not (yet) sticking to the rules, creativity, exuberance.

Provenance plays a role in language too. For Mukarovsky (1964b [1940], pp. 338–339) archaisms, "foreign expressions," "dialect words," and "the intermingling of standard with folk speech, of written with conversational speech" have an aesthetic effect as they can disrupt the "automatization" of the "standard language" and draw attention to language itself—but they of course also introduce the ideas and values associated with the period from which the archaisms come, the groups which speak the dialects, and so on. Leech (1968, p. 57), too, recognized this as an important aspect of poetics and used an example from *John Lennon in His Own Write*: "Henry was his father's son and it were time for him to go into his father's business of Brummer Striving. It werst a farst dying trade which was fast dying."

Machin and van Leeuwen (2007, pp. 138–148) describe the writing style of *Cosmopolitan* magazine as a hybrid of advertising style, fashion caption style, expert style, youth street style, and conversational style which connotes what the magazine seeks to be and do—promoting consumer goods and fashion as a passport to identity, glamour, success, sexuality, etc. (advertising and fashion style), providing reliable and trustworthy information and advice (expert style). Being up to date on the latest trend and a touch provocative (youth street language) and providing vicarious companionship (conversational style). Accents and dialects are often used for purposes of characterization in drama and movies, or for purposes of persuasion in the language of advertising (see for example, Whyte Kelstrup, 2010, on the use of regional dialects in advertising), sometimes using only some salient aspects of the accents or dialects, rather than authentic versions. We might add to this the use of "crossing" into different languages that is increasingly common in multilingual cities, not only in movies and advertisements (e.g., the "*Vorsprung durch Technik*" slogan of Audi), but also in the language of young people who are often already highly skilled in this, as has been described by sociolinguists like Rampton (2005).

The importance of provenance in aesthetics means that aesthetic literacy is not only a matter of understanding the affordances of different semiotic modes and of recognizing rhetorical figures and parallelisms, but also of recognizing cultural references. Advertising has of course always drawn on such references, but this does not mean that audiences have to be consciously aware of them. But active aesthetic literacy means developing awareness of such cultural references, building collections of culturally salient dialects and accents, color schemes, fonts, and graphic clichés (there exist reference books for graphic clichés for design training), rehearsing their cultural background, and exploring their affordances for a creative use in contemporary contexts. To give an example, Honeywill (1999) explored the use of Mayan hieroglyphics for the design of contemporary computer icons, noting, for instance, that these hieroglyphs often included a hand as one of their components. Clearly, he said, the Maya understood the ability of hand gestures to signify "doing something." He then applied this to computer icons, but this was not the only way hands were used in those icons; they could, for instance, also show the scattering of blood from the hand to signify "it ended" (pp. 24–26).

## Conclusion

In the course of the twentieth century, many important genres of writing have radically changed, and, today, continue to change further. These new forms of writing are thoroughly multimodal and combine functional regimes with an approach to aesthetics that is harnessed to the expression of the values that constitute personal and corporate identity, and to ensuring writers' and readers' affective engagement with the text. Because of the importance of these new forms of writing in the contemporary workplace, they can now be regarded as important life skills that should begin to be developed well before young people enter the workplace.

While the mastery of increasingly homogeneous and mandatory genres is an important part of this, in this chapter I have focused on aesthetic literacy, arguing that this is an equally important aspect of what might be called the new literacy, and I have also argued that this requires an approach that is at once creative and exploratory and reflective, at once attentive to form, and to the creative and context dependent way in which it can set up meanings.

I have also argued that the new literacy is intricately connected to digital writing technology, and should take a creative but also critical stance toward it, ensuring an awareness both of its affordances and its constraints. What I have called the new writing was well underway before the digital age began, as a result of the rising social and cultural importance of marketing and advertising, and of global corporate culture generally. Digital writing technology has merely democratized it, making it accessible to all. The new literacy is therefore not, or at least not only and not in the first place, digital literacy—the ability to confidently use digital writing technologies—but multimodal literacy, the ability to use multimodal expression in ways that are both functionally and aesthetically effective, whether digitally mediated or not.

The next step will be developing pedagogies for including aesthetics in the teaching of writing generally, and in the teaching of functional forms of writing specifically, for instance through appropriate apprentice genres that can prepare learners for the literacies required in the contemporary workplace.

## References

Addison, P., Albert, T., Bickham, C., Melissas, S., & Wood, J. (2011). *Pearson history*. Melbourne, VIC: Pearson.
Barthes, R. (1977). *Image-music-text*. London, UK: Fontana.
Cook, G. (1992). *The discourse of advertising*. London, UK: Routledge.
Durand, J. (1970). Rhétorique et Image Publicitaire, *Communications, 15*, 70–93.
Dyer, G. (1982). *Advertising as communication*. London, UK: Methuen.
Eco, U. (Ed.). (2002). *History of beauty*. New York, NY: Rizzoli.
Facebook. (2016). *Reactions now available globally*. Retrieved August 27, 2016, from http://newsroom.fb.com/news/2016/02/reactions-now-available-globally/.
Hawkes, T. (1972). *Metaphor*. London, UK: Methuen.
Honeywill, P. (1999). *Visual language for the worldwide web*. Exeter: Intellect Books
How to Erase your Dating Mistake (2004). *Cosmopolitan magazine*. November Issue. New York, NY: Cosmopolitan.
Iedema, R. (1992a). *Media literacy*. Write it Right Research Report 2. Sydney: Disadvantages Schools Project, Metropolitan East.
Iedema, R. (1992b). *The language of administration*. Write it Right Research Report 3. Sydney: Disadvantaged Schools Project, Metropolitan East.
Iedema, R. (1997). The language of administration: Organizing human activity in formal institutions. In F. Christie and J. R. Martin (Eds.), *Genres and institutions* (pp. 73–100). London, UK: Equinox.
Jakobson, R. (1960). Closing statement: Linguistics and poetics. In T. A. Sebeok (Ed.), *Style in language*. Cambridge, MA: MIT Press.
Kress, G. (2003). *Literacy in the new media age*. London, UK: Routledge.
Kress, G. (2011). *Multimodality: A social semiotic approach to contemporary communication*. London, UK: Routledge.
Kress, G., & van Leeuwen, T. (2001). *Multimodal discourse: The modes and media of contemporary communication*. London, UK: Arnold.
Kress, G., & van Leeuwen, T. (2006). *Reading images: The grammar of visual design* (2nd ed.). London, UK: Routledge.
Leech, G. (1969). *A linguistic guide to English poetry*. London, UK: Longman.
Locke, J. (1972 [1706]). *An essay concerning human understanding* (Vol. II). London, UK: Dent.
Machin, D., & van Leeuwen, T. (2007). *Global media discourse: A critical introduction*. London, UK: Routledge.
Martin, R. M., & Ellis, M. (2001). *Pasos: A first course in Spanish*. London, UK: Hodder and Stoughton.
Milic, L. (1970). Connectives in Swift's prose style. In D. C. Freeman (Ed.), *Linguistics and literary style*. New York, NY: Holt, Rinehart and Winston.
Mukarovsky, J. (1964a [1932]). Standard language and poetic language. In P. L. Garvin, (Ed.), *A Prague school reader on esthetics, literary structure and style*. Washington, DC: Georgetown University Press.
Mukarovsky, J. (1964b [1940]). The aesthetics of language. In P. L. Garvin (Ed.), *A Prague school reader on esthetics, literary structure and style*. Washington, DC: Georgetown University Press.
Palmer, M. (1998). What makes news. In O. Boyd-Barrett & T. Rantanen (Eds.), *The globalization of news*. London, UK: Sage.
Pastoureau, M. (2008). *Black: The history of a color*. Princeton, NJ: Princeton University Press.
Rampton, B. (2005). *Crossings: Language and ethnicity among adolescents*. Manchester: St Jerome Publishing.
van der Heyde, K. (1958). *Latijnse Grammatica. Vol. II: Syntax*. Groningen: J.B. Wolters
van Leeuwen, T. (2005). *Introducing social semiotics*. London, UK: Routledge.
van Leeuwen, T. (2006). Towards a semiotics of typography. *Information Design Journal, 14*(2), 139–155.
van Leeuwen, T. (2011a). *The language of color: An introduction*. London, UK: Routledge.
van Leeuwen, T. (2011b). The semiotics of decoration. In K. L. O'Halloran & B. A. Smith (Eds.), *Multimodal studies: Exploring issues and domains*. London, UK: Routledge.
Whyte Kelstrup, J. (2010). How regional dialects shape advertising. Retrieved August 28, 2016, from www.utalkmarketing.com/pages/article.aspx?articleid=17596&title=how_regional_dialects_shape_advertising/.

# Contributors

**Albers, Peggy**
Georgia State University, USA

**Alvermann, Donna E.**
University of Georgia, USA

**Arola, Kristin L.**
Washington State University, USA

**Bailey, Chris**
Sheffield Hallam University, UK

**Buchholz, Beth A.**
Indiana University Bloomington, USA

**Burnett, Cathy**
Sheffield Hallam University, UK

**Cope, Bill**
University of Illinois, Urbana-Champaign, USA

**Curwood, Jen Scott**
The University of Sydney, Australia

**Dovchin, Sender**
The Centre For Language Research,
The University of Aizu, Japan

**Exley, Beryl**
Queensland University of Technology,
Australia

**Gallard, Cristina Salazar**
Teachers College, Columbia University, USA

**Garcia, Antero**
Stanford University, USA

**Godley, Amanda**
University of Pittsburgh, USA

**Golden, Noah Asher**
Chapman University, USA

**Graham, Phil**
Queensland University of Technology,
Australia

**Haas, Christina**
University of Minnesota, USA

**Hall, Matthew**
The College of New Jersey, USA

**Harste, Jerome C.**
Indiana University, USA

**Hollett, Ty**
Pennsylvania State University, USA

**Hull, Glynda**
University of California, Berkeley, USA

**Kalantzis, Mary**
University of Illinois, Urbana-Champaign,
USA

**Kellner, Douglas**
University of California, Los Angeles, USA

**Kerr, Kristine Rodriguez**
New York University, USA

**Ladwig, James**
University of Newcastle, Australia

**Lammers, Jayne C.**
University of Rochester, USA

**Leander, Kevin M.**
Vanderbilt University, USA

**Lewis Ellison, Tisha**
University of Georgia, USA

**Loring, Ariel**
University of California, Davis, USA

**Losh, Elizabeth**
College of William and Mary, USA

**Luke, Allan**
Queensland University of Technology, Australia

**Magnifico, Alecia Marie**
University of New Hampshire, USA

**Medina, Carmen Liliana**
Indiana University, USA

**McGrath, Megan**
University of Minnesota, USA

**Merchant, Guy**
Sheffield Hallam University, UK

**Mills, Kathy Ann**
Learning Science Institute Australia, Australian Catholic University, Australia

**Pandya, Jessica Zacher**
California State University, Long Beach, USA

**Pennycook, Alastair**
University of Technology Sydney, Australia

**Phillips, Nathan C.**
University of Illinois at Chicago, USA

**Ramanathan, Vaidehi**
University of California, Davis, USA

**Robinson, Bradley**
University of Georgia, USA

**Sefton-Green, Julian**
Deakin University, Melbourne, Australia

**Smith, Anna**
Illinois State University, USA

**Stornaiuolo, Amy**
University of Pennsylvania, USA

**Tate, Tamara**
University of California, Irvine, USA

**Unsworth, Len**
Learning Sciences Institute Australia, Australian Catholic University, Australia

**van Leeuwen, Theo**
University of Technology Sydney, Australia; University of Southern Denmark; Honorary Professor, Learning Sciences Institute Australia, Australian Catholic University, Australia

**Vasquez, Vivian M.**
American University, USA

**Vasudevan, Lalitha**
Teachers College, Columbia University, USA

**Wargo, Jon**
Boston College, USA

**Warschauer, Mark**
University of California, Irvine, USA

**Wohlwend, Karen E.**
Indiana University, USA

# Index

Abbott, R. D. 130
Abrams, S. S. 177
academic outcomes and computer usage 67
active externalism 127
*Active Worlds* 189
activism: collaborative composing and 264, 269–72; hashtag 17
adolescents *see also* children; youth: digital writing and 161–70; fan-based online affinity spaces and 173–81
*Adventure Author* 188
advertisements and images 225
aesthetic literacy 250
aesthetics 8; in the digital age 285–99; return to communication 286; separation from meaning 285
aesthetic writing and newer forms of 286–91
affinity groups 117, 204
affinity spaces 200, 204; fan-based 124
affinity space theory 175, 177
African Americans: counter-narratives on Twitter 117; critical race theory and 113; digital literacy practices of 61; digital participation and 79–80; Internet access 64; male youth and intersectional identity 83; police killings of suspects 76; stereotypes of masculinity 83; time spent with media 68
African American women: digital narratives of 93; embodying themselves in digital tools 95–6; as knowledgeable agents 88–96; literature on 91–3; negatively stereotyped 90–1; rewriting histories and their images 92; shaping the digital worlds 92; use of digital tools to cope with trauma 92, 93; writing identities 93–4
after school alternative to detention program (ATDP) environment and writing 264, 266–9
agency 228; among youth 264; collaborative composing and 270; transfer during gaming 208; writing and 271
agential realism 228
Aguilera, E. 226
Akil, Omari 158
Albers, P. 186, 226
Alexander, J. 40, 78
algorithms in digital writing 241
*Al Jazeera* webpage 105
Alvermann, D. E. 123, 162, 163
American Indian 8, 249; approach to digital ethics 275–83; philosophy 278–80; rhetoric 278–80
Ames, Morgan 69

Andrews, R. 236
Androutsopoulos, J. 211
Anishinaabe peoples 8, 249, 275–83
anti-migrant sentiments 103–5
Antin, Judd 84
anti-racist counter-movements 111
anti-racist engagement in digital texts 116–19
anti-Semitism 102
"A Pedagogy of Multiliteracies: Designing Social Futures" 169
Arab Spring of Middle East 78, 255
Aristotle 28, 126, 281
Arola, Adam 282
Arola, Kristin 249
Arroyo, S. 39
Artemesia 188
art in digital texts 186
Asians connecting digitally with others 117
assemblage 185, 191, 195; authenticity and 278; spatialized literacies and 141–2
asylum seekers and media coverage of 102–5
audience: for collaborative composition 270–1; in fan-based affinity spaces 175; online 177; theories of 177
augmenting place 155–6
Augsburger, A. 130
Austin, J. A. 256
Australian Indigenous communities preserving heritage 114, 117
authenticity in writing 276–8
author: blurred with consumer 3; function of 52
autoethnographic writing practice 16, 18
automated essay scoring (AES) 242–3
avatar-based diversity representation 115–16, 117
avatars linked to gender and racial stereotypes 83

Bailey, Chris 185
Baker, P. 102, 104
Bakhtin, M. 161
Balsamo, Anne 82
Banet-Weiser, Sarah 83
Banks, A. J. 281
Banterbury Library 191–4
Barad, K. 228
Barthes, Roland 289
Bass, T. 162
Beach, R. 179

Bean, T. W. 166
Beavis, C. 189
Behm-Morawitz, E. 116
Behrens, J. T. 243
Beltrán, C. 16
Benhabib, Seyla 254, 259
Benjamin, Walter 3
Bennett, J. 195
Benton-Bai, Edward 280
Berninger, Virginia 128, 130
Berry, M. 156
*Beware of the Bears* 33
BFT *see* Black feminist thought (BFT)
bias of communication 258
Bienkowski, M. 241
big data 240–1
big G Game 201–2
Bishop, S. C. 176
Black, R. W. 175
Black feminist thought (BFT) 88–96; literature on 91–3
Black Lives Matter movement 17, 19, 61, 76, 77, 85, 91, 255
#BlackLivesMatter movement 17, 111
Blacks *see* African Americans
Black Twitter 117
black women *see* African American women
blended learning 73
blogging 267–8
BlogSpot 93
body: duality with the mind 28; embodiment and 142–3; enhancing literacy learning 32–4; interacting with the world 149; regulated for literacy learning 31; role in communication 26; role of 11
Boggs, G. L. 163
Bogost, Ian 83, 203
Boldt, G. 38, 169, 178
book production in *Minecraft* 191–2
borders of country and refugees 104
Borgmann, M. 179
Boulton, A. 150
Bourdieu, P. 11, 50–3
Boyd, d. 177, 240
brain activation during handwriting 129–30
Brandt, D. 161, 162, 163, 170
"Breaking Point" campaign 118
breath in digital practice 11
Brexit referendum 118, 255
Bronowski, Jacob 132
Brown, Michael 17, 20
Bruckman, Amy 83
Bruning, R. 131
Buchholz, Beth 123
Buck, A. 151, 214, 221
Buckingham, D. 53
build books 191–2
burden of proof to establish as a refugee 100
Burnett, C. 151, 185

Cain, C. 51
Cain, E. 54
Camara, S. K. 89
Campano, G. 17, 179
Canagarajah, S. 41, 213
Cantor, M. 208
Canvas 168
capitalism: driving Internet participation 229, 230; literacy and 70

Carbone, N. 277
Carpentier, N. 230
Carr, N. 161
Carrington, V. 189
Cartesian mind/body duality 28
Castells, Manuel 78
Castile, Philando 76
Center for Solutions to Online Violence 85
centrifugal cultural forces of writing 166–7, 169
centrifugal schooling 166
centripetal cultural force of writing 166–7
Chalmers, D. 127
Chandler-Olcott, K. 175
Chandra, V. 167
changing ambience with picture book apps 30
#Charleston 82
#CharlestonSyllabus 82
Chartrel, E. 129
Chavez, V. 269, 270
children *see also* adolescents; youth: collective cultural imaginaries of 141; generating digital texts 226; Internet usage by 65–6, 173; making imaginaries of 136–45; playful literacies and 136–45; sensorial literacy of 28
Chouliaraki, L. 14, 16, 19, 22, 23
Christensen, C. A. 130
Chun, Wendy 78, 82
citizen journalism 77
citizenship 101; legal *vs* de facto 107; use of term 102–3
civic interaction through use of digital media 54
Civil Rights movement 91
Clark, A. 127
class-based aspects of identity 219–20
classroom: critical image analysis in 227; division with the world 167–8; not embracing fandom literacies 179; play and making in 136–45; study of fanfiction practices 176; use of games 207
Clinton, K. 236, 265
*Club Penguin* 189
cognitive subversion 50
Cole, M. 70
Coleman, Beth 82
collaborative composing: activism and 269–72; agency and 270; spaces for 270–1; by youth 264, 269–72
collective cultural imaginaries 141
Collins, A. 179
Collins, Patricia Hill 90, 91
color: intersectionality identity of 79; marginalization of 4
colorblindness racism on the Social Web 112–13, 115–16
color in writing 292–5; differentiation of 294–5; luminosity, luster, and luminescence 294; modulation of 294; saturation of 294; temperature of 294; value of 294
Colton, J. S. 282
Comber, B. 227
comment sections as writing 168–9
commodification of Internet users 6
Common Core State Standards 51
Common Core State Standards (CCSS) for English Language Arts (ELA) 165, 168
Common Sense Census 68
communications: in gaming 204; political economy of 257–8
communicative ethics 251–60
communities of practice 177, 200
community building in virtual play 187
composing: as culturing 282–3, 291–2; culturing and 279–83
composition 291–2; capability of mobile devices 151–2

compositional fluency 40
computerized assessment of writing 242–3
computers: content consumption on 67; content creation on 67; interest-driven uses of 67; usage at home 64, 67; usage at school 66–7
conduit model for Internet access 70
connected civics 117
connected learning 178, 204
Connected Learning Massive Online Open Collaboration (CLMOCC) 144
connective ethnography 241
connectivity: growing relevance of 67–8; in typography 296
Connelly, V. 130, 132
Connor, J. M. 176
Consalvo, Mia 84
Consortium of School Networking 65
consumers blurred with authors 3
content: consumption on computers 67; creation on computers 67
contexts, imaginary of play 140
Cook, G. 297
Cook, M. S. 189
Cooper, Anna Julia 89, 99
Coover, Robert 198
Cope, B. 186, 225, 236, 238, 240, 241, 243
coping metaphor for refugees 105
copy-and-paste (CP) strategy 131
Cordova, V. F. 279
Cosmopolitan Critical Literacy 166–7, 169
cosmopolitanism 117; challenges to 15; in education 14–15; in networked writing 16–17
Couldry, N. 240
counterfactual ideal 258
counter-mapping 41, 236
counternarrate inequality 18–19
counter-narratives of race and racism 116–18
counter-stories of people of color 113
Crawford, K. 240
Crenshaw, Kimberlé 79
Cresswell, T. 149, 158
crisis mash-ups 153
critical computing 83
critical image analysis 223–33
critical literacy 228; based on social justice 254
critical media literacies 53–7
critical race theory (CRT) 62, 111; race in digital spaces and 112–13
critique of relations of power 17, 21–2
Crooks, A. 152
Csordas, Thomas 127
Cuban, L. 69, 207
cultural capital 51
cultural computing 83
cultural context of play 204–5
cultural duping 56
cultural forces in ecologies of writing 161
cultural hegemony 5
cultural references in writing 299
cultural scripts 254
culture: as active process of production 3; influencing gaming 201, 202; linked to language 1; participatory 3, 5
culturing and composing 279–83
Current Population Surveys (CPS) 63
curriculum: development by teacher study group 144; digital ethics and 251–60; personalization and individualization of 71

curvature in typography 295–6
Curwood, J. S. 124, 175, 176
Cutler, C. 277

Dahlgren, P. 229, 230, 232
Dark Souls video game 208
data exhaust 237
data journalism 81
data mining 237
data traces in education 235–44; mechanisms of producing 236–40
data visualization 81–2
Dawson, S. 241
de Certeau, M. 157, 158
deep writing 161, 170
de facto citizenship 107
Deleuze, G. 185, 191
Deloria, V. Jr. 279
Denmark and polylanguaging of youth talk 213
density of usage 66
de Souza e Silva, A. 155
Development, Relief, and Education for Alien Minors (DREAM) Act 264, 269, 270, 272
DeviantArt 174
device ownership model for Internet access 70
Devos, P. 26
DeVoss, D. N. 277
Dewey, J. 137, 259
DiCerbo, K. E. 243
Dickey, M. D. 189
Diemand-Yauman, C. 132, 133
differentiation of color 294–5
digital: defining 38; physical spaces and 150–2; relationship with geographies 150
digital actions and their impact 253
digital culture 258
digital devices usage 224–5
digital diversity 6, 61–2
digital divide 113; definition 63; expanded notions of 69–70; statistics on 63–7
digital dossiers 80
digital ethics 6, 7–8, 249–50 see also ethics; American Indian approach to 275–83; curriculum and 251–60; ideology and 257; social relations and 257
digital futures 6, 11–12
digital geographies 123, 148–58; literacies and writing within 150–2; mobilities and 149–50; relevance of 148–9; writing with 152–6
digital inequality 61
digital layering of place 152
digital lifestreaming 43–6
digital literacy: awareness of necropolitical abuses and 81; Black feminist thought in 88–96; counter-narratives of race and racism in 116–18; defining 77–8; detracting from intrapersonal relationships 55; digital rhetorics and 40–1; ethics and 275–83; on Facebook 211–21; games and 198–208; importance of 68; intersectionality and 78–80; necropolitics and 76–86; perspectives on 38–9; practices of African American women 88–96; race and racism 111–19; rhetorical perspective of 39–40; schools embracing 263; Whiteness as property 112, 113–15
digital lives 7, 123–4
digital media: access to 61; composition 123; increased access to 265; reporting on migrant groups 103–5
digital metroliteracies 211–21

digital narratives of African American women 93
digital necropolitics 80–2
digital production gap 73
digital representations of physical places 152–5
digital rhetorics 12, 39–40, 61, 85; digital literacies and 40–1; literacies and 37–8
Digital Songlines Project 114
digital spaces 7, 185–6; images in 223–33; participation in 229–30
digital surveillance 80
digital technology 38; inclusion in 61; in schools 71–2; complexity of 72; performativity 72; workability of 72
digital texts: ability to express identities 268; meaning making by 200
digital traces of writing 235–6
digital writing 235–44; adolescents and 161–70; ethnographic studies of 42–6; mobility 41; multimodality 40; as a postprocess theory 38; praxis 41; techne 40–1; youth as global citizens and 165–9
Dinerstein, J. 112
Disadvantaged Schools Project 286
DiSalvo, Betsy 83–5
discursive consciousness 281
disfluency 132
disidentification 46
distance learning 71
diversity: digital 6, 61–2; of peoples and communicative forms 4–5
Dobrin, S. 161, 162, 163
Dodge, M. 152
Donovan, Joan 76–7, 81
Dooley, K. 33
Dovchin, S. 185, 212, 214
doxa 50
Doyle, Sarah 82
DREAM Act organizations 269
DREAMers 264, 269–72
Drummond, D. K. 89
Duffy, J. 39
Durand, J. 298

e-books 26
ecological theory of writing 163
ecologies of writing 161–70
economic capital 51
Ede, L. 177
Edminston, B. 179
education: cosmopolitanism in 14–15; global interaction by youth 165–9; Maker Movement in 137–41; performative experiences in 142–3; role of emotion in 142
educational data mining 241
educational justice 249; conceptualizing 264–5; digital youth and 263–73; multimodal composing and 266
education data science 241
Education Superhighway 2015 report 65
edutainment 5
Eglash, Ron 79
Ehret, C. 128, 152
ekphrasis 40
elaboration activation with picture book apps 30
elaboration explication with picture book apps 30
electracy 11, 37–47; defining 39; ethnographic studies of 42–6; experience in digital writing and 40–1
Electronic Literature Organization (ELO) 236

Eli Review 238
elitist identity enacting on Facebook 219–20
Ellison, Lewis 61
Elwood, S. 153
emancipatory literacies 54–6
embodied mind 127
embodiment 142–3; of reflective action 280–2; theories 126–7
Emerson, Lori 84
Emerson, Ralph Waldo 41, 276
enchantment 195
Engelhardt, L. 129
Enlightenment 27
epidermolysis bullosa (EB) 92
equitable relationships 19–21
E-rate program 65, 71, 168
essentialism 119
ethics: digital 7–8, 249–50, 257, 275–83; for pedagogy 94–6; of representation 40; for writing 11, 13
ethnic identity enacting on Facebook 217–19
ethno-mining 241
Eurocentric notions in digital literacy 113–14
Every Student Succeeds Act 71
"everything is related" maxim 279
Exley, A. 117
Exley, Beryl 11, 32, 33
expansion in typography 295
experience in digital writing 37, 39, 40–1
extension with picture book apps 30
extratext interactivity 29
Eyman, D. 39

Facebook 7, 174, 185, 225, 231; anonymous environment of 214; counter-narratives on 117; digital literacy on 211–21; enacting elitist identity on 219–20; enacting ethnic identity on 217–19; enacting sexual identity on 215–17; fixity and fluidity on 212; identities related to off-line identities 214–21; Mongolians' literacy practices of 212–20; re-entextualization on 211; re-semiotization on 211–12
Facebook Live 76, 78
Fairclough, N. 205
Fairlie, R. 69
false logic of identities 44
fan-based affinity spaces 7, 124, 173–81; in the classroom 179–81; definition 174
fan-based literary practices 173–81; theories of 176–8
fandom literacies and tension with school experiences 179
fandom practices 175–6
Fanfiction.net 174, 175
Federal Communications Commission (FCC) 65
Feld, S. 27
Felderman, C. 227
feminist and digital literacy practices of 61
Feng, M. 241
#Ferguson 82
field, defining 50, 51–3
field of power 51–2
Fields, D. A. 189
Figment.com 174, 175
figurative language with technology 92
filmmaking 227
Fiore, Q. 57
fire object 193
Fisher, D. 126
fixed identity markers 213–14
fixity and fluidity on Facebook 212

Fleer, M. 190
flickering 190
Flickr 174
fluency of text production during handwriting 130–1
Ford, A. 54
*Forged in Fire* 229
Foucault, Michel 232
fractional objects 151
framing of text 292
Fraser, Nancy 254
Freire, P. 14, 15, 41, 228
Fuchs, C. 229, 230
fusiform gyrus 129

Gabrielatos, C. 102
Gallardo, Cristina Salazar 249
Gamboa, M. 177
Gamergate 199, 201
games 7; classroom use of 207; defining 199, 205–6; digital literacies and 198–208; as digital texts and cultural domains 200; embodiment within 206; intertextuality of 204–5; mediated by the world and mediates one's understanding of the world 201; platform of 203; shaping learning and identity 198–9; socialization within 206
gaming 185; agency and transfer 208; cultural dimensions of 201, 202; ecosystems 201–2; writing and production 206
gaming literacies 82–5, 198–208; layers of 202–5; reading practices of 205–6; writing and production 206
Garcia, Antero 185
Garcia, N. 130
Garfield, Richard 201
Garner, Eric 20
Gasser, Urs 80
gay sexual identity enacting on Facebook 215–17
Gee, D. 130
Gee, J. P. 77, 84, 100, 117, 174, 177, 200, 201
Geertz, C. 3
gender: inclusion of 6; role in gaming 201
gender-bending 217
gendered identities through images 225
geocomposing 41, 236
geofences 148
geolocate 4
Giang, M. 115
Gibson, W. 150
Giddens, A. 281
Gillen, J. 2
girls and digital literacy 84
Glitch Game Testers 83–5
global citizenship 14, 165; of students through digital writing 166–70
globalization 15
Global Positioning System (GPS) 148, 153
Godley, Amanda 62
Goffman, E. 5
Golden, Noah Asher 12
gold farming example 206
Goodes, Adam 111
Goodwin, O. 156
Google 229, 230, 231, 232
Google Classroom 168
Gordon, E. 155
GPS 148, 153
Grabill, J. 238

Graham, M. 150
Graham, Phil 249
Graham, S. 130
*Grand Theft Auto: San Andreas* 83
Grant, Oscar 80, 81
graphic design in writing 295–6
Grasmuck, S. 214
gratuitous additional action 29–30
Guattari, F. 185, 191
Guo, L. 270
Guzzetti, B. 177

Haas, Angela 278–9
Haas, C. 123, 128
Habermas, J. 256, 258
habit in typing 128
habitus of agents 50, 51
Haffaker, D. 268
Hall, Matt 11
Hall, Stuart 257
Hall, T. 93
Halverson, E. R. 137
Halverson, R. 179
*hana* 129
handwriting 126 *see also* writing; aiding composing text 130; cultural power of 125; fluency of text production 130–1; haptics of 123, 125–33; letter recognition 128–30; phenomenological accounts of 127–8; retention and learning 131–2; sensory dimensions and 31–2
Haney-Lopez, I. 111
Hansen, D. 41
haptics 6, 11, 26, 29; literacy and 127; of writing 123, 125–33
hardware: access at home 64; access in schools 64; as a language 92
Hargittai, E. 73
Harlow, S. 270
Harrell, Fox 82–3
Harrell, Sneha Veeragoudar 83
Harste, J. C. 186, 228
Hart-Davidson, W. 238
Harvey, A. 225, 236
hashtag activism 17
hashtags as syllabi 82
Hayes, E. R. 201
Hayes, J. R. 128, 130
*Heart and the Bottle, The* (Jeffers) 29
Heath, S. B. 148
hegemony of vision 126
Hensher, P. 125, 127
Hessdorfer Experiment 84
Hickey, D. T. 176
Hicks, M. 162
Hicks, T. 179
Hidi, S. E. 178
Hines, M. B. 176
Hispanics: density of computer usage and 66; time spent with media 68
Hodgetts, K. 189
"Hole-in-the-Wall" project 68
Holland, D. 51
Hollett, T. 123, 128, 142, 152
home: access to hardware for the Internet 64; access to the Internet 65–6; computer usage at 67
Honeywill, P. 299
Horrigan, J. B. 68

Howes, D. 27
Huc-Hepher, S. 241
Hudson-Smith, A. 152
Huizinga, J. 199
Hull, G. 11, 38, 117, 118, 170, 179, 268
humanizing 14–15, 19
Hunt, B. 179
Hurley, K. 201
Hutchins, E. 127
hyperlinks analysis 231

idea of multiplicities 194
ideational meaning 30
identities: African American women writing in variety of texts 93–4; digital 230; digital metroliteracies enacting 215–20; enacting sexual identity on Facebook 215–17; expressed in digital texts 268; false logic of 44; fan-based online affinity groups and 176; games shaping 198–9, 208; linked to language 1; literate in fan-based online affinity spaces 173–81; performance of 6; power and 79; represented in images 226
identity artifact 142
identity kit 77
identity markers 213–14
identity politics of public writing 5
ideology: digital ethics and 257; represented in images 226, 227
Igo, L. B. 131
images: critical reading of 223–33; definition 223; gendered identities through 225; intra-action with 228–9, 232; mulitimodality of 226–7; representing ideologies 226, 227; universal access to 225; viewing as an active act 225
imaginaries: of children 136–45; multisited collective 141
imaginative play 123
imagining 136
imbrication and digital geographies 151
Immigrant Rights Movement 162
immigrants: media coverage of 102–7; writing about their experiences 16, 264, 269–72
immigration 62; use of term 103
immigration reform and writing 269–72
impossible possibles 11, 50–8
income: Internet access and 64, 65; student usage of school computers and 66
India and cosmopolitanism in the digital space 117
2015 Indiana Digital Rhetorics Symposium 37
Indigenous communities being preserved 8, 114, 117
infomediaries 6
information visualization 81–2
in-game learning and socialization 207
injustice 21–2
Innis, H. A. 258
Instagram 231; usage by race 113
interest-driven uses of computers 67
Internet 3, 39; access at home 65–6; access at school 65; access by race 113; access statistics 63–7; amount of information on 223, 224; commodification of users 6; controlled by Whites 113; density of usage 66; hardware access at home 64; hardware access in schools 64; participatory culture of 229; as a public stage 5; resources for access 70–1; unequal access to 63; usage by children 173; usage by race 113–14; used for learning 68; visibility on 232
*Internet-in-practice* 73
Internet of Things 4, 40

interpersonal meaning 30, 288
intersectionality 78–80, 119, 164
intertextuality of games 204–5
intratext interactivity 29, 30
inward national focus 15
in-world chat 189
iPad and image analysis 227
ironic spectator 23
Ito, M. 84, 117, 178

Jacks, D. 241
Jakobson, R. 285
James, K. H. 129
Janks, H. 227, 228, 232
Japanese handwriting 129
Jeffers, Oliver 29
Jenkins, H. 5, 175, 229, 236, 265
Jocson, K. 117, 118
Johnson, J. M. 93
Johnson, L. L. 162
Johnson, Robert 281
Johnson, S. 163
Johnson-Eilola, J. 276, 277
Jones, D. 130
Juhasz, Alexandra 80–1
justice: enacted in space of interactions 265; through writing 263–73

Kabali, H. K. 224
Kachorksy, D. 226
Kafai, Y. B. 189
Kajder, S. 179
Kalantzis, M. 186, 225, 236, 238, 240, 241, 243
Kaluli 27
*kanji* 129
Kato, C. 129
Kazakh identity relocalization 218
Kellner, Douglas 249
Kelly, P. 227
Kerr, Kristine Rodriguez 249
Kerwin, L. 227
keyboard and ergonomic interaction with person 126
keyboarding 125, 129–30
keyboard note-taking 131, 132
kinesis 26
kinesthetic focalization 30
King, Coretta Scott 95
Kirk, J. 226
Kirkland, David 92, 93
Kitchin, R. 152
Klein, Lauren 82
Klein, Naomi 254
Knobel, M. 268
knowledgeable agents: of Black women 88–96; of the digital 88
Korean education system 21–2
Kress, G. 292, 298

Lachicotte, W. 51
Ladd, H. F. 69
Ladson-Billings, G. 112
Ladwig, James 249
Lam, W. S. E. 117
Lammers, J. C. 124, 175, 176, 177
language: by hand 128–32; ideological nature of 1; linked to culture and identity 1; literacy and 211; proficiency determining nationality 100–1

Lankshear, C. 268
Latino/a: critical race theory and 113; digital participation and 79–80; intersectionality of 164; writing as part of acclimation process 162
Lave, J. 177
Law, J. 151, 193, 194
layered presence 190
layering place 152
Leander, K. 38, 123, 142, 148, 150, 169, 178
learning: being enabled by technology 71–2; blended 73; connected 204; games shaping 198–9; gaming and 207; making as productive learning 137; retention and handwriting 131–2
learning analytics 241
Learning Analytics and Knowledge Summit (LAK) 236
Learning Management Systems (LMS) 168
#leave hashtag 118
Lee, J. E. R. 116
Leech, G. 297, 298
legal citizenship 107
Lemke, J. 41
#Lemonade syllabus 82
Leppänen, S. 211
lesbian, gay, bisexual, transgender *see* LGBTQ community
letter recognition 128–30
Lewis, C. 56–7
LGBTQ community 43–4; violence on in gaming 201, 204
Liberman, A. 128
lifestreaming 43–6
linguistic ethnography 214–15
literacies: affective dimensions of 4; critical media 53–7; within digital geographies 150–2; digital rhetorics and 37–8; emancipatory 54–6; gaming 82–5; globalism and 165–9; ideological nature of 1; linked to social practices in digital cultures 3; maker 144–5; as multi-spatial practices 266; participation and social inclusion of digital youth 265–6; research 2–6; sensory dimension to 11; spatial 200; spatialized 141–2; virtual play and 187–95
literacy: concerns with global refugee crisis 99–107; definition 100; digital technology access and 70; haptics and 127; language and 211; for new writing 291–9; role in refugee crisis 62
literacy learning with sensorial engagement 32–4
Literacy Playshop 144
literate arts of the contact zone 15
literate identities: definition 173; in fan-based online affinity spaces 173–81
"Little g" game 202–3
local level of meaning-making 56–7
locative media 156
Locke, John 289
locomotion 26
Longcamp, M. 128, 129
Loring, A. 62, 102
Los Angeles Unified School District iPad roll out 69
Losh, E. 61, 78, 79
Luke, A. 31, 249
luminosity of color 294
Lunsford, A. 177
Lurcat, L. 129
Lynch, C. 241
Lyons, S. R. 279

Machin, D. 291, 298
machine learning 242
machine-mediated feedback 243
Magnifico, A. M. 124, 175, 177
Magno, C. 226
Mahar, D. 175
Mahiri, J. 117
maker literacies 144–5
Maker Movement 137
makerspaces 144
making 137–41; *Beast Quest* 138–9; as productive learning 137; writing about it and 139–40
Malcolm X 90
Malkowski, Jennifer 81
Mangen, A. 127, 129, 132
mapping, interactive 153
marginalization of color 4
marginalized groups 6; counter-narratives and 116–18; subordination of 1
markers of identity in images 226, 227
Markham, A. 40
Marsh, J. 189
Marsh, V. L. 176
Martin, D. B. 157
Martin, Trayvon 17, 111, 113
Martinez, E. 69
mash-ups, crisis 153
Masny, D. 170
Massey, D. 157, 158
master narratives of people of color 113
material anchors 127
*Matrix, The* 228
Matsuo, K. 129
Matthew effect 67
Mbembe, Achille 81
McCrudden, M. T. 131
McEnery, T. 102, 104
McGrath, Megan 123
McLeod, M. 238
McLuhan, M. 57
McWilliams, J. 176, 179
meaning-making 4, 26; of digital texts 200; in gaming 208; with picture book appls 29; process 56–7
Means, B. 241
media activism 80
media coverage: of global refugee crisis 99–107; role in refugee crisis 62
mediated discourse analysis (MDA) theory 141
Medina, C. L. 123, 141, 142
memory and handwriting 131–2
mental illness stigma 18–19
Merchant, G. 151, 185
Merleau-Ponty, M. 127
metagame 201–2
metrolingual identities 213–14; Facebook literacies and 215–20
metrolingualism 185, 213–14
metroliteracy 7
microblogging 167
migrants and media coverage of 102–7
Miller, Paul D. 278
Mills, K. A. 11, 26, 62, 117, 165, 167, 227
Minard, Charles 81
mind/body duality 28
*Minecraft* 7, 140, 142, 185, 187–90; building books in 191–2
minorities 17; violence on in gaming 201, 204
Mirra, N. 54
Mirzoeff, Nicholas 78
Mitchell, W. 150

MIT Media Lab 84
mobile devices' compositional capabilities 151–2
mobile storytelling 156
mobility 41; digital geographies and 149–50; place-making and 157
Mockingjay.net 174
modal aesthetic 46
modulation of color 294
Moje, E. 41
Mongolians' Facebook literacy practices 212–20
Monroe, B. 282
Montfort, Nick 203
Moodle 168
mood of enchantment 195
Morey, S. 39
Morrell, E. D. 54, 80
motion sensing technologies 28
motor activation in handwriting 128–9
movement and handwriting 128–9
Mueller, P. A. 131
Muhammad G. E. 93
Mukarovsky, J. 285, 298
multiliteracies: framework 175; perspectives 178
multimodal composing 249, 264; contexts for 266–7; educational justice and 266; making the self known 267–9
multimodal interaction analysis (MMIA) 226–7
multimodality 40, 266
multimodal literacies and race 111–19
multiplayer online games 115–16
multiplicity of realities 151
multisensoriality 26–34
multisited collective imaginaries 141
[Murmur] 156
MySpace 93

Nakamura, L. 82, 115
Napier, John 126
National Assessment of Educational Progress (NAEP) 66
National Broadband Plan 71
National Center for Education Statistics 64
National Education Plan 67
National Education Technology Plan (NETP) 71
national script 125
National Telecommunications and Information Administration (NTIA) 63
National Writing Project 140
naturalization to become a U.S. citizen 101
natural language processing 242
necropolitics 61; digital literacy and 76–86; resisting digital 80–2
Negroponte, Nicholas 84
Nelson, M. E. 179, 268
neogreography 152–3
Neopets 175
Netherlands producing counter-narratives 117
netnography 214–15
networked writing 13–14, 15; cosmopolitanism in 16–17; critiquing systems of power 17, 21–2; to express solidarity 16–17, 19–21; to negotiate visibility 16, 18–19
New Literacy Studies (NLS) 177, 200
New London Group 4, 169, 175, 178, 202
new mobilities paradigm 149
nexus of practice 141
Nishi, N. W. 116

No Child Left Behind Act 71
nonvisual senses 26
Norman, D. A. 126
Norris, S. 226
*34 North 118 West* 156
note-taking 131
NTIA Data Explorer 63
Núñez, A. M. 164
Nuñez, K. 93

Obama, Barack 80
ocularcentrism 27
off-line self influenced by online, networked self 212, 214–21
Ojibwe 279–81
olfaction 26
Olmanson, J. 239
O'Mara, J. 190
on-and off-line integrated 212
One Laptop Per Child initiative 69, 84
Ong, W. 126
online affinity spaces 173–81; community-building and socializing in 177–8; definition 174
online identity influenced by off-line self 212, 214–21
online metrolingual identities 213–14
online surveillance 6
online violence 85–6
on/off screen activity blurring 190
OpenStreetMap 154–5
Oppenheimer, D. M. 131, 132
oppression 7, 119, 164
Orbe, M. P. 89
organic pheminist framework 93
orientation in typography 296
#Orlando 82
Otsuji, E. 212, 213

Padgett, E. 175, 176
Pahl, K. 226, 227
Palfrey, John 80
Pallasmaa, Juhani 126
Pandya, Jessica Zacher 12
Papert, S. 137
parallelism in writing 297–9
participation: in critical media literacies 54–5, 58; in digital spaces 229–30
participatory culture 3, 5, 265
participatory politics 6, 12
Pastoureau, Michel 293
Pea, R. 241
Pearce, C. 188
pedagogy of collegiality 269, 270
Pennell, H. 116
Pennycook, A. 185, 212, 213
people of color: counter-stories of 113; subordination of in digital media and 113–16
performance of identities 6
performative experiences in education 142–3
performativity 5–6; of digital technology in schools 72
Perry, M. 142
Persson, Markus 187
Pew Internet & American Life Project 64
Pew Research Center 224
Phillips, N. 38, 123, 148, 170
philosophy of the American Indian 278–80
Phyak, P. 212

physical spaces: digital representations of 152–5; digital spaces and 150–2
picture book apps 28–31
picture postcards 2
Piece, J. 157
pinkification projects 84
Pinterest 231
place: augmenting 155–6; digital layering of 152
place-making 41, 123, 142; as bundling 157; racism and 157–8
placement of text 292
plagiarism 276–8
plagiarism detection services 276–7
platform of the game 203
Platial.com 153
play: defining 136–7, 199; imaginative 123; sociocultural contexts of 204–5; virtual 7, 187–95; writing and 192–4
player, manipulation and interaction of 203
player affinity groups 204
playful literacies 136–45; making 137–41
playing the text in virtual games 189
plunderphonics 277
podcasting 227
Poetry 4 U Project 156
*Pokémon Go* 158, 226
police abuses 76, 85–6; documenting 80
police killings of Black suspects 76
political economy of communications 257–8
political subversion 50
Polling for Justice 54
polylanguaging 213
Poniewozik, James 76
popular media characters 225
pop-ups generated by search engines 231
Porter, J. 37
power 50; being critiqued by networked writing 17, 21–2; dynamics 11; inequalities 16; oppression and 4; relations 164
practical consciousness 281
Pratt, M. L. 15
praxis 41
presentation of self in everyday life 5–6
"Press Here" (Tullet) 31
pretend digital props 140
privacy and its loss 5–6
private paradigm shifts 163
process drama 33–4, 190
produsage 5
prosumption 152–3
provenance in writing 298–9
public advocacy events: agency and 271–2; storytelling at 272; strategic disclosure at 271
public authoring 156
Purushotma, R. 236, 265

quantification metaphor for refugees 104
quantified writer 186, 235–44
queer exemplified in lifestreaming 42–6
QWERTY keyboard 126, 128, 130

race: being marginalized in digital media 113–16; counter-narratives of in digital literacies 116–18; definition 111; density of computer usage and 66; digital literacy and 113–15; in digital media 111–19; inclusion of 6; representation in video games 114–15; student usage of school computers and 66; time spent with media and 68
racial colorblindness on the Social Web 112–13, 115–16
racial stereotypes and videogames 83
racial theme parties on social networking site 115
racism: definition 111; in digital media 62, 111–19; to maintain political control 81; place-making and 157–8; in schools 112; syncretic 102
radio broadcasts 269
Ramanthan, Vaidehi 62
Rampton, B. 299
Ramus, Peter 285
Rault, Jasmine 79
Rawls, J. 264
reading: analysis of reading navigation 231; with gaming 205–6; images 223–33; reciprocal relationship with writing 170; sensorial dimensions of 26; the world 200, 201
reciprocal relationship 19–21; between reading and writing 170
re-entextualization on Facebook 211
reflective practitioner 280–2
refugee crisis and media coverage of 99–107
refugees: anti-migrant sentiments expressed towards 103–5; coping metaphor and 105; country's borders and 104; described as a problem 104; described as dangerous water 103–4; described as large numbers 104; described as tragedy 104; displacement 6; promoting inclusion of 106; tensions in the resettlement process 100–1; as transaction with a country 104; understanding special needs of 106; use of term 103
regimes of visibility 232
regularity in typography 296
reinterpreted fairy tale 33
relatedness of things 279
relationality 279–83
relationships, imagining equitable and reciprocal 19–21
relocalization 57, 214; of ethnic identity 218; on Facebook 212; of Russian 220
remix culture 277–8
Renninger, K. A. 178
re-semiotization on Facebook 211–12
resettlement process for refugees and literacy 100–1, 107
restory 17
retention and learning with handwriting 131–2
revelation in picture book apps 30
Revision Assistant 242
Reynolds, Diamond 76, 77, 78, 80
rhetorical velocity 277
rhetoric of the American Indian 278–80
rhetorics and digital literacies 39–40
Rhodes, J. 40
Richard-Bossez, A. 32
Ridolfo, J. 277
Riley, T. 93
Robinson, A. 236
Robinson, Bradley 123
Robinson, J. 69
Robison, A. J. 265
Rojo, Martín 102
Roozen, K. 176
Rowe, D. W. 142
Rowsell, J. 226
rural areas and Internet access 64

Saes, K. 162, 163
SafeAssign 277
Salen, K. 199, 200
salience of text 292
sandbox video game 140
Santa Ana, O. 102, 103
saturation of color 294
scaffolding for digital learning 72
scale in media literacies 57
schizophrenic context 270
Scholar software 238–40
schools: access to hardware for the Internet 64; access to the Internet 65; computer usage in 66–7; digital strategies of 253; embracing digital literacy 263; providing digital technology 71–2; technology initiatives in 68–9
Schools and Libraries Program of the Universal Service Fund 168
school-to-prison pipeline 91
Schultz, K. 38
Scorza, D. A. 54
*Scratch* 188
Scribner, S. 70
search engine analysis 231
*Second Life* 116, 188, 206
Sefton-Green, Julian 249
Selber, S. 276, 277
self and understanding of in relation to others 41
selfie existing in a context 78
Sen, A. 264
senses: in communication 26; nonvisual 26; regulated for literacy learning 31–2
sensorial engagement with literacy learning 32–4
sensory dimension to writing and literacies 11
sensory literacies 26–34
Serafini, F. 226
Sesame Street effect 67
sexual identity on Facebook 215–17
Seymour, Richard 103
Shannon, P. 225
shared humanity 14
Sharma, B. K. 211
Sheridan, K. M. 137
Sherman, T. 212
Shipka, J. 40
Siemens, G. 241
sight being dominant sense 27–8
Silverstone, R. 15
Singleton, V. 193, 194
Skinner, D. 51
slavery 91
slope in typography 295
slow-motion 228–9, 232
smartphone: access to the Internet 64; apps 28; picture book apps for 28–31
Smith, A. 12, 38, 170, 186, 236
Snow, John 81
social connections of digital technology 67–8
social inclusion being increased by digital devices 69–70
socialization within games 206, 207
social justice 6, 7, 17, 54, 252, 254
social media 255; usage by race 113; as writing ecology 163; youth being global citizens 166–8
social movements 61, 79
social relations and digital ethics 257
social space 123

sociocultural contexts of play 204–5
Soep, E. 269
software functioning as expressive media 82
software spaces 241–2
solidarity expressed in networked writing 16–17, 19–21
Sontag, Susan 77
sousveillance 81
Space2Cr8 project 166–7
Spain, D. 201
spatialized literacies 141–2
spatial literacies 200
spatial repertoires 213
special needs students having access to digital technology 71
Speno, A. G. 116
stacking stories 195
Staehr, A. 214
statactivism 76, 81
Steinkuehler, C. 189
STEM and sports video games 84
Stephansen, H. 240
Stewart, M. A. 162
Stornaiuolo, A. 11, 16, 38, 117, 170, 179, 188, 269
storytelling 272; mobile 156
Streeck, Jurgen 126
Street, B. 3, 56
structured data in writing environments 238–40
subjective computing 83
subordination of marginalized groups 1
Sudnow, D. 127, 128
suffering represented in the media 22
Sullivan, P. 37
Sultana, S. 212
survival English 106
Svelch, J. 212
syllabus using hashtags 82
syncretic racism 102
Syrian crisis 167
systemic functional semiotic (SFS) accounts 29, 30

tablets 26, 28; picture book apps for 28–31
Taguchi, Lenz 195
Tate, Tamara 61
Tate, W. 112
Taylor, K. H. 148
teachers' education in literacy methods 144
teacher study group 144
techne 40–1, 281
technical knowledge and preconceptions of 79
technocultures 62; racism and 112–19
technologies blurring distinctions between authors and consumers 3
Technology and Engineering Literacy assessment 66
technology initiatives in schools 68–9
technomissionary efforts 83–4
television usage by race 113
Tellagami 117
temperature of color 294
test parsing 242–3
text: fluency of production 130–1; framing 292; image being complementary and 289–90; placement of 292; salience of 292
text sense 128
textual meaning 30
thick data 241
Thomas, A. 175
Thomas, E. E. 16

Thompson, B. 115
Thorne, S. 212
time and its manipulation 229
Tomlin, D. D. 226
Tosenberger, C. 175
touch 6, 11–12, 28
touch design 29
touch screen technologies 28
tragedy metaphor for refugees 104
train-as-established-sequence trope 42–3
transcription during handwriting 130
transgressive behavior 199, 266
translanguaging 213
translingual practices 213
transliteracies 170, 241
trauma being handled with digital tools 92, 93
Treuer, Anton 281
Truth, Sjourner 89
Tubman, Harriet 89, 95
Tufte, Edward 81
Tullet, Herve 31
Tumblr 174
TurnItIn 242, 277
Twitter 174; counter-narratives on 117; usage by race 113
Tyeklar, N. 107
Tynes, B. 115
typewriter separating body and word 128
typography in writing 295–6

Ulmer, G. 37
undocumented youth and writing 16, 103, 264, 269–72
United Nations High Commissioner for Refugees (UNHCR) 99
universal design for learning (UDL) 71
unstructured data 236–7
Unsworth, Len 11, 29
urban annotation 156
Urban Word NYC 42
U.S. Immigration and Nationality Act 100

value of color 294
van Leeuwen, T. 102, 250, 291, 292, 298
Vasquez, V. 186, 227
Vasudevan, L. 151, 249
Vaughan, E. B. 132
Vee, Annette 85
Velay, J. L. 127, 129, 132
Velghe, F. 211
Vic, S. 277
videogames 28, 198; racial stereotypes and 83; social construction of race and 114–15; STEM learning and 84
Vigdor, J. L. 69
Vinter, A. 129
violence in gaming 201, 204
virtual play 187–95; assembling 191; writing from the world 189; writing in the world 189; writing the world 188–9
virtual worlds 185–95
visibility, negotiating 16, 18–19
visual being dominant sense 27–8
Voices 266–9
Volunteered Geographic Information (VGI) 153–4
Voxmob 156
Vygotsky, L. S. 176

Wajcman, Judy 82
Wakeford, S. 150
Walsh, E. 130
Wargo, Jon 12
Warschauer, M. 61, 179
Watkins, S. Craig 79–80
Wattpad 174, 176
wearable technologies 4, 38, 40
Web 2.0 3
webs of significance 3
Weigel, M. 236, 265
weight in typography 295
Weintraub, N. 130
Wells, Ida B. 89
Wenger, E. 177
Wenimont, Jacqueline 79
Whiteness 79; mobility and 158; as property in digital and online literacies 112, 113–15
white noise 79
Whites: affects 79; density of computer usage and 66; identities in video games 115–16; time spent with media 68
*Whyville* 188
Wikimapia 154
Williams, B. 161, 166
Williams, D. 115
Williams, Fannie Barrier 90
Williamson, B. 81, 241, 242
Wilson, Frank 126
Witness organization 80
Wittkower, D. 254
Wodak, R. 102
Wohlwend, K. E. 123, 141, 225, 227
Womack, E. 93
women: African American as knowledgeable agents 88–96; African American digital literacy practices of 61; violence on in gaming 201, 204
workability of digital technology in schools 72
world: division with the classroom and 167–8; intertwining with digital technology 148
worldmaking 269; in Minecraft 140
Write4Change (W4C) online writing community 17, 23
WriteLab 242
writer, quantified 235–44
writing *see also* handwriting: about immigration reform 269–72; about it and making it 139–40; agency and 271; background 2–3; being done by youth 263; centrifugal cultural forces 166–7, 169; centripetal cultural force 166–7; color in 292–5; composition 291–2; computerized assessment of 242–3; cultural references in 299; deep 170; definition 38, 266; with digital geographies 152–6; within digital geographies 150–2; digital traces of 235–6; embodied practices of 127; emerging directions in 3–6; empirical studies of 128–32; ethics for 11, 13; gaming and 206; haptics of 123, 125–33; homogenous functional structure of 290–1; justice through 264–73; literacy for new writing 291–9; as a matter of justice 263; multimodality of 266; newer forms of aesthetic writing 286–91; parallelism in 297–9; perceived loss of 263; personal nature of 290; phenomenological accounts of 127–8; play and 192–4; provenance in 298–9; reciprocal relationship with reading 170; sensory dimension to 11; typography and

graphic design 295–6; by undocumented youth 16, 264, 269–72; virtual games and 189; virtual play and 187–95
writing ecologies: case studies of 162–3; as emerging theory 163
writing environments: collating learning process data 238; structured data in 238–40
writing hand 126
writing trace data 240–3
writing trade routes 41
writing tutors, computerized 238

Young, C. A. 179
youth *see also* adolescents; children: activism 16; agentive and just spaces for 272–3; becoming visible through writing 273; being digitally connected 68; collaborative composition practices of 264, 269–72; creating media texts 265; digital and educational justice 263–73; digital media composition and 123; educational justice and 263–73; empowered with media literacy 54–5; interacting as global citizens 165–9; lifestreaming of 43–6; participation and social inclusion through literacies 265–6; writing 12; writing by undocumented 16, 264, 269–72; writing ecologies of 161–70
YouTube 93, 174

Zhao, S. 29
Zillien, N. 73
Zimmerman, George 111, 113
Zimmermann, E. 199
Zook, M. 150